few are quite so powerful, evocative and immediate as Ian Denys Peek's personal memoir'   *Soldier* magazine

'The controlled fury which underpins Peek's harrowing and moving account of his captivity gives his memoir a depth of intensity which historical records can only hint at'   *Yorkshire Post*

'Peek is a natural narrator, sharing an account of suffering with grace and expertise . . . an evocative book, not always an easy read because of the horrors of its content, but mesmerising in its intensity'   *Big Issue*

'An astonishing and enthralling account . . . the book's power lies in the immense detail that Peek has been able to recollect . . . his writing captures the desperation, suffering and bravery of life in the camps and stays with you long after you've finished'
Bookseller

'A shocking and deeply moving personal account . . . eloquent and powerful'   *South Wales Evening Post*

'*One Fourteenth of an Elephant* is not just haunting, it evokes the very best that man can rise to when faced with adversity beyond comprehension. Its lesson . . . is told with raw passion'
Scottish Legion News

'Others have written books about the railway . . . but Peek's incredible eye for detail stands as a triumph of memory and passion'   *Weekend Australian*

'Peek has forged a diamond out of the terrible degradation of the past'   *Saturday Age*

'Brutally frank and beautifully moving . . . a story that once read won't be forgotten. It is a tale of suffering and bravery, of anger and humour, of inhumanity and dignity, of comradeship, ghosts and miracles'   *Adelaide Advertiser*

The son of English parents, Ian Denys Peek was brought up in Shanghai but educated in England. After leaving school, he and his brother were reunited with their family in Singapore. He joined the Singapore Volunteer Corps following the declaration of war in 1939 but was taken prisoner in 1942 after the Fall of Singapore. Although repatriated at the end of the war, Denys Peek returned to the Far East, where he worked as a harbour master before moving to Australia in the 1960s. He lives in Perth, Western Australia.

www.booksattransworld.co.uk

Acclaim for *One Fourteenth of an Elephant*:

'Written in the present tense, like a loose-limbed diary, his account of what he saw and suffered . . . is touching, vivid, angry and utterly compelling. It is also exceptionally well written'
Sunday Times

'This is a horrifying and extraordinary book . . . When a few years ago the Emperor of Japan visited London, a number of old men who had been Jap POWs lined the Mall and then turned their backs on him and the state procession. There was some criticism of their action. It was, some people said, time to let bygones be bygones, time to forget. The former POWs couldn't. Anyone who reads this book will understand why'
Allan Massie, *Literary Review*

'At first I thought 50 pages of prison-camp horror would be enough, but Peek drew me in with his detail, his lack of sentimentality and his downbeat account of kindness, comradeship, brutality and cowardice' *Guardian*

'With the steely courage he displayed as a captive during World War II, Peek revisits his past . . . recreating the gruesome heat and the smell of death, he tells his story with delicate outrage and bone-chilling humility. Readers are left only to question the path our world took to arrive at such brutality' *Good Book Guide*

'Peek's first-person present-tense narration gives immediacy to the everyday horror of POW life . . . Peek tells the truth as he experienced it, and there is no doubting the vivid power of his telling' *Books Quarterly* magazine

'One of the most compelling accounts of life on the Burma-Thailand Railway . . . a valuable record' *Spectator*

'There have been many harrowing accounts by prisoners-of-war of life (and death) constructing the Burma-Thailand railway . . .

One
FOURTEENTH
of an
ELEPHANT

A memoir of life and death on the Burma–Thailand Railway

IAN DENYS PEEK

BANTAM BOOKS

LONDON • TORONTO • SYDNEY • AUCKLAND • JOHANNESBURG

ONE FOURTEENTH OF AN ELEPHANT
A BANTAM BOOK : 0 553 81657 8

First published in Australia by Pan Macmillan Australia Pty Limited 2003
Published in the UK 2004 by Doubleday
a division of Transworld Publishers

PRINTING HISTORY
Doubleday edition published 2004
Bantam edition published 2005

1 3 5 7 9 10 8 6 4 2

Set in 11.5/13.5pt Garamond by
Falcon Oast Graphic Art Ltd.

Bantam Books are published by Transworld Publishers,
61–63 Uxbridge Road, London W5 5SA,
a division of The Random House Group Ltd,
in Australia by Random House Australia (Pty) Ltd,
20 Alfred Street, Milsons Point, Sydney, NSW 2061, Australia,
in New Zealand by Random House New Zealand Ltd,
18 Poland Road, Glenfield, Auckland 10, New Zealand
and in South Africa by Random House (Pty) Ltd,
Endulini, 5a Jubilee Road, Parktown 2193, South Africa.

Printed and bound in Great Britain by
Cox & Wyman Ltd, Reading, Berkshire

Papers used by Transworld Publishers are natural, recyclable
products made from wood grown in sustainable forests. The
manufacturing processes conform to the environmental
regulations of the country of origin

Dedication

This book is written as a humble tribute to those thousands of friends and unknown mates who died in appalling circumstances while building the accursed Siam–Burma Railway in 1942–45.

We all suffered physically and spiritually, and those of us who survived were in no way more deserving to live, we were just a bit luckier.

Death came bearing a dismal shroud of utter loneliness, which sealed off dying men from all those they had loved and who had loved them, warmed only by the intense compassion of those few friends who were with them at the time.

We must never forget them, or allow them to pass from their people's memories. Indeed, our constant remembrance is our own personal thanksgiving for our survival.

If this book helps to put flesh on all those bones lying in Thailand's cemeteries, then I shall have achieved something worthwhile.

Denys Peek

I offer my very deep personal thanks to Dorothy Rose, the 'girl in my dreams' whose visitations were such a wonderful help to me, as a prisoner of war, in such stressful times.

It was she who persuaded me to convert my memoirs into a book, then affectionately 'nagged' me to keep on writing when I tended to slow down, until it was finished.

Without her unfailing encouragement and faith in my work, this book might well never have been written.

Contents

Author's note

This book is entirely my own work, compiled from my own memories, occasionally verified by talks with friends who were there. Beyond checking a few dates in the chronological sequences, I have drawn nothing from any other book. Accordingly, there is no bibliography. The events described are just as I remember them. They were not forgotten and dredged up after fifty years; they have been part of my life ever since they happened.

NAMES

I have avoided surnames and have used pseudonymns for personal names. They do not affect the narrative and there is no point in identifying individuals. I have no desire to hand out praise or blame. The purpose of my writing is simply to say how I saw things that happened.

If the reader was never there, the absence of surnames should not affect his or her perception of my story. If the reader was there, he or she will recognise the men in the story.

PLACES

There were many camps other than those that I tell about. Some of them were truly horrific and far worse than those I encountered. It is for others to write about them.

The spelling of place names has varied in books I have

read, which again is of little importance, for anyone who was there will know them and lack of precision in the English rendering does not alter any facts. Of note is that we sometimes referred to places with a familiar abbreviation. The most prevalent is our shortening of Kanchanaburi to Kanburi.

Siam, as that country was known to us who lived in that part of the world, changed its name to Thailand some little time before the start of the Japanese war. In the confusion of those times this seemed not to have been widely adopted immediately, and amongst us the familiar Siam persisted until well into our captivity. Newly arrived soldiers were told its name was Thailand and used it from the start. The name Thailand was internationally recognised in 1949.

Incidentally, the word 'Thai' means 'Free', and in fact theirs is the only nation in the East which has never been conquered and ruled. So our experts tell us, and apart from Japan I cannot think of any exception.

About 1947, I think it was, the word 'Asiatic' fell into disfavour and was replaced by 'Asian'. I have kept to Asiatic in my narrative because that's the way it was – no disrespect is intended in any way.

CURRENCY

As the currency in Singapore and Malaya was in dollars and cents, the Siamese tical (or baht) was frequently referred to as a dollar or buck, and the sattang as a cent.

FOREIGN WORDS

Foreign words occur unavoidably; I have included them to give authenticity and colour. Our roll-call parades – tenko – were conducted in Japanese and I can still recall the basic military parade commands used on these occasions. After all, I heard them often enough! Beyond counting heads in Japanese numbers, there were relatively few words necessary for us to get along well enough with our Japanese and Korean camp guards – amplified by ingenious pantomime when necessary – such as:

arigato	–	thank you
asta	–	tomorrow
bango	–	number
benjo	–	latrine
boom-boom	–	war
bushido	–	fighting spirit; absolute loyalty to one's master unto death
changkol	–	hoe-like tool for breaking earth. It had a heavy steel blade with a sharpened cutting edge fixed to the end of a long, stout wooden handle
damme	–	no good. Emphasised by repetition
dozo	–	please be so kind as to (accept a gift, do something)
fundoshi	–	a minimal version of a Japanese loincloth
gunso	–	sergeant
heitai	–	soldier
hikoki	–	aircraft (sometimes heard as 'skogi')
hiru	–	sun (today)
hiru meishi	–	midday rice meal
howdah	–	(Indian) the passenger box on an elephant's back
kwali	–	rice cooking pot (encompassed all sizes from a small family kitchen pot to our twelve-gallon, cast-iron circular pans)
mateh	–	wait
meishi	–	rice
mizu	–	water
orru	–	the Japanese pronunciation of the English

word 'all'. The Japanese tend to substitute an 'r' sound for 'l' and have difficulties with words that end in a clipped consonant, preferring to add a vowel sound to the end

pisang mas	–	(Malay) literally, golden banana
saiyo hajumei	–	stop work
sampanu	–	sampan, small rowboat
shoko	–	officer
skoshi	–	little
takusan	–	(pronounced 'taksan') more, plenty
tenko	–	parade for counting, or simply calling everyone together
tonga	–	a stretcher made from two hessian rice sacks threaded on two bamboo poles, used for carrying earth (or bodies)
yasumi	–	stand at ease, rest, holiday

MEASURES

The Japanese used the metric system. Weights were in kilograms and grams, which were entirely meaningless when given to our medical officers for use as their official scales of food rations since they were never fulfilled. Distances were in kilometres, holes drilled for dynamite in centimetres. We used both metric and imperial systems freely as appropriate.

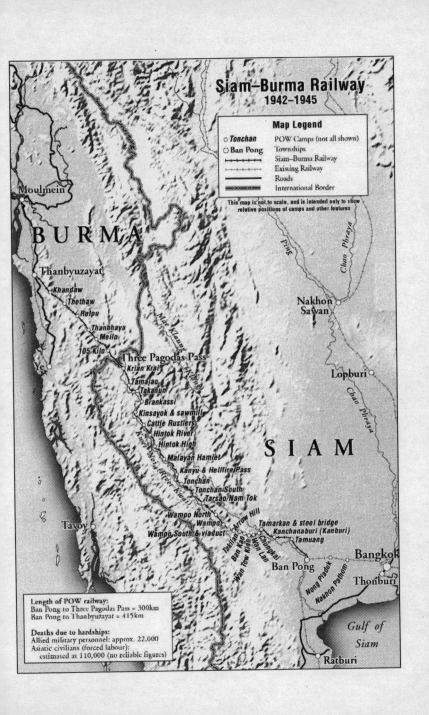

Siam–Burma Railway
1942–1945

Map Legend

○ *Tonchan*	POW Camps (not all shown)
○ Ban Pong	Townships
⊢⊢⊢⊢⊢	Siam–Burma Railway
⋯⋯⋯	Existing Railway
══════	Roads
▬▬▬▬	International Border

This map is not to scale, and is intended only to show
relative positions of camps and other features

BURMA

Moulmein

Thanbyuzayat

Khandaw
Thethaw
Reipu
Thanbhaya
Meilo
105 Kilo

Ye

Three Pagodas Pass
Krian Krai
Tamajao
Takanun
Brankassi
Kinsayok & sawmill
Cattle Rustlers
Hintok River
Hintok High
Malayan Hamlet
Kanyu & Hellfire Pass
Tonchan
Tonchan South
Tarsao/Nam Tok

Wampo North
Wampo
Wampo South & viaduct

Tavoy

Tardan
Ban Kao
Wan Tow Kien
Wan Lan
Arrow Hill
Chungkai

Tamarkan & steel bridge
Kanchanaburi (Kanburi)
Tamuang

SIAM

Mae Khlung

Kwai Noi River Kwai

Ping

Chao Phraya

Nakhon Sawan

Lopburi

Chao Phraya

Ban Pong

Bangkok

Thonburi

Nong Pladuk
Nakhon Pathom

Gulf of Siam

Ratburi

Length of POW railway:
Ban Pong to Three Pagodas Pass = 300km
Ban Pong to Thanbyuzayat = 415km

Deaths due to hardships:
Allied military personnel: approx. 22,000
Asiatic civilians (forced labour):
estimated at 110,000 (no reliable figures)

1

Ban Pong Transit Camp

OCTOBER 1942

It is dawn on 17 October 1942, and the train has stopped at a small station displaying the name BAN PONG, in Siamese script and in English. We have been cooped up in steel goods wagons since leaving Singapore four and a half days ago, sweltering hot by day and chillingly cold at night, with a few brief halts along the way to allow us to leap out of the wagons to deal with nature's calls, and a stop once a day at some Nip army post for a ration of rice and tea.

The international railway line runs northwards from Singapore, crosses from Malaya into Siam (recently renamed Thailand – 'Land of Free Men') and, after some 1,200 miles, turns east near Ban Pong and continues to Bangkok, thereafter curving southwards down the far coast of the Gulf of Siam to the French Indo-China capital of Saigon. All this information comes from a couple of our men who, in peacetime, used to do the journey at regular intervals for their trading companies. Both have a fair knowledge of the local language, one of them even being able to read the complicated alphabet to a useful extent.

Having watched the night sky, we have noticed our eastwards swing and have an accurate reckoning of where we are on the map. There are some 1,600 men being transferred to

Siam from two camps in Singapore, one in River Valley Road and the other from what used to be the Great World Amusement Park, the two being separated by a small creek. Our own lot comprises some 200 ex-civilians from Singapore and the Malay States, all members of various Volunteer (capital V, Straits Settlements and Malayan) units, some of the older men reaching back to the trenches of the Great War. There are a couple of hundred Australians, some regulars from the British army, and the rest are from the British 18th (East Anglian) Division – thrown into Singapore only a matter of weeks before the capitulation. A mixed bunch indeed!

The ride up from Singapore has been desperately uncomfortable. The railway is built to the smallish one metre gauge, so the trucks are accordingly scaled in size. Dumping our kit on the floor at Singapore station we distributed ourselves as best we could, thirty-two men in our cramped steel box. In the mornings the right-hand side took the full glare of the sun, which swung over to heat up the left side in the afternoons, with such power that it was beyond bearing to lean against the steel sheeting. If you stood up to ease cramps, you found your head in a steamy layer of almost unbreathable sweaty fumes trapped under the roof. Unable to lie down or to lean against the sides, we sagged against each other like stuffed dolls, naked except for shorts, our bodies glistening with sweat and quivering like jelly as the train shuddered and rattled along.

Against Nip orders, we keep the central sliding doors open to bring in some fresh air – which also allowed those suffering from dysentery to project their bums outside while being firmly held by the wrists and ankles. After a somewhat startling near miss, somebody would keep a watch ahead to look for bridge parapets, poles and other items having only a minimal clearance from the trucks. The absence of any kind of toilet paper added to the unpleasantly thick atmosphere, and no one has had a wash since leaving the Singapore camps.

So it is a great relief to find that Ban Pong is our destination, and we are escaping from those awful steel cells. We pick up our gear and fall in on the road behind the station, to be counted. What should be a simple operation becomes confused when the train guards hand us over to Nips from the Ban Pong camp and their separate counts do not agree, but eventually things are sorted out and we march off under our new escort. The village is a shabby collection of huts and shophouses, the people much in keeping and showing little interest in us, and after a quarter of an hour we find ourselves approaching the entrance to a fenced camp which, surely, must be the most depressing dump we have ever seen. Our working camp in Singapore was slummy enough, but this place has an aura of menace and ill omen. This may be due to those sights immediately catching our attention. One is a Siamese man curled on the ground, being savagely bashed by a group of Nips. The second is the sullen, sour-faced cluster of Nips at the entrance gateway, staring at us with frank hostility, and the third is the dozen or so vultures perched on the roof of the guardhouse. These revolting-looking birds are eyeing us with the interested anticipation of gluttons waiting to be turned loose on a heap of food. God, they are unwholesome creatures, but in Siam they are necessary to local hygiene for they tidy up rubbish and are therefore under government protection.

Despite having been counted only fifteen minutes ago by guards from the camp, we are now required to form up again on an area of dried mud within the camp for a tenko. Presumably, we have now officially come into the custody of the camp and our numbers have to be formally recorded in the guardhouse. The Nips indicate to our officers which huts we are to occupy, and the parade breaks up. We find that we have been standing on the only dry patch of ground in the camp. All the huts are wallowing in water – stagnant water full of mosquito larvae and (from the stink) the contents of over-flowing latrine trenches, and the air pulsates with the drumming of mosquitoes and flies. The place is empty, some of the huts leaning over in a state of collapse.

The huts are constructed of bamboo poles with a thatch of dried palm leaves, which the Malays call 'attap'. Laid on at close intervals attap provides a serviceable roof, but in these huts daylight comes through everywhere. And so does the rain, as a heavy monsoon squall passes over while we sort our kit on the split bamboo sleeping platforms built down each side of the huts. These platforms are hard and uncomfortable, but they do keep us above the filthy soup below. To make up for this, however, the slats are full of bugs which leave irritating spots where they feed on us and a foul stench when they are squashed.

But the sudden downpour has us all scrambling outside, standing naked in the sweet cleansing rain bucketing down from the lowering clouds. Just as the thick smelly film of train-sweat slides off us, so are our spirits rinsed clear of the despondency which has crept over us in the hour spent in this unwholesome paddock, laughing and chattering with relief as we rub ourselves down with the bits of clothing which we have just taken off, and washing them through at the same time. We make the most of the warm shower despite the chilly breeze sweeping across the camp, until the sky lightens and the rain eases to a stop.

We have been performing our ablutions (as they say in the army) on the parade ground simply to avoid standing in the muck around the huts. What had been dry mud is now, of course, wet sludge, but we would far rather stay here than return to our huts where we can expect to find a rancid swamp thoroughly stirred up by the rain. The choice is not ours, however. The Nips, emerging dry and in a foul mood from their snug guardhouse-cum-living quarters, screech and bawl at us with energetic arm-waving which, we gather, means we have to return to our huts.

Squelching back into the malodorous and buzzing atmosphere, we hang our wet clothing over the bamboo framework inside and resign ourselves to a thoroughly uncomfortable wait for something to happen. We haven't eaten since yesterday afternoon's brief train-halt (the only meal of the day), and someone remarks that he has not seen a cookhouse – indeed, where could a cookhouse stand in such a place? Also, where might there be a water supply? Any well would be filled with overflow from the latrines. Having worked all this out we lapse into torpid semiconsciousness, the only movement being men wading out to open spaces to cope with the stresses of dysentery and diarrhoea. The humidity is overwhelming and the temperature must be well over 100° F. We are stretched out like glistening corpses.

An hour before dark a shout of 'On parade, mess tins and mugs!' brings us out to the parade area, from where we are funnelled out of the gateway along the road to a bamboo and attap shelter where tubs of rice are lined up with 44-gallon drums of tea. Inside the shelter is a party of British soldiers ready to issue the food. One of them shouts out, 'You'll have to be quick. Line up and move off, if there's time we'll be able to talk to you, but they'll be back to pick us up in a few minutes and there's no time to waste.'

The ration is rice with a scrap of dried fish (salty, strongly flavoured, and most welcome for that) and a mug of plain tea which is at least hot and wet, and immediately after it has been served out we start talking to the men. They are not from any one unit but are a collection of oddments who were captured early during the up-country fighting in Malaya and ended up in Siam. They run a cookhouse a mile or more down the road where there is a shallow well of fresh water, this being the only source of clean water they know of. Their job is to cook for parties in transit, such as our lot, which means that they can usually 'fiddle' enough to keep themselves from being hungry, but apart from that they have very little.

A smallish, isolated group of men, they are bored silly with each other and with their dull lives, and are desperately eager to hear any news we can give them: events, units, names, rumours – anything. In return they tell us there has been talk of a railway to be built from Ban Pong to Burma, and it could be that we are the first labour battalion to go into the hills for the construction. And we remember that, stopping at Prai (on the Malayan side of the Siam border), we had seen Malay railwaymen sticking Ban Pong labels on our rake of wagons, and they had told our men that the Japs had already sent up a mass of railway lines, dogspikes, fishplates and sleepers. So maybe we shall soon be heading westwards!

The cooks' truck rolls up and our conversation comes to an end. The cooks load their bits and pieces and are carted off. Instant response to Nip orders seems to be the way of things hereabouts.

Back in camp we perch on our bamboo platforms in the unlit huts and gather together our combined ideas of the territory between us and the Indian Ocean. From the main mass of Burma to the north a narrow strip of Burmese territory runs some 500 miles south of Moulmein, down into the Kra Isthmus, with the Andaman Sea on the west and its border with Siam to the east. The coastal plain is narrow and the east is heavily forested mountain country, being the tail end of an offshoot of the mighty Himalayan range. This whole coastline, from the Bay of Bengal in the north to the Andaman

Sea at our end, takes the full force of the south-west monsoon from May to November, and is one of the heaviest rainfall areas on earth. Somewhere down the spine of these mountains is the Burma–Siam border.

Someone contributes a recollection that the British army, at the request of the Siamese government, sent a party of engineers to survey a route for constructing a road and railway in the area, some time around 1912, before the Great War. The difficulties of the terrain, transport and climate put a stop to the venture, but the most important factor was that the Siamese and Burmese refused to work in the area because of its reputation for disease and hard living. Siam being a country of plentiful food and easy-going Buddhist village communities, no man in his right mind would even think of heavy physical labour in such conditions! Is this what we can look forward to? We thank our knowledgeable informant for his encouraging little discourse, and settle down to sleep.

There is a sudden medical emergency: a soldier has developed agonising appendicitis. With no proper facilities available, our medical officer has no choice but to operate. Despite the appalling conditions – the MO and his helpers standing shin-deep in filthy water, the patient lying on bare bug-infested bamboo slats, and a single coconut oil lamp giving feeble illumination – the diseased appendix is successfully removed with a straight razor and the briefest whiff of chloroform from the MO's scanty kit.

An hour after the patient is carried out, the hut collapses.

Five days of intense boredom – relieved only by the brief evening outing for our one meal of the day, amid the all-pervading stink and insects – come to an end with an announcement that we are to march out next morning. Our medical officer has permission to leave behind a party of some twenty sick men who would not be able to manage the march ahead of us, some of them from our own unit. We are most upset at the idea of leaving them behind in this filthy camp, and they would rather face any problems to stay with us, but the hard fact is that they are not fit enough to march. The distance is some sixty-five miles, to somewhere called Tarsao, westwards towards the Burma border, and who knows? In staying behind they may turn out to be the lucky ones.

The Nips have ordered us to be ready to move two hours before daylight, so that we can make a fair distance before the heat of the day. A good idea, so in the dim starlight we are assembled with all our personal gear, ready for tenko. Our officers warn us that we must not drink from our water canteens until we get permission to do so, because we have no information whatsoever about our route and do not know about water supplies for refilling.

The rest of the night passes, the abrupt dawn lightens the sky, and we are still standing on the parade ground. The Nips count us, and disappear. Two hours after sun-up they are screaming for a tenko, despite the fact that we have been standing on the same spot for four hours without moving.

Our friendly vultures are in their usual places, and give us a disappointed stare as we move out of the camp. The road is bitumen and the sun already uncomfortably hot. On our backs we are carrying all our worldly possessions. Some have very little, others a kitbag, one has a piano accordion wrapped in his groundsheet. Can he play it? No, but it might come in useful for cheering up the lads and he has almost nothing else to carry.

There is no pretence of holding any kind of march formation. Those who can get ahead do so, others lag back, and the army habit of stopping for ten minutes of every hour is abandoned. The column straggles over so much road that our Nip escort gives up trying to keep us all together. The heat builds up, the road shimmers ahead of us, the countryside is mostly flat rice fields with groups of houses and trees dotted over it, there is no shade on the road and we are sweating profusely. But, sticking to orders, we do not touch our water canteens.

Getting up after a few minutes' rest on the grass verge I am dizzy and my vision is blurred. I start marching, and my brother, Ron, who is also part of our group, turns me round because I am heading back the way we have come. Others are showing similar signs of distress from heat exhaustion and dehydration. Cramps, trembling limbs, disorientation, slurred speech – it's obviously time to forget orders and uncork our water canteens. A pint, swallowed slowly, gets us back on the road, but we have had nothing to eat since yesterday afternoon (and that wasn't much!) and have marched some twelve miles in the full sun and have no idea how far there is to go. Until, at sundown, we find ourselves turning off the road into a group of bamboo and attap huts. The short twilight passes and it is night by the time we have dumped our kit and found the cookhouse. After hot tea, a ladle of rice and something unidentifiable in the dark, we strip off our sweat-saturated uniforms and flop, exhausted, into unconsciousness.

We are roused before dawn, given a dollop of rice and salt fish, and are able to fill our canteens with tea. This camp, we are told, is called Tamuang, yesterday's march was twenty miles and we now have the same distance to Kanburi. After tenko we move off, stiff and aching in every joint, our rancid clothes chafing and rubbing on prickly heat rashes.

Some three miles along we pass through the small village of Tamuang, pleasant little homes and open-fronted shops already astir. But it is a couple of miles beyond that we enter an extraordinary experience. Both sides of the road are lined with villagers, mostly elderly men and women and small children, with rows of charcoal braziers on which pots and pans bubble with rice and vegetables, eggs, banana fritters, fish and peanuts; fresh fruit in baskets, limes and papayas, small sweet bananas (which the Malays call 'pisang mas' or golden bananas), coconuts and acidic star fruits. And these are offered, not for sale, but as friendly gifts pressed on us with unlimited generosity. The polite dignity of the old men, the betel-stained smiles of comfortably stout mums and grand-mothers thrusting rice puddings wrapped in banana leaves at us, and the shy offerings of children running amongst us with trays of savoury food, bring the whole column to a standstill, everyone milling around, pushing wrapped parcels into haver-sacks and filling mess tins with what has to be eaten straight away. The air is full of Siamese chatter and 'Thank you, thank you' from our men, until someone shouts out, 'Keep moving, keep moving, the Nips are coming, keep moving!'

Three Nips arrive and, in their usual arrogant fashion, they start to bawl and scream at the villagers. In a moment these smiling people surround them, shouting and gesturing angrily from all sides. Their black hostility is unmistakable, the women in particular giving out their opinions with great vigour. The bewildered Nips, not used to this kind of response, hurriedly push their way out and retreat. Puzzled by this, we come to the conclusion that maybe the military occu-pation of Siam is not too popular with the citizens, even though it is by treaty with the Siamese government. Any such reaction by us, or by civilians in Malaya or Singapore, being countries occupied by conquest, would have resulted in severe punishment. So, possibly the Nip soldiery has been ordered to avoid ructions with the local people.

Our spirits marvellously uplifted by the morning's show

of ordinary human decency, we continue our slog towards Kanburi. In the late afternoon I begin to hear regular squeaky noises, faint but quite definite. I stop walking, and the noises cease. When I start walking again the squeaks resume, and they keep time with my paces and the movements of my arms. All my joints feel dry, as if an oilcan would be useful. The others in our group, when I mention it, feel the stiffness and hear the same persistent little sounds. We are still being careful with our water supply, but a drink is indicated. Half a mile further on, we are squeaking audibly as we march and the dry joints are worse. Walking is beginning to become noticeably painful, our joints starting to swell.

At this point we meet a small group of Siamese youths who press on us little parcels wrapped in newspaper, murmur good wishes in English and pass on. The package given to me has in it two waxed paper tapes each holding a dozen aspirin tablets, and about a pound of greyish lumpy crystals which taste like salt. We all take a small pile and lick it out of the palms of our hands. Nothing ever tasted so good! A swig of water to help it reach our muscles and joints, and within minutes, literally, we are swinging along squeakless and with every joint lubricated, and at twice the speed. Pains disappear and swellings fade away.

Now who was it that arranged for us to be met by a party of young Siamese who gave us exactly what we needed, at exactly the time when we needed it desperately? We are so struck by this incident, and by the spectacular benefit of salt, that we immediately make a firm decision to build up a stock of it with priority over everything else. Ron and I, and our friends George and Wally, decide we will always aim at having at least a pound between us, before we buy even eggs. Are we just lucky, or is someone keeping an eye on us?

This day's march ends far more cheerfully than

yesterday's. We have covered some forty miles from Ban Pong in two days, carrying all our possessions, and despite not having had a decent meal in the fortnight since we boarded the train in Singapore, we are physically in fair condition. The camp area on the outskirts of the small town, Kanchanaburi, has a few huts and is clean and dry. We pass a couple of days relaxing and are told to be ready to move early next morning. It will be a rough country march and we are to carry only minimum gear and leave the rest to follow by boat, with a party of our sick who will look after it. Naively, we pile our kitbags as directed.

An early start sees us filing through close bush and bamboo, along narrow paths and in constant gloom as the rainy season asserts itself. In the afternoon we come into cultivated land, walking along the raised bunds which divide fields of tall rice, and arriving at a pleasant little rural village.

The houses are arranged on the four sides of a large rectangle, which is centred on a substantial Buddhist temple, and clumps of trees. The people look at us with quiet curiosity, and we feel it must be a bit of a shock to them to have to accept (presumably with neither warning nor choice) such a large group of scruffy strangers of a race totally unknown to them.

But the Siamese are by nature, and by their Buddhist religion, a friendly and generous people, and the monks indicate that we are welcome to use the temple as shelter. As we gratefully settle down out of the rain, young boys bring us local fruits and cooked rice in banana leaves. Their spontaneous hospitality gives our morale a big boost.

In the brightening dawn, we witness an aspect of Siamese village life which fills us with admiration. It seems that the monks do nothing to feed themselves, relying entirely on the people around them, and this morning they line up with their food bowls held at waist level to receive contributions, their eyes turned steadfastly downwards so that they see neither the food nor the faces of the givers. All over the village, Siamese women and children emerge from their homes carrying silver and wooden dishes of steaming rice, vegetables and fruits, all carefully and artistically arranged. The children scoop food into the bowls, a few words are murmured, and the women move on to the next line.

This is in no way a slapdash soup kitchen affair. The housewives are beautifully dressed, as are the children, and all is done in a pleasing ceremony of mutual respect and harmony, smiling faces and goodwill, dignity and peace. The Christian attitude to begging and charity suddenly seems shabby and unworthy, adversarial rather than a willingness to help others, far too condescending on the part of the fortunate and demeaning for the recipients. It is a subject of discussion amongst us as we plod along. The simple dignity of the monks in their saffron robes, shaven-headed and with calm expressions, impresses us greatly, and our nickname for them, 'The Mustard Club', is affectionate and in no way unkind.

The medical officer with our party happens to be the MO of our Volunteer battalion. His family is in the Canary Islands; he is part Spanish and takes the ethics of his calling very seriously. The health of his men is paramount, and the sick are given every care he can offer within the hopelessly inadequate means available to him. On this march he has probably walked twice as far as any of us, ranging up and down the straggling column and doing what he can to ease blisters and cramps. As far as possible he pushes to the head to check water in streams and pools, swilling it around a silver goblet to look for signs of pollution. A piece of paper on a stick says 'DO NOT DRINK' or 'POTABLE' (why doesn't he write 'CAN DRINK', which everybody would understand?)

and then he is away back to his patients. Septic sores on bare legs are becoming frequent.

It's a thoroughly miserable day; the Nips apparently haven't planned to feed us until we reach our destination, a Jap military camp called Tarsao, which is the main base camp for the railway itself. We are due there tomorrow.

Today ends far worse than it began. In the near darkness of a late afternoon monsoonal downpour we reach a river to find a wooden barge pulled up broadside to the beach. A plank provides a gangway up which earlier arrivals are being herded, each man receiving a thwack across his shoulders from a heavy bamboo cane, swung by a Nip counting his cattle – 'Shi ju goh, shi ju roku, shi ju suchi, shi ju hachi, shi ju ku, goh ju, okay'. The boat poles across the river with its complement of fifty men with bruised backs and another takes its place. It's our turn – 'Ichi (whack), ni (whack), san (whack)' as we negotiate the sloping gangway, slippery with rain and mud, and jump down into the cargo space. The distance across is only some sixty yards, but the swollen current is fast and takes us downstream until the boatman is able to work us across to the quieter far side, where he has to pole us back upstream to the landing area. If it were not for enormous log fires blazing on the banks, we would be in total darkness by now.

The boat nudges into the beach, the plank is put in place, and as we start to file down it we observe, standing in the flickering fire glow, a sight we have not seen for months. A British officer is watching us, a major's crown on his shoulders, full uniform (shirt, shorts, boots, hosetops with ankle puttees, brown leather harness, cap), very smart, trim moustache, even a swagger stick under his arm. Before we can decide whether or not we should salute this shining specimen of our army he bawls at us, 'Hurry up there, get a move on! Your life's not worth a damn this side of the river so don't waste time!

Get moving, up that slope there!' Someone in the distance shouts at him in Japanese, he springs to attention calling back, 'Hai, hai,' and is off at the double, into the shadows.

An angry, sarcastic voice drawls, 'Well, he's a friggin' 'appy liddle Ovaltiney, innee? I just 'ope I catch up wiv 'im sometime, I'll fix 'im good an' proper.' The venom in his voice is shared by all of us.

We claw our way up a sticky slope in the streaming rain, about 100 yards, to a clearing lit by several towering fires. Nobody is interested in us, there are no huts, no latrines, only thick mud and silent trees lit up by the fires. All we have to do is wait for daylight, in the rain and sludge, maybe fourteen hours. A sleepless night is made all the more uncomfortable by empty bellies, with no breakfast in sight.

During the night the rain stops and early morning sees us moving out. At midday our Nips decide to cook themselves a meal and have a siesta which lasts three hours. We make the best of it, and stretch out for what rest we can get. Late that night we come to some huts. This is Tarsao. We are exhausted by hunger and all the stresses since leaving Ban Pong. The huts are not for us, we stay in the open, but at least we can light small campfires which are comforting.

Fortunately, we have three days at Tarsao to recover. The rain holds off, we can dry our kit, and we do get fed now and again. We are not called upon to do anything while we wait for boats to take us downriver to our working camp, where it seems we shall start on the railway.

Eventually the boats are here, and we have a serene drift downriver until we pull into the left bank and scramble up the slope. We have arrived! There is a guardhouse for the Nips, and stacks of bamboo and attap thatching lying around.

The name Wampo filters through to us. Fate now seems to have nailed us down.

2

Wampo Camp

OCTOBER TO NOVEMBER 1942

The colonel's voice rings out over the 1,600 men assembled in a patch cleared in the forest, on the left bank of the mud-brown river running swiftly and silently some thirty feet below at the foot of a steep bank: 'The name of this camp is Wampo, W-A-M-P-O, and it takes its name from a small village a little way over there.' He points northwards over our heads. 'That village is strictly and absolutely out of bounds to everybody.

'The Japanese say they will shoot without hesitation any man either found there, or seen talking to the people, and I have no doubt they mean what they say. The river is the Kwei Noi. The Japanese commandant is Lieutenant Tanaka, and I am senior British officer in this camp.

'You will be organised into three labour units of 500 men each, leaving 100 officers and men for camp administration, cookhouses, medical and sanitation services.

'We are to build a section of a railway that will eventually run from Ban Pong through this area to somewhere near Moulmein in Burma. Three days from now, you will start on its construction, and you have until then to build a camp to live in.

'Obviously, there is not a moment to waste in putting up huts and cookhouses, and in digging latrines and refuse pits. And, of course, our priority is to get the sick under cover.

'I warn you, this is going to be an extremely difficult time for all of us. You are going to need the utmost self-discipline among yourselves to see you through the coming months, in adjusting to new conditions which you have never experienced in the past. Never forget that you are still soldiers with high standards of personal behaviour. Above all, maintain your sense of humour and of obligation to your fellows.

'At tenko, all orders and numbering will be in Japanese, as you have already learned back in Singapore.

'Break off now, and start work on the camp. Do not wander off outside the camp area, or you may find yourselves in serious and unpleasant trouble, in which I may not be able to help you.'

The mass of men loosens and quickly coagulates into groups around their officers to be told what is to be done and where to do it. A small party of our own men arrived a day or two ago and marked out sites for living quarters and so on, and piles of bamboo poles and attap thatching are stacked on the river shore. The Nips must have been here for several days as their own huts and a small house for their officer have already been completed. Within minutes we are sorted into working squads and start clearing trees and undergrowth, and carrying bamboo and attap to where they will be needed.

The Nips have provided a totally inadequate quantity of miscellaneous tools – rusty saws, blunt axes, sledgehammers, picks and shovels – and ragged strips of stringy tree bark to lash the bamboo frames together. The huts themselves prove very simple to erect, but we frequently come to a standstill because there are not enough tools. The main problem is cutting bamboo to two-metre lengths for the sleeping platforms. Several hundred lengths will be needed per hut, each one to be split down its length and hammered flat, and all spiky bits trimmed off.

Our Volunteer sergeant, a resourceful former rubber plantation manager with years of labour management behind him, sorts out the problem by imperiously commandeering saws, axes and sledgehammers and handing them to groups of men. 'You lot will do nothing but saw bamboo into lengths as fast as you can. You fellows with axes will trim and split them, and you with the hammers will bash them out flat. The rest of you will keep the squad supplied with bamboo and carry the finished lengths to the hut builders who will draw on them as needed, for all the huts. And don't put your tools down, keep them in your hands all the time, or you may lose them.'

Postholes are dug, mainframes lashed together on the ground and hoisted upright to stand in them, roof stringers and attap tied in place, and the split lengths of bamboo laid over bamboo posts and rails knee-high above the earth floor.

The huts are long rectangles with an opening in the centre at each end and midway along each side. The sleeping platforms run down the sides from the ends to the centre doorways, and a quick bit of mental arithmetic tells us there will be twenty-two inches width per man to lie on, so there will be no tossing and turning at night. One of the men, a professor of English with a never-failing sense of humour, puts it in simple terms, 'There will be no turning over in bed! That is an order! If you should wish to change your position to face in the opposite direction, you will have to rotate your body around your fixed longitudinal axial alignment!'

Fifty yards away the medical orderlies have pitched four British army bell tents ('Other Ranks, 12, for the use of'), canvas contraptions with a circular base and conical in shape, held up by a central pole and steadied by guy ropes pegged all around. Because it has started to rain, they have begun putting up the tents without first clearing the ground, in order to get the sick under some sort of cover at the earliest moment, and when the central poles are upright they go inside and start to pull up the small shrubs.

In moments they are out again, yelling, 'Look out for scorpions!' The tents are hastily dragged aside, and in one space they find fourteen hefty specimens, stirred up and thoroughly angry with their tails curled high and forward, ready for action. The other tents produce several more. They are big creatures, about fourteen inches from pincers to tail, cased in blue-grey armour, and they scuttle around to dodge the frenzied spade swipes aimed at them. Three of the bodies are dangled from bamboos stuck in the ground as a warning to everybody to look out for them. They make us nervous, wondering how we shall be able to see them after dark as we move around the shrubbery still standing in the camp area. We must have happened on a colony of these dangerous little nasties, but who knows how many more are tucked away in the virgin undergrowth.

At the end of the second day it is announced at evening tenko that work will start on the railway the next morning, a full day early. The Nips say that the huts have not been put up as quickly as they should have been, therefore we cannot be interested in completing them, so we can start tomorrow on our real work. Obviously we have tried to take advantage of their generosity in allowing too much time for setting up the camp, and they are very angry at our ingratitude and in future they will not be so kind-hearted. Their lousy tools and the almost constant rain, of course, have nothing to do with it.

So, on the following morning the work parties go off for the first time to the surveyors' trace line of the projected railway, and start felling and clearing trees and undergrowth along a wide swath through the forest. The sick men attend a parade where the medical officers decide who is fit enough to continue with the hut-building and clearing the ground.

I have a painful big toe on my left foot, caused by a hard wrinkle of leather inside the toecap of my boot, which has pressed against the nail and dragged it almost free of its anchorage. Continuing to wear the boot has of course aggravated the injury but I hadn't liked the thought of going barefoot with those scorpions around. The MO directs me to his sidekick, Corporal 'Sadistic', who grips the loose nail with a pair of tweezers and, without warning, twists and tears it off. My yelp of pain is met with 'Got to be firm, no sense in fiddling with it.' He has no antiseptic or dressing, and as I limp away he calls after me, 'Keep it clean, now!' How the hell can I do that? The nailbed on my toe is pulpy, bloody, oozing pus, and throbs like hell, I can't put my boot back on, and in a few steps my foot is smothered in wet mud. I pull off the other boot and join a squad working on a hut.

With their usual incompetence, the Nips don't seem to have made any calculation of the quantities of materials required to build the number of huts needed for the camp, and we are starting to run short. Their theory seems to be that they provide a big heap and we have to make it go round. The sticks of attap thatch should be laid not more than three or four inches apart to keep out rain, and we are having to space it out to such an extent that the rain drips through every-where. Stripping attap from walls and transferring it to roofs goes a little way towards improving the roofs but allows rain to drift in at the sides – the lesser of two evils.

The really sick were moved into the first hut to be roofed on day one, and by the end of day four everyone is under some sort of protection from the weather, but camp sanitation is the next problem. Getting the living quarters erected as fast as possible means there has been no labour available for extend-ing the first hastily dug latrines and cookhouse swillpits, and the start of work on the railway has left us with almost no men in camp physically capable of digging trenches. The latrines are filling rapidly, and being without roofs the heavy rain has aggravated their condition. Most of the tools have gone to the railway sites and we have nothing to dig with.

Men with lesser problems, such as myself, are held back by the medical officers as unfit for work outside the camp. In any civilised situation, we would be classified as sick – persistent diarrhoea and septic sores, for example, all requiring treatment – but a few hours after we start digging we are noticed by the Nips. The sight of men able to use a shovel being kept in camp instead of being in the railway gangs infuriates the Nips and there is immediately an outbreak of shouting and bawling and face-slapping.

Fortunately for us our colonel hears the uproar and comes to investigate. The Nips calm down because they know that the colonel is held in respect by Lieutenant Tanaka, who used to be a schoolteacher and speaks good English. Eventually, Tanaka is persuaded that the risk of fly-borne disease would be as dangerous to his own men as to ours, and we are allowed to complete our digging but are not permitted to put up roofs over the trenches. So the new trenches will fill up quickly, but of greater concern to us is that, when dysentery and diarrhoea compel their use, sick men will have to squat in a downpour of rain while stabbing pains rack their guts, wet and chilled and with no means of drying and warming themselves on return to their huts.

What a depressing dump this is! Heavy purple-grey monsoon clouds seldom allow the sun to shine through, almost constant rain and dripping trees cast gloom everywhere. Steamy heat brings out sweat in streams, and we are worried that the severe deficiency of salt in our rations will result in dehydration and muscular cramps. Our only source of drinking water is tea, which does nothing to replace lost body minerals and is limited in quantity by the simple fact that there are not enough containers to boil the quantities we need.

We who have lived in Singapore and Malaya for some years (some of our men used to travel frequently to Bangkok on business) understand the monsoon cycles and find the climate easier to tolerate than the men who have only recently arrived from Britain and Australia. We know the wet season will dry up by the end of November, and tell them so, but they feel that the bucketing rain (which is far beyond their past experience) will go on forever. They are in a totally alien environment, thousands of miles from home and cut off from even basic civilisation, and at the back of everyone's mind is the depressing knowledge that the war cannot possibly end soon. We have a long haul in front of us. There can be no doubt of that.

The Nips, too, are becoming short-tempered and touchy, and bashings are more frequent as they work off their irritations on us. We Volunteers, having more experience of Asiatics, are better able to assess their moods and catch warning signs of temper, but the other men have not had time to adjust and they get into trouble over minor things, and stoically endure having their faces slapped in Japanese fashion. This is the normal form of summary punishment in the Japanese army – the miscreant is expected to stand at attention and take it in silence and without flinching, and there appears to be no requirement for it to be appropriate in severity to the offence. The slaps are not casual admonishments but are solid blows delivered with an open hand and full straight-arm swing from the shoulder. If you try to roll with it, or fall over, the Nip flies into a screaming rage and really gets to work as a punishment for cowardice.

This morning there is such an incident in the camp. The

matter is trivial but the punishment is savage and gets out of proportion. It is witnessed by one of our junior Volunteer officers, one of the very few junior officers (apart from the MOs) who have shown any real concern for the welfare of their men. We have no choice but to stand around without any show of emotion while the Nip works off his foul temper on his helpless victim, but our officer starts to boil up at the injustice of it all. Marching forward he shouts at the astonished Nip, 'Stop that, you bandy-legged ape!' and heads off towards a Nip sergeant who has been a disinterested spectator nearby. His cheeks flaming crimson with indignation, and without even a tactful salute, he starts to harangue the gunso while gesticulating in our direction. Two minutes later he comes back to us, his cheeks and ears now an even brighter scarlet from the gunso's unfriendly and heavy-handed response. Though defeated, he holds himself straight-backed and is morally a victor (or maybe, a martyr). Someone says quietly as he passes by, 'Bad luck, sir. You did your best and we appreciate it. Thank you from all of us.'

We watch him march stiffly back to the officers' hut. Most of our officers are careful to stay in their part of the camp, out of sight during the day, keeping away from work parties and leaving their men to make out as best they can. True, they visit the men's huts in the evenings, just occasionally, but the men reserve their welcomes for those few who take a genuine interest in their problems, and clearly show that they merely tolerate the others. On the one hand are cheerful smiles and conversation, on the other blank faces and cool politeness.

We feel this morning's beat-up may discourage some of the decent officers from letting themselves become involved but, really, would they achieve anything worthwhile by trying to step between us and the Nips? In practical terms no, they wouldn't, but they would earn our respect if that is of any value to them. Looking after their men is, of course, their prime duty, but this concept quite obviously does not, in their eyes, cover such abnormal circumstances as these. The average British officer, with his lifelong background of social superiority, must find it very difficult to adjust to being confronted by some ignorant barbarian bully who has complete power over him and enjoys using it. Considering the point, we conclude that it might well be better for all concerned if the officers stick to camp administration and the welfare of the sick, leaving the men to develop their natural cunning in day-to-day contact with the Nips. But in fact the officers don't even try to ease the lot of the sick. Their appearance in the 'wards' is a rarity.

At the end of the first two weeks the camp has settled into a defined shape and daily routine. After morning tenko the work parties move off along a track through the forest, about a kilometre to the railway site. In the camp the medical officers hold sick parades consisting, at present, of some 200 men daily, but the numbers are steadily increasing. Nearly every man in the camp is having painful trouble with his bowels, which is not surprising. The rice is filthy and gritty, and the cooks have no facilities at all for washing it. It is boiled in water carried straight from the river which, at this late end of the rainy season, is thick with brown silt and polluted with every kind of refuse from upstream villages, and with dead animals and other rubbish swept off the banks as the river rose when the rains started. There is no means of straining or filtering the water, so every meal and every mug of tea is packed with a wide variety of irritants which scour our innards on the way through.

Diarrhoea, as we now experience it, is no schoolboy joke. Apart from the constant griping pain there is loss of body fluids and salts that cannot be replaced, resulting in increasing debility, cramps and weakness. Heavy physical work puts a severe strain on the whole system, and frequent visits to the latrines at night mean that sleep is reduced to brief snatches between hurried trips outside in the pouring blackness. Just a few days of this is exhausting – two or three weeks may well be fatal. There is no medication and part of the standard treatment is to avoid solid food, which is all very well in a healthy and restful environment but, for us, being told not to eat when we are already starving is sheer nonsense and psychologically unsound.

Our rations come by river, some fifty kilometres (as far as we can judge) from Kanburi, this being the only access route to the camp. There is, we hear, a track linking the camps along the railway trace, but it is absolutely impossible for wheeled traffic in the wet season. We can be provided only with such foodstuffs as will keep long enough to survive the journey, which translates to rice, sweet potatoes, marrows, and Chinese radish – and not much of these – frequently well on the way to rotting by the time they reach us. Dirty rice is served three times a day, sometimes a half teaspoonful of sugar at breakfast, nothing extra at lunch, and in the evening half a pint of smelly hot vegetable water with, maybe, a few shreds of something floating in it. Not very appetising but there is nothing else, frequently not even salt, which makes us especially thankful for our earlier resolve when we were in Kanburi to buy salt in preference to more tempting items such as eggs and fruit.

This totally inadequate diet is bringing men on sick parade with festering sores which will not heal, starting as simple scratches from handling spiky bamboo and growing larger day by day. What look like healthy scabs turn out to be crusts of dried pus floating on thick oozing discharges of disgusting appearance and odour.

45

Most of the men use the river along the camp frontage to rinse off the day's sweat and dirt. There being no soap, they rub themselves down with handfuls of sand, and it helps to refresh and relax their bodies. The Nips have reserved for themselves a stretch upstream, and ostentatiously relieve themselves in the water which will pass through our cookhouse water points, giggling as they do so like the mindless idiots they are. Below the cookhouses is the men's ablution area and the narrow strip of beach is thronged every evening with tired men trying to get themselves clean and wash out their ragged bits of clothing. Even after being sluiced down with clean rain, we can still roll tiny pellets of dirt from our skin by rubbing our fingertips over it. Still, we manage to keep ourselves looking reasonably clean, and at least we don't go to sleep smelling of stale sweat! That indeed would be most unpleasant, lying packed together in our twenty-two inches of bed space.

Some twenty of us, however, have discovered a pleasant little circular cove a couple of hundred yards downstream, secluded and peaceful and reached from a remote corner of the camp area. The sandy beach slopes gently into the water, which is some fifty or sixty metres in diameter, and the river runs in a curve on the far side, creating a slow swirl in the bay and keeping the water fresh. Lying in the shallows I can feel tiny little fish nibbling away at the pus on my toe, crowding in on each other to get at this tasty delicacy. Bless their morbid little appetites! By sprinkling a little crushed rock salt on my toe I am gradually shrinking the lesion, with the unexpected help from my hungry fishy friends.

I am now able to join my brother and friends in the railway gangs, and have my first view of the construction area. It is impressive. From the point where the track from the camp reaches the site a cleared strip runs to left and right, some forty metres in width. Along each flank are the pits from which earth has been dug and carried to form an embankment, the dimensions of which are shown by bamboo poles tied into frameworks indicating height, and widths at top and bottom, and the slope of the sides. A few hundred metres on the far (eastern) side of the cleared strip a high rocky tree-covered ridge extends on either hand.

The men walk along to yesterday's digging spots and get to work, shovelling earth onto stretchers made from rice sacks and bamboo poles, to be carried up on the embankment and dumped. Our group moves on ahead to fell trees and clear undergrowth. It is reasonably pleasant work, for the trees in this open type of forest are not too big and can easily be brought down, trimmed, and dragged to the sides. The difficult obstacles are the clumps of bamboo, anything up to eighty feet tall and thirty feet through, their stems tightly interlocked by small spiky branchlets from bottom to top. If you chop through the outer stems, they are held up by the mass of the clump and cannot be pulled free, so the inner stems cannot be reached. Even a tank wouldn't be able to push them over, so the effective method is to set fire to the stands in the late afternoon, letting them burn themselves out during the night. Bamboo burns with a furious heat, and the tall clumps blaze in a most spectacular display with showers of sparks shooting out amid sharp explosions as the hollow sections explode, crackling like a Chinese fireworks festival.

The saws are rusty with broken teeth, the axes blunt, and we have no rope, but work progresses steadily. Some of our men who are working with the Nip surveyors ahead of us have told us that the ridge which runs parallel to the railway trace curves to meet the river a few hundred metres ahead and it is there that we can expect to run into real problems.

Back in camp we hear some good news at evening tenko. The colonel announces that he has been informed by the Nip commandant that we are to be paid for our labour, ten sattangs a day for privates and fifteen for NCOs, commencing from the first day of work on the railway. Every tenth day will be a rest day, when we will be paid, and contact has been made with local Siamese boatmen who will bring tobacco, eggs, sugar and whatever else may be available. The first rest day will be next Saturday, the thirtieth day, when we will receive all pay due to us, and it is hoped that some supplies will be brought into the camp by then.

'But,' continues the colonel, 'I have ordered that a small deduction be made from each man's pay as a contribution to a central camp fund from which we will purchase necessities for the sick, extra food and, if possible, medical items. I understand very well that you will not like to lose any part of your pay, which is small enough, but we must all help each other, and the simple fact is that there is no other source from which we can raise money. The officers are also being paid, and I am requiring them to accept substantial cuts from their pay as well. I assure you that a welfare fund is absolutely essential, and it will be administered under my personal supervision.'

We have all heard by now that the colonel was a POW in the Great War for over three years, and have no doubt that his experience of that period will be influencing his thinking in the present circumstances. His upright character and real interest in us have become evident during these few weeks, and we are quite ready to accept his ruling as being for the good of all of us.

Even amongst the habitual grumblers and grousers the thought of pay produces a quite dramatic lift in our spirits, and as we brighten in our thoughts and attitudes we realise how we have, without being aware of it, drifted into lengthy silences and humourless conversations. In other words, the situation has been getting us down somewhat, and now something so basically trivial is enough to spring us back to normality. The prospect of money in our hands and 'luxuries' to buy has us all looking forward to Saturday.

When did we last have anything at all to look forward to with any degree of interest?

Friday afternoon comes, and three small Siamese barges pull in to the Nip beach. The Nips have first pick, then our purchasing party is allowed to offload baskets of duck eggs, bananas, packets of tobacco, small cakes of brown palm sugar and sundry other items, to be carried into the cookhouse store for safekeeping. Now isn't that odd? The purchasing party is composed entirely of officers, humping loads from the barges to the store. It is the first time we have seen them doing any kind of manual work (voluntarily at that!) – maybe they feel that ordinary soldiers, who are known to be a thieving shower of rascals, are not to be trusted within reach of such temptations. Or maybe the officers don't want us to know what there is, and want to have first dip after the Nips. Interesting speculations, arising no doubt from our poverty-induced cynicism towards everybody in a more privileged position. Should we be thankful that, being at the end of the queue, our personal consciences will not be put to any test? Can we be sure that our morals would remain as firm as we like to think they would, faced with such an opportunity to get in first?

Saturday morning, we are all awake at dawn as usual, but some clot has decided, without telling us, that reveille will be half an hour later than usual, presumably in honour of the holiday. As a result we are restless and fidgety waiting for breakfast and tenko. Every day we have to get up early when we don't want to, and today we are held back when we want to get started early! It could be that the Nips decided to have a lie-in, and ordered tenko for half an hour later. God, what a lot of fuss about nothing!

Breakfast – a scoop of dirty rice with a bare teaspoon of crude sugar and a mug of plain tea – doesn't take long. Tenko is also brief, a simple count of heads and no sorting out work gangs and tools, and the Nips are still half asleep. Then back to our huts for the important business of the day.

We receive our pay in Siamese currency, which has 100 sattangs to a tical (about thirty-five cents Singapore money, or ten pence sterling, or one shilling Australian), so a private soldier is due one tical for ten days of hard, sweaty labour, less the welfare deduction leaving ninety sattangs to spend. NCOs, with a slightly higher rate of deduction, end up with one tical twenty-five sattangs. We won't get fat on that, but when you have nothing even a tiny bit extra is important.

Right at the start there are problems. The Nips have given the camp administration our pay in random denominations of notes, so it is quite impossible to give every man the exact sum due to him. Also, the goods available are insufficient to set out as in a shop for sale to the public. So the answer is to divide everything as evenly as possible between the huts, where the men form themselves into groups and sort out the money amongst themselves. The smokers, already tightly strung up from weeks of almost total deprivation (some have had small stocks acquired at Kanburi a month ago), say that all the tobacco should go to them. The non-smokers object, claiming entitlement to a fair share which they can pass on to friends or sell. Or, they suggest, smokers should have all the tobacco and non-smokers all the eggs, sugar, etc.

The mood of happy anticipation starts to change rapidly into bad temper and futile squabbles about fair shares and greediness. Weeks of stress, due to our miserable living conditions, come to explosion point, and the hut is full of quarrelling, swearing men working off their frustrations, until a stentorian bellow tells them to 'SHUT UP! QUIET! Pay attention! There are 160 men in this hut, that is sixteen groups of ten men. The stores have been divided into sixteen lots, share and share alike, and they cost nine bucks fifty each lot. Come up in groups of ten, hand over your money, and take your pile out of the hut. When everybody is through you can come back in. And I'm not having any argument from anybody, is that clear?'

The voice of authority brings the men back to tolerant good humour. They have had their outburst and now are content to wait their turn.

Soon the air reeks with fumes from shaggy Siamese tobacco, acrid and biting, and eggs cooked in mess tins filled with tea boiling over small fires. There is an acute shortage of paper for rolling cigarettes. The best by far is pages from Bibles and prayer books, which brings objections from many men who feel strongly that these books should not be used for such a demeaning purpose. But religious principles give way to the desperate need for tobacco ('I'll only use the pages we won't need, like the marriage service.' 'Well hang on to the funeral section, we'll probably have to use that before long.') Those with a pipe fill the bowl smugly, but the tobacco's super-hot embers soon have them gasping and choking with the others.

Duck eggs, bananas, and sticky toffee-tasting palm sugar – sheer luxury and almost intoxicating after living so long on insipid, unpalatable rubbish. You can actually FEEL them doing you good. We need so little to cheer us up, which must be a fair indication of how much pressure there has been on us. Tomorrow we shall go back to work with our spirits much revived. With the prospect of a yasumi day with pay at regular intervals, the future looks more tolerable. Just a little.

What we miss, very badly indeed, is mail from home. Do our families know anything about us? Has the Red Cross been able to pass out any information at all? Are our families okay?

What about bombing raids at home? Any casualties among families and friends? Those of us who were living in Singapore and Malaya have particular concern for wives, children and friends now in Japanese hands – it is impossible to be optimistic about their circumstances. And on the last Friday, 13 February, two days before Singapore capitulated, it is known that a fleet of small ships, coasters and launches attempted a final evacuation – what happened to them? Not knowing anything at all is most depressing, but it is pointless to think about it too much. But how can any one of us *not* think about it?

Part of our personal gear left behind at Kanburi has been dumped on our beach. It has been badly looted, and what is left is green with mildew.

In the evenings when it's raining and we can't gather outside around a cheerful fire, we lie on the bamboo slats in our dark huts and take turns in providing some sort of entertainment. No compulsion, but boredom is a great destroyer of morale, so we all try to think of something to contribute which might be of interest or make others laugh. Our George, for instance, has a very pleasant Irish tenor, and his singing of Irish folk songs such as 'Danny Boy' is always very easy to listen to. His own favourite, however, is 'Macushla', which seems to run to at least ninety-nine verses, all of which must be sung from beginning to end without interruption. A bit tedious, but never mind – it's the willingness that counts.

There are any number of personal yarns, childhood events, adventures, party occasions of one kind or another when Uncle Joe disgraced himself or Aunt Agatha embarrassed everybody. Ron and I contribute bits of our life in Shanghai in the 1920s, such as being chased by water buffaloes (which left me scared of ordinary cows when we came to England), and how we wore genuine bearskin overcoats and hoods during the ferocious Shanghai winters which blew down direct from Siberia. We Volunteers, some of whom have lived in other parts of Asia and have travelled widely, have a background which provides all kinds of tales.

Our slats are uneven and knobbly and not at all comfortable, but we have become used to them, and I find that the shadowy atmosphere allows me to either listen to what's being told or to relax with my own thoughts. After a day's heavy physical slog in sticking mud and drenching rain, it is pleasant to be able to mentally detach myself from our surroundings, and drift away on a soothing murmur of voices.

We are well into November, nine months in captivity, and things have definitely deteriorated as time has passed. From being confident soldiers of a proud empire bearing the torch of civilisation, we have become coolie slaves of a brutish nation which has not yet dragged itself out of its medieval sludge.

It has become quite apparent to all of us that we have been, by force of circumstances, reduced to living like animals in many ways; but only in our physical lives, for we remain in spirit determinedly human beings holding tightly to personal pride and dignity. As our living conditions deteriorate, so do we become increasingly obstinate in keeping our spiritual values high.

It is almost incredible that we are still on our planet, so absolute is our severance and isolation from practically every aspect of civilisation. Our world has shrunk to a few acres of forest and rocky hillsides and the brown river winding through them. There are no voices – telephone, radio, newspapers or mail – from outside, and the world beyond does not know where we are, or even if we exist. A few crude hand tools, the occasional launch or barge on the river and the Nips' rifles are all we have to remind us of man's ingenuity. Silence, apart from our own voices, wraps us in a thick shroud.

The crude side of life is inescapable. Like work animals in some remote and primitive corner of the earth we sweat and toil all day in return for miserably poor food and a dirt-floored leaky shelter. At work we relieve ourselves wherever it happens to be necessary, moving away a distance (collecting a few leaves as we do so) and, like a cat, we dig a hole to bury our droppings. The sun scorches our unprotected hide and the tumultuous rain sluices off it almost unheeded. Cold tea is the only remedy for eyes irritated by the glare and dust, and if your nose needs clearing just press a fingertip to one nostril and blow.

We have almost none of the small items that we used to consider essential for personal comfort. The Nips have provided absolutely nothing, so each man's possessions are precisely what he brought into camp with him. My brother and I each have a toothbrush and a comb, a pair of nail scissors between us, and these are rare treasures. Sharing is a thing of the past. A few men have a cut-throat straight razor which is useless because there is no way to keep a proper edge on it, and in any event no kind of soap. If anything is lost or broken, or rots or falls to pieces, you manage without it. If your spectacles crack you must get along with poor eyesight, and the Australian soldier who (in front of me) sneezed violently at the latrine and catapulted his dentures into the trench may even be glad there is nothing to chew in his food. (Incidentally, he did manage to retrieve them, fishing with the splintered end of a bamboo wand. He boiled them in his mess tin for hours before putting them back into his mouth. He gave me a great beaming smile to prove it!)

Despite adventure yarns in *The Boys Own Paper* of our schooldays – God, was it only six or seven years ago? – teeth cannot be kept bright and white with the frayed end of a green twig, nor can shoes be made from tree bark. Nor can we find sharp-edged chips of flint to shave, or fish bones to comb our hair.

Necessity being the mother of adaptation, the absence of replacement clothing has compelled us to resort to use of the Nip-style fundoshi, a kind of much-abbreviated loincloth (or slightly enlarged G-string) as standard wear for all occasions. A rectangle of cloth, cut from a shirt or trousers and tied at the waist, provides minimal decency, and a spare gives you something to change into to sleep at night. One does like to be as civilised as possible!

So our appearance at tenko parades would break the heart of any visiting regimental sergeant-major. Hundreds of bare-footed men, gaunt and wearing nothing but a fundoshi and a hat (any kind of protection from the sun and shade for the eyes), with weeks of unkempt beard and hair, uncleaned teeth and broken nails (fingers and toes), all this decorated with sundry scabs and weeping sores dotted over undernourished bodies. It is the same for everyone, philosophically accepted as our current way of life, because there is no choice and that is simply the beginning and end of the matter. We have no alternative but to come to terms with this most uncomfortable and unpleasant situation.

There is no fence around the camp; none is needed. Any man can walk out at any time, but where would he go? Thousands of miles from his own people and allies, and standing out starkly in the local population who would be rewarded for his recapture, there can be no thought of escape.

Apart from these trivial discomforts and other problems we really have nothing to complain about. After all, we are fed three times a day, have sufficient work to keep us from being bored, and do not have to put up with well-meaning but tiresome attentions when we are sick. And no nagging wives, jealous girlfriends, mothers-in-law, or taxation officials can bother us. On top of all that our kindly hosts count us at least twice a day to ensure that we are not foolish enough to be tempted to leave this paradise for somewhere less comfortable. Well, that's one way of looking at it!

God, stay with us! If you know where we are. Could we have some indication that you do? Please?

I have been doing some reminiscing. We all do it, but this time it started with a hazy thought in the back of my mind, scenes from when I was some eight years old, in the late 1920s.

During the last few years of my childhood in Shanghai, we lived on the far edge of the residential area of the International Concession, in a block of flats near the junction of the main thoroughfare into the city itself, Yu Yuen Road, and Kinnear Road coming in from the eastern suburbs. Before us was open countryside, farming land with yellow mustard and white cotton, a high embankment carrying the main railway line and station half a mile away, and only a few hundred yards to the right was the gated entrance to Jessfield Park.

In the open space between our flats and the road junction was a pond, with not-too-clean water, and a clump of shady trees. There was little motor traffic, but a busy flow of pedestrians to and from the villages just beyond the railway embankment. Sturdy Chinese peasants carried heavy loads on springing bamboo yokes shaped to fit across their shoulders, rickshaw pullers trotted with passengers and goods, farm produce was brought in and manufactured goods taken out. Squads of soldiers straggled past, and funeral processions were frequent.

What I noticed in particular, however, was that the grassy area and shady trees tempted people to stop and rest for a while. The labourer would lower his two bundles and buy tea or noodle soup from the little swarm of portable stalls, coffin-bearers and mourners would stop for refreshment, soldiers fall out for a 'smoko' and to form rings for throwing cards and dice. And in doing these things, everybody – men and women, ancients and children alike – folded their legs into the same position. With their feet flat on the ground, knees bent so that the backs of their thighs pressed against their calves, they squatted comfortably and rose upright easily and without any sign of cramps, even after extended periods of crouching.

I think now how useful it would sometimes be to assume this posture but when I try to do it myself, I find that I fall over backwards and can only keep my balance if I lean forward on my toes with my heels clear of the floor, and within two minutes my ankles and knees are aching intolerably. Sometimes I can't straighten up and have to fall over sideways before I can get up.

Thinking back over those days, a dozen or so years back, I decide there must be a way to adapt. Obviously the first requirement is to stretch the tendons above the heels and around the knee joints, so we begin to practise during our evening chat sessions around the campfire, using a small branch under our heels to support our body weight. Gradually it becomes possible to lengthen the period without pain, and to use a thinner branch.

The benefit of being able to do this Asiatic squat is astonishing. If you are physically tired from pick and shovel work, standing up gives no relief and there is nowhere to sit because the ground is streaming with rain, so the squat is the answer. We find we can squat, balanced and comfortable, for lengthy periods while we eat rice, talk to each other, smoke a fag, even doze off, totally relaxed and yet able to straighten up without a twinge or even any effort. It enables us to straddle a latrine trench without wobbling or the risk of falling in, without strain on the feet and legs – and, if you think about it, the position must be helpful in emptying the bowels! It's all truly remarkable – such a simple thing and so beneficial. We take note of even the smallest thing that contributes to making our life a little easier.

It is a good idea for those, such as ourselves, who have been accustomed to commonplace objects like chairs and tools, to take a good look at the way things are done by people who have never had these advantages and yet manage to grow crops and shift heavy loads, and make themselves reasonably comfortable, with only muscles and ingenuity to work with. Their capabilities, developed over centuries of patient trials, should most certainly be admired rather than looked down upon as primitive and crude. To accomplish much where there is little on hand to work with is indeed an achievement in itself. In our Western societies we have gone for practical inventions whereas the Chinese have preferred to create works of art of incredible delicacy and beauty. Maybe we shall all be sufficiently intelligent to learn from each other at some time in the future.

We have also come to understand fully, and to respect sympathetically, the Asiatic peasant's deep feelings for rice, which he holds as sacred. A vast amount of backbreaking labour – creating nurseries and planting out each young stem separately in its paddy field, irrigating and harvesting – is behind every meal. Millions of people are totally dependent on the success of each year's crop, for often it is almost the only food available to them. Home-grown vegetables and occasional fish from rivers and ponds are valuable supplements, but ducks, chickens, eggs and pork are special treats for they usually have to be sold to bring in cash for clothing and household goods and are not so plentiful as to provide more than an infrequent treat. So rice is the basic stomach-filler, the provider of warm food in the belly and energy for work. Without it, they starve. It's as simple as that! Not a single grain may be wasted!

As a matter of interest, there has never been sufficient land to spare in China for raising cattle and sheep – unless you go right up north to Manchuria. Consequently, these meats are entirely unknown, and there is no dairy industry, so milk and cheese have never appeared in Chinese meals.

We, in our present circumstances, are similarly dependent on rice for all our bodily needs, but in our case there is little or no supplement provided by the Nips, yet they expect us to do heavy physical work. The rice which they give us is of the poorest quality, frequently swept off the earth floor of a rice store, and a torn or nearly empty bag is issued to us counted as a full bag. Rotting vegetables are not recognised as uneatable, diseased meat is considered wholesome. We are now in a state where food, food, food saturates our collective consciousness.

We are shrouded in a depressing helplessness, we cannot expect any improvement, and we are fully aware that if it goes on for too long, we shall exhaust our reserves and die.

I know of no man who finds support in his religious faith – rather, there is cynicism and deep disappointment at the total absence of comfort – yet a few do adhere to their principles. One of us is a Jew in his early thirties, and he has a big personal dilemma. What little food with any flavour the cookhouse can give us is usually a greasy riceball fried in pig fat. This, of course, is totally unacceptable to him, and he has refused to eat his ration. But it is the only palatable item we have, not very often at that, and having to do without is a serious matter and demands a strong will.

None of us can contemplate missing out on a large proportion of any meal – our minds and bodies protest urgently at the very thought. But our Jewish friend always gives away his riceball, sometimes accepting plain rice in return. All of us are glad to have the extra mouthful, but at the same time we are reluctant to see him depriving himself.

Religion can be curious in its demands. What is binding on some is looked upon by others as quaint, unnecessary, even amusing. But Charles is adamant, his upbringing is too strong for him to disobey. Our medical officer gets to hear of this and talks to him about the absolute need to eat every available scrap of food. Charles has no rabbi or spiritual adviser to consult, and eventually he decides to follow the MO's advice. He will eat a riceball fried in pig fat and hope that our stringent circumstances will justify his decision and that some kind of spiritual cleansing will, eventually, make him whole again.

He finds it to be a traumatic experience, overcoming his strong reluctance to break the kosher laws of his people, and it takes over an hour to force the objectionable rice down into his stomach. I think he is murmuring prayers all the time. But he doesn't sleep that night. He feels that he has fouled not only his body, but also his soul. Never again will he submit himself to such enormous stress. He will starve rather than offend his religion if that is the way it is to be.

We can understand his feelings, and have real sympathy for him. What we cannot figure out is how a religion can continue to enforce rules which may have been practical a couple of thousand years ago, but nowadays are not really necessary.

And in this we do not confine our thinking to the Jewish faith alone, or to food only. Christianity seems to us to harbour a lot of beliefs which may have impressed illiterate generations in the past, but have no real relevance to today's better educated adherents who really cannot accept them. But then, lots of highly intelligent folk do accept them – it may be that they draw some inner strength from their beliefs which we more cynical fellows do not know about. Whatever the truth may be, it is, I think, important to feel comfortable with your beliefs, accepting and rejecting as seems right to you.

I wonder if this attitude might have resulted from the determined efforts of our school chaplain to stuff religion down our throats so that it came to be uninspiring, of less interest to us than our classroom studies, interfering with what should have been our free time, resented as meaningless. I remember our chaplain – a most unprepossessing and unlikeable man in his person – bemoaning during a sermon the fact that in his sixteen years at the college, not a single boy had gone into holy orders after leaving. We could have told him the reason!

Clearance of the trees along the surveyors' line has been completed, and all working parties are now employed building the foundation to carry the sleepers and rails. In the Wampo section, this requires a continuous earth embankment some thirteen kilometres in length to provide a constantly level surface for the track. The height to which we must build varies with the dips and slopes of the land itself. Generally it's between one metre and three metres, and therefore not really a problem for a properly equipped and organised workforce.

Such a workforce we definitely are not. The soil, washed down from the rocky limestone hillside over the centuries, has never been broken before our arrival and has compacted to concrete hardness. Without heavy boots you cannot drive a spade into hard ground, so it must first be broken up with a pick, which will not penetrate if its point is blunt. Beneath the surface lies a tangled mass of tree roots which must be chopped through with a sharp-edged spade before any earth can be dug out. Our equipment is as basic as it can be and of poor quality, a miscellany of spades, shovels and pickaxes for digging, and changkols, which are new to us. Changkols are similar to a hoe, but with a heavy steel blade fixed at right angles to a long stout handle. They combine the qualities of a spade and a pickaxe, and are remarkably effective in chopping into the earth and, with a twist of the wrist, you can toss your load almost as far as with a spade. They are used by barefoot farmers from India to the Philippines. Tongas (stretchers made of jute sacks and bamboo poles) carry the spoil from the digging pit to be dumped on the embankment. Tonga loads are not easily carried up a muddy slope in streaming rain by men with bare feet which cannot get a grip, so that even a short climb becomes a slogging, slithery scramble, which is physically and mentally exhausting. So much, so impossibly much, human effort to dump a few shovels of earth in place!

It must be obvious, even to the thick-brained Nips, that this relatively simple work could be done much faster by well-fed men with good tools, but of course they see things differently. At evening tenko it is announced that work is behind schedule, we are lazy and do not have the Japanese soldier's spirit of bushido, which inspires him to overcome difficulties and to achieve his objects. So we cannot be allowed to continue to work at our own speed, and in future we shall be required to dig and dump on the embankment one cubic metre of earth per man per day. This will be measured and must be completed before returning to camp at the end of the day. Further, we have been taking dishonourable advantage of their lenient and generous treatment of us, whose lives (we must not forget!) we owe to the Emperor. We have been keeping men in camp pretending to be sick, and more men must be turned out to work in future. It shows ingratitude to the Emperor.

Well, quite plainly our concept of the spirit of bullshito (sorry, bushido), which we first heard about way back in Changi, is not the same as theirs, so we shall have to see how things develop. We sort ourselves out into squads of six, which means excavating a pit two metres by three metres and one metre deep, and carrying the soil on to the embankment. A Nip will measure each pit when we claim we have completed our quota.

Having assumed that we have been working too slowly, we are now surprised to find that by the midday rice break we are actually ahead of schedule and have now been ordered to do less than we were when working at our own pace, when we didn't have a set minimum! The word rapidly passes along to slow down for the afternoon and spin the work out until four o'clock, and tomorrow to adjust to an easier rate. No difficulty here since the Nips, having been relieved of the need to watch us all the time to prevent slacking, have moved into the shade of the trees alongside the track to doze off, knowing that we cannot leave until we call them to check our digging pits.

Late this afternoon we have our work measured with a bamboo pole notched at one-metre lengths. Each pit is meticulously square at the corners and the walls and floor are shaved to a millimetre – we are not digging a spoonful more than necessary. In a week or so we shall be able to tidy up old pits and pass them off as today's, shovelling earth straight into a nearby pit, which is much easier than carrying it up to the top of the embankment. The big difference is that the old way required earth to be put where it was wanted, whereas now we merely have to produce a suitable sized pit. The heavy rain quickly blurs outlines, and since there have to be some 200 new pits every day, the Nips can easily be fooled.

Then it all goes wrong, within a couple of weeks of settling in to our unexpected good fortune. Some of our men are so blindly stupid that they cannot see a good thing when they are standing in it. In their blatant selfishness (or simple-mindedness) they have to spoil things for everyone, including themselves. Among us we have coalminers from Wales and Northumberland, born with a pickaxe in one hand and a big pan shovel in the other, and they have formed themselves into elite teams capable of knocking over their quota in quick time. Their sick and weaker fellows are left to fend for themselves.

The totally predictable result is that men are returning to camp at midday, and this becomes noticed by the Nips. Why are fit men roaming around the camp area so early, while others are straggling in just before evening tenko? The retaliation is immediate and the workload increased a straight fifty per cent. Those responsible are cursed richly and with great feeling.

In imperial measurements, this works out at two tons per man – that is twelve tons of earth for each squad to dig, lift, carry and dump. According to conditions, a squad might have two diggers and two tongas or, if the earth is difficult, four diggers and a single tonga. In the latter arrangement the work is slow and backbreaking and twelve tons in a day is a hell of a lot to shift. It is intensely hot and humid, and since we are always in the open we have no protection from rain or sun. The strain starts to tell on us, some squads not being able to get back to camp by tenko time, which upsets the Nips in the camp. It also means that the Nips at the worksite have to wait there and become irritable and unpleasant.

The Nips, of course, have a solution. Every morning they will set up a marker at the further end of the track, and the embankment will be filled to this point before anyone leaves. We shall still work in convenient groups, but now the responsibility for the day's quota will rest on everybody. In theory, this means that the strong will help the weak, but in practice, selfishness rules and many of the fit men deliberately dawdle through the day out of sheer bloody-mindedness. But some, indeed, do work steadily, then cheerfully move along the track and help out where they are needed. A few of the senior NCOs and warrant officers who know the men well remind the slackers that the new rules have everybody under our own discipline again.

This is, of course, really a matter for the officers to handle, but as has been the case since we arrived at Wampo, they show no interest. I have seen officers on the worksite only twice. One of them had his ears warmed up by an irate Nip and that was the last of them. Through necessity, we have sized up the Nips and Koreans and know reasonably well how to cope with them. The officers in general, however, seem absolutely incapable of adjusting or comprehending, and we have a strong suspicion that the stumbling block is their inability to accept the hard fact that their rank means absolutely nothing to the lowest Nip private soldier. Rather than learn how to deal with them, they hide away in the officers' huts, keeping out of everybody's way. The prominent exceptions are our commanding officer, the colonel, and his immediate group of senior officers, and the medical officers, who stand out as men of conscience and determination. Too often it's a case of 'In action he was a first class officer, but as a POW he is just bloody useless. Too worried about his personal dignity.'

A few of our lads with experience in land surveying have been working with Nip engineers, laying out the alignment for clearing the ground and setting up posts with painted markers indicating the height of the embankment to be built.

Pushing their way through the forest to find the markers already set up by Nip railway engineers, they have found two surveyors' cairns identified as having been erected by British army engineers in 1912. The distances shown are some twelve kilometres less than the Nip distances, indicating either a different starting point or another route.

Two of our older men who have worked in the timber forests up north around Chiang Mai tell us they heard of this project when the British army carried out a preliminary investigation, at the request of the Siamese government, into the possibility of a railway link with Burma. The purpose was to shorten the trade route from the Indian Ocean to the Far East by eliminating the 3,000-mile sea voyage down the Straits of Malacca to Hong Kong. A canal through the Kra Isthmus had been a similar idea. The railway project was abandoned when serious difficulties were found – rainfall amongst the highest known in the world, mountainous terrain with thick forests, no food supplies available in the area and prevalent diseases such as malaria, seasonal cholera and hookworm. Further, no labour force could be raised locally, because the natives already knew of these unpleasant facts.

The significance of this bit of history does nothing at all to cheer us up. Before leaving Singapore we had heard rumours of a major sea action in which the Japanese fleet had been crippled. The situation is now clear to us. If Japan becomes unable to supply her armies in Burma, on the massive scale required, by sea to Rangoon, a railway linking Saigon and Singapore to Burma is the one and only answer. There are no roads across the border, anywhere. Therefore our railway is top priority and we and other POWs are the unlucky bunnies who will have to build it. Great news indeed! May a multitude of blessings, preferably in the form of heavy bombs, fall on Emperor Hirohito's head!

And there's more! Ever optimistic, someone points out that when the Nips are inevitably driven out of Burma, an awful lot of Nip troops, in a foul temper, are going to retreat into Siam along our railway, and we shall be right in their way. And when they build defences in Siam, they won't want thousands of Allied soldiers in the same area. Logic has it that we shall all simply be killed off.

With these comforting thoughts in our minds we stretch out on our knobbly bamboo slats and go to sleep.

The rocky ridge running along our eastern flank takes a curve southwards until it meets the river. The end of the ridge falls sheer to the water, leaving no ground where the railbed can be carried through. The alternatives appear to be a tunnel of several thousand feet in length, or a massive cutting across the ridge from the crest down to the level of the railway.

The Nip commandant wants to know whether we have men experienced in digging tunnels, but we suddenly find that we were all office clerks and shop assistants in our previous lives. It gives us the shudders to think of all that digging – mostly rock, it would be – with primitive tools and a total disregard for safety, lighting or ventilation, slithering around on bare feet in the last few weeks of torrential monsoon rains.

Malnutrition, undernourishment, starvation, call it what you will. There may be medical or technical variations in what should be understood by each word, but for us they are all the same, even (you might say) rolled into one, and the consequences to our health have become visible, painful, smelling, contagious – every man has some, or all, of these disagreeable and uncomfortable symptoms and we have nothing whatsoever to alleviate them.

The deficiencies in our diet result in open sores which will not heal, intestinal problems which trouble us day and night, blurred eyesight and uncertain balance, drumming headaches, and skin sensitive to the hot blast of the sun. Without a clean water supply, or soap, or antiseptic, or dressings, broken skin quickly develops running lesions and ulcers. Ringworm spreads alarmingly in dull rainbow arcs, scabies intensifies from itching to fiery little pustules.

The monsoon rain is both a curse and a blessing. It adds to the sheer physical effort of our work on the railway, but it helps to wash our bodies. On days without rain, our sweat irritates open sores and carries dirt into them, the sun burns the raw patches and brings out the big blue-green flies to feed upon them.

Your personal situation is a matter of luck, it seems. Every man has some kind of problem, some only a few and others more than a fair share. One of the gunners has a multicoloured shawl of ringworm starting under his chin and swathed over his shoulders, halfway down his chest and back, as if he had been attacked by a mad tattooist with octopus arms. Others have small circular designs dotted around at random. There is no consistency about it.

By far the worst afflictions are those resulting from beri-beri and pellagra, both of which have long lists of symptoms that seem to strike haphazardly. There is no sequence by which you progress (if you can call it that) from one stage to the next. Any symptom can appear along with others at any time, and one man will differ from another in his sufferings.

With pellagra, the skin discolours where the sun strikes most, resulting in blotchy mauve patches separated by dry and scaly brownish streaks. The roof of the mouth burns and the sensitive fine tissue of the palate peels off in shreds which dangle on your furred and aching tongue. Even cold tea is painful to swallow, and cold rice is torture – like hot gravel. Only raw eggs can slip down without too much discomfort. But eggs from outside don't become available often, and even then the quantities are small and the medical officers have priority for the sick. The sick? We are all sick, of course, but things are relative here and they are in a worse condition than we are, God help them, so they must come first. We don't complain.

I think beri-beri is, in some ways, even worse. I have had spells of both, like scores of other men, and really there is no ground for comparison, but most of us seem to feel one thing in common. It could well be that one particular aspect is so personal, so intimately involving one's basic instincts for survival and siring children. It is variously referred to as Sore Balls, Red Balls, Itchy Balls, Burning Balls, Fiery Balls, and (in a despairing scream) Oh God, My Flaming Balls, and other imaginative imprecations.

The first sign is an itching in the scrotum, which quickly intensifies. The skin thickens and loses its softness, cracks appear and a thick serum starts to ooze out. The adjacent skin in the crotch then begins to sweat a sticky film, the whole area takes on a brick-red hue, and there is a vaguely unpleasant odour. I cannot find a word which comes anywhere near describing the sheer intensity, the depth, of the burning irritation of this affliction. It is, of course, a naturally sensitive area of the body and therefore particularly liable to magnify an itch.

There is nothing you can do to ease it. Scratching is not only ineffective but provokes waves of even worse pain, and is also very likely to introduce infection. In desperate moments I almost wish I had a razor blade to slash away the torment, but then I'm thankful no blade is handy or I might really be tempted!

Then – mysteriously, because we have had no improvement in diet – the awful itching fades and life is bearable again. But it is hell while it lasts!

Also prevalent is avitaminosis. The most usual manifestation is deteriorating eyesight – weak and blurred vision – in which the Nips are not the slightest bit interested. There is often nothing outwardly visible so they simply do not accept that anything is wrong. It takes careful juggling on our part to keep afflicted men out of the danger areas, because the Nips watch the numbers in their gangs and it is risky to slip away into another squad. So far we have been able to avoid accidents, for which we are thankful, but there is a real risk always hanging in the background and there is nothing we can do to lessen it. We can only cope with whatever happens when it happens.

One possibility which has worried our medical officers but has not yet occurred, as far as I know, is that the lack of boots raises the risk of hookworm, a most unpleasant disease which results from bare feet picking up parasites from the earth. The result is intestinal problems and anaemia, against which we have no defence and no treatment. Since it is a common disease in this part of the world, we are indeed fortunate – perhaps it is due to the fact that we are working on previously untouched soil, and the parasites are not established. Who knows?

When our shirts and trousers started to rot a few weeks after our arrival in Wampo and some men started to cut them up into Nip-style fundoshis, our officers accused them (quite seriously!) of being 'Jap-happy', going native, letting the side down! Within a week the whole camp followed suit – no pun intended – because it was so obviously sensible and practical.

Wearing only a fundoshi and hat, we are free from acidic rashes from sweaty clothing, and from chafing seams and belts, which would inevitably turn into septic sores – of which we already have more than enough!

Looking back, if we had obeyed our officers and continued to wear such items of clothing as we had, everything would have rotted away beyond the point of being useable, and we would then have been, quite simply, absolutely naked and totally without any means of doing anything about it. There's no point in saying that, in such circumstances, the Nips would have had to supply clothing – the plain fact is that the Nips never *have* to do anything for us! Ordinary humanity is unknown to them.

The officers themselves, of course, lazing in the comparative coolness of their huts all day, do not have our problems and are unable – not interested? – to see the simple hard and inescapable realities which decide how we live and work. Isn't it odd that the rank and file, not very well educated for the most part, seem to have far more insight and recognition of practical issues, and respond more sensibly to problems than their well-educated officers, who have difficulty accepting – and adapting to – new and awkward conditions? Maybe the officers are too accustomed to throwing items away and buying replacements and cannot 'make do'.

And while I am thinking of education, why is it that nobody knows of a single officer who has *learned* to speak Japanese, when communication between us and the Nips is such a critically important factor in our lives? There are a few who lived as children in Japan and grew up speaking Japanese, including that unpleasant bastard we met when we crossed the river near Kanburi. But the interpreter in our camp back in Singapore (and he is here in Wampo) is one of us Volunteers, a private soldier. In the early days in Changi, there were four of our fellows learning from books which had turned up from somewhere, one of them being a White Russian refugee from the communist revolution who had come to us via Shanghai.

Maybe we Volunteers have a special ability to see different aspects. All of us are men of university or similar education, or have professional qualifications – otherwise, quite simply, our employers would never have sent us out to the East – yet the way things have happened, we are all in the ranks, never having had any chance of obtaining a commission. So we are uniquely placed to observe, talk to all and sundry, and criticise, and I see no need at all to apologise for our conclusions and opinions. The sheer waste of brains and talent – scientists and professional men toting a rifle as private soldiers – is typical of the panicky irresolution of civilian and military chiefs in Singapore.

I have had the great good fortune to have access to a most interesting book. Because of its highly technical nature, I have had to read through it several times in order to acquire a fair understanding of its general principles, its detailed reasonings and findings being outside my experience. It belongs to one of our Volunteers, a highly qualified food chemist who used to work for a big food processing company in Singapore. Before that he worked in the laboratories of one of Britain's major dairy and small goods producers and, aside from that, represented Britain as a breaststroke swimmer in the Berlin Olympic Games in 1936.

The book, *The Chemistry of Nutrition*, is the latest professional summary of the relationship between various foods and human health and diseases, and is written by two research scientists presenting and evaluating all that has so far been published in scientific papers. It seems that the first real studies in this field were prompted by attempts to find out why beri-beri is so prevalent in some areas of Japan, its causes and effects, treatment and residual damage. From these investigations developed a whole new field of sciences: the discovery of vitamins and their importance in physical and mental health; the values of a long list of minerals; and the consequences of deficient supplies to the body, their interaction and mutual stimulation, the bodily organs which store and utilise them, and the length of time for which a properly nourished body may hold them to protect against periods of inadequate replenishment – a complicated mass which has become more and more complex as research has probed more and more deeply.

So far there is working knowledge of vitamins A, B1, B2, C and D, and there are firm indications of many more to be discovered. In relatively few years of research, a lot has been found, together with the knowledge that it is only a beginning and that there is no way of estimating how much there is still to be learned.

The book tracks the progress of different foods from the moment they are put into the mouth, through being broken down by this or that bodily secretion, their transformation into new substances suitable for absorption and utilisation by specific organs, and their part in the overall harmonious functioning of the body. Chemistry was never my good subject at school, but at least I can follow the reasoning well enough.

While I find all this intensely interesting, it is also more than a little depressing. I now understand why my balls itch with a fiery intensity and why my mouth is raw inside. I also know what is needed to put things right and, further, I know bloody well that the Nips will not provide it! The logic is that my condition will – quite inevitably – worsen until I either disintegrate or simply drop dead. The book does not go as far as telling me how the end will come, but I'm not really interested in knowing. I cannot ignore the symptoms, they are too painful for that, so I have no choice but to be philosophical and hope for the best. In the meantime, like every other man in the camp, I have no option but to survive as best as I can.

But, Jesus Christ – and he doesn't seem to be helping – it's a dismal prospect.

Another change in routine is ordered by the Nips. Instead of walking back to camp for midday rice, then returning to work, we shall have breakfast served before daylight and carry rice to work, thus saving good working time. The lunch break will be signalled by the Nips, knocking off and starting again, the rice cold and insipid.

And today a nasty surprise, so unpleasant as to be literally stomach-turning. We ate our breakfast in the dark, and at midday pick up our mess tins to find the rice full of boiled white maggots and black pellets which are clearly rat droppings. Did we eat this muck for breakfast? Without noticing it, in the pre-dawn blackness? We are accustomed to river silt and dirt in our rice, but this is disgusting. There is far too much to pick out and throw away, maggots and rat shit are distributed throughout, clinging to the rice grains so that removing them would also remove two-thirds of your meal. Already well on the way to starvation, we simply cannot afford to lose that much food.

Some wag says, 'Well, I suppose it's thoroughly cooked and sterilised!', as we reluctantly poke around trying to force ourselves to spoon it into our mouths. And there's more – pale remnants of the cobwebby nests which rodents like to build inside the sacks of rice, the strands running everywhere, almost invisible. Without any doubt, this is rice swept from the floor of a storage godown, fouled stock which is normally destroyed as inedible. Sheer hunger wins out, as it must do when a man is literally on the edge of survival. There might even be proteins in it!

What's on the menu? Dirty rice with boiled maggot and ratshit garnish! I must recommend it to the chefs at the Savoy when I get back to London. They will never have dreamed up anything so exotic, even to relieve monotonous wartime rationing!

Back in camp this evening we find that all the latest delivery of rice is the same, so we are stuck with eating this filth for at least a fortnight. We cannot possibly do without it for so long. There is nothing else to eat; we do not have any choice.

We also discover that some pigs have been supplied, brought to the camp by barge. These wretched animals are stuffed into long tubular open-work baskets, unable to move, and sometimes stacked three deep in the boat. Those on the bottom are crushed, with broken ribs and legs, too exhausted to squeal after several days of torture, and most have fearsome ulcers. Probably they have had neither food nor water; their condition is pitiful. And they have been gnawed by rats.

Our medical officers have looked at them, thoughts of anthrax in their minds, and most of the pigs are condemned as unfit for our consumption. The Nips may claim they have supplied meat, but that doesn't do us any good if we can't eat it. Like the nauseating rice, we suspect the Nip quartermaster has done a deal by buying cheap rubbish and pocketing the difference. There is not even a rumour that a protest might have been lodged by our administration. It would have been futile anyway.

Our contempt for the Japanese nation is now absolute. If this sort of thing represents the attitude of the army command, what sort of future do we have?

Well, surprise, surprise! The Nip camp commandant has said we may organise a concert for an evening before a yasumi day in the near future and the colonel calls for anyone who wishes to perform, or to help as stagehands, to come forward. It seems that we have amongst us officers and men with experience in professional shows, as producers and players, and some also can sing – and there's that fellow who carried a piano accordion from Ban Pong, for someone who could play it. There is also a bugle and a trumpet, and a quite surprising miscellany of instruments which can be tooted, banged and twanged, all ingeniously put together in the camp from bits of this and that – including telephone wire unknowingly contributed by Nip army signals.

A raised earth platform is shovelled up to form a stage, and bamboo matting taken from the cookhouses to make a backdrop and side screens. The matting is daubed with white ash and soot to depict an Italian-style villa with a terrace, a low stone balustrade with urns and statues, and poplar trees dwindling in perspective into the background. In the flickering orange glow of two heaped fires, one off each front corner, the whole scene has a pleasing moonlit effect. It is nine o'clock, a calm dark night soft with the warmth of the tropics.

The colonel and the Jap commandant seat themselves centre-front on a bamboo bench, a few Nips flanking their officer, and our own officers alongside the colonel and filling the second row. Looking at them, most of our officers are complete strangers to us. We haven't previously seen them either at work or even during the evenings or yasumi days. Maybe our welfare is of no interest to them, whereas we had always understood that it was one of an officer's prime responsibilities.

At the end of the front row, however, near where I happen to be standing, a space has been left and the reason for this becomes apparent. Just before the concert is due to begin, seven pairs of men appear, each pair being one man walking stiffly upright and staring blankly ahead, with the other man alongside holding the sleepwalker's arm and guiding him to his place. These seven are men whose minds have been unable to cope with the enormity of the changes that have destroyed their previous lives. Their fuses have blown in shock. They have been brought to the concert in the hope that music and singing, laughter and chatter, will stir memories and provide a linkage by which they might pull themselves out of their mental vacuum. The colonel rises to his feet, turns towards them and snaps to attention while the seven men are seated. The Nip commandant glances over, a flicker passes across his face and he turns away. There is total silence!

The concert opens with an Australian corporal lustily singing 'O Sole Mio' and 'Come Back to Sorrento', and several other Neapolitan folk songs, accompanied by the piano accordion. He has a full melodious tenor, and obviously loves the warm lilting passion of the music. The songs, richly mellow and plaintive, pour in a nostalgic flood over the rapt listeners.

It is the first real singing voice we have heard in nearly a year filled with unpleasantness and stress, and when the singer falls silent, tumultuous applause shatters the night with clapping, whistles, and shouts of 'More, more!' and (from the Australians) 'Good on yer, mate! Bloody good on yer!' Even the Nips join in with grins and hand-clapping, after first looking to their officer to copy his reaction. But the stricken seven have sat bolt upright with blank unmoving faces throughout the singing, and even now are totally unresponsive to the deafening racket around them.

The singer grins and shuffles his feet as the applause breaks over him, shy and somewhat overwhelmed by the sheer enthusiasm of his audience. He will never have had such a wild reception back home in Yackandandah, in the village hall at a Saturday night social hop. When he can be heard again he repeats a couple of songs, and leaves the stage to give way to a group of eight young men carrying a weird assortment of homemade instruments.

These are Eurasian boys from Singapore who joined the local Volunteer force despite being well under age. Living in the Colony, they were keen to do their bit in (quite literally) defending their own homes and families, and now they are here in Siam, with no means of knowing how their people are faring at the hands of the Japs. Knowing of the unbelievable savagery of the Jap troops in China, of which we used to be well informed by the local press, they must suffer private agonies unknown to the men from Britain and Australia who, indeed, have their own worries about air raids and so on, but not the intensely personal despair from knowing that a barbaric enemy has absolute power over family and friends.

Tonight, stimulated by a shouting, whistling, laughing crowd of 1,600 men letting off steam, they plonk and plunk, toot and bong their way through their program, then take off spontaneously with songs and funny stories until they are exhausted. For sheer morale and high spirits they have the admiration of all of us.

Our resident (involuntary!) theatre professionals follow with quite splendid readings from Shakespeare and the

Victorian poets, some from memory and some from an assortment of books carried from Singapore. There are, thank heaven, men who will always value their cultural heritage above material things. And there are haunting melodies from Ivor Novello, sketches and farces from the London stage, all delivered with such skill and flair that even the most lowbrow amongst us enjoys them. And, of course, jokes – clean, coarse, bawdy, subtle and crude, unprintable but not unsayable, and all stations in between.

One persistent fellow is totally unfunny and doesn't even know it! There are plenty of laughs during his turn, not as a result of his long-winded meanderings, but because of the vigorous and cheerfully abusive advice shouted at him from the audience. Undeterred, perhaps even encouraged by thinking it is his jokes bringing applause, he canters steadily through his repertoire, unstoppable, laughing and gesticulating, and finally he thanks his audience for being so appreciative! How can he do it? How can he fool himself that everybody thought he was funny when they were telling him quite plainly that he was not, and to shut up? It must be the mood of the evening – every man is determined to enjoy himself and goodwill flows strongly to the performers. There is a big welcome to anyone willing to have a go at entertaining us.

Well after midnight the Jap commandant stands up. The concert is over. He and our colonel exchange salutes and polite smiles, and when the Nips have left the colonel goes up to the stage and thanks everybody for their efforts. Then he asks us all to stay in our places for a few minutes 'while our sick friends are helped back to their quarters'. The sad little procession eases through the crowd, an oddly moving end to the evening's hilarity. It's a chilling thought that any one of us can end up just like that.

But tomorrow is yasumi day, with ten days' pay due.

There will be a few hours to relax and unwind. As the night's boisterous mood fades we shall sleep well. The excited chatter dies away, the huts fall silent.

The first death within the camp has occurred, and it is a personal tragedy for our small group because he was our close friend. A radio engineer, he had served for years in the chain of wireless stations between Britain and the Far East, receiving and relaying messages in Morse code which he tapped out and read at incredible speeds. In Singapore he had run his own radio business, and being in the Singapore Volunteer Armoured Car Company with us he had installed experimental equipment. My brother Ron, who had built receiving sets while still at school, operated the car set.

Older than the rest of us and already run down by dysentery and malaria (those mosquito-breeding pools at Ban Pong), Geoff reported sick with abdominal pains which were diagnosed as acute appendicitis. Immediate surgery was necessary, done in candlelight with a cut-throat razor, sewing needle and cotton thread, in the most primitive conditions. For a few days Geoff progressed well, until struck by a severe malarial rigor. The violent shivering tore stitches and there was internal bleeding which could not be stopped and which resulted in his death. The Nips have given permission for a small funeral party, and indicated a site for the grave beyond the railway embankment.

So here we are, six of Geoff's friends, the camp chaplain and the bugler who calls reveille every morning. The medical orderlies have made a stretcher of bamboo, laid his body on it and wrapped it in attap thatching. Creepers bind him in place. We hoist the stretcher to our shoulders and start the kilometre trek to the grave site, the chaplain in front and the bugler behind. No one feels like talking, but our thoughts are on the new realities now becoming apparent with Geoff's death and all the circumstances of it. We are now faced with the fact that, unpleasant as life has been so far, it will in all likelihood become a lot worse.

The dull morning has darkened with grey-purple monsoon clouds, and as we leave the camp area the deluge comes down on us. We are used to it and pay no attention to the rain, being concerned only with keeping upright on our bare feet. The possibility of slipping and dropping the flimsy stretcher, and having it break apart, is a worry. As we walk, the only sounds are the rattling of the heavy drops on our friend's shroud of dried palm leaves, and the soft shuffle of our feet stirring the sodden leaves on the forest floor.

The grave has already been dug, and the two men with shovels are waiting to one side to fill it in after we leave. We have no straps to lower the stretcher, so two of us drop into the trench to take it and settle it on the bottom. We are hauled out awkwardly, the sides are slippery with rain and we want to avoid putting a foot on the corpse. The chaplain has tucked his prayer book under his soaking robe to keep it dry, and recites the words of the service. The bugler sounds the last post, then, after a brief silence, reveille. There is no dust to toss into the grave, only clods of soggy mud which does not seem to be appropriate. The rain pours down and floods into the grave. The bamboo stretcher, with its lightweight burden, begins to float. We signal the grave-diggers to start work and set off back to camp, wrapped in our own thoughts.

I am a few months past my twenty-first birthday (which happened in River Valley Road Camp in Singapore) and this is my first attendance at a burial. I have childhood memories of funeral processions in Shanghai, where I spent my first ten years, passing along the street to the cemetery. There was always some kind of public display of grief, mourning, reverence, solemnity, pomp, wreaths and trappings in purple and black. We took our hats off as the coffin passed by, standing silent and respectful. But just now I looked down on a bamboo raft with my friend's body tied to it under a covering of dried leaves, floating in a muddy puddle at the bottom of a wretched hole in the ground, in a forgotten corner of a foreign country. The minimum of ceremony, and all I could say was, 'Goodbye, Geoff. Sorry we can't do any better for you.'

What a dismal affair, the sagging clouds which barely permit daylight to reach us, the sombre dark-shadowed trees standing in silent indifference, the rain thrashing odours of decay from the saturated earth and its mat of rotting vegetation, the smothering atmosphere. Is this perhaps more in keeping than civilisation's ostentatious ceremonials? They are, after all, nature's contribution to continuing life, taking her child back into her care. And we, a puny little group of near-naked, unshaven and scabby men, have stood proclaiming our determination to hold to our belief in the renewal of our souls after bodily death. It doesn't matter that the chaplain's prayers, and our own thoughts, and the bugle's melancholy notes, will not be heard beyond the circle of trees. We know that the spoken words of our faith will soothe the gentle spirit of our sleeping friend and bring comfort to his dreams. Indeed, if we cannot believe these things, what point is there in trying to stay alive?

Dear God, did you even notice our subdued little ceremony? Did it do any good at all? To our friend's body? To his soul? To our souls? Did the chaplain really feel he had achieved something worthwhile? But we had to try, didn't we? Never before have I examined the social conventions relating to death, with which we have all uncritically grown up.

Geoff has died and we have laid his wasted body in the

earth, prayers have been intoned and the army's traditional salute has been sounded – the barest minimum of ceremony. The personal feelings of each of us are held closely within during the return to camp. Maybe we will loosen up and talk together later. As for me, deep within my consciousness I am aware that every aspect of this funeral has been etched into my memory. Not a single detail will ever fade or be lost. To the last of my days, the clear poignant notes of the last post will softly immerse me in those damp earthy odours, the heavy silence, and I shall look into that muddy slit in the ground, with the gleaming rain sliding down the sides and lifting Geoff's poor body off the bottom.

I know it. The haunting has already begun and will hold me in its grip until I die.

In the army's lowest ranks there is a well-founded saying: 'Never volunteer for anything!' If your sergeant comes along and asks for volunteers for a special job, then he is simply trying to avoid his responsibility (for which he is paid more than you are) to name four men. If it turns out to be a cushy job he can be accused of favouring his friends; if bad, he will have dumped it on those he doesn't like. Either way he is in the wrong, but he can avoid this if any man is sucker enough to stand forward. It's a symptom of the subtle hostility between privates and those with stripes on their arms.

Amongst us Volunteers, the situation is different. Not having been subjected to army practices and bull (thank heaven!) we are still more civilians than soldiers, and prefer to work on a basis of friendly cooperation. So when it is announced that a party of four is wanted to go to Tarsao for a couple of days, my brother and I look at George and Wally, and say, 'Okay, we'll go.' And that is why we four are now standing in the belly of a wooden barge, waiting for our escorting Nip to turn up. When he does, swaggering towards the boat and smirking with self-importance at being in charge of this trip, we wish we hadn't been so stupid as to volunteer. It's that horrible little bastard Putrid, we guessed badly wrong and it's going to be a bloody awful outing.

Putrid is the youngest of the fifty or so camp Nips and seems to be the lowest in the pecking order. All the others treat him with contempt, even in front of us, and he has a nasty habit of taking out his humiliation on us. He's a spiteful little bully who knows that we cannot retaliate. His nickname, however well suited to his personality, really comes from his private cluster of flies, a dozen or so which constantly circle above his shaven head. They never land on him and never go away, so something attracts them. Like all the Nips, Putrid keeps himself personally clean, so there is nothing visible to attract flies – maybe his mental distress causes some kind of emanation which puzzles the flies. Or imaginably, they could be a black halo to attest to his unpleasant personality!

Anyway, our towboat starts its pom-pom-pom-pom and pulls us away from the riverbank, and while Putrid sits cross-legged under the stern canopy we four stand up in the bow as far away as possible. Going upstream against the current, now running strongly in the last few weeks of the rainy season, we reckon on some eight hours to reach Tarsao. Subconsciously we are waiting for trouble to start, and scarcely are we round the first bend and out of sight of Wampo than Putrid shouts, 'Hey, Ingerishu,' which means us. We brace ourselves and turn to face him. To our surprise he is giving us the friendly Asiatic gesture of welcome – right arm extended, palm downwards and fingers waggling to beckon us to come closer. In his left hand he waves a packet of Siamese cigarettes, and his teeth show in a beaming smile.

We warily move to the stern, where Putrid hands out cigarettes to the Siamese boatman and to each of us in turn, with polite nods and a hissed 'Dozo' which, in my scanty knowledge of Japanese, means something like 'Please be so kind'. This display of formal Japanese good manners is an ironclad indication of friendly intentions and, not to be out-done, we give him a small bow and an 'Arigato (Thank you)'. Our unexpected show of social niceties delights Putrid, coming from barbarians such as us, and he rummages in his army haversack to produce a packet of biscuits, which he hands round to another polite exchange of courtesies. His face almost split by a happy smile, Putrid visibly relaxes and chatters away while we listen with carefully intent faces.

I have heard that the English language is taught in nearly all Japanese schools, and bits of rudimentary English occur in whatever it is Putrid is telling us. I must admit that his small acquaintance with English is a lot more than my bits and pieces of his language, which I have picked up in occasional chats with the camp interpreter, who used to run an import/export business in Singapore and speaks fluent Japanese.

It is extraordinary how happy chance and unlikely co-incidence can come together to shape a situation. We gather that Putrid wants to know if any of us has been to Japan, and it happens that Ron and I have. We lived in Shanghai all through the 1920s until we went to school in England in 1931, and during Shanghai's unbearably hot and muggy summers, we had twice spent several weeks in a holiday resort at Unzen, in the mountains behind Nagasaki, and at Obama on the shore of the Inland Sea. Putrid is absolutely delighted. With sign language and his minimal English we learn that he is a farmboy from somewhere near Nagasaki, and he knows of Unzen with its volcanic hot springs. The pantomime to convey this is fascinating. 'You rike (like) Japan?' 'Hai, taku-san okay (Yes, plenty okay).' His eyes fill with tears and he lies back on the deck mumbling to himself in a soft singsong, wallowing in homesick memories.

We withdraw tactfully to the bow and talk about the complexities of the Japanese character, which has this surpris-ing yeast of sentimentality buried in an apparently impenetrable mass of savage brutality totally devoid of human decency. It is an amazing situation. Ron and I must be about the only men in Wampo who have been to Japan, and with luck it will keep Putrid in a good mood for the rest of this visit to Tarsao.

Wally reckons that Putrid could have been scared of us when this trip started. After all, we are four to one and could easily knock him off and dump him ashore somewhere, and say he simply disappeared, which is probably why he gave us cigarettes and biscuits, to show he is a good fellow after all. He surely must know that his previous bullying treatment of us can hardly have made him popular, and that this trip gives us an ideal opportunity to get rid of him. Well, he may indeed be missing his old mum and dad and the comforts of home. He could also be relieved at being free of the bullying of his fellows, but we still think that he is a nasty little specimen.

Pulling in to the bank at Tarsao, we wait in the boat while Putrid reports to the guardhouse. This is a main administra-tive base for Nip army movements in the area, and it is evident that every boat on the river is scrutinised by the sentries.

Putrid calls us ashore and points out an empty Jap army tent in which to leave our kit. He puts his mess tin on a plank outside a small cookhouse, indicating that we should do the same. No time to waste, we are off to a huge pile of bamboo and attap thatching. He tells us (with pantomime), 'Asta, hiru finish, sampanu finish, go backu Wampo,' which translates as

'Tomorrow by sundown, boat must be loaded, go back to Wampo'. So we have the rest of today and all tomorrow to fill the boat with bamboo and attap, and we don't see any problem in doing that comfortably. In fact, by the end of the day, when Putrid calls, 'Yasumi, meishi ichi ji (Stop work, rice in one hour),' we have half filled the boat and have time for a splash in the river.

We examine our Jap army tent with interest and growing surprise. It is mud-brown in colour, spacious, rectangular with a low-angle pitched roof, and would sleep ten men along each side with a walking space down the middle. There is a lace-up door flap in each end wall. What causes our surprise is that George, who is somewhat of a connoisseur of the good things in life, declares that the material of the whole tent is silk! Treated for waterproofing, but undoubtedly silk! There are only four poles, the tops held in reinforced pockets, and the ridge and walls are stiffened with sewn-in rope. The whole tent is braced taut with outside guys, the roof panels extend slightly beyond and clear of the walls and are held by guys, leaving a long narrow ventilation space. In one corner of the tent is a neatly strapped pack with four poles – obviously a spare tent. We pick it up and it is so light that a couple of men could carry it all day, in addition to their personal gear, without being fatigued.

The British empire's poor bloody infantry tramping all over the world on active service in every imaginable terrain and climate is provided with tentage in various shapes and sizes as developed over centuries of hard experience. The great importance of keeping troops in good health has long been recognised, and you might expect that careful thought had been given to producing the best possible in field accommodation. You would be sadly wrong. Our tents are bulky and clumsy to erect and strike, and seem to have innumerable iron-tipped poles. They are so heavy that ox-carts or trucks are needed to transport them, which can be impossible in rough country campaigning. They are made of thick canvas-like material that is quickly saturated by rain, which doubles its already considerable weight. If not dried out before it's folded up, which requires an age of continuous fine weather, it soon becomes stinking and mouldy. The British army, which professes to take pride in the health and welfare of its men, is content to use this rubbish. The Japanese army, poverty-stricken and not caring a hoot about the living conditions of its soldiers, provides lightweight go-anywhere tentage which does what it's supposed to do.

There is a Nip transport park about 100 yards away from our tent, where trucks are being re-fuelled, repaired and prepared for transporting men or stores, and men start to drift out of it towards us, chatting and laughing amongst themselves as they enter their hut and strip off to wash away the day's sweat and dirt. Just like men in any army, they make themselves as comfortable as primitive conditions allow. They notice us, but show no curiosity.

There is a shout from the cookhouse and the Nips line up their mess tins alongside ours and walk away. The cook ladles out the food and the men come back to pick up their individual items, the system ensuring that there is no favouritism. No titbits or extras for the cook's friends! Our rations are exactly the same as theirs and, to us, quite marvellous. Siam produces some of the world's best rice, and this is high quality long grain, dazzlingly white and steaming fresh from the kwali. Piled on top are several pieces of meat and beautiful savoury-smelling vegetables and gravy.

The cook is a tubby, cheerfully grinning fellow, and when we take our mess tins we are careful to say, 'Arigato,' which makes him positively beam with pleasure. The Nips group themselves in a circle, squatting comfortably on their haunches, and when we move away to eat they call us over to join them. So there we are, four of us amid some thirty of them, sharing a meal without the slightest hint of awkwardness. Putrid, full of importance at being in charge of us all on his own, is busily answering their questions about us.

Inevitably, some of the Japs have a few words of English to try out on us. Putrid points to Ron and me as having been to Japan, and they are delighted. The Japanese seem to have a passion for learning English. I remember them coming up to my father, students and young people especially, saying, 'Prease, you herrup me un'erstand Ingerishu?' Even at railway stations they used to do this, while waiting for a train, and in hotel lobbies.

One wag is inspired to produce chopsticks (we have been using spoons), challenging me to eat with them. I don't know when I first picked up a pair of chopsticks, certainly well before my fifth birthday, and my dexterity causes so much merriment that men from nearby units come over to see what's happening. Our cook, obviously a man who takes pleasure in feeding people, brings his tubs of rice and vegetables with three more pairs of chopsticks, and refills our mess tins. We four, of course, having lived in Singapore for some time, all handle chopsticks with ease.

A slightly crazy situation gathers momentum. We quickly dispose of our second helpings, then our thirds, which empty the tubs. The cook stares at us unbelievingly, but not to be outdone he dashes off to another cookhouse and brings us extra food. We demolish this lot, and off he goes again. The meat runs out but the vegetables are far too good to refuse. By the sixth helping we are slowing down somewhat and the cook is having to forage further afield to find more food, which gives us welcome extra time for digestion. We are very careful of our good manners.

There is now a definite atmosphere of challenge, their hospitality versus our extraordinary appetites. We are the centre of a noisy circle of grinning brown faces, and see money changing hands. They are laying bets on whether we will give up eating, or they will run out of food. The seventh helping is rice with an omelette of tinned fish, peanuts, soya sauce and ginger, obviously concocted with malicious intent! On top of what we have already had, it proves to be our limit and we have to decline the eighth serve. It is an honourable defeat, and there is an outburst of good-humoured applause as the men disperse.

The cook picks up his tubs with a few cheery words, and we retire to our tent. How did we do it? None of us has ever eaten such a huge meal, but there is no discomfort, just a contentedly full stomach for the first time in far too long. There is an unfamiliar bugle call that must be the Jap army 'lights out', the camp quietens and we settle down to sleep.

During the night we are disturbed, not by overworked stomachs but by a heavy downpour of rain. Instinctively we look for drips in the roof, to shift our kit if necessary, but our silk pavilion doesn't let in a drop!

Our cook greets us in the morning with a big smile, a pile of snowy rice, an omelette and a piece of oily dried fish – a good start to the day. By carefully pacing our work we hope to fill our barge too late to return to Wampo that night, and the sun is starting to sink towards the mountains of Lower Burma by the time the boatman signals he will not take any more. Our idea, of course, has been to stay for another good dinner.

But the Jap army is as inexplicably stupid as ours. Despite the obvious facts that we cannot get back to Wampo before nightfall, and that the Siamese boatmen will not move on the river in the dark when they cannot see obstacles and currents well ahead, Putrid hurries from the guardhouse, shouting and waving his arms and pointing to the barge. We grab our kits and perch ourselves on the stack of bamboo, resigned to a hungry night tied up at the bank just downstream, and knowing that we shall arrive at Wampo too late for breakfast. Our pom-pom winds up its engine and pulls us out in the stream. Savoury smells from the boatman's brazier settle over us with the evening shadows. A dim oil lamp hangs under the aft canopy.

Putrid, however, has not forgotten us after all. As we pull in to the bank and moor to a pole shoved into the sand, he produces a woven rice-straw parcel which he hands to us. Inside are eight substantial cold riceballs with a chunk of sour pickled cucumber embedded in each. Not bad at all! His face lights up as we all politely say, 'Arigato,' and we retire to the far end of the boat.

Hardly have we finished when Putrid calls out, 'Hey, Ingerishu,' and we see him beckoning us with one hand and waving a bottle in the other. 'Whisukee, whisukee!' This isn't the nasty little runt we knew and loathed a few days ago – this new Putrid with a beaming smile is asking us to join him in a drink! Alcohol is strictly against the rules and, for all we know, a firing squad offence, but refusal could be taken as an insult, so, somewhat warily, we pick up our mugs and step carefully along the bamboo poles. Chattering away happily, Putrid sloshes generous tots into our mugs and lastly (such good manners!) into his own china bowl. With toasts all round we take a cautious sip – gawd, it's powerful stuff. Certainly not whisky, but some crude distillation of hooch. By the third sip it slides down smoothly, warming the belly and, we hope, shrivelling up those dysentery bugs clinging to our intestines. George has a whimsical vision of them unhooking themselves and scrambling for the exit when the fiery blast hits them. Not to mention cauterising stomach ulcers! Maybe even alcohol poisoning for malaria parasites in our bloodstreams!

Our genial host, already warmed up by several slugs taken with his dinner, starts to sing in an off-key whine. The songs are obviously sentimental as tears roll down his cheeks and the words become slurred. He seems to want us to join in but, of course, we can't do more than make sympathetic noises. With unsteady hands he tips the last of the bottle into his bowl and swallows it at a gulp.

The hooch can hardly have had time to explode in his stomach before he is out like a switched-off light. Our Siamese boatman is on the launch with his mate, we are alone with a poleaxed Nip and not all that sure what might happen if he is still out cold in the morning and a Nip boat comes by. So we straighten Putrid out to lie on his side so that he won't choke himself to death if he pukes, and take ourselves off to roost on the attap cargo, almost floating in the warm afterglow of our medicinal hooch.

It is still dark when we are awakened by loud splashing and watery gurgles. Putrid is floundering in the river, the oil lamp just able to illuminate the swirls and flying drops. The current is taking him away steadily – luckily we are moored on the slack bank of the river, or he would have disappeared into the darkness by now. In an instant we are over the side and thrashing after him, hauling him up the sandy beach and turning him on his belly, head down the slight slope so that he can rid himself of any water he might have swallowed. We do this not simply out of humanity, but because we are mindful of the consequences of arriving at Wampo without him, and trying to explain what happened. Presumably he was trying to relieve a bursting bladder over the side of the barge and, still unsteady from his boozing, toppled into the water. When he stops heaving and moaning, we dump him back on the deck and leave him to recover as best he can.

With daylight we gaze dispassionately at a haggard Putrid trying to reassemble his scrambled wits. He is shivering from the aftershocks of his boozing and chilled from sleeping in his soaking uniform, and, no doubt, nauseated by a churning belly. The Siamese boatman steps across from the launch and, irritated by Putrid's bleats and moans, lays into him with a blast of angry talk and gesticulations, to show how we pulled him out of the river and put him back on the barge. Putrid slumps in a heap of misery.

The Siamese signals to us to pull up the mooring pole and take in the rope, the pom-pom cranks up and we glide into the stream.

Somehow a thought must have seeped into Putrid's muddled brain. In a short time he will have to face up to his tough disciplinarian gunso and report in a soldierly manner on our trip to Tarsao. In a panic he strips off his uniform and tosses it on the canopy to dry, and hauls buckets of water from the river to pour over his body, rubbing himself vigorously with a small towel to induce some degree of sobriety. The sun comes out strongly; he puts on his uniform and, almost back to normal, sits cross-legged on the deck and gazes smugly around him. Then, suddenly, where the hell's his rifle? His panic is truly theatrical.

We know where it is but deliberately watch him work himself towards a seizure. We are not telling him – after all, how should we know what is bothering him? After fishing him out of the river, we slipped his rifle down the face of the bulkhead amongst the bamboo poles, where it is almost invisible – not quite out of sight, as it must look as though it fell there accidentally and was not deliberately hidden. It had occurred to us that, coming out of his hangover, he might have been in a belligerent mood, touchy and nasty.

We perch up at the bow enjoying the scenery and listening to the pom-pom's regular beat and monkeys hallooing in the thickly forested hills. This really would be a pleasant place for a peacetime camping holiday! In the dry season, of course.

Without the least sympathy, we watch Putrid work himself into a high state of nervous alarm, worried that he might have dropped his rifle over the side while he was drunk. When we are nearing Wampo, we make our way aft and enquire solicitously, 'You okay?' And then suddenly notice his rifle – quite by accident, of course – and fish it out with an air of surprise. 'This belong you-kah?' Well, after all, he has been decent to us on this trip, but we are trying to time his relief at recovering his rifle to carry over into our arrival at Wampo, so we mustn't be too early. We must look after our own interests!

His reaction is comic to watch. Incredulity, relief, surprise and joy all burst forth, worry and panic vanish, and our innocent expressions convince him we are his friends and won't give him away. We have gauged it nicely – in twenty minutes we nudge into the beach below Wampo's steep bank.

Dutifully we march with Putrid to the guardhouse and stand to attention like good soldiers while he makes his report. Dismissed from the guardhouse, he marches us off out of sight of the gunso and makes a little speech, which we take to be a thank you. We respond with dignified politeness, telling him what a horrible little creep he is, and how we would much rather have left him to drown. Not understanding a word, he smiles happily, we exchange small bows (this being, after all, somewhat of a special occasion) and, with honour satisfied all round, we break off.

A moment later we see Putrid heading for a sanitation squad digging a new latrine. It is nothing to do with him but he is already celebrating his return with an outburst of screaming and bawling. He has reverted to type without wasting any time.

Well, it has been a change from the usual routine. But it might easily have been quite different!

It has quickly been realised that marking off a length of embankment to be completed daily is not a practical way to work, and the Nips have decided to change to three- or four-day tasks. This means that we are spread out more conveniently along a stretch of two or three hundred metres at a time, depending on the amount of earth to be shifted, and the scene changes daily as work progresses.

Day one is the easiest. We are faced with the cleared way through the forest, bamboo markers already in place. We distribute ourselves in gangs along both sides and start digging close enough to the strip to be able to shovel earth directly onto it. The green surface becomes covered with dark red-brown spoil from the excavation pits, and by afternoon we have to introduce tongas to dump spoil where it is needed as the level rises beyond shovel-throw. Knowing that the following days will require greater effort, especially in the heavy slog of tonga-carrying, we put in a full day's work at this early stage.

It is of great importance that, when the last day is reached, we are faced with a task which can be accomplished without a gut-wrenching grind to finish off the heaviest part of the work in time. Always, however, we must be careful not to let the Nips get it into their heads that we could have done more in the scheduled time. On the other hand our judgement can be upset by heavy rain slowing us down or, say, an inadequate allocation of tools by the Nips. The tool store is in the charge of a Korean who seems to issue items entirely according to his own irrational whims, and when he shuts up shop in the morning, nothing more comes out for the rest of the day. Every tool is counted back into store in the evening, and he is totally deaf to any request to retain a spade for improving stormwater drains around the huts. The perfect petty bureaucrat!

By the end of the last day, the section of embankment lies completed, its flat top and smooth flanks clean-cut and glowing in the late afternoon sun. Up until now it has been thickly dotted with toiling men trudging to and fro over its snake-like body, and swinging picks and shovels alongside. Finished, it looks smug and relaxed, a long serpent warming its terracotta body in the sunset.

The men, walking back to camp, have acquired much the same colour. Dressed in their working gear of fundoshi and hat, carrying digging tools and mess tins and water bottles, they are heavily tanned all over – behind the ears, between the toes, under the arms . . . no bit of skin can escape the burning sun except for the minimal area covered by a fundoshi. They glisten with perspiration, and on every man's back are white crystals of salt, exuded by his skin and carried down by running sweat to form small crescent moons. And between his shoulder blades below the brim of his hat, a spatter of earth which fell from the tip of his pickaxe as he raised it for the downward swing. These are the hallmarks of our labouring.

Today has been particularly trying, the sun's heat hammering through the heavy atmosphere and no breeze to take the edge off it. We spend most of the working hours bent forward as we dig and lug tongas up the slope of the embankment, and our backs have acquired a deep brick-red hue overlaying our already dark tan. Sweat rolls out of us, and the supply of tea has been quite insufficient to replace the lost fluids. Even the Nips, slumped in the shade alongside the track, grumble amongst themselves as they wipe their wet faces. In the humid air, our sweat cannot evaporate and our clogged skins suffocate our muscles and we move sluggishly, breathing heavily as we push ourselves to complete the day's quota. Our group is at the front end of the section, and behind us are several hundred men labouring to get their work done, some leaning on a spade motionless except for heaving chests while they gather strength for the last hour. In the sun the temperature must be 125° F (52 by the Nip's Centigrade reckoning), and except for the midday rice break, we have toiled without any respite since early in the morning.

Suddenly, from way back, comes a shouting and hallooing. We look down the line to see men straightening themselves and turning round and round with their arms held high. A breeze has come, and we can watch its front approach by the responses of the men as it reaches them. Then it comes to us, blessed cooling relief as it soothes our bodies with fairy fingers. Even the Nips come out from under the trees, grinning and loosening their cotton trousers and pulling off their shirts. We do not have even a rag to dry our eyes, smarting from sweat and sun glare; even taking off your fundoshi and wringing it out doesn't help much. When I want to put down my shovel I find I cannot let go of it. My fingers are clamped tight around the shaft and no effort on my part will straighten them. I have to prise them open with my other hand. My first move on returning to camp will be to swallow a spoonful from our priceless little hoard of salt, even before I go down to our secluded beach to slide into the water.

We haven't seen soap for so long that we have almost forgotten what it feels like to be really clean. Your scalp is itchy with the day's sweat and your hair stiff and ragged, far too long

97

for the hot climate, and without soap will not come clean.

Today is a yasumi day, and early in the afternoon we are called to stand by our bedspaces to receive a cake of soap per man – a whole new cake for each of us! Parading us in our huts is the only way to ensure that each man gets his issue and no one can cheat for extras. It is that beautiful pink 'Lifebuoy' soap, with its fresh carbolic scent, the one that a few years ago made the nation conscious of 'body odour'. 'Do you have BO? Do you offend those close to you? Do you notice that they move away from you? Use Lifebuoy and be sure your friends won't turn their noses up at you!' Or something like that.

This brand of soap is supplied to the Royal Household and therefore carries the appropriate insignia with the words 'By Appointment' impressed on one face. The sight of this familiar emblem is enough to provoke thoughts of home, families and friends, and nostalgic chatter, so deprived are we of everything that was a normal part of our lives such a short time ago that it takes very little to bring on an attack of home-sickness. We have no idea where this soap has come from – it certainly won't be a Nip issue.

Everybody hurries off to the river except our little group, which sidles off to our private pool which, to our grateful surprise, has not yet been discovered by others. Privacy is quite impossible in camp life, and we value our secluded hidey-hole for the odd hour of personal privacy which it offers us, a precious time to be as nearly alone as our situation permits. In the cramped press of men in the camp area and at work, it is quite possible to feel lonely, but to be alone is quite a different matter – there is an important distinction here which we, in our group, recognise and which, I am sure, is not understood by many.

After a cooling soak in the shallow pool we soap ourselves all over using our fundoshis as washcloths to work the glorious clean-scented suds all over our bodies and scalps and scrubbing each other's backs. It is an extraordinary feeling, the skin coming alive and tingling, and all of us give out small exclamations of sheer pleasure. We are all reluctant to go back into the water to rinse off this deliciously stimulating foam, and afterwards we stand naked in the breeze to dry off. The air all along the beach is redolent with the soap's perfume. We breathe it in as if it were a woman's fragrance, making the most of it.

My near-sensuous reverie is dispersed by our Welsh friend Taffy. He has a physique honed by generations of deep-coal miners, he hasn't had a shave or haircut for months, his black hair stands out spikily and a shaggy pelt covers his body and limbs. Standing ankle-deep in the water, his eyes modestly downcast, he has struck a coy pose with one knee slightly bent and his big hands joined in front. In a simpering voice he says, '*Do* look at me, fellers, now I have a beautiful schoolgirl complexion *all over*.' He is, of course, imitating the well-known pretty girl in the Pears soap adverts telling everybody about her perfect skin, and although the words may be the same, the image could hardly be more in contrast!

We are a cheerful group as we walk back to the squalid discomforts of Wampo Camp. So little can do so much for us!

With our sleeping arrangements, lying close side by side on a split bamboo platform, you do not 'get out of bed' in the usual way. You have to sit up and work yourself feet forwards to the edge of the platform with a heels-hands-bum movement until you can lower your feet to the earth floor of the central passageway.

This morning, getting up at daylight, the soles of my feet seem to explode with intense pain the moment they touch the ground. My immediate thought is that I have been stung by a scorpion, or bitten by a venomous snake. The shock leaves me unable to move for several seconds until I am able to gather my wits. I realise that the burning sensation is in both feet simultaneously and therefore a snakebite cannot be the cause.

Working back into my bedspace, I find that, with my legs horizontal, the pain eases a little. Ron examines my feet but can find no sign of injury, no swelling or discolouration; there is nothing he can see to account for it.

Carefully I try again and at once the burning sensation flares up the instant my feet take any weight. Picking up my mess tin, I dance on hot coals to the doorway and out into the pouring rain, hoping the puddles will cool my feet while I line up for rice. They don't, and I hop from one burning foot to the other, collect rice and tea and start a sprightly polka back to the hut with everyone else to eat breakfast out of the rain, splashing half my tea on the way.

At tenko I fall in with the men needing to attend sick parade, a sorry-looking lot suffering from the effects of mal-nutrition and dirty food and water, and blotched with septic sores that won't heal. No one has had a shave or haircut for months, it is difficult to remember that – only a year ago! – these were trained soldiers who took such pride in their bear-ing and appearance. Their self-respect is as strong as ever, but circumstances have forced them to let go the old outward symbols and to adapt to surviving on the barest minimum of everything. Their belief in themselves is undiminished, only their outward appearance is deceptive.

The medical officer tells me I have one of the less common symptoms of beri-beri: the nerves in the soles of my feet have become acutely sensitive to pressure. It seems to come and go unpredictably, and while I have it, I shall simply have to put up with the pain. I am given two days' sick leave and do an elegant skip-dance back to my sleeping space where I can stretch out horizontally.

Putting men on the sick list can be a very tricky business for our doctors. Too many men off work can bring down a lot of unpleasantness from the Nips, who are not the slightest bit impressed by the visual evidence of weakness from disease and malnutrition. The only exception is beri-beri, which they know well from its widespread incidence in their homeland. If a Nip questions you about your presence in camp and you can tell him you have beri-beri, the odds are that he will be sympathetic – but if you are visibly shaking with a malarial rigor, he is quite likely to smack you around for slacking!

I find that our POW sense of humour has labelled my burning feet 'happy feet', from the apparently light-hearted way in which we sufferers hop and skip around. I don't see anything funny in it at all – try squatting over a latrine trench while your feet are twitching and jumping uncontrollably! Why is it that so much of our time is concerned with our bowels!

We are nearing the end of this phase of our overall task. The footpath from our camp to the line of the railway is the dividing point of an unbroken embankment running south (where we have been working) and north, which has been built by the other half of Wampo's labour force. The embankment runs close to the foot of a steep rocky hillside which curves to meet the river at each end, and we are told that new camps are being set up to house us workers. Only fit men will be sent to these camps, which are intended for work only. Anyone falling sick will be sent back to Wampo Central (as it will be called) and because the work will be heavy, the rations to the working camps will be increased.

Of course, everyone wants to go to the new places! There are two enormous attractions – one is the prospect of better food, the other is the thought of getting away from our present dismal surroundings. Anything new must be better, and as for the 'heavy' work which will be required of us, what have we been doing until now? By far the most important consideration is food, which fills our thoughts but not our stomachs. As someone said: 'We are not living in this camp, it would be far more accurate to say that we are all slowly dying in it.' Not a cheering thought, but the plain truth nevertheless.

The camp itself has become steadily more depressing as the rain-soaked weeks have passed. The huts in which we sleep have deteriorated. Poorly built in the first place with insufficient materials (particularly roofing attap), they have not had any patching up because we have had nothing to use. The ground has become a muddy slop with thousands of bare feet slipping and sliding over it, and the end doorways (no doors) and side entrances are always wet from rain dripping off men passing through. There is nothing we can do about any of this: we cannot produce something from nothing.

Without consciously doing so, we have become aware of the phases of the moon. When it is not obscured by monsoon clouds, it is very useful to know at what times of the night it will be shining, so that when your bowels start protesting you can open an eye and see whether you will be able to find your way to the latrines. Maybe you can wait for the moon to rise, maybe it has already set, and maybe you should scramble out quickly to catch its last rays.

During any expedition of this sort, you need to watch the ground carefully. Some men cannot contain themselves between their hut and the latrine, and are forced to dump their mess on the way. It is easy to accuse them of simply being too lazy, but once you have experienced their desperate agony, you will be inclined to sympathise. Nevertheless, having dropped their load they can do nothing whatsoever to clean it up, and if you step in it you cannot even clean yourself up. If you slip and fall in it, you really are in difficulty – you cannot go back to your bedspace. If you take your water bottle with you, at least you can rinse your feet with tea before re-entering your hut, but anything more than that is impossible. There is just no water supply in the camp, and the river is strictly out of bounds at night. Except, of course, if it is raining you can take a shower under the dripping eaves of a hut.

God, what a bloody awful life! Not only is there a total absence of the most ordinary civilised comforts, we cannot avoid constant preoccupation with life's most squalid aspects. We are forced to live with them, and it is intensely frustrating to know that, left to ourselves to use our ingenuity, we could make considerable improvements – nothing much, maybe, but at least our living conditions could be tolerable.

It is absolutely essential to have friends to support you when you are sick or going through an attack of the heebie-jeebies. Most of us have started to withdraw into our own little fortresses, linked closely to those of particular friends. Around us is the comradeship of battalions or regiments, the kinship of everyone in the same mess. The Australians are very strong on this – if you're an Aussie you are inside the laager, no exceptions, and will always have someone to offer a hand when you need it. Their loyalties within units are very firm. There are, I think, somewhat over 200 Australians in Wampo out of a total of 1,600 men, which may tend to induce a close 'family' attitude. We Volunteers and many of the British have found them somewhat difficult to get to know; there is a vaguely standoff 'laager outlook' towards those outside, but maybe this will change as we continue to live and work alongside each other. I hope so – we should all be friends.

If you are sick or depressed, your friends will jolly you along until you recover your spirits. Every man's survival is going to depend on his own inner spiritual toughness and resilience, for we are realistic enough to know that things will only worsen, and each one of us is going to have to rely, at some time, on his friends – without them it could well be too easy to give up when too much piles up on you. And luck. Even the most determined will need luck to see him through. Courage alone may not be enough.

It is now definite, 500 men are to be selected to go to each of the new camps, Wampo South and Wampo North. When you deduct officers, cookhouse and administration/medical personnel, and the sick, that means that just about every able-bodied man will be moving. It takes only a matter of minutes to get our personal gear together. We are counted and set off down the track through the forest, then walk along our brand new embankment southwards to the river.

It is a beautiful day. The faintly discernible changes in the weather over the last few days now seem to have settled on us. The air is drier and definitely fresher, the skies clear and marvellously blue. We are leaving behind us the stifling gloom of Wampo, the weather should improve rapidly, and the huts in our new camp should be free of bugs. It is a day for cheerful optimism, and we step out in better spirits than we have felt for God knows how long.

The embankment stops short of the point where the curving hillside falls sheer into the river. The idea of cutting a ravine through the rock has been abandoned (thank heaven!), and instead a ledge will have to be hacked out of the rock face of the bluff to carry the line several hundred metres across the face of a cliff, to level ground on the far side.

Some sixty feet below us the river flows fast and thick with brown silt, while on the opposite bank we see our new home. A narrow sandy beach rises steeply to a plateau slightly lower than where we are standing – all lovely clean sand, no muddy sludge! Just beyond another ridge clothed in forest makes a green backdrop and the bamboo huts with their brown attap thatching sit snugly blending into the scenery. To our left, beyond the blunt nose of the bluff, the face of the cliff recedes in a hollow curve, its vertical face patchy with bare rock and thick vegetation and the lower half covered with a sloping area of boulders and shrubbery down to the river. All in all, a pleasing scene.

Below us is a typical wooden river barge, the Siamese boatman holding it into the bank with a long pole. An officer tells us to put our gear into the boat and swim across to the other side of the river. Non-swimmers can ride in the barge, but if we all want to ride we shall be here until nightfall. The river is not particularly wide, maybe some fifty metres at this point, but poling the barge across the current and back is slow and time-consuming.

The slope is so steep that it is not a question of walking down. We have to grab at bushes and slither from one holding point to another. It's surprising how many of our regular soldiers can't swim, and the barge has to make two trips – the first with all the baggage (not much, really, for 500 men) and the men who can fit around it, and the second with all the rest of the non-swimmers packed in tightly.

Now, I would have thought that the army would train every man to swim. What happens in a campaign where infantry come up against a river, and there are no boats or rafts? Does everything come to a standstill? I think back to the sight of thousands of troops on leave in Singapore city, bored crazy with nothing to occupy their spare time, and no one the slightest bit interested in finding them something useful to do. At the Swimming Club, an officer said to friends of mine, 'Useless bloody lot, they spend all their time getting drunk or in brothels,' in a sneering tone, and when he was asked what else was available to them on their miserable pay packets, he replied, 'Don't know, don't care, not my job.' Most of the men couldn't even drive a truck, which meant that if the trained driver was killed, the truck had to be abandoned. What a lousy state of affairs in an army which had already been at war for over two years when the Japs arrived.

3

Wampo South

NOVEMBER 1942 TO MARCH 1943

Anyway, we collect our kit and settle into clean huts. The cooks and a working detail get a meal organised, other squads start digging the inevitable latrines, and we are called for the likewise inevitable tenko. The Nips have a hut between us and the river. There seem to be eight of them under a gunso, who is known to us as a tough (but reasonably fair) disciplinarian. The Koreans are housed on the opposite side of the area, close to the trees and well clear of us – and clear of the Nips, who despise them and are deeply hated in return.

The British officer-in-charge introduces himself to us. He is a gunner from 18th Division, and the mere fact that he must have volunteered to come with us is a big point in his favour. As a captain, there are many senior to him in Wampo and the officer should certainly have been selected from among them, but we can imagine them thinking up excuses to avoid being sent. For our part, we would far rather have a junior officer with the strength of character to step forward than some reluctant senior who only wants a quiet time playing bridge.

The Nips don't require us to start work until tomorrow morning. In a very short time there are small fires dotted all over the area, and men are boiling eggs and drinking coffee –

well, it's not really coffee, it's bits of charred rice which colour the water and put in some kind of a roasted flavour – and trying to find something to talk about which hasn't already been done to death.

I find myself remembering the voyage to Singapore. When Ron and I finished schooling in England, we moved into a totally different environment. For the previous two years Dad had been working in Singapore, after more than twenty years in Shanghai (where Ron and I had spent our childhood), and in March 1939 our parents took us out to Singapore as a family reunited after more than seven years.

We sailed from Liverpool in the Blue Funnel *Aeneas*, a typical no-nonsense freighter-cum-passenger ship in a fleet running regular schedules to Japan. With a capacity for 12,000 tons of cargo and 150 passengers in comfortable (but by no means elaborate) accommodation, these ships were very popular with travellers, especially young people. Free of the snobbery and stuffiness of the big passenger express liners, full of senior civil servants with their superior airs and pomposities, life on board was a friendly and informal affair, everybody mixing easily. In particular, no busybody pests came around insisting ruthlessly on you being organised into taking part in deck games by day and whist or bridge sessions at night, because 'if you don't join in, other people won't be able to make up a proper competition, so you really have a social obligation, don't you?'

One of our fellow passengers was Wally, a Scot from Glasgow, in his mid twenties and on his first venture overseas, also bound for Singapore as an accountant for an import/export company. He is with us now in Wampo, one of our close-knit group, and on the *Aeneas* he joined a bunch of us young folks spending a couple of hours a day trying to learn Malay from a primer and vocabulary picked up in London. We remained friends in Singapore, except when he played his bagpipes in the lounge after dinner!

We acquired a teacher, who happened to come across us struggling to form sentences without knowing if we were right or wrong. Miss Stokes recognised our problem and simply sat down with us to help. She was a truly delightful lady, on her way back to Borneo, where she was born, to join her elder brother in the deep jungles. Between them they ran a small organisation which distributed medicines and supplied education, and Christian teachings to those who wanted them.

They were a quite extraordinary pair, both of them totally familiar with Malay and able to read and write the language (Jawi script, linked to Arabic through their Muslim religion). They were both qualified medical practitioners, with expertise in tropical medicine, and were absolutely devoted to the welfare of the jungle people amongst whom they lived. It also came out in conversation that both Miss Stokes and her brother were certificated pilots of a seaplane, which they used for keeping in touch with the Iban and Dayak river settlements. They operated so far into the interior that a seaplane was in fact the only practical means of crossing the jungle, setting down on the rivers where their friends lived. Of course, they had to be mechanics too.

There was nothing whatever about Miss Stokes to conform to the general public perception of a po-faced do-gooder carefully attired in unattractive clothes. The bright colours she wore proclaimed her shining happiness in her life of caring for the headhunters of British North Borneo, and in her Christian faith. Generous in her time freely given to help us, she had a fund of fascinating yarns about her unusual work and experiences far away from our kind of civilisation. Personally, I am thankful to this delightful lady for my modest fluency in Malay.

I often wonder how the Japanese invasion of Borneo affected these two dedicated and unique people. Did they fly out in the seaplane? Or did they elect to stay with the wild tribespeople with whom they had spent their lives? I have no doubt at all that they would have chosen, unhesitatingly, to stay in the jungle to help their friends to the limit of their ability. That would certainly have been in her character, and therefore in her brother's too.

Does she, nowadays, ever think of our studious little group trying to learn Malay? I feel quite certain she will have remembered us, and have prayed for our safety and wellbeing, just as I have often prayed for her and her brother. It seems now like another world, but it was only three and a half years ago, easy to recall but somehow difficult at times to accept as reality. I think we are all developing protective walls to blur the past so that it doesn't hurt too much, a self-induced form of insulation, and a careful detachment.

I was drawn into this bout of reminiscence before falling asleep last night by thinking that the north-east monsoon has definitely arrived. The connection was that it popped into my mind that Miss Stokes had informed us that our word 'monsoon' quite possibly comes from the Malay/Arabic 'musim', meaning season or seasonal, being descriptive of the great wind systems. This simple recollection brought with it a maze of stored memories and perceptions – sunny days on a glittering blue sea, unbelievable flaring red and gold sunsets which brought everyone on deck, the thrumming vibration of our ship's coal-fired engines, dolphins and flying fish, even a spouting whale, and the constant hissing wash of the great bow-wave sliding along the ship's sides, frothing and swirling as it rode over the ridges of overlapping steel plates and rivet-heads, to rejoin behind the stern and stretch right back to the horizon. Serene days, deck games, shy romances in the evening shadows, truly a Shangri-la like world!

And those two suntanned Australian girls who came on board at Colombo (their mum and dad ran a sheep station in the backblocks of New South Wales and were taking the family on an extended holiday cruise) – gee, did they cause a commotion amongst us! Attractive, lissom and athletic, bursting with the sheer exuberance of being turned loose on the world, they tossed themselves into our so-English little community like two bundles of dazzling fireworks. Spirited and generous with their affections, being kissed by them left me weak at the knees and incoherent for a full quarter of an hour. I was seventeen, and not used to such heart-zinging attentions!

But I must (reluctantly) bring my thoughts back to the monsoons, in order to explain to Taffy how they blow and create our climate. Taffy, our Welsh friend, was at one time a coalminer in the deep tunnels with his father and brothers. We reckon he must have started at an early age and when he grew up enough for his head to touch the tunnel roof, he continued to grow sideways. Bandy-legged, broad across the shoulders and with hands like the proverbial leg of mutton, he had come across us in the early days of pick and shovel work. We thought we had developed reasonable skills from zero experience, but his professional conscience was provoked: 'Hey, boyos, you're making a dog's breakfast of that! Mind if I show yer?' And he did show us, earning our lasting gratitude, how to shift the maximum quantity of earth with the minimum effort, an invaluable skill in our circumstances. In return, we do our best to help him develop his neglected education; someone amongst us could usually find answers to his questions, which ranged over a wide field, reflecting his innate intelligence.

So I'm explaining to Taffy that monsoons are not to be confused with the trade winds he learned about in his school-days. The word monsoon really applies only to the massive movements of atmosphere across the Indian Ocean and sub-continent and southern Asia, which occur at regular times of the year.

In the northern winter (which we are now entering) the winds blow from north-east to south-west and change to the opposite direction, that is from south-west to north-east, in summer. We who lived in Singapore and Malaya know that the north-east monsoon sweeps in to the east coast, bringing rain and thundering surf from the South China Sea, making the fishing villages haul their boats well up the beaches. Here in Siam, however, the winds come across mainland China and they are dry for the whole season, from mid November to mid May, with an occasional thunderstorm lasting only a brief period. These rainstorms come quickly and without warning, spiking the air with crackling displays of lightning, switching off just as suddenly, and dumping rain in buckets for just an hour or two. So the same monsoon brings totally different weather patterns to different latitudes.

In the northern summer the south-west monsoon sucks up moisture from the Indian Ocean and pours some of the world's heaviest rainfall on India, Burma and Lower Burma, and on coastlines to the south, as we have experienced since our arrival in Siam up until the last week or two. And I can well believe it is the heaviest in the world! Our local mountain range, though not particularly high, is sufficient barrier to bring the whole lot down on our heads.

When we fall in for our first tenko at our new camp on the western bank of the Kwei Noi, we stare across at the face of the cliff along which a ledge is to be cut in the sloping scree. Opposite us is the blunt nose of the cliff, which falls perpendicularly to the river, and a hell of a lot of rock will have to be hacked away down to the level marked out by the surveyors. Several hundred yards to the south-east, the other end of the arc of cliff slopes down into the riverbank and only minor work (in comparison) will be required. In between these two butt ends of the cliff we shall dig a ledge, pour concrete slabs, and set up bridge timbers to carry the railway line to the embankment which we have just completed. The distant end is the southern limit of Wampo's responsibility. There are other camps working up from Ban Pong to join up with us.

Morning tenko is soon over and work tools are collected from the idiot Korean storekeeper and piled into the boat. Those who can't swim are ferried across and toss the tools out on the other bank, where they are picked up by those who have swum over. It's all a slow and cumbersome business, geared to the boatman poling his barge to the edge of the shallows until he can no longer reach the bottom, then working his way across the deep section while the faster current carries him downstream, until he reaches the far side and can offload.

It is quite amazing how the gloom of the old camp has lifted! The combination of suddenly brightened skies, a new bug-free camp with open vistas, an expectation of better rations, and a distancing from the depressing effects of intrusive Nips all over the place – all these have contributed to a lifting of our spirits. We scramble up to our new work area in a mood of cheerfulness which we have not known since coming to Siam, to start our first day on our new project.

It's not going to be as simple as it looked to be from across the river. A railway, of course, cannot have up and down slopes except as very shallow gradients, nor can it negotiate curves except on a long radius. The irregularities of the cliff face and the scree are such that it is not possible to align the track direct from one end to the other. It will have to follow a flat curve to the left, swing right-handed, then left again around the bluff at the southern end. The face of the cliff is vertical, part bare rock with hardy trees and thickets of shrubbery clinging to crevices in it. The earth sloping down to the river is packed hard, with rocks and boulders embedded in it, all held tightly together by the roots of trees and bushes massed all over. Fortunately for us, all the spoil we will have to shift can simply be tipped down the slope and will not have to be carried anywhere.

The midday rice break is a bit tiresome as we have to return to our huts and the cookhouse. For the swimmers, it provides a refreshing dip in the river, but for those having to use the one and only boat, it means that no sooner have they eaten than they have to queue up for the return trip. But after a few days on the cliff face in the blazing sun, we find we welcome the shade of the huts and the chance to stretch out in the cool breezes.

By the end of the first few days we have scratched out a definite shape for the basic ledge. The level is established, we have dug into the shallow curves to the necessary width of the floor of the ledge, and cleared off all the trees. We now have scores of rocks to be shifted, some small enough to be levered out with crowbars and rolled down into the river, others bigger and more stubborn, and two in particular which sit squarely in the way. One of them is our problem, being in our section of the ledge, and it is big enough to be called a boulder.

We have shovelled away the earth on each side, exposing a smooth face which protrudes from the vertical back wall into the width of the ledge. It is oval in shape, like a giant mango seed, fifteen feet tall and nine feet across at its widest, its tapering base set in the floor of the ledge. Had it been only a few yards further back, it would not have mattered, but it stands squarely in the way and must be removed.

Despite our pantomime that it could cause the boulder to come adrift, our Nip insists that we excavate around the sunken base in an attempt to find the bottom. About two feet down there is a rounded tip which could be the rock's low point, but without being able to guess at the shape bedded in the earth behind, we cannot be sure. So at this stage the rock is suspended vertically above a small pit, held in place by whatever grip it may have on its rear face.

In readiness for the mid-morning smoko, someone has gathered a few twigs and lit a fire on the bare apex of our rock, to provide burning tapers for lighting cigarettes. The welcome shout of 'Yasumi' runs along the sweating labourers, and as the smokers crowd into the tiny patch of shade at the base and start rolling their fags, I climb up alongside to fetch a few burning twigs for them. Someone calls up, 'Don't put your foot on the rock, it don't look too safe,' so I carefully avoid doing so, leaning over to reach the fire. As I stretch out downwards, the whole mass starts to lean slowly away from me, and I am left crouched on a crumbling lip of earth, my instant thought being that if it gives way and I fall into the widening gap and the rock then settles back, I shall be as flat as a slice of ham in a sandwich. For a moment, both the rock and I teeter precariously, then I pull back and the rock drops with a thud into the pit. I have a fleeting vision of the men below me hurtling outwards to safety, to the sides and down the slope, scrambling frantically to gain distance before the boulder makes up its mind what to do next.

Almost in slow motion, the boulder tilts towards the river. Halfway down the scree, Hughie has managed to stop somersaulting and looks up the slope to see the great monster toppling straight towards him. Its smooth face strikes the downward slope with a massive thump, the base kicks up into the air, and immediately the whole mighty slab is sliding juggernaut-style at increasing speed, rapidly catching up on Hughie, who has now reached the tangled mass of tree trunks and bushes at the foot of the scree and can move no further. The swirling cloud of dust thrown up by the boulder's rush prevents us from seeing anything, then the movement ceases and we all slither down with thoughts of finding Hughie's mangled body. Picking our way through the dust cloud, we find Hughie, our Irish comedian, standing upright with an outstretched hand placed against the nose of the boulder, a beaming smile splitting his grazed and bleeding face, calling out to us, 'There, I managed to stop it for you, with just one hand. It shows what a daily pint of Guinness will do for you! It won't be more than twenty tons, all in a day's work for an Irish navvy!' Is there just a tiny tremble in his voice and body?

The other big boulder is a different problem. Earth has been dug out all around it and it stands free, an almost spherical thing some thirty feet in diameter and several hundred tons in weight. The obvious way to shift it would be to dig away the lip of the ledge until it can roll down the slope under its own momentum. The Nips will not go along with this though, because it would leave a large crater in the floor of the ledge, which could not be filled satisfactorily to carry the weight of the upperworks. This is a relief to the men working on the site – who would want to be shovelling out the last of the supporting earth when the monster started to roll?

The solution is typical Nip thinking. Dig a tunnel underneath, right to the rear face. Pack the far end with dynamite, lay a fuse to the front and stuff all the excavated earth back into the tunnel to contain the blast. That, they reckon, should heave up the rear side sufficiently to start the boulder rolling.

It is accepted by all of us that some jobs are more unpleasant than others, and you take your luck as it comes. So we have no qualms about thanking our stars that someone else has to cope with this chancy business of hacking out a tunnel just large enough to wriggle in with a small spade, and scooping loose gravel back out beyond his feet. As the tunnel lengthens, of course, another man has to slither in behind to keep the earth moving back. Another time, it could be our turn.

It is slow and laborious work. The men engaged in it swap positions frequently, for the air at the far end is quickly fouled and full of dust, it is unbearably hot; the whole naked body is grazed and scraped against grit and stones. It is claustrophobic, no illumination, with all that rock just inches overhead and nothing to support the wall of the tunnel, and exhaustion is an ever-present concern – in fact, a number of men have simply stopped working in a state nearing collapse, and have had to be dragged out feet first through the rubble to be revived. This is a working camp, therefore, in contorted Nip logic, no medical staff or supplies are necessary. The men manage as best they can, relieving grit-scratched eyes with tea and rinsing dirt and blood off their lacerated skin in the cooling waters of the river.

Detonating the dynamite is to be a ceremonial occasion. The Siamese boatman has been warned to move his barge out of harm's way, we have an evening tenko in the last of the afternoon sun and we are kept on parade to watch this stupendous proof of Nip engineering technology. The Nips swagger around gesticulating for our benefit how the great boulder will be toppled into the river, the gunso shouts across to his mate waiting with a box of matches, and the Korean bugler sounds off on our side. The dynamito-man, fumbling his matches all over the ground in his nervousness, at last

117

gets the fuse to flare and takes off along the ledge like a frightened jack rabbit.

Half a minute passes, there is a dull whump and dust rises as though from a beaten carpet. For a split second nothing more happens. Then there is a great roar, and an enormous quantity of gravel is ejected at high speed from the mouth of the tunnel, travelling across the river in a flat trajectory. In another split second, all 500 of us are dashing smartly to our right as the hail of earth and stones (looking much like a comet's tail) smashes squarely into the Nips' hut.

The tunnel shaft had become the barrel of a giant cannon, the solid hillside behind the stacked dynamite and the mass of the boulder on top had confined the whole of the explosion's force along the shaft, and the packed gravel had been hurled out like grapeshot from an old-fashioned naval gun. The boulder continues to sit there impassively, astride a blackened and smoking trench.

The stunned Nips rush over to their ruined hut to salvage their belongings, chattering and gibbering to each other. It doesn't seem to occur to them to blame us – indeed, why should they when they had directed the whole operation? Except, maybe, to save all-important face? How were they to know that our men doing the tunnelling were gunners from the heavy coastal artillery regiments which manned Singapore's fifteen-inch guns? Knowing exactly what the effect of the explosion would be, the alignment of the tunnel had been most carefully aimed to find a satisfying target, and the men's scarred faces wear grins of quiet pride in their achievement.

While we have been cutting our ledge, which is now nearing readiness for the next stage of construction, a gang has been working on the face of the bluff at the northern end. There is a mass of rock to be dynamited, and they have been pecking at it in a somewhat futile manner by drilling small holes with hand-held drills struck with a four-pound sledge-hammer. The deepest they can go is less than a metre, and two holes in the hard rock are about all a pair of men can manage in a day. Because the bluff is smooth-surfaced and slopes downwards everywhere, work is possible only at the top rear end which, to start with, provides a small platform which will increase in area as the level is brought down. Even bringing in more pairs of drillers, as the space widens, will not speed up work appreciably.

So it is with great interest that we observe a pom-pom coming upriver from the south, towing a pontoon with a big air-compressor on its deck. It pulls in to the beach below the camp and at the end of the day, after evening rice, we are able to have a close look at it. The company I used to work for in Singapore imported these British-made plants designed expressly for mining. On a heavy steel base frame is mounted a petrol-engined compressor, pumping air into a big steel tank feeding air at high pressure into a manifold of eight outlets, into which airlines for pneumatic drills can be plugged. The whole piece weighs well over a ton. Obviously, this efficient chunk of machinery is here to boost the drilling of dynamite holes in the bluff.

The intriguing question which we toss around our little group is, how is it to be hoisted up the face of the riverbank to the only place where it can operate – that is, in the flat area between the end of our old embankment and the bluff itself? We know the height, it is nineteen metres above the river, sixty feet of earth studded with projecting rocks and shrubbery. There is no crane or any other kind of lifting gear, nor any material from which even a simple pulley and boom might be constructed. Anyway, that will be somebody else's problem, and it will be interesting to see how they cope with it.

In the morning, we find out. It is to be *our* gang's problem, so we shall see from right close up how it is done! We are absolutely dismayed; not one of us has had any experience whatsoever in this sort of thing. We hadn't been accustomed to swinging a pick and shovel all day either, but that is a totally different matter. Even with a proper crane or hoisting machinery, some degree of technical know-how is needed to ensure safe transfer from low point to high. Who the hell chose us? Well, we weren't exactly 'chosen' for our professional skills; our own pet Nip simply marched us down to the beach after morning tenko, pointed to the pontoon and said the magic word, which sounds like 'Hurrooshi' and, we have gathered, means 'Nothing to it, just get on with it'. Full of confidence, he is. Being too dumb to have the smallest notion of the difficulties! We, on the other hand, have a very good perception, and consequently no confidence whatsoever.

The pom-pom brings the pontoon and us across the river in no time at all, and we have to pull our wits together very smartly and decide how we are going to go about the job. It is a really serious problem, how to manhandle this bulky mass of steel machinery up a sixty-foot slope rearing above us at eighty degrees, nearly vertical, and setting it in place, without any damage, on the flat space at the top. It has to be controlled by one man to ensure coordinated effort, so that we shall all heave and shove together in the same direction and at the same time. Otherwise, we shall all be at high risk of injury, even death. And if the machine breaks loose and falls into thirty feet of river, we shall probably all qualify for a firing squad, for sabotage – provided, that is, we aren't carried into the river with it!

There is, of course, a big problem to be solved even before we start. How is the thing to be transferred from the pontoon to shore? On the outside curve of the fast current, the pontoon will have to be held close and absolutely firm against the bank, and as the load is edged from the centre to the side, the pontoon deck will tilt downwards. If it tilts too much, the compressor will slide into the river; there will be no holding it. We are filled with gloom and despondency (which the army says you should never allow to happen when in the face of the enemy, however bad the odds may appear). I think this might be classified as a different situation.

The British army is a versatile body. If you need somebody who can pick locks, poach pheasants, or recite the marriage ceremony of horsemen on the Mongolian steppes, somewhere there will step forward a man who is perfectly able to do it. In our present dilemma, it is our squeaky-voiced Eddie, former manager of the Ford vehicle assembly works at Bukit Timah (it was in his office that the capitulation of Singapore was concluded between Yamashita and Percival). Eddie is Australian, with the ingenuity born in him from his pioneering forebears, and it is a matter of personal pride that we shall not be defeated by the problems of this particular job, not in front of the Nips. It's an odd thought but, had this been a real Australian army project, a squad of Australian soldiers would very likely have sat back with smokos and a billy of tea until someone higher up produced the right materials. But they also have a bloody-minded obstinacy which, in our present difficulty, gets Eddie going.

Jumping aboard the pom-pom and waving our Nip and a bunch of us to come with him, we cross the river to the tool-shack, leaving the Nip to squabble with the Korean storekeeper while we collect crowbars, axes, ropes, sledge-hammers and spades and pile them in the boat. Our Nip seems to be catching on to the spirit of the game. He comes down to the boat grinning all over his face while the Korean is in danger of blowing all his gaskets at the insult to his authority. Their hatred of each other can occasionally be used to our advantage.

The machine is on a base of heavy steel girders turned up at the ends so that it can be dragged like a sled, and there is a hoisting hook welded onto each corner. It is sitting on two heavy slabs of timber laid on the deck of the pontoon. While the two boatmen rope the pontoon hard up against the bank, Eddie explains how we are going to do it. Not how he hopes we shall manage with luck and God's help, but how we will do it with our own efforts and by working as a team on his orders. 'Get that, you lot? Anyone doesn't do exactly as he is told, someone gets killed! Right? Let's get started!'

The morning is spent finding stout bamboos and sawing them to lengths. Bamboo's thick walls and close-set joints make it incredibly tough, and by levering up the ends of the timber slabs we are able to push pieces underneath to act as rollers, until finally the whole of the machine is poised ready to be moved off the pontoon onto a convenient rock shelf. The boatman noses his pom-pom up against the side of the pontoon to hold it in close, and slowly, inch by inch, the mass is edged forward until the timber bearers form a bridge to the shore. Heaving on ropes at the front hooks and levering with crowbars at the rear, precisely coordinated by Eddie's directions, we manhandle the steel monster broadside to the base of the cliff.

While this is in progress, others have been digging out a series of steps up the face of the slope, big enough to lodge the machine and at height intervals something less than four feet. So far, so good. Tomorrow we shall tackle the next bit.

Tomorrow comes, bright and sunny. And we come too, reluctant and apprehensive, having lost some of yesterday's confidence gained in getting that bloody thing ashore, and knowing that today will be far more risky. There is no way we can slacken bolts and nuts to dismantle the machine and take it up in pieces. There is no avoiding having to hoist it up as a deadweight lump.

Eddie's plan is to do it by stages, ledge by ledge. The load is to be lifted clear of the heavy timbers, which will then be slipped upright against the face of the slope. As the load is hoisted, it will slide over the timber surfaces, and when it nears the first ledge the lower ends will be lifted to help support the weight and tip it into the recess. The men hanging on to as many ropes as can be slung around will be standing on the next ledge up. When the machine is safely lodged, everyone moves up a step and the procedure is repeated. The floor of each ledge is strengthened with bamboo sections packed close together.

There is no point feeling nervous about personal safety – indeed, it would put yourself and everyone else at risk. Concentrating solely on doing the job, we find that it progresses smoothly. Watching every move with close attention, listening for Eddie's voice and all moving with precise effort, we develop confidence and (unexpectedly) pride in our achievement. By the end of the second day, the compressor is at the top, intact and ready to go. Eddie is our modest hero, accepting our congratulations with self-deprecating comments, but his relief at getting the job done without accident is obvious. What, I wonder, inspires a man to come forward and accept such responsibility, voluntarily? No one even said, 'You'll have to take charge, Eddie, you're the only engineer among us.' He could simply have kept quiet and let things take their course. Luck has indeed been on our side.

The brilliant winter weather seems to have set in properly. It is in fact winter although you might not think so, for the sun blazes serenely in a cloudless sky and the air is dry and crystal clear. And unlike a winter sun in Europe, there is tremendous heat in it. Here the rains fall in summer, with swollen purple-grey clouds for days on end, the sun coming through in occasional breaks and the air sodden and stifling.

With the cessation of rain in the mountains up-country, the level of the Kwei Noi has fallen rapidly, the current has slowed and the silt settled to the bottom. The water is now as clear as if it came from a civilised tap, reflecting the unbroken blue of the sky. Ron has a small atmospheric thermometer which today shows 135° F (57 degrees Nip style) in the sun where we work. The shade temperature is of little interest to us except in our huts, where it is 105° F at midday rice time. The dry atmosphere makes the heat bearable, but the rocky cliff behind us reflects heat to add to the sun's rays. There is no respite during our working hours, for the morning sun catches us and stays with us all day. The narrow strip of shade thrown by the ridge doesn't reach far enough to cover our worksite. From early morning until sunset we are in the full blast of the day's maximum heat, which is tempered only by the friendly little breeze that drifts down the river valley. A fundoshi and hat do not provide much protection for the skin, and this breeze is more than welcome.

The work gangs keep to the same area each day, and we are at the extreme northerly end where the bluff towers over the river. Our air-compressor is on the far side, not yet in use, waiting for air hoses and pneumatic drills to arrive. Just above us is a tiny shallow cave in the cliff face, and we scramble up there during the smoko breaks. About ten of us can squeeze into its shade. From the stink we know it was the habitat of the monkeys whose hooting and hallooing ring out through the forest around us. Sometimes we see a group moving down the riverbank to drink, only 100 yards or so away. One of the Nips takes potshots at them but, even with his rifle resting in a forked branch stuck in the shingle, he has not been able even to frighten them.

The midday rice break is a relief to look forward to. Before leaving our workplace we bury all our tools in the dust, or they will be uncomfortably hot to pick up an hour later. Even wood-handled spades absorb so much heat, and steel crowbars are untouchable.

Traffic on the river is not frequent. We can hear pompoms coming up an hour or more before they reach us, the bellow of their exhaust bouncing around the hillsides as they wind around the bends, making only a few knots against the current. From upriver there is faster movement, some launches towing three or four barges, which demands particular skills from the pilot as he is compelled to travel faster than the current or he will lose his steering power. With the bargemen standing alert with long poles, the string swings and sways through the curves, fending off rocks and beaches to disappear round the far bend. It looks so easy!

Occasionally there is a barge with a different cargo. It's just the usual type of wooden vessel for carrying goods, but these have thirty or forty women standing upright, packed together, all Asiatic and ranging from weathered old women to girls of maybe fourteen years old. Some look cheerful, some don't. When we wave at them and call out rude comments they wave back and shout equally rude (presumably) remarks, often accompanied by laughing and unmistakable hand signals. Do they feel sorry for us, being out of reach? Are they all voluntary contributors to the wellbeing of Jap troops at Tarsao and beyond, or are they shanghaied slaves? On the whole, we pity them.

Our Nips demonstrate to us with spectacular pantomime what these ladies are required for, as if we hadn't guessed. I think they are trying to rub in to us that we shall not be invited to the parties, crude bastards that they are. As a matter of fact, I do not know of any man who is in the slightest degree interested, beyond seeing what goes on and cracking a casual joke or two. Maybe we have just dried up as a result of nearly a year spent barely above starvation level, and our depleted bodies simply do not send urges to our senses. Just as well, because there is no opportunity to do anything about it, and if we did have normal feelings, what a desperate and unruly mob we could be. So it is probably a real blessing (at least in the current term) that we do not get excited and over-wrought. As with everything else, we simply accept matters as they are.

There is, however, a serious side to this and some men have discussed it with the medical officers. If our circumstances persist for another couple of years (which to those of us who can think objectively is more than probable), will there be permanent damage? Will we, on returning home after the war, be normal again in our relationships with wives and the girls we shall meet and marry? Will we be capable of becoming fathers? What shall we tell these women, in all honesty? The medical officers can't help – so much depends on age, past health record, future deprivations, how long before we are released, so many factors which cannot be fore-told. Some men are becoming really depressed, wondering about producing deformed babies or becoming mentally unstable themselves. And there is nothing, nothing what-soever, that their mates can offer to cheer them up.

God help us all in our problems. For what man in our circumstances can, by taking thought, influence his own future?

'Hey, fellers, just have a look at that!' We straighten our backs and look upriver to see something quite extraordinary. Emerging round the curve that is the limit of our view northwards is a great white cloud following the course of the river. Moving just above the surface and maybe fifteen feet in diameter, it is not a vapour yet not solid, and the whole mass pulsates with tiny movements.

As the head of the column comes nearer, we can see what it is – an enormous swarm of white butterflies held in close formation, and still drawing more length around the curve. Millions, tens of millions, of fluttering little creatures making their way purposefully downriver. We can see, as they pass only a few yards from us, that the pack is solid right through, every butterfly only inches from others all around it. The shape of the column is uniform throughout its length, and it not only keeps a steady height above the water but, having come to us round a left-hand bend it now curves sinuously to the right to follow the river. Only a few at the very front end will be able to see where they are flying, but somehow their leading controls all the others.

The rear end of the mass, when it come past us, is neat and perfectly formed. There are no stragglers or odd bods trying to catch up, and every tiny creature has beaten its way along its allotted path, with no deviation from its private little spot in either speed or position. All those busily thrashing wings, and not a sound audible to us!

Work has come to a complete halt, with every man (even the Nips) standing in silent wonder gazing at this manifestation of nature's marvellous powers. We watch the leading end faithfully swing around the far bend, and our foreshortened view from behind shows that there are no short cuts across the curve – the alignment is kept perfect over the whole length, which must surely be well over 400 yards. The living creatures fade into a powder-puff rump disappearing from our sight, and the spell is broken. But, for me at least, never to be forgotten.

How did all these minute muscles keep those wings

beating at such a constant rate, for such a long time, for they must already have flown some distance before reaching us and there were no signs of flagging as they went past? Such incredible stamina! I doubt if any one of us could jog-trot such a distance without being winded and stressed, and having to stop for a breather. As I get back to thumping my pickaxe into the earth, it occurs to me that my muscles, a hundred thousand times their size, do not produce anything like that ratio of efficiency. And we are supposed to be the 'intelligent' species on this planet?

In the last few days a new hut has been built on the camp side of the river, a couple of hundred yards downstream. It is for storage of the bags of cement that will be required for the concrete foundations to carry the bridge timbers. To protect the cement from the weather the hut is built far more carefully than the huts in which we live, the cement naturally being of more importance! The thatch is thick and the walls go right up to the roof, to keep the interior dry.

At the present time no cement has reached us, but nevertheless the hut is not left unused. A bargeload of prostitutes arrived four days ago and was towed away this morning. The women looked weary from insufficient sleep and excessive activity, but the Nips, having been the cause of their problem, are lively and cheerful and far less of a bother to us. Sorry, ladies, we sympathise with you and also offer our thanks for improving the tempers of our overseers!

I witnessed an interesting little scene after their departure. Our Nip was so full of joie de vivre that, during our lunchtime break in camp, he came over to our group to tell us all about it. 'Orru Korea weemeno! Japan weemeno nai! Korea weemeno takusan jig-a-jig!' With a lot more in Japanese unintelligible to us, but not to one of the Korean guards standing nearby, whose black scowling face showed just what he thought of the Nip army's use of Korean – but not Japanese – women. Not that such thoughts had prevented the Korean from visiting the cement hut on several occasions, as we had observed (it was impossible not to observe!) in the general flow of traffic. Maybe he simply objected to Japanese clients, while himself being appreciative of his countrywomen's 'plenty jig-a-jig' qualities.

We can't help having disquieting feelings on the subject. We Singaporeans used to read frequently about the barbaric behaviour of Japanese troops in China, being kept informed by news sources reporting through Hongkong and in the great English language newspapers published in China. Being so close, and having a large Chinese population there and in Malaya with very good reason to hate the Japanese, we were far better placed than people in Britain to know what had been happening in China during the thirties. We had little doubt that the Jap army would have had no compunction whatsoever about forcing Korean girls into their brothels. Conquered nations have no rights at all in the Nip philosophy. Their capture demands that they become totally obedient to the Sons of Heaven.

Many of our men have wives and children in Jap internment camps in Singapore, and our Eurasian boys have whole families under Jap authority. Even the mere fact of menfolk being in the Volunteers could, for all we know, bring heavy and unpleasant treatment on all those related to them. There is no way of knowing and maybe it is better not to know.

Five troopships brought the British 18th Division to Singapore in the latter half of January 1942, four of them reaching the docks safely. They sailed nearly empty owing to the Governor's refusal to approve the evacuation of women and children or to issue permits for them to leave. And this despite the captain of one ship calling personally on the Governor, saying his ship and the others could take thousands. The Governor's attitude, apparently, was that European women and children should not have special consideration over Asiatics, and if the Asiatic population couldn't be wholly evacuated, then no one would be sent away! What an incredibly inhuman attitude, from a man simply unable to grasp realities, way out of his depth and unable to cope, but refusing to recognise his weakness.

We heard about this, at the time it happened, when a man in our unit was told by our CO to take his family to the docks and get them aboard if he could. He spoke to army officers at the wharf who told him that they had been given strict orders not to allow Europeans to board any ship, but in defiance of these orders they were helping all they could to get away. Our fellow succeeded but very few others got away, out of the thousands who should have been helped to leave. Sadly, those who paid heed to the Governor's decision suffered accordingly, while those who ignored it were able to give their loved ones a chance of escape to safety.

These four ships sailed clear, but others were not so fortunate. My friend's father, who had served in the 1914–18 war and was in charge of security at Government House, was ordered out on a special permit. He sailed on the *Kuala* with forty other small coastal vessels, everybody an official evacuee, on Friday 13 February 1942. Black Friday indeed! Thirty-seven of those ships were sunk, by bombing and deliberate shelling by the Japanese navy. The *Kuala* was in company with the *Vyner Brooke* which carried a large contingent of Australian army nurses. Both ships were sunk but some men and women were able to reach the shore. There the Jap army found and murdered hundreds out of hand, including twenty-two nurses who were machine-gunned from behind, having been ordered to wade into the sea.

This news was brought to us at Changi in March 1942, when my friend's father (having been captured on Banka Island) joined us. I shall never forget the look on his face when he walked into our area and saw that his son was alive and his friends with him.

There is no reason to doubt the truth of this. It is merely one aspect of the uncivilised brutality of the Japanese nation – are not their serving officers supposed to be of the highest social standing in their homeland? If so, what can you expect from the rest? In our view, having personal experience of them, they are proof that you cannot make a heap of dung look good by trying to put polish on it. It is still smelly shit underneath.

The Korean ladies having moved further along in their sad life, the cement store is now available for its original purpose. Now that the river level has fallen, there is a long upward slope to carry the bags from the barges which have started to bring in supplies. We cannot understand the Nip decision to put the cement store on the camp side of the river. Maybe for security. But every bag now lugged up the slope will in due course have to be brought down again, loaded into a barge, poled across the river, unloaded ashore, and finally be carried up the face of the scree to where it is to be mixed. Just beyond the southern end of our section, there is plenty of flat land for a store, on the correct side of the river, which would save a hell of a lot of work. It could be, however, that it would officially be beyond our construction boundary and therefore common sense would not be taken into consideration.

We also have a change of work, and have struck lucky. The barge is allocated to us to take over two loads of stone in the morning and one in the afternoon, for concrete mixing. By the time the barge has taken non-swimmers across for work, and done the two midday trips, our job has to be done in the time left in between. It turns out to be pleasant and not unduly hard. The beach below the camp is really shingle: pale yellow river sand with masses of pebbles underneath. The Nips have provided timber frames with chicken-wire netting to sieve out the sand. The netting lasts an hour or so before disintegrating under the weight of shovelled sand and stone, so we simply shovel the stuff into the shallow edge of the river and let the sand wash off. The pebbles vary in size from hen's eggs to ostrich eggs, smoothly rounded from being rolled through sand by the river currents over the years.

Good concrete should have jagged stone chips of fairly small dimensions, but the Nips seem to be unaware of this – which is just as well, or we would find ourselves having to hammer every pebble to pieces. When the barge comes over, we scoop up a load of stone into small flattish cane baskets and tip it into the boat. The Siamese boatman poles his craft across the river, we swim over, and on the other side we form a chain up the slope. Baskets are filled and passed up, man to man, to be dumped on the ledge, the empties being tossed down to the barge. A slow and tedious process, but we don't have anything else to do, and because the boatman strictly limits the quantity we can put in for each trip, I doubt that we are moving more than a ton and a half in a full day's work. No matter, we can easily adjust our rate of work to fill in the time.

We have completed our second trip for the morning and the barge, well overloaded, is collecting its passengers to take over to the camp for midday rice. Halfway across, a swirl of the current catches it and in a few seconds the hull is floating upside down and dozens of men, none of whom can swim, are floundering around in the water and being carried downstream. Amid a good deal of shouting and yelling, everyone is pulled ashore safely. A search has been made under the barge, and while our men in the open cargo space were able to scramble clear as the hull heaved over, a Nip under the aft canopy was trapped. He was found by one of our men, a Scot who had been in the Aberdeen constabulary and obeyed his old training, pulling the Nip out and applying first aid on the beach. A curious situation: the Nip, naturally grateful at being rescued but not wanting to acknowledge his indebtedness to a red-haired foreigner, finally gives the Scot a grudging 'Arigato'.

Not that the Nip can be accused of a lack of civility. In Japanese social conventions (which are usually very strict) you have an unending obligation to a person who saves your life, a debt which can never, in fact, be settled. How can the Nip acknowledge this when his benefactor is an enemy soldier? But, to his credit, he at least has the innate decency to make an effort, which must have twisted his rigid upbringing painfully. And further, later that evening he brings a packet of cigarettes as a symbolic gift, handed over with a small bow and a grunted 'Dozo'. In their intricate system of social relationships, this may well have been intended to indicate 'signing off' the matter, leaving no feelings one way or the other in the future.

Despite our efforts to fill in our day and still look busy all the time, the Nips have increased our daily quota to three morning trips and two in the afternoon. This creates no problem in the workload, we can still do it, but the problem is the availability of the one and only barge. From now on breakfast and tenko will be earlier so that non-swimmers can be moved across sooner, and at the end of the day the barge will not bring them back until our second trip is completed.

A new shed is to be put up on a strip of flat beach below the camp, and a sawmill installed to provide planking for forming concrete slabs. In a few weeks or so we have piled heaps of stone along the full length of the ledge and are assigned to finding and felling suitable trees to feed the sawmill. In the perverse way of these things, such trees are all on the northern side of the river and the trimmed bare logs have to be tossed over the cliff into the river where our swimmers manhandle them across to the sawmill. Because they land in the swift current side, some vigorous swimming is needed to avoid losing them downstream.

In the first instance of intelligent Nip planning to come to our notice, a boatload of Nip army engineers turns up. Busy as a small swarm of ants, by the end of the day they have rigged up a sheerlegs on the high side of the riverbank, where the best trees are to be found, carrying a cable down to the lower bank where another sheerlegs is erected. A grapnel to carry logs is slung on wheels, so that trimmed tree trunks can now be sent down the cable in moments. They have also brought petrol for the air-compressor for a brief test run. It seems that our quiet solitude is to be disturbed by the racket of rock-drilling.

Next day a squad of our own army engineers joins us from Wampo Central, to examine this new equipment which they will use. They note that the machine is new and in good condition, but the pneumatic drills are clapped out and the airhoses are soft rubber when they should be reinforced. They give us their collective opinion in typical army all-purpose adjective and single-noun style, which is informative, if free of technical details.

Meanwhile, we have tried out our new aerial runway. The Nips didn't think of providing any kind of braking system on the hurtling logs, and on the third run the sheerlegs on the lower end is battered into collapse. Eddie, of the Ford factory, comes to the rescue again. We all swim across the river and rebuild the sheerlegs under his direction, then go back up to the top end where he ties a rope to the grapnel cradle so that its run down can be controlled. The Nip engineers weren't so smart after all.

Our own people have got their drilling equipment assembled, and the sergeant-in-charge has tried to explain to our Nips that the hoses are no good – 'damme'. The Nips, of course, refuse to accept that there can be anything wrong with their stuff, so the drills are connected and the hoses split open as soon as the pressured air is let through.

Three days later new hoses arrive – heavy reinforced material that functions perfectly. Shot-holes are drilled all over the bluff and there is to be a ceremonial firing of the first blast. The Nip commandant himself will attend. Even one of our own officers turns up to check everything. He is the only officer (apart from the captain in our camp) that we have seen at Wampo South. Working at our sheerlegs, we overhear a conversation between him and his sergeant:

'I say, sergeant, those shot-holes you've drilled, aren't they in the wrong place?'

'No, sir, they're exactly where the Nips told us to drill them.'

'But when the charges go off, the rock will blow out all over the compressor!'

'Yes, sir.'

'But, I mean to say, you shouldn't do that, should you?'

'No, sir.'

'Then why are you doing it?'

'Sir, the *enemy* wants it done that way.'

'The enemy? But surely they don't want to damage their own machine?'

The sergeant is losing patience – can't this twit

understand?' 'I wouldn't know about that, sir, but it's how they have arranged things.'

The light dawns on the officer. 'Oh, I see! What a damn good joke, eh? Hee, hee, hee!' And he walks back to Central chortling away nineteen to the dozen, no doubt to tell his friends how clever he is.

Next day, when we are all in camp for lunch, the great moment arrives. The inspecting party is in place, standing well back from the bluff, the shot-holes have been filled with dynamite and fuses laid. We are called to attention, the Korean bugler toots his serenade to the gods, the fuses are ignited and smoke plumes sizzle up the face of the rock.

The charges detonate, the rock bulges for a brief moment, then splits outwards amid clouds of smoke and dust. Chunks of rock soar upwards, then curve down gracefully all around the compressor. Not as much damage as we had hoped, but a satisfying burst of flame from the petrol tank, and blazing fuel running down to the ground. The nearest water is sixty feet down the cliff in the river, and the few Nips who form the demolition party have to improvise. Shirts are torn off to beat out the flames, one man actually tries to urinate on them but can't get close enough, and the fire goes out of its own accord when the petrol tank has emptied itself.

Even this farce doesn't discourage the Nips. Determined to get something done right, there is to be another ceremonial parade to watch the dislodging of our old friend, the Great Boulder, for the second time. The next day, at evening tenko, we all parade to watch. More bugle tunes, a rumbling explosion, the earth around the tunnel collapses and the great bulk starts to tip over the edge and roll down the scree. With a majestic splash, it settles in the river, pushing a rolling swell across to our side. Before the boatman can do more than jump to his feet, his barge is tossed up high and dry on the beach.

The boulder is so large that, bedded in the deepest channel of the river, the top is well above the surface. And a permanent navigational hazard has been set up in the most awkward spot, right in the traffic lane.

There are only a few lumps of rock thrown up by the blast. One of them comes across the river and crashes through the roof of one of our huts. There are only a few men with malaria inside, lying on the sleeping platform, and one of my friends is in precisely the wrong place. The fist-sized chunk of jagged rock strikes him squarely on his left cheekbone. It looks to be a very nasty laceration, which may have damaged his eye.

There is no field telephone on our side of the river, and the only way to call the medical officer from Wampo Central is to send a runner. During the waiting period the Australians demonstrate their talent for quick reaction to an emergency – while our people tend to wait for orders, they simply start to get things organised.

The barge is shoved back into the water and poled across ready to bring the medical officer over. A stretcher is made up of bamboo poles and rice sacks, and squads of four men stand ready as stretcher-bearers. The MO arrives and stitches up the patient's face, the man is strapped to the stretcher and taken across the river in the boat, to be carefully carried up the cliff by the waiting four men. Two other squads have already positioned themselves along the embankment to act as relays, and our injured friend will be in Central Camp as soon as is possible, moving at a steady pace without pause except briefly for relay changeovers.

He has had nothing to relieve the pain of the injury and having it cleaned of grit and sewn together, and the unavoidable jolting of the journey to Wampo Central will not help things. Nor is it likely that he will get any better treatment on arrival, but we have done our best for him.

* * *

There must be an area upriver from Wampo where bamboo grows in masses near the riverbank, for we occasionally see great rafts of this incredibly useful wood. Maybe it's not technically correct to call it 'wood' – our agricultural experts say it is, botanically, a form of grass – but most of its uses are those associated with timber. Growing in thick clumps amongst the trees, which we have had to clear for the railway, we have found it in lengths of sixty feet and more. It is extraordinarily tough, hard and resilient at the same time, easy to saw and split, and it burns with a fiercely hot flame even when green. The young shoots are a favourite vegetable with Asiatic peoples, crunchy to bite and with a delicate flavour, but so far we haven't been able to find any to supplement our insipid rations. Maybe we just don't know where to look.

We have seen several great rafts of bamboo floating down our Kwei Noi; there must be thousands of stems lashed tightly together to form solid pontoons. The flat decks have two or three bamboo and attap huts, where the boatmen's families live, women and kids, dogs and cooking braziers, in a cosy domestic display of contented village life sliding round the river's bends.

Usually there are three or four of these rafts in close procession, silently carried in the fast current along the outer curves and swinging across as the river changes direction. The boatmen on each raft keep control by fending off the banks, a seemingly effortless operation, but one that actually requires considerable skill. A momentary lack of concentration could easily result in a raft swinging broadside across the river, which in our particular spot is not wide, and a piling up of the following rafts, for there are no brakes on these craft and the river stops for no one. It must be that these voyages can be undertaken only about this time of the year, when the fast torrent of the wet season has subsided and there is still sufficient depth of water over the sandbanks before the end of the dry winter weather, when they will be exposed as the river falls to its lowest level before the next monsoon. A jam of colliding rafts would be a disaster. There must be a considerable tonnage there, and extricating them in the teeth of the current, with only muscle-power available, would be a formidable task.

The people wave and call out to us in friendly fashion, and we pause in our work to respond. Our Nips don't interfere; there is only a break of a few moments before they are swept into the downriver bend. For us, it's a small patch of interest in our lives – anything that is different and gives us something to talk about is more than welcome.

Several of us think that, after the war, we would like to come back – hire a motorised barge and go upriver for a week or so, then quickly back with the current to Kanburi. A few books, a camera, maybe a fishing line, would be all that we would need for comfort and to pass the time in peaceful relaxation. It's a good thing we can look beyond the present and appreciate the scenic qualities of our surroundings, despite the dismal facts of our situation.

It's near enough to Christmas (our first in captivity) for us to have nostalgic thoughts of home and family festivities, especially for those of our troops who, this time last year, were about to embark for North Africa and, while at sea, found themselves diverted to Singapore. They arrived at the end of January 1942, went into action straight away with no knowledge whatsoever of the country and unable to distinguish between the many Asiatic races, and relatively unfit after some thirteen weeks at sea. In our opinion, it was politics and not military necessity that brought them to Singapore – they were far too few to retrieve an already doomed Singapore and they now suffer the consequences of Whitehall's inability to face unpleasant facts. The 18th Division should have gone to Rangoon, where it could very possibly have held things together until further reinforcements could be brought in, instead of being uselessly sacrificed to the gods of disaster and to the puffed-up self-esteem of gutless politicians.

We have had plenty of time to think about the war, free of the obfuscations of propaganda and the pressure to support those in control for the sake of patriotism, able to review events and argue openly and form opinions. In the case of the 18th Division, sending the division to Rangoon, where it would have been ready for action a critical fortnight earlier, would have meant admitting the inevitability of Singapore's capitulation. But no one had the guts to make such a decision, and a fine division was deliberately destroyed for the sole purpose of fending off damage to spineless reputations. We may be wrong, and we may have developed a cynical standpoint, but looking back over the unbroken series of disasters, we do have cold logic behind our reasoning. As some historical personage said, if you are under an immediate sentence of death, your mind is wonderfully cleared (or something to that effect), and are we not in a comparable situation?

Even to us Singapore Volunteers, Christmas is associated with snow and cold weather from our early days and, quite without warning, we find night temperatures falling to 45 degrees (8 degrees Nip). Which is decidedly chilly after a day's work on the rock face, being a drop of ninety degrees in a few hours. Our knowledgeable fellow says it is the usual pattern for some three months from mid December, for brief spells of a few days to a fortnight. Well, after all, it is winter, and may have something to do with the passage of the monsoon winds over the high mountains of south-west China.

Many of our men sold their army blankets to the Siamese villagers on the march from Ban Pong, thinking that they were not necessary in the tropics. They must regret it now; it's no joke being naked when the night temperatures are little above freezing point, sleeping on bare bamboo slats which rattle audibly as the men shiver.

There has, however, been a comic aspect to these wintry nights. The cold has induced a moistness into the early morning air, and today I wake up to find myself totally wrapped in a cool milky mist, so thick that I can hardly make out my neighbours less than a foot away on either side. Looking up, nothing but cloud. Sitting up, my head just breaks through and I have the slightly weird sensation of gazing over a flat cloud top. The roof and its supporting poles are clear, and here and there up and down the hut other heads are looking around in surprise. I have a momentary vision of a satanic gathering of the victims of execution by beheading, coming together for a ritual dance. The heads seem to slide along the opalescent surface as the invisible bodies slither (heels, hands and bums) off the sleeping platform to stand upright in the central passageway, when chests and shoulders appear.

Outside the hut the cloud stretches unbroken over the parade ground, the valley of the river is filled with mist, the boatman and his barge (presumably) somewhere down below, invisible. The sky is blue and cloudless, the top half of the cliff face shining in the clear early sunlight. It's all quite unusual, beautiful and fascinating.

Now the problems arise. The mass start-of-the-day promenade to the latrines hesitates, then comes to a standstill. We all know where they are, but since we cannot see precisely

141

where, it is immediately apparent that a careless step could drop you into a trench. And anyone who does manage to locate it would be out of sight from above as he squatted over it below cloud level, so you might unknowingly blunder against him and tip him in, quite possibly going in with him yourself.

The cooks bring the rice tubs into the huts, standing them on the sleeping platforms so that they can see to ladle out breakfast. Tenko is a slightly comic affair: with our sun-burned skins we resemble lifelike head-and-shoulder carvings in dark-stained timber, decorated with sprouting whiskers and an odd assortment of hats, bedded on cotton wool. The Nips, being shorter than us, float around like disembodied heads.

Work is plainly impossible, but our unexpected yasumi is not of much use to us because we have to remain standing up. Our officer takes the opportunity to tell us that, last night, the Nip railway engineers told him that we are not working hard enough and progress is too slow. He replied that our food was 'damme damme and too skoshi (no good and not enough)', and that they should tell the Koreans to give us more, which had been promised when we came to this camp. He hoped this tactic would bring results, especially as he had taken the visiting Nip officer to our cookhouse to see our food for himself.

It takes over an hour for the sun to disperse the mist, and we are back at work. The first log is sent down the cable, the gang on the lower end releases the jaws of the grapnel and drags the log away while we haul the grapnel back and clamp another log in place. It is a restful easy-paced job that can't be speeded up, and we are quite happy to do it, but even the Nips must see that, as suitable trees become harder to find, there won't be enough logs to produce the timber they will be needing. Most of the forest hereabouts is small stuff, and the far side of the river doesn't look any different.

I think our working party must have impressed the Nips after our handling of the air-compressor and aerial cable, because we have now been switched to a new project. We are to work in the sawmill, which will slice up the logs that we have delivered as well as timber which is to be brought in along the river. Maybe the Nips have noticed our Eddie's familiarity with things mechanical.

A pontoon arrives with massive slabs of timber, already cut and drilled, to be bolted into a heavy saw table. A circular blade is set into a slot in the centre, coupled to a broad pulley-wheel underneath. This in turn carries an endless loop of conveyor belt, which drapes over a similar pulley-wheel behind a petrol engine. Eddie reckons the engine came from a Dodge truck, about a 1924 model, and when he has started it up, he announces that it is so worn that it should be scrapped. The drive pulley is mounted behind the clutch housing, which can be switched by a lever from neutral into gear. Our Nip is full of admiration for Eddie's skill in putting everything together, and wants a demonstration of it all functioning as a unit.

Eddie has already explained to us that three things are critical to its successful operation. First, the two pulleys must be exactly in line and squared off with each other. Second, the distance between them must be precisely matched to the belt, which cannot be adjusted in length. Thirdly, the engine must be set at a dead right angle to the belt as even the smallest deviation will throw the belt off the pulley.

He has also pointed out that it can never work properly. The belt is a massive thing, far too long and heavy for the job and it's beyond the clapped-out engine's capacity to drive. Its sheer length and weight will cause it to sag in the middle and it will drag the engine (which stands on loose sand and cannot be anchored in place) out of alignment. In addition to that, the whole set-up has to be done by eye, which is nowhere near accurate enough. So Eddie warns us to stand well clear when the belt is being driven. He will keep the test run as brief as possible and hope the Nip will be satisfied, and switch off before anything goes wrong.

It all goes wrong. Eddie's cautious revving of the engine gets the Nip all excited and he wants a log pushed onto the circular blade. We heave one up on the table, whereupon our Nip seizes it and shoves it forward with a total disregard for the absolute need to align the log perfectly with the saw. The blade is bent sideways and splits. Luckily the sudden strain throws the belt off the pulley before the saw disc can splinter and hurl jagged bits at us.

The horrified Nip turns an interesting puce colour, but remarkably quickly he grabs a spare blade from a box full of bits and pieces. There's even a spanner to release the busted blade and fit a new one. The Nip army seems to grow in efficiency day by day!

This time he will drive the engine, and we will handle the log. He's not going to be caught making the same mistake twice, and he's right – this time he stuffs it up in a different way. The belt is manhandled into position, he pays no attention to Eddie's warnings to keep the revs down but races the engine to full throttle, then engages the clutch with a slam and signals to us to push the log onto the saw.

The pulley behind the engine jerks madly, snatching at the belt as it tries to get a grip. The pressure of the log on the saw blade tugs the belt back; the belt itself slaps wildly then gives up and jumps free. Steaming with rage, the Nip can scarcely control himself while Eddie, with masterly pantomime, demonstrates how the stresses have combined to dislodge the belt. Then he points out that the weight of the belt has dragged the engine slightly out of alignment, and it will have to be pushed back into place before it can be used again.

Dazzled by science though he is, this is something the Nip can grasp. Seizing a six-foot steel crowbar, he stabs one end into the sand under the pulley, puts his shoulder under the other end and, in true Nippon bushido style, gives a great heave. The engine moves, but too far. Never mind, a repeat effort from the other side will get it right. We loop the belt on once again (it is so heavy that four of us are needed to manipulate it), and all is ready for another try.

The engine is started, the clutch engaged, and the belt leaps off almost immediately. Eddie shows the Nip that the pulley is now not spinning smoothly but is wobbling with a definite eccentricity. The Nip's spirit of bushido was evidently too powerful, for the drive shaft has been bent out of true by the crowbar levering against it. It is now a job for an engineering workshop, and the sawmill will be at a standstill until further notice.

Eddie has never seemed to us to be a man of subtle thinking, but when we look back, we can see how he led the Nip into responsibility for everything that went wrong, while we were not only blameless but actually tried to warn him against making mistakes. No doubt the Nip will get hell from his own people, but that's his problem.

We have been hearing rumours of other camps upriver where conditions are far worse than ours. Where these bits of gossip come from we don't really know, certainly not from the Nips, so there must be some form of communication between our people, but we haven't seen any actual evidence of it.

We do know that parties of men make their way northwards from time to time, which will be to establish new camps or to reinforce existing camps. Even in this there is no actual contact that we know of. They must march (as we did) direct to Tarsao from Kanchanaburi. If they move by river barge, they would have to pass through our area, and that has not happened. Or they could come through on foot via the camps downriver, which are working up to connect with our stretch, but there have not been any such movements.

Apart from this kind of local chitchat, we have items of war news; usually fuzzy in outline and never with any dates, frequently obviously fabricated, and never reliable. Maybe the local Siamese traders pass it all on to us; so many of them speak passable to fluent English, as we found during our march to Tarsao. In fact, we have seen definite signs of their dislike of the Nips, and there has been occasional proof of their sympathy towards us.

The paper bands wrapped around hanks of tobacco that came in recently are an example of the latter. The outside has the brand name and decoration, but the white inside surface is printed with what appears, at first, to be a casual kind of doodle. Of course, we inspect it closely (having little else in the way of intellectual exercise) and it suddenly becomes clear. The wiggly slanting line down the left-hand side is the Lower Burma coast, and the long inverted U at the bottom right is the head of the Gulf of Siam. A straight horizontal line from west to east with the number fourteen at one end indicates the fourteenth parallel of latitude, and the hardly noticeable black dot, left of centre, identifies the location of our camps. No Nip officer would touch this rough shag tobacco, so would never be likely to see the sketch, and any Nip soldier who did see it would be too ignorant to realise what it is.

We who lived in this general part of Asia are able to explain the significance of the drawing to others, pointing out that fourteen degrees of latitude corresponds to a distance of about 1,000 miles, and if they are thinking of trying to escape, they should keep in mind how far we are from any friendly territory. Apart from sheer distance, a Westerner stands out amongst Asiatics too plainly to be disguised or concealed, and in all probability there would be a reward offered by the Nips for handing in an escapee.

Despite their complaint that we are not working hard enough, the rate of progress seems to satisfy the Nips, and so far we have been able to keep to a regular daily schedule. Rousing ourselves at daylight, we go through a settled timetable until evening tenko, without too much unpleasantness from the Nips. It is a far better place than Wampo Central, and everyone works steadily to avoid being sent back there.

After evening rice, we are left to pass the time until 'lights out' in our own way. The weather being quite delightful in the evenings, everyone sits in groups over the parade ground and chats, making small fires to brighten the scene and to boil mess tins of charred rice 'coffee' or an egg. Conversation is relaxed and tends to be patchy – after all, what is there to talk about beyond the day's incidents? Without news and books, we have long ago exhausted most past events in our lives, and it is becoming difficult to find subjects for discussion. I also think that the unreality of our situation, so totally cut off from families and friends and from the daily doings of a normal life, has tended to make us intellectually tired, maybe disinclined to make the effort to recall, and thoughts do not slide around our minds with the old facility. It could well be that malnutrition has something to do with it, our brain tissues not being properly nourished in some vital way.

Last night was somewhat different. Presumably as a result of his conversation with our captain about rations, the Nip gunso emerges from his hut and marches purposefully to the Koreans' hut, returning with the senior Korean. They disappear inside and there is immediately an outburst of furious shouting and thumping of fists and boots on flesh. After several minutes the racket dies down, the gunso comes out and bawls at the other hut. Two Koreans come over to drag their comrade away, unconscious and sagging. Maybe the rations will improve now.

In our group of Volunteers are two men from a government experimental farm near Kuala Lumpur, where they were engaged in experiments to try to improve local crops and to find new plants which would suit local conditions for commercial production. These two highly qualified scientists are, consequent upon the wise decisions of the civil service, now private soldiers. But their skills have found two edible plants; not very plentiful, it is true, but nevertheless a welcome addition to our diet for those who can spot them. One is a creeper that is sometimes found growing over bamboo clumps; part of the passion fruit family, it is not particularly appetising. The other is what they call Bombay spinach, a small dark green bush that grows here and there along the sandy beach close to the water. The leaves are covered in tiny prickles which draw blood from your fingertips when you pick them, and when you boil them the water turns an intense green. I imagine rusty nails would produce the same flavour, but if that indicates iron, then they are worth eating and drinking.

Tucked away in my kit, and kept out of the sight of the Nips when they conduct searches, I have a Rolex Tudor wristwatch, a birthday present from Mum and Dad in happier days. For some reason it stopped working while we were in River Valley

Road Camp way back in Singapore, but I have hung on to it in the hope it will still be with me when the war ends. Now, however, seems to be a good time to try to exchange it for whatever cash I can get, so I am waiting for an opportunity to turn up.

The Nips allow the occasional barge to stop at the beach, it being by the Nip commandant's permission that they call at Central. And, of course, they extract a toll from the traders. Slipping into the shadow between two barges nosed into the beach, I reach up and put the watch on the deck by the aft canopy, where the boatman is sitting talking to his mate. It is quite safe to do this; the boatmen are absolutely trustworthy in their dealings with us. A couple of minutes later a voice says something, I reach up and feel a small packet.

Back in my hut, I find forty ticals, a fair price for a non-working watch, equal to more than six months' pay, half going to my brother. When eggs are next available, there will be 'presents' to my particular friends.

Welcome news from Central! Lieutenant Tanaka has said we can have a concert before Christmas and the whole camp is permitted to attend. In practice this means only those who can swim across the river, because the boatman has taken to pushing off on his own after completing his day's duties. That's tough on those not able to go, but there's nothing we can do about it.

Amid remarks such as, 'Damn, I've run out of polish for my evening shoes,' and, 'Do you think a black tie will be appropriate with my fundoshi?' we have a tenko to count how many are going. There will be 100 plus of our men staying in camp, and they cannot be left unguarded, so the Nips perforce will have to stay. They are in an unpleasant mood, scowling blackly and shouting at us, and counting us several times. It is impressed on us that we must be back by 'ju-ichi ji' (eleven o'clock), 'Orru man, ju-ichi ji.' Probably they don't want to be kept up late for tenko on our return.

Dismissed from counting, we swim over and climb up the other side, jog-trotting along the embankment to dry off. We wear nothing except fundoshi and hat, but I don't think any one of us feels that it is just a little bit weird to be going to a Christmas concert in this style. We take these things in our stride nowadays.

On arrival our doughty captain reports to camp administration, making a point of the necessity for our party to leave in good time to get back before eleven o'clock, or there could be trouble with our Nips in such a foul mood. Word comes back that Lieutenant Tanaka says we can stay to the end of the concert, whatever time that may turn out to be, and he will notify Wampo South. Since none of us has a watch, our only indication of time passing will be the position of the moon, unless an officer who has a watch lets us know.

The concert is simply marvellous. The previous one was good but hastily put together at short notice, while this is the result of effort put in by an unofficial (but Tanaka-approved) working party comprised of officers with professional experience (surprisingly many) and enthusiastic helpers. Some turns are from memory, others have been pieced together from a pool of recollections, and some are original. As before, the stage is lit by big bonfires in front at each side, throwing a rosy flickering illumination which lets us see what is going on but, fortuitously, is not bright enough to show the makeshift scenery and costumes.

The 'girls' are glamorous in wigs of teased rope and a little Mercurochrome lipstick, with rice-flour cheeks and sooty eyebrows, their rice-bag dresses trimmed with leaves. By necessity, the play takes place in an officers' mess, since only khaki shirts and trousers are available for the men.

The faithful accordion plays dance music, and couples drift around the stage in waltz and foxtrot time. Waiters hover, the crooner drools on about moonlight and perfumed nights and there is an entrancing atmosphere of romance, hand-holding, and intimate whispers. It is all overwhelmingly nostalgic, the audience so lost in soft recollections of the past that the playlet ends in total silence while the men emerge from their private dreamlands. Then the applause is deafening. The illusion continues for the rest of the concert, singers and comedians, readers of verse and musicians with their homemade instruments all being clapped and cheered in a great outpouring of thanks and appreciation for the magic moments which they have given us.

Time to go home. We suspect that it is getting late, but we have to be officially 'signed off' before we can leave. In the confusion and general exhilaration, it is difficult to find an officer who will help us to check with Tanaka. No one is in the mood for formalities, and we are called together to move out without further delay.

As we trot down the embankment, we see by the moon that it is well past our deadline, and when we emerge from the river and form up for tenko, it is obvious that the Nips are furiously aware of that too.

We count ourselves, the number is correct, and the captain reports to the gunso, to be slapped across the face with a heavy right hand followed by a left. The gunso has (in true Nip style) worked himself into a rage while awaiting our return and is now almost out of control. His Nips and Koreans are ranged behind him, glaring at us in conformity with his mood. We have been disobedient and must be punished.

Our captain tries to explain that the Shoko Tanaka told

us to stay until 'finisho', but the Nip is so mad with anger that even Tanaka's name does not penetrate. He bashes our captain twice more, then raises his fist again.

The unfairness of all this has its effect on us, all 400 or so standing at attention and watching the performing ape. Our tempers have been building up pressure, and at this point a great roar of anger bursts from us. It is quite extraordinary. Without any word of command, we all shout at the same instant, some critical point of control having been reached at which we all, every man of us, simultaneously detonate.

A bellow of rage from 400 men at the same instant must have a startling impact on the recipients. A moment of frozen immobility, then two things happen. Our sergeant-major snaps around to face us and, in a voice that carries all his authority, he shouts, 'STAND FAST! EVERY MAN, STAND FAST! *QUIET!* COME TO ATTENTION!' The second thing is the Koreans dashing into their hut a few yards away and coming back with their rifles, pumping a round into the breech. The gunso is transfixed, and his Nips cannot go for their rifles without coming close to us.

In half a minute the crisis is over. We are all standing blank-faced, at attention, the Nips have had a fright (despite their rifles, they are only a handful against us) and maybe even realise that they were in the wrong. Not that being in the wrong matters in the Nip army – it is the authority conferred by rank that counts, even at the lowest levels. Or, possibly, an instinct for self-preservation tipped a cold douche over them.

We are dismissed as if nothing had happened, to our great relief.

Our two months or so at Wampo South have brought quite remarkable changes for the better in our spirits and in our physical condition. It may or may not be relevant, but the huts are quiet at night, there are no sounds of pain and distress or mumblings in sleep – indeed, not even snoring – and no constant movement of men in and out. I sleep lightly but restfully.

Permeating every aspect of our daily lives has been the change in seasons, from saturating wet to bone dry in a matter of a few days. The lowering, steamy and utterly depressing gloom at Wampo Central has given way to daylong brilliant sunshine and clear blue skies, in itself a tonic to every one of us. The days are intensely hot, but the dry heat is far easier to bear and an occasional cool breeze ripples over us as it runs down the valley of the Kwei Noi. Nights are a pleasant relief and our huts are (so far) free of bugs. Even the clean sandy floor is something to be appreciated after the brown, always damp, earth at Central. During smokos, at the lunch break and in the evenings we are able to freshen up in the river, now clear and serenely ambling along.

Rations have improved – not a lot, but even a little is noticeable and thankfully received – possibly as a result of the Korean being bashed recently. Our rice and tea are now cooked and brewed in clean water, which not only improves their palatability but means that our intestines are no longer irritated by silt and grit. Being able to sleep through the night without having our rest broken by half a dozen visits to the latrines is, in itself, marvellously restorative. In the absence of even the simplest and most commonplace medical treatment, a night's peaceful relaxation is our one and only resource for repair and healing of our bodies and minds, and in consequence is invaluable. And the sale of my watch has enabled me to buy extra duck eggs, bananas and limes as they become available from time to time.

There has even been some entertainment, such as the gunners' bull's-eye of the Nip hut and the damage to the air-compressor and sawmill. And no recriminations from the Nips either! Laughter had become rare at Wampo Central.

Even the Nips and Koreans have become more manageable. I like to think that our confrontation with them after the concert has something to do with this, making them realise that we are still men of spirit and might well boil over if pushed too far. One thing we can be sure of, the incident will certainly not have been reported to Central because of the serious loss of 'face' which our Nips would have suffered. Further, they must know that, in the event of any enquiry, we would point out that Lieutenant Tanaka had expressly given permission for us to stay on at the concert, and that our camp Nips had disregarded that when we told them – such an insult to an officer would have brought down severe punishment. So there has come into being a carefully balanced truce, where we do our work steadily and they moderate their attitude towards us.

Bright days are followed by brilliant nights, with all heaven's magnificence displayed above us. Situated as we are, well within the Tropic of Cancer, our sighting extends far into the familiar north and, at this time of the year, deep into the southern constellations. Sleeping outside the huts, we can watch their vast, slow, majestic wheeling through the depths of space, timeless and somehow comforting.

The Australians, who tend to claim the Southern Cross as their own personal and national property, stare nostalgically at this glittering symbol of their homeland. The distinctive outline of Orion's Belt they affectionately call the Old Iron Pot.

Sunsets are always colourful, frequently spectacular to a degree which fascinates and entrances the mind. Due west is a high mountain, standing solitary above the lesser ranges which lie north to south between us and the Indian Ocean. It has a broken-tooth crest and, with the vivid flaring sun behind, it stands in black silhouette against furnace crimson on the skyline, shading lighter overhead and eastwards. Ten to fifteen minutes only to enjoy such glorious beauty, and the show is over until the next day.

Oh, a relatively tiny occurrence which caught the attention of all of us! A couple of weeks ago, while we were waiting on the parade ground for tenko, an odd-looking bird flew directly overhead in an undeviatingly straight and level path precisely due north to south. It was not very high above us, so we could clearly see small details of its body, which was compact like a plump sausage, and had a neat narrow fan of tail feathers. Its neck, tube-like and stretched rigidly forwards, was almost as long as its body, its smallish head spherical with a strong beak curved to a hook. Its feet were tucked up close, its whole body maybe thirty-six arrow-straight inches from beak to tail, and its wings beat with a curious clockwork regularity – two beats, and a pause in which its wings remained outstretched and motionless. And during this pause, it uttered a staccato cry – 'tok-tok' – so the rhythm of its flight was 'flap-flap, tok-tok'. Only a minute or so and it was gone, but it has repeated its flight every day, at precisely the same hour and in the same manner, its dark plumage a glowing ruby in the setting sun. Nobody can identify it, but it has caught our imagination and we have fondly christened it The Tok-Tok Bird. This endearing little creature shared part of its life with us until two nights ago when it failed to appear. We have not seen it since and are whimsically saddened, and hope it hasn't come to any harm.

We do have a human need for a living creature to which we can offer affection (as distinct from the comradeship which binds us all together), and the Nips certainly don't qualify! This bird, with its quaint appearance and mannerisms, touched and stirred some buried emotion in us, and we are grateful.

Some soul-less bastard suggests it might not have been a real bird after all, but a mechanical robot with a camera spying out the railway construction. Damn him, he may be right for all we know, but he soon shut up under the dirty looks we gave him!

Despite this being the dry season, we have in fact had some rain here at Wampo South, a thunderstorm a month ago and another last night which swept up on us in the small hours. A few distant rumbles and pale flickerings woke me, then the storm smacked into us in a shattering bombardment, shot through with jagged lightning of such intensity and frequency that the hut's interior was constantly stark-lit with blinding blue and white flashes, some of which seemed to sizzle in one side and out the other. The unpleasant odour of burning was noticeable, a hot electrical stink in the atmosphere, but nothing could possibly have been on fire in the massive deluge hammering on our attap roof. Spears of rain drilled into the sand outside, glittering and scintillating in the lightning's frantic slashing.

The onslaught continued for an hour or more without slackening, then suddenly it was quiet, as if switched off. The sand was wet and beaten firm, totally different from Wampo Central where the mud would have been lapping over everyone's ankles and the cookhouse fires in all probability flooded out.

The air was fresh and cool, the firmament's jewels again scattered generously overhead, and sleep came back easily.

The shrinking of the river, which is now some fifteen feet lower than when we came to Wampo South, has exposed a new area of flat land, two or three acres in extent, just beyond our downstream boundary. Almost immediately this sizeable patch has become covered with new green vegetation, reeds and grasses and shrubs all growing vigorously. The fertility is incredible!

Mid morning today there is a high-pitched trumpeting sound, vaguely familiar from somewhere back in the childhood memories of some of our Londoners. Looking downriver, we see two mighty elephants emerging from a gully in the face of the escarpment, which backs the new flat patch. Each has a rider perched high up astride its neck, and the great beasts push into the shrubbery until they come to a halt at some spot which appeals to them. The riders slide down and the elephants begin to graze. The memory clears – this was the sound made by the elephants at London's great Regents Park Zoo as they patiently carried small children in howdahs on their backs at tuppence a ride.

At evening tenko, our captain tells us that they have been brought in to work with logs for the sawmill, and we shall probably be in close contact with them. He warns us, 'Don't get too near them to start with, give them time to get used to you. You will look strange to them, and probably smell peculiar too, and they may not like you. Just be sensible, and don't try anything stupid.'

Eddie has been up to his sly tricks again. Removing the grapnel from the aerial runway to grease the wheels, he hands the piece back to our Nip to put it back on the wire. Our Nip loves being included in these highly technical little jobs, and grins like a child when given something to do. Unfortunately, he fails to notice that Eddie has run the nuts off the bolts which hold the apparatus together, and in a few moments it has jumped off the wire and fallen into the deep channel of the river. This kind of mishap either drives a Nip into frenzied panic or paralyses him with fear. Luckily ours is the manageable, quiet type. We scramble down the cliff and engage in duck-diving, finding the grapnel almost immediately and carefully hiding it in a crevice from where we shall be able to retrieve it in two or three days' time. This period we happily fill in by diving for big shellfish, somewhat similar to abalone, which we came across on the first dive. The meat is as tough as truck tyres, but the broth from simmering it must, surely, have some value. Our Nip is almost embarrassingly grateful for our efforts, especially when we point out in pantomime that the great depth is painful for our ears but, nevertheless, we want to do all we can for him. It's almost a shame to mislead him like this, taking advantage of his naivety.

So in due course we have our aerial log delivery service back in action, and soon clear the small pile which has accumulated. Then exciting news reaches us. There is to be an inspection of work by a party of very senior Nip army officers, coming down by boat from Tarsao, and our runway is to give a special demonstration! How about that? Our Nip will be the star performer, and will himself operate the passage of a log! Which gives Eddie something to think about.

On the grapnel is a lever which is clamped into position to bite the prongs securely into a log, and on reaching the bottom end of the run, this lever is pulled back to free the prongs and release the log. Eddie demonstrates how, with a long wire fastened to the lever, the log can be released before reaching the far end, to fall free and dive into the sand at the river's edge, from where it can be quickly floated down to the sawmill. Our Nip is fascinated, and we lay on a demonstration. A log is sent down, released, and the grapnel smartly hauled back for reloading. The second log is on its way, and then the third with record speed. Our Nip is delighted –

surely this will earn promotion for efficiency and ingenuity! Four logs are carefully selected and put in place to await the momentous occasion.

The great day arrives, we hear the pom-pom-pom-pom of the boat approaching from upriver, and our Nip is tense with excitement. As the boat noses around the bend, we see Lieutenant Tanaka pointing towards us for the benefit of the group of high-ranking officers standing on the forward end of the launch. Our Nip jumps to a salute, then sends off the first log to a perfect landing. The second and third follow rapidly, and as we hook on the last one Eddie pinches up a notch in the wire controlling the release lever. The kink jams in the top pulley, the wire is jerked taut and the speeding log swoops down like an aerial torpedo.

Eddie's judgement was excellent. What went wrong was that the boat's pilot, to ensure a good view of the last log, had slowed down, and the log plunged into the river ahead of the boat.

We turn to look at our Nip. He is lying on his back in a dead faint. Maybe he is dreaming of firing squads, poor little bugger!

When we came to Wampo South most of us had open sores which would not heal, the result of inadequate nutrition and the absence of antiseptics and dressings. These lesions were nearly all on our feet and shins, from going about with bare feet and coming up against twigs and so on while clearing trees and bushes. Scratches, from bamboo thorns in particular, always became septic and were aggravated by sweat, dirt, flies and repeated knocks. There isn't much flesh on the shins, and even small sores fester unpleasantly.

Inadvertently, we seem to have found a form of

treatment. Our lads working with concrete have found that cement dust packs into their sores and can't be rinsed out, binding with the mucous into a hard scab-like protection. After a week or two these cement patches fall out of their own accord, leaving a clean surface ready for growth of new skin.

Cement, of course, does not actually 'dry' out, it sets hard by chemical reaction between its lime constituents and the water mixed into it. All such reactions produce heat, and lime has been used for centuries in the disposal of dead bodies, so possibly these factors account for the destruction of putrefaction without harming living tissues. Anyhow, our conversation leads to this conclusion, right or wrong, and either way the evidence is in front of us because we have all applied the cement powder to our own oozing sores with success.

We do not meet the elephants for a couple of days. Apparently they have walked a long distance to get here and are tired, so they are taking a lengthy yasumi. Somehow I don't think we could work that one on our Nips for ourselves, we being mere human beings.

Meanwhile, the aerial runway has been dismantled (I wonder why?) and our squad has a pleasant time wading in the shallows while we retrieve logs coming down in the current and stack them near the sawmill shelter. We are still waiting for the straightened shaft to come back from Tarsao.

It has always been the practice of the timber companies to fell trees in the northern forests, trim them, chop their brands into the base, then shove the trunks into the rivers to find their way downstream to be claimed by the mills. This procedure may take years as the logs get caught up in thick bushes and become stranded in the dry months, then carried a stage further on the next floods. So the timber we are salvaging must be stolen from its rightful owners, unless it used to belong to our people, in which case it is spoils of war.

Occasionally we are switched to humping bags of cement from the store into the barge, then up the far side bank to where the concrete gangs are mixing and pouring the slabs, which will be the foundations for the big timbers. River water has to be carried up in buckets and wooden tubs, and the mixing of sand, stone, cement and water is all done by hand-shovelling – slow, laborious, heavy work in the full glare of the sun and heat reflected from the face of the cliff. Work has commenced from the southern end where the ledge has been dug to our camp boundary, and is gradually progressing to the bluff, which is now rapidly being chewed down to its designated level, thanks to the powerful air-compressor and dynamite.

The bluff seems to be hard limestone, glaringly white when the weathered surface is blown away, and our men are perched on flat steps here and there with pneumatic drills preparing shot-holes for explosive charges. The whole site is enveloped in drifting clouds of white dust. The men are coated thickly as the particles stick to their sweat, they breathe it in all day, and the racket from eight hammering drills and the compressor's engine is stupefying in such a small space. Their eyes are red with irritants and sun glare, and their feet and legs nicked by flying chips of stone for, like the rest of us, they have no boots to protect them. At the end of the day they are exhausted from the slamming impact of heat, the juddering clamour of the jackhammers, and from dehydration, which is aggravated by the clinging stone dust which clogs their pores and prevents their skin from breathing properly.

After blasting, our squad goes up to the site to clear loose rubble by dumping it in the river, and since this is usually around mid afternoon, we get the maximum reflection of heat and light from the blinding limestone. A couple of hours are more than enough, and the men on the drills have our full sympathy.

One morning after tenko we are walking to the toolstore when we see the two elephants moving across their flat campsite towards the river. Each rider is sitting up high, a short spike goad in one hand while the other holds a rope looped around his animal's head.

As the big beasts wade into the shallows George comments, 'I've never heard of elephants being able to swim. I suppose the mahouts know the depth of the water? It must be far too deep for them to walk across.'

The deep channel in this right-hand curve of the river is on the far side and the elephants steadily progress until the water is up to their jaws, their trunks held up clear of the surface. Without any hesitation, they press on until they disappear entirely from sight, submerged except for the tips of their trunks protruding above the surface with the nostrils aimed to their front, like a submarine's periscope. Their riders, still holding their ropes, are towed along the surface while the elephants breathe comfortably as they move over the riverbed, which rises steeply to a narrow strip of shallow water before coming to our bank.

The great grey shapes emerge, glistening wet in the bright sunshine as they climb upwards and move to the bushy slope of the bank, their mahouts once again settled in place on their necks. The mahouts (an Indian word, I don't know what the Siamese call them) cry out commands and press their knees behind the elephants' ears, and there is a moment's pause while a route up the slope is chosen. The massive heads swing from side to side as the long-lashed eyes take in the ground, and all of us cluster above them watching every detail with utter fascination. When they start to move, we hastily shuffle off to the sides to give them clear passage.

I am instantly entranced by this remarkable and beautiful coordination of intellect and power, of tremendous muscles swelling and relaxing, the liquid flowing procession of movement unbelievably graceful and controlled. How can such a huge bulk be carried up a steep uneven slope with such silken ease, as if it were without effort?

My friends are also struck with admiration, and during the rest of the morning's labours we talk about our perceptions. An elephant's eyes, being set as they are, will give him a good view only forward and to the sides; we doubt that he can see his front feet very well, and he cannot turn his head far enough to see behind his shoulders. His great size and weight make it essential for him to be sure the ground will support him safely – an unseen hollow could result in a broken leg and slow death, a bog could mean drowning. So his sensitive trunk, like a blind man's white walking stick, probes and tests the ground in front to the breadth of his body, and his brain analyses every detail sent up to it, including the leading foot's assessment of the solidity underneath. While each foot is receiving instruction as to exactly where it must be placed when its turn comes, there is an increasing inward flow of fresh details being sorted out and transmitted with the elephant's forward movement, the steps ahead being investigated and signalled back.

What seems outwardly to be a simple matter of walking on four feet is seen by us, discussing the creature's special circumstances, as a fascinatingly complex interplay of intelligence and sheer strength. This is no clumsy, lumbering and dull-witted beast, but a marvellous living power plant, with all the rhythm and grace, poise and confident balance of a ballet dancer.

The riverbank has the incline of a splayed-out stepladder, and the elephants unerringly spot the diagonal traverse, which we have formed over the past few weeks climbing up to the level ground above. It is a steepish slope, especially at the foot, and the water dripping off when you come out of the river makes it slippery as well.

The elephants haven't finished demonstrating their special capabilities. I have a close-up view of them coming ashore because I have carefully positioned myself near the water so that, if they object to our presence, I can get away in the shortest possible time. But there is no problem at all – we are majestically ignored.

The near beast turns to start his ascent and the other swings behind him. It is quite incredible to watch. With his trunk hanging down vertically he rolls up the tip until the underside of the roll just brushes the ground. As he moves forward at a slow walk, his trunk sways from side to side across the width of his feet and nudges gently against the rising slope in front. Continuously his trunk rolls and unrolls, shortening and lengthening as it explores every change in the ground's contours. It tells him exactly where to place each of his feet, and this he does with delicate precision. The front foot is put down in two stages: the bent knee lowers the flat pad to contact the ground and test it for firmness, then the full weight is allowed to come down. As the weight is applied a thick cushion bulges out at the ankle, apparently a kind of shock absorber, and the thrust of the hindquarters pivots the leg forward to vertical. But most of the weight is held on the other three legs until the test has been completed.

The other foreleg finds its own spot a little in front, the hind legs move up to their selected placements, then the whole cycle is repeated smoothly and without pause.

* * *

The brilliant dry weather continues, hot as hell up on the ledge mixing concrete and manhandling heavy timbers, but bearable if you can get into the river now and again to rinse off dust and cool your body, which is usually possible during the brief smokos which the Nips allow when work is going ahead to their satisfaction. They also allow us to brew tea in whatever containers are available. It's an odd situation – whatever excuses they can think up for not providing food, there always seems to be tea available. It comes in small leafy branches, which go straight into the dixie, dull greenish leaves and tiny twigs all together. It is refreshing and of quite pleasant flavour.

Nevertheless, cases of heat exhaustion do occur. There seems to be little warning of its onset, possibly because most of the symptoms are a normal part of our general discomfort and our bodies cope as best they can. Then suddenly the combined stresses of white-hot sun glare on unprotected eyes, inadequate salt in our food, heat beating back from the cliff rocks and heavy physical demands on undernourished bodies all overwhelm the system's natural defences. The stricken man's movements become uncertain and jerky, his eyes stare, and in moments he is prostrate, inert and streaming with sweat, mouth open and breathing in harsh desperate gasps, his heart visibly pounding against his ribs, totally unconscious and in a state of severe shock.

You must not put liquid into the mouth of a man in this condition, even though fluids are what he urgently needs. In reality, there is nothing we can do for him – he requires hospital attention and the nearest medical aid is at Wampo Central. A friend crosses the river and brings back the man's blanket, which is soaked and wrapped around him while a stretcher is quickly put together. A squad of bearers is assembled, and trots off down the railway embankment trying to avoid jolting the patient as far as possible. It is some six kilometres to the point where the track leads off to Central, and another kilometre to the camp. The poor fellow will be lucky to get there alive. Facilities for treatment at the so-called 'hospital' hut will be at best minimal, more likely non-existent, but the medical staff will do their best for him. His chances of survival are not good; there is too much against him and too little in his favour.

Our gang has settled in to working full-time with the two elephants, to my great personal delight as it enables me to watch these wonderful beasts close-up, and I am continually marvelling at their displays of sheer strength and, more than anything else, their sagacity. There is an air of calm competence in the way they move around and carry out their tasks in response to the high-pitched cries of their mahouts, who rarely use the goads which they always carry.

Logs arrive mostly by river barge, a few still floating down on the current for us to retrieve. We unload the barges by rolling the logs into the water, then pushing them far enough up the beach to hold them in place before positioning them for the elephants to pick up. A trimmed log, of course, is thicker at what was its base end and tapers gradually to the other end. Its point of balance, therefore, is not at the midpoint but towards the base. I have never seen an elephant misjudge his selection of the point of balance, pushing his great tusks underneath the log at exactly the right spot and strapping the log firmly into place with his trunk laid over the top and curled down. Unhurriedly, he then ambles over to the sawmill and rolls the log off his tusks neatly into place on the stack.

Early every morning, the elephants cross over from their home on the far side of the river, wading in deeper and then submerging themselves completely except for the tip of the trunk held above the surface to breathe. I never tire of watching this performance, which is followed by the steady climb up the riverbank as directed by the sensitive contour-tracing of the rolling and unrolling trunk.

We work comfortably with these magnificent creatures, talking to them quietly when we are close to them and being careful to keep within their vision. The Nips, in contrast, stay at a respectful distance and eye them warily, frequently muttering amongst themselves.

It seems clear to us that our elephants' placidity is not the product of an obtuse or dull intellect, for they are quite obviously fully aware of everything happening around them. They swing their heads from side to side to see as much as possible, fan their ears to listen, and test the atmosphere continually with their trunks. With their limited field of vision, they have to ensure that nothing is going to take them by surprise.

That they can become annoyed, and even dangerously angry, was demonstrated yesterday. At first light we heard a launch start its engine downstream, its loud pom-pom-pom-pom echoing around the hills. In the silence of this river valley, these boats can be heard anything up to an hour before they come into view around the bend below our south boundary, chugging slowly up against the current. This particular launch must have been lying up for the night below the bend, for it appears just as the elephants are stepping into the shallows.

By the time the elephants are chest-deep, the launch is closing in on them with its rowdy engine blabbing away, and the boatman is lolling in the stern gazing sleepily at the scenery. Both elephants come to a standstill, turn to face the intruder, then in the same instant decide they don't like it. Trumpeting with rage, they start to thrash through the water, in a few paces speeding up to a pounding run which throws up a surging bow-wave around their shoulders. Fifty yards to go, and maybe the boatman hasn't heard their war cries over the noise of his engine, but his early morning sleepiness vanishes quickly enough when he sees the behemoths charging straight at him. Whipping his boat into a turn, he opens up the throttle, but they gain on him until his boat picks up enough speed to draw away. Our last view of him is of a frightened face staring back pop-eyed over the stern of his launch. It has been a very close thing.

The two mahouts are shouting and yelling, smacking their goads into the elephants' skulls in their attempts to bring them under control. The animals stop their headlong rush and quietly resume their crossing of the river. Tragedy having been avoided, I see the incident as entertaining and try to imagine the elephants' thoughts: 'Well, we saw him off, all right', or 'Better luck next time', or 'Makes a change to the start of the day'. This outburst hasn't given us cause for concern. We are still happy to be working in close proximity to our friends. I feel that in some subtle way the elephants have accepted us, which I find curiously satisfying!

There are fourteen of us, all Volunteers in the Singapore and various up-country Malayan units, who form the regular working party with the elephants. The Nip in charge of us is Hasegawa, who is selfconsciously proud of his title 'elephanto man', and this morning we are walking along the beach near the water's edge, lagging some little distance behind one of these massive creatures. In between, Hasegawa is walking backwards, having turned to shout at us to hurry up, when the elephant drops three great steaming turds on the sand. Before we can warn him, Hasegawa trips over the first heap, sprawls across the second, and shoves his face into the third.

It doesn't do to laugh on such an occasion, the loss of face to an Asiatic is too important, so we rush up all solicitous and concerned, picking his spectacles out of the muck and rinsing them in the river. We can laugh about it later, but our attitude at the time helps to build up an easy-going relationship with him, and that is well worthwhile. Being 'local' men we have a far better understanding of their natures than do the troops from Britain, and such simple deceptions are no problem. In fact, we have come to regard ourselves as somewhat of a special group, spending our days in a harmonious relationship with the elephants. They are privileged workers: when the afternoon sun is considered by their mahouts to be too hot, they are simply taken off the worksite to lie in the river shallows, where they spray themselves with water from their trunks and the mahouts carefully scrub their hides with coconut husks.

And when the elephants approach a log they consider too heavy to tackle, they just turn and walk away, and no amount of persuasion by the mahouts will bring them back to that particular log. We have tried shifting a rejected log to another position, but to no avail – it is recognised and ignored. In such instances, Hasegawa shouts and waves to us to take over the job. In his view seven pairs of men, each with a bamboo pole and a rope sling, are a sufficient substitute for an elephant. Maybe he thinks the animals are not imbued with the proper spirit of bushido and service to the Emperor. We aren't either, but can do nothing about it!

So we lay our slings on the shingle and lever the log to lie across them, slip the poles through the end loops and bend our knees to get our shoulders under the bamboos. Straightening up in unison we move off with the log slung between two files of seven men. There is an art to doing this. We pair ourselves off in similar heights so that the load is evenly distributed as it hangs from the poles across our shoulders. To prevent the heavy weight from swinging, each man keeps in step with the man in front, but the two files walk in opposite step (outside feet, inside feet), while the taut ropes are gripped as far down as possible to control swaying. It is surprising what can be lifted and moved with primitive gear. The secret lies in smoothly controlled and coordinated effort.

We have developed a certain pride in our ability to do this heavy work, and by mutual agreement we consider each one of us officially rated as 'one fourteenth of an elephant'.

A small party of Nips has arrived with the repaired shaft of the sawmill engine, which they fit into place. After a few trial runs during which the heavy belt is frequently thrown off the drive pulley due to its excessive weight dragging the engine out of alignment on its shifting sand and gravel foundation, they do what we had deliberately avoided doing. They build a small solid platform of logs held securely in place by stakes driven into the beach, and mount the engine on top. The sawmill then functions efficiently, trimming logs for heavy bridge timbers and thinner scantlings for making up concrete forms.

In several weeks our squad has produced exactly eleven planks, and we watch this smooth output of sawn timbers with some apprehension. What happens to us if someone decides to ask why we hadn't been able to achieve the same results? But it seems that these Nips are mechanics and not sawmill operators, for they disappear after sorting out their problem.

We have put together a map of our local geography, as accurately as we can from our own observations and from deductions and assumptions. Of course, our own Singapore/Bangkok/Saigon travellers have been able to contribute personal knowledge, but their own experiences were not really in this area where we now find ourselves.

We know we are on latitude fourteen degrees north, a little over halfway up from the equator to the Tropic of Cancer, and we arrived in Siam just at the autumn equinox. Kanburi would be somewhat north of due west from Bangkok, and Tarsao westerly of Kanburi. These relativities have been obvious from sunrises and sunsets as they appeared on our march from Ban Pong to Tarsao (which is on the Kwei Noi river some fifteen kilometres upstream from us) on a metalled road from Ban Pong as far as Kanburi, and on a mud track from there onwards.

At our first river crossing (where the British officer/interpreter was considerate enough to inform us that, having crossed over, our lives are worth nothing), the course of that river was southwards. Here at Wampo South, the Kwei Noi runs south-easterly, and presumably flows into the first river, which would continue south into the head of the Gulf of Siam. And, somewhere in that area is a sizeable town called Ratburi through which we passed by train coming up from Singapore.

Our camp administration officers occasionally go to Tarsao on camp business, and meet officers and parties of men from other camps. We hear that the terrain between Kanburi and Tarsao is too difficult for the railway, in the absence of heavy machinery for tunnelling and similar problems. So the track is being built southwards from Kanburi bearing right-handed to Wampo South and then north-west to Tarsao. From Tarsao, it is to continue north-westerly along the left (eastern) bank of our Kwei Noi, eventually linking up with the Burma railroad system at its most southerly terminus, which is at Moulmein or (as someone conjectures) at a small town a bit to the south, called Ye.

A thought tossed into our pool of discussion is that, once our Siam-to-Burma length is completed, the Japanese army will be in control of an unbroken railway communication from, say, Harbin in Manchuria through Peking, Shanghai, Nanking, Canton, Saigon and Singapore, Bangkok, Moulmein, Rangoon and north to Mandalay. This is a quite staggering concept; there must be some 12,000 miles of main line, and with all the branch lines running through the countryside along its length, surely this constitutes an all-time record for a railway system under a single management. Should we be proud of our contribution, small as it may be in actual length but absolutely vital in its location? And what will be its contribution – to world trade patterns when the Nips have been thrown out? On further thought, we doubt whether it will in fact make any contribution – it is so ramshackle in our own section, and doubtless just as poorly constructed along the whole length, that it may well simply fall to pieces.

Trees felled in the jungle are trimmed, squared, and put into place, still green, within a few days. Some creosote was splashed on for the first day or two only, but no kind of pre-servative since then. And the concrete foundations have had so much junk thrown into the mixes (when the Nips weren't looking) that they must be totally unreliable. And although there will not be a single bridge actually crossing the Kwei Noi, there will undoubtedly be several hundred small structures spanning watercourses carrying stormwater from the flanks of the mountains to drain westward into our river, and every one of these will be shoddily built and will be a weak point in the line.

The latest rumour is that the camps between us and Kanburi have progressed to the point of laying sleepers and rails, though we have no idea how close they may be to us. This, of course, means that the first river has been bridged to carry trains, for there would be no other means of bringing such heavy and bulky materials to the railhead for laying the next section.

These camps will not be situated on our river, but strung along an alignment through virgin jungle and the lumpy, rocky hills which we passed through on our march to Tarsao. We hear that they have had to dig out deep cuttings through solid rock, backbreaking work with crude tools, and have suffered far more casualties than we have.

Due to being downstream from the Nip headquarters at Tarsao, we are out of the main traffic stream (Kanburi to Burma) and, in consequence, relatively isolated. But our peace and quiet have now been shattered by the irruption of a Nip railway engineering battalion. So far they have made no contact with us, so presumably we have not been allocated to them for work, and we thank heaven for that. We have never seen such a mob of eager beavers as they are, never still for a moment, shovelling concrete like madmen and heaving big timbers into place! No one seems to wait for orders. When one job is finished, these Japanese army engineers actually go looking for something else to do and get stuck into it. The worksite changes hourly in its appearance, with new structures rearing up continuously. We are profoundly grateful that the river lies between us, they being all on the north side while we contentedly work with our elephants at their more leisurely pace.

We have named our gracious and sedate friends Pooh and Bah, titles which have a vaguely Siamese tone to them, not having been able to discover what their mahouts call them. They are no less fascinating to me than they were on the first day of our acquaintance. We talk to them quietly and pat them on their trunks, always being careful to approach them from the front so that they see us coming towards them. The mahouts have given up trying to shoo us away. The elephants accept our friendly overtures with small nods and movements of their trunks, which we like to interpret as their recognition of our admiration. The mahouts are nervous, the Nips stay well out of reach, and we enjoy our favoured relationship.

But we discover they can be startled very suddenly out of their normal placidity, and can become dangerous and unpredictable. Pooh is plodding along the narrow strip of flat beach one day and I am paddling through the shallows a few yards away, keeping pace with his right eye so that he can see where I am. On his left side is the steep twenty-foot slope of sand and smooth pebbles rising up to the level where our huts stand.

We have just passed the sawmill when someone pushes a log crookedly onto the circular blade. The sudden harsh scream of twisted steel and ripped timber startles Pooh. Hearing the noise, I turn towards him to see him heave up on his hind legs, trunk raised and shrieking in panic. As his front legs come down, he breaks into a run, heading into the steep bank. It is an incredible sight! I have long ago given up climbing this slope – the shingle falls away under your feet and the steepness of the gradient exhausts you by the time you reach the top. It is preferable to walk 100 yards or so along the river's edge and go up an easier incline.

But Pooh plunges straight at it, his great feet ploughing deep holes and sliding down in the loose sand so that he gains hardly any height with each lunge. His skin, usually slack like an oversized suit, is suddenly packed with mighty bulging muscles straining, swelling as he shoves and pulls his great bulk upwards, dislodged sand and pebbles showering down. And all the while he trumpets his anger while his mahout clings on desperately to Pooh's almost vertical spine.

Sheer massive strength takes Pooh to the top of the bank, but he doesn't stop to rest despite his enormous expenditure of effort. Gaining the level parade ground, he heads off for the far side in a smooth, pounding rhythm. Scrambling up the slope in his wake, I see him disappear into the scrubby bush, his mahout still perched in place.

What an extraordinary and wonderful sight to have seen so close by! An afterthought: what if I had been walking on the beach on Pooh's left flank instead of paddling like a child in the river?

We are formed up for our usual morning tenko, and it is immediately evident that something has happened. Instead of being counted off in work parties, we are told by our captain that this is to be a yasumi day. The Nips have been informed that our work has been satisfactory and the holiday has been ordered in recognition. Further, the Nips have said that they have some spare dynamite and will blow the river for fish.

Never having seen any kind of fish except tiny tiddlers in the shallow edge of the water, we are sceptical of the results, but any prospect of getting something to eat is of tremendous interest, so we are content to wait around while the Nips get themselves going. A number of small bundles of dynamite sticks are taped together with a detonator and slow-burning fuse, and tossed into the river upstream from our camp. The charges go off with muffled thumps, dislodging splodges of brown mud from the bottom, and suddenly there are hundreds of fish dotted all over the surface of the river, being carried down on the current. In a moment we are in the river, but catching the fish is not so simple. They float on their backs, heads pointing downriver and mouths open, stunned and immobile, but the instant you try to grab one, it comes back to consciousness and slithers out of your hand, turning right side up and swimming strongly. The trick is to shove your thumb into the gaping mouth and your fingertips into the distended gills, then hold the wriggling, flapping fish out of the water while you work your way to the shallows and hand it over to one of the non-swimmers before going back to midstream to catch another. Taking one fish in each hand and kicking for the beach on your back doubles your catch.

In ten minutes or so it is all over. The current has swept away scores of fish that we couldn't catch in time, but it has been a good haul. We concentrated, naturally, on the bigger specimens and there is a surprising variety of shapes and colours: creamy yellow, blue and brown stripes and dots, reddish tinges, and one quite spectacular specimen – flattish and deep-bellied, sooty black with broad golden vertical bands – ranging in size from about eight ounces to a plump pound and a half. There is plenty for everybody, and since fish won't keep for long in this climate, it has to be cooked and eaten as soon as possible.

Possession of any kind of knife is strictly verboten, but nearly everyone seems to have one when it comes to scaling and cleaning our catch! Cooking is unavoidably simple – just straightforward boiling in a mess tin because nothing else is available – not even salt can be spared from the scanty cook-house stock – but our group benefits from the small supply built up by purchases from the local traders. Some of the fish is spoiled by intense bitterness from a gall bladder ruptured by the underwater explosions, but there is enough to share around and no man needs to go short. Who would have thought that fish were so plentiful in our river, totally unsuspected until then? And so sweet-tasting, too.

And, two days later, an even bigger (literally) surprise.

Men poking around in thick shrubbery growing at the water's edge find two enormous fish, dead and caught up in the branches spread out over the water. The fish are brought to the cookhouse; they are so big that each has to be carried between two men with a hand thrust into the gills at shoulder height. The heads of the fish are taller than the men, and their tails drag on the beach! But the cooks cannot use them – after two days they are no longer fresh. Disappointment.

We shall be careful to wear our fundoshis in the river from now on. Nobody is going to risk losing his most prized assets to predators such as these!

It is now the last week in March 1943. We have been captive for just over a year. Pooh and Bah have gone, and in our genuine affection and admiration we wish them well in return for their friendly acceptance of us. Personally, I know that I shall never forget them. I don't know why they had a special appeal for me, but am content simply to accept it. And in some faintly mystic way, I feel gratitude to them, too, just for knowing them. It has been a great privilege.

We have been told that we shall be moving back to Central in a day or two, leaving the completion of our viaduct to the Nip professionals and, no doubt, a new batch of POWs. We are to work at Wampo North.

The dry season will be ending in six weeks or so, and the prospect of entering six months of wet monsoon at Wampo Central fills us with dismay. Gloom, mud and more mud, pernickety Nips and Koreans, dreadful rations, not to mention leaky bug-ridden huts and overworked latrines. These are not prospects to anticipate with any enthusiasm at all!

4

Wampo North

MARCH TO MAY 1943

Our forebodings about life at Wampo Central are dismally accurate as far as they go, but it's not long before we discover that they were not nearly pessimistic enough. Every aspect that we can think of takes us depressingly downwards, and the next few months become a doom-laden prospect which we prefer not to look at too closely.

At Wampo South we were more or less isolated, there being no toing and froing of men and only occasional visits by our medical officer. Now we hear plentiful rumours/news, from the men who stayed at Central, of upriver camps run under barbaric conditions, with rations even more wretched than ours and deaths counted in hundreds. The name of one particular Nip, a horrific bastard nicknamed The Tiger, keeps cropping up as being in command at a camp called Tonchan, the first on the far side of Tarsao. What are we to believe? There is no reliable way of sorting out truth from rumours – frequency of repetition, of course, does not prove anything.

I am sure that after the touch-and-go incident at South Camp following our 'late' return from the concert, the Nips there became far more circumspect in their dealings with us. On our side, a very careful recognition of the situation kept everything in a delicate state of balance, in which we were doing sufficient work to keep them from bugging us without putting ourselves to excessive effort. Every man was, relatively speaking, fit to work, there were no sick men officially, but we were all well below par.

And there was a marvellous 'open' atmosphere at South Camp. Looking southwards the mountains diminished into the far distance on our right, but on the left they curved away eastwards affording us a vast prospect of lesser-forested hills fading to the southern horizon. Nowhere was there the smallest sign of a human presence beyond our little collection of huts, and the scarred cliff face where we worked. In contrast, Wampo Central is hemmed in by trees and the mountains. The only open space is the parade ground where we assemble for tenko, facing westwards towards the Nip guardhouse which is on the edge of the riverbank where all river traffic can be seen. Immediately in front of us, across the river, the view during tenko is abruptly cut off by steeply rising rock and forest. In the middle distance is a prominent mountain standing well above its companions, the same jagged top that we looked at from the South camp.

We guess that there are some five or six distinct ranges running north and south between the Kwei Noi and the Indian Ocean, only maybe 120 miles away. But to reach the ocean would be quite impossible on a direct westerly line – it is totally out of the question to consider the idea. On clear afternoons the sunset sky can blaze with furnace reds and brilliant yellows and oranges, the mountain ridge-tops and the 'big tooth' standing out in black silhouette. I have nostalgic memories of these magnificent soul-dazzling sunsets, seen from the deck of the ship carrying us from schooldays in England to the start of a new life in Singapore. A new life, yes indeed! But the visual splendour and sweet-sad memories bring warmth to my spirit and I welcome them. Only four years ago . . . such unimagined changes!

Wampo Central is a camp of sick, dispirited men. All those fit to work live out at Wampo North, leaving the weak to fend for themselves with a totally inadequate number of medical staff to look after them. There is no water supply (except the river which is beyond their strength), no decent sanitation (and to reach even those primitive facilities, again beyond their strength), no light after dark (so they have to rely on the moon to move outside their huts), and – more destructive to morale than anything else – *nothing whatsoever to do!* Being sick and therefore unable to contribute to building the railway, they are on half rations, which literally means a starvation diet. In the Nip view they are malingerers whose spirit is too weak to keep them healthy, so starvation will encourage them to make themselves fit again! The result is that these wretched men lie inert and dirty on their knotty bamboo slats all day, all night, with no bedding or clothing, racked by malarial rigors and gut-stabbing dysentery, no bedpans or drinking water, their wasting flesh rubbed into ulcerous bedsores for which there is no treatment. Many have reached the stage where months of malnutrition have reduced them to the early stages of beri-beri and pellagra, with the typical symptoms of dragging apathy, both mental and physical.

The medical officers and their orderlies do everything they can to help, but the Nips will not permit the allocation of more men to look after them. We who work have deductions from our pay to create a hospital fund, but the purchase of eggs and other foodstuffs is erratic, dependent on local boatmen and the whims of the Nips.

Of course, there are in fact a number of perfectly fit men in the camp – I understand maybe sixty or thereabouts – who could help in many ways if they chose to do so. These are the younger officers whose hut is set somewhat apart from ours, and they stay out of sight. If we did not know they were there, there would be no evidence of their presence. They are not required to be at our tenko, being counted in their own area. Our colonel has brought together a small group of dedicated older officers for camp administration, and they do a fine job in most difficult circumstances, but the rest (according to our medical officer, who is totally disgusted by their selfishness) 'sit around on their bums all day, playing bridge and reading and complaining about not being able to get decent pipe tobacco'. These men could give time to visiting the sick and just talking to them, or reading from the big store of books that they brought up from Changi in their kits (carried by somebody else, naturally). Or, if water containers can be found – admittedly a big problem – they could bring washing water from the river. The sick men have gone through weeks of tropical heat without the comforting touch of cool water on their bug-bitten skins.

The privileges of rank endure to some extent even in our pinched circumstances. There are sick men being forced out to work, but the Nips allow a number of batmen to wait on the officers and wash their clothing (who else has any?) and these batmen come to talk to us in the evenings, so we are kept informed about what life is like in their part of the camp. To their credit, most of them are ashamed of their more comfortable situation, but many of them are older men who were batmen in earlier days, and we do not in any way begrudge them their good fortune.

The chaplain makes his duty rounds, dressed in his religious robes, but the men are not interested in what he wants to talk about. It is plainly obvious to them that the chaplain's God is not making the slightest effort to help them in their desperate need against a heathen enemy, and the chaplain's confident reassurances and readings from the Bible and prayer book are meaningless. An all-powerful God who lets Christian men suffer like this? Don't make us laugh, it hurts too much! The chaplain cannot even draw a response, earnestly as he tries to reach them. They simply stare at him in stony silence until he gives up and goes away.

Real grief and disappointment show on his face – he has failed and does not know how to cope with the problem. If he could hear the men's muttered imprecations after his departure he would feel even worse, for he is known as a decent and genuinely sympathetic man. But his training and experience have in no way equipped him to triumph over these circumstances, poor chap; in his helplessness, what can he offer to comfort us? The discouragement must be agonising. No doubt he will pray to his God for enlightenment and strength to endure. His faith is his life and if he cannot communicate his faith to the men in his care, then his failure is deeply personal. The men's cynical hostility must not be used as a facile let-out; it would be shameful even to think of that. The deeper their depression, the more vigorously he must try to lift them up. It is his duty, his God must have put him amongst us for that very purpose. The cross he bears must be heavy.

We have our first look at the work going on at Wampo North. The familiar embankment runs to the northern end of Wampo's area, but the last few hundred metres are on a bigger scale, owing to the fall of the land. The greatly increased pick and shovel work and earth to be carried higher and dumped have been an enormous strain on the men. It is still nowhere near finished, and this is our job – to get the work back on schedule.

The arc of the rocky hillside ends in a massive bluff with a sheer vertical face falling to a narrow beach between its base and the river. A ledge has been cut at the required height of nineteen metres above the river level, wide enough to take the sleepers and track to be laid along it. Creating this ledge has meant blasting out all the rock above it working down from the top, mainly with hammers and hand-held drills. The blasted face must be some eighty feet high in the centre. About 200 metres along the ledge is a great natural fissure, cutting in from the face of the bluff well back into the mountain. Wampo's responsibility extends to preparing the railbed as far as this fissure and building a timber bridge across the gap – some ten metres.

Establishing the ledge on our side involves the blasting out (we calculate) of some 8,000 cubic metres of rock. On the far side most of the ledge has already been cut out, while our people were still building their embankment. We understand that this was done by a labour force consisting mostly of Australians working south towards Wampo from a camp upriver, but our men never saw them and they appear to have been withdrawn before finally tidying up, which (in the mysterious planning of the Nips) has been left to us. The beach at the foot of the bluff is littered with chunks of broken rock from the blasting, and the newly exposed limestone face is blindingly white in the afternoon sun.

The massive embankment cannot be built right up to the face of the hillside, which has acted as a sluice draining the heavy monsoon rains down into a wide stormwater gully leading into the river. This gully has to be bridged from the end face of the embankment to the solid rock of the ledge, and to keep the bridge timbers to manageable size, a concrete culvert has been constructed to form the foundation of the bridge and to allow the floods to pass underneath. The gully has been dry since the end of last year's rains, and a good deal of timber construction has already been completed.

It is a two-layer bridge, with seven inward-sloping uprights on the deck of the culvert with a crossbeam along the top to hold them in place. Sitting on that are five uprights with a crossbeam. There are two of these frames resting on concrete, and a third of one tier only bedded in the earth of the embankment. The timbers are massive – fifteen inches square and thirty feet long – with the top ends sawn to leave projecting pegs which fit into square holes chopped into the crossbeams. The dressing of the timbers is being done by Siamese carpenters, who have a hut and cookhouse to themselves on the site. We see them at work, drawing chipping lines with chalked string along logs laid on stumps, then crouching down to form flat faces with patient strokes of an adze, working along the chalk lines and rotating the logs as each face is completed. For such a slow form of work, their daily output is surprising, possibly because they seem to be using relatively softwood trees. Green timber without any wood preservative!

The crossbeams are overlaid with similar lengths of timber, butted into the embankment face and the hillside rock, the whole structure being braced by diagonal struts bolted to the uprights and to each other at crossover points. The crudity of design and construction causes a good deal of sceptical comment as to its ability to carry locomotives and goods wagons, but our Australian friends assure us that they build railway bridges in Queensland just like that! Maybe with more suitable timber and so on, but basically the same in appearance.

The excavation pits, which provide earth fill for the embankment, are having to be dug further and further away from the base, which means we have to carry our tongas over long distances with an exhausting climb up the flank to dumping points. The Nips continue to require a full day's quota, still measured here as one and a half cubic metres per man excavated before they will allow us to go back to camp. Lugging tongas some sixty or seventy yards, zigzagging along the walls between old excavations, is too much like hard work, so we resort to being clever. The Nips never miss knocking off for lunch, and our opportunity comes during the hour they are out of sight. By now we are digging close to the edge of the cliff that falls down to the river. We take things easily all morning then dig like maniacs to dump earth over the edge. In the afternoon, we resume plodding back and forth, but well over half our day's output has gone into the river during the mid-day rice break. At a suitable time we call our Nip over to check our gang's pit, and then walk back to camp. When we are moved to a different spot, we simply dump our loads into the scores of holes between us and the embankment. It saves us a great deal of effort!

Down the face of the riverbank, the falling river level has exposed an opening in the rock from which a spring of cold clean water spouts all day. We cannot get into the river itself, but by scrambling down we have a marvellously refreshing source of water for drinking and pouring over our sweating bodies. Filling your hat and up-ending it over your head is really good.

One morning the Nips announce that it will be the Emperor's birthday on 29 April. There will be a present for each of us from His Imperial Majesty to show his appreciation of our work, and it will be a yasumi day with sporting contests. We are all expected to enjoy ourselves and give thanks to the Emperor for his unfailing kindness and interest in our welfare! And, of course, for his generosity, which turns out to consist of a blackened can without a label, salvaged from a fire. Inside is well-cooked pineapple – in our opinion a fair expression of His Majesty's view of us.

The Nips have decided that the sporting events will be between us and themselves with the Koreans, which poses an interesting question – what is our attitude to be? Do we try to win, and risk having the Nips say that our rations are obviously too good and can be cut? Or, worse, that we can clearly work harder than we have been doing? Or do we lose, and let them consider themselves superior to us in sport as in war?

As it turns out, the competitive spirit prevails. In our group of Volunteers, we have two men who represented England in swimming and skiing at the Berlin Olympics in 1936, two university rugby blues and a couple of long-distance cross-country runners. The Nips and Koreans are all physically fit and well-muscled, full of energy and determination to win, but they have no experience of competition techniques. Rocketing off the starting line in the foot races, they carry off the short races, but in the longer distances they cannot keep up the pace.

The longest race, 1,000 metres round and round the parade ground, ends up with a few very awkward minutes. There are three Koreans, tall fellows with long strides, who seem to have a plan in which two of them tear away at top speed in the hope of running us off our feet, while their chosen winner cruises along in the pack until a late spurt brings him to the front. All goes well for them until the last fifty metres, by which time most of the runners have had to drop out. The Korean champ is belting along with a big grin on his face when a skinny, ginger-haired POW slides up past him effortlessly for a clear win. The three Koreans are furious, and for a few moments it looks as if they might lose control over themselves and give the winner a bashing, but they manage to restrain themselves — the fact that it is the Emperor's birthday may have compelled them to avoid a display of bad manners. But the Jap gunso, who supervises tenkos, has something to say: why is it that our man can run a long-distance race but is too sick to parade for tenko? For weeks the gunso has checked the bed-down sick cases to count them (these cases being confined to bed and excused from all duties), and our man has always been sitting on his bedspace with an ulcerated foot.

We all know Jaunty, whose life has been spent as much in civilian gaols and army detention barracks as out of them. A regular soldier of many years, he has a record of petty convictions for indiscipline and unruly behaviour. His chums say he has always been one of the regiment's best athletes, and the military police have never been able to catch up with him when he has had a chance to run from the scene of a crime! Out of sheer bloody-mindedness, he has been carefully cultivating an ulcer on his foot, keeping it from healing up, just to avoid going out to work for the Nips. But he has never been known for his intelligence. For his cunning, yes, but not brains.

The swimming races, back and forth across the river, were easy victories for us. Some of the inexperienced Nips ended up well downstream, not having allowed for the current by swimming in a curve, but aiming directly at the opposite bank.

The festivities end with the Nips tossing dynamite into the river, giving us a big haul of fish for the sick. They have one of their army riverboats, a simple plywood craft with a big cargo space and a diesel engine under a canopy at the stern. Drawing about a foot of water fully loaded, and with sufficient speed to push against a strong current, it is a thoroughly practical and effective boat.

On this occasion a bunch of Nips have crowded into the stern with a few bottles of beer, happily boozed up and singing tearfully. Every few minutes they chuck a stick of dynamite over the stern as the boat chugs upstream, until one of them, in a state of maudlin enthusiasm, tosses a stick forward over the bow. Now this is interesting. They are using short fuses and with a bit of luck the charge will detonate exactly as the boat passes over it.

But we are disappointed! The helmsman is sufficiently sober to realise the situation they're in and jams the throttle open. The boat surges forward and the dynamite explodes just clear of the stern. Amidst a welter of swinging fists and screamed abuse the drunken twit is hurled overboard and left to flounder ashore as best he can. What fun it must be in the Nip army! The culprit is, naturally, our idiot friend Putrid.

The start of the rainy monsoon season can't be far away, and our medical officers are worried by the knowledge that cholera is an unfailing scourge in this part of the world every year. During the dry winter months the river level falls maybe forty or fifty feet, and the exposed banks collect a mass of rubbish – decaying vegetation, dead animals of all kinds, waste from the upstream villages – which rots in the hot sun and breeds flies. When the water rises, all this mess is washed downstream and the rivers become carriers of unpleasant microbes of which the most deadly, and most feared, is cholera.

In our utterly primitive living conditions, we depend entirely on the Kwei Noi for cooking, drinking, and keeping ourselves reasonably clean. Within the next few weeks we shall lose the luxury of Wampo South's clear stream, and be back to the muddy rice and tea boiled in brown silt-laden water, with its attendant bowel and intestinal irritations and pains.

So, after evening tenko we are addressed by the colonel and medical officers on the perils and problems which will soon confront us. The Nips, worried about the possible wipe-out of their labour force, are providing cholera serum with which we shall all be inoculated, one injection now and two more to follow at weekly intervals.

When tenko is over we hang around on the parade ground while our medical officer and his assistant set up a charcoal brazier with a tray of boiling water to sterilise the needles. There are three needles: one in the syringe, one already sterilised ready for use, and one lying in boiling water. The process is hampered by the need to inject, take the needle out and put it in the steriliser, fit the readied needle to the charged syringe, and take the third from the boiling water to allow it to cool. There is no choice of equipment – the MO has to use what he has got, and the syringes and needles are big and clumsy. The needles are blunt to start with, and will become more so as they are applied to 1,600 arms in Wampo Central and in the North camp. And there will be two more injections to follow! We shall have a good idea by then of what it must feel like to be stabbed with a bayonet.

Our two pharmacists are helpful, and tell us that the vaccine bottles are labelled for Bangkok's Chulalongkorn Hospital and are dated 1916 – twenty-seven years old! We have no choice but to use the stuff and hope for the best.

We have taken to sleeping outside the huts; the bugs are beyond all bearing. They lodge in the crevices formed where lengths of bamboo cross and are tied with stringy tree bark. From there they cannot be got at even by flames from burning bamboo torches – which, of course, cannot be held in place very long or the whole hut would go up in flames. And the stink of charred bugs is even worse than when they are squashed.

The few men still sleeping inside are mostly malarial cases, trying to smother their shaking rigors with borrowed blankets and groundsheets. The bamboo sleeping platforms and framework of the huts can actually be heard rattling when a number of men start their fevered shivering at the same time. In the morning, they are drenched with sweat and exhausted from stress, lack of sleep and dehydration, but even so they may find they have to turn out for a day's work because the Nips think there are too many sick.

Finding that their accustomed food supplies have moved away, the bugs start to converge on the few men still inside the huts until they, too, are driven outside. A few nights later we are being bitten, and in the moonlight we can see dark patches moving purposefully from the huts in search of us. We can't win.

Our expected move from Wampo Central to the North camp is announced at morning tenko. It takes about three minutes to pick up our worldly goods and move out along the track we have followed every morning these last weeks, going to work at Wampo North. Our only regret at leaving Central is that we shall not have a bathing place as pleasant as our little pool.

We choose our bedspaces in the huts already standing at the North camp. Apparently they have not been occupied for some time, and within seconds we are attacked by hordes of voracious bugs looking for their first blood-meal in weeks. Sitting on the edge of the bed-platform for only a few moments produces a mass of irritating bites from the rump down to the calves – our fundoshis give no protection at all – and the air is full of the foul decaying stink of squashed bugs.

This is not going to be a pleasant place to live in. The wet monsoon is due within the next few weeks and we shall not be able to sleep outside in the open. The roofs are dilapidated and will leak badly.

Someone high up in the Nip hierarchy must be getting impatient, for our Nips are starting to become difficult. The big embankment is now finished, as is the timber bridge connecting it to the cliff ledge, apart from some cross-bracing being put into place to stiffen the whole structure. Under the bridge is a rock-lined culvert to carry stormwater from the far side of the embankment into the river.

Our gang is told to lay a facing of rock over the end section of the embankment, to hold the earth in place when the rains come. This means picking up chunks of rock from where the ledge was dynamited, and fitting each piece in place. It is easy work and by convincing our Nip that it must all be done with great care, so that the pieces interlock properly, we are able to make it last a whole week. The final result is, in fact, a neat and well-finished drystone sloping wall, and our Nip actually shows he is pleased!

We have been hearing rumours that a rail-laying party is close, that the viaduct at Wampo South has been completed with rails already in place. Our isolation is so thorough that we do not get real news, even of events so close to us, only rumours. As at the South camp, not a single officer at Central can be bothered to stroll over to us to tell us what is actually happening only a few kilometres away. So we are taken completely by surprise when our work is interrupted by the triumphant hooting of a steam locomotive. And there it actually is, a real hissing and puffing engine, about 200 yards away just outside of the curve which aligns the track onto the bridge. We hadn't even known that the rails had been laid so close to us! 'Thar she blows!'

Our emotions are mixed. For six months we have sweated and endured privations, near-starvation, and mental stresses. We have always known that we were building a railway, but somehow it has always had an air of unreality, as if we were sure it would never happen. We have been living in a state of limbo, going about our daily work and coping with problems as they come along, almost totally deprived of even the simplest aspects of civilised life. We have performed with unexpected ingenuity, doing tasks with the crudest tools and not even enough of those. We have overcome the thick-headed ignorance and stupidity of the Nips and Koreans, and found within ourselves sufficient mental resilience to adapt our philosophic outlook to keep both our sanity and our sense of humour. Our bodies have retrained themselves to extract the utmost from the wretched food provided for us, so that we can do our work adequately.

But we know that we have been losing ground. We have thirteen dead, who need not have died had they had the most ordinary medical treatment and food. We have a daily sick list of several hundred, and the rest of us (so-called healthy) are below par by any normal standards. And now, with such sudden effect, a steam whistle has pricked our bubble of unreality! 'Thar she blows!' Yes, indeed! The outside world has found us and we are back on planet Earth.

We unravel our thoughts round a fire during the evening quiet, flickering like the firelight shadows over the events of the last few months. Despite the fact that the railway is being built to sustain Jap armies in Burma, and we have therefore contributed to our enemy's strength, we are finally in agreement that, having had no choice in the matter, we are entitled to take pride in our achievement. In living conditions akin to those of beasts of the field, we have endured, adapted, persisted – and finally triumphed – by simply refusing to admit defeat. And that, we feel, is something to be proud of in itself.

We have been put to clearing rubble off the rock ledge, to expose the solid bed on which the sleepers and track will be laid. Chucking lumps of shattered rock down to the bottom of the cliff is easy work, and there are a few humps still to be chipped down to the general level. We reach the big cleft running back into the hillside, and our Nip indicates that we are to cross the ten-metre chasm to continue clearing loose rock on the other side. What he hasn't worked out is how we are going to get across.

The ledge is about five metres in width, a vertical smooth face falling nineteen metres to the beach on one side, and another vertical face of blasted limestone rearing up (at this point) twenty-five metres on the other. Back at the embankment, we would be able to scramble down to the beach, but would not be able to climb back to the ledge. Or we could climb up the flank of the mountain from the same point, but would be unable to get down to the ledge. On the far side of the cleft, the ledge runs away into a right-hand curve half a kilometre away, and there is no knowing how far we would have to go along the beach, or the hilltop, before finding an access route up or down to the ledge.

Eventually, picking his way deep into the cleft, our Nip finds a point at which fallen boulders jammed in the split allow us to reach the other side. We had been having unpleasant thoughts of doing a tightrope style of crossing on planks nailed together, not at all a happy prospect when malaria and beri-beri are upsetting your sense of balance and fuzzing your eyesight.

Starting at the lip of the chasm, where the bridge

abutment will be laid, we clear away loose rubble down to the solid base underneath. A surprise – it is a clear metre below the level on the Wampo North side! Well, that's not our business. We shall leave it to the Nips to find out for themselves.

We work out what we think may have been the cause of this discrepancy as we shovel tons of loose rock over the lip. Wampo was the first camp to be established on the Kwei Noi itself, and the surveyor's trace and level markers would have been set up about last September, when the river was in full flood in the wet monsoon. We know that the floor of the railway bed was fixed at nineteen metres above the water level of the river, which would have been to conform to the trace through the hills from Kanburi, and this would have been carried through from the South camp zone to the crevice which had been fixed as the limit of Wampo North's area.

Nip surveyors working from the north towards this same point probably took their measurements a few months later, after the start of the dry season when the river level had already begun to fall, still obeying the 'nineteen metres' instruction and thus working down to a lower level.

We are nearing the far end of the ledge when the loco-motive's whistle echoes along the cliff face. It has crossed the timber bridge and brought sleepers and rails to be laid along the ledge itself. The engine shoves a couple of flat wagons in front of itself as far as the end of the track already laid, the POWs lift the sleepers off and carry them along the railbed, dropping them in place one by one. They are trued up in their spacing and alignment while the ten-metre steel rails are brought forward and laid on top, bags of dogspikes and connecting fishplates are dumped in convenient spots, and the loco retires for another load while the rails are positioned, checked for gauge, spiked to the sleepers and bolted together.

It is a slick and well-organised operation, obviously done by experienced gangs.

The men are all Dutch army, mostly (as we find out when talking to them in the evening) Javanese with a good number of European and mixed bloods. They live in roofed wagons, which are part of the train, as a mobile camp moving up constantly behind the railhead. In sharp contrast to us, they are well fed, healthy and actually wearing uniforms that are clean and in good condition! Up to this point in their work they have been operating in the farming country between Ban Pong and Kanburi, with access to local food supplies and luxuries such as soap and tobacco and – good God, toilet paper! It seems that they are a self-contained unit within the Jap army railway regiment, with their own supply arrangements, and they have little contact with (and take no orders from) other Jap troops in the area, including the Nip POW administration.

Thus it is that they lay their sleepers and rails to within a few metres of the great split in the cliff, without realising that not only is there no bridge, but there is a considerable step down on the far side. In true bushido fashion, they have kept their noses firmly down on the work immediately being done, oblivious to anything around them.

In an hour, a bunch of Nips are on the spot, running around like chickens with a fox amongst them. There is really no choice. The low side cannot be built up so they will have to lift some 200 metres of newly laid track and carry it back to the embankment, while the high side is blasted down and cleared, and the track then put back in place. Even then track-laying will not be able to proceed, because the span across the gap cannot be started until new abutments have been formed. It will take weeks.

A complication is that the massive timber bridge

connecting the cliff face with the embankment cannot be altered in any way. The new level will therefore have to be tapered to fit at both ends and trains don't like much deviation from the straight and level. To do the job properly would require a new instrumented survey to establish the corrected gradient, and careful removal of overlying rock down to that level.

But the Nips can be original in their thinking. The fact that their originality ignores, or disregards, good engineering practice doesn't matter − the insistence is on speedy construction and that overrides all other considerations.

We see a flat wagon being pushed along the track, with the air-compressor from the Wampo South viaduct sitting on it. Within minutes the blatting roar of the compressor is echoing off the cliff as the drills stab into the surface of the ledge. The engineers are actually drilling shot-holes between the sleepers and under the rails! Obviously, they intend to pack the shot-holes with dynamite and clear the shattered rock from underneath the sleepers and rails, which will then drop neatly into place! The drills bite into the limestone, and by the end of the day drilling is complete. As the compressor is withdrawn, a gang of Nips stuff sticks of explosives with detonators and fuses into the holes. The overall length has been divided into three sections of about seventy metres each, as is indicated by the long fuses standing up at the far end of each section grading down to short lengths at the near ends. Nothing so modern as simultaneous electrical detonation; the long fuses will slowly burn down as the engineer moves through his section, touching off each fuse until they are all lit, giving him sufficient time to get clear before the whole lot detonates more or less at the same time. It is a crude method, the timing being dependent on the roughest of calculations combined with plain guesswork.

After morning tenko we move out as usual to the site, and are held back to watch the fireworks. As seems to be the custom of the Nips on these occasions, there is a small ceremony to mark it as a special event – and maybe also to impress us with their technical skills. There are about 1,000 of us, gathered in a mass on the embankment.

To our surprise, there are only three men detailed to ignite the fuses, and they are not engineers but Korean camp guards who, as far as we know, have no experience at all with explosives. Yesterday evening, as we stepped back to camp along the sleepers, we made a rough count of the number of charges laid. By our reckoning there were nearly 300 altogether, so each Korean will have to set off 100, one at a time, and make sure that each is fizzing steadily before moving on to the next.

The three brave warriors set off across the great bridge, each to the far end of his section, the first two waiting until the third (who has the longest distance to walk) is in place. Incredibly, they all light cigarettes and begin to touch the burning tips to the ends of the fuses. The fellow at the far end is the big Korean who didn't win his race at the Emperor's birthday sports carnival, and he is putting on a show for our benefit. Maybe he didn't win his race, but by golly he's not frightened of dynamite, no sir! After lighting a dozen fuses, he stops to enjoy his cigarette, gazing with studied nonchalance at the scenery before carrying on. When his cigarette has burned down, he takes his time lighting another, moving deliberately down his area and leaving a growing patch of blue smoke spirals behind him. What he has not realised is that right in front of him is a near 200-metre stretch of spluttering blue smoke which he will have to cross to reach safety. The other two Koreans dealt with their fuses as fast as possible and sprinted off the site in quick time.

Looking on as spectators, the implications are immediately apparent and a buzz of conversation arises. Close to me, a slow Australian drawl: 'D'ya reckon he'll make it? A dollar says he won't!' is answered by another: 'Yer on. But I hope you win! It'll be a pleasure to pay up!' Nobody shouts a warning – who cares if this idiot kills himself? The tension rises as the critical seconds slide away.

The Korean lights his last fuse, straightens up and tosses away the stub of his cigarette. Reaching into his shirt pocket for another smoke, he faces down the track and what he sees freezes him into immobility – but only for a split second before he leaps forward and bolts into the forest of swirling smoke. He is a tall man, and his long legs stretch out in such tremendous strides that he hardly seems to touch down, almost flying at low level! His footing is railway sleepers bedded in broken rock, awkward even for walking over, but he skims across at incredible speed. 'Jesus, if he'd run like that at the races, he'd have cleaned up everything!'

He is almost clear of the danger area when a few of the charges start to detonate. Fifty yards ahead of him is the big air-compressor and he flings himself down on the far side just as the majority of the charges go off in scores of irregular explosions. The straw-mat sunshade fixed over the machine tears loose and is whipped up into the air like a kite in a gale.

The blast reaches us just in time to bring our fascinated attention back to the mass of flying rock hurled up and now starting to come down. Most of it is carried towards the river by the blast bouncing back from the cliff face, but some of it is heading straight for us. It is the only time in my life that I have been thankful for all those tedious hours on the cricket field at school. Watching the chunks of rock curving up in our direction, it is easy to identify which are going to come close and, resisting the temptation to catch one and toss it back, to step aside to avoid it. My brother is holding a pick-axe in front of him, the steel head resting on the ground, when a low trajectory googly comes in undetected through the crowd and smashes itself against the socket. Without this protection his feet would have been pulped, for the rock was travelling like an artillery shell – I saw it only in the half-second before impact. The slimmest margin of luck can make such a difference!

The Korean picks himself up, a very shaken man. The steel mass of the compressor sheltered him from serious injury, as is shown by hefty dents all over it. Well, that's his good luck. We are completely indifferent as to whether he lives or dies; he simply does not matter to us.

The nights have been providing blessedly cool relief from the overpowering heat of the days. Months of dry weather have laid a brownish tinge over the forest trees, and a few nights with heavy dew are sufficient to bring back a young green to their leaves. To dodge the persistent bugs, I have taken to sleeping on a spare bridge timber lying in our area. This is a tree trunk some ten feet long, chipped by adzes to four flat faces, resulting in a bed fifteen inches across and a foot above the ground. It is hard and unyielding but clean and beyond the reach of bugs, and as long as I'm careful with turning over in my sleep so as not to roll off, I am reasonably comfortable. And the fresh dew settles sweetly all over me in the early hours of the morning, which is relaxing and reviving. The sparkling sky is calm and friendly in the quiet time before dawn.

The laying of railway lines has brought both benefits and problems. We are now only a few hours from civilisation, and there has been an immediate improvement in rations such as fresh vegetables which could not last over the slow boat journey – purple eggplants, long white Chinese radishes, pumpkins and tiny reddish onions. And duck eggs – fresh, wholesome, lifegiving – costing only five sattangs apiece and worth their weight in gold!

The cheerful fresh-faced Dutch, healthy and with clothes to wear, have money in their pockets to buy anything we care to offer. Signet rings, wedding rings, anything in precious metals, watches, fountain pens, English and Straits Settlements currency – they will take it all after haggling over prices. The goods go back to Kanburi where they are sold for three or four times what we are paid, as we soon find out. The way we hear it, the Dutch in the Dutch East Indies did not fire a shot in opposition to the Jap landings, but drew all their cash out of the local banks while waiting for the invaders to arrive, and as POWs have been able to live comfortably in the meantime. With their private train running back and forth, they have the means for a profitable trade in our personal possessions one way and in luxury goods such as soap, tobacco, tinned milk, toilet paper, pepper and chilli sauce returning to us. Blankets, groundsheets, eating utensils, all are available to be purchased at their exorbitant prices.

After the first excitement of selling and buying and discussing experiences amongst ourselves, we begin to have niggling doubts about all this. Most of the European Dutch speak English, and we Volunteers are able to talk to the Javanese in Malay. We do not object to them making a degree of profit for their trouble, but we do also think it reasonable to expect them to be moderate about it in view of the circumstances. The Javanese chatter freely to us largely, we feel, because the white Dutch are taking most of the trade and leaving only the crumbs for them. From what they tell us, there is an unwholesome familiarity between the whites and the Nip train personnel (who are also the equivalent of our camp guards), which no doubt satisfies all concerned in profits, bribes and, in British army slang, lurks and perks all along the line. But there is something immoral in their greed for exorbitant profit from their position of advantage over our helplessness.

The problems are in the disruption to our hitherto carefully regulated relationship with our own Nips, who are low-degree, line-of-communication troops with no real fighting qualifications and no real knowledge about anything at all. We have been doing just enough to keep them happy while still maintaining a neutral attitude towards them, thus holding our personal dignity intact while being careful not to antagonise them. We are cooperating without crawling, obedient as far as may be necessary to avoid unpleasantness, and so far the results have been satisfactory. Matters such as food and medical supplies are, of course, outside our scope, but in everyday contacts at work the system functions well.

But now our ordered existence is shattered. The Jap railway regiment troops, seen at a distance at Wampo South, have caught up with us, and life is now dominated by a new word – speedo! – which is shouted and screamed at us all day long, accompanied by streams of orders and abuse in Japanese which, naturally, we do not understand. Which is no excuse apparently – failure to jump to it instantly is rewarded by a hefty bash. Very rapidly we start to look for something which needs doing and get stuck into it. If we guess correctly all is well, otherwise we are 'encouraged' to think again. Better still, we keep an eye open for a quieter area where we can slide off, which is possible because we no longer work in gangs which can be controlled. The railway engineers work at fanatic speed and simply grab anybody within reach to help, so that in the overall dizzy confusion, it is possible to be dragged in at one point and slither off unnoticed at another. It needs nerve (or maybe desperation!) and cunning to do this, because if you are caught, you will suffer for it as some men have painfully discovered.

The loosened rock under the track already laid on the ledge is dragged out and chucked over the cliff at frantic speed. Splintered sleepers are pulled out and replaced, and irregularities in the ballast are levelled by bashing with a sledgehammer. The rails, slightly buckled here and there by the dynamite, are in surprisingly good condition, and the whole lot is rammed back into place by the locomotive being slowly driven back and forth until it compacts the rubble into some semblance of stability.

Building a bridge across the chasm in the ledge should be a relatively simple matter but becomes a nightmare in the hands of a berserk bunch of railway engineers. The irregular tapering walls going down sixty feet to the beach have to be squared off to form a step on either side, where the base timbers will be laid to carry the upperworks. It's difficult enough working with crude tools and in the cramped space of the cleft, but it becomes plain bloody dangerous with screaming Nips trying to get started on the next stage before the essential preparations are completed. Lumps of rock, dogspikes, anything handy, are hurled down from upstairs to attract attention to their incomprehensible gibberish orders. There is no secure footing while we work, and a tumble to the bottom of the cleft would result in serious injury or death. In the total absence of any kind of medical treatment, even a minor injury is to be avoided. As it is, many of the men suffer from dizziness and blurred eyesight, consequences of prolonged malnutrition, but since there is nothing visible to prove it, the Nips don't accept that these problems even exist.

At the midday break on the second day, we have had enough. Observing a raft coming into the beach with a big hand-cranked winch on its deck, we work our way down the cliff face and offer to help get it ashore. We are right opposite where we had been working, but as far as we can see our absence has not been noticed, our positions simply being filled by eager-beaver Jap engineers.

News, good or maybe not so good. Tomorrow we move out of Wampo North, which is in itself good, but we had hoped that having completed our stretch we would get out of the hills and into the more civilised country around Kanburi. Not so. We are marching north to Tonchan, upriver from Tarsao, a hike of some twenty-five miles all in one day, to help out because the project has fallen seriously behind schedule.

Tonchan is ruled by that fearsome Jap sergeant-major known as The Tiger, whose reputation for sheer brutality has reached even our isolated area. So maybe our relief at getting away from Wampo will turn sour on us — as always, we shall see in due course, and accept what we find as philosophically as we can.

We had heard, vaguely, that a motor road was under construction alongside the railway, as a more efficient means of bringing materials to the construction camps than the river, and also for Jap army movements to Burma. What we find is a mud track hacked out of the forest, in poor condition at this end of the dry season and destined to become a quagmire in the rains. Unlike a railway, which has to be kept more or less level with only slight gradients and wide curves, a road climbs and falls and has tight bends. In the monsoon storms (which will start any day now) the slopes of this road will become muddy torrents, gouging the surface and flooding the hollows, for there is no sign of drainage preparations.

The march is exhausting, the day scorching hot and the alignment of the track keeps us full in the sun for most of the day. The shady forest on each side is out of reach except when we fall out for ten minutes every now and again. The cook-house gear is shared amongst us, the twelve-gallon iron rice kwalis being distinctly unpopular, slung from bamboo poles over the shoulders of four men. Stumbling over the rutted ground, these awkward loads swing all over the place.

We stagger into Tonchan well after dark, to be paraded and counted in front of The Tiger. There is no food prepared for us, no tea, only a roaring lecture (through the camp interpreter) to the effect that we shall be punished severely if we do not behave properly. We are dismissed to an area which has a few tents, into which the sick men are placed. The rest of us bed down where we can on the ground in the open.

The senior British officer in the camp does not put in an appearance to welcome us. Maybe he is sick, or maybe just not interested.

During the night we find out the cause of the oppressive heat of our march – the wet monsoon arrives. In pouring rain we gather our kit and find what shelter we can under the eaves of huts, or simply huddle together in the swirling pools which quickly fill every hollow and rut, and wait for daylight.

Welcome to Tiger territory.

5

Tonchan Camp

MAY TO JULY 1943

The darkness of the night intensifies and the rain continues to bucket down on us without any sign of diminishing. In a strange camp we have no idea where we might find shelter, and it is essential that we stay together. The leaky huts at Wampo were bad enough, but nothing has prepared us for this. Wearing nothing but a hat and a fundoshi, we are fortunate that the rain is warm and there is no wind to chill us. It is simply a matter of endurance until daylight.

But we have had a tough day's march with no food since breakfast rice. We have no shelter and cannot lie down in the muddy slop now inches deep around our feet. Our bodies cry out for sleep, our empty bellies nag us, there will doubtless be a day's work demanded of us tomorrow, our officers in the camp either don't know (or don't want to know) that we are here, and daylight is eight hours away. We are all more than a bit fed up as we prepare to pass the night with whatever patience and philosophy we can summon up.

Daylight crawls in, yellow-grey and looking as dispirited as we feel, but we do not see the sun, which is somewhere on the far side of the dirty purple clouds lowering over us. The rain lightens but continues to stream over us as if it will never stop.

Our own cooks have not yet been able to set themselves in place, and the camp cooks can do very little to cope with 1,600 men suddenly dumped on them. Breakfast rice is scanty and half-cooked, and there is nothing to take with us for a midday meal at the worksite.

Tenko is held under the malevolent glare of The Tiger, who is introduced by the camp interpreter as Staff-Sergeant Furobashi. The head count is quick, once only instead of the usual repeated count and disagreements. Maybe the Nips prefer to accept our figures rather than risk The Tiger's wrath at any appearance of inefficiency!

Furobashi disappears, and his place is taken by a British lieutenant-colonel who calls us to attention before addressing us. We know his rank because he is in full uniform, badges of rank, Sam Browne leather all polished, cap exactly right on his barbered head, clean shaven this morning, boots polished and everything laundered and pressed – we haven't seen anything like him for so long that we can't believe our eyes! In this jungle setting, he is just ludicrous. And to preserve all this studied perfection his batman (also in full uniform) stands just behind his left shoulder, holding a large Chinese oiled-paper umbrella over his head to fend off the disrespectful rain!

Sheer amazement causes us to miss most of his speech, but if the first part was in the same vein as the bit we heard at the end, then we weren't bothered: '. . . and therefore expect you to take proper pride in yourselves as British soldiers, in particular to make every effort to maintain our army's high standards of personal hygiene and neatness in dress and appearance, and to preserve your dignity in the face of the enemy at all times and in all circumstances!'

His measured parade ground tones are a trifle blurred by the rain drumming on our hat brims, but it is very clear that he means every word of it. Yet although he says we should have pride in ourselves (do we really need to be told this?), it is quite obvious that he has nothing but contempt for us. There is unmistakable sneering disdain and cold hatred in his face as he surveys us. Immense disgust projects itself over us, a spray of venom from a baleful snake.

The colonel stalks off, under the shelter of his batman's umbrella, and a fully dressed junior officer takes over. He stays with us just long enough to point to a group of huts where we can dump our kit, and we have ten minutes to be back again and formed up ready for work. Every man is to be here; there will be no sick parade this morning. Having delivered his speech of welcome, he disappears at a trot.

When we come back we join a squad of men who fall in to the side. After tenko, they mix with us as we move away to collect tools. There are exactly thirty-two of them and they are the total workforce available this morning from a strength similar to ours at Wampo – three labour battalions of 500 men each and a group of 100 for camp administration and internal duties, 1,600 in all.

Where are all the others? We are told that about 800 are dead and buried (more or less!) 'over there, under the trees', and 700 are laid out on the bedspaces in the huts, too far gone for even The Tiger to roust out (which means that they are as near dead as makes no difference). There are no medical supplies whatsoever, and the rations are abominable under the Nip reasoning that there is no point in feeding men who are not fit to work and, anyway, nearly dead already.

It has taken only four or five months for this awful situation to come about – all those deaths and the hundreds who will most certainly follow.

'Look at us! All that's left able to stand on our feet and get to work. Thirty-two today, and we're all well on the way to joining the others. The Nips won't allow us to dig graves, the sick men can't stand upright so they can't do it, we shall all end up lying in the mud where we fall or underneath the huts as they collapse! There must be scores of bodies lying around on the ground, unburied.'

He is right – they are all extremely sick men, moving with the sluggishness and weary effort resulting from starvation and exhaustion. With sunken eyes, tight skin over shrunken bodies and stringy muscles, they are little more than skeletons. God, what must the 700 look like? Some have the muck of dysentery and raddled bowels trickling down their legs, washed away by the pouring rain. They don't pay any heed to it. It has been their condition for so long, they are past caring and can't stop it anyway. And they simply have nothing to wipe the mess away – not a bit of rag or anything else.

The speaker's eyes burn with intense feeling, his voice quivers with passionate anger. 'If I live through this, when I get home I'm going to fix that bastard colonel properly! He's personally responsible for what has happened here, and I'm going to make bloody sure that every newspaper in England knows about it. I'll write to the Prime Minister, the War Office, my Member of Parliament – everyone. I'll see him tried, convicted and shot! Bloody hell, I will. I owe it to every man who suffered and died here.'

The outburst of anger brought him to a standstill, his thin chest heaving and tears streaming down his cheeks. Then he went on, speaking quietly and with great emphasis: 'And if I come to think that I won't survive to get back home, I shall kill him myself with a pickaxe, right here, before I'm too weak to do it, and every man in this hellhole will cheer me on – even the dead will stand up and thank me! I give you my word, I'll do that.'

We are the first men from outside Tonchan he has been

able to talk to about this foul death camp. He and his friends have been desperately afraid that every single man in the camp will die, and that nobody in the other camps will ever know their story. More than anything, they want justice for their fellows by having those responsible exposed and charged in public – and that includes our own people just as much (or even more so!) as the Nips. After all, you don't expect much else from the Nips, but our own people do have responsibilities towards us.

Once the talking has started they all join in, their dammed-up emotions released by having new people to listen to them. We can have no doubt as to the truth, and it is not until the end of the day that we can sit around a fire and sort it all out, piece it together. The rain eases during the day, and stops.

We had thought Wampo was a tough camp, and our thirteen dead and daily sick list of between 200 and 300 pretty bad, but in the face of what we have learned today, it really was a Boy Scouts' Jamboree! All those rumours about some of the upriver camps, even about The Tiger – they had been true. Less than the whole truth, even, because we had never heard any details, only general gossip. And nothing quite as awful as this reality now exposed to us.

We settle down to sleep with disquieting thoughts about our future. It is something to be enormously grateful for, the ability to get to sleep whatever the day's problems, to have a mind untroubled for a few hours, and peaceful rest for the body. We all seem to have acquired this gift. It shows how we have adapted to circumstances, and we know that to lose it will lead to decline, even to death. Wipe out today, do not think about tomorrow!

We hear, by the way, that there are no officers amongst the dead or on the 'dangerously ill' lists.

In the coming days we are told that the *entire* stock of medical supplies in this camp consists of one bottle of Epsom Salts! Nothing else, not even dressings. No antiseptics, no disinfectants, no soap! In all the camps I've seen the medical supplies have been woefully inadequate, but given the number of dead and dying men here, this defies belief.

We are told that the problems started right at the beginning, when Tonchan Camp was established. The men had marched all the way from Ban Pong, as we had, as far as Tarsao where they turned north upriver. The site of the camp was some distance from the Kwei Noi, and high up, so that the river could not be used as a water supply. In the dry season, which has just ended, they relied on natural springs which provided good clear water for cooking, but in the total absence of buckets or piping, these springs were simply not available for personal washing. The huts, as usual, were inadequate and bug-ridden, medical supplies almost non-existent, rations rotting and fouled and by any standards insufficient.

The Nip in command of the camp was not even an officer, only a staff-sergeant, Furobashi, a professional soldier and typical of the type to reach that rank in the Jap army. His only duty was to maintain efficiency and discipline, and he succeeded by freely indulging in a natural talent for overbearing brutality. He said little, and what he did say was roared out in a ferocious voice – hence his nickname, of which he was well aware for he spoke some English, and he came down heavily on our men when he overhead them complaining amongst themselves.

It seems that early on, when the bad conditions had become established as the camp's normal conditions, the colonel had gone to see The Tiger to discuss improvements. A soldier from the Great War with a Military Cross to his credit, the colonel found himself confronted by a scruffy hulk with no civilised manners at all and, worse, with not the smallest sign of respect for a British officer of senior rank who displayed campaign and personal medals on his uniform, indicating long and honourable service, which would be recognised and command a proper response in any decent army.

From reports of this interview which leaked back to the men, the colonel was given no opportunity to say anything. Through the camp interpreter, The Tiger bellowed that the British troops were lazy and pretended to be sick, did not work satisfactorily and took advantage of Nippon's leniency, which showed a lack of proper gratitude towards the Emperor! If there was no improvement, discipline would be tighter, working hours increased, and rations reduced! The colonel was dismissed, deeply insulted and seething with rage at having had to endure such treatment from a barbaric savage.

As far as was known, he had never been able to bring himself to request another interview with The Tiger. He had occasionally been summoned to receive a raging storm of complaints (this being Furobashi's standard way of imposing his senior position), but never said a word more than was unavoidable. He considered that it was beneath his dignity, as a senior British officer and gentleman, even to acknowledge the presence of such an ill-mannered oaf! So, no complaint was ever formally made.

It is the duty of every officer in the British army, emphasised during his training and after receiving his commission, to take a real interest in the welfare of his men. He is the last to fall out on a route march or while campaigning, moving amongst his men during breaks to enquire as to their fitness and wellbeing, checking the cookhouse and seeing to distribution of food and water. A good officer is familiar with his men's personal circumstances, families and homes, and is always available for a quiet talk and such helpful advice as he may be able to give. It is a solid tradition and has an enormous effect on morale and the unit's cohesion.

In the Jap army, as far as we can see, an officer never talks personally to his men. He issues orders through his immediate juniors and every man is expected to do as he is told. The gap between officers and rankers is wide and inviolate. But that is the way they choose to run things, and has no bearing on us.

So, this is the big question. To what extent is the colonel's obsession with his precious self-dignity responsible for the camp's abysmal squalor, the hundreds of deaths already and the hundreds more which will surely happen? Would he have achieved anything if he had pressed his complaints? Who knows? If The Tiger had boxed his ears and humiliated him, would that have helped? It certainly would, say his men. It would have gained him enormous respect from them!

Even if he had not managed to make any improvement, at least he would have tried, and his men would have appreciated that. As it is, his men have nobody else to look to for help, and he has done absolutely nothing, not even made an effort, and they blame him with deep angry resentment. To them he is, despite his Military Cross, a moral coward at the lowest level, putting his personal dignity before their desperate needs, and prepared to watch them suffer and die in filth and degradation rather than force himself to make any effort. 'Bugger his dignity. Ours is trampled on every day! And why should we suffer like this, and die like this, to protect his tender feelings?'

But there is more to it than this. The colonel has formed the opinion that the men are scum, that they have allowed themselves to degenerate to their present condition, they have no morale, no stamina, they are incapable of bearing up under hardships, they have only themselves to blame. They have let themselves go to pieces, they are not fit to be British soldiers, they deserve what is happening to them. The colonel has in fact said all this, on a number of occasions, to the men themselves. The word is that, to his officers, he has added: 'Why should I humiliate myself to a Japanese warrant officer to help men like these? It is demeaning to me, and the men not worth it.' Word has trickled out through his batman and others.

It all ties in with that awful look on his face at our first parade in his camp. We, scruffy, near-naked, with scabby sores dotted all over us, were just another rabble pack come to add to his wearisome troubles. Well, maybe he does recognise, but simply cannot overcome, his deep-seated prejudices, and has conjured up a kind of antidote to anaesthetise a troubled conscience.

We wonder what his fellow officers, junior to him in rank, really think of him. And if they should have an uneasy feeling that he is dreadfully in the wrong, do they remain quiet and hide (thankfully, maybe?) behind his senior rank? Army protocol is very powerful, but surely the enormity of the humanitarian issues involved must justify action by somebody? Apparently not.

But then, we are told that the officers do not even visit the sick to bring a little comfort, some reassurance that someone cares whether they live or die. There is no doubt that the huts where the sick are lying are dreadfully unpleasant to enter, as we find out for ourselves, but a few hours' visiting is nothing compared to the horrors of being condemned to lie there in hopeless agony, slowly dying as the days and weeks drag past, and knowing that the effort to stay alive is useless because death is coming and will take its own time.

We know how we feel about all this, without any doubt; 1,500 dead and dying men, in shocking conditions of neglect, degradation and callous disinterest, are far too high a price to pay for any one man's personal sense of dignity. And these men are a shameful shadow over the moral values of those who should know better.

This is how we see it, and we shall not forget.

Our work at Tonchan is mainly drilling shot-holes for dynamite. Because of the disastrous rate of sickness and death, the labour force diminished rapidly and the whole program in Tonchan's area is way behind schedule. It is typical of the Nip attitude that, instead of doing what is required to maintain workers in reasonable condition, they will allow them to die from neglect and then send for replacements. There is no intelligent logic at all, only waste through sheer stupidity – the human casualties, of course, don't matter!

We, the replacements, will presumably be expected not only to catch up on the lost time, but also to carry everything forward to meet deadlines. The railway lines will soon reach Tarsao, and if the track-laying comes to a standstill because the Tonchan section is not ready for it, then the Nip High Command will be out for blood. Our medical officer, a captain who accompanied us from Wampo, has confronted The Tiger with a list of rations required if a productive work-force is expected, and the rations have in fact improved. We all have a tremendous respect and admiration for our MO, who is in charge of our Volunteer battalions' medical section, having come to us from a government hospital in northern Malaya. He is always prepared to stick his neck out on our behalf, usually with notable success, and inevitably we make comparisons between him and the haughty colonel, who could (and should) have tried to protect his men.

A swath has been cleared through the forest along the floor of a shallow valley, but the earth lies in a very thin layer on top of irregular rocky formations which prevent the usual pick and shovel method of clearing. The general level has to be taken down a couple of metres, which means doing it in two layers since our drills cannot go over a metre deep. The rock is unusual, as if it has been poured molten in the hollow of the valley and then been subjected to tremendous rain. The surface is pitted and dimpled with spherical hollows, cracks run like crazy paving in all directions and there are ridges and hollows everywhere. And it's as hard as hell! And ragged and tough on bare feet!

We work in pairs with a steel hexagonal drill bit and a sledgehammer. There are no tongs: the drills have to be hand-held firmly vertical by one of us while the other thumps it with the hammer. The drill has been beaten out to an edge at one end, so that the cutting tip is slightly wider than the stem. After each strike the drill has to be rotated slightly to prevent the tip from jamming and to make it cut more effectively. We work out a routine of fifty blows with the hammer and change over, at which point the dust has to be lifted out from the bottom. If it is raining the dust becomes a sludge which can be picked out with the frayed tip of a slim bamboo or twig. If it is not conveniently raining, you can sacrifice some tea from your bottle, or simply piss into the hole. Crude, maybe, but effective!

We start with an eighty-centimetre hole per pair, which is not too bad, but after a few days this is stepped up to two holes, which is a bit tough, and then to three holes, which is just bloody impossible. So a little ingenuity is needed. The system is that when you have completed a hole you call a Nip to measure it. He drops in a bamboo with a notch at the correct depth, says okay, then you stuff a wad of grass into the hole. This tuft of grass shows the dynamite men where to drop in their sticks of explosive. The weakness of the system is that, with 600 pairs of men boring three holes each, at the end of the day's work no less than 1,800 charges (with detonator and slow-burning fuse in place) must be inserted and set off. The few Nips cannot possibly put so many charges together and place them, so nearly all this is done by our own people.

With the Nips' total unconcern for safety measures, we are all crammed into a stretch of some 200 metres of track, and the shot-holes are so close together that most of the explosive will be wasted. But this does give us the opportunity to cheat, which is done by completing one hole to full depth and having it measured and topped with a grass marker. A second hole is then started and, when halfway down, the tuft of grass is moved across to it and a Nip (if possible, a different Nip) is called to measure the first hole again. The sheer number of holes makes it most unlikely that the deceit will be spotted, and it does save us an awful lot of tiring labour!

As the explosive charges are completed by pushing a detonator and slow-burning fuse into the stick of dynamite, the shot-holes are stuffed, our men putting a single stick in the short holes and cramming the surplus in the deep ones. At the end of the day there is a small forest of white fuse lengths sticking out of the floor of the cutting, long ones for first lighting and short for the last.

We are not sent back to camp while the charges are detonated. We have to wait and watch the fireworks. Dispersing ourselves amongst the trees we look for trunks thick enough to shelter behind, but they are all small and even our skinny frames are not protected. All we can do is peer round whatever trees we can find and watch the explosions – if you have a shovel you can hold it up over your head!

The timing of the fuses can only be approximate at best, and for an unpleasantly drawn-out minute or so there is a continuing rumble of irregular explosions hurling out thousands of lumps of shattered rock all over the place. All we can do is keep an eye on the pieces that look as if they are heading for us, and ignore the swarm of projectiles whizzing past at all angles – being careful, of course, not to step aside from one chunk into the path of another! Exhilarating it may be, but we would rather do without it. Thank heaven, there are no casualties.

Clearing up the loosened rock and dirt is done by the highly technical method of picking and shovelling into small half-moon wicker baskets, which are carried to the side of the cutting and emptied up on the rim. This tedious business is enlivened by finding unexploded dynamite sticks buried in the debris, even bringing them up speared on the point of a pickaxe! If there is no detonator embedded in it there is (so we are told, reassuringly) no risk of explosion. If there is a detonator, you won't have to worry about it – which is also supposed to be reassuring.

Because we can't bear to see anything wasted, when the Nips aren't looking we retrieve lengths of telephone wire torn by flying rocks off the poles alongside the cutting. Working it to and fro until it snaps, we soon have tongs for holding the drills and dipping sticks for lifting out powdered rock from the holes. So far no one has lost finger joints, which is quite miraculous, but some men have had ragged fragments of steel pinging into their skin from the burred tops of drills, and we are worried at the possibility of being blinded if struck in the eyes.

Mid afternoon we are joined by a group of some fifty men – not reinforcements, but turned out of the cookhouses by The Tiger. This means that the cookhouse routine of collecting firewood and water has been interrupted, and there will be no evening rice waiting for us when we go back to camp at the end of the day. The cooks will then have to turn to, and we shall have to wait for a late meal.

The Tiger has warned that if our work is not more productive he will send the cooks out every morning, including the night duty shift who stoke the fires and cook the breakfast rice. It seems that a feeble protest was attempted by the colonel's adjutant, but even that was taken by The Tiger as an insult to his authority and he immediately threatened to order all the officers out as well, to work on the track. The prospect of such an absolutely unthinkable (almost blasphemous) situation galvanised the officers into protesting in a body, talking about the dignity of the officer class which was, after all, of the highest importance in the Japanese army. The Tiger, apparently, was not in the slightest impressed and told them the matter was in their hands.

We can see, agree and sympathise with the officers' argument, but if it really comes to the pinch, we are damned if we are going to work harder than we already do just to save their egos.

In the event the whole affair seems to fizzle out. The cooks go back to their normal duties and the officers to their bridge-playing and books. That Tiger sure is some smart negotiator – he has scared the poop out of all concerned and that will keep them on their toes for a long time.

Even in The Tiger's camp it is not always just work and no play. A Jap army film unit visits us and stretches an enormous screen over an ingenious bamboo frame on the parade ground. Luckily it is a balmy evening with no rain, and by making ourselves comfortable on the ground behind it we not only avoid the company of the Nips and their privileged guests, but can chat freely amongst ourselves. We have a perfect view since the images are as clear from the back as from the front, and the sound is very good.

The program lasts from 9 pm to 3.30 am, starting with a propaganda film about the assault on Singapore Island, with

Jap artillery banging away and troops rushing everywhere with fixed bayonets and ferocious expressions. There is also footage of the British troops running away helter-skelter; obviously staged after the surrender because so much was in close-up.

There is also a musical comedy of shenanigans in a hotel, with people popping in and out of rooms and getting all mixed up. Although the dialogue is in Japanese, the story and plot are easy to follow. There is an attractive sequence in which every step on a broad curving staircase gives out a soft bell-like note when trodden on, and everyone runs up and down accompanied by a pleasing melody.

News sequences (all of victorious Jap troops storming ashore and being deliriously welcomed by the local people) and sundry bits and pieces fill in the rest of the time, then – would you believe it? – tomorrow is declared a yasumi day!

Sorting out work parties after morning tenko one day, volunteers are invited to go to Tarsao to pick up rations for the camp. Anyone interested? Ten men – how about you lot? Well, okay, we'll give it a go, a ride in a truck and humping bags of rice will be a change and get us out of the camp for a day.

We are all Singapore Volunteers, and a couple of Nips march us off to The Tiger's hut. He barks his orders in fractured English, but they are clear enough. We walk to Tarsao, collect twenty cattle and drive them back to Tonchan. Take water and rice bowls, we will be given 'hiru meishi' (midday rice) at Tarsao. We are to be back by dark, or we will be strongly hurt. He flashes his big teeth in a bellow of laughter, and dismisses us.

What the hell have we let ourselves in for? No transport, twelve kilometres on foot to Tarsao along that mud track, round up twenty Siamese cattle (which are muscled like racehorses and anything but placid), drive the animals twelve kilometres uphill, all during about ten hours of daylight – who worked this out, if anyone did?

Half an hour down the track, sweating uncomfortably in the hot sunshine, we hear a truck coming up behind us. Our Nips wave it to a stop and we climb in but very soon wish we hadn't. The truck must be some sort of special purpose vehicle, maybe a field workshop, for it has a sheet steel box body. The interior has been stripped of everything except permanent fixtures such as brackets, hooks and a multitude of other hard protuberances. The driver goes like a crazy Jehu, hurling the vehicle at breakneck speed over the ruts and channels. Because the track is downhill most of the way, he is almost out of control as we slide wildly through the bends, bouncing and rocking and jarring heavily on the springs. We are flung bodily around like dolls shaken up in a box, coming up against every single one of the steel projections, unable to find a grip or keep our footing. Thankfully, we are put off before coming within sight of Tarsao's main gate and guardroom – possibly the driver is not supposed to give lifts and doesn't want to be seen doing so. There is no part of us that doesn't ache and feel bruised; even the Nips who travelled in the cab look a bit shaken.

We have heard that there are actually two camps here: the one called Tarsao is the base for POW activities all along the river while the other, Nam Tok, is Jap army and concerned with troop movements and military stores. The guardroom at which our Nips present us for inspection is obviously Nam Tok: the men inside have a positively frontline look about them which is quite different from the sloppy bunch of slackers to whom we are accustomed.

There is a bamboo fence with a gateway wide enough for two-way vehicle traffic. We pass through and follow a mud road for about a kilometre before coming to several acres of open grassland with, at the near edge, a corral of tree-trunk fencing enclosing a herd of cattle. One Nip goes off to find the quartermaster or cowherd while the other calls us to 'mateh' (wait) in the shade. We do so, dozing off for well over an hour before our Nip returns, accompanied by a quartermaster who is clearly in a foul temper.

The two enter the corral. The cattle immediately shuffle to the far side and nervously eddy around as the men come closer and the haggling starts. Some of the animals are emaciated and a few cows have young calves with them. As far as we can tell, the cowherd wants us to take all his sick beasts and to count a cow and calf as two. Our Nip refuses – possibly the looming threat of The Tiger's displeasure at having third-rate goods brought to him gives him the courage to stand up to the cowherd's bullying.

The shouting gets louder, the cattle become more restive, and the interior of the corral is choking up with yellow dust. Another half-hour gone and we are not even started. Eventually the quartermaster holds up both hands, fingers spread: we can have ten only. Our Nip spies a rope dangling over the fence, grabs it and heads for the biggest beast. Maybe he thinks that this will be a leader and the others will follow when he brings it out. The cattle must have seen this rope trick before – they all break into a zigzagging canter and the dust thickens.

Our Nip abandons his choice and manages to throw a loop over the horns of another animal. As he drags it towards the entrance our second Nip slips the loose poles aside to let him come out. With him, bucking and wild-eyed, come all the others racing out into the wide open spaces, the quarter-master lumbering after them, screaming with rage. We just keep well out of everyone's way.

Our Nip, keeping the rope taut, comes close enough to his captive to shift the rope loop around the animal's neck. It keeps backing away from him, mean-looking and snorting. The Nip slackens the rope and quickly turns it around his wrist to anchor it. Unfortunately this means that he can't let go when the beast, feeling the rope fall loose, turns around in a flash and gallops off across the open ground. Our Nip, unable to free himself, lengthens his stride until he is being towed horizontally through the air, his toes flicking the ground as he loses altitude.

About 100 metres away, where the trees start, a fallen trunk lies on the ground. The animal hurdles it with ease, the Nip hits it like a torpedo, we hear the thwack clearly. We trot to the spot, unwilling to have anything to do with it but unable to see how we can stay clear. Expecting to find a body with a fractured skull or broken neck, we are astonished to see that the Nip is conscious and rubbing himself over to check for damage. Some spots are obviously painful, but nothing seems to be broken. A drink from his water bottle, and he is ready for another try.

The cattle, having said their piece, allow themselves to be rounded up without much trouble and we head for the camp exit. The cowherd can look for the rest of them, and we haven't signed any forms for the ten animals which we are taking away. The sun is well over to the west, so our Nips are anxious to start home and haven't time for such trivialities.

We make steady progress with our little herd, but just as we come close to the gateway, a string of army trucks rattles up, the drivers hooting at us to keep out of their way. In an instant our beasts are startled out of their wits and race off in all directions. Chasing them would be futile, and in any event we are in a Jap military area and cannot be allowed to run loose.

Our Nips see discretion as the safer choice, check us out at the guardhouse, and we start the long plod back to Tonchan. Also, we are thinking, back to face The Tiger well after dark and having failed dismally to carry out orders. We are in a philosophical mood – after the day's events, nothing will surprise us – but our Nips are already looking worried and muttering to each other in nervous tones.

Stumbling dog-tired into camp (we have walked well over twenty kilometres today) and forming up outside The Tiger's hut, we await our fate. Furobashi stamps out with a lantern, scowls at us and roars something in Japanese. Presumably: 'You're late, and where are the cattle?' Our Nips seem to be in a paralytic funk, and there is a moment's dead silence until one of them tries to explain. He is actually stuttering in his nervousness, something we have never heard before, then the other joins in with a rush of words, and they both break into waving of arms and excited pantomime. Furobashi's scowl turns to astonishment, he bursts into great shouts of laughter and goes back into his hut, hooting and roaring. At the doorway he turns and waves us away, in great good humour. Well, we had heard he was unpredictable.

The relief of our Nips is such that they take us to their own cookhouse for supper. Not such a bad day, after all!

At tenko one morning we are told to collect our kit ready to move to a new camp a couple of kilometres down the track/road towards Tarsao, to be nearer the site where we shall be working.

When we left Singapore, we were formed into three labour battalions, labelled 'D', 'E' and 'F', which comprised the labour force at Wampo. Here at Tonchan we are in the same formations, and it is our 'D' battalion which is moving today, now a few less than the original 500 men. In this life we never know what is ahead of us, but we have become a good group to be in, attuned to our circumstances and self-disciplined, in good humour and high in morale, and physically in reasonable condition (for the grim circumstances) because we are sensible enough to take whatever care is possible in personal hygiene and so on. We are all under-nourished, the symptoms are with us all the time, and we simply do what we can to look on the positive side of things.

Anyway, it is a relief to get away from the main camp at Tonchan, out of The Tiger's sight if not out of his reach, and away from the British colonel and his brooding, hostile glare.

Our new campsite is off the west side of the road. There is a hut and cookhouse for the Nips, of bamboo and attap, and a bare muddy patch for us. A shallow stream some four paces across and knee-deep is the water supply. Near the road is a mound of mildewy and rotting canvas which we are told consists of British army tents for our use and we have until midday rice to set them up.

The rolls and folds of canvas cling together with mould and have to be peeled apart. However carefully we try to separate the layers, the rotten material splits and tears, the stink is awful, and we have only a limited time to rig up our shelter for the night. It starts to rain again, a typical wet season's downpour, which is almost unheeded by us and actually helps to open up and rinse the canvas a bit cleaner.

There is a haphazard mixture of conical bell tents and various sizes of rectangular tents with pitched roofs. The latter are supposed to be in two pieces: an outer cover without ends that protects an inner sleeping tent which has lace-up flaps to form the end walls. It is soon apparent that there are not nearly enough sets to go round, and not only will the doubled types have to be used as two units, but each will have to accommodate as many men as can be stuffed inside. There are not enough tent poles, and we have to find branches from the surrounding bush – not an easy job as we have neither saws nor axes.

After midday rice we are sent out to work, and luckily it is felling and clearing, which means we can trim a quantity of branches to take back with us. The camp has become a great muddy bog, and we do our best to get the last of the tents rigged in what is left of the gloomy saturating day.

There really isn't much point in all our efforts, as it turns out. The outer sections have twelve men packed in like sardines, the rain swirling through the open ends on the chilling night breezes, while the small two-man tents hold eight with the flaps open and the interior similarly sprayed. These tents should have floorboards but, of course, there are none, and everybody simply lies naked in the mud – on a groundsheet (if he is fortunate to have one), although in fact it makes no difference whatsoever, and rolled in a blanket (ditto-ditto). The only protection from the rain is to put your hat over your face. It does help, a bit.

While we workers were thus occupied our cooks were digging earth emplacements for the big rice kwalis. Without any roof over their heads they managed to defy the streaming rain by building roaring fires to produce rice and tea, a great comfort to us, God bless 'em!

After a few days we have still not been favoured with a visit by our colonel or any of his minions. Would the sight of his immaculate turnout (including umbrella, naturally) and cold sneering face be a boost to our morale? As our resident comedian puts it: 'He'd only be a wet blanket, and we have plenty of them already!' Wry smiles all round, but a humorist should never be discouraged.

In total contrast is our medical officer, who is dedicated

to our health and general welfare. He has inspected our camp, held sick parades, and gone straight back to The Tiger's den and told him what he thinks. A man of tremendous character and courage, and a real sense of humour, we count ourselves fortunate in having him in our battalion.

He has traced the source of the stream which is our precious water supply and found, to his horror, that upstream from us is a camp of Asiatic labourers drafted up from rubber estates and tin mines in Malaya, which had ceased production after the Jap occupation. They had been promised (as we had) good pay and working conditions with plenty of food available, and are now living in the most appalling state of squalor. With a complete absence of organisation – no discipline or comradeship, no proper issue of rations, no medical supplies at all – they are in the most desperate straits. But the MO's great worry is that they have no facilities for (or knowledge of) camp hygiene. The whole area of their camp is fouled, and the stream is badly contaminated. The risk to us is obvious, and there is no possibility whatsoever of any improvement. We have no choice but to adapt to suit conditions.

An absolute ban on the use of the stream for any purpose is unavoidable, except for the cookhouse, which will ensure that all water drawn from it is thoroughly boiled for tea and in cooking food. The almost constant rain looks after personal washing adequately, but in non-raining (I really can't say 'dry') intervals we shall have to put up with the discomforts of not having a water supply.

Walking to our worksite, we simply find our way over the flank of the hill which, in this weather, has a number of tiny streams running down its slopes. Backtracking up one of them we find its source springing directly out of a small hollow – clean water fit for drinking – where we fill ourselves and our water bottles on the way back after work.

I am sure that the strip of earth where our people are building the railway has never known the presence of man. It lies between the Kwei Noi river in the valley floor and a ridge of low mountains on the east, and as we fell trees and clear the surface we find no footpaths or cultivation, or even signs of old timber-collecting. The few villages are groupings of only a dozen or so scruffy huts situated on the bank of the river, with a flock of ducks and chickens, and banana plants. All movement must be by boat, small sampans or the noisy pom-poms, which we can hear in the distance although the river itself is out of sight from Tonchan.

This strip must, by now, also be one of the best manured you could find anywhere. The tribulations of the wet monsoon are again with us: painful bowels that have to be relieved frequently. There can surely be nothing more uncomfortable and dispiriting than having to stop work every hour (or less) to hurry off the track into the trees with a spade, scratch a hole and squat over it with the rain streaming cold down your body. When 500 men are at the same site for a week or more, the ground is soon used up close by, and you have to trot a good distance to find an unused spot. Not funny when your guts are nagging urgently!

The camp latrines are impossible to use. The Nips refuse to let us have bamboo and attap to rig up even the simplest shelter to keep the rain out, so the trenches are constantly filling up and overflowing. We prefer, if our lacerated plumbing will allow, to perform outside the camp area. Sick parade has echoes of the early days at Wampo – 'Twenty-eight times, wet and sloppy', 'Only twelve times, a bit more solid', 'Every few minutes, just water', 'Some spots of blood and a blot of mucus'. There seems to be little point seeing the medical officer except that it does give him a picture of our condition. He can offer nothing by way of treatment, The Tiger will not allow time off from work to rest, and if you get anything to eat it will be gritty rice and muddy tea, which are the basic cause of it all.

Working in the rain during the day, lying down in wet mud at night, deprived of sleep by both discomfort and the stabbing pains of diarrhoea and dysentery, we are all steadily deteriorating – losing weight, finding it harder to swing a pickaxe or hammer, feeling lethargic and showing signs of snapping tempers. Every one of us instinctively understands the interconnection of mental and physical health, and knows that to let go mentally is to start a downward slide that, in our circumstances, can end in a grave before you can again get a grip on yourself. We have only to consider all those dead and dying men a few miles away to realise how deceptively the slide can start, then gather impetus until it is beyond stopping. And we are sure it can be contagious – a few men give up hope, gradually lose their self-pride, wonder if it's worth the effort to stay alive (what is there to live for?), feel that nobody cares anyway, cannot see any likelihood of help coming, and just want to go to sleep and escape it all – and the mood is picked up by others who succumb to the slow erosion of their resistance. Call it what you will – inadequate temper in one's psyche, despair for the future, pain which will never cease, sheer loneliness, absolute isolation from everyone and everything which was ever dear and comforting, the massive uncertainty of getting back to it – these are the over-whelmingly oppressive factors.

All the men from Britain have families and friends at home, and have had no news for nearly two years. Some are in the forces – are they dead or wounded? Some live in cities which are bombing targets – are wives and families, friends and sweethearts still alive? Old folk and new babies – who is looking after them? Is the army still paying wages to dependants, or have we all been officially written off in the absence of recent proof that we are living? We worry about others as much as about ourselves.

We exist in a totally sealed and seamless void. We cannot look out and nobody can look in. And it will stay this way for as long as it takes, and if we are still alive at the end of it all, we may well be killed off and never get home, so why bother to struggle through now?

There is no news whatsoever of the interned wives and young children of many of our Volunteers, but the reputation of the Nips towards captives is appalling – don't we all know that? – and these men live in a continuing private hell of their own.

Whatever your personal circumstances, the burden is awful and will become more oppressive as time goes by. The essential thing is to concentrate on the survival of yourself and those around you, which is in any event the only area in which you can have any effect at all, everything else being out of your reach. It may sound selfish, but it does limit the strain to a bearable degree if you can remove from your mind all responsibility for people outside your range. Think of them occasionally, yes, but if possible in a detached way. Simply accept that you can do nothing about it.

Now, there is of course another attitude to take. Trust in God! Hand over all your problems to him, and all will turn out well while you relax with a mind at peace! In all our endless discussions during our time in captivity, at work and in the evenings, this concept has been discussed but only as an abstract sort of idea to fill in time, and never as something of present concern to be seriously considered. Yet we are all from Christian communities, and have grown up hearing and accepting the church's teachings uncritically. Perhaps that has a bearing on our indifference – we were fed assurances which have not materialised and it doesn't surprise us. If a man came into our present circumstances without a firm faith, there will certainly have been no inducement for him to acquire and develop such a faith. Those already with a strong belief in the tenets of Christianity must be finding it very difficult to persist in their faith in the face of what is happening to them, for they are no better off than the rest of us. It's a complex matter, and we certainly don't have any answers. But heaven does seem to be totally indifferent to our problems. Imagine being expected to forgive our captors!

The camp area becomes steadily worse as the days go by and the rain continues to pour down. The slippery surface mud conceals hard lumps and ruts which can easily turn an ankle, bare feet being almost useless in these conditions. The unavoidable traffic of men walking to and fro creates a quagmire which will not drain away. We cannot even dig channels to divert the flood from our tents, because after dark they would be a dangerous hazard to men stumbling around to and from the latrines. God, our lives seem to be centred around the awful weather, the miserable tasteless food, pains in the guts, and latrines. The cooks have managed to get a roof over their kwalis, but we still have to eat standing in the downpour – our hot rice going sloppy with cold rain in moments, so we are denied even the small comfort of hot food in our bellies.

When the rain stops, as it actually does at times, the sun cannot penetrate the heavy grey clouds and the humidity is overpowering. We cannot dry or freshen our blankets, but only drape them over our tents to get some air to them because we know that if they become mildewed they will rot and fall apart, and there will be no replacements.

No man reports sick unless it is absolutely unavoidable. Those who cannot work are sent back to Tonchan, on

Furobashi's strict orders. Anyone other than cooks found in camp during working times is rounded up, so we take our sick fellows out with us and bring them back in the evening. If we are going to die we would prefer to do so amongst friends rather than fade away in the mass anonymity of that dreadful camp, where The Tiger is chief hyena, and our colonel tells himself that everything is our own fault anyway and there's nothing with which his conscience needs to bother itself.

Opening up a new area of forest this morning we have unpleasant surprises. Tonchan, all uphill from Tarsao, must be several hundred feet above the Kwei Noi. There is a lot more green grass and small shrubs, the trees are taller and more substantial and more conducive to plant growth. The surprises are snakes, hidden away in the undergrowth. While they're not very big (up to, say, four feet in length), there are hundreds of them. Luckily for us they immediately take fright at our intrusion. Quite probably we are their very first contact with man and they prefer to get out of our way in order to size us up, rather than stay and challenge us. As we disturb the bush they wriggle away in dozens, seeking fresh cover and causing the hurried retreat of dozens more.

Thank goodness they are not aggressive. With bare feet and no protective clothing at all, we are not keen on close contact. Nor are we the slightest bit interested in killing them. There is far too much suffering and death in the neighbourhood already, and it is we, after all, who are invading their territory and not the other way round. So we pick up small branches and carefully prod the undergrowth to scare them away. We cannot avoid destroying their nests and eggs, but we do what we can to spare their lives.

Our tactics seem to be successful, for after a couple of days we do not see any more of them. Our agricultural scientists say they are pythons and not poisonous, and not

231

likely to be aggressive unless we provoke them. We must be thankful for such mercies!

We never know in advance of anything that is about to happen. It is an ordinary end-of-day (except that the rain has stopped for a time), and in the half-light of early evening we suddenly find that a large body of men has stopped on the 'road' running past our camp. They are as surprised to see us as we are to see them, and immediately there is an exchange of calls to find out who we all are, where we're from, where we're going, and any other news, all of which is of intense interest to everybody.

Their Nip escorts run up and down all agitated, shouting and bawling, presumably telling us that there is to be no talking to each other. We do not try to mix because almost certainly there will be a tenko at any moment, with unimaginable confusion, but it is only a matter of waiting patiently, and we are very good at that. Their Nips confer with ours, who presumably warn the newcomers that stumbling into Furobashi's presence at a late hour could be unpleasant, and a night's stopover is decided. There is a tenko and the new arrivals move into the scrub on the far side of the 'road'.

It doesn't take long to skip over from one side to the other, and when we see that the Nips have noticed the toing and froing and don't seem to be bothered about it, there is a general mixing.

These men turn out to be part of 'F' Force, 7,000 men in all (half are Australian and half British), sent up from Changi to reinforce the labour battalions on the railway. They came up by train to Ban Pong, as we did, and, we discover, have marched along the same route via Tarsao. With the usual total incompetence of the Jap army administration, they passed out of Changi Command into Siam Command without any arrangements for rations or anything else. In consequence no food has been supplied to them from Ban Pong onwards (and precious little during the long train journey from Singapore). Had it not been for the generosity of the local people along the road to Kanburi, and the little they could buy with personal funds (British Singapore currency only, the Siamese won't touch the Japanese paper rubbish), they would by now be incapable of marching.

They have slogged nearly 100 miles on foot in five days, without shelter at night or even facilities for boiling water for safe drinking, and with no medical treatment of any kind. Sick men have had to be helped along simply because there has been nowhere for them to rest before catching up later. There are other big groups following, and a daily distance must be covered to keep them separate.

They have no idea how far they still have to march, only that it will be a long way. We cannot offer much information, except that we know of several camps at intervals of fifteen kilometres or so, which suggests that they have at least another 100 kilometres ahead of them. Unless, as is the case with us at Tonchan, there is a camp so depleted by casualties that they will go in to make up the numbers.

These men have had a year and a half on the most scanty rations in Singapore, and even less since leaving there and reaching Tonchan. They have found themselves in conditions of great severity and cannot expect any improvement; they are exhausted physically and under heavy stresses. Nevertheless, they are in quite remarkably good spirits, refusing to be beaten, and meeting us has lifted morale on both sides.

Among them is a large party of Singapore and Malayan Volunteers – we very quickly find each other and eagerly swap news and gossip. And then there is news verging on the miraculous for Ron and myself – an old friend comes to us and hands over a piece of paper which he has carried from Changi on the off chance of finding us somewhere in Siam (we are on a list of names kept by administrative staff at our Changi Headquarters of men sent to Siam from River Valley Road Camp in Singapore). The paper bears a brief message from Mum, broadcast over Radio India well over a year ago, picked up on a secret radio in Changi, written down and kept until a means of delivery could be found, and then handed to our friend and finally passed to us. Out of date it may be, but at least Ron and I now know that Mum reached safety in her last-minute escape from Singapore. Our gratitude to those dedicated men who risked their lives operating a secret radio is unbounded, as it is also to others who took the trouble to trace us and get the message through. We are immensely cheered.

There is no recent news of Dad. All we know is that while we were at River Valley Road Camp he was seen, at a distance, in a working party of civilians at the Singapore docks way back in June 1942. Like us he was a Volunteer, and worked at Fortress Headquarters in Singapore in a signals cipher unit. To have been seen in a civilian party we can only presume that, because of his age, he was discharged just before the capitulation and thus has been interned as a civilian, avoiding the rigours of being a military prisoner of war. We can only speculate.

While all this has been going on our cooks have drawn on our scanty stock of rice and tea, and produced a hot meal (well, a miserable excuse for a meal, but the best we can manage) for our visitors, the first for a week and accepted with grateful thanks. It will, of course, mean reduced rations for us, but nobody has the smallest objection to that. Sharing with our own people is an unquestioned priority. We shall do what we can to give them another meal before they leave in the morning, but the hard fact of shortage of stock will not allow us to give them rice to take with them. We can only hope that the Jap army quartermasters will wake up soon, but we wouldn't bet on it.

That night sleep isn't important – we make the most of being with friends. They are new to the Siamese forest, and we can give them tips on how to look after themselves. Nothing very effective, of course, but every little bit is valuable.

At daylight we watch them move off, not without forebodings of an unpleasant future ahead of them. When we first came to Wampo we had no idea what we were facing, but now we have no delusions at all regarding Nip callousness and sheer inhumanity in their attitude towards us prisoners. At Wampo we had a Jap officer as camp commandant, and this may have helped us to some degree, but upriver the camps seem to have ignorant rankers in charge, with neither qualifications nor the authority to do anything.

We do not know of any Nip medical staff, which is why our guards come to us for treatment. In fact this has come in handy as a way to rid ourselves of particularly unpleasant characters, for our medical officer used to have his orderly obtain a good steaming fresh dab of dysentery excreta on a bamboo spatula, which he then carefully wiped off well down the Nip's throat. A useful number of bullying bastards disappeared to Tarsao for treatment of explosive dysentery, and it was several weeks, even months, before we saw them again. A welcome relief.

Walking back to camp at the end of a day's work my eyes, quite suddenly, start to play tricks on me. Everything becomes blurred with double or treble outlines, floating towards me and receding as I try to regain focus. Trees and men, even the ground, shift around in a weird fashion, and distances change so that my footing becomes uncertain. I grab Ron's shoulder to steady myself, and tell him what is happening. After standing still for a few minutes my vision steadies itself and, although I still see double, I am able to walk without help.

Tucked away in my haversack is a tiny bottle of halibut liver oil tablets, our one and only reserve against total malnutrition. There are twenty-four of these irreplaceable little nuggets of vitamin A, which is exactly what I need for it is a shortage of this particular vitamin that causes eye problems. Other men have already suffered faulty vision, and since there is nothing available to treat it they have had to cope as best as they could. Ron and I decide to take one tablet each per day for twelve days to build up some reserve, this being a vitamin the body can take in quantity and store away in the liver, which releases it over a long period – unlike the B complex vitamins, which will last only some ninety days and need periodic replenishment or the result is beri-beri, from which every one of us presently suffers to some extent.

The benefit from taking halibut liver oil is immediate. Overnight my vision starts to clear. In forty-eight hours it is back to normal, and we both find that our small open sores are showing signs of healing. But once the bottle is empty, we shall have nothing at all.

There is a change in the pace of work. Whereas the Nips on the worksite used to lounge in the shade and leave us to produce enough to keep them happy, they now keep moving among us. To encourage us to work harder, they screech and gibber as we fell trees or dig, swiping with bamboo canes at any man standing still for a few moments. It's all very tiresome, but we learn to keep moving around and, even if there is no purpose to it, the Nips are satisfied. These Nips are an ignorant lot. They have no idea at all about work outputs. They are obviously being leaned on to get more out of us and are opting for the simplest way to do it.

Where do rumours come from? The latest is that a long stretch of track was cleared and prepared for rail-laying when Tonchan was set up, but it was found that all the work was wasted because it had been done in the wrong place.

The Jap army seems to operate in watertight compartments, nobody knowing what others are doing. As with the farce of different levels at the Wampo North cliff face, it seems that the Tonchan surveyors laid their trace northwards to their side of a high ridge. On the other side of the ridge the surveyors worked southwards, the theory being that the two traces would meet, whereas they ended up several kilometres apart. We think that possibly, under the original alignment, a tunnel could have been required, but without suitable equipment to build one, the north-moving side diverted to come round the end of the ridge, a sensible decision which was not communicated to the Tonchan surveyors. The result is our present stampede to cut a new alignment to the end of the ridge, and to do it in a hurry to bring the schedule back into shape.

Aren't we clever! After our speculations over the rumours, we have found ourselves standing at the beginning of a mountain slope rising high on our right and falling in a vertical precipice to our left. At the foot of this precipice (maybe 800–1,000 feet below us?) a flat green carpet of treetops spreads westwards to a silvery river, which can only be our Kwei Noi. Beyond the river the mountains rise steeply, the ridge running north and south as far as we can see into the distance. To our left, way off, is the familiar broken-tooth hump from our Wampo days, and northwards the crests are higher. As we remember it, these mountain ridges start in the Himalayan massif and come down through eastern Burma, past where we are standing and on to the south, splitting into the central Malayan highlands and the Sumatran chain which continues in an eastward sweep through Java to New Guinea. We are impressed by the immensity of this picture, and only wish that our insignificant little patch were not causing so much trouble. The view really is splendid!

We know that the Indian Ocean lies beyond these steep ridges, not really very far away as the crow might fly. But we are not crows, and we know that it would be quite impossible to attempt to walk to the coast. The only method of travel would be along the valley rivers, all of which (like the Kwei Noi) must be watched by the Nips. Tavoy lies directly west.

Anyway, a little more thought shows why the railway bed has been brought so high above the river, the upper reaches of which will undoubtedly run between vertical rock walls (such as the precipice at our feet), leaving no alternative but to climb above the obstacles. The slope on our right leans well back, and we can see the surveyor's poles and markers sticking up in the rocky soil. We shall have to dig out a flat railbed at the level of the top edge of the precipice, wide enough for the rails to be laid with a sizeable stormwater trench to carry off the monsoon rains flooding down the slope.

It is a peaceful scene, the rain is holding off, and the distant mountains are softened in a haze. It will be a pleasant change to work here in the clean freshness and open space after the gloomy humidity of the forest. And, almost without ceasing, echoes float up to us of monkeys hooting and hallooing in the trees far below.

Allowing for the fact that we have no choice but to work

for the Nips, we do indeed have a happy week labouring on the new site. The rocks are mostly small enough to be levered out and shoved over the edge, the boulders are drilled and dynamited into chunks, and the loose soil and scrubby vegetation are no problem at all. The Nips, too, are less bothersome. I suspect they get soured by the oppressive forest and respond positively, as we have done, to a more pleasant scene.

The precipice is so near to vertical that rocks and debris chucked over the edge fall clear to the treetop canopy hundreds of feet down. It's tough luck on the creatures living down there. We hope we do not do too much damage to their homes and families as the cleared strip gradually lengthens. Howls of rage float up to us after each dump.

The Nips have permitted us to detail a small number of men to make tea for the workers mid morning, at midday rice time and during the afternoon, and we arrange this prized quiet day on a roster system so that we shall all have a turn at it. After a week or so, Ron and I come to the head of the queue, and collect four four-gallon cans and tea from the cookhouse. These cans originally contained cooking oil and were 'souvenired' (as the Australians put it) from the Nip kitchen, the wire handles being contributed unknowingly by the Jap army telephone service. Slung on a couple of sturdy bamboo poles, filled at a clear stream on the way to the cliff, we hoist them onto our shoulders and carry them to where the men are working. A gallon of water weighs ten pounds, so we have a load of 160 pounds between us, stumbling along the uneven path and trying to steady the cans from swinging uncontrollably from side to side.

Doing this three times a day is probably heavier labour than working on the track, but that's not the point. It's a pleasant change to be on our own, collecting firewood and brewing tea. In addition, you knock off early and have a couple of hours in camp to air blankets or whatever.

Looking forward to this more relaxed period, Ron and I are close to the camp when we come across a small group of cooks. They have devastating news for us – a man with cholera was brought in from a small timber camp during the afternoon. He was dead within an hour and two of our people in camp have already developed symptoms! The cooks have collected a pile of bamboo and every man coming in from work is to bring in as much as he can carry, for sterilising fires. Annoyed at first that this had to happen on our precious free day, the shocking implications gradually sink in as we continue on our way, dragging four lengthy bamboo poles which we hand in at the cookhouse with our tea cans.

Our medical officers have spoken to us a number of times over the past two months, after evening tenko, to warn us of their worries that cholera might strike us: 'This is a *known* cholera area. It is not a matter of maybe it will and maybe it won't. It comes *every year without fail*! It never misses a year. When the rains swell the rivers, and that includes this river, all sorts of muck is washed down from where it has accumulated on the banks during the dry season. Dead animals, decayed rubbish, village cesspits, all highly dangerous material.

'Your safeguard is that you catch it *only* by swallowing the bacteria, taking it in through your mouth or up your nose. You won't get it through skin sores or up your arsehole, or through your ears. And you don't need to swallow a great dollop of contaminated substance – the merest trace, which you can't see without a microscope, is sufficient. Remember that, think about it! *The merest trace is enough to kill you!*'

Optimistically, we have been pushing these warnings to the back of our consciousness – maybe we already have enough to put up with and don't want to worry about some new menace which might not happen. With so many burdens already on our shoulders, surely the gods will relent and give it a miss this year!

'If you are careless, or just plain unlucky, and catch the bug, you can expect to die in very considerable pain because we have no treatment. It needs only *one* man to become infected and *every single man* in the camp is immediately at risk. If there is an outbreak, we shall not be able to stop it. *Think carefully* about these consequences, and follow instructions for your own safety and that of your mates. There will be *no* second chances. If cholera hits us your *only* protection is to avoid it!'

So there it is. Cholera *has* hit us and we shall have to cope with this new risk as best we can. The cooks point to a small column of greasy black smoke a few hundred yards away. 'The Nips found a can of petrol, and that's the man who died. Every spare man is to go there to clear space for cholera cases and set up some kind of shelter.'

There are no Nips there. They are always frightened of disease and the word 'cholera' has thrown them into a panic. They are all gathered outside their hut, faces masked with squares of cloth and staring fearfully around. For shelter for patients they have provided a single canvas tent, rotted and leaking; obviously the idea of comfort for dying men has no meaning for them.

By the time it starts to get dark the tent is crowded with ten cases, all of them in agony and soaking wet for it is raining again, the typical steady downpour of the wet monsoon. Word was sent to The Tiger many hours ago, but so far nothing has reached us. No disinfectant or soap, no drugs for pain – nothing whatsoever. All our MO got from him was raving abuse, because it was all our own fault.

Cholera is a disgustingly horrible disease, incredibly painful for the victim and distressing for the helper or onlooker. The symptoms are frequently violent, fluid of greyish-white colour being ejected forcefully in vomiting and diarrhoea as if the kidneys are trying to rid the body of invasive poisons. The result is rapid dehydration with accompanying muscular cramps of such intensity that muscle fibres can tear apart as the body writhes and twists in wrenching spasms. The pale colouring of the fluid is due to the mucous lining of the whole intestinal system disintegrating into tiny shreds and particles that are scoured away and flushed out, leaving the inner surfaces raw and unprotected.

The first signs of infection are sunken eyes in a pinched and drawn face, unnaturally cold breath from abnormally low body temperature, and cold and clammy skin with the fingertips wrinkled and purple as the kidneys draw fluids from the extremities to try to repair damage to the vital organs. If a man shows these signs there can be no doubt that the violent ordeal will follow – sometimes mercifully brief and sometimes drawn out. The only treatment is replacement of lost body fluids, and if the infection is moderate the patient can be given tea, which helps if he can hold it down. For several weeks our MO has been planning for just such an emergency, and has put together a crude but effective water distillation plant for intravenous salines – the difficulty here is in inserting a sharpened bamboo needle into collapsed veins. But his apparatus saves lives, quite miraculously. Their thickened blood is like dark treacle.

There is no more petrol after the first can, and massive quantities of firewood are needed for cremations. By the third day we have over 200 cases, and hygienic disposal of the bodies is critical for flies can carry and distribute infected matter all over the place, such is the rate of infection.

We are warned not to touch our mouths with our fingers, and at meal times every man dips his mess tin and spoon (we have no use for knives or forks) into a kwali of rapidly boiling water before moving on to the serving point. The cookhouse is responsible for bringing rice to us in covered containers, and we must be especially careful not to allow flies to settle as we eat.

The Nips stop work on the railway for two days while we do our best to cope with the emergency. We have sent some of our tents to the cholera compound to accommodate the terrible increase in victims, and crowd ourselves even more tightly into the others, but nobody complains.

On the third day, it is announced that railway work will resume tomorrow, but some of the sick will be allowed to stay in camp for the 'light work' of cremation and grave-digging! Not surprisingly, nobody wants to report himself as sick – the gruesome work in camp doesn't appeal at all! But disposal of the dead is obviously beyond the resources of those marvellous men who have volunteered to work in the cholera compound. They have far too much on their hands, and help is absolutely necessary. So the so-called 'light duties' are allocated on a rota basis – everyone will have to take a turn.

The whole camp quickly settles into an ordered and disciplined routine, the success of which must owe a lot to our background of comradeship within the army framework, supplemented by our deepening hatred of the Nips which binds us solidly together in our determination to *survive* and see them punished as they deserve, when we have won the war. We all have to rely on each other, and we must have full confidence that every man will pull his weight at all times.

Not far away, however, is the camp holding Asiatic labourers who have no such bonding to encourage them to work as a community. We hear that they were lured to join parties of labourers coming to Siam. They are mostly un-employed rubber tappers and the like from estates which, once prosperous but now unproductive under the Jap occupation of Malaya, can no longer support them. They are mostly Tamils and Southern Indians, and left their families and womenfolk behind on a Jap promise that they would soon follow. We don't know how many men there are in this camp, but it could be between 2,000 and 3,000.

Miserable as our conditions may be, theirs must be far worse, as they are totally without any form of medical aid or anybody to speak for them, and they must be performing forced labour similar to ours on rations and wages at much the same level, or even lower. These hapless people are now hit with cholera and are totally helpless, with no idea how to deal with it and no facilities. A Nip medical orderly has been sent from Tarsao. We have glimpsed him across the road dressed all in white, with a face mask and gumboots, and his solution is to have the Asiatic sick carried to our side of the road and left there for us to bury.

There will be tens of thousands more of these wretched people along the railway. We must never forget them, name-less and suffering and dying in squalor, their kinfolk not even knowing what has happened to them.

On the third day (I am not quoting from the Bible about rising from the dead!) I am in a grave-digging party near the cholera tents. By morning smoko there are twelve Tamil bodies laid in a neat row for burial. It is not raining, and we are digging a pit some twenty feet long by six feet wide (the Tamils are, in general, small in stature). The problem is that there should be a clear six feet of earth above the bodies, since maggots can work their way up to the surface from lesser depths and develop immediately into lethal cholera-infected blowflies. The deeper you dig the more difficult it becomes, in terms of physical effort, to throw the earth clear of the rim of the pit.

By midday rice there are some forty corpses laid out, and when we return after a quick meal in camp, another twenty have been added. We grimly mark out an extension to the mass grave, and get to work. There is no fixed amount of work to be done by the end of the day. The digging continues in the darkness because every corpse must be buried. Fires are started to provide light.

When it is too dark for the 'search and pick up' stretcher-bearers to find more bodies in the Asiatic camp, the men help out in the burial process. They bring each corpse to the end of the pit, where two hefty fellows (wrists and feet, swing – one – two and heave) pick it up. The bodies are stiff, and con-torted into the final grotesque poses of cholera death, and as we dig at the far end we hear the regular chant: 'One, and two' – thump.

We cannot always keep our backs turned to it, and it is a hellish sight when we face it: the flickering firelight, the deep pit gloomy with shadows but its grisly contents visible, staring eyes and teeth exposed between lips shrunk away in pain, torso and limbs twisted and emaciated. In the background our men, naked except for fundoshi and hat and the firelight slid-ing over their sweating bodies, bring corpses to be tossed in. They are coming to an end; ninety-three have been counted.

It starts to pour, the rain-glossed bodies in the pit acquire shimmering firelit haloes, and all the earth we have so laboriously dug out now has to be shovelled back before we can leave. We have never had such a heavy day's physical toil, and we drag ourselves into camp for a mess tin of hot rice (bless the cooks!) and a mug of plain tea, standing in the rain.

We are absolutely buggered, and tomorrow will be worse. In the words of Samuel Pepys – 'And so to bed!' God almighty, what a life! I shall have my twenty-second birthday in ten weeks, if I live that long. Just at this moment, it looks decidedly uncertain.

Yesterday evening I thought today would be worse, and I was right. In fairness to everybody the work to be done each day is rotated so that the dirty jobs are shared by all in turn. This we can do because the Nips don't want to leave their hut area, and we can organise ourselves as we wish. This morning we are to take stretchers into the Asiatic camp and pick up corpses, carrying them to the grave-diggers who will be working next to yesterday's great pit.

As we cross the 'road' in pairs, each with a stretcher made of two bamboo poles shoved through a couple of jute rice sacks, my stomach starts to show signs of nervousness at what I expect to be faced with in a few minutes. The men who did this unpleasant work yesterday did not want to talk about it – they were screwed up so tight with shock that they only wanted to be allowed to unwind in their own time. Plainly, we are going to have a stressful day. Thankfully, no Nips accompany us, so we won't have them screeching around in panic. Nor does a single one of our officers appear from Tonchan main camp, although they must be fully aware of what has happened. Well, maybe it's common sense for them not to expose themselves, but we do feel that it is their duty to be with us nevertheless. Be that as it may, we have to get on with the job.

It may sound simple picking up corpses and taking them to the burial place, but the circumstances here are such as to tear at our sensitivities so that, on entering the camp area, we all come to an involuntary halt together. The weather doesn't help at all. It is not actually raining, but the sun cannot penetrate the bulging grey and purple clouds hanging low overhead, the temperature must be well over the century mark, and the humidity so high that our sweat slides off in streams. The subtle and insidious effect of this kind of wet monsoon day has to be experienced to be believed. Not only does the body have difficulty moving (possibly because of its pores being clogged and unable to breathe), but the mind's processes can become muffled and less agile. Stupefied. The heat is altogether overpowering. In a way, though, the oppressive gloom is in keeping with what we see. I have the odd thought that bright sunshine would in some way be incongruous.

What we see is utterly dreadful. The atmosphere is thick with pain and distress and the foul odours of human degradation and decay. It is as if the joys and beauty of the miracle of life have never been known in this awful place, it is so saturated with misery and death. We are a little too far from the inmates to see them clearly, but there seems to be nobody on his feet – every man is stretched out on the ground or slumped sitting against a tree or a tent pole. There is no movement, only an inert stillness.

We walk through a slippery, muddy bog, similar to the one at our own camp, towards a ragged awning slung between trees. Under it several men lie listlessly on the ground amongst a pile of grubby sarongs and bedding. They watch our approach without interest. There were men like us here yesterday and our stretchers show what we have come to do. It doesn't really matter to them one way or another.

We are going to need their help and must approach them in the right way. They are Tamils, probably from Ceylon originally, and Hindu in religion. If they have been brought from rubber estates in Malaya they may well understand the pidgin form of Malay in common use by the many non-Malay communities throughout the territory. Because these men are not Malays, I decide not to use the traditional address: 'Greetings, is the news good?' The reply is, 'It is good!' even if the news is in fact dreadful. I remember having heard that because Almighty Allah arranges all things to the smallest detail, it would be criticism of his will to say the news is bad; even the worst suffering must be accepted with serenity.

So I start with, 'Tabeh, kawan-kawan (Greetings, friends all),' and there is an immediate brightening of faces and stirring of bodies. Their innate politeness, being spoken to in a language they can understand, brings the response, 'Tabeh kawan, selamat berjumpa (Greetings, friend, blessings on this meeting),' and it encourages me to continue: 'Kita askar English. Kita misti chari semua orang mati. Ada lain askar korek lubang di-sana, didalam orang mati itu boleh tidor senang (We are English soldiers. We must collect all dead men. There are other soldiers digging a pit over there, where these dead men may sleep in peace).' They give us smiles of understanding. 'Mintak ma'af, kita misti kreja terus sekarang (With your permission, we must get to work without delay).'

They all rise to their feet, eager to help. There is a part of the camp, well away from the living area, where those stricken by cholera have been helped to go – but having pointed this out to us, our friends will come no nearer. With polite smiles and gestures they retreat to their shelter. After a moment's glance at the scene in front of us, none of us can blame them one little bit.

The ground is dotted with shrubs and hacked trees; probably everything that will burn has been taken for cooking fires. Lying all over the place are bodies – stretched out flat on their backs, faces in the mud, collapsed into bushes, leaning against tree stumps, twisted in the contortions of a painful death, eyes shut, eyes staring, teeth bared, limbs sticking out stiffly. Dozens of them, and these are just last night's victims. No doubt there will be more brought out during the day as we work.

We know what we have to do, but we need a few moments to brace ourselves so that we can face up to it. A quiet voice says, 'Come on, lads, let's get started, before the flies turn up in full strength. The sooner we begin shifting this lot, the better.'

There is no possibility of avoiding the frightening risks of infection as we pick up corpses and lay them on stretchers. These poor men have vomited and defecated uncontrollably until they had nothing more to get rid of, and their rags of clothing and the ground around them and their own bodies are all heavily contaminated. We have no means of picking them up except by grasping them with our bare hands. Everything we touch may infect us and our bare feet are ankle-deep in bacteria-infested mud. There is no water supply, no soap or disinfectant, and whatever we unavoidably pick up on our skin can be moved around our bodies by the ever-present film of sweat that covers us.

The corpses have to be buried as quickly as possible, for decay sets in immediately in this climate. Just how quickly we soon discover when we come across rotting flesh missed by our men working yesterday. The stench is awful, because it soon becomes evident that this is an old latrine area for the camp. With no organised camp hygiene, nobody dug trenches for everyone to use, so this fringe of the campsite became a midden until its surface was so fouled that another area was used. Weeks of sun, and more recently rain, have broken the muck down so that it has saturated the ground. Our bare feet squelch in it, and we are all keenly aware of the consequences of slipping and sliding under the weight of a stretcher, and falling full length in it. If this disgusting mess should splash onto your face, how would you get rid of it? No water, not even a rag to wipe it away from your mouth and nose – and what if it were actually to splash on your mouth? How do you remove it without risking that you will edge some between your lips? 'It needs only the merest trace!' The words are frightening.

In general Tamils are small in stature and wiry in physique, and as we lift them from the ground we find they weigh even less than we expected, because they have lost so much moisture. So it is possible to carry two, or even three, at a time, which will reduce the number of trips to the burial site. We have to lay the corpses across the stretcher instead of lengthways, which looks undignified but niceties must perforce give way to hard necessity. But we still retain our sense of reverence for the fact that only yesterday these were living men who had done nothing to deserve such desecration.

As expected there is a steady flow of victims during the day, some already dead and some staggering on their own in the agonies before death. We have asked our friends to direct others in the camp to take their dead to the 'road', where it will be a shorter carry for us, for we shall be exhausted by the time we get to them all.

Making use of the first day's experience, the grave-diggers have not been digging the whole area at the same time while the corpses accumulated. Today they have dug a short section to full depth, and then utilised it for burials while the next section is excavated. A third section is then started alongside the first, the new spoil being shovelled directly over to cover and fill the pit. A great deal of laborious work is saved compared with the first day when we had no idea of the size of the task in front of us.

We talk very little as we work. Comments on what we are doing are superfluous, and idle chatter to take our minds off it seems out of place. In any case it would not succeed – nothing can possibly lessen the tragedy which stares us in the face. All we can do is plod grimly through the wearying hours. There will be no fixed time to stop; we shall continue until every corpse is buried. We blunt our sensibilities as much as we can, and do not allow ourselves to be overly worried about infection. If it happens, it happens.

This fatalistic attitude is something we have acquired gradually during the past year. It has been an invaluable protective shield against going right off the mental rails, allowing us to preserve our personal dignity and sense of humour. We all accept that there is a long time still in front of us, and if we are to survive sane and unbroken, we must not let our inner selves be corroded away by our circumstances. All the nastiness must slide off as far as may be possible, disregarded.

Today's nauseating labours would have proved quite beyond us, I am sure, if we had not been able to approach them without an attitude that verges on disembodiment – this is not really happening at all, not to us anyway, and at the end of it we shall be able to be our normal selves again. In fact, I have had the somewhat weird experience today of becoming two distinct beings. One of them took up station above my left shoulder, some fifteen feet up, and quite dispassionately watched my own body and all the others going about their work while making sympathetic and encouraging remarks: 'Come on, it's not really as bad as that!' 'Don't slack off, there's a lot more to do!' 'Keep going, it won't last forever!' A bit weird, maybe, but helpful nevertheless.

I can see myself in clear outline and detail, slightly foreshortened from my overhead viewpoint, sunburnt and naked except for hat and fundoshi. How is it that I know exactly what I look like from behind, the muscles moving under my skin, the glistening sweat rolling down my back into my grubby fundoshi, the streaks of mud splashed up the backs of my legs? No man can actually stand behind himself to view the back of his body, yet I have this perfect image of myself and can even talk to it, although I don't seem to get answers! My spiritual self is the one 'upstairs'; my physical self is sweating on the ground. Other men tell me they have had this same 'disembodied' experience, when it all looks like becoming too much to bear.

Is this what seers and mystics do, when they go into a detached state? Can it be deliberately achieved, or is it only a random condition brought on by severe stress? Does it happen to everybody, or only to those who happen to be attuned and receptive, perhaps unknowingly?

By late afternoon we have cleared the Asiatic camp open areas, and now must go through the tented section to bring out any bodies which are being kept out of sight by grieving relatives and friends. There are no women or children here, the men having been told that they would follow when camps in Siam had been established and conditions settled. The sheer mindless cruelty of the Japs is beyond comprehension. People other than their own simply do not matter; there is an endless supply in the conquered territories, to be used up with unbelievable callousness.

Accustomed though we have become to living in primitive conditions, what we now see is human misery and squalor on a heart-wrenching scale. Our Tamil friends come with us, courteous and quietly spoken, telling us how they have been worked until they collapsed, brutally beaten for no reason except that the Nips enjoyed it, starved, not paid wages, isolated from human contact, weakened and destroyed by malaria and all the diseases familiar to us, but with never a pretence of medicines or treatment.

With no organisation to bind them together, and no one

to speak up for them, their society has disintegrated until nobody has the will to do anything. We cannot estimate the number of men here, our friends don't know either, but we can see hundreds lying around under tattered canvas. Most are emaciated, nearly all are totally unresponsive to our presence, almost in a state of coma, and so still that life and death are hard to distinguish.

We take leave of our friends, pick up our last loads and head for the pits. Our contributions are tossed in, and we are at last free to go back to our own camp which, miserable as it really is, is so much better than the dreadful slum which we have just seen. In all, we brought in 137 corpses.

Suddenly, as if an order to halt had been shouted, we all come to a standstill. Here we are on the edge of our camp, and the question strikes us all simultaneously – how are we to go into the camp when we are, every one of us, contaminated with muck from the Asiatic camp? We have known all day that we are personally at risk, but we cannot possibly move in amongst our fellows in this condition.

We cannot wash ourselves, we have had nothing to eat since early morning, our water bottles are empty and we are thirsty. We are nearly dead on our feet (and could well be truly dead within twenty-four hours), we cannot get to the cook-house or to our eating things (and you can't eat hot boiled rice from your bare hands). Quite simply, we are ready to fold up and give way to the screaming meemies. If only we could get ourselves clean!

Have the gods been watching us with a sympathetic eye? With an impact that nearly throws us off our feet, the murky purple-grey gloom hanging over our heads detonates with blinding lightning and a shattering crash of thunder, and the sudden weight of rain makes us stagger. In seconds the warm needles of rain have scoured our bodies clean. We laugh and chatter in the drumming twilight, stretching out our arms and taking off our fundoshis to rub down every inch of skin. Who cares that we cannot dry ourselves? Our spirits, too, are washed free of the day's depressing sludge. We are altogether revived, almost exhilarated! Clean! Clean! Clean!

The inside of our tents offers very little improvement on the outside. The rain sweeps through the open ends and nothing is dry. We think of those hundreds of poor bastards in the other camp, and are thankful that we have a pint of hot rice in prospect.

What will happen when this cursed bloody railway is completed? Will the Nips move us elsewhere to other work, or will they leave us in our camps along the Kwei Noi to rot and die? This is something we have just learned they are quite capable of doing. I have never felt hatred for any man, not even a strong dislike, but I have developed a frighteningly intense loathing of the Japanese nation as a whole, and its military people in particular, and a limitless contempt for their brutish arrogance and callow disregard for everyone else. And I hate them for being responsible for creating this festering sore in my soul. I don't like it, I don't want it, but it is there and I can't get rid of it. By the time the war ends it may well be permanent, ineradicable, a black scar on my mind.

On the fourth day of the cholera epidemic we are informed that the Nips have decided that work on the railway must continue. Already three days have been lost due entirely to our own slackness and weak spirits, and we must ask the Emperor's forgiveness by working extra hard to make up for it! This sort of bullshit, of course, does not impress us in the slightest; it only confirms our view that the Nips are a bunch of uncivilised and ignorant thugs.

In our labourings over the last two days, we have been too fully occupied in the disposal of the casualties in the

Asiatic camp to keep in touch with what has been happening amongst our own people. The days have been long, we have been exhausted by the end of them, and the almost continual rain has made campfires impossible and discouraged social gatherings before bedtime – in fact, as soon as we have swallowed our evening rice we have settled down to sleep in our muddy wallows. Sleep is of the utmost importance to us. Without medicines, it is the only help we can give our bodies to repair damage and gather strength for the next day. And if you miss out on sleep you find yourself so much more behind the start line, and a correspondingly greater effort is required to get your mechanisms functioning again. In normal health sleep is a valuable restorative, and if you miss out you can always catch up on it. In our circumstances it is the essential thread holding the fabric of mind and body together.

So today we hear that there have been some 200 cholera victims in our own camp. They have been carried to our isolation area, where most of them have died. The corpses have had to be buried in mass graves, for we cannot possibly bring in enough firewood to dispose of them in hygienic flames, so there is no alternative to mass burial, all heaped together just as the Tamils were. Religious conventions and preferences have all had to be pushed aside to allow us to cope with the problem – and the problem will continue in-definitely. Our inoculations at Wampo were not very effective, were they?

And not one of the bloody Nip bastards has been infected! They have carefully kept themselves at a distance, leaving us to do all the unavoidable dirty work, from which most of our casualties must have picked up the disease. Now, with their total lack of understanding of the situation, they say the worst is over and we must get back to the railway! There have not been any Nip casualties, which proves that if we take proper care of ourselves we won't have any more in future! Nip logic would make us laugh if it didn't turn our stomachs.

However, they do permit a small squad to remain in camp to do whatever may be required of us while everyone else has gone off to work on the railway, and today I happen to be part of it. We are digging new latrine trenches (the joys of living in a Nip camp are too numerous to list) when there is a commotion on the Tarsao 'road'. A mass of Tamils has swarmed out of their camp and is starting to walk down the 'road' towards Tarsao, shouting and waving their arms. We see our friends of yesterday, but they are shouting in the Tamil language so we do not understand the words. The meaning, however, is clear – they have had enough and are going to Tarsao! Well, the best of luck to them. I call out 'Nasib baik (Good fortune),' and get a wave in reply. Our collective opinion is that they won't get far – our Nips will telephone ahead and there will be a roadblock of tough frontline Jap troops to bring them to a halt. Tarsao is a military base for the Burma armies and all the troops there are fighting men – no nonsense about them. The combination of mutiny and the risk of bringing cholera into Tarsao will make the Nips absolutely implacable, and we shall be very surprised if a single Tamil is left alive.

During the day we are able to look into our isolation area. Like our camp it is a morass of sticky mud in which our barely living sick are huddled under a few rotting and tattered tents and tarpaulins. Our medical officer's rudimentary apparatus for distilling water for intravenous salines has done wonders, and has undoubtedly been responsible for saving lives, but it cannot cope with the numbers. Apart from this there is no medicine or treatment available, and all that can be done for those still living is to try to bring some comfort to them in their last hours. Physical comfort, of course, does not exist, but there is no doubt the dying men are grateful for the mere fact that, in their severe distress, someone is there to talk to them and, if they can find a scrap of paper and a pencil, to write down messages to send home after the war.

Unbelievably, there are men who have gone into the cholera compound of their own accord to bring such comfort as they can. They know full well that they will not be allowed to leave until the cholera outbreak has cleared, and that there is a big risk of being infected and dying while inside. There are also many helpers who have survived an attack, and have voluntarily stayed there to be with their mates. True heroes, these men are just ordinary men who feel for their fellows.

As deaths occur the bodies are carried away to be laid tidily by the pit. There is no minister of religion (of any denomination) at Tonchan South. If there are any at the main camp they have not come to us. As far as we know, cholera is only present in our immediate area so far, but there have been rumours of outbreaks in camps further upriver. It is, of course, in the headwaters of the rivers along the Burma–Siam border that the epidemics start, every year without fail.

Tomorrow I shall probably be back on the railway work. I never thought that I would be glad to do that!

We have settled to a very strict routine of personal hygiene as it is the only defence we have, but casualties from earlier infection are still occurring. Apparently you can carry the bug in your system without even knowing, which makes you liable to be struck down at any time, although it also may never develop and will eventually fade away. The quarantine period, we are told, is twenty-one days clear after the last case. So we shall not know for some time whether we are winning or losing, and meanwhile must do what we can.

It doesn't help us to know that the dreadful monsoon rains will continue until November. What with that and our current abysmal circumstances, it is difficult to maintain an optimistic attitude, but we do. Against all logic we continue to have easy conversations, swap yarns and tell jokes and, above all, we do not allow our tempers to fray at the edges. It is a testing time indeed, and who can know in advance how he will behave when such a time confronts him? You will have to cope with it when it happens, and I think we can all take modest pride in keeping our sanity and sense of humour intact.

At this point the Nips decide to close Tonchan South and move us all back to the central camp. We move with relief, away from that horrible place, but taking cholera with us.

This last week has left us physically exhausted, emotionally stressed, and spiritually numbed.

I have been back in the railway gangs for three days, and have found the deep silence of the forest to be healing and restful. It is not quiet all the time, of course – the sounds of work and occasional dynamite explosions go on throughout the day – but the vastness of the tree-clad hills is soothing, calming the nerves and offering tranquillity, particularly during the walk back to face the spiritual desolation of the camp.

Deaths have continued, but in lesser numbers than during the last week, which is a hopeful sign. But cholera is unpredictable, ebbing and flaring up at random. A single case can start an epidemic.

One of today's victims was an officer whom we all knew, not very well on a personal basis but well enough to exchange occasional chitchat. He was (for the British army) a somewhat unusual man, a regular soldier who joined the ranks of the heavy coastal artillery regiments manning the fifteen-inch guns that defended Singapore. Rumour has it that every man in these units has a criminal past and has served time in prison, either as a civilian or in army detention centres, and indeed that is why they are stationed in Singapore, which had been regarded during the 1930s as the place to which bad boys could be posted, well out of everyone's way. I really don't know the truth of that, but the rumour persists and never seems to be denied.

Be that as it may, this particular soldier was seen to have leadership qualities and was commissioned from the ranks as an officer. At the time of his death he had been promoted to captain. Evidently he had performed well, and his men told us of their respect for him. An officer commissioned from the ranks (a rare event) is normally posted to another regiment, to break him away from the men with whom he used to mix, but the problems of wartime had kept him with the same men. So they knew him well, and approved of him, and believe me there is no soldier more critical of his officers than the British ranker. But, as is the way of things, men so promoted are not popular with their fellow officers who have Sandhurst or some military training college behind them. He is not of their social background, and is usually at a serious disadvantage in his personal finances (which can make his mess bills a problem). In fact he 'lets the side down', and this can never be excused or even disregarded.

Two other things made this particular officer socially unacceptable to his fellow officers. The first was that he had a Jewish-sounding surname, and titbits brought back to the men by mess orderlies and batmen made it clear that this was a minus. (Why is it that officers ignore the fact that their military servants have ears, and delight in passing on gossip which they were not supposed to be capable of hearing and understanding?)

The other thing was much more serious. At some early point in his career, presumably when he was on a boozing spree with his mates, he had a truly magnificent tattoo done on his back. From his shoulders, right down his back, galloped a group of red-faced horsemen in full hunting pink rig, following a pack of tail-wagging hounds, close on the bushy tail of a fox disappearing between the cheeks of his bum. Obviously he had never expected to become an officer! The existence of a tattoo was bad enough in itself. Such an ostentatious tattoo was a step worse. But what put it right out of social bounds was the scene depicted: a derisory 'two fingers up yours' attitude towards that holy symbol of the aristocracy – the fox hunt. When the captain joined us at our private pool back in Wampo, we all inspected and admired the artistry in this extraordinarily complex and detailed masterpiece. He was an outgoing chap, cheerful and with an earthy sense of humour, and he was devoted to his men. Maybe all that told against him too.

The reason I am recounting all this is that, coming across an officer we knew to be in the captain's group, we stopped to offer our sympathy. His response at first surprised us, then annoyed us, and finally aroused such a rage in us that we told him what we thought of him and those who thought the way he did. Too flummoxed to reprimand us for impertinence to an officer, he stood there gaping at us when we pushed past him. He was lucky not to have been belted with a shovel blade. He represented social snobbery at its worst.

It seemed that the captain was one of an official party escorted by the Nips to buy canteen supplies from a riverboat. These purchasing missions are quite frequent now – the Nips and the Siamese have reached agreement on bribes and kick-backs, therefore the more often the better. On the way back to camp the captain had been seen eating a raw papaya fruit, holding it in his hands and licking juice off his fingers. In an hour or two he was ill, cholera symptoms showed up, and within twenty-four hours he was dead. The papaya was blamed.

'Stupid fellow, we warned him not to eat anything not cooked, but he told us to mind our own business. Of course, a proper officer would never have been so careless. What can you expect from an ignoramus from the ranks? Should never have been given a commission. He's never been one of us at all! Serves him right for accepting a commission, he should have known better and refused it! Ignorant bumpkin! Serves the bugger right – he would still be alive if he had stayed in his proper place! No bloody right to have the presumption to join us! Mean to say, have you seen that awful tattoo on his back? Perfectly ghastly!'

Throughout this tirade the emphasis was entirely on the social aspects of the captain's elevation from the hoi polloi to the realm of his betters. There was no reference to his military competence which, surely, is of far more importance in wartime? And this pink-faced prick in front of us, yapping away about his nauseating snobbish prejudices, what has he done for his men in the last eighteen months in general and six months in particular? We certainly have not seen him on any worksite, or visiting in our huts.

A man has just died an agonising death, one of hundreds it's true, but each man is an individual person in his own right. And his brother officer has nothing to say except that he was a fool to bring death on himself, something to be expected (naturally) because he was not a 'proper' officer.

The senior British officer (our haughty spectacle of parade-ground elegance) has not seen fit to visit our part of the camp to enquire as to our situation. When he runs his cold stare over us at morning and evening tenkos, we just stare stonily right back at him, bolshie lot that we have become! Unkempt and near naked we may be, but we prefer our kind of pride in ourselves to his distorted vanity. We don't really want to speak to him anyway.

We do, however, have a message from him, conveyed by his batman and delivered in a halting and shamefaced manner as if the man wished he were elsewhere. Why do we not respond to bugle calls summoning each unit's duty corporal to his tent? Bugle calls? Duty corporals? The batman explains that the colonel was originally a cavalry officer and uses cavalry tunes, so maybe we didn't recognise them, but the colonel is very keen on keeping up army procedures, so would we please send someone along when the bugle sounds? In the interests of good army discipline?

The wretched batman is so obviously embarrassed at having to pass on all this rubbish to us, we send him back with soothing reassurances which we have not the slightest intention of keeping. And that is the last we hear of it. The colonel must be bloody mad – right round the bend!

The cholera compound at Tonchan South has been kept functioning while the rest of us were moved out. Presumably it will continue until the last corpse has been disposed of. What will happen then to the survivors and orderlies, who will undoubtedly be carriers of the disease? Will the Nips simply bring them here to rejoin us? The medical officer is the only one we have, we can't afford to be without him.

News comes from them that the Tamil party was met a few kilometres down the 'road' by several bursts of machine-gun fire across their front. Nobody was hurt, but they got the message and walked back to their miserable hovels, looking as if they were on their last legs. Maybe the Nips should have shot them – a more merciful death than the one they can expect in their camp. Poor buggers, alone and helpless – only death in its foulest form awaits them. The thought festers in my mind.

We have by no means completed all the necessary work in our area when we are told the welcome news that we are to move out of Tonchan to another camp upriver. Going further north would normally not be a cheerful prospect. There are so many rumours that conditions become even worse (is that really possible?) the further you go, and the gossip is so persistent that some of it must be true. Anyway, at the moment we are (literally!) so deep in muck that it can only be a relief to move somewhere else – anywhere else – and we are thankful to be going. During our stay at Tonchan there has been a steady daily procession of bodies to the cemetery, maybe even including some of the thirty-two men still on their feet when we arrived, for we have not seen any of them since then.

The expression 'death camp' should not be used too readily. Didn't we think that Wampo might be called that, with thirteen deaths, only a couple of months ago? But Tonchan has forced us to think on a new scale. There could well be 1,500 men buried here, and we mustn't ever forget to bring those wretched Asiatics into the total. Surely we now know what the words 'death camp' mean?

The clouds have emptied themselves and we are grouped around a great blazing pile of wood, enjoying the sight of clear starry skies and the toasting warmth of the fire. There is some kind of relaxing magic in the crackling flames as they leap up from their glowing bed of shifting reds and yellow. Our ancestors probably had just the same feelings when night came down on their caves. With all our education and familiarity with modern technology, we have not broken away from some of our primitive reactions – thank heaven for that!

The talk is of our experiences over the last few days, since cholera struck us. We discuss events that have had a horrific impact on our unshielded sensibilities, but do so in a totally dispassionate manner. Calm voices recall gruesome situations; there is a matter-of-fact acceptance of sights which once would have turned our stomachs. Might it be that our civilised responses to the human condition are, perhaps, being insidiously distorted into new patterns of indifference to the sufferings of others, to deaths of innocent people, to mindless brutality? It is an unnerving thought.

But the very fact that we are able to debate the point, quietly and without undue alarm, is in itself proof that we have not changed at all in our basic principles. We still have our old instinctive sympathies, possibly even intensified by our present personal circumstances, but if we are to stay sane and perceptive, it is essential that we blunt our sensitive edges. We must not turn our eyes away, but we must not allow ourselves to be so pained that our mental defences collapse. Only by sealing off the horrors can we keep our personalities intact and able to function normally, waiting patiently for the time when we shall be able to revert to being our true selves. It is most important to believe totally that such a time will indeed come again, and we shall be once more whole and intact. We must stay alive to be there when it happens.

The key to this process of holding our souls together in one piece is to recognise the inevitable, to accept that unpleasant things will happen and we shall be unable to prevent them – therefore, if we cannot do anything about it we must face it and accept it. Very simple, very difficult. Unendurable, but must be endured. Very frustrating, but let it pass and hope for something better. Be part of it if you cannot avoid it, but remain detached. Life at its simplest!

We have amongst us a Jew, in his late thirties and formerly a businessman in Singapore. He is the only one of his race in our group, and has always offered witty contributions to our evening campfire chats and debates. Tonight he observes that although we have all been brought up as Christians, he has noticed that we do not (at least, not openly) seem to derive any comfort or strength from our religion. We do not offer prayers, or call upon God for relief from our tribulations or for courage to bear them. And is it not one of the mainstays of Christianity that earnest prayer will be heard and answered? Is not the Bible full of reassurances to this effect? On the other hand, we do not revile the Christian God, or accuse him of failing us – work that one out!

For his part, he always manages to find a few quiet minutes every day for prayer and meditation and feels all the better for it. He feels that his troubles are known by someone who sympathises with him, and lifts his pain from his shoulders.

It is an interesting comment, but the hour is late and the bugle calls 'lights out' for all good cavalrymen. Tomorrow, provided the river barges turn up, we shall set off on our holiday cruise up through the glorious scenery along the Kwei Noi, and it will be something to talk about as we lounge lazily in the sun, sipping a long cold gin and tonic! The motto of Nippon River Cruises might well be 'Passengers Who Complain Will Be Bashed Wholeheartedly To Our Entire Satisfaction'. Who could ask for more?

6

Kanyu Camp

JULY 1943 (TWO DAYS)

For a couple of hours our flotilla of wooden river barges has been moving serenely upstream on the Kwei Noi river, muddy now and fast-running with the first weeks of the monsoon rains. We have seen no habitation, and the absolute silence of the rocky hills and thick forest on either bank is broken only by the rhythmic pom-pom-pom-pom of the small launches towing us smoothly against the current.

For all of us it is a blessed, if brief, interval of peace, free of that miserable camp called Tonchan and its equally unpleasant adjunct Tonchan South, where fearsome cholera first struck us. In particular, we are out of the grip of that ferocious barbarian Warrant Officer Furobashi. We have had no new cholera case for eighteen days, and three more clear days will see us officially out of quarantine. Moving out of that infected area, we are hopeful that this curse may be lifted, although we are well aware that the whole length of the Kwei Noi is highly dangerous in the wet season. Even if we come clear in the next three days, a new infection can hit us at any time.

Today the weather is kind to us, and there is little talk as the men doze in the warm sunshine, relaxed even in the cramped discomfort of the barges. Looking idly ahead I notice that hills lying along the riverbanks curve towards each other and almost meet a few hundred yards directly ahead of us, separated by a narrow gorge the walls of which rise vertically several hundred feet above the river, leaving the interior gloomy and sunless. Suddenly I am aware that the river is pouring out of the pinched gap in a high torrent, and our barge is beginning to sway and tilt as it enters the brawling turbulence of the river finding its new level, spreading out into our wider stream.

Expertly catching a strong swirl running out to our right, our tug pilot swings to the right into an extensive bay of quiet water, and soon the echoing pom-pom-pom-pom dies out and the barges drift on to nudge gently into a sandy beach. In a few minutes the men are all on the shore with the scanty camp gear stacked ready to move, waiting for orders. The beach is only some fifty yards across to the foot of a steep and forbidding rocky face dotted with shrubs and scraggy trees, and several hundred yards away to our right we can see the huts of a typical camp. The sun is behind our mountain, and the whole area is shadowy and depressing.

Our Nips are muttering to each other as if undecided about what to do next, scratching their heads and armpits for inspiration. The launches have restarted their engines and pushed off with the empty barges, so we are on our own. It is time to be philosophical.

Suddenly the Nips reach a decision, and with a lot of shouting and flapping of arms they indicate that we are to go up the mountain speedo speedo. What! Up that cliff? Carrying tents and cookhouse kwalis and bags of rice? What about the camp just along the shoreline?

Like agile apes in scruffy uniforms, the Nips start scrambling up, finding toeholds and pulling on the vegetation. We, with bare feet and hampered by heavy gear, make the best of it, shoving and hauling the tent bundles and iron kwalis and rice sacks, hoping not to be underneath if a kwali breaks loose from fifty feet further up the slope. Every step is an effort, every upward heave is a separate struggle over an obstacle, but in our group we have long since learned to work as a team and there are no slackers. By the time we reach the top we are near exhaustion, and thankfully dump everything while we have a breather. According to one of us whose hobby used to be climbing in Wales, we have dragged our loads some 700 feet above the river. No wonder we are a bit puffed.

We have reached a flat area with a muddy track running left and right, rutted with lorry wheel marks, a little way back from the edge of our cliff. Further back the mountainside again rises vertically, bushes and trees all over its face. As soon as we are all assembled here, our particular Nip, fresh after a half-hour rest, is impatient to get moving again. He starts off easterly, changes his mind and trots off to the west, stops and has a think (scratching his bum to activate his brains), then comes back to us looking distinctly worried. It is mid afternoon and presumably he has to deliver us somewhere specific before dark, so we can understand his predicament without really giving a damn how he solves it.

Three cheers, he has decided to go east, and by the time we have sorted out our loads he has disappeared along the track. Those of us who manhandled the gear up the mountain travel light, and we follow the new porters to give a hand if it becomes necessary, as some of them are not too fit. So it happens that a group of us, about a dozen including my brother and myself, are at the tail end of the march.

We are all Singapore Volunteers, some of us knew each other well in peacetime and now we are all close friends and spiritually comfortable with each other. So when we follow a curve in the track and find ourselves looking at a number of huts, we all come to a collectively instinctive standstill and gaze around. There is something unusual in the atmosphere, and everyone senses it. We are wrapped around with an extraordinary feeling of calmness and serenity, and for some minutes not a word is spoken. Peace and tranquillity soak into me, and I want to do nothing but stand quietly and absorb them. I am in a kind of trance, relaxed but with all my senses sharpened and taut, expectant, waiting for something – something unusual – to happen. For me it is a totally new experience, but I feel no surprise or concern whatsoever. I know with an odd certainty that I am about to be the recipient of some unusual sign of grace. It will be benevolent and I am completely unafraid and receptive to it.

The layout of the camp in front of us is the usual one: bamboo and attap huts on three sides of a parade area, with a Nip guardhouse on the side nearest to us, close to the lorry track. All of the huts have collapsed and small shrubs grow in the open spaces, so clearly it has been unoccupied for some time. And there is something we have not seen in any camp so far: a formal entrance to the parade ground, made of tree trunks put together somewhat in the style of a traditional Japanese gateway, by the guardhouse.

And again, something different. Between the track and the looming mountain face in the background and to the right, the flat surface is peopled with tall trees quite unlike the stunted growth familiar to us at river level. The trunks are straight and neatly barked and tall, with the first branches reaching out some sixty feet above the ground, providing a shady canopy dappled with sunlight. They have a haughty nobility, a stately presence which claims my full attention. With all the other men, I wait.

Clear as a bell, from the shady recesses a voice calls to us, strong and resonant, two words only: 'Ron! Den!' A pause for a few seconds, and the call is repeated: 'Ron! Den!' It is no surprise to me that the voice is totally familiar, and that the words are the names of my brother and myself.

The spell is broken, our bodies are eased from their still-ness, and we turn to each other. Did it happen? You cannot fool a dozen intelligent men all at the same time, not in these circumstances. Did they hear what I heard? We are all thoughtful, considering and remembering what has just happened, and no one seems to think it was in any way eerie or weird.

'Did you hear that voice?'

'I did. I thought it came from the trees, somewhere up in the air.'

'I heard it too. From the space above the huts and below the branches.'

'No doubt about it. But there's certainly nobody here but us. The camp's totally deserted.'

'But there definitely *was* a voice! I heard it clearly, and more than that, I'm sure I recognised it. It was Bill Hatton's voice.'

'That's what I thought. I've known Bill for years, and I couldn't be mistaken.' Wally turns to Ron and me: 'And it was your names that he called out, and you two were particular friends of his.'

Wally was right; Ron and I had met Bill and his young brother and parents shortly after our arrival in Singapore. Mum and Dad had known Grace and Bill senior for several years.

There is a brief discussion, matter of fact and with no expression of wonderment or even surprise, and it is unanimous: there *was* a voice from the empty space, it *was* Bill's voice (to those who knew him), and it called out Ron's name and mine. And it hasn't struck any one of us as being in the least other than normal. Have we all been under some kind of spell?

A different voice, our Nip bawling down the track, brings us back to realities, and we move on. My state of mild trance has given way to a tingling elation, and I am waiting with a pleasant sense of anticipation for the next sign.

Soon the track bends to the right, curving in a long downward sweep to the riverbank. Lo and behold, we arrive at the camp which we had seen in the distance when we landed on the beach. The inevitable tenko is finally completed when our intelligent son of Nippon has counted us five times and actually arrived twice at the same total.

When the head of our party reached the camp the cooks turned out to provide rice and wishy-washy 'stew', so we line up for the evening meal. As the mess orderlies bring the food to us from the cookhouse we become aware of a deep humming and thrumming sound, and in the failing light we see swarms of flies, millions of fat blue-black flies, buzzing and zizzing around them. The sheer mass of them penetrates everywhere, clinging thickly to surfaces and zooming in swirling shoals around the rice buckets. We are familiar with flies in the primitive conditions of hygiene forced upon us, but these dense swarms are way beyond our experience.

The mess orderlies keep the food containers covered with bits of matting as closely as possible as they scoop out the rice, and we hold our hats over our mess tins as the rice is dumped in. But the flies are so thick and moving so fast in all directions that complete protection is impossible. They settle immediately on our skin and on our hats, our arms and hands are layered with the disgusting creatures trying to slither into our mess tins. Eating is an unpleasant business, the first spoonful is blotted from view before it reaches your mouth and has to be thrown away, so we eat with our mess tins held close to our mouths, shovelling rice in under the protection of a hat. There is very little – a quarter of a pint mug each.

We are told that this has been the situation for some weeks. There are no fit men and no shovels for sanitation, the latrines are full and overflow in the heavy rains, and the flies live in the filth and migrate at meal times to the cookhouse. After that they disappear to snug down in the latrine trenches, as we find when we have to go there ourselves. This rich diet accounts for their obscene size and numbers. The only benefit seems to be that they don't bother the men in the huts – presumably they are not worth the trouble of visiting!

We are told to make use of one of the empty huts for the night, but most of them look dangerously ramshackle and we prefer to bed down in the open. We pull bamboo and attap from one of the more tumbledown huts and start some blazing fires to brighten the place up, then walk over to an occupied hut to see if there is anyone we know in the camp.

Our cheerful bustling entry is met with silence. The hut is in darkness except for the flickering light from our fires, and we are able to make out some fifty or sixty men lying on the usual split bamboo platform. They have the languid attitudes of the desperately sick and dying. Worse than thin, they are skeletal with sunken eyes, and the hut has an unpleasant odour of unwashed bodies and sour breath, bugs and decay. Very few have a blanket or groundsheet, their skinny bodies resting directly on the uneven slats. The shock of the awful scene brings us to a wordless standstill; we are looking into a death-house where all these men have been left, without even the smallest form of comfort, to die. We move in to see what we can do.

There is someone we know, but he is difficult to recognise. Months without a shave or haircut (and obviously without a comb), half his normal weight and with dirt in the wrinkles of his shrunken skin, Freddie is barely alive. As we stand at his feet calling his name, he pulls his eyes into focus and realises that we are talking to him, and with a tremendous effort he drags himself to a sitting position, panting with exhaustion even with our help to support him. His smile of welcome shows that his teeth have had no attention for a long time, his nails are ragged and broken, and his only clothing (as is the case with all of us) is a Nip-style fundoshi or skimpy loincloth, grubby and threadbare.

Throughout the hut there are stirrings and voices, and the creaking of bamboo slats as the sick men bestir themselves to talk to us. We are the first new faces for weeks, and many of us are old friends, but even strangers are warmly welcomed. It is so long since anybody took any notice of them, and weeks of mind-shrivelling loneliness and despair now give way to a tremendous urge to talk, talk, talk, and feel like a human being again. Freddie gives us a quick rundown on events.

This camp by the river was the original working camp, Kanyu, and the men had to climb up the cliff every morning to work, come back down for midday rice, climb back up for the afternoon shift and then down again at the end of the day, which was no joke in the dark on the rain-slippery slope. The Nips said this was unavoidable because the camp had to be on the river for its water supply. The combined physical stresses of climbing and labouring knocked out so many men, and so much time was wasted going to and fro, that eventually the Nips agreed to establishing a camp higher up, where the water supply was inadequate, and then they increased the workload. So there had been, in fact, no improvement in conditions and the men were nearing total exhaustion. As the sick list grew, the Nips became even more brutal and men began to die in increasing numbers. Then cholera struck and the death rate rose until disposal of corpses became a problem because the Nips still demanded a maximum number of men for working parties. If you were fit enough to dig a grave you went out to work – simple logic!

The situation became so bad that even the Nips had to give in. The high camp was closed, men who could lift a shovel formed burial groups, and the rest came down to the river. Obviously, the camp up above was the abandoned collection of huts which we had seen.

I ask him: 'Tell us, Freddie. You used to know Bill Hatton. Was he here or in the high camp?'

'Oh yes, I've known him for years. He was here and then up the top, but he had a very bad time with diphtheria, almost went out of his mind, delirious and raving, about as close to dying as you could get without actually going over the side. Because he was so ill he was in the first party to be sent down here, and was evacuated downriver. Chungkai, I think, some weeks ago, I'm a bit vague about time.'

I tell Freddie about the voice, Bill Hatton's voice, ringing out of the tall trees, about the strangely serene atmosphere, and how none of this was my imagination because all our group had also experienced it individually. And how we had all discussed it amongst ourselves and agreed on the details, with no one seeming to think there had been anything odd or unusual at all.

Freddie looks at me thoughtfully, and I feel a sudden surging excitement. I know that I am on the verge of something extraordinary.

'You know, that doesn't really surprise me either, somehow. When I was too sick to work I was put on to grave-digging with a number of other fellows. At least we were able to work at our own speed without any bloody Nips shouting at us, and as long as we kept up with the number of bodies coming in, we could rest when necessary. I used to sit on the ground leaning back against one of those trees, and relax. I used to think how beautiful those trees were, soothing and comforting, and that the dead would be able to sleep peacefully beneath them. There must be over 800 men buried there, under those trees. May they rest in peace.'

And in a single instant I *know*, I *understand*, with absolute clarity and certainty, what happened to us that afternoon at that deserted camp. More than 800 men had been murdered, sacrificed to that accursed railway, and had been buried under the trees. Their outraged spirits hovered over them, and our small party, unknowingly receptive to their aura, had halted in reverence, sympathetic and silent. In acknowledgment of our instinctive courtesy, the spirits hailed us in the voice of a man we knew who called out the names of two of us. What were they really telling us? I knew the answer to that, too: 'You who have felt our presence without even having known that we are here, do not forget us!'

I feel a deep sense of privilege, and a certainty that I shall survive this captivity under their benevolent protection. Their memory will be held faithfully in my consciousness until I die. Fanciful? Do the others feel as I do? Or was I specially chosen as being receptive to them, the others being brought in to prove to me that it really happened, that I had not dreamed it? Why were they not even puzzled, but accepted and discussed the experience as simple fact? For myself I have no doubts at all. Something in my consciousness has been touched with mystery and brought to life, and I am fully content to acknowledge it and let it remain so. But this is not the time to discuss it all with the others; we must see what we can do to help these friends of ours in their distress.

Freddie tells us that the men in his hut seem to be victims of a typical Nip organisational foul-up. As far as he knows they

275

are the last group in the camp set aside for evacuation, several hundred having already been lifted out, and a lot of men having died while waiting. They themselves were supposed to have gone a couple of weeks ago, but no barge came for them. The Nips must have assumed they had gone, so no rations were allocated and, presumably, there would be no barge either. So there they were, in a sort of limbo, hoping that someone would wake up and do something for them.

There are a couple of Koreans in charge, and they disappear occasionally, probably to collect their own rations, and now and again a little rice comes in from somewhere. The cooks never know how long it has to last and dole it out in small quantities, but even so there have been days with nothing at all. Water is short because there are so few men fit enough to carry it from the river, and cooking must have priority – there is none for personal hygiene. Nor are there any containers in the cookhouse for storing water. Every bucket goes straight into the kwalis and the tea boilers as it is brought up from the river. The cooks and rations are intended for the rest of the camp – all desperately sick men – and officially our friends are simply not there.

'So you see,' concludes Freddie, 'we are still waiting, and if we aren't taken out within a few days we shall simply fade out. In fact, I doubt whether any of us would survive a trip downriver anyway.' Our faces must have shown our concern, for he went on: 'You mustn't worry about us. We have had plenty of time to read the signs and get used to the prospect. Really, after these last months it will almost be a relief. We have all passed beyond pain and will slide away quietly in our own time.'

'Can we do anything to make you more comfortable? How about a wash in the river?' We are not supposed to go into the river, because of the cholera risk, but in the circumstances that doesn't seem to be of much consequence as long as we are careful not to let the river water get into our mouths.

The word goes round quickly, we carry the dying men (they feel like sacks of loose sticks) to the river and lay them in the cool shallows. There is no soap, but we do what we can to get them clean, sloshing water over them gently and washing away the accumulation of sweat and dirt. Their few bits of blanket and groundsheet are shaken, while a couple of lads pass blazing torches under the bamboo sleeping platform and the stink of singed bugs and lice wafts out of the hut.

The night coolness makes itself felt and our patients begin to shiver; there is so little body warmth in them. We have nothing to dry them with, so carry them close to the fires. There is little talk, the evening's excitement has come near to exhausting them, but their gratitude is plain.

Suddenly the peaceful scene is broken by a cry of intense pain. Our friend Freddie is rolling on the ground doubled up with severe stomach cramps, his arms and legs twitching and jerking as his muscles seize up. Then his body erupts with vomiting and a violent forced rush of fluid from his bowels, whitish fluid the colour of rice-water. We have seen this before, it is cholera without a doubt, but this attack is unusually ferocious and sudden, the fluid forced in hard jets out of his body by the fierce bunching of his muscles, agonisingly painful.

Tim is the first to jump to his feet and hurry towards the sick man, but as he leans over him he is sprayed with contaminated muck as poor Freddie goes into uncontrollable spasms and rolls around, the discharges being flung everywhere. His own body is splashed all over and is dangerous to touch, and the ground around him is infected within seconds.

The authoritative voice of Bertie, our sergeant, cuts in:

'Tim, get into the river! Scrub yourself with sand, but for God's sake keep your mouth shut. And you others, get the other fellows clear, we don't want anyone else contaminated. Everyone stand clear of Freddie, well clear. There's nothing we can do for him, just leave him alone. Keep away from him!'

There is, of course, exactly nothing that can be done for Freddie but to wait for him to die. In his emaciated condition he has little flesh and will dehydrate very quickly beyond hope of survival. Mercifully, within a few minutes he lies still, his body bent and his limbs outflung just as the last wrenching contractions twisted his body. His eyes are rolled up and his lips drawn back over his teeth, and risk of infection means that we cannot even offer the decencies of trying to compose him for burial. The loathsome flies are already finding him, and we must move quickly.

The sudden commotion has brought one of our Nips to investigate, bad-tempered, scowling and muttering. Sergeant Bertie, unflappable and resourceful, marches straight up to him and halts squarely in front so that the Nip is brought to a standstill, and barks, 'Ichi man die!' Pointing to Freddie's body. 'Cholera!' He holds up his hands, palms close to the Nip's face, and repeats, 'Cholera! You understand? We want two shovels, at once! Ni shovero haiaku!' Shrinking away in panic from those two supposedly infected hands, the Nip sprints away and returns with two shovels, which he tosses towards us from a safe distance. Cholera is a word all the Nips know, and it frightens the stuffing out of them.

Sergeant Bertie picks up the shovels and hands one to the nearest man. 'This won't be pleasant so I'll take one. We can't move Freddie, so we'll bury him right here. Then we'll spread fire over the area to sterilise the ground. Some of you collect bamboo for the fire, the rest of you get the sick men back to bed. They've had enough for one day.'

We all know we have to be strictly practical in this matter – sentiment cannot be allowed to override precautions against cholera breaking loose amongst us. To catch it is virtually a death sentence, and one single case will put every man in our party at risk. Our sole protection is to avoid being infected. But sentiment is nevertheless present, and we mourn for Freddie's ordeal and sad death, and a new measure is added to our already massive hatred of and contempt for the whole foul, savage, barbaric and uncivilised Japanese nation.

We dig in clean ground close by and tip Freddie's contorted body into his grave, cover him up and scatter fire all around. It has not taken long – he was alive and talking to us an hour ago. Then we paddle in the river, dragging our feet through the sand in the hope that it will scour away any infection we may have walked on.

Knowing that we have an early start tomorrow, we say goodbye to our patients, wishing them well and leaving with them such few luxuries as we have – duck eggs, tobacco, palm sugar – then settle down for the night.

Sleep does not come readily; I am filled with a leaden sadness. We know that in a day or two our sick friends will start to die, there will be nobody able to bury them and their bodies will lie alongside their living companions. In a week or two the huts will contain only decomposing corpses and flies, flies, flies. The Koreans will slip away and report the camp empty, and nobody will care a damn.

But we shall remember. How can we ever forget? No man in that camp in any way deserved such a wretched, squalid fate. May the Japanese be cursed forever.

Funny thing, nobody says prayers any more, at bedtime or any other time. It really seems quite pointless. We all had our own thoughts as we slid Freddie into his private hole in the ground, but it didn't seem to have occurred to anybody to say a prayer out loud. We used to do so, in the early days. Maybe we have come to think that no one listens. Certainly no one seems to bother to help us.

Shut your eyes, don't brood, go to sleep! You'll need it tomorrow.

The next morning we are astir before daylight, the smouldering fires are revived and we eat the scanty cold rice held over from last night. In the pre-dawn quiet we become aware of a peculiar sound from the west, a squealing, grunting, screaming which is weird and slightly unnerving.

We are ready to move when our Nips appear for tenko, expecting to march out by the easy track along which we had come down into the camp – that would give us another look at the mysterious group of huts up above. But the Nips head off along the beach towards yesterday's cliff face, and with muttered imprecations we pick up our loads and follow. Soon we come to a scene that fills us with disgust: an area some fifty yards square bounded by a waist-high fence. It's a pigpen with a dozen or so pigs inside, and we have found the source of the screaming.

The wretched animals stand belly deep in a thick foul-smelling black ooze, unable to lie down or they will drown, and with nothing to eat or drink. And then we see the reason for their tormented, high-pitched squealing. Their backs are raw with open sores and ulcerated wounds smothered in blood-streaked mud, and huge rats are scampering over them, chewing and gnawing at the living flesh. The pigs try to dislodge them by submerging their bodies in the liquid mud, but they have to keep their snouts above the surface and the rats merely run to their heads and gnaw at their faces, or swim over to another animal. Some pigs have empty eye sockets and torn snouts running blood, and cheeks ripped away from their jaws.

The Nips have walked past without a second glance, but

are forced to return to us when we come to a standstill and look at this sickening place. The Nips observe our concern (fortunately for us they do not understand our angry comments) and giggle, but when we pantomime that they should shoot the pigs they become hostile and bawl at us to move on. We have no choice but to obey. There is nothing we can do – it is just another example of Nip indifference to pain and suffering. These pigs had probably been destined for their cookhouses and then abandoned when the camp was evacuated. Uncivilised bastards, all of them.

We arrive at the foot of our mountain, and work off some of our ill-temper as we claw ourselves up to yesterday's ledge, this time marching off to the west. But I cannot burn out the deep, nagging sadness at having been forced to leave our doomed friends back there by the river. I am filled by a stupefying frustrated rage at having to obey the orders of such an ignorant, insensitive, less-than-human, barbaric bunch of savages, which is not lessened by the thought at the back of my mind that an equally unpleasant fate might be mine at any time. Human decency is not enough to provide a shield, it can only be its own reward – the gods don't give a damn. Our only strengths are our personal pride, our sheer contempt for the Nips, and our unwavering certainty that our people will thrash the Nips and rescue us, so that we can all go home.

But then, of course, what will our position be when our troops throw the Nips out of Burma, and thousands of us find ourselves right in the next war zone behind the Nip front line? We have discussed this situation, and it is totally clear to us that the Nips will start a massacre to remove us as a threat. There will be nothing we shall be able to do for the sick, immobilised and helpless in their camps, and we ourselves will have precious little chance of escaping. Maybe the Siamese army will help, but who knows what their attitude will be?

What a horribly foul war we, personally, are having. Nothing whatever to do with soldiering, reduced to a squalid and degrading existence as slaves, a bloody awful present and decidedly uncertain future. Really, one's capacity for remaining philosophical can be severely strained.

Thinking such thoughts and chatting to each other as we hike along our carefully straggling column, we notice that the altitude not only induces a pleasant coolness in the air, but the trees seem stronger than those at river level, the bamboo is more slender, with smooth stems and without thorny branchlets. The river, far below on our left somewhere, is not visible, and there is no habitation nor any sound except occasional hooting and calling of monkeys on the steep, forested slopes.

By late afternoon we are thinking that we must be due at a staging camp when we find that we have closed up on the men in front, and the Nips are waving at the virgin bush and shouting, 'Campo, campo!' What, right here? Apparently, yes.

We have had a small breakfast, no lunch, and obviously there will be no evening rice or breakfast tomorrow either. And we cannot see any water supply, but it is beginning to rain steadily and a few shallow pits will produce drinking water. The raggedy tents are quickly pitched and huge blazing fires built from the scrub as we clear it. Bamboo, fortunately, burns fiercely even when wet, once you get it started.

Hungry though I am, and despite the rain dripping through my rotting tent, sleep comes easily. It has been a long tiring day. Any man having to go to the trench latrine chucks fuel on the fires as he passes, so that there is light to see his way around. It is just before dawn, the rain has stopped, and I see Ken emerge from the next tent and look around the camp area. 'What's up, Ken? Something wrong?'

'I don't know. Tim was sleeping next to me but he went out some time ago and hasn't come back.'

Then we see Tim, shovelling embers from a fire and lurching away a few paces to toss them on the ground. He is staggering as if in great pain as he turns back to the fire, and as we hurry over to him he collapses, doubled up and twitching as his limbs are seized by cramps. Ken takes his hand and feels the fingertips. They are cold and wrinkled from dehydration. It can only be cholera. Poor Tim. His reward for trying to help a sick man is catching the infection.

Tim's sickness is confirmed (if that were necessary) by his hoarse voice, his vocal chords shrunk and dried out by cholera's expulsion of moisture. 'I'm afraid I wasn't able to get to the latrine, and I've shit all over the place. I couldn't walk straight. I found a shovel, and I think I've managed to cover all the places with fire.' He passes into a faint for half a minute, then opens his eyes and whispers, 'Sorry to be such a bother to you.' And then he dies, quietly, as if not wanting to bother us any further. An unassuming fellow, he was helpful to everyone and well liked by all. Typically, right up to the moment of his death he was concerned firstly for the safety of his friends.

Ken says he will find a Nip to verify the death officially, so that the tenko figures will be correct, and would I attend to checking on the patches that Tim had covered with embers, keeping an eye open for any others. I rouse the others in my tent and tell them what has happened, and by the time the Nip arrives a grave has been started. The Nip nods and grunts as he views the body, and we are able to complete Tim's burial.

A small crowd has gathered meanwhile, and despite the informality of the funeral there is real emotion and sorrow apparent in the onlookers. I give a brief thought to the formalities and extravagancies of funerals in our society at home, and wonder whether it is all necessary. All those elaborate trappings and surely, sometimes, hypocrisy and ostentation. Different circumstances, different conventions, I suppose.

We strike camp and move on without delay, and the track starts to fall steadily towards the river. In a couple of hours we have a vertical mountain face on our right, and to the left a flat area with the usual bamboo and attap huts in rows. After tenko we disperse and look around. The huts are full of bugs, and according to the sick men in one of them, this camp is called Hintok and the Nip in charge is a right bastard. On the far side is a forty-foot escarpment dropping down to a narrow flat strip with the Kwei Noi river beyond. The lower area is thick with trees, and the cookhouse is on the riverbank. The mountain wall is repeated on the far side of the Kwei Noi.

A gloomy, cheerless dump. There will be nothing to eat until evening, and the rain is coming down in torrents. And cholera is with us again. Oh well, it could be worse.

7

Hintok Camp

JULY 1943

The only thing we can find in favour of this place is that the verminous huts are an improvement on the ragged mildewed canvas at Tonchan. At least we sleep on a bamboo platform clear of the ground and the roof doesn't leak too badly, but there is no escaping the bugs that have survived since the departure of the previous occupants and now welcome us, as a fresh food supply, with open jaws. The unending rain prevents us from sleeping outside, and even passing burning torches under the platform doesn't kill all of them. The malodorous stink of burned bugs fills the hut, but enough avoid the flames to continue to make life uncomfortable for us.

The huts occupy some two-thirds of the flat area while the other third is covered with tall trees and lush green grass that is a breeding ground for millions of mosquitoes, which add to our discomfort. We sometimes seem to be itching all over, and the risk of malaria must be higher than ever. So far, however, our group has been lucky indeed, with none of us yet infected.

The camp staff have managed to put up a bamboo and matting shelter over the latrines, located fifty metres away from the end huts and close to the mosquito area, this being the only available spot, but it means that men from the far end have over 200 metres to walk – no joke in the pouring rain at night. But some clever lad knows that blowflies are not keen on darkness, so the matting has been blackened with soot to discourage them. The result of this intelligent thinking is that on a moonless night the structure is invisible! When your bowels are straining for relief you don't have time to stumble around in a lengthy search, and a work party has to be turned out every morning to clean up the fouled ground. This is not what you could call a comfortable camp!

The daily work output has been stepped up. There is now no specific quota or requirement, but the pressure is on from daylight to whenever the Nips decide we can stop. Supervision has tightened up, and the Nips on the worksite are bad-tempered and continually barking at us. We don't understand what they are saying, but volleys of jagged rocks frequently accompany the screeching and we keep ourselves busy and move around as much as possible to be more difficult targets!

Excavating a cutting can be slow work, a lot of effort being put in before results become apparent. The soil is a thin layer on top of irregular rock formations, requiring tedious scratching and scooping away to expose the rock for 'hammer-and-tap' drilling for dynamite. After the explosions, the loosened debris has to be shovelled up and carried up the sides of the cutting to be dumped. As the cutting goes deeper, lugging tongas of earth and rock up to the rim becomes more and more laborious. The Nips, of course, are not the slightest bit concerned with our problem and simply scream for faster work and throw more rocks at us.

One of these missiles hits my brother just below his right knee, splitting the skin through to the muscle. He is not allowed to return to camp, and the wound is soon smothered in sweat and mud. The medical officer has no treatment and, by Nip standards, the injury is not enough to keep him in camp.

In two days Ron has a full-blown tropical ulcer, a nasty lesion in the form of a circular crater, raised like the rim of a volcano, about two inches across and filled with a thick yellow ooze. This is not ordinary pus from infection; it cannot be washed or wiped out. It is dead tissue, still firmly attached to the living underlying flesh, removable only by scraping or slicing away at the adhering surfaces. The ulcer itself is extremely painful, so treatment by excision is agonising without any form of anaesthetic, but there is no alternative in the absence of drugs.

The medical officer puts Ron on the sick list and arranges for me to work in the cookhouse for a time so that I can stay in camp with him. I am put on the night shift, which means that during the day I can search the riverbank, where there is a short stretch of beach, for wild Bombay spinach. The plant grows only in sand and is of solitary habit, not found in groups. The bush itself is small and scattered, and I can find only a few, which give me a bare half a hatful of leaves at the cost of bleeding fingertips from the tiny barbs which cover the stems. Simmered in water for ten minutes they produce a deep green soup, which tastes of rusty nails but has an extraordinary effect on Ron's ulcer. The slough starts to dry out and shrink, and little fragments can be picked out, and the pain lessens, all within twenty-four hours.

Back at the beach I search through other shrubs in case there are spinach bushes hidden amongst them, but there are none to be found. Yesterday's bushes have not had time to put out new growth, so I break off the side stems in the hope that they will be helpful. The need is really urgent. There is not time to let unhurried nature grow more foliage.

We are trying to cleanse Ron's ulcer when one of our Volunteers joins us and has a close look. 'Jeez,' he says, 'that's a nasty-looking thing. Here, try packing it with this.' And he hands over a white May & Baker 693 sulpha tablet, adding, 'Just keep quiet about where it came from. Don't tell anyone at all I gave it to you.' We are speechless, only just able to thank him before he leaves us. A whole tablet with M & B impressed on one face and 693 on the other. It's real, no doubt about it! Manna from heaven! Priceless, where gold would be worth nothing! We have heard that its efficacy is incredible.

We have seen hundreds of small jungle sores, and every one of us has several, caused by scratches and nicks on bare skin developing into septic wounds which cannot be kept clean and take a long time to heal, owing to our under-nourished condition. But Ron's ulcer is something else again, a runaway horror that makes your guts heave just to look at it.

Bits of medical knowledge can come from anywhere, and we always pass around every little scrap that comes our way. Our Volunteer battalion medical officer, who has been with us from the beginning, is now the camp MO. He is (deservedly) extremely popular with us, and we have had endless conversations with him, from which snippets of medical lore have been accumulated. He is the one from the Canary Islands, Spanish in background, and his brother was personal pilot to General Franco in the Spanish Civil War recently ended. Having to cope with battle wounds with totally insufficient medical supplies, the Spanish doctors pioneered a system of packing infected wounds with crushed sulpha tablets and encasing them in plaster for ten to twenty-one days before renewing the dressings. Contrary to the expectations of orthodox doctors, who changed dressings daily, the results were marvellously successful.

So, being pledged to absolute secrecy as to the source of

this magical gift, we do not tell the MO where it came from but manage to elicit his advice as to how to make the best use of it. We carefully scrape half the tablet so that the powder covers the whole of the infected surface, then protect it with a pad and bandage from a well-boiled shirt. Now we can only wait for results.

Camp cooks have always been suspected of holding back more than their share of rations and of keeping the least spoiled vegetables for themselves, which I suppose is inevitable. Everyone thinks they have an easy life boiling rice and a few sweet potatoes while we slog our guts out doing heavy physical labour. And, indeed, the cooks do seem to be in better bodily condition, but then they are not so exposed to the mental stresses of working under short-tempered Nips all day, and maybe that makes a difference. And, of course, they work at their own speed, unsupervised.

I very soon find, in my sojourn in the cookhouse, that the cooks all put in a full day's work with plenty of sweat and labour, but the relief from being on our own is enormous.

Working on night shift is, for me, a matter of keeping fires going under the big rice kwalis and the 44-gallon drums of water for tea, the actual cooking being done by the more experienced men. There is no provision for storing water, so it has to be brought up from the river as and when required. There is not enough of anything, there is no water supply point within the camp and no means of filtering the mud out of the silt-laden river, which is now running at full flood and thick with dirt from upstream. The Nips will not allow us to build any kind of pier to enable us to take water from out in the stream; we have to fill containers in the muddy shallows. A full six-gallon army kettle weighs some seventy pounds, and has to be carried up a slippery slope studded with rocks and tree roots exposed by the sluicing rain, the men sliding and stumbling on bare feet.

Our low quality rice continues to be full of rubbish. Some bags are not too bad but others have obviously been filled with sweepings from an earth floor. There is no way it can be washed or picked over, and anyway the river water is so dirty that washing would be a futile exercise. Some of the grit can be scooped out with sieves made from old jute rice bags, when the kwalis are boiling hard and throw it to the surface, but the fine mud passes through.

The so-called motor road which runs more or less alongside the river is still a rutted morass, difficult for trucks even in the dry season and totally impassable in the wet. As a result, as was the case at Wampo, our rations can be brought up only by river-boats, and perishable vegetables cannot survive the slow journey, so we are restricted to sweet potatoes, Chinese radish and (infrequently) pumpkin. There is so little of even these that they cannot be doled out as a vegetable, but can only be issued by chopping them very small and serving them as a watery, tasteless brew which is beyond identification. Meat simply does not exist. Live animals cannot be driven along the 'road', nor brought by river, and arrive in good edible condition.

Once again, as at Wampo in the last part of the wet season, we are not living in this camp but, more truly, slowly dying. And we don't have the promise of an approaching dry season, but several more months of torrential monsoon rains and depressing sunless days and thick dark nights with the moon blotted out. There seems to be absolutely nothing but gloom in our future.

Coming off night duty does not mean that I can get my head down and catch up on sleep. The day cooks take over to finish boiling the breakfast rice and getting the tea ready, and in the interval before breakfast we take axes into the forest to bring in bamboo to replenish stocks. After that we eat our rice and I can see Ron.

His ulcer, of course, is still bandaged and cannot be inspected, but he is daily more comfortable and we take this as a good sign that it is healing steadily. And over the past few days we have been able to trace the origin of the M & B 693 tablet, that quite marvellous gift. We remember that, back at Wampo some time about last November, a party of men carrying several basketwork panniers came into the camp with a Nip escort. The panniers were stowed in the rice store with a Nip sentry on guard, and the men were put into a hut on their own. At evening tenko we were told not to approach the rice store or to talk to the men, on pain of severe punishment. Obviously, something of interest was going on and (one POW being indistinguishable from another) it was no problem to meet our guests and find out what it was. Nothing much, just a quantity of medical supplies being taken up to Burma, eighteen panniers in all.

It was our medical officer who recognised that these were the standard packages for British army hospital drugs, presumably seized in Singapore. Quite rightly he decided that the contents were still our property, and that night he collected a squad of four Volunteers to break into the rice store to investigate.

With typical Nip thoroughness the door was padlocked, but there was no difficulty in sliding in through the attap wall at the back. A very useful quantity of various drugs was removed and buried under the MO's bamboo bunk, the empty boxes being put back in the panniers to appear intact. Next day, the carrying party hoisted their loads and departed.

There had been rumours of this episode at the time, probably started by the sudden appearance of drugs for sores and dysentery for a short time, but the secret had been well kept and only whispers had passed among us. There can really be no doubt that the precious M & B 693 tablet was a gift from personal 'souvenirs' acquired by one of the raiding party.

The medical officer, who organised the whole thing, must have had a quiet laugh to himself when we asked him how to use the tablet!

It seems the human spirit, though it has no substance, can be as tough as a manilla hawser, capable of absorbing enormous stresses and then regaining its original form and elasticity. This thought comes to me after a brief outburst of humour, totally unpredictable yet somehow entirely spontaneous throughout our group of some fifty men walking back through the forest to camp.

It has been a difficult day, even more so than usual, the Nips putting on an unending display of nagging petulance which made life most unpleasant. Even the weather has seemed hotter and steamier, the sodden earth clinging stickily to shovels, and streaming slopes at the sides of the cutting made even more slippery than usual to climb. So it is that when the sullen and bored Nips have themselves had enough discomfort for the day, they decide to let us finish. Thankful we are for that, and we start the hike home with desperately tired bodies and in a mood of deep despondency. We are exhausted and there is little enough comfort to look forward to when we reach camp.

All the men in the group are just ordinary fellows, raked into the army by the necessities of war and without any pretence of ensuring that they are at all suited to the hardships of soldiering, or to the life that we all now have to endure. Yet this day, after so many months of daily physical and mental strains far beyond anything they would ever have imagined, has not subdued them.

One man starts to sing, one of the trivial, drooling dance-hall tunes once familiar to us, and immediately it is picked up by others. From there it swells into the early wartime jingoistic drivel about rolling out a barrel and hanging out our washing on the Siegfried Line. The lightened mood just naturally leads to a booming climax in 'Rule Britannia, Britannia rules the waves, and Britons never, never, never shall be slaves!' These bombastic words – pompous, boastful and now, to us, absolutely ludicrous – catch our sense of humour.

So the cheerful singing develops a sardonic edge as the words are bellowed out. There is a moment's silence, then a shout of, 'Three cheers for Britannia, lads,' followed by an emphatically sarcastic, 'Hip hip hip hoo bloody ray,' and, 'Hip hip hip ha frigging hah,' and sundry other earnest comments. 'Must 'ave got on the wrong flamin' bus, there ain't no ocean waves here, maybe that's the trouble.' 'The bloke wot wrote that oughta be here for a spell, that would change 'is mind!' Imprecations of considerable ingenuity are sprinkled liberally everywhere, but they are familiar and commonplace and do in fact help to relieve tensions.

We walk into camp in a far better frame of mind, our hearts uplifted by the simple act of singing together, and our sense of humour tickled by the sheer inanity of our songs. Abstract, weightless and invisible the human spirit may be, but you can hang all the weight of your troubles on it and, for the time being, walk away from underneath.

Working in the cookhouse at night has its moments. Being down at river level, at the foot of the escarpment, it seems darker than ever in the shadows of the great tall trees outside the dancing glow of the fires. Last night there was a tremendous thunderstorm, lightning blazing ferociously almost without ceasing in a shattering cannonade. And close enough to lift our scalps in fright, three trees were struck and came crashing down right by the cookhouse. The pelting rain and fireworks continued until daybreak, while we kept the fires going and hoped that Thor and his playful mates had done enough tree-felling in our neighbourhood.

In these conditions everyone is worried about the difficulty of carrying food from the cookhouse to the top of the escarpment. The Nips won't allow the rice to be served at the cookhouse, and have refused to provide tools for cutting steps reinforced with timber in the face of the steep slope. Footholds scraped out simply disappear in the sloshing rain, and lugging a seventy-pound dixie up to the camp level is plain bloody hard work. Only two men can handle the container and it has to be kept horizontal to avoid spilling the contents. It takes gut-straining effort to manhandle it up the slithery slope where bare feet can find no real grip.

No food is served until all the dixies have reached the top safely. There is a good reason for this: any rice lost on the way up is not replaceable, and nobody can be made to go without a meal as a result. Whatever reaches the top safely has to go around to feed everybody. It happens with distressing frequency that a dixie gets out of control and takes itself and its bearers tumbling down to the bottom, in which case nobody blames the men but accepts a smaller issue of rice philosophically.

Nobody likes being detailed as mess orderly; the responsibility for safe delivery sits on your conscience as heavily as the load in your hands, notwithstanding the sympathetic attitude of your mates. Every spoonful is too important. So the job is rotated as fairly as possible, among those fit enough to do it. Just one more of the many stresses which we all have to carry.

It is ten days since we packed Ron's ulcer with half the sulpha tablet. His leg is now reasonably free of pain so it is with optimistic feelings that we ease off the dressing. The improvement is quite amazing, and we are delighted to see that the crater rim has subsided and is filled with healthy pinky-red flesh. The yellow muck of decayed tissue is now stuck on the underside of the dressing, inactive and odourless. Another piece of shirt is sacrificed and boiled, and the last part of the tablet is carefully packed in. It is a marvellous relief to me to know that in another week or two the healing should be complete.

In the background someone has been keeping an eye on my job in the cookhouse, and now that Ron's ulcer is no longer a cause for worry, I find myself back in the workforce. Nothing has changed, the Nips shriek and gibber as usual and the occasional flick of a thin bamboo across my back encourages me to keep moving. The rain buckets down most days, but there are occasional breaks when it is not actually raining, although the air is still heavy with moisture. At least the rain keeps us clean and cool, and the sun cheers us up. We can never get it right – when it rains we wish it would go away, when it doesn't we wish it would, and when we have weeks of unbroken blazing sun we long for sweet refreshing showers!

Unexpectedly, we are given a yasumi day. Maybe even the Nips want a break for relaxation, a change from the mindless boredom of supervising us at work, a chance to sort out and clean their kit. We are down by the river, soaking in the shallows, when a pom-pom swings a raft into the beach. On it are three British Bren-gun carriers, captured during the campaign, which a squad of Jap troops manhandle ashore.

At the north end of our camp area is a steepish slope which rounds the end of the escarpment. In this wet weather it is a morass of soft mud which has a man bogged to his knees in a few paces. Full of the spirit of bullshito, the Japs set the little tracked machines at this innocent-looking slope. In moments they are brought to a standstill, resting their flat undersides somewhere deep in the slop while the engines scream at full throttle and the tracks thrash madly and uselessly.

It gives us something new to talk about. What were the Japs trying to do? They must have captured scores of these machines in Singapore. Were they to go to Burma for use by the army? In our opinion they were totally useless as a weapon in battle (we had trained in them with the Gordon Highlanders in Singapore, and had no faith in them whatsoever; they were death-boxes). At a maximum of five miles to the gallon they would each need 100 gallons to get to Moulmein (if they didn't fall to bits on the way), and even then they would be totally worn out. Maybe the Japs thought they could be used to carry stores, in which case wouldn't it be obvious that their three tons of armour plate should be removed beforehand? And why choose Hintok to get them onto the 'road', when bringing them by train to Tarsao would have been the sensible way? We cannot fathom Jap thought processes; logic and advance planning do not seem to be a part of them.

The three Bren-carriers, by the way, are from our old carrier platoon of ten machines. The British army identification numbers are still on the sides and the camouflage paint is still exactly as we sprayed it on.

I come back to camp at the end of an exhausting day to find an extremely disturbing situation. After the departure of the working parties this morning, some little yellow turd in a white medical gown came into the camp, called out all the sick (about 400 men) on parade and split them into two parties. Without any pretence of sorting the men into medical categories – malaria, dysentery, ulcers, etc. – he ordered one lot to go to Tarsao and the other lot to stay at Hintok. Purely by chance, Ron was in the Tarsao lot, and with totally unprecedented Nip efficiency, they were moved out in half an hour, with no opportunity to shuffle themselves around from one group to another. So, with devastating suddenness, men were separated from friends with no likelihood of meeting up again – a heavy blow to morale in a situation where personal ties and mutual support are essential to wellbeing.

All the news which we have heard about Tarsao is bad. Supposedly a hospital camp, it has a reputation for being a place where men are sent to die, the Nip commandants of the working camps upriver using it as a convenient way of getting useless men off their strengths and thus making their figures to headquarters look better. Once they reach Tarsao, these wretched men, already seriously ill and unable to do useful work, are considered to be not worth food or medical treatment, and as far as the Nips are concerned they can rot and die. We have even heard it said that the British administration at Tarsao has long ago given up trying to change the Nips' attitude, and simply lets things drift from dreadful to even worse. This is only a rumour, but it is profoundly disturbing. Our recent experience at Tonchan reminds us that it can and does happen.

Wally, George and several others try to comfort me with optimistic reassurance, but they don't really help. After all, who actually *knows* anything? The corrosive fog of ignorance and uncertainty seeps into my heart, and dark foreboding suffuses all my thoughts. I have no possibility of moving to Tarsao to be with Ron, and not the smallest chance of hearing any news of him. He will simply be one of thousands in that dreadful place, and I shall very probably move further and further upriver, quite possibly to die myself in some godforsaken spot, and neither of us will know anything of the other.

My father is, presumably, in Changi gaol with civilian internees, if he hasn't been moved elsewhere or died. It is over fifteen months now since one of our unit saw him humping bags of rice at the Singapore docks. He was fifty-two years old then and not really fit enough for that kind of heavy physical work. My mother is, also presumably, somewhere in India, but may well have moved, and worrying about her three men will not have done her health any good at all, especially as a refugee who has lost her home and all her possessions, and is achingly alone and without support.

We are now, all four of our family, widely dispersed and completely out of touch with each other. The chances of ever being reunited as a family are slim and shrinking all the time, and if any one of us survives this war, what is the possibility that he (or she) will ever know what happened to the others? I fall into a black rage at the injustice of it all and at my help-lessness to do anything about it. God, how I hate the mindless savagery and inhuman barbarity of the Nips – and, for that matter, I haven't so far found God of much use either.

It is not a good mood to fall into, and I must pull myself out of it, get back to that detached mental attitude where only the present is important and has to be endured, and all other worries which are beyond dealing with right now are pushed to the horizon. Otherwise you are liable to blow all your fuses and fizzle out.

Far more than sufficient to each day is the evil thereof! Every day!

* * *

It is a curious fact, which became noticeable soon after setting up our first camp at Wampo, that the huts are so quiet at night. The standard hut, long and narrow with a doorless entrance at each end and another each side at the midpoint, accommodates 160 men (more or less) and five million bugs (give or take a few million). A platform of split bamboo, about knee-high from the mud floor, provides our total living space, so we sleep forty men in each quarter section of the hut, which allows some twenty-two inches for each man to stretch out but does not allow for restless sleepers to roll around or even bring their knees up when lying on one side.

It may be that this unavoidable proximity, where we lie like a row of toothpicks laid out on a strip of cardboard, touching each other, has caused us to impose strict discipline on ourselves, even in sleep, in order to avoid adding to the discomfort of our immediate neighbours. When we turn from one side to the other we come half-awake to hitch ourselves over, careful not to deviate from our central axis and nudge the next man, then drift back to sleep. And usually we have a forearm in front of our face so as not to breathe/cough/sneeze into the face twenty-two inches away. These things are a matter of mutual courtesy, for everyone's benefit. No one had to be told how to behave, it simply came about of its own accord.

The curious fact is that nobody snores! Or grunts, or puffs and wheezes, or even snorts, or talks in his sleep! Discussing this phenomenon, it seems that none of us even dreams, except very occasionally, and then it is usually just nonsense and nothing to do with the present (of which we have more than enough during the day) or with the past (which we deliberately try to hold off at a distance). Is this self-control or, as we think to be more likely, a subconsciously developed protection? It may help that, with all our multiplicity of diseases and the consequences of prolonged malnutrition, nobody ever seems to have a common cold! No stuffy noses or painful sinuses – there must be a reason for this, just as there is for everything else that either does or does not happen.

So when I find myself waking up during the night, or not getting off to sleep easily, I am not dreaming about Ron but worrying about him. Sleep is the one and only restorative we have, and if the day's wear and tear is not repaired during the night you start the next day with a handicap. After several such days in a row the accumulated effect becomes noticeable, work is even more of a wearying drag and the simple business of living through the day becomes more and more of an effort. My friends take off me as much of my labour on the track as they can, and try to ease the despondency which is settling over me, but it is not a matter of persuading myself to shake it off – that just does not work.

In this unhappy situation, from which I feel unable to break free despite concentrated mental effort, release comes in an entirely unexpected form. At the heart of my despair is (I know it) sheer loneliness – not only being without the companionship of my brother, but in the wakened recognition of the heart-wrenching dispersal of my family, all four of us scattered in limbo and quite possibly never to be reunited or even to have news of each other.

It is after dark and we have been chatting as usual in the moonlight when I suddenly feel unbearably saddened and want to be on my own. I retreat to my bedspace and stretch out, dreading the creeping despair which I know will come but not knowing what to do about it – in itself a new source of worry, which I recognise but cannot prevent. But instead I find myself relaxing, mind and body being eased unhurriedly into a state of calm, silken placidity. I have no thoughts or pain, all the many oppressions slide off me into nothingness, my brain becomes clear, my spirit lightens, my body is weightless, my innermost soul surges back to full power.

Floating on this dreamstuff cloud I become aware of her presence, her closeness to me, I can see her dear face, she is looking steadily at me, her eyes full of compassion and a small smile on her lips. No words, just that flow of tender warmth, invigorating and reassuring. I know with certainty who she is although we have never spoken to each other or even touched hands, for I fell in love with her only two years ago. It was an odd happening, not so much something new but more as if it were a renewal of a great love – even of many such loves between us – in different lives in past ages.

Two years ago, in Singapore, I was in a group of onlookers at a function concerned with war charities, raising funds for wounded Allied servicemen, and she was introducing honoured guests to the assembly. Without at first recognising it I found my attention concentrated on the petite, slender girl, her graceful form set off by a simple dark evening gown and a sparkling collar at her throat. A strapless dress it was, never before seen in staid Singapore, which brought forth acid mutters from a number of stuffy matrons near me.

I have always thought that love should come like this, not striking you from outside, but waiting within you for that magical touch which brings it to life whole and rounded, complete and unquestioned.

For several days I had drifted in a mist of happiness, letting it fill and saturate my whole being, unable at first to believe that love had really come to me so quickly and so smoothly. I had heard, however, that she was 'spoken for', so I decided to let it ride for a time while I thought out what might be done.

But the events of the time beat me to it.

The sudden and quite unexpected removal of so many of our friends, and their despatch to a place totally beyond any possibility of contact or news, has been a severe shock to all of us. Since leaving Singapore we have become a closely knit body of men – losing a few to death and leaving behind a small group of sick at Ban Pong. We are used to each other and have drawn great strength from our mutual comradeship. We do not all know each other's names, but the faces are familiar and we have all come through tough times together, creating a morale-sustaining bond throughout. Irrespective of different personal backgrounds, we work and live together in the most trying conditions, and do this easily and without friction.

We are now faced with the fact that this might happen to us again at any time, without warning. Not only could we lose sick men, but fit men could be detached to help out at any other camp where construction of the railway has fallen behind schedule, totally at random, at the whim of the Nips and without any say on our part. It is another worry to be pushed away and ignored, because as usual there is absolutely nothing we can do about it and there is no point in brooding on it.

A small event today has cheered us up immensely. It is not of any real import, but it does make us feel good to put one over the Nips in a subtle way without their realising we have done it.

Since moving upriver north of Tarsao we have, on a few occasions, seen parties of Jap frontline troops on the so-called road heading towards Burma. In the dry season these men stumped determinedly through the heat and thick dust, weighed down by kit and weapons and ammunition pouches, their uniforms saturated with sweat and their faces haggard with exhaustion. They seemed to move in small units, a platoon of about thirty with a warrant officer or sergeant at their head, and must have foot-slogged at least from Kanburi. In the wet season, ploughing through the muddy slush is a hell of a lot worse.

By late afternoon they would be knackered, the warrant officer obligated to march at the front of his squad to set the pace and prove his worth as leader, while the rest trailed behind and kept going as best they could. The warrant officer would call a rest halt, loosen his load and take a disciplined short drink from his water bottle, and wait for the tail to catch up. Just as the laggards (obviously the most affected by the stress of the march) threw themselves down gratefully, he would tighten up his equipment, jump to his feet and boot the latecomers solidly in the ribs. Refreshed and energetic, he would set off up the track without looking back, knowing that his men would be there even if only to avoid another belting at the next stop. It's a tough army!

Today we meet a larger than usual party, headed by a young officer, as we are returning to camp just before sundown. Seeing us he brings his column to a halt and comes over to us. After a polite exchange of army salutes he tells us, pleasantly enough, to yasumi – stand easy – and introduces himself in English. All civilised and polished.

He wants to know, 'Is this Booruma?', which takes us by surprise as, surely, he should know where he is if he is taking a body of troops to Burma. Being an officer, wouldn't he have been briefed before setting off as to distances, timetable, feeding and watering points, overnight stops?

George sees the opportunity immediately. 'You are going to Booruma? You have a long way to go.'

A shadow passes over the Jap's face. 'Long way? How far, do you know?'

George points northwards: 'From here to Burma, 400 kilos. To Moulmein, more 200 kilos. To Rangoon, more 1,500 kilos.' He draws figures in the mud, in a column so that they can be added up. 'You want to go beyond Rangoon? To Mandalay?'

'Yes, to Mandalay. Our armies are fighting near there. We are going to help them.' Adding proudly: 'We shall march all the way.'

'Well, that will be extra 2,500 kilos.' George adds the figure to the list and totals it all up. 'That's 4,600 kilos from here to Mandalay.'

The Jap officer's face, which has been twitching with anxiety at each stage, has gone pale. 'To Mandalay 4,600? You not wrong?' He can't – doesn't want to – believe it.

George simply can't resist it. 'Well, maybe little wrong.' And as the Jap's expression brightens: 'Maybe 5,000, I'm not sure.' We all watch the eyes widen and the mouth fall open in dismay. We put on our solemn, trustworthy faces.

A brief exchange of salutes, and we move off. 'Poor little bugger, he's probably marched only 300 kilos and is already fed up, now he finds he's faced with another 5,000! I'll bet he's not been an officer for long, he looks green.'

A bright moment at the end of a hard day, we talk it over with happy chuckles all the way back to camp. We don't really know the distances to Mandalay with any accuracy!

* * *

Four of us, all Volunteers, have found a secluded little beach where we can relax for half an hour away from the crowded camp area. We are now out of quarantine for cholera, no new cases having appeared for a clear twenty-one days, but that doesn't mean that the river water is safe, only that we can reasonably hope that there will not be a new outbreak unless it is brought in from outside.

Walking to our beach we find an elderly Tamil standing in the shallow water, still wearing his sarong while he washes himself as is the way of his people while bathing in a public place. Greeting him in Malay, we start a conversation and find that there is a camp of labourers not far from Hintok, working on the motor track. They have been warned by the Nips not to have any contact with us, and so far we are the first Europeans he has seen.

Coming out of the water, he scoops up a tiny pile of fine silt on a fingertip and carefully polishes his teeth with it, bending down to rinse his mouth with a handful of river water. We tell him that the river is the source of cholera and the water is highly dangerous to swallow, or even to take into the mouth. He smiles politely and says he knows that, but he is doomed to die and wants to be clean and presentable when it happens. Taking a comb from a little cloth bag he tidies his grey hair and then shakes out his damp sarong, rewinding it around his waist.

One of us offers him tobacco and paper from a tin which used to hold anti-gas ointment (these small flat tins being waterproof, and easily tucked into a fundoshi, are consequently highly valued). The Tamil accepts gratefully, saying he hasn't had a smoke for several weeks and apologises for his inability to offer anything in return.

He used to work on a rubber plantation, one amongst thousands drafted up to Siam to work as labourers. At first they were told that Siam was a good country to live in, plenty of food and schools for the children. This bit about schools was apparently thrown in because the men were reluctant to leave their families behind, the news having gone around that earlier drafts of men only had not been followed up (as had been promised) by their womenfolk and children.

But the rubber estates were not working, there was no money or anything to buy, and the food rations were very poor and getting worse. The Nips, faced with their continuing lack of enthusiasm to move, then cut off all food supplies so that the estate labourers had no choice but to agree to go to Siam, and were allowed to take families with them.

His camp is full of people in the last stages of despair, helpless and hopeless, starved and sick, without protection from the weather and with no medical facilities whatsoever. Many have already died, first of all the older folk, then new babies. Some of the younger children are being kept alive by mothers sacrificing their share of food, but the end is inevitable and will come soon. Everyone is now listlessly waiting, too weak and apathetic to be able to make any effort.

We are all much impressed by his personal dignity and calm acceptance of his fate. Between us we offer him all the scanty luxuries we have with us – a few pinches of tobacco, some paper, a hard-boiled egg, a couple of limes. They are not much, but we want to show our sympathy. We have to press him to accept. He says he knows we also have very little, but takes our gifts on our assurance that our friends back in camp will be glad we have been able to offer him something, even so little.

He leaves us with a grave salaam, which we return with sad hearts as we watch him slowly walking off down the path, leaning on a stick, to rejoin his wretched and doomed community.

After dark, the rain having stopped, we are gathered round a comforting blaze and relate our encounter with the Tamil gentleman. His personal composure, knowing that death is near and facing that fact unafraid, has left us with troubled feelings. Something beyond a natural sympathy for someone in his situation, and for all the others in his company of abandoned men and women, youngsters and infants.

We have been put into a work party finishing the construction of a timber bridge. A cutting has been completed, and sleepers and rails laid in it, and the bridge crosses a deep stormwater gully to a ledge already cut into the flank of the rocky hill opposite. The bridge has two tiers and is built in a curve. The outer rail is banked up a few inches so that trains will lean over slightly as they take the bend, and this requires the structure to be strengthened by props supporting the inner timbers. So far, the rains have brought raging torrents down the gully and it has not been possible to put the props into position.

Our job is to clamber down into the bed of the gully, receive the thirty-foot tree trunks lowered from above, and set the bases firmly into the rock-strewn bottom and fit the top ends into the bridge timbers. We have had a couple of days without rain and the gully is dry, but the rushing waters have scoured out every trace of soil and we have to try to create footings for the props in a jumble of boulders and smaller rocks wedged together on a solid rock base. We shall need drills and dynamite, and at least two full days' work, to do a proper job.

We are wondering how we might communicate all this to the Nips when screams of abuse from above, and a few random chunks of rock hurled at us, decide us to abandon all ideas of 'a proper job'. Grabbing the bottom end of a prop we drag it to a point where it can be jammed against a boulder, while above us, clinging to the bridge timbers wherever they can find a footing, others try to control the top end as it swings on a rope. A thirty-foot tree trunk, still fresh from the forest and full of sap, is heavy and awkward to manipulate, but we manage to align it so that it leans in against a bridge trestle. It is not actually giving any useful support, but from the high rim of the structure the top end cannot be seen, and provided no Nip comes down into the gully to make an inspection, we might get away with it.

Having done the first prop we can manage the others more easily. There are ten to put up, and by early afternoon we have set eight into place. While we have been doing this, a Dutch crew has been laying rails along the deck of the bridge, and from the thumping of sledgehammers on dogspikes, we can tell they have reached the far end.

We are wrestling with prop number nine when we hear a rumble of steel wheels way up above us, and a creaking and sighing of big timbers coming under stress. Looking up we see a rake of open-top steel wagons rolling slowly along the bridge, a locomotive at a panting stop in the mouth of the cutting having given the necessary shove to the wagons. Obviously, the Nips are testing the bridge to see if it will carry the load, ignoring the fact that there are still two props to be put into position. And to ballast the train, every wagon is full of our men, scores of them! The wagons come to a halt, we gaze up at the men some fifty feet above us, and they stare down at us. Then one of them calls out, in a ridiculously exaggerated aristocratic drawl, 'Ay say, you fellahs dahn theah, ay doo apologise in case anything goes wrong! You will have the most dradful bluddy headaches if we come dahn on you!'

The test being successful, the loco creeps forward, adding its weight while we retreat as fast as we can from the danger zone. It hooks up to the wagons and backs away slowly. Our eight props are still in place and we set about fixing the last two, while our pale faces recover their normal sunburnt complexion.

I suppose men are easier to use than sandbags as ballast – they climb in and out of the wagons themselves.

The monsoon's purple-black clouds are with us again, swollen-bellied even after they have emptied unbelievable quantities of rain on us. From memory, this eastern shore of the Indian Ocean has the heaviest rainfall in the world, receiving something like 600 inches in a year – that's about 15,000 millimetres in Nip reckoning – which falls mainly in the six months from May to November, give or take a week or two at either end.

An impenetrably black night when the rain buckets down is not the best time to develop gripes in your bowels. Without the faintest glimmer of light, I put on my hat and work my way down my narrow strip of bamboo until I can lower my feet to the earth and stand up. Turning right, and keeping a firm clamp on my burning bowels, I head for the end of the hut, fumbling for the edge of the sleeping platform and the upright bamboo poles as I go, to keep my direction to the doorway.

Outside, I am immediately under the full weight of the downpour and cannot see even as far as my feet, slithering and stumbling over rutted ground, ankle deep in a running flood. Heading for the sooted shelter over the latrine trench, hoping to find it in the equally sooty blackness of the night, I am totally lost within a minute. Blundering around, my bowels ever more urgent, I can hear muttered curses from other men in the same plight, but I can't see them. Then I feel long grass

ONE FOURTEENTH OF AN ELEPHANT

against my legs, so I have gone beyond the end hut into the tall trees clear of the camp area. It will have to do. I squat and relieve myself thankfully, tipping my hat back so that the water spouts from the brim down to my rump to clean myself as well as might be. God, what a bloody miserable way to live! Rainwater, swirling inches deep over the ground towards the river, carries the mess away instantly. You must, of course, remember to face uphill, to avoid fouling your feet!

The pressure is gone – for the time being anyway – but the stabbing pains are still there. They will be with me possibly for weeks, nagging continually and frequently flaring up and demanding to be eased. My urgent problem now is, how do I find my hut? I know it is the third from this end, but I quickly lose my sense of direction. Coming up against a tree – which tree, where in the camp? – I am exhausted. The pains of dysentery, my overall weakness, the solid blackness, the rain drumming on my hat and chilling my skin are too much for me. I fold on my haunches on the lee side of the tree for what little shelter it can give me, and slump in an Asiatic squat to wait for daylight. How long that will be I don't know. There's no moon to help me to guess, so I shall just have to wait. It works out to be well over four hours.

I am tired, hungry and in pain, wet and chilled to the bone, almost ready to give up.

Last night a number of empty barges were towed to our shore, and at tenko a few hundred of us are kept back while the rest move off on work parties. We are to collect our kit and be down at the river in ten minutes for moving out of Hintok.

This is the second time some bloody Nip has arbitrarily split us up, with no choice as to who goes and who stays. Close friends are separated, with no hope of getting together again, regimental groups are broken up – there is nothing deliberate about this on the part of the Nips, it just does not occur to them to give the smallest consideration to us. But if they simply told us to provide a certain number of men for a move, then we could arrange matters much more happily.

As usual we have no idea where we are going, but as soon as we are on board the barges are pulled upriver. This depresses me as every move northwards takes me further from Ron, with less possibility of getting back to him. There is, of course, no way of passing information in either direction, but rumours of dreadful conditions at Tarsao have persisted and I am filled with gloomy foreboding.

My friends do their best to cheer me up, but when someone suggests that 'no news is good news' I snap back an irritable, 'What a damn stupid thing to say!', followed by a despairing apology. We are all subject to spells of irascible behaviour, and nobody takes offence, but an apology makes me feel better by proving that I still like to observe the ordinary courtesies of civilised society. It is very important that we do so, because it helps to maintain our philosophical balance.

Thoughtfulness and compassion for each other – without these, we may as well give up.

8

The Cattle Rustlers Camp

AUGUST 1943

The riverside scenery doesn't change much, the thickly forested hills rising steeply on either hand with bare rock showing in places. We are now well into the wet season, the river is brown with mud carried from its upper reaches and the fast current keeps our progress down to little more than walking pace. There are frequent twists and turns, making pleasant variations to our view upriver, with small sandy beaches on the insides of the curves where the current is slacker. Only the launches' staccato pom-pom-pom-pom disturbs the absolute quiet, echoing back from the hillsides, and we don't find that to be intrusive. For us the journey is a brief time of peace and restfulness, almost totally lacking in comfort though it may be – but who expects to be comfortable nowadays? We have long ago learned to accept whatever turns up and simply make the best of it, thankful if it is not as bad as it might have been and not even bothering to curse if it is worse – there is just no point in doing so. We are not in any way cowed; we have fully adjusted ourselves to looking squarely at hard facts without the faintest edge of wishful thinking.

There must be about 400 of us standing crammed together in the open cargo holds of wooden Siamese barges. Nobody can sit down, we are on our feet for as long as the voyage might last, and there will be only the tea in our bottles, nothing to eat, until we are put ashore. We do not expect anything else and don't let it bother us. We are content with the moment – it's not even raining!

Swinging in towards the bank we take a look at our new campsite, and a comment 'Lovely spot for a picnic' is indeed appropriate. Instead of the usual narrow beach the shore is a big level area only a foot or so above the river waters, carpeted with lush green grass and dotted with tall trees throwing a pleasant dappled shade. We haven't seen such luxuriant grass anywhere along the river, and the trees are quite different from the scrubby growth which covers the hillsides. Standing straight and smooth-barked, they are close enough together to allow only filtered sun to pass through their canopies, but with plenty of space for us to pitch tents in between.

And tents there are! One of the barges has carried our kwalis and bags of rice, together with sufficient British army tents for every man to sleep under cover, and without too much crowding. After the horrors of Tonchan South, it is almost too good to be true. Our group bags a spot close to the river, at the corner of the site, and our tent is pitched in quick time. Even the midday rice ration is more plentiful than normal, and there is a piece of oily dried fish to go with it. We are really in danger of being spoiled. The rest of the day is ours, we are told. Some railway regiment Nips will come tomorrow to get us working.

We are camped in an area as flat as a table top, stretching from the river for several hundred yards to the foot of an almost vertical rocky face, where trees and bushes grow wherever their roots can find a grip. Near our tent there is a split which looks as though it might provide a route through the hillside.

The rest of the day is spent lazing around, after bringing

firewood for the cookhouse. We have only a handful of Nips with us and they are looking after their own comfort and showing no interest in us. We soak in the river, dry our kit in the sun, lie in the grass and doze, sit around fires and chat. It is a brief time of spiritual healing and we make the most of it.

Next morning we come back to reality, but not too abruptly. We have our breakfast rice and wait for someone to take an interest in us.

Two Nips turn up and we fall in to be sorted out into working parties. These men are noticeably different from our camp Nips and Koreans. They have a brisk and competent look about them, no shouting and gibbering, but an air of getting things done. A quick count of numbers, and we all hike off in a body through the ravine which takes us to the far side of the hill. We are in a valley running in the general alignment of the Kwei Noi, a swath of trees has already been cleared down the centre and hammers and drills are laid out ready for us. There is also a group of Nips preparing dynamite charges with detonators and fuses. It looks all very professional, so there is no possibility of getting away with funny tricks such as undersized shot-holes.

We are given a bunch of thin bamboo notched to show the depth for drilling, so that we can check our work as we go along, without supervision. The 'dynamito' Nips distribute themselves amongst us, priming holes as they are completed. There is no set number of holes to be completed by each pair of men before knocking off. We work steadily but without interference until late afternoon. It is a full day's work, but not excessive and without stress. If it continues like this, we shall be quite content.

The charges are detonated after we have left, which means that we have not had to stand around ready to dodge flying chunks of rock. We are not used to such consideration for our safety!

Next morning some of us clear loosened earth and rock and dump it at the sides, while the rest start drilling further along the line. Again, nobody shouts at us while we work, but it is clear that our progress is constantly watched for, as the cutting begins to take shape and depth, small groups are detached to drill where the underlying rock has not broken up, hammers and drills already laid out on the spot. These Nips know how to plan ahead and to provide the equipment needed in sufficient quantities, and as long as we produce a satisfactory flow of work, they let us get on with it. Breaks for morning and afternoon smoko and tea are punctual, and there is a full hour for midday rice.

At the end of the day we are handed back to our camp guards, who count us at the usual tenko and then forget about us. In comparison with the last few months it is such a pleasant time that we are able to unwind and relax mentally and physically. The rations are still miserably poor in every respect, but at least we are getting enough rice to feel reasonably satisfied. How we have changed – we no longer hanker after meat and such luxuries. All we ask is enough rice to fill our bellies!

One thing has struck us as odd. We are excavating a cutting along which the railway track will eventually be laid, but we have not seen any sign of connecting with another camp, not even survey markers. Our smooth-floored cutting with its stormwater drain along each flank simply starts and ends in virgin forest. And that's how it is on the eleventh day when our engineer Nips tell us, 'Worko finisho. Asta worko nai (Tomorrow no work).' After tenko that evening our camp Nips are all smiles. 'Worko finisho, orru man yasumi san shi hiru (all men rest three four days). Mateo boato (Wait for boats).'

There is a perfunctory count after morning rice, and we find ourselves in a totally unaccustomed state of idleness. Our Nips are cheerful still – they must have had a pat on the back from the engineers for providing such a good labour force. When someone asks for permission to walk outside the camp area, there is a casual wave of the hand, and within a few minutes the energetic ones are out of sight while the rest of us settle down earnestly to being plain lazy. Who wants to go scrambling over rocky hill slopes in bare feet?

We are disturbed by the barking exhaust of a launch heading in towards us. We recognise a Nip from Hintok, and one of our officers who has news for us. The local Nip shoko (officer) in charge of railway construction is so pleased with our work and good behaviour that he has sent us a few bags of rice and dried fish (the yellow oily kind, which is our favourite because you can fry a duck egg in the oil) as a thank-you 'presento'. Not only that, he has brought all our back wages owing to us and there will be a Siamese trading boat coming along shortly! This really is a day to remember!

The Siamese floating shop duly arrives, with duck eggs, green limes, bananas, brown palm sugar cakes (the Malays call it jaggery or gula melakka), and (for the addicts) hanks of Siamese tobacco (known to us as hag's bush) and paper for rolling cigarettes. What more could we want?

Our Nips get their cut from the boatman, in the form of several bottles of Siamese hooch which will keep them in a happy mood for a few days.

In half an hour the campsite is blue with acrid tobacco smoke – how can human lungs stand up to it? – and the powerful odour of stinkfish sizzling in hundreds of mess tins. The cookhouse boys have produced a double ration of rice, and we stuff ourselves with a rich mixture of rice, fried eggs, greasy dried fish with palm sugar (it takes the edge off the fish), followed by a hand of deliciously sweet thumb-sized golden bananas.

The rain, which falls most days at this time of the year, holds off, the sun shines benignly on us, our stomachs are full (but will still accept an occasional banana or lime), all is peace and serenity, and we doze stretched out on the grass. We haven't had a day like this since God knows when! Bliss, perfect bliss! A beer or two, well chilled, would be good, but you mustn't expect too much.

Someone is shouting, but it takes a long time to penetrate into our consciousness, largely because we don't want to hear it. Slowly we become aware that they are not Nip voices but our own men's, and the words are, 'Meat! Tons of it! Come and get it!' Really, are we expected to believe that?

An appetising smell of cooking meat drifts over us. There is a hubbub of voices over at the cookhouse. The odour overcomes our inertia, and we go over to see what it's all about. There it is, chunks of beef waiting to be cut up, and thick slices being boiled, fried, grilled, and charred by the impatient into burnt offerings. 'Help yourself, mate, there's plenty of it!'

The problem is how to go about it. Nobody has needed anything more than a spoon to feed himself for so long. We are just not equipped to tackle chunks of raw beef. Some of us have a table knife and fork tucked away in our kit (unused, but we don't throw away anything at all), but these are useless until meat has been cooked. Then we see one of the cookhouse lads taking off slices and handing them out to all and sundry, and we find places around a fire. Our stomachs, comfortably full a couple of hours ago, easily take in half a pound or so of grilled beef and, no doubt, will be ready for evening rice (double rations!) and stinkfish when the time comes. How wonderfully efficient and adaptable is the human stomach – indeed, the whole body!

We soon learn how the beef came into camp. Some of the men exploring the back slopes of the hill came across cattle droppings, then saw a number of animals browsing amongst the trees. Catching them was not easy – the men had no ropes and the bullocks were agile and fast moving. But the hungry hunters were determined and persistent, and eventually a beast was cornered and dragged back to camp. The cooks quickly dealt with it, the hunters were given the first choice of meat and our surprised Nips were offered a large piece. In return, the Nips found some lengths of rope which made it a lot easier to capture and bring in two more animals. The herd must have been strays from groups of cattle being driven north to feed Nip troops upriver.

It has been a marvellous day, and there is the prospect of two or three yasumi days to follow, with an abundance to eat and nothing to do!

A boisterous hunting party is away immediately after morning tenko. They bring in five bullocks within a couple of hours. Two are turned loose, because we simply cannot use more than three in a day, and meat won't keep for long in this climate. To avoid fly-breeding, the skins and other material that we cannot immediately use are buried deep. There is beef stew available all day, whenever you want it, and another boat-load of extras from a Siamese trader. For us it is a miraculous interval of food in plenty and total rest.

Does every ointment have to have a fly in it? To take the edge off what would otherwise be perfection? Throughout the kingdom of meat-eating animals it is entirely natural to kill other living creatures for sustenance. And, of course, there is an ever-present risk of being killed and eaten in turn. The killing methods are invariably painful and seldom quick, but I wouldn't think that any wild animal has a worried conscience about that. The need for food has to be satisfied, and the means of obtaining it are dictated by the tools provided by nature. All very straightforward. But human beings, despite being animals in a physical sense, are different in that they think, and analyse their thoughts. In general we try to distinguish between right and wrong, and this can conflict with natural urges.

Today we witnessed (inadvertently, but the closeness of camp life compels you to see everything that happens) the slaughter of the three bullocks which were unlucky enough to be caught. Our animal instincts, and our undernourished bodies, demand that they be killed, while our human thinking regrets the necessity and requires that it be done as painlessly as possible.

The Nips refuse to shoot them or to provide us with a rifle and three cartridges. In the cookhouse we have two Australians who grew up in Queensland cattle country (they dealt with yesterday's kill) and it just happens that we are in the vicinity when they go to work. The unsuspecting animal stands quietly, its head snubbed up closely to a tree with a length of rope, and an expertly swung sledgehammer strikes it precisely in the exact centre of its forehead. Instantly its legs collapse, and a length of thick steel wire is rammed through its ear into the brain. Death is immediate and the timespan for pain can only have been a second or two, but the sheer crudity of the method upsets us badly as we hurry away so as not to see the messy processes which must follow.

A little later, when we are able to talk about it, we recognise that in fact the kill was conducted with great skill and, if the necessity was accepted, in as humane a manner as was available to us. Which may make us feel somewhat easier but, of course, did nothing at all for the victim except that it suffered far less than it would have done had it been overtaken by some natural predator.

It has been a troubling experience, and I think we found it so because it was our first close-up view of death by sudden violence. We have all seen our own people die, but this has always been a slow linking of starvation to malnutrition, to disease, to disintegrating flesh in ulcers and internal organs. During the campaign, it happened that we did not see mutilation or death. The impact of witnessing the abrupt destruction of life is different from watching slow agonising decay after which death comes as a relief.

A point is raised during discussion: 'The Catholic church says that animals do not have souls, therefore no wrong is done by killing them for food.'

'But what about killing them for sport, or for trophies?'

'Well, that might be a matter for individual perception, but in the eyes of the church it might be deplorable but not sinful.'

'Doesn't that dodge the question, which is to distinguish between necessary taking of animal life and its frivolous destruction? All life is God's gift and must be respected.'

'Did our Christian forefathers declare that it was no sin to kill animals because they do not have souls? Or was it the other way round? Were they simply greedy for meat, and did they seek to exempt themselves from sin by declaring that animals had no souls, and therefore could be killed without compunction?'

'Doesn't the Bible say that God has given man total dominion over other creatures?'

'And precisely what does that mean or imply? Does anyone really know? Or is it deliberately vague enough to be fitted into anybody's conscience?'

'Should there not be a clear and definitive answer to all these queries? Why can we Christians not accept the church's assurances without uneasy feelings? And if we do have doubts in this, what other attitudes should we look at sceptically?'

My thoughts go back to my school's chapel, five years ago, where we attended services twice a day from Mondays to Saturdays, three times on Sunday, plus a fourth if you went to Holy Communion at 7 am. There was a hymn which stuck in my throat. I refused to sing the words because I found them intolerable in their bland smugness:

> As pants the hart for cooling streams
> When heated in the chase,
> So longs my soul, oh God, for thee,
> And Thy refreshing grace.

The mindless comparison between the agonies of a hart driven to exhaustion by hounds and horsemen (quite probably plump clerics!) with the spiritual maunderings of some self-abasing friar, always struck me as cruelly inappropriate and quite nauseating – a prime example of smug, self-righteous thoughtlessness continually stuffed down our throats in our religious guidance and development.

'Come to think of it, if the cattle which we are slaughtering may fairly be considered as sacrifices to our need for food, how should we see our own present situation? Are we not being held as beasts of burden, to service Japan's determination to build this railway to sustain her armies in Burma? To be worked even to death with absolute indifference – doesn't that mean that we are also sacrificial objects?'

'And those of us still alive when the railway is completed, as it will be – we can be sure of that, whatever the difficulties – will we simply be wiped out? We all know that the Nips are quite capable of that!'

Oh dear! There's no point trying to think this through. We shall have to see how things turn out and do our best at the time. And so to bed. There will be beef stew again tomorrow!

Two more days of luxurious idleness, and we are told to be ready to move out early tomorrow. Not by river, but on foot to the next big camp, which is called Kinsayok. As usual we are given no information as to distance, but what does that really matter anyway? We shall keep going until we get there, we shall be provided with nothing at all on the way, and we need not expect anything when we arrive. A routine move, in fact, except for two things – a boat will come to pick up tents and kwalis, for which purpose a small party will stay behind and travel by boat; and our Nips have agreed to our catching bullocks in the scrub and driving them to Kinsayok to contribute to camp rations. On our last day we manage to bring in fifteen animals, though I really think nobody expects to see them in our cookhouses once the Kinsayok Nips get their hands on them.

It has been an unusual experience, working with real engineers instead of our usual bunch of incompetent idiots. An honest day's work meant a complete absence of bashings and irritating harassment, there was proper concern for our safety when dynamiting, and (totally unexpected) a handout of extra rations in recognition of satisfactory work.

We know we are supporting our enemy's war effort by building this railway, but we don't have any choice in the matter. We shall have to leave it to the RAF to destroy war stores as they arrive at the far end, after the railway starts to function. In the meantime we would find life a lot easier if the Nips would treat us with even reasonable decency.

Even the weather has been kind to us. There must be a catch in all this, somewhere – it's too good to continue for long.

9

Kinsayok Camp and the Sawmill

AUGUST TO OCTOBER 1943

Boosted both in morale and in the flesh on our bones, we set off for Kinsayok, soon finding ourselves on the mud-track 'road' which, after several weeks of monsoon rains, is now almost impassible on foot. Even a slight upward gradient is difficult in bare feet, which cannot find a proper grip in the sloppy mud. Our bullocks, each attended by one of our men with a rope round its neck, plod along in the rear.

Rounding a bend we find ourselves coming into the area of a Jap army bivouac, brown tents dotted amongst the trees. It is a cavalry or mounted infantry unit, men rubbing their horses down and generally attending to them. Beyond a casual glance at us as we move through, the men show no interest in us.

There is a sudden outburst of noise, a horse screaming in pain and fear and a Jap furiously shouting. The horse is at one end of a taut tope, plunging wildly in the slippery mud, its teeth bared and eyes staring white. At the other end of the rope is a yelling Jap soldier clutching a long and whippy bamboo with which he is thrashing the animal with all his strength.

Our reaction is immediate. Every one of us stops walking

323

and turns towards the Jap and his terrified horse, and a deep-throated growling swells into a steady roar of disapproval. Angry voices, Australian accents loud and clear – 'Yer flamin' baboon, yellow bastard, stinkin' cowardly creep, bloody mongrel, dungheap, flat-faced lump of shit, miserable son of a whore' being only some of the more polite insults hurled across the road.

The Jap troops are suddenly quiet and still. They are puzzled and don't know what to make of it all. Surprise and uncertainty show on their faces – probably they have never had contact with POWs. The man who caused the ruckus is staring at us with his mouth gaping, his horse still trying to back away. He is the focus of several hundred pairs of eyes glaring at him, and must be fully aware that all the hostile shouting is aimed at him personally. The effect is almost comic. The bully-boy's bravado drains out of him, he drops the cane and rope and shuffles off into the trees, glancing back nervously at us as he goes. The horse stands trembling, head hanging.

Our shouting and growling stop as if switched off, and there is dead silence. Facing left we resume our march and the Jap soldiers, as if coming out of a trance, get on with grooming their horses.

It is a weird feeling. We exposed ourselves to the possibility of an unpleasantly painful reaction, but nothing happened. Our outburst was totally spontaneous, yet it was initiated and controlled as precisely as the swirling flight of a flock of birds obedient to mysterious signals. In some extraordinarily subtle way, each one of us received and responded to commands without even being aware of them – and where did those commands come from?

I think back a few months to our confrontation with the camp guards at Wampo South, when 400 of us sprang, instantaneously and as if with a single mind, to a fine point of readiness for violent action. We really have no concept of the intellectual forces that surround us and motivate us, individually and collectively. Which is, perhaps, just as well.

It is not a long march to Kinsayok, but we have had to keep to the pace of the little herd of cattle – which, as we expected, is appropriated by the local Nips and led away as soon as we arrive. Counted up and dispersed to the usual bamboo and attap huts, we set out to look for friends amongst the men already there. It is too early for work parties to come in, and the sick who have been allowed to stay in camp are mostly in a bad way. The Nips have been ruthless in sending out every man who can stay on his feet – some who are unable to walk as far as the railway site have to be carried there by their mates. The Nips say that if they are not able to dig or carry earth they can still do hammer-and-tap drilling, for which they do not even need to stand up! The sheer callousness of the Nips still defies our understanding, even after eighteen months.

We are warned to be very careful in our behaviour on the worksite as the Nips are short-tempered and do not hesitate to bash any man for any reason whatever. They have set up a workshop with a forge, to hammer new cutting edges to drill bits handed in at the end of each day. The work is exhausting and goes on all night without cessation. Our men are worn out by morning. Smiths are men of muscle and their work demands a substantial diet, but the Nips expect us to function fully on the miserable rubbish which they provide. And when these night-workers are trying to rest during the day, the Nips frequently turn them out to dig latrines in their own area, and to bring in firewood and water for their cookhouse. So we have nothing pleasant to look forward to when we parade next morning for our first tenko.

Damn right, the Nips make special efforts to ensure that we new boys learn the rules very quickly. Careful as we are to work steadily, Nips walking among us indiscriminately hand out painful whacks with bamboo canes to encourage greater effort. There is no set task which would allow us to go back to camp when it is completed. We start work soon after daylight and finish when we are told we can stop, which is usually after dark.

We are now about halfway through the wet season and the heavy strain of drilling shot-holes and shifting sodden earth, stumbling on bare feet through the gluey mud and jagged rock, is telling on us. The food is still indescribably poor and dirty, with the inevitable consequences of scoured guts and wasted muscle. Dripping forest trees, gloomy skies, rain bucketing down incessantly, leaky and bug-infested bamboo slats to sleep on – really, we would appreciate something to cheer us up, just a little!

Our daily lives are ruled by daylight and darkness which, in this part of the world, does not vary much throughout the year. The clock doesn't really mean anything. We are out of step with Siamese reckoning anyway, as our Nips operate on Tokyo time, which is two hours ahead of us – a six o'clock sunrise is eight o'clock camp time – and nobody has a watch; they were all sold to the Siamese long ago. So we have gradually developed our own personal methods of assessing time as we used to know it, in the daytime by a glance at the sun and during the night by the moon, its position in the sky or whether it has not yet risen or has already set. Though rough and ready, it works well enough. Anticipating meal times is not so reliable – our stomachs tell us all day (and night) that the next meal is overdue!

At Wampo Central we had a bugler, whose dismal wailing dragged us into consciousness in the last of the night's shadows. By now we have all developed an unfailing ability to wake up and get on our feet just before daylight, ready for the day's excitements and pleasures. It is a useful discipline that helps us to mentally tune in, right at the start of the day.

At the first glimmers of watery light, we are standing at the edge of the parade area, waiting for the call to line up for tenko. Our huts are on our right hand, the Nips and Koreans live over to the left. Kinsayok has more of a military atmosphere than our previous camps, and this morning we watch as a young officer comes into view. He looks as if he is the duty officer of the day, with his uniform clean and pressed, cap on precisely straight, left hand on the scabbard of his two-handed sword to prevent it swinging, and a definite no-nonsense air about his bearing. The Jap guards are already in place, their efficient gunso has seen to that and calls them to attention. With only the briefest acknowledgment, the officer strides on to the Koreans' hut, calling the gunso to come with him.

We have gathered that Koreans have an unusual status in the Jap army, being in uniform and armed but having no military rank at all. They are simply 'Koreans', of lesser standing than the lowest Jap recruit, and subject to abuse by all and sundry. In return they look down on the whole Jap nation with towering contempt, holding that they were civilised way back before the Japs came down from their trees. Well, what nation could have any other opinion?

To return to this morning's events, the Korean guards haven't yet put in an appearance – maybe it is still not yet time to parade? While the officer waits outside, the gunso, roaring and bellowing, stamps into the hut. In moments the Koreans are out and shuffling into some sort of line, hurriedly pulling their bits of clothing together and coming to attention. The gunso barks at them, then the officer gets started on the first man with sledgehammer slaps to the head, right hand, left hand, backhand. When the officer moves on to the next Korean, the gunso adds his own contribution to the first. Any man who falls down is booted solidly until he gets back on his feet. Not a man escapes punishment.

It has been a display of deliberate brutality, stony-faced, ritualised, cold-blooded, sickening. And humiliating – this is obvious, and as we realise that we slide out of the area to another part of the parade ground. These Koreans will be with us for the rest of the day, in a foul mood, and we definitely do not want them to recognise us as having witnessed their humiliation. Loss of face is all-important!

Their bruises come out beautifully during the day, and we manage to keep out of their way reasonably well. Our feelings are mixed between satisfaction at seeing our guards at the receiving end, and disgust at the use of savage bullying as a disciplinary measure.

The Nips have discovered the word 'speedo' again and use it incessantly, at full volume. They know we cannot pretend not to understand it, and we very soon learn that it is unwise to ignore it. Where the rumour comes from we don't know, but we hear that the whole of this accursed railway is now being pressed forward with ferocious intensity as a giant 'speedo' project. It is said that upriver camps have been addressed at tenko by senior Jap officers that death and sickness are now of no consequence, work must be completed regardless of casualties. We must be prepared to die, as Japanese soldiers are, in the service of the Emperor, who has decreed that the railway must be operating by the end of September. This year, not next year. And August, according to our men familiar with Siam, is the worst of the rainy months – we ain't seen nuthin' yet!

There is worse to come. Bashing our drills into limestone rock, shovelling earth and rubble into tongas and lugging them to the side, we are joined by a group of men whom we immediately recognise. They are the camp cooks (including the night shift) and sanitation squad, who have been ordered out to work on the track. The Nips say they will not return to the cookhouses until our output of work has improved. Meanwhile there will be no cooked food for us. If we still continue to be lazy and uncooperative, the sick will be turned out as well. The situation appals us. The sick allowed to remain in camp are in such bad shape that they can hardly stand, but we have no doubt that the Nips will not hesitate to clear them out, even though it would mean death for every one of them.

What are our officers doing about it? Surely this must have stirred them up enough to protest strongly? We don't really think that protests will actually get anywhere, but at least they should make a determined stand to protect their men in such an extreme situation.

Well, yes, maybe they did, but if so we haven't been told. What we do know is that the Nips threatened to turn them out to work on the railway, and that really did arouse them. There are limits, after all! The upshot was that the officers agreed to dig new latrine trenches (a never-ending health necessity, for the Nips as well as for us), which would release the sanitation squad. Exactly how true all this is we cannot tell, but the cooks are vehement in their condemnation of the selfishness and indifference to our welfare displayed by our officers. Looking back over our months in Siam, it does seem to be part of a pattern.

It is our Nips' whim today that we return to camp before sunset. We are in a thoroughly bloody-minded mood, dog-tired, with no evening meal in prospect and fuming with resentment towards our officers as much as towards the Nips. And what do we see as we come into the camp area? It brings us to a halt, staring in amazement.

There are three shit trenches, dug to hip depth. Shovelling out earth are some fifteen men, with a few more standing at the rims to scoop up the dirt and scatter it about. This is ordinary enough. The spectacle, in our eyes, lies in the appearance of the workmen, which is so unusual that we need a few moments to sort it out.

They are wearing shorts or trousers and boots, their bare torsos and arms are an unblemished white, their faces clean-shaven or with neat moustaches, hair brushed and trimmed, and with more flesh on their bones than we have seen for ages. The penny drops. These are the officers who sportingly took on the undignified work of digging latrines in order to release the regular sanitation squad (composed of 'light sick' men) for slogging on the railway! How kind and compassionate of these officers, showing such concern for the welfare of sick men, to their own disadvantage!

What is their reaction as we stand gawping at them? Not a cheery greeting, making a joke of it, but angry glares and snarled orders – 'Don't stand there staring, move on!' – and similar friendly remarks. Is their personal discomfiture so great?

The contrast is too much. We didn't know that there were such men in the camp, practically untouched by the privations of being POWs. From our bunch of thin to skinny walnut-stained scarecrows, blotched with sores and shaggy with wildly sprouting hair and beards, comes a beautifully elegant and modulated voice: 'I say, you fellows, do you see what I see? Here in this remote jungle, far from any civilis-ation, we have stumbled across an unknown tribe of white men, whose occupation appears to be to dig trenches in a cleared space in the jungle. Gad, sir, it's almost impossible to trust my eyes! I must report this to the Royal Geographical Society the moment I get back to London!'

The spell is broken. We start to giggle, then laugh uproariously as we walk on into camp. Angry shouts of 'bloody impertinent' and 'filthy rabble' follow us as we go. Who cares? We don't! It's not our pride that has been bruised!

The situation is, however, extremely serious. Having had our laugh, we know we are facing a crisis. The Nips cannot retreat from their demands and we cannot agree to seriously sick men being forced out to work – it will kill them quickly just as it is killing us slowly. Totally unresponsive to argument and the basic decencies of humanity, the Nips need only with-hold food supplies to break our resistance. They still need us to complete their bloody railway, and this is our only strength, but they are quite capable of leaving us to die off once the rail-way is running through.

We don't know of any other big project which might induce the Nips to keep us alive as a labour force. Even if there were something of the kind, would we simply slave on that job, and then be killed off? If so, we might just as well bring everything – both the railway and ourselves – to an end right now.

It is curious how we can think along these lines. We have a nearly hopeless present and a totally unpredictable future, and there is absolutely nothing we can do to influence events. Yet we are able to discuss matters calmly and rationally, no hysteria, no despair, just a thoughtful recognition of facts. The single conclusion we can reach is that, if the situation deteriorates beyond any possibility of recovery, we shall have to take to the bush and make the best of things after that. But we all know that such action would undoubtedly bring on the immediate slaughter of every man in the hands of the Nips (my thoughts go to my brother at Tarsao). What is the alternative – if there is one?

Wait and see, do what you can when something has to be done, and hope you can achieve something. There's no point losing sleep over it.

We don't know what has been going on behind the scenes. We are the people most affected, but no one tells us anything. The rumour is that our medical officers have told the Nips that they have sent out every man who is even partly fit to work and will not send out any more. If the Nips insist on more men being turned out, they will have to visit the 'hospital' and point to every man who, in their opinion, can work. The results will be reported to the Red Cross after the war, and the Nips will have to take full responsibility for their actions.

Astonishingly, this highly dangerous strategy works. Our doctors get their faces slapped for being uncooperative, but the Nips can save face by saying that they have nobody with medical training who can pick out men fit enough to work. In the background, we feel, is the totally overriding demand from high up that work on the railway must be kept up without any slackening, and even one day at a standstill will bring down wrath on the Nips responsible.

Normal conditions are resumed. The officers dig latrines for a few more days so that we all know who is the boss, and our hearts bleed for them! Respect for our medical officers, so often at the sharp end of our troubles, is unbounded and genuine. The cooks are back at their kwalis, and again we have to listen to the familiar tedious rantings of our Nips in the bush. There is no opportunity for slacking off even a little; those interfering little bastards are continually moving around swishing their canes, and by the end of the day we are dead beat. Our morale, nevertheless, is as good as ever – some people say that, like the soul, morale has no actual substance, but I think it could be made of old truck tyres.

The old regular yasumi day – every tenth day, when we were paid – which originated for us in Singapore in the working camp at River Valley Road, but was never regularly upheld until Wampo, was abandoned when we left Wampo. Since then it has been a haphazard event, sometimes with weeks in between, usually announced at evening tenko for the following day. Possibly it is granted when funds arrive in camp for our working pay which, at present, is equivalent to just over three pence a day in sterling.

Right in the midst of the 'speedo' maelstrom, a yasumi day is announced. Not only that, our pay is brought right up to date, weeks of it! And, to our absolute amazement, our contingent from the Cattle Rustlers Camp has been awarded a special payment of ten ticals each, a bonus solemnly labelled by the Nips as 'Danger Money' for our good work with dynamite at that camp. It seems to be given on the recommendation of the Nip engineers, who not only behaved decently towards us but also gave us a 'presento' of extra rations. By twisted Nip logic, we are being paid 'Danger Money' for working in perfectly safe conditions, while we now get nothing extra for blasting rock despite imminent risk of injury and death every day!

Ten ticals, fifty days' pay, all at once! We are rich – it's a heady feeling.

Kinsayok has a fairly well-stocked canteen, with Siamese boat traders calling frequently with a good variety of foodstuffs and plenty of their crude tobacco. There are high quality Virginia-type cigarettes made and packaged in the country, but they are expensive and to our men, who have become accustomed to shag tobacco, they are almost tasteless. Not having any cash at all we have, nevertheless, looked in at the canteen occasionally, unable to buy anything but driven by the same urge that brings a penniless urchin to a sweet-shop window. It hurt, but we had to do it!

Now we descend on the canteen like locusts. Duck eggs, palm sugar cakes, bananas, limes, a bottle of runny pig fat, chilli sauce, precious rock-salt, a little bit of everything to ease the awful monotony of our rations. But what are those things tucked away in the shadowy back corner of the hut? Good God, rolls of white toilet paper, tins of strawberry jam, small packets of paper for rolling cigarettes! George and I spot them at the same time, look at each other and cannily move a few paces away from the cheerful mob making their purchases. 'Nobody else seems to have noticed them yet. Let's wait until the crowd clears, otherwise the whole stock will disappear before we have a chance to get at it.'

When everyone has hurried away with his treasures to light fires and start cooking eggs, we front up at the counter. The man on the other side is a big fellow, and when he sees us staring past him he moves his bulk to block our view. Before we can say anything he tells us, 'Them's not for you, them's for officers only!'

'How much are the bumf and the strawberry jam?'

'Too expensive for you. I told you, officers only!'

'My bum may not be as soft as an officer's, but it's just as sensitive. And I like strawberry jam. How much are they? My money's as good as anyone's.'

Reluctantly, he tells us. A dollar a roll, a dollar a tin. That's five days' pay, each item! A lustful surge builds up in me, shoving aside the thought of such sheer extravagance. We deserve just a little luxury, we've earned it the hard way, dammit we *need* it, to hell with the cost! The decision to spend so much on trivialities is a big effort. Holding my breath to stifle my conscience, I say, 'I'll take one bog-roll and two tins,' and George (in much the same tense state) says, 'Same for me.'

There, it's done! Fifteen days' pay from each of us! Back in our hut we sit on our bedspaces and stare at each other.

'How could we have been so absolutely bloody stupid?'

'Like greedy kids!'

'And we don't even have a tin-opener!'

'Let's return it all, see if we can get our money back?'

I'm beginning to tremble; I can't reconcile my conscience with this shocking extravagance. Eighteen months of starvation, every cent to be hoarded and spent with exacting self-control, and here I am tossing whole dollars away for one roll of toilet paper and two tins of strawberry jam! I could burst into tears, I really could, at my weakness.

George produces a Boy Scouts clasp knife from its hiding place in his haversack. 'We do have a tin-opener. Let's see what the jam is like.'

The moment he punctures the lid and starts to lever it up, we catch the gorgeous aroma of strawberries and sugar. My nerves immediately steady themselves as I inhale the rich scent, and my self-confidence snaps back into place. I am totally satisfied that I made the sensible decision in treating myself to a little luxury. After all, I remind myself, the money came from a bonus and was therefore not wages! A little sulkily, my self-reproach admits defeat and retreats.

We would have been glad to find the jam to be of even mediocre quality, but this is by any standards magnificent. The tin is crammed with big berries of a beautiful colour, whole and unblemished, the tiny spaces between them filled with sugary strawberry pulp of the same standard. The label is printed in Japanese characters only, so it must be imported from the homeland. I have never seen such perfect jam under any label, even from Switzerland. It really is a solid strawberry and syrup pack.

While we slowly spoon up the so-delicious jam, taking our time to get the utmost pleasure from it, several of our friends dash off to the canteen. The officers will have to go short!

Dreamy nostalgia clings to me until tenko jerks me back to reality just before sunset. After evening rice I find I am disinclined to join the others around a fire, and stretch out on my knobbly strip of bamboo slats to relax and, if I am lucky, to fall again into the spell of the past.

I make no effort to recall events, I simply unwind and make my mind receptive to whatever may drift in. And there she is, my dear love, although she has no knowledge of it, for I saw her and my heart went out to her instantly, but I had no opportunity to approach her and we never met before the Jap invasion. But my heart must have reached her, for here she is, close but out of reach, of her own will because I cannot summon her, and her expression is full of sympathy, which soothes and illuminates my soul.

This is her second visit. She brings me tranquillity and renews my strength.

A man comes out of the darkness into the flickering light of our small campfires. 'Everyone down to the river. There are several boats full of our people so sick they can't climb out. Bring them up here and do what you can to help. I'll see if the cookhouse can find something for them.'

Hurrying down in the early evening gloom we can make out several wooden barges nosed in to the beach, silhouetted

General Percival surrenders to the Japanese, Singapore, 15 February 1942.

Japanese troops parading near Fullerton Square, Singapore, 1942.

Top: Prisoners of war marching up-country to Kanyu River Camp (also known as Konyu), Thailand, 1942.

Right: POWs building the railway 'bund' (embankment) in the jungle at Kanyu, 1942.

Bottom: A Japanese survey group on the Burma–Thailand Railway, c.1943.

Left: POWs manhandling railway sleepers, Takanun, Thailand, c.1943.

Below: Australian and British POWs laying track, Ronsi, Burma, c.1943.

Bottom: POWs being moved into railway carriages at Slim River, a stop on the railway journey from Singapore to Bampong in Thailand, 1942.

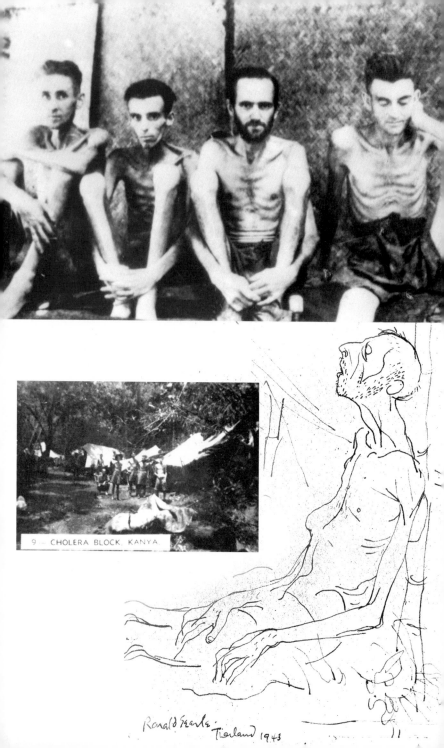

9 - CHOLERA BLOCK, KANYA

Ronald Searle
Tïland 1943

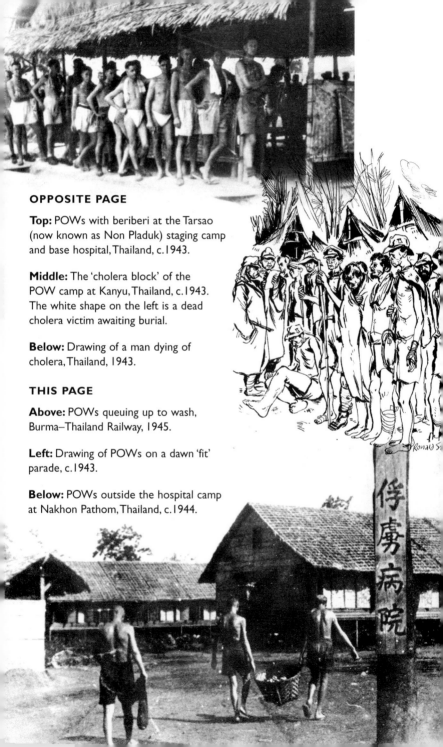

OPPOSITE PAGE

Top: POWs with beriberi at the Tarsao (now known as Non Pladuk) staging camp and base hospital, Thailand, c.1943.

Middle: The 'cholera block' of the POW camp at Kanyu, Thailand, c.1943. The white shape on the left is a dead cholera victim awaiting burial.

Below: Drawing of a man dying of cholera, Thailand, 1943.

THIS PAGE

Above: POWs queuing up to wash, Burma–Thailand Railway, 1945.

Left: Drawing of POWs on a dawn 'fit' parade, c.1943.

Below: POWs outside the hospital camp at Nakhon Pathom, Thailand, c.1944.

Left: One of six trestle bridges built between Kanyu (Hellfire Pass) and Hintok, Thailand, c.1945.

Opposite page: RAF aircraft attacking the Burma–Thailand Railway.

Above: Liberators flying low over the hospital area at Changi Gaol Camp, Singapore, dropping leaflets announcing the end of the war, 28 August 1945.

Left: Graves at Lower Kanyu.

Above: Two former POWs of the Japanese with an English nurse after liberation, Thailand, c. September 1945.

Left: Edwina Mountbatten meeting convalescing former POWs at the 2/14 Australian Hospital, Singapore, October 1945.

against the faint sheen of the water. Outlines of heads, some broad-brimmed Australian hats, but no movements. The men are slumped against the sides of the boats and against each other. In the usual Nip mode of river travel, they have been packed in so that all have to stand. There is no room to sit except for those who have been able to stay upright no longer and have collapsed, their mates making such tiny space for them as they can.

A few have managed to get to the beach where they have collapsed, exhausted and gasping. This is not a matter of supporting them to walk. Every man has to be carried, with his small pack of personal kit, up the slope to our huts where we lay them on our own bedspaces – we can sleep outside, but they must have shelter. Feeding them will absorb most of our midday rice ration for tomorrow, but no matter.

We have to make several trips back to the river before all have been brought in. They are the British and Australian men from 'F' Force, which came up from Singapore a few months ago. Sent up as urgent labour reinforcements, 7,000 men in all, they were only 'on loan' from the Jap Singapore Command to the Siamese military area, and in the typical farce that is the Jap army, no arrangements were made for rations, medical supplies or transport in the handing over. In consequence the Siamese Command provided nothing whatever, leaving the railway organisation to cope without funds or any other form of assistance. The 7,000 men had had no issue of food since their train crossed the Malaya–Siam border, and they had marched over 300 kilometres from Ban Pong – in the incessant rain of the wet monsoon – up that dreadful morass of a track to their designated working area, spending the nights without shelter wherever they happened to be at sunset, trying always to care for their sick.

On the route they passed our established camps

(including Tonchan South, where we last saw them) but were forbidden to make contact with the men in them. However, they managed to do so here and there, and it was only the food (necessarily scanty) that our people were able to slip to them that kept them alive. Their Nip escorts picked up food from their own people at these camps, but were totally indifferent to the needs of their prisoners. In truth, there was probably absolutely nothing they could do, so they simply did not let it bother them. Sick and exhausted men could not be left behind at our camps. The only way to fall out of the march was to die and be buried in a hastily dug grave alongside the track.

In appalling weather the survivors finally dragged themselves into their upriver working camps, fatigued to the limit of their endurance. With no time allowed to recover, they were expected to start without delay in the heavy labour of railway construction, often working sixteen hours at a stretch with a total disregard for meal times. With the mud track frequently impassable for motor transport and the swollen river sometimes running too fast for boats to move upstream against the racing current, rations were irregular or even non-existent, but that made no difference to the 'speedo' work demanded of them. Sleep, when it was permitted, had to be found in dilapidated huts; overcrowded, leaking and open-ended tents; or on bare, saturated mud in the full force of the monsoonal downpours. Without any pay they could not even buy food from the Siamese, even if they had the opportunity.

These wretched and unfortunate men are so emaciated that, in the darkness, they resemble young boys in their slight frames. Close up, the difference is shockingly apparent. Their ribs and joints protrude and their skin is stretched tight. Carrying them is like picking up a sack of loose sticks, and we have a horrible feeling that any small jolt might cause their joints to fall apart, the whole skeleton separating into individual bones. Gaunt faces, sunken eyes, ragged hair and beards, but still they do not accept defeat and have spirit enough to thank us for our ministrations. Not that there is much we can do beyond sharing our tea and whatever we have in the way of eggs and tobacco and other oddments, and washing the sweat and dirt off their bodies.

Their voices are hoarse and weak, and telling us their story draws heavily on the small reserves of strength left in them. We have to piece it all together later. They reckon that already half of them have died. They are now on their way back to Singapore, presumably in their river barges to Kanburi, then by train to Ban Pong and onwards to Singapore. We calculate ten days at best, but anything up to three weeks, for men in this condition an age of pain and suffering which will surely claim more lives.

Before daylight we rouse them and carry them back to the beach, helping them into the boats. We are reluctant to wake them so early, but we know that once our own working day starts we shall not be able to help them, and getting themselves back to the river will be beyond the strength of some.

We part as we met, in darkness, gratitude and sympathy flowing between us. We have not even seen their faces clearly, but they are brothers in this dreadful time. Their courage and endurance and firmness of spirit are an inspiration to us. We may think we have had a tough deal – and it may be so – but these men have our real admiration. And the whole Japanese nation has our deepest contempt and detestation.

What God thinks about this sort of treatment of decent men we have no idea; we have seen no signs. After this we don't really care anyway. It doesn't seem to matter one way or another, so it would be pointless to worry about it.

Our pain and anger have to be buried deep if we want to preserve the balance of our minds. Brooding, combined with frustrating helplessness, will only corrode our humanity, which we will need again when we return to civilisation. The war must end, and we must hope to be alive when that happens and must be fit to go back to our families and friends. We cannot avoid living like captive animals for the time being, but it will be a matter of personal pride, for each one of us, to come out of our imprisonment as whole and civilised men, in some ways wiser, perhaps, but in no way misshapen, our sanity and sense of humour intact.

The impact of pain and hurt can have odd effects. In the flush of having a few dollars in my (non-existent) pocket, I have bought a cake of soap from the canteen – two days' pay, and only the second piece of soap I have had in eighteen months. I could not resist the luxury!

Standing under the eaves of our hut to soap myself, I see a fat frog hopping about around my feet, enjoying the wet mud and bucketing rain. As I step out to place myself under the water spouting off the attap roof he moves with me, and by pure mischance a stream of soapsuds falls directly onto his upturned bulbous eyes. In an instant he is in pain, frantically wiping his eyes to rid them of irritation. And I, although unwittingly, have done this to him! The sight of this innocent little creature's agony triggers an immediate reaction. Tears spring from my eyes, paralysing remorse sweeps through my whole body, I have a strange sensation flooding outwards to my fingertips and toes, I go weak and have to grab hold of the side of the hut to stay upright.

It must be a full minute before I am again in control of myself. The weakness fades and I finish rinsing off soapsuds. The frog has disappeared, poor little fellow. I hope desperately that he is okay.

What brought all that emotion to the surface? In all the mass of suffering and death to which we have become accustomed, the hurt caused to a frog, infinitesimal in comparison, knocked me silly. I can see only one explanation – the mass has been unavoidable and my thoughts about it suppressed, but the small hurt was unnecessary and could have been avoided. It did happen, though, and the genie sprang out of the bottle and I wept not just for the frog, but for all of us. You will not know it, little frog, but your pain has shown me that I have not lost my precious human quality of sympathy for others. It has not withered away in the harshness of our living. Thank you!

Kinsayok is obviously a big camp with a large population of prisoners, but I really have no idea as to its extent. Morning tenkos are held in the murky grey light of dawn, the sun not showing itself through the dense clouds, and in the evening the visibility is no better. The work parties disperse out of sight of each other in drenching rain, and come back to camp too tired to do much more than collect their rice from the cookhouse and stretch out quietly to rest. This must be the worst of the wet monsoon months. What we have experienced so far has been bad enough, but this is beyond belief!

The rain slams down with demonic intensity. Day and night our lives are filled with its drumming on attap roofs and slapping into the saturated earth. Everywhere there is the gleam of water sliding rapidly along ruts and gullies, down slopes, off the massed trees. Mostly it comes down vertically, not in drops but in thick unbroken columns, with a velocity that pounds our exposed bodies. The bare earth floors in our huts are continually wet from water draining off men as they come inside, and from drips through the attap roofs. Nobody has a towel and drying off is simply a matter of perching on your bamboo slats until your skin has shed its moisture, which drains away through the splits in the bamboo without, however, disturbing the armies of bugs.

Even in the shelter of the huts the skin cannot dry properly. The day temperatures must surely be over 100° F and at night cannot fall below 85 degrees, the muggy atmosphere inducing a perpetual film of sweat. A quirky sense of the ridiculous tells me that at least we don't have to worry about clothing and boots going mouldy and rotten, surely the only benefit of our primitive living conditions!

Whether we are digging a cutting or building an embankment, earth has to be picked and shovelled up to be carried in tongas in one direction or the other, and the physical effort required is multiplied several times over when the ground is sodden. It sticks to the shovel instead of sliding off freely, which puts severe stress on your abdomen and spine, and rain-weighted tongas are almost unmanageable as you slither around on bare feet. But the rain is warm and there is little breeze, so it could be worse!

The Nip way of doing things (I can't use the word 'system' because that implies at least some degree of logical thought) is beyond comprehension. We are switched from one area to another without finishing what we were doing, digging one day and drilling rock for dynamite another, humping bags of rice, bridge building – all over the place.

I hope we shall never have to travel by train over any section of track where we have worked – the standard of Nip engineering is abysmal and we have never made any effort to improve it. There must be hundreds of bridges, high and low, lengthy and short, along the track, carrying the lines across stormwater gullies and ravines which take the mighty run-off from the hill slopes into our Kwei Noi which, as we have seen at Wampo and along various stretches, rises forty or fifty feet to accommodate the summer monsoon rains. The lower section of the river, where we have been working, also has to cope with the colossal floods pouring down from the upper reaches.

When there has been an overnight lull in the rain we have made our way to work through rocks and scrubby trees, scrambling down and up the almost vertical sides of ravines slashed into the steep flank of a hill, to find on walking back to camp that rain during the day has filled these gullies with foaming torrents leaping and tumbling in mad excitement down to find the river. They are too wide to jump across, and wading is impossible because of the steepness and volume of the falling water, which would toss you to death far below. The only way is to climb the hillside to find a route above the head-waters. At the end of a long and tiring day this is a hardship we would rather not have, and because we carry no lights it is essential that we get back before dark, as the terrain would be far too dangerous to negotiate afterwards. The prospect of a night exposed to downpours in the open, with no food, and the complications of not being in camp for evening tenko, are enough to keep us moving.

The necessity to make use of local resources has demanded some unorthodox thinking on the part of the Nips in managing without proper tools and equipment, and on our part in how to put such novel ideas into effect. In the Nip army it seems that someone high up has an idea, which he then passes on to sub-ordinates without the slightest notion as to how (or even whether) it can be done. The 'how' is part of their job too, but if they can't work it out they simply pass it on. We, at the bottom of the ladder, are stuck with it. Possible or not, the order is to do it or take the consequences of failure. There are no excuses.

Take bridge building as an example. We are presented with a shallow depression between the hill slopes, rocky slabs and outcrops everywhere, and gather that a bridge is needed. Searching the scrub in what appears to be likely spots, we find survey pegs which we point out to our Nip. We don't think he really understands their significance, but he grunts in a semblance of intelligence and puts on a pantomime act to indicate that he wants two towers erected, one here and another over there, somewhere, more or less. Not a big job.

Our work party consists of some 300 men, and we have lugged tonga-loads of cement with us to this spot. Most of the bags are torn, the contents now in rocky lumps instead of dry powder. We find a stream in the forest but no sand, so ordinary soil will have to suffice. It is a totally useless mix for making concrete, but that is not our concern. We split up into groups and get to work.

Two squares are marked out for pouring concrete slabs, trees are felled and trimmed, rocks gathered and piled. Holes are dug at the corners of each plinth, tree trunks are set upright into them. Logs are laid along the sides, log-cabin fashion, and as these are built up the interior floor is covered with rocks tossed in. Concrete is shovelled over them and we have our foundation. More logs at the sides, more rocks thrown in – smaller as the floor rises – until eventually we have two towers consisting of green tree-trunk walls packed with stones, standing on woefully inadequate foundations. There is not a nail or dogspike in the whole construction. Only the corner posts hold it all together – if they collapse outward under the pressure of the stones, the towers will fall apart.

Our Nip looks at our work with satisfaction and signals to us to go back to camp. Fervently we hope that we shall not come back to work on the top decking. Except for the fact that we have been careful to line up the towers with the survey pegs, they have nothing in their favour. As engineering structures they are plain dangerous – the logs are green and will dry out and be a feast for white ants within a few weeks – but just now they look reasonably good, and that is all that matters. When this railway is finished, may God help those who travel on it – except, of course, for Nips, who are welcome to fall into the ravines when the bridges collapse underneath them.

We have long ago learned to absorb frustrations or, even better, to disregard them. We no longer mutter about incompetence when given a tedious or apparently pointless piece of work to do. The philosophy is that if you are not being bored here you might well be bored somewhere else. So, stop wishing you were somewhere else and make the best of where you are. It is a useful way to look at things. It stops them getting under your skin and drawing off emotional energy which you really can't afford to waste like that. Bend with the wind, wait until it has blown past, then straighten up again – an old piece of Chinese wisdom.

Today has upset me, almost frightened me. I came within a hair's-breadth of losing control over myself.

By the end of yesterday our squad had finished what it was doing, and this morning we should have been allocated new work. But someone forgot to arrange for this, so we find ourselves back on the same site, with nothing specific to do. To keep us busy, our Nips set us onto pointless jobs such as shifting piles of earth which did not need to be shifted, pushing felled scrub around, and so on.

All on my own, I am told to dig a hole inside a circle scratched with a stick. It is not raining, the sun is burning hot in the thick moist air and any effort results in a flood of sweat.

Just behind me is a small shade tree, which is why the Nip has chosen the spot, so he can be in the shade and watch me sweat in the sun.

I dig for an hour or so, piling the excavated earth on my left. No good, the Nip wants it on the right. I shovel it all across, and start digging again, throwing out earth to the new position. No, that earth should be over on the left. And all the time the Nip is carrying on in a whining dirge, he wipes his face with a small cotton towel. I begin to feel irritated.

I enlarge the bottom of the hole, because it is easier than digging deeper. No, the hole must go down further. I am already hip deep, and there is not enough room in the hole to swing my spade properly. I get an angry 'speedo, speedo' which is quite impossible without enlarging the hole. I can't make the stupid bugger understand this, and can't make too much fuss because he is, quite plainly, starting to work himself up into a rage.

My irritation, fuelled by his own mood, moves into anger. I can see the danger clearly. I am losing my grip on myself, and if he goes much further and takes a swipe at me, I am just so short-fused I might wade into him with my shovel.

The idea takes hold. Let's give it some thought. I know exactly where he is, squatting on his haunches just behind me. If I shift my hands on the shovel, just precisely so, I can bring the blade up in a round-arm slash which will catch him right under his chin, splitting his throat wide open. What a marvellous idea – he won't even see it coming, it will be so fast!

I can't dig, I am trembling so much with the effort of not doing what I want to do. The whining and snivelling go on and on, fraying my nerves. What better way to shut him up than slashing his throat? That would keep him quiet! I am breathing heavily, and my heart is pumping violently. I am working up to the point where something is going to have to break. My body is rigid, my hands clamped on the shaft of the shovel, when a tiny voice tells me to hold on tight.

Staring down into the hole I see a shimmering patch, but there is no water. The Nip's face appears in it, gazing up at me. It starts to flush pink, then reddish, then blood-red. I think: I'm seeing red, actually seeing red! I have to kill him! I've got to kill him! Blood pounds through my head, my eyes ache, all my perceptions are incredibly sharp. I move my hands into position. One sweeping slash and it will be done. He will be dead and I shall be free! I am exactly poised, ready to do it, and turn my head slightly to verify precisely where his throat is.

He's not there. The whining has stopped, and he is walking away. He has cheated me! The bastard, after all my effort getting ready to kill him he has just walked away!

My disappointment is huge, but a few moments later there is a total deflation, an enormous sense of relief. My whole body goes quiet, relaxed. I lean my rump against the rim of the hole and let myself unravel.

Well, if the Nip has gone I see no point continuing to dig this useless hole or filling it in. Looking around I see that everyone else has knocked off and found some shade to lie in, so I join them. Wally asks me: 'Are you all right? Your eyes look awfully bloodshot!'

We are working in a new area a few kilometres from camp, out of the forest and on the bare flank of a hillside sloping down to the Kwei Noi, a kilometre or so distant. The fall is moderate and the earth is gravelly, not the solid hard rock we have previously had to deal with.

Earlier gangs have had no difficulty in excavating the

railbed and have moved on elsewhere while we have been brought in to do the final work to have all in readiness for the rail-laying people. We cannot fathom the sense in the Nip habit of shifting men before they have completed a stretch, and having to find new gangs to take over.

The problem we encounter is a number of sizeable boulders which were exposed when the hillside was dug away. These sit squarely in the track alignment, some of them taller than a man and of considerable circumference. It isn't possible to estimate how deeply they are bedded in but some of them look as if they could go down a long way, in which case they cannot be dug out – it would be far beyond our capacity to roll them out of the way. Even the small ones would leave very large pits that would have to be filled in, causing soft patches that would not support trains passing over. Even our thick-headed Nips seem to have realised this, and their solution is to break up the boulders down to ground level and remove them in chunks.

So we spend the days lugging bamboo and wood to be heaped in great piles around and over each boulder. This means felling trees and bamboo clumps in the forest area, which suits us because we are out of sight of the Nips for most of the day and can work at our own pace, while the Nips huddle in whatever shade they can find in crevices and gullies. As long as the colossal bonfires can be lit by the end of the day they are satisfied. The fires blaze for hours, the bamboo burning fiercely and exploding in showers of sparks to get the heavier timbers going.

The next day is spent searching the rock surfaces for hair-line cracks and bashing at them with sledgehammers while more firewood is brought up. It is tedious work but fills in our days without us having to overexert ourselves, and as the boulders do not break up easily under our puny attacks, we can see several weeks of reasonably endurable work ahead of us. No complaints on that score!

We are not helped by the fact that we are at about the midpoint of the wet season and it is, as always, hot and uncomfortable. But as we know, bamboo ignites easily even when wet and sets off even wet and sappy wood with its blow-torch heat. Our worry is the possibility of septic wounds from hacking down clumps of bamboo while moving around with bare feet and legs. Their tough thorns and sharp splinters easily tear the skin.

Today the sky is bright blue. It's going to be a real scorcher, and with no shade at the worksite we shall find the rocks uncomfortably hot to touch and the ground blistering to walk on. Eating our midday rice, a Korean comes along with one of our officers to tell us and our Nips that there is a high-ranking officer group coming to inspect the camp, and no working parties may come in at the end of the day until permission is received.

Our own fellow doesn't even stay long enough to ask how we are getting along. He simply delivers his message to us as his first contact and tells us to pass it along the line. Muttering something about perspiring uncomfortably in his shirt and trousers and how hot his boots make his feet, he heads back to camp. Our hearts bleed for him in his distress!

Back to work, and the killing heat of the afternoon begins to bother even our Nips. Mopping sweat with the small cotton towels most of them carry, they grumble to each other and quite obviously are just as keen as we are to get back to a cool hut and a soak in the river. But orders are orders, more so in the Nip army than in others, and no one dares to take the initiative and release us. An hour after the usual knock-off time the sun is still tormenting us, and our work slows without any reaction from the Nips.

One of the Eurasian lads asks, 'What's that expression the Nips use to stop work? Something like "Saiyo hajumei"?' We agree that it sounds like that, and he steps into a small cleft in the hillside where he can't be seen, telling us to keep moving. A moment later his voice rings out, 'Saiyo hajumei,' up and down the line. It is picked up by our Nips and shouted out further off. There's a chorus of cheers from our men, and in half a minute the whole crowd is moving towards camp, the Nips laughing and chattering cheerfully in relief – it doesn't seem to have occurred to them to wonder where the first shout came from. Frankie's cheeky grin could tell them! Score a point for our side!

When we get back to camp we learn that the inspection group walked straight through the camp, looking neither right nor left and speaking to nobody. It took them less than five minutes. And our own officers couldn't be bothered to bring word to us to come in!

As I have said before, it is an understood rule in the British army (and, for all I know, in any other army) that you do not volunteer for anything. However, we in the Volunteers see things differently. We want to know and discuss all available details and then we will decide and accept the consequences of our choice.

We are told that there is a small sawmill camp a few kilometres upriver, run by Jap army engineers, and a party of fifteen men is required to work there. It is thought that it would be best if the party were made up of men who have been working together rather than of individuals picked out at random, and the suggestion is that in an isolated camp we Volunteers might be best suited. So the opportunity is on first offer to us.

A privilege indeed – who can resist such subtle blandishments? The pros and cons are obvious, but nothing can be held as certain so discussion cannot really lead to a good decision. It will have to be a gamble based on optimism/pessimism/hell why not/anything to get out of this dump/it could be a lot worse/Nip engineers are usually a lot better than these camp bastards/but not always – and so on, getting nowhere. The big question is uncertainty about the future – once separated from our friends we might never rejoin them, and this is a serious matter. On the other hand, we might be sent off in different directions at any time, as has frequently happened. Our life is full of uncertainties.

There is nothing to be gained by lengthy and repetitive talk, and soon it develops that some of us are willing to take a chance. One of our officers, from a Kuala Lumpur unit, will be in charge, the idea being that an officer just might give us some standing in a Jap professional camp. The captain could be a good choice – in the Malayan campaign he showed up well in action and, for what it may be worth, he cultivates a thick bushy Field Marshal Kitchener moustache which (he must hope) gives him a military bearing to complement his parade ground strutting around. He looks solid and dependable.

Next to him in rank, also from near Kuala Lumpur, is a company sergeant-major (CSM), an Australian built like a steer from his native Queensland, and formerly a rubber estate manager, brisk and efficient.

By their very appearance these two inspire confidence, so we raggle-taggle thirteen feel reasonably optimistic when we agree to form the new party. Next morning we are in a barge being towed upriver by a pom-pom launch, pulling in after an hour to an almost invisible gap in the shrubbery growing thickly on the riverbank. Our Nip leads us a kilometre or so along a narrow track until we find ourselves in a small encampment tucked away in a basin at the foot of our familiar hills.

There are two small huts of the usual bamboo and attap construction, a cookhouse, and an open-fronted hut with a truck parked under the roof at one end and a timber workbench with sundry tools, all neat and tidy, at the other. A dozen or so Japs are lounging around or tinkering with bits and pieces of equipment. Nobody pays much attention to us as our Korean, puffed up with the ceremonial importance of handing us over, lines us up for tenko. The Jap gunso deflates him with a casual wave and a look that clearly says, 'All right, I can count to fifteen, piss off and leave us in peace'. He gives us a friendly grin, points to one of the huts and calls out, 'Okay, you go house-o,' and we are dismissed.

Our 'house-o' is far superior to anything we have yet seen. The steeply pitched roof is so closely layered with attap that it will keep out even the heaviest downpour, and it is supported by tree-trunk poles down the centre passageway. The sleeping platforms are solid timber, well fitted together, there are even timber duckboards laid on the earth floor, and the attap walls go up near enough to the eaves to stop rain from drifting in. The entrance doorway is the only opening in the walls, and is protected outside by an attap canopy.

Altogether a cosy living room, with space to spare for everyone. There is even a raised platform in the corner by the doorway, as a private apartment for an officer, screened off and reached by a short ladder. In the Jap army officers are a superior category of men, keeping themselves physically separated and aloof when circumstances permit – in fact, I have not seen an officer speaking directly to private soldiers but only through a senior NCO – but, as we all know, when the troops go into action officers are right up front setting an example. We dump our kit and go outside.

Hygiene being always at the head of our priorities we convey to the gunso that we need spades to dig a benjo (latrine). He seems a bit surprised, points to the toolshed and leaves us to get on with it. We select a site some fifty yards downwind and away from the cookhouse, help ourselves to a few bits of sawn timber and wire, and soon have a neat latrine with a flyproof lid, the first we have been able to construct in any camp. The Japs, it is soon apparent, simply wander out a short distance into the scrub to relieve themselves, which accounts for the thrumming clusters of flies all over the place.

The gunso comes to look at our handiwork and is clearly impressed. He calls over a couple of his men and they, too, frankly admire it. Would we build one for them? Over there, near their hut? No, not there, over this way – we indicate unpleasant smells, buzzing flies, and the cookhouse. They catch on at once and say, 'Okay, okay, arigato, you fix-o.' With little effort we have been able to establish a friendly and easy-going relationship, a fact of tremendous importance to our wellbeing.

There is a contradiction in this Jap ignorance of very basic field hygiene and their own high standards of personal cleanliness. They are fastidious in themselves, but accept the stench of ordure lying in the open and the clouds of bluebottle flies resulting from it. I remember how, during my childhood in Shanghai, the family would drive out of the city area to Hungjao to give our dog a run in the countryside. Mum always carried handkerchiefs damped with eau de cologne to wave around as we passed through villages and fields of crops, in a vain effort to defeat the stink of human waste fertiliser tipped into the soil. There were always ox-carts with barrels collecting household waste – in fact the 'honey-pot' men actually bought it from the villagers, it was so valuable for fertilising the vegetable and cotton fields. Dad said that some of these fields must have produced crops continuously for several thousand years, made possible only because of the careful utilisation of nature's cycle of growth, waste and regrowth. When holidaying in Japan the same farming method had been pungently noticeable, so for Jap troops it would simply be a familiar background to their lives.

A shout of 'meishi' brings us to the cookhouse, where we set out our mess tins on a shelf for the cook to fill. Clean, good quality rice with a chunk of dried fish, the same ration as for the Japs. A good sign for our stay in this camp, we begin to think we made a lucky decision to come here. The flies must also think this is a good place – the serving of food brings them in thousands, so thick that it is difficult to keep your hat over your mess tin and lift spoonfuls to your mouth, and they swarm to our hut with us.

After lunch one of us is picked out to stay in camp and help the cook. The rest of us are provided with axes and saws, bamboo poles and ropes, and led out into the forest by a Jap who selects trees to be felled, trimmed, and carried back to the sawmill. It is easy work, and there seems to be no urgency. We work steadily and efficiently, the Jap has no complaints and even the rain has held off. It's as good as a rest camp.

The evening meal is even better: a little fresh meat and some vegetables, beautiful rice and any quantity of tea. We can be happy here! Except for the flies – we must do something about them!

Camp routine settles into a comfortable pattern which is marvellously beneficial to our overstressed bodies and mental processes. We have an easy day's work, which passes the time pleasantly, and we are free of harassment by gibbering Koreans who have nothing better to do. In fact, we have even managed to persuade the Japs that we can work unsupervised, and the man who used to accompany us to find suitable trees to fell no longer bothers to do so.

This arose from our CSM saying 'Damme damme (No good)' when the Jap pointed to a tree, indicating that it was rotten all up the centre of the trunk. The Jap insisted nevertheless, and the trunk was found to be black and decayed in its core from the butt end upwards. The Jap's amazement was almost comic, and from that moment on we have been left to ourselves. A cluster of diseased leaves in the crown of the tree was the giveaway.

The camp is required to provide planks for making forms for pouring concrete slabs and supports. The saw is an ingenious contraption, being a steel band with teeth all along one edge which is mounted on a steel pillar bolted to the rear end of their truck. The band passes over pulleys top and bottom and is driven by a power takeoff from the truck's transmission system. The teeth face to the rear and a log is pushed up against them as the band is whizzed round at high revs.

The local trees being of smallish diameter and soft wood, the bandsaw works efficiently and peels off planks with no trouble at all. All we have to do is bring in a sufficient number of logs to keep the mill busy, and there is no difficulty in doing that for the supply is all around us and the trees are felled and trimmed easily. The Japs have a small machine which automatically pushes the bandsaws through and hones every tooth, and the crosscut saws and axes which we use are checked and refurbished frequently. After the blunt tools hitherto supplied, it is a pleasure to work with this outfit.

The camp atmosphere, too, is relaxed and informal. As we assemble for morning rice (with a bit of something tasty) the Jap gunso saunters across, salutes are exchanged almost as a casual 'good morning' rather than as army protocol, we are counted where we stand with a wagging forefinger, and that's that for tenko. After our meal we collect saws and axes, bamboo poles and ropes, and take ourselves off into the forest to bring in logs at intervals.

The comfortable workload, the improved food and, most of all, the absence of daily harassment very quickly have a beneficial effect on us. These last few months, with the start of the depressing rains and the onset of the vicious speedo, we have all become tightly wound up. We have endured the heavy physical stresses of overlong hours of work on starvation rations and insufficient sleep in appalling conditions, and we have been faced with the truly awful circumstances of cholera outbreaks. We have helped mates worse off than ourselves, and gratefully accepted the help of others when we needed it. We have watched friends sicken and waste away without even the most rudimentary medicines. In daily talk we have heard of this or that number of deaths in our own camp and in others along the river, but burials are done during working time so nobody can attend them except the grave-diggers, who are drawn from the so-called 'light sick', and the stretcher-bearers, who are so enfeebled that they may well be looking at themselves in a week's time.

More than anything else, we have been compelled to be as bystanders to all this. We are totally unable to do anything about it, displaying a docile and obedient attitude towards our loathed and despised captors, putting on blank/disinterested/polite faces to suit all occasions. Showing our feelings would be construed as insulting – the Nips and Koreans have very tender susceptibilities! – and would invite a ferocious bashing.

This unnatural and insidious cramping of our individual personalities has forced on us a degree of self-control which is hardly credible. Accepting things as they are (totally outside any man's experience) while holding to a firm faith in the future (against all logic) and somehow distancing the soul from unpleasant daily reality, these are all essential to maintaining sanity, our personal wholeness and pride, and the determination to behave as civilised and intelligent men. It's a sort of carefully controlled and operated split personality, switching seamlessly on demand to suit circumstances.

Amongst ourselves we keep our conversations matter-of-fact, carefully avoiding angry and contentious discussion. Thankfully we can, after all this time, still talk in an equitable style, and find something amusing to relate. But I tell you what: if any of our piss-begotten politicians from the last twenty years (and that includes all our current lot!) were to drop in for a chat, we would take them to pieces savagely, in the plainest language, for their negligence in having allowed Britain to fall to such an abysmal state of weakness. I really think we have more contempt for those men than we do for the Japs, they having always claimed to be intelligent and patriotic. Maybe we are slightly prejudiced – but then, who wouldn't be? We are no longer under the influence of propaganda of doubtful truth and moral standards. We can talk freely, carefully analysing known facts and disregarding all the camouflage and whitewash of official versions. It's going to be interesting, after the war, to hear all these inept politicians trying to justify their policies, or even claiming with bare-faced hypocrisy that they were always right!

In all this turmoil of bodily and mental stress, I have still not come across a single man giving thanks to God for anything at all nor, on the other hand, have I heard anyone railing at God for seeming to be completely indifferent towards us. We have become strictly practical – something helps or causes problems, it exists or it does not, it is a fact or it is dismissed, you can do something about it or you cannot. Our existence is today, even tomorrow may not be predictable, and our future is totally outside our control. Under these circumstances you would expect that some bulwark of spiritual/religious strength would be welcome, to lift some of the weight of uncertainty and daily suffering, but it is not so. We all started with it when we entered this valley of shadows eighteen months ago, but it has withered away and we no longer look for it.

One of our thirteen has been detailed to help as a general dogsbody in the Jap cookhouse and camp area. The remaining twelve can be handily sorted into two gangs for heavy logs or three gangs for light loads. The CSM, who is responsible for tree selection, comes with us. Our officer occasionally wanders around – apparently the Japs leave him to his own devices. True to his devotion to military correctness, he is in full uniform – shorts, shirt, hosetops and boots, cap on straight, badges of rank on his shoulders, even a bamboo swagger-stick – with his Kitchener moustache bushy and neatly trimmed, strutting around in ceremonial parade style. It is said that he knows the history of every regiment in the British army, he has immersed himself so thoroughly, since he was a boy, in military knowledge.

The dogsbody job is rotated occasionally, and my turn duly comes up. The main duty is to assist the cook in preparing food, carrying water from a nearby spring and bringing in firewood – pleasant enough, for the cook is a cheerful and easy-going fellow. The other is to heat water in an oil drum in time for the gunso to have his hot bath at the end of the day.

Not being sure how long it takes to heat thirty gallons in a steel drum, I set a fire under it during the afternoon to give it plenty of time to become really hot. I had imagined that the gunso, and maybe others, would bale it out to pour over themselves, but what happens is quite different. Coming out of the cookhouse to check the water temperature I see the gunso trotting up to the drum, stark naked. All in one athletic movement he steps up on a flat rock next to the drum, places his hands on the rim, springs high with drawn-up knees and drops plumb into the hot water. A split second later he gives a loud screech and shoots up vertically, rosy pink from ribs to toenails, to fall in a heap beside the tub. Grabbing a bucket of cold water I run across to pour it over his parboiled body.

That no damage has been done is pure luck. The water was far too hot for comfort but not so hot as to cause blisters, and instead of a bashing for carelessness I am thanked by the gunso for my prompt action in cooling him off. Any Nip in the big camps would have given me hell!

We have been able to learn a very valuable lesson. Two days ago a small group of Siamese villagers brought into the camp a party of twelve Sakai tribesmen and a woman, all roped together and looking very dejected. The Sakai are mountain peoples of northern Malaya, aboriginal tribal folk living in the thickly forested high ranges which run down the country's centre. They have a primitive agricultural system, clearing and burning patches to grow crops, fishing and hunting. Occasionally they come down into Malayan villages to buy supplies, and to do this they speak a simple form of Malay. It was while on one of these visits that this group was rounded up by Jap troops and brought up to Siam with a large force of conscripted labourers. The Sakai are a free-living lot, totally unreceptive to organised labour and being told what to do. Being forest hunters they move silently through woodland, and had no difficulty in breaking out of their camp and disappearing. We learned these details on their first evening in our camp.

Visiting the latrine at dusk, I hear a voice speaking softly in Malay, and when I reply a pair of dark brown bodies materialise close to me. We begin to talk.

Life in a Nip railway construction camp had been, from the start, unhappy and difficult for them, then quite impossible. They could not adapt and decided to escape, living off the jungle and rivers while they made their way back home. With no idea of the distance involved (close to 1,000 miles) they knew they must head south. After some fifteen days they had to admit defeat. Despite all their jungle skills they could not feed themselves and hunger forced them to go into a Siamese village and offer to work in return for food. A farmer took them in, and reported their presence to the nearest Jap army post, which was this camp. The next day the farmer roped them together and brought them in, no doubt collecting a reward.

Our Japs (so apparently civilised compared with our loathed Nips and Koreans) had tied the men to trees just outside our camp area and taken the woman into their hut where we heard her crying out as they abused her without cessation. There has been no food or water for any of them.

I am in camp carrying out my dogsbody duties when, inevitably, a squad of stone-faced Kempei-tai arrives. These degraded troglodyte monsters, the Japanese army police, chill the air around them by their mere presence. Answerable only to themselves, brutalised by training and totally ruthless, the ordinary Nip soldier seems terrified by their presence alone. Without a word they check the Sakais' bonds and lead them away. I have a last glimpse of sad, beseeching eyes turned towards me, and the poor wretches disappear into the trees. Ten minutes later I hear a muffled volley of shots.

When my friends come back into the camp I tell them of the fate of the Sakai group. We are all saddened, as much as anything by the utter futility of their experience, from being torn from their families to their savage death, all totally pointless and unnecessary. And from this moment we have a different view of Jap army frontline troops, seemingly so much more civilised and easy-going than our slovenly Nip and Korean rubbish. They are just as mindlessly cruel and barbarian, only not quite so crudely open about it.

The important lesson for us in all of this is that if the Sakai cannot feed themselves in the jungle, even for a few days, then it is quite out of the question for us even to think of trying to do so.

The rain continues to pour down in torrents, with occasional gaps of steamy humidity, while the big fat bluebottles swarm in reverberating clouds. They settle in millions on the long plank set up outside the cookhouse, where the cook chops up vegetables and meat. I notice him using a kerosene blowlamp to start a fire in wet wood under the big kwali, and with suitable pantomime get him to open the flame to a broad fan and pass it over the plank. The blowflies do not hear the hissing flame, and are instantly shrivelled in the blast as they seethe several layers deep. The cook is delighted, and next day we rub a piece of meat all over the surface of the plank. The flies again swarm thickly and are destroyed. One more time, and we must have wiped out the whole bluebottle population within sniffing distance.

For several days we haven't seen a fly.

I have my very first attack of malaria, and it is really quite extraordinary that I have so far escaped it when so many thousands of men in the same camps have been afflicted. We have all been exposed to exactly the same degree, and none of us has had any protection from mosquitoes. It may be pure luck, but it has been noticeable that we who have lived in the Malaya/Singapore area for a time seem to be less susceptible. We see nothing logical in this when the cause of infection is considered – it is just a thought, but maybe living in the tropics we have developed a skin aroma which is imperceptible to us but sufficient to deter mosquitoes. Maybe years of Sunday curries have something to do with it? And wouldn't a real hot curry go down well right now!

The attack is mild, thank goodness, for there is no treatment of any kind available in this small and isolated camp. A queasy stomach, sundry vague aches and pains in the head and joints, occasional dizziness, sudden periods of chilly shivering despite the day's heat, and finally rigors, when every muscle in the body tightens up and uncontrollable shaking seizes me. At this stage there is no choice but to lie down until the rigor has run its course. The usual treatment then is to pile on anything available to promote warmth and induce heavy perspiration – 'to break the fever' – so your friends chuck over you every blanket or whatever else they have. I find it distinctly uncomfortable and emerge exhausted, not so much, I feel, from the fever as from the loss of body fluids from excessive perspiration.

The Jap gunso takes a sympathetic look at me and says I can 'worko campo', which will give me an easy day or two to recover. The last thing I want is to be sent back to Kinsayok in exchange for a fit man, but in this sawmill camp it is essential to have all twelve men working.

Late yesterday afternoon a young Siamese came into the camp leading a bullock, which he tried to sell to our Japs. After some haggling he departed, taking the animal with him while our CSM (who is Australian and has had some experience with cattle) gazed after him thoughtfully: 'You know that feller must come from a bunch of cattle being driven north along the track that runs between us and the river. At this time of day they will be making camp for the night, and he brought the bullock in hoping to make a sale. What say we sneak out after dark, two or three of us, and see if they have been careless enough to leave one of them straying a bit?'

Sure enough, this morning two of the cattle herders turn up and despite the language problem they make it clear that one animal has disappeared from their bunch, and they think our Japs must know something about it. Oddly enough we prisoners are not under suspicion – the Siamese and the Japs must assume that we have all been good little boys and stayed within camp bounds. It is the Japs who are being accused! The voices become heated, the Japs obviously taking offence at being accused of stealing, until the gunso has had enough. He stamps into his hut and comes out with a rifle, pumping a round into the breech and bellowing with rage. The Siamese take the hint and depart rapidly.

Off we go to our day's logging, the CSM leading us in our search for trees in a wide circuit towards the river where we find the Siamese campsite, now deserted. Satisfied that they have gone, the CSM wheels back a mile or so into the bush and there we find the missing bullock grazing at the end of a long tether. The trio of rustlers grin at us innocently. The rest of us had no inkling of the operation, which was why we were able to appear genuinely ignorant at this morning's confrontation.

The CSM says, 'We'll leave it here tonight, in case the Siamese send someone back for a look-see. Now we had better put on a bit of a speedo to catch up on our quota.'

Sure enough, we spot our Siamese slinking around the camp outskirts at evening rice time, but there's nothing for him to see.

Next morning we bring the animal into camp with our first logs, and the CSM marches up to the gunso, throws a cracking salute and says, 'I you presento this burrocko!'

The gunso's look of amazement gives way to roars of laughter as the funny side hits him. All the Japs join in, chattering and laughing. The cook grabs the burrocko's halter and his rifle, and we hike off to work amidst cheerful back-slapping from admiring Japs.

Midday rice is accompanied with strips of beef done sukiyaki style, well remembered from my childhood, although it is a bit tough because the meat has had no time to age. In the evening we have a bucket of thick stew with vegetables in a Japanese flavouring which also brings back memories.

Of course, meat does not keep for long in this climate, and in the wet season the occasional sun does not persist long enough to dry it properly for preservation, so we have to eat our way through the supply as quickly as we can. As a bonus, the Japs do not seem to like offal, so all these choice bits are handed to us!

I have been lucky with my dose of malaria. This disease comes in three types, we understand, all of them serious to different degrees. The mildest is BT (Benign Tertian) which I have. Next, and most unpleasant, is ST (Sub Tertian), while the third is MT (Malignant Tertian), which in our circumstances is usually fatal as it attacks the brain.

Without facilities for blood-testing, the first two are identifiable by the time periods between the shaking rigors and the duration of an attack. Not that there is much to be gained by knowing which type you have – there is no treatment for either except by pure chance that our medical officers have managed to acquire drugs. You simply (literally) sweat it out and hope for the best. If you have MT you will probably not know much about it consciously. The burning temperatures bring delirium from which you are unlikely to recover.

In our state of chronic malnutrition our bodies are further weakened by the destruction of red blood cells, which our miserable diet cannot replace. This loss is serious, and you can monitor your downhill slide by noting the colour of your urine. As the dead corpuscles are collected and passed out of your body, your urine steadily changes from pale yellow through darkening hues of orange, coming back to normal as the attack spends itself. Some men have a morbid fascination in watching this process and discussing the implications, but mostly it is mentioned casually in conversation and dismissed, it is so common. In three days I am back at work.

A swollen spleen often accompanies malaria – the heavier the fever, the more painful and prominent the swelling. It subsides when the attack passes.

The Nip gunso has told our officer that he and his men will be having a booze-up this evening – 'takusan beero' – and we must stay inside our hut after 'hiru go sleepo'. The 'plenty' beer, as far as we can see, consists of some two dozen bottles to be shared amongst all the Nips – hardly enough for a wingding.

But orders are orders, and shortly after the 'sun has gone to sleep' there are loud sounds of the Japs working themselves up into a state of maudlin drunken yowling. We have noticed this a few times in other camps – either the Japs can get sozzled on very little alcohol, or they are told to get themselves paralysed on whatever is available and, however small a quantity that may be, they obey orders and work themselves up into the required state of falling-down inebriation.

A thought – could it be this capacity for self-delusion that inspired them to attack us and America, believing that they could win? If the capacity is there, amongst the high-placed men who run the country, what would be the top limit of their fanatical dreams?

We are in fact discussing this theory, sitting on our sleeping platforms and leaning our backs against the walls, when our tranquil evening is disturbed in a most unpleasant way. Through the doorway at the end of the hut lurches a Jap soldier, so unsteady on his feet that he has to lean against a doorpost to hold himself upright. His eyes glare around the hut, his teeth are bared and he holds a rifle, with fixed bayonet, well forward in the aggressive stiff-armed attitude taught in any army when hand-to-hand fighting is about to begin. Sodden with alcohol, his mood and next move both unpredictable, he looks murderous and thoroughly dangerous.

All this is plainly obvious to all of us in a split second, and in a swift slither we are all off the sleeping platforms and standing rigidly to attention. From my spot I can see, by squinting to my left, both the Jap in the doorway and right alongside him the elevated cubbyhole occupied by our officer, whose face is in full view. His appearance is no credit to him – his cheeks are deathly pale and his mouth gapes slackly open, his eyes bulging. It is he who should have called us loudly to attention and presented himself with a smart salute, but instead he is obviously terrified and paralysed, incapable of action.

The Jap gathers himself into a crouch and moves slowly up the central walkway, bayonet rigidly forward and sweeping from side to side, looking for a target, his finger inside the trigger guard. If he has put a cartridge up the spout then every man in the hut is in danger. We are tightly tensed up, waiting.

The change in his attitude is almost imperceptible. The effort of concentrating his foggy brain to enable him to move into the hut has been too much to sustain. His scowl starts to lose its shape, his bleary eyes fill with tears and his rubbery legs wobble, his rifle and bayonet droop – but his finger is still close to the trigger.

Coming to a swaying standstill the Jap makes an effort to pull himself together. Our officer peers like a stunned codfish out of his hidey-hole while we, having nothing else to do, simply stand fast and hope that this nasty menacing little dollop will go away.

Muttering and whining to himself, as Jap soldiers seem to do when dealing with mental contortions, the Jap gathers himself into a lurching leap forward, bringing his bayonet up into position. From the corner of my eye I see that he is coming straight at my left side. I just have time to turn to face him, moving fractionally to my right so that his bayonet slides past just above my left hip. I feel the blade's cold touch against my skin. His forward impetus, not meeting the expected obstruction of my body, throws him off balance, and his fuddled brain needs a few seconds to get him under control again. It gives me just long enough to assess my situation, which has become decidedly delicate.

In his drunken condition it would be easy to disarm him and knock him out, but this is out of the question. Whatever the rights and wrongs of the matter, it would mean a firing squad for me. I shall have to take advantage of his mental confusion to dodge his bayonet in such a way as to leave him thinking he has misjudged his thrust, and hope that he will lose interest or, maybe, collapse on the ground.

Our hut is unusual in its construction, having a tall pole

in the middle of the walkway to support the ridge of the roof. While the Jap has been getting himself upright, I have edged to my right so that I am partly protected by the pole.

Working himself up into a fury he comes at me again, and misses. Keeping my feet together, and not taking actual steps, I can do a kind of softshoe shuffle which puzzles him because he has not seen me move yet has not been able to hit me. I think he must be seeing several bayonets and images of me, and cannot match up the right pair.

I find myself absolutely calm and clear-headed, my reactions razor-sharp and precise. Our pas de deux goes on for several minutes, though I am not concerned with passing time. He pauses to size me up or makes repeated lunges which keep me (literally) on my toes, and I see with relief that he is tiring. But he still has his finger near the trigger of his rifle, and a single shot would bring the gunso and all his mates.

Despite my concentration on my own situation, I clearly hear one of my friends calling out to the officer to intervene. Just as clearly I hear his reply, stuttering in fear: 'I – I – I c-can't! He-he-he mum-might slap, slap, my f-face!' Which draws an angry threat. 'You'll get more than your bloody face slapped by us if you don't do something very quickly! Call the gunso!'

At this point, fortunately, the Jap gives up trying to stick his bayonet into me. Maybe he is frustrated, or tired out, or has just lost interest. With tears streaming down his face, muttering incoherently, he makes for the doorway, hardly able to stay upright and holding his rifle by the muzzle while the butt drags along the ground. There is just enough light for us to see him, flopped in a heap and vomiting uncontrollably. The rain is bucketing down in torrents – good!

We all get back to our bedspaces. There is no knowing whether he will come back, on his own or bringing someone with him. We settle down to normality, picking up our conversations, and wait (as always) to see what will happen next.

The CSM moves his belongings to an empty space in our area, leaving the officer to reflect alone on his disgrace. We shall not speak to him again, and when we rejoin our friends in the main camp we shall make sure that everyone hears what happened. In the British army it is a prime responsibility of an officer to see to the welfare of his men, and being a prisoner of war in no way relieves him of this obligation. But to demonstrate personal cowardice while failing in his responsibility as an officer, that is something that none of us can condone.

Reflecting on last night's episode while we fell and trim trees for the sawmill, we are all relieved by this morning's normality in all things. The Japs seem to know nothing, which means that 'Little Turd' (the nickname has quickly come into use) has not reported the incident, and (most certainly!) we are not going to lay a complaint. In fact, Little Turd looks so woebegone that it is quite possible that he has no recollection beyond picking himself up out of the mud and his own mess, with an enormous hangover. The other Japs all look a bit haggard, but Little Turd was really sodden with booze.

My own reaction at the time interests me. I was never in the least scared, only tense and watchful, and at the end just plain bloody angry at having had to submit to such risk at the hands of such a miserable piss-begotten wretch whom I could have disarmed and disposed of with ease. It is, of course, very probable that Little Turd's plainly drunken state shaped and influenced our attitude, it being obvious to us that he could well fizzle out provided he did not go berserk before reaching that stage. Our instinctive tactic was to keep him going without upsetting him, in the hope that his strength and determination would fail. An irritating episode which could have ended badly, but didn't – fortunately.

The real casualty is our officer, shown to be a coward by his lack of action and disgraced by his own appallingly feeble words. He will have to live with it amongst his fellows for the duration of our imprisonment, and in his own soul beyond that point. Personally, it doesn't matter a damn to me – he is not worth a second thought.

It was an unusual way to celebrate my twenty-second birthday!

Our daily workload is not excessive – it's well within our capacity, in fact – and we are well practised in doing enough to keep the Japs happy without giving them the notion that we could do more. Being left alone in the forest away from camp we work at our own pace, ignoring heavy timbers and felling only smaller trees which can be trimmed and carried in comfortably. This creates no problems with the gunso, who is required to provide light timber planks for concrete moulds, not heavy beams for bridge structures, nor will his bandsaw tackle anything but softwoods. The Japs keep our tools in professional condition, the rations are far better than in the big camps, we live in a rainproof bug-free hut, life has indeed become easier and, as far as we are concerned, can so continue for a long time.

I am, therefore, more than a little puzzled when I find that our daily log-carrying is becoming increasingly demanding in effort. The usual loads that I handled with ease as part of a team weigh down on the bamboo pole across my shoulders more and more heavily. In a few days I cannot simply lift the pole onto my shoulders – I have to bend my knees to get underneath the pole and then straighten up to bring the rope sling taut. The sheer effort has my heart thumping, blood pumping around my head, my eyes aching, limbs and body leaden. In a fit of anger I shout out to my friends: 'Hey, you chaps, for Christ's sake pull your weight – don't leave it all to me!' I glare at them in fury while they look at me in complete surprise. Someone says, 'What's wrong, Den? This isn't like you! What's the matter, you not well?'

I stand there, chest heaving and limbs trembling with weakness, full of hot shame for what I have said and know to be wrong, trying to find words of apology and unable to say anything coherent because my throat has seized up. My friends do not take offence but look at me sympathetically, trying to understand.

'Let's all sit down for a few minutes.' Willy puts his hands on my shoulders and gently pushes me down to sit on a rock. He looks at my legs, presses his thumb against my shins in several places, making dents which do not recover. Everybody looks at the hollows in my flesh, and we all know exactly what they mean – beri-beri. 'Short temper, irascible behaviour, unreasonableness, and these dents, they're all symptoms of beri-beri. I'm afraid that's what's wrong, old son.'

Beri-beri! Two small words of fearful import. I am shattered by the knowledge. And there can be no doubting the signs, we have seen them all too often in other men and watched the slow deterioration that inevitably followed. Our medical officer has said that in itself beri-beri is not usually the actual cause of death, but other problems we have – malnutrition, dysentery, malaria and so on – so that recovery becomes progressively more difficult. Or, to put it a little differently – progressively less likely! Or, plainly, it makes it more likely that you will die rather than recover. It's all very simple; those dents in my shins mean that I am now beyond all the old preliminary afflictions from which we have all suffered and (to some degree, at least) recovered – ferociously irritating balls, burning feet, sores that won't heal. I am at the stage where the disease has established a grip that will only become tighter.

The others carry the last logs of the day back to camp while I walk on my own, not really hearing their friendly attempts to cheer me up as I get my thoughts and feelings into shape. I am partially in shock. For a year and a half I have coped, with reasonable success, with all the physical and mental stresses and hardships of our situation, just like everybody else (except, of course, for those who found it too much for them and died), and now, without warning, I have slid past the point of no return and there is nothing I can do about it. Nor can anyone else do anything. For the first time, death is a hard and real possibility – even a probability.

When we reach camp I am in a state of black depression, realising at the back of my mind that I must pull myself out of it, and making an enormous effort to respond to my friends' sympathetic attitude.

A mug of hot tea with the evening rice, and sitting up on my bedspace while my weary legs rest themselves, bring me back to normal. The shock has worn off and I have recovered my equilibrium – only a small nagging ache and a new puffiness above my ankles remind me that I still have a problem to deal with. Thankfully, I have no difficulty in falling asleep. A night's rest is so important at all times.

It is in the morning that I realise that my condition has worsened slightly. Our diet of boiled rice and tea, and thin 'soup', puts so much water into us that the first act of the day is always a good relieving piss, but I am noticeably short of quantity. My night's rest, which should have encouraged my puffy shins to subside, has allowed fluid to seep into the leg tissues and the swellings this morning are more obvious than last night. By the time we have had our morning rice and tea and are ready for work, my legs and feet are aching and I know that I shall not be able to last the day.

Our CSM speaks to the gunso, who comes to me to see for himself. A Korean guard at Kinsayok would probably have bashed me for trying to shirk and sent me out in a work party, but the gunso immediately shows concern. In their homeland beri-beri is common and they know the signs and seem to respond sympathetically, whereas they have a brutal indifference to any other form of illness. In fact, every soldier is given a daily dose of yeast tablets to provide vitamin B1, which demonstrates how seriously their army views this disease. But apparently there is none to spare for our doctors, despite their pointing out that a healthier labour force would produce a better rate of work.

The gunso tells me to stay in our hut and, to my surprise, comes in a little later with four yeast tablets as a 'presento'. He gives me to understand that he will telephone Kinsayok to collect me, which I find most upsetting although I realise that he has to do it. This is a working camp, with no place for men unable to put in a full day. Meanwhile, I am to rest in the hut.

I swallow all four yeast tablets. They have a brewer's yeast flavour which is very pleasant but doesn't go too well with the mug of tea that washes them down. Within a couple of hours my bladder is full and I get rid of all the fluid trapped in my legs in an extraordinarily lengthy pouring out. All that is needed to defeat beri-beri is an adequate intake of vitamin B1, the effect of treatment is immediate, and a small daily supply prevents it altogether. The vitamin cannot be stored in the body for lengthy periods, and sustained deprivation over several weeks uses up all reserves.

The sudden draining of fluids from my legs leaves the flesh soft and flabby. It will take a little time to recover elasticity. But in my whole self, physically and mentally, there is an astonishing improvement. By the end of the day I am almost hopeful of being able to stay in camp, but overnight the puffiness returns with its dull aches and lassitude – and despondency.

I say goodbye to everyone as they walk out of the camp for the day's work. During the morning my replacement arrives from Kinsayok and I board a pom-pom sliding downstream to that hated place.

During the short river trip, I try to revive my drooping spirits by thinking that at least I shall be back amongst my own crowd again. Even if I am in a 'hospital' hut I shall be able to see them in the evenings.

I am dismayed to find that Kinsayok is now almost empty, all fit men having been moved out while I was at the sawmill. The population now consists almost entirely of sick men, and they are in such a poor state that even the Nips have to acknowledge that they are incapable of work. Which means that they are in a pretty desperate condition. Which I realise, with a nasty jolt, must include me!

Checking in at the administration office I am told which hut to move into, and there I find a bunch of complete strangers. Friendly enough, but not a single familiar face. I dump my pack in an empty bedspace and sit on the edge of the platform, feeling my spirits drain out of me and leaving a black void of despair and hopelessness. The walk from the boat into the camp, then to this hut, has exhausted me and I have no reserves, either physical or spiritual.

A hand on my shoulder and a quiet voice saying, 'Come along, chum, time for lunch,' bring me back to reality, and with an effort I pick up my mug and mess tin to be taken to the food queue. There is very little movement in the area. The only men in sight are converging on the cookhouse and they all move slowly and seem to sag or move their legs with difficulty. Another jolt – I must look just like them! The meal is a small scoop of rice and a mug of tea, both plain and without flavour, totally unappetising. Did I hope for anything else? The Nips have told us that sickness and inability to work are due to criminal lack of willingness to work for the Emperor, to die for him if necessary, and are an abuse of his kindness and generosity towards us, therefore we shall be on reduced rations until we reform ourselves and go back to work. Nor will there be any pay – if we don't work, we mustn't expect wages.

There does, however, seem to be a slight change for the better, according to my new friend. The railway has been laid past Kinsayok, trains are rolling through and the pressure has been eased. All fit men have moved north to replace the hundreds of sick who have come down from up-country, some staying here but most going south to Tarsao and Chungkai, which are now used as base 'hospitals'. In his opinion that just means that Nip commandants to the north are getting rid of as many sick men as possible, so that they will die in some other camp. The death rate down there is said to be terrible, not only because the men are so weak but also the camps themselves are so awful.

My brother is in Tarsao (as far as I know) with his shocking leg ulcer, which is a distressing thought. We could both die without being able to help each other or even knowing what was happening. I fall into such a deep despondency that I cannot listen to any more talk, and have to stretch out on my bamboo slats to rest. The humid afternoon heat presses down; we all lie quietly until the evening coolness comes to our relief.

Next morning I attend sick parade. As a new patient I have to be examined officially and have my illness diagnosed by a medical officer. Not that there is anything that can be done for me medically, but I do benefit in two ways. Firstly, the MO tells me that beri-beri has a strong tendency to induce feelings of depression and loss of appetite, and I must, repeat must, make every effort to overcome these symptoms – no one else can help me, I must do it entirely on my own. Secondly, since I can stand up and move around to some degree, he will officially put me onto light duties so that I can walk about with a broom and, in consequence, claim wages.

The completion of the railway through Kinsayok's area of responsibility has, apparently, earned our Nips a pat on the back and lifted a great weight of stress off them. Taking advantage of their happier mood our MOs have been able to get them to agree to paying sick men who do something useful. So scores of bamboo brooms have been made and these are now being used in camp hygiene to bring pay to people like me. As always, deductions are made (ten to twelve per cent) to go into hospital funds to help those too sick to qualify for pay. Nobody objects to that – our people control the distribution of monies and purchases. And the canteen is still functioning, although only on a small scale because there is so much less money in the camp after all the fit men were moved out, but at least we have occasional supplies of eggs, bananas and so on. With the sparse rations, these extras are invaluable – indeed, they keep us alive and boost morale.

Kinsayok is now a camp of sick – and mostly dying – men. There are, I hear, some 1,200 of us and if our present conditions of inadequate food and medical attention continue without improvement, then none of us will last more than a few months. Already there is a hut full of men who would probably not survive a move downriver. Even though the MOs give them priority in the foodstuffs purchased through hospital funds, there is nowhere near enough of the right foods to strengthen their bodies to resist the consequences of prolonged malnutrition. Medical supplies simply do not exist.

There are men in advanced stages of beri-beri who have so much fluid locked in their tissues that they cannot be allowed to lie down. Bamboo backrests have been fashioned for them to lean on. They must be kept upright day and night or their hearts and lungs would be choked with fluid. Their swollen legs are stretched out on the comfortless bamboo platforms, their testicles enlarged to the size of pears as oedema accumulates and moves into their abdomens. If it reaches their hearts, all is lost.

Some men have been unable to stand on their feet for weeks. They are trapped on the bedspaces without a shred of comfort, or hope of recovery, their bodies saturated with pain, helpless in their natural functions, and with nothing but death in prospect.

And they are bored, bored, bored. No books to read, conversation subjects long since exhausted (and requiring too much effort anyway), no news of their families. Homes may have been bombed, parents and sisters killed or died, brothers lost on active service. Their past lives have been blotted out and they themselves have disappeared into limbo. Who knows what records concerning us prisoners will survive to tell the world what has happened to us?

Every day or so someone has to give it all up and die. The others watch as the medical orderlies check their patients as soon as it is light enough to see properly, and bodies are lifted up and taken away. It is an awkward procedure. The orderlies have to kneel on the platform on either side of the corpse to get their hands underneath the body, disturbing the sick men on either side, and then gradually shift it feet first to the central gangway. Unavoidably clumsy, it upsets everybody.

The Nips have refused to allow us to construct individual beds, and even doctor's examinations have to be conducted by crawling up between patients to use a stethoscope. This is but one aspect of the Nips' total indifference to human suffering, and their absolute refusal to permit even the simplest means of alleviating it. Saying 'no' seems to be their response to any request.

I cannot think of words to adequately describe our utter contempt for these barbarous and inhuman people. Stories of atrocities committed by the Japanese army in China, reported in the Singapore press and possibly thought to have been exaggerated by Chinese propaganda, are entirely credible to us with our close-up view of Nip brutalities. I remember reading of a prominent Japanese saying in public that his people were civilised when Britons were dressed in crude skins and painted themselves blue. I will add that at least we have progressed steadily since then, while the Japanese have determinedly gone backwards.

For several days now, my beri-beri has steadily (far too rapidly!) worsened. The puffiness above my ankles has crept up my shins and I can make a row of persisting dents like the holes in a flute. Pains of different kinds have developed, twinges and sudden stabs up into the groin, hot soles on my feet, aching joints and intermittent numbness, all against the ever-present dull, soggy slow throb of a heart trying to push blood through obstructions. And a creeping onset of lethargy, and an evaporating will to do anything about it. Such a tremendous effort is needed to do even the simplest things, I think there is no point trying. I may as well lie down and wait for death. We have all seen so much death in these last six months it is no longer a distant stranger. It moves amongst us, picking and choosing almost at random so that you cannot plan how to avoid its touch.

The medical officer's warning suddenly snaps into my consciousness. Who put it there? I don't think I could have made such an effort, or maybe my instinct for life is still in a fighting mood and is trying to jerk me out of my morbid attitude. Hooray for me, I shall get a grip on myself and throw off my pessimism! Starting right now! Where's my broom?

I find I am huddled in a patch of shade, leaning against an upright pole in the side of a hut. Without really being aware of doing so, I must have stopped to ease my weariness and then slumped to the ground. It's just as well the Nips aren't bothering to supervise us, to ensure that we are actually earning our generous twenty sattangs a day. I have been resting at frequent intervals during the last few days because of the awful dragging tiredness. Despite my new determination it is an unbelievable struggle of flesh and spirit to force myself up on my feet. I have to hang on to the pole to steady myself while my body gradually stops trembling, then my drained will has to push me out of the shade into the heat of the sun.

There is, of course, nothing at all to sweep – I simply have to go through the motions. When the rain slams down it is out of the question and when the ground is dry there is only dust, for every trace of grass and other vegetation was trampled out of existence months ago. Inside the huts there is no rubbish whatsoever – nobody has ever had anything to throw away, so nothing is discarded – and the earth floors are as clean as it is possible for them to be.

It is self-pride that gets me back into gear and finds sufficient energy to keep me sweeping, not too energetically but enough for me to tell myself that I must do what I can to justify being paid. I will *not* allow myself to become a bludger (that marvellously descriptive word learned from the Australians), not even on the Nips. Especially not on the Nips! I will *not* take money from them as a handout, so bugger them!

I feel I have reached a turning point and am now facing the future with optimism. I recognise it as a change of the utmost importance as I have so often seen men fade away because they lost the will to stay alive. On the other hand, the most courageous men have not been able to fend off death despite their gritty fight right up to the last moments. I am absolutely convinced that there is a vital interaction between our physical and psychological powers that involves each helping the other when needed, to the furthest limits. Without the will, the muscles cannot function and without bodily response, the will is ineffective in circumstances such as ours.

The mental effort to get started on each day's routine is now easier, but increasing physical weakness is becoming more of a burden. After evening rice I am desperate to lie down and have to wrestle within myself to be sociable until lights out. As it happens, we are all strangers to each other, a mix of men from different regiments and parts of Britain. Normally this would make for easy conversation but now that is just too much trouble. We cannot think of what to talk about and our attention wanders.

One night I give up early and go to my bedspace to get my feet up, to lessen the aches. With the reduced camp population there is plenty of room in the huts and we are no longer laid out side by side like sardines. I have the hut to myself, apart from a small group down the far end quietly singing popular songs from the far distant never-never land of two years ago. The atmosphere is restful, moonlight washes in soothingly, and there is an occasional buzz of conversation from outside. Peace and serenity lap over me and I doze off.

A sudden, urgent, stir of alarm within me brings me sitting bolt upright, my whole body chilled and sweat running down all over me. I have a moment's panic while I try to find the cause, but the hut is quiet as before and singing still floats up from the far end. Nobody else seems to be concerned.

Then, with absolute clarity, I see my brother Ron, head and shoulders against a dark background of attap, just beyond my feet. His face is thin and drawn, his eyes full of pain. He is staring straight at me. His lips move and his voice comes to me clearly: 'Den, Den, I need help. Come and help me. Come and help me, Den!' and I hear myself answering, 'I'll come, Ron, I'll come, as soon as I can!' The vision fades and is lost. I am looking across the centre passage and sleeping platform on the other side of the hut, at the placid moonlight under the overhang of the roof.

I am shaken and thoroughly disturbed, thoughts racing through my mind as I try to sort out and lock into my mind every tiny detail of what I have seen and heard. For I have not a shadow of doubt that I did see Ron and hear him speak, and that I answered him. I have no idea what woke me so abruptly, I do not have any recollection of bringing myself upright nor any idea as to why I should have felt so cold yet perspire as from a fever – I still am chilled and my skin wet. My mind is seized with his staring eyes, and with the desperate urgency in his voice, and with my promise to come to help him.

He is, by my reckoning, some ninety kilometres away for any bird stupid enough to fly across the jungle – probably 120 by river. But his communication with me was absolutely undeniable, intelligent, positive and *real*. I do not even think of questioning it and I *know* he heard my answer and understood it. I am sure that a tiny flicker of relief showed in his face.

Men come in to settle down for the night, and the small bustle gives way to moonlit silence. I cannot relax. I have had no news of Ron since he was sent out from Hintok last June and now, suddenly, I know that he is in serious trouble and needs my help. Is he dying? His words could mean just that.

How did he reach me? By what power? Is such power available only in drastic circumstances, when an almighty gathering and explosion of mental energy must be made? And how about my reply? I spoke normally, as if on a telephone, but he heard me. Did he exhaust himself, ill as I know he is, and have to fade away immediately after I spoke, unable to stay with me any longer? Is there any way in which I may reach him, and talk further? If so, how can I find it and exercise it?

I am almost felled, as if by a lightning strike – I promised to come to his help, he heard me and was relieved by it. He will be relying on me to keep my promise, but I have no say in my life. I cannot ask to be moved to Tarsao, I have no way whatsoever to influence things! Oh God, what have I done, what can I do? My promise was a natural reaction to his appeal, no other was possible, but how am I to keep it?

I have an uneasy, disturbed night, my mind unsettled by thoughts and half-thoughts, doubts and frustrations. Right now the four members of our family are isolated from each other, without news of any kind. The death of any one of us cannot become known to any other until after the war, and even then the circumstances may not be ascertainable. This is a new worry. It has been hanging in the background for over a year and has now been shoved forcefully into prominence by the fact that death is now a distinct possibility for two of us. I have to face it squarely, while being fully aware that there is nothing at all I can do about it. It is not even a dilemma, because there is no actual choice open to me, but I cannot dismiss the thoughts and they fret at my nerves.

Dozing and waking, my mind never at rest, I attend sick parade in the morning dog-tired and emotionally drained. Clear and dominant in my consciousness, however, is the certainty that Ron and I have been in intimate contact, and that I must watch for a chance to act and take it. I have to wait only ten minutes, to my astonished surprise.

The medical officer joins our group. 'I have some bad news for you, I'm afraid. The Nips have decided that there are too many sick men in this camp, and we have to find 400 men to go down to Tarsao. Now, we know perfectly well that Tarsao has a dreadful reputation and that no one is keen to be sent there, nor do we like the idea of having to pick and choose, but it is a firm order from the Nips and 400 men will have to go. So, if any one of you has any reason for wanting to transfer to Tarsao, we will put him on the list – and, I will add, be grateful to have our unpleasant task reduced by that much. Well, any volunteers?'

Immediately I put my hand up and everybody stares at me in surprise. 'I want to go, my brother has been there since last June with a tropical ulcer and I want to be with him.'

'Fair enough, come to the admin office with me after sick parade, and we'll make sure you're in the party.'

As simple as that, so far anyway. The chances of joining Ron look reasonably good, I just hope that I shall get to him in time – the dark foreboding is still settled on me – but on the whole I am immensely cheered. As the Malays say: 'Siapa orang tahu nasib-nya? (What man can know his fate?)' Indeed!

I am duly listed, apparently the one and only willing passenger for Nippon River Barge Jaunts to Tarsao Holiday Camp. Be ready for departure at short notice – who needs more than three minutes to pack? – tomorrow or the next day. It's really on! My morale soars.

I sweep close to my hut – not only is it less tiring but I can grab my pack in the shortest possible time. Always, my ear is cocked for someone shouting, 'Tarsao party, ready to fall in and leave immediately!'

I wait through one day, two days, a full week. The shine on my optimism starts to dull. We all know from experience that the Nip organisation is an absolute shambles, and the others may be glad of the delay, even hope for cancellation, but I find myself starting to fret and lose heart. In part this may be due to the daily worsening of my beri-beri. We have seen in other men that if the soggy puffiness creeps up the shins above the knees, then you are not likely to recover. You may have six to eight weeks left, steadily deteriorating, and then simply waiting to fade away.

The spongy finger-dents are nearly up to my kneecaps, and I now have a new worry. If our departure is delayed too long I may be found to be too far gone to travel, for I would only be a burden on the others who, of course, are themselves very sick and weak and without the strength to look after someone near death. It would not be fair to ask it of them.

Depression, a symptom of beri-beri, deepens.

Quite suddenly, I am tipped nearer to the edge of the final downward slide. At morning rice I find that I cannot eat. It's not that I have lost my appetite (which I have been warned may happen) but I simply cannot put rice into my mouth. The sight of it is repellent, my stomach heaves, and the smell revolts me. I don't want it, can't face it, and won't eat it.

This is ridiculous. Food has been a daily preoccupation for eighteen months, nobody turns away from a meal. You can't afford to miss even one because you are always existing on such a slim margin, and hunger itself is a psychological problem. I force myself to take up a spoonful of rice, but I can't lift it to my mouth. My elbow locks rigidly, my shoulder too. No effort I can make produces the smallest movement. I take the spoon in my other hand, my right arm immediately relaxes and my left seizes up solidly.

I put my spoon back into my mess tin, an effort in itself, and at once my joints are loose again. Laying the mess tin on my bedspace I try to work it all out. Try again – pick up the mess tin with both hands, and both arms are paralysed. Put it down again, back to normal.

Call one of the others, tell him the problem, ask him to pick up my spoon and feed me. He obliges, but as the spoon comes close to my mouth my teeth clench tight. Try to pull my jaw down with my fingers, cannot move it. Think I might try to take rice from the spoon with my lips, and work it in somehow around my teeth, but they tighten up even more firmly and pain develops around the hinge of my jaw. I'm scared something might break under the intense pressure, and wave the spoon away – my tongue doesn't function and I can't even speak because my whole face is clamped solid. The spoon is put down, everything loosens, but a small ache in my jaw reminds me I have a problem.

The implications suddenly hit me hard. I cannot feed myself, I cannot be fed, the doctors have nothing to offer me: the consequence is plain and unavoidable and horribly close – Christ, I'm scared to panic point.

There must be *something* I can do, or I'm dead. Literally! The canteen, that's it! Maybe some bananas or limes, fruit with vitamins, maybe I can manage to get them into my mouth. But the canteen doesn't open nowadays until after evening rice, and in the meantime there will be midday and evening meals to tackle.

I give away my breakfast and report to the MO at sick parade. He is sympathetic, having seen it before, but he has nothing to help me. He says it sometimes fixes itself as suddenly as it starts. I must keep trying to eat, take my ration at meal times and persevere, see if there's anything in the canteen – limes, peanuts, chillies, eggs, bananas – whatever is there, buy some and keep working at it however long it takes. I can see that it pains him to have to go through all this rigmarole, his doctor's instincts thwarted and deeply offended by having nothing to hand out except transparent verbal placebos when there is so much he could do with a few basic foods. All the MOs suffer this frustration, we know from talking to them, and it shows in their voices as they deal with us. They are wonderful men – despite their inability to help, their mere presence amongst us is good for morale.

Midday rice is served. I am hollow with hunger and screw myself up for the struggle to eat but the result is the same. I have to admit defeat, fuming with anger at not being able to control my body.

By the evening it has occurred to me that I should try a more subtle approach: refuse to be aware of any problem, simply take my rice and eat it without thinking of it, talk to somebody to keep my mind elsewhere. That doesn't work either. The hunger pains will not be dismissed and I am filled with an overwhelming aversion to rice. My body rejects it, absolutely.

The canteen has nothing to sell and doesn't open. I am ravenous, frustrated, depressed, sluggish, and totally exhausted, muddled in my brain and aching everywhere. I can drink tea, thank goodness, and the cookhouse has plenty for the dragging effort of walking to it for my water bottle to be filled. I know I must drink it, but think of how much is staying in my swollen legs.

For most of the night I lie inert, dozing on and off, always aware of hunger and sundry pains coming and going here and there. By daylight I have had no useful rest. The following couple of days and nights follow the same pattern but, inevitably, I am losing ground. My body is feeding on itself and I am noticeably losing weight which I cannot spare.

* * *

We have been given official news that the railway has been completed, and that trains are now running in both directions. The final connection was made at a ceremony attended by high-ranking Jap officers and civilians on 17 October at Takanun Camp.

Unofficially we have also heard that a selected group of our fittest-looking men, dressed in new clothing and boots, was photographed in front of a stack of rice and tinned food. Immediately afterwards everything was taken back and was not seen again. This bit of cheap cover-up does seem to indicate that the Jap command, somewhere in the depths of their minds, do acknowledge that their actual treatment of us must be concealed from the world. But I am really far too tired, worn out, to give all this any real thought. Working in our isolated patches of the line, knowing almost nothing about progress elsewhere, we have known that the last rail must be due to be laid about now, so it's really no surprise.

Good news: it should mean a great – and welcome – lifting of stress and, maybe, an improvement in our living conditions. Bad news: this railway will help our enemy's war effort, but we had no choice in the matter and the RAF will have to deal with that. It is simply beyond my strength to summon up intelligent thoughts about it all, one way or another, beyond a vaguely felt sense of relief and thankfulness that the worst must, surely, now be behind us. It is done, and that's the end of the matter. The future will bring what it will, and we shall just have to cope with it, as usual.

It is five days since I have eaten. My empty stomach must have given up asking me to feed it – in fact nothing much seems to be of interest to me beyond passing the tedious days and nights. It takes all my determination to go around with my broom, sweeping ineffectually when it is dry and simply carrying it around in the frequent torrents of rain. I am indifferent to the downpours, actually finding them somehow soothing and comforting. The really important thing is to keep moving, not allow myself to slump into a heap as I could easily do. I wonder if it is worth the huge effort, just delaying the end. Only the possibility of seeing Ron again sustains me. I have to try, do what I can.

Bananas! The canteen has bananas! It takes me several minutes of slug-like shuffling to get there, stopping to ease the hammering of my heart and driving on again.

Only a few bananas, three per man, and nothing else. I buy three, hold them up in my hand, look at them. No reaction. Pull the skin off one, take a bite, chew, swallow. No problem at all! My stomach shouts for them, all three at once, but I resist it with all my willpower. Two now, keep one for tomorrow morning. Stuff comes into the canteen entirely unpredictably, at the whim of local Siamese boatmen. There may not be any more for days.

To bed, oddly comforted, my last banana deliberately within easy reach to compel me to exercise restraint. In the morning I peel and eat it slowly. Nothing has ever tasted more delicious. A couple of these a day, an egg or two sometimes, a few limes, I shall come back to life!

The canteen remains empty and closed.

In the last twelve days I have eaten only those three bananas, and drunk gallons of plain tea. My body has wasted away. I can circle my waist (all but a bare inch) with my thumbs and index fingers, ring my thumb and finger around my upper arms. In contrast to my grossly swollen legs (still below the knees – did the bananas stop the oedema rising further?) my torso and limbs carry hardly any flesh, the skin stretched smooth and taut. My hair hasn't been cut for three months, nor have I had a shave in that time. I must look like some weird brown-skinned hairy ghost. So do many of the men in this camp. I don't need a mirror to know what I look like.

The long awaited shout comes: 'Tarsao party, ready to leave immediately. Fall in at the river, boats are waiting!'

Soon after midday we nudge into the river beach at Tarsao. An uncomfortable journey, 400 very sick men packed into wooden barges, standing room only, upright sardines, candles in packets, no moving until we arrive.

We crawl and heave ourselves out of the barges, helping each other where possible. In front looms the usual thirty- to forty-foot cliff – no steps, just work your way up as best you can. Dragging my pack I put myself into mental bottom gear and go to it.

Word of our arrival has gone around the camp and helpful hands are with us to struggle up the top half. Everyone looks for familiar faces – friends are of first importance. One of mine rushes up to me: 'Gee, I'm so glad you've come. You're just in time! Your brother's having his leg off tomorrow!'

The way he put it almost makes me want to laugh, but I can see the real concern behind his greeting.

10

Tarsao 'Hospital' Camp

OCTOBER 1943 TO MARCH 1944

It takes only ten minutes or so to walk through the camp area from the river to the Nip guardhouse at the main gate where we are to be counted and handed over to the Tarsao administration, but it is quite long enough for us to become aware that this is a truly dismal place.

Apart from those men who came to the river to help us ashore, the inhabitants take little notice of us. There are not many men in the open, and the faces turned to us from inside the huts as we pass by do not seem to have a smile or a word to say. In any working camp the arrival of a party from outside immediately attracts a great buzz of attention, with lively chatter and enquiries about friends and units, welcoming recognition of mates, even before the newcomers have been checked in and released into the camp. Here there is a heavy silence. We all feel it.

Our own admin staff write down our personal details, allocate us to huts (they call them 'wards' – after all, this is supposed to be a 'Hospital'!) according to our medical status, and we are left to settle in.

My friend Alec rejoins me. 'Your brother has a dreadful tropical ulcer, and agreed this morning to have his leg taken off. They have fixed to operate tomorrow morning. There have been so many in the last few months. I'm so glad you've come – he'll need all the help you can give him.'

As we walk along a line of huts I become aware of a disgusting odour, a thick foul stench hanging in the muggy air.

'Oh, you've noticed it! It's the dysentery wards. And in a few moments we'll come to the ulcer wards. It's even worse there – different, but worse. And the poor buggers inside live in it, day and night. Most of them can't even walk outside to get away from it.'

He hasn't exaggerated. It is different, and it is worse. The first lot, after all, was somewhat familiar – the stink of open trench latrines. But this is new to me. I haven't experienced it before but I know without doubt what it is – the stench of decaying and rotting flesh, held around the huts on a humid windless morning, clogging the nose and throat and seeping down into the stomach. Big blue flies hum around, revelling in it.

Alec stops. 'We go in here. Brace yourself, and try to keep a cheerful look on your face! Ready?'

I can't take a deep breath to steady myself; it would make me throw up. I nod to him and we step into the hut's shadowy interior, which is the same as in any other hut – a central walkway, split bamboo sleeping platforms knee-high along each side, with a crosswalk to doorways halfway along, built to hold some 160 men in cramped discomfort. And this is a hospital ward? There is, as usual, neither water supply nor toilet provision for men unable to walk outside. The floor is earth, trampled down the middle and in loose clods under the platforms. And, of course, no form of lighting.

Ron is in the further half, which means that I have to walk between the rows of sick men who stare at me with vague interest, an occasional smile and a few words here and there for a new face. For my part I am quite unable to put on a cheery smile or even call out a hello. The effort is beyond me, my spirit is paralysed.

During the admission process Alec had hurried off to tell Ron of my arrival, and to warn him of my changed appearance. Nevertheless we are both shaken – two skinny wraiths staring at each other after months of separation, both near death and recognising that fact in the other's face.

He is sitting well back on the platform, leaning against the flimsy attap side of the hut, his left leg out straight and his ulcerated right leg drawn up. I have to kneel on the edge of the platform to reach his hands in a firm clasp.

'Hello, Ron. It's been a long time, but I'm here at last.'

'Hi, Den. I knew you'd come.'

'Alec tells me that your leg is bad, and you've agreed to have it taken off?'

'Yes. It's been getting worse all the time. This morning the MO told me gangrene has set in, and if they don't amputate I shan't last more than two or three days. So I agreed, and they operate tomorrow morning. Even then, my chances are not good. They've taken off over 200 legs here in the last few months, and hardly anyone has survived. But it's my only chance. Anyway, I've had as much as I can stand. It'll be a relief one way or the other.'

His voice is quiet, his words matter-of-fact. He has been through too much pain for too long to be under any illusions. No man in this dreadful place, suffering his own personal hell and watching all the others around him in theirs, and counting the corpses carried away almost every day, can avoid accepting realities.

'You'll pull through okay. I'll be with you, together we'll do it.'

'You look as if you can do with some help yourself! Being together will make all the difference – I can face it better now.'

Leaning over his drawn-up right leg I am aware of the awful smell coming from it. The shin is wrapped in what appear to be bits of old army blanket, stiffly caked with patches of what can only be old pus.

'Den, this is Ted.' Ron gestures to the man next to him. His right leg is similarly covered. 'Ted has been a marvellous friend. I know I would have died if he hadn't been here to cheer me up and keep me hanging on.'

Ted grins. 'Nonsense, Ron's a tough old bird, and now you're here he'll be up and hopping around in no time.'

Alec intervenes to say that it's time for lunch, and we mustn't miss it.

'Back in an hour.'

'See you then.'

I draw my ration of rice, as usual cannot eat it, and hand it over to Alec. The stink hasn't killed his appetite: 'You get used to it. Can't afford not to eat every bit you can get – there's little enough and frequently even less than that.'

Back to Ron's hut. Ted's there but Ron isn't. By now everyone in the hut knows that I'm Ron's brother, and the medical orderly comes along at once: 'Your brother's being operated on now, instead of tomorrow morning. Another chap died, so the surgeon has brought Ron forward to this afternoon. A good thing, it will save him waiting the rest of today and all night thinking about it. Don't you worry, he'll come through okay now that you're here to support him. The others had nobody special to be with them. They lost heart and gave up. It makes all the difference. And the surgeon's first class, top of his year at Edinburgh. Your brother's lucky, they've got some ether, some of the other poor buggers didn't. Stay here and talk to Ted. I'll fetch you when it's all over and take you to the convalescent ward.'

I appreciate that his bright chatter is intended to reassure me, but I'm not really in a mood to respond. I sit down on the edge of the platform and Ted treats me to another big grin. He must be from original Anglo-Saxon stock, straw-coloured hair, tall and big-framed. Every hefty bone now stands out clearly under his taut skin, there's so little flesh to cover them. He can just hobble out to the latrine and that's about the only exercise he gets. His wasted muscles won't allow anything more than, perhaps, an occasional move around the hut to talk to the others. It's several months since his shock of yellow hair was trimmed, he is whiskery, and there has seldom been enough water available to wash himself.

He is, nevertheless, a cheerful chappie with a remarkable aura of serenity which captures my attention. Easy to talk to, interested in everything, Ted is in a Field Ambulance Unit (where else?), and it doesn't take long for me to realise how lucky Ron was to have him lying next to him. Ted's unfailing good humour must have been a real tonic. Even in this first hour spent with him, I look into his lively blue eyes and feel his serene power seeping into me. It is a quite extraordinary experience, absorbing a soothing calm which washes my tensions away.

Ted's mother had been the cook at one of England's aristocratic country houses, and he grew up in the lovely countryside of Berkshire. The lady of the house knew person-ally every man, woman and child in the three villages on the estate, provided a complete set of baby necessaries at every birth, remembered all birthdays, helped with funerals, and followed each child's progress through school. When Ted was old enough he was taken into the kitchens, became a footman (I can imagine how impressive he would have looked in his livery!), butler's assistant (from which he learned about wines), and finally gentleman's valet. He was, in fact, valet to one of Australia's state governors when war broke out, and he joined the Australian army as a volunteer, this being the quickest way to get involved. So this English country boy has ended up as a Digger in a prison camp in a remote patch of Siamese jungle, with a horrific tropical ulcer on his leg.

'Would you like to have a look at it?' He starts to peel off the bits of old army blanket. 'It's coming along beautifully.' I really don't want to see it, but Ted keeps stripping. 'Not as bad as Ron's was, but pretty bad.' The last tatty bit of blanket is laid aside and there is only a piece of khaki shirt over the ulcer. I feel I might easily throw up. The odour grabs my throat.

A bright smile: 'There, doesn't that look good?' It looks absolutely bloody dreadful. From below his knee almost down to his ankle is a raw mess, swollen to twice its normal size, a dull sheen of mucous fluid all over it. I manage (only just) to control a spasm from my stomach. I mustn't let Ted feel that I am sickened by the sight.

'See that?' He points to a pinkish area. 'Healthy tissue beginning to form. And here, new skin growing along the edge.' He looks up with a cheerful grin. 'Won't be long before it heals all over!' His optimism is incredible. How can such a foul mess ever get better?

Ted's blue eyes look straight into me. 'You'll never see Ron's ulcer, be thankful for that! It was far worse than this ever was, and it never showed a sign of improvement. Now you will have some idea of what he has been through. He has shown tremendous courage, wouldn't have lived otherwise. Now, I know you're sick yourself, but you *have* to help him. He'll very probably die if he doesn't have your support. You must be with him every possible minute. He's in a critical state, understand that? You'll have to keep at him to pull himself through – don't let him get depressed!'

Ted starts to wrap up his leg again. 'And I know you'll find that encouraging him will be good for you too. It will help you strengthen your own willpower and fight your own problem. You will help each other.'

The medical orderly comes up. 'I'll take you to Ron now. He's not clear of the anaesthetic yet, but he'll want to see you there, right next to him, when he comes round.'

Another of Ted's confident sunshine grins. 'Off you go! Best wishes to Ron from all of us here. We're all rooting for him. Tell him so when he wakes up.'

Every man in the hut knows what is happening. Their dulled faces are transformed by friendly smiles and cheerful words of encouragement as I follow the orderly out.

Patients convalescing from amputations and other surgery are lodged in a hut of their own. It is exactly the same as any other except that in one section there are individual beds instead of the usual sleeping platform, which allows the MOs and orderlies to stand alongside the patient rather than having to crouch awkwardly on a platform. The word 'beds' is not really accurate, they are just narrow tables made of bamboo poles tied together with strips of tree-bark, hard and uncomfortable and totally without any kind of 'give' or flexibility. A sloping backrest allows the patient to lean back, which is slightly better than lying flat if you don't have a haversack or something else which can be used as a pillow. Few men have even that. There is nothing at all, not even a groundsheet or blanket, between a man's skin and the hard corrugated surfaces of the bamboo, unless he or his mates can produce something.

I have plenty of time to look around while waiting for Ron to wake up. The orderly from the ulcer ward looks in and checks him quickly, tells me he is through the anaesthetic and sleeping quietly, the signs are good and I must let the convalescent hut orderly know immediately Ron opens his eyes. 'Come and tell us how things go, we're all very interested.' And then he has to get back to his ulcer ward.

Ron has lost a frightening amount of flesh since leaving Hintok. His thin body is stretched out flat, his haversack under his head, his breathing is shallow but, thankfully, regular and he seems to be free of pain but no doubt that will come back in due course. The stump of his right leg, taken off above the knee, is neatly bandaged and there is no blood showing through it. I am suddenly struck with the realisation that it is the first new and unused bandage I have seen in any camp. He is wearing only a fundoshi, but it is a warm and humid afternoon with the temperature in the high nineties. I find the orderly and tell him I can let Ron have my blanket if he needs it, maybe tonight if it's cooler. I sit on an empty bed-space opposite Ron, and wait.

Not feeling too good myself, I am half dozing when I become aware of a tall fellow hopping up to me on one leg, moving from one upright pole to the next. He is very tall and so thin that when he turns to sit alongside me I nearly lose sight of him. His voice is quiet, with a pronounced Australian accent. 'G'day, mate, my name's Arthur but everyone calls me Splinter, obvious why!' I introduce myself. 'Yeah, thought you must be Ron's brother. Word gets around quickly. I was in the same hut. They took my leg off three weeks ago. There's twelve of us down the end there, Aussies and Poms. When your brother's recovered, they'll bring him down to join us. He'll be number thirteen. Lucky number, hey? Come along and see us, any time!'

Standing up and moving carefully to try to ease the aches in my podgy legs, I see Ron's eyes open and quickly move alongside him. He seems to be fully conscious and recognises me immediately.

'Hi, Den, glad you're here.' We grip hands tightly; I can feel strength flowing between us. His voice is weak and tired.

'How're you feeling? The orderly tells me it all went well.'

'Much better than I have been. Can you lift me up a bit?'

I raise his shoulders and he looks down to where his right leg was. 'Thank God I've got rid of that bloody thing, it was killing me. Not to have that terrible pain any more, you wouldn't believe the relief.'

I lower him carefully. 'I'll call the orderly. He wanted to know as soon as you wake up. Be back in a minute.'

The orderly takes Ron's pulse. 'Feel rested? No fuzziness, mind clear? Pain gone? It'll come back, I'm afraid, not the same as from your ulcer but from the amputation, but we'll do everything we can to help you. Right then, nothing to drink for a time, sleep some more if you can. I'll be around to keep an eye on you.'

He turns to me. 'You don't look too bright. Go back to your hut, get your feet up for the rest of the afternoon. Your brother knows you're here, he'll sleep easily. Come back after evening tenko.'

I'm glad to take his advice. I'm desperately tired with stress and being on my feet so long. I had hoped that the fillip of being back with Ron would do something to bring back my appetite, but I find that I am still unable to get any rice into my mouth. By now I am past feeling hungry. My belly simply aches all the time. The oedema in my legs is up close to my knees, but instead of creeping up further the swellings are increasing above my ankles, making the skin unbearably taut over so much soggy flesh. Walking anywhere requires deliberate thought in advance, to collect sufficient determination to get myself moving.

But I now have motivation (didn't Ted say so?) and I set off across the camp to Ron's ward more easily than I have been able to move for some time. He has rested well during the afternoon, greets me cheerfully and has a livelier appearance than when I saw him this morning. The anaesthetic has completely worn off – it had been only the barest minimum for the operation – and he has been able to eat some rice and a boiled egg. The egg, according to the orderly, was from hospital funds and not a generous gift from the Nips.

We talk quietly for an hour or so until Ron becomes sleepy, then I walk over to the ulcer ward to let Ted and the others know how he is getting along. They are all intensely interested and give me messages of goodwill to take back to him. They are also interested to hear that I had a brief meeting with Splinter. It suddenly occurs to me that these ulcer cases are unable to move out of their hut, and Splinter and his lot cannot hop on one leg all the way over to see them, so I offer to take messages to and fro at any time.

Surely this is a simple thing for our camp administration to have organised? Something the officers, passing the time in boredom in their hut, could be doing? Doesn't anyone care for the suffering of these men? Is no one sufficiently interested to take a look at how things are? No one here can recall a single officer (apart from the doctors) putting in an appearance during the past several months.

Ron has told me how Ted helped him through the bad patches of his time in this dreadful camp, when his ulcer deepened and spread and his whole being – body and spirit – was saturated with such pain that he was close to giving up. Ninety-seven days from his arrival from Hintok until today, living in agony for which there was not even an aspirin, unrelieved discomfort and boredom, and a total absence of any hope of improvement. The other men in the hut, of course, have all suffered in the same ways, but no one is helped by knowing that others are as badly off as he is. He can sympathise, but that doesn't reduce his own problem – he is merely an individual item in the great overall mass of suffering.

I offer to Ted Ron's, and my own, heartfelt thanks for the constant care and support that he gave despite his own problems. Ron reckons that, had he not had Ted's support, he could easily have given up and died. Certainly he would not have lasted until today, but would have faded out as so many others have done in this same hut, overcome by prolonged starvation and the added strain of their fearsome ulcers. Most, of course, were also burdened with the weakening effect of additional diseases – avitaminosis, dysentery, malaria – to make life even more difficult.

Next morning I am back with Ted, Ron's orderly having asked me to leave while the MO was doing his rounds.

'You know,' says Ted, 'how big a coincidence it is that you just happened to arrive yesterday, only an hour or so after Ron had told the MO he agreed to have his leg off? The MO told Ron that his leg was now in a critical condition, gangrene had set in and death was only a few days away. But they had enough anaesthetic to amputate, which would at least give him a chance. He would not amputate without Ron's permission; the decision would be entirely his. So Ron thought it over, then said he would take the chance and get rid of the bloody thing. It was fixed for today, but they came for him just after you turned up, as you know.'

Ted pauses for a moment to collect his thoughts. 'Now, there's something I want to tell you. It seems weird to me but I think you should know. It must be about three weeks ago, after dark, and I was dozing here when Ron suddenly woke me up. He was all excited, and saying, "Ted, look, my brother's here!" I couldn't see anything, but Ron insisted: "There, standing there, can't you see him?" No, I still couldn't see you or anybody else. There was no one there.'

Ted goes on: 'You know, it gives me a bit of the creeps to think back on it. There was something uncanny in Ron's insistence that he was looking at you and talking to you. Then Ron said that he had told you he needed help and wanted you to come here, and you said you would, as soon as you could, then you disappeared. I thought maybe Ron was going round the bend a bit, but he seemed to be perfectly clear-headed and was absolutely definite about the whole thing. Then he lay back and went to sleep, calm and relaxed, the first real sleep he had had for weeks. Next morning he was bright and cheerful and said that you would be here soon and everything would come good, and he's been sort of expecting you to walk in at any moment. And right on the dot, here you are!'

My hair feels as if it's trying to stand up on end, and Ted's eyebrows are arched up as if he still can't believe it. So I tell him, in detail, how in Kinsayok, at what must have been precisely the same moment, I had a vision of Ron calling me to help him and of my promise that I would come to him. And how, totally out of the blue, there was the announcement next morning that a large party of sick men was to go downriver to Tarsao and I had asked to be included. I also thought that if I had not developed symptoms of beri-beri at the time I did, I would not have been sent back to Kinsayok and would not now be here. Ron's ulcer would have deteriorated as it did, and without the spiritual strength which he gained from our brief 'communion', he could well have died. And, come to that, if I had had to stay at Kinsayok with my beri-beri, I would most likely be dead by now. It was only the hope of rejoining Ron that kept me resisting the insidious urge to give up and get it over and done with. I had seen it happen with others.

So many links in a fragile chain of incredible chances, every one of which was a miracle in itself, strung together in the right sequence to achieve a specific purpose – keeping Ron and me alive! Neither Ted nor I can accept that we have just been lucky, that it had all been a matter of random events. Some power must have been in control – but then why had it been necessary for Ron to have his ulcer in the first place?

We can't make it add up – I can only feel intensely grateful that Ron and I will now survive. For some reason I am absolutely sure of that, even though there is no foundation at all for such confidence – except, perhaps, for that brief moment at Kanyu, near the empty camp and the graves of so many dead soldiers, when I felt such certainty that I would survive.

Tarsao is the first camp I have found with a boundary fence along three sides and a large guardhouse (with pole and Jap flag) at the formal entrance/exit gateway. The fourth side is, of course, the river Kwei Noi, running at the foot of an embankment some twenty or more feet high, with a small guardpost (also with flag prominently displayed) overseeing all traffic moving along the river.

It has changed a lot since we passed through on our march to Wampo a little over a year ago, when it was not much more than a bivouac-style transit camp. Now it is the headquarters and base area for the railway system and for all Jap troop movements and stores to and from Burma. This explains the need for a fence to keep us contained in a specific area, separated from the Jap army which is under a totally separate administration. The military zone is called Nam Tok, and it is full of movement of trucks and men – and we can easily see the difference between soldiers of the frontline units and the slovenly rabble who infest our camps.

The fence is constructed of bamboo (what would we do without this marvellously versatile species of grass?). Thick poles set in the ground at intervals support a continuous screen of thin sticks laced with bark strips to horizontal rails.

It is, in fact, little more than an unnecessarily elaborate marker to show our boundaries, for a few quick slashes of the bindings at the main posts would allow the whole length to fall flat on the ground.

My hut is one in a row of about twenty, laid out at right angles to the fence and spaced close together. They are simply attap roofs on bamboo poles, no walls along the sides, so that I have a curious view: it's as if I were inside a dense bamboo forest populated by hundreds of men lying and sitting on their sleeping platforms, and moving about in the shadowy interiors.

A big problem is created by the fence: the Nips insist on latrine trenches being located in the narrow strip between the fence and the ends of the huts. We have no choice in the matter, our medical officers are simply overruled by some stupid Nip or Korean soldier, who points to a spot and says, 'Benjo.' Any protest sends the Nip into a screaming tantrum, with bashed faces all round. They simply have no concept of field hygiene.

With maybe a couple of thousand men in this part of Tarsao, the latrines do not take long to fill up; there is nowhere else for the men to go. The monsoonal downpours flood the contents out and swill them around everywhere, the flies are thick, and when the rainwater soaks into the ground, the residues are left on the surface. Requests to draw shovels from the toolstore are ignored, so we cannot even dig new trenches or drains to carry away the floods.

Walking around in bare feet, especially if the skin is broken with open sores, is a disgusting experience, especially at night. For the men living and sleeping at the ends near the fence, the discomfort is unending – even the ever-present bugs in the sleeping platforms have become a minor irritant in comparison.

There is no water supply unless you can get yourself down to the river, which is several hundred yards away. There are no containers such as buckets to carry water from the river for sick men to use. The river water is too muddy (and certainly is contaminated) to use a water bottle because it would be impossible to sterilise afterwards.

I am told that there are some 3,000 men in Tarsao. The number increased with the completion of the railway in mid October, when the working camps sent seriously sick men downriver. There is another 'hospital' camp between here and Kanburi, called Chungkai. It is the subject of numerous rumours which say it is both far better, and far worse, than this place. Why is it that we never get real news about other camps?

I spend as much time as possible with Ron. The improvement in his condition, day by day, is quite remarkable. The medical officers are able to provide him with an egg most days, and his starved body makes the most of it. The nourishment that had once been used ineffectively to fight his ulcer is now available to build up his strength, and the release from constant saturating pain is a tremendous help in his recovery. His dull cheeks now show a patch of pink, his eyes have brightened, and he talks much more easily.

When I comment on this, Ron tells me he has noticed it himself and has been having some thoughts about it. Some three months ago the Nips issued quinine in large quantities to be given to all patients in daily doses as protection against malaria. This quinine came in the form of tiny crystalline needles, the dose being a level teaspoon once a day. The stuff was incredibly bitter (as I knew from being similarly dosed at Wampo, at the beginning of the wet season) and difficult to swallow. It would not go down in one lot, instead spreading all over the tongue, palate and throat, bitter as hell, and clinging for hours. Mixing it with tea didn't help. The hut's 'wardmaster' couldn't be bothered administering each man's dose individually, so he put a dollop of crystals into a canteen of tea, shook it up, and told the men to swallow a mouthful and pass it on. He then disappeared.

The mixture was so vile that each man pretended to drink and handed the canteen to his neighbour. Ron, the last man at the end of the hut, found himself compelled to drink the lot when the wardmaster came to collect his tin and saw it had not been emptied. The man was a habitual bully, loathed by the patients in his care, and he stood over Ron shouting and swearing until he had drunk far more than he should of this disgusting mixture. In his weak state Ron simply couldn't resist him.

The result was that Ron took several times more quinine than was medically desirable, in completely random and unmeasured doses, over a long period. Discussing this with his new medical orderly, Ron has been told that quinine has to be administered carefully. Dosages must not be exceeded and, after ten days at the most, treatment must be discontinued for a time. Excess intake leads to quinine poisoning, resulting in deafness, dizziness, slurred speech and other troubles.

I tell Ron that when I first saw him I was very worried by the fact that he seemed to have difficulty focusing his eyes on me, couldn't speak clearly, and did not seem to hear me very well. I had put these symptoms down as side effects of his ulcer and prolonged pain, but it now looks a bit different. It could well be that the overbearing wardmaster, who couldn't be bothered to look after his patients properly, was responsible for Ron's deteriorating condition, which was noticeable in comparison with Ted and the others.

Ignorance, bullying, concealing laziness and in-competence behind badges of rank – these occur in all armies,

I suppose, but I hadn't expected to find them in a professional medical service.

Back with Ted, I pass on my discussion with Ron. He had noticed Ron's symptoms, but had not realised their probable cause. Nor had the medical officer, come to that! He will see if he can have a quiet word with the MO about the wardmaster and the consequences of his negligence and crude behaviour.

In the last twenty-two days I have eaten nothing at all except three bananas, early on, and drunk gallons of tea (which won't have had any food value). I don't think I have any more weight to lose, unless my internal organs start shrinking. Do they do that? If so, has it already started to happen? I doubt if I weigh much more than eighty pounds. I used to be around 170.

When I go to see Ron and Ted I have to make a real effort to liven myself up and make conversation. I know it is good for me to make this effort. If I didn't have to do so I could very easily – even thankfully – lie down, go to sleep, and simply not bother to wake up again. My body is close to surrendering, but my spirit is determined not to give in, like the old saying: 'The spirit is willing, but the flesh is weak'. How true, but while the flesh can be kept functioning, by willpower, through incredible odds, the spirit does have to have a home to live in. At some point there must be a simultaneous failure, a cessation of both functions. I don't think I have become depressed, which is really a mental condition. My problem is in my body, a nagging tiredness that tempts me to rest, to relax, to drift off, just for a little while until I feel stronger, to give all the aches and pains a chance to let go.

So far I have been able to sleep at night without any worry about whether I will wake up in the morning. Now I'm beginning to wonder, during the day, if tonight I shall fade out and not wake, so maybe I should try to stay awake all night. But common sense tells me that won't work. I must just go to sleep and wake up as usual. I need the sleep not only for the rest it gives me but because it blots out the day's miseries for a time, and strengthens me for the next day.

Standing in the queue for evening rice, there is an announcement. The hospital has bought some rice polishings, two spoonfuls for every man. 'This is a very valuable food, collect your ration with your rice.'

When I reach the serving point I don't take any rice – I know I won't eat it – but I have my polishings dumped in my mess tin. Many men look at the reddish-brown powder and refuse it – 'Not going to eat that muck' – so I push my mess tin forward and take their share. By the time serving-out is completed, I have quite a pile.

Same trouble as before – my arm locks and my teeth clench tight. Tip some into my mug of tea, drink it quickly before I realise I have fooled myself! It works! Same again, refill my mug and drink until the whole pile has gone.

A couple of hours later my bladder is shouting at me. As fast as I get rid of urine my bladder tops itself up, a continuing stream that goes on for several minutes. The fluid in my legs seems to be draining out, too. I do go to sleep, dashing out at intervals to lose another pint or two. By daylight I'm a different person, new life is stirring vigorously and, God, am I hungry!

Breakfast rice goes down, and I hang around in case anybody is too sick to eat his ration, striking it lucky with a few extra spoonfuls. Still ravenous! My legs look deflated, flabby and soggy with being nearly drained, but the real improvement is in my mind. Confidence and optimism have come back; I am ready for the future.

Ron and Ted both notice the change immediately, as does the MO at sick parade. Twenty-four hours, it's a miracle!

It's going to be a long wait until midday rice comes up. No man awaited his lover with as much urgency as I look for my next serve of rice! I fidget with longing!

There is a stirring throughout the camp, an air of activity that contrasts sharply with the apathy and inertia that were so noticeable when I arrived at Tarsao.

Our party of sick was under the command of an Australian medical officer. He is an imposing figure, some four inches over six feet, and big physically. I am in a hut which has mostly Australian troops, and this MO came into the hut to meet his fellow soldiers. Their welcome was tremendous, enthusiastic. He is a real hero to them. He served in the disastrous Greek and Crete campaigns, and in Egypt before ending up in Java. A man of enormous energy and dedication to his men, he has come down from the Burma end of the railway and frequently been in trouble with the Nips for speaking his mind about conditions in all the camps.

At least twice in his brief time in Tarsao he has been subjected to severe punishment, but it has not discouraged him and now he is back in action. In this context 'severe' punishment is in fact deliberate torture.

Ted has given me his firm opinion – and it is supported by every man in his ward – that the dreadful condition of the camp is largely due to the disinterested attitude of the senior British officer, a lieutenant-colonel in the British Royal Army Medical Corps, a career professional with long years of service behind him. The opinion is that he has given up trying to obtain improvements from the Nips. It is said that he just cannot bring himself to talk to Japanese coolies – it's beneath his dignity! – so he has turned his back on the hardships of his wretched men, spending his days down by the river indulging in his hobby of fishing. Meanwhile the camp has steadily deteriorated, rations are terrible and hospital supplies almost nil. There is no canteen functioning, camp hygiene is abysmal and morale is at rock bottom.

All these defects were, of course, immediately apparent to the Australian MO when the British colonel showed him around the camp. Indeed, the shockingly bad conditions would have thrust themselves onto the attention – and up the nose – of the most unobservant passer-by. The listless sick men (nine out of ten pocked with septic scabies sores), the cook-house litter heaped in the open, the unsanitary latrines, the flies in swarms everywhere, the absence of normal activity and movement – all these added up to a demoralised slum area.

Word has quickly gone round that the Big Australian, as his men proudly refer to him, made a number of pointed remarks and finally asked the SBO point-blank how such a dreadful state of affairs had come about. Affecting surprise, the SBO replied, 'Really, is it as bad as that? I'm afraid I hadn't noticed!' Which provoked a wrathful outburst recommending the SBO go back to his fishing and leave the camp to be run by someone who was sufficiently interested to do so.

Interested bystanders, fascinated by this public dressing-down of a senior officer despised by all as being responsible for their misfortunes, lost no time in passing on their stories to their mates. Whether or not the SBO could actually have achieved anything by standing up to the Nips, his great sin is that (as far as we know) he has never really tried to get anything done. If he had pressed the Nips for improvements and had his face slapped, at least he would have earned respect. But it seems that he gave up at his first rebuff, unable to bring himself down low enough to talk to such unpleasant people, and preferred to pass the days down by the river, fishing. We do know that his batman carried his fishing gear to Tarsao, all the way from Singapore. That's how we all see it.

The Big Australian, however, is made of far tougher material. The Nips are an unpredictable lot, and it is quite possible that their 'Samurai' heritage admired his courage during his two punishment ordeals, which occurred within his first few days in Tarsao. This, in turn, may have induced them to hand out a few useful items.

Not very much – empty oil drums (to be scrubbed out with sand), shovels, axes, buckets – but they had not been provided previously, and to us that is significant. We are also allowed to make up parties of fitter men to bring in water to fill the drums and firewood to boil it, to sterilise every item of clothing and bedding. Cookhouse refuse is buried and new latrines are dug.

On the medical side we have obtained some crude lump sulphur and animal fat to make up ointment for scabies. The skin is first scrubbed with hot saltwater until the pustules come away and blood dribbles cleanly from the spots, which are then smeared with the sulphur goo. Painful, but remarkably effective.

The huts are dealt with systematically. While the stark naked men of the first hut are attending to the sterilisation boilers and passing blazing torches around the joints in their hut, the men next door are carrying everything out ready for their turn.

Stupefied by endless weeks of boredom, the men get going with a will. Sick men are carried out into the sunshine and given a hot water wash, something it has not been possible to do for them for months, while their rags are boiled up. There's no soap, of course, but the hot water is a treat and helps them to feel like human beings again. There isn't a leaf within reach inside the camp, and for months these wretched men have not been able to clean themselves properly after a bowel movement, so they are unpleasantly crusted with dried excrement. Not their fault at all – and I'll bet the SBO has never given such problems a thought. It wouldn't have occurred to him because he has never taken any interest – none at all. All kinds of pox on him!

My roll of beautiful white toilet paper, bought on an extravagant whim at Kinsayok, is still unused because you can't carry it around in the rain or even use it on a wet bum! Ron can have it. Used sparingly, it should see him through until he is on his feet – foot – again. There, I knew all along it would come in useful! I'll take it with me on my next visit, a Christmas present in advance. He'll never have another one quite the same!

Counting their actual years these men are young, mostly around twenty-two or so. But in their shrunken physique and haggard bearing they look to be in their fifties and sixties, undernourished and in the poorest health at that.

They cannot hold themselves properly upright. Their walk – if indeed they are able to walk – is shaky and pain-ridden. They talk only when there is a need to do so. Their speech is slow and difficult, the effort too tiring.

Only in their eyes do most of them show defiance and grim, stubborn determination not to give in. In some, though, there is only despair beyond the reach of friends, and defeat that will surely lead only to longed-for release in death.

In which of these men does our God of Mercy reside?

Ron continues to make good progress. He not only looks a lot better in his face – brighter and more cheerful – but he moves

411

more easily and speaks clearly now the quinine poison is being eliminated. His hearing has also improved, and he is eating all he can get.

On the seventh day, though, everything changes. I find him lying back listlessly, his face lined with pain, his morning rice almost untouched. The medical orderly sees me and immediately comes over: 'It's just what we call post-operative relapse, nearly every case has been through it. The stump of the leg starts to hurt, probably the internal cotton stitches beginning to break up. It seems to bring on a period of depression. Be with him as much as possible, try to get him to talk, keep his interest up. And make him eat, get that rice into him however long it takes, keep at him. It depends on you. Once he starts to slip it will be difficult to pull him back again. I see you're looking a lot better yourself, good for you! You'll have to watch your brother carefully. Call me anytime. Start with his breakfast rice, push it into him! However long it takes, I say!'

It takes nearly a couple of hours to do that, talking to him continuously to keep him mentally active, urging him to feed himself. He is still very weak physically, from those awful months when his ulcer drained away all the scant nourishment from his food and left nothing for the rest of his body. But he is determined not to give in. I can see the tremendous effort he is having to make to take in each separate mouthful of rice, and to swallow it rather than spit it out. It is painful to watch, but with my own so-recent experience of nearly starving to death, I will not allow him to ease up.

I visit Ted frequently, and talk to the men around him. There are very few with ulcers on their arms or torsos, nearly all are leg cases with dreadful lesions on shins and ankles and most of these men are unable to move from their bedspaces.

Along the length of the hut, on both sides, some 120 men spend all day sitting up on hard bamboo slats, leaning back against the framework of the hut wherever a support can be found, their good leg stretched out flat and the bad one drawn up. Conversation dried up a long time ago – what is there to talk about? They have talked about their lives at home until they can talk no longer, homesickness sets in and adds to their bodily pain. They lie there, gazing across the hut at someone equally distressed, simply waiting for time to pass, unable to bother about what it will bring.

And every morning the medical orderlies come in to work on their ulcers. It is a time of intense fresh pain which leaves each man stretched to the limit of his fortitude. There is no medication whatsoever, treatment can be nothing more than the crudest attempts to clean out muck and pus, dead flesh and rotted fragments of tendons and tissues. Tropical ulcers start with a patch of mortified tissue, which does not break away from the underlying healthy flesh but remains firmly attached and eats into it. The deadened tissue cannot be wiped off, so with no drugs to fight it there is only one way to remove it: by scraping and slicing through the attached surfaces so that it is cut away, leaving the healthy flesh clean and bleeding, and raw.

The sheer horror of these festering ulcers turns the stomach of anyone seeing them for the first time; they are beyond anything a normal person can imagine. Yet the men who suffer – such an inadequate word! – from them are forced to look at them every day when the pus-blotched pieces of old army blanket are peeled off.

They get used to it, inspecting their own ulcers intently to look for signs of improvement or worsening. They examine those of their neighbours, pointing to this or that bit of something and making comments in matter-of-fact voices. A malarial rigor will set it all back overnight, red blood cells destroyed by fever and the poor diet totally unable to replace them, weeks of tiny signs of healing obliterated by angry new infections, weeks of tiny hopes shattered.

But good signs, hardly noticeable to anyone less deeply concerned, are hailed with optimism. The almost invisible new skin beginning to form around the edges brings out cries of joy and congratulation from everywhere. In this close community of pain and despair there is a powerful bond of sympathy for bad news and encouragement for good. No man is alone and the comfort it brings is beyond measuring. But nothing shifts the enveloping stench of decaying flesh.

The men are familiar with all this, but it is new to me and my first time, as onlooker, I have been screwed up tight with horror and nausea. Ron's ulcer at Hintok was the first we had seen, and it horrified us. But the dreadful ulcers here are so appalling, beyond any imagining, that what I saw earlier is almost as nothing. Ted hadn't warned me, and my imagination has nowhere near prepared me for the shock, and he notices my reaction: 'Bit gruesome, isn't it? You get used to it, like the smell, in time.'

The men at the end of the hut are treated first, the others await their turn in resigned patience. The orderlies have a sickenly difficult job. There is no point at all in trying to be gentle because it only prolongs the agony rather than achieving anything helpful. The men agree with this, and the orderlies scrape and slice briskly to get each man done as quickly as possible. A busy chatter goes on all the time, and insults are traded: 'You learning to be an apprentice butcher?' 'I tickle my girl like this, and she loves it!' 'Didn't know you fancied hippos!' 'Well, some of them are better looking than you!' It helps to smother the cries of pain.

How do they think of something new to say, after so

many weeks and months? The courage of these men is extra-ordinary. After all, any soldier can get used to being shot at, but this is quite different and demands very special spiritual strength. Not only do they endure pain at intense levels, they are all well aware that in the end it may all have been for nothing. Ron is the thirteenth amputation survivor from 228 operations – that is, sixteen died for each one that lived.

The surgeons have a terrible decision to make. Short of anaesthetic in particular, and of every other item, they cannot amputate while a man is still strong enough to cope. They have to keep the numbers needing amputation to a minimum, and must operate only when death is very close, when the patient is at his lowest ebb and least able to bear the shock. Some have died, of course, simply because nothing was available when needed, and even a last-hope operation could not be done.

The voluntary orderlies do a wonderful job, many of them having started by looking after a friend and then staying with it. Although they have no medical background, they deal efficiently with their patients, their days filled with such unpleasantness as I would be unable to bear. There are others in the dysentery wards, working in primitive conditions and nauseating squalor, and many have become infected and died. This is the heroic side of human compassion, attainable by only those few who respond instinctively to calls from the helpless. I don't think anyone can, simply by careful thought and consideration of all the circumstances, choose to involve himself in work so offensive to all human senses. There must, surely, be deep inner springs of sympathy and love and care, and an urge to help which will not be denied.

It is a severe ordeal for Ted and the others at the far end of the hut, having to watch and listen to others receiving their 'treatment' until the orderlies reach them. But this is not the end of the matter. After the orderlies come men (mostly voluntary helpers, for there are not enough trained RAMC personnel) with hot foments. These are quite disgusting squares of old army blanket, fished with bamboo tongs out of four-gallon cans of very hot water and slapped onto the newly exposed raw flesh to draw out any residual infection. The pain must be shocking, and the men's faces show it.

These bits of blanket have to be reused continually. They cannot be thrown away because there is nothing to replace them. There is no soap to wash them clean after use, no disinfectant, and they are sterilised only by prolonged boiling. Every one seems to have old pus patches clinging stiffly to the fabric – boiling does not dislodge them and they cannot be scraped out. The foments are left in place, gradually cooling, until the next morning's torture session. They cannot be removed because there is nothing which can be used in their place as a dressing against flies. They come off coated with new pus, for further use. There is no choice in the matter. What is being done is simply the best that circumstances allow.

To receive 'treatment' each man has to work himself forward so that his leg is accessible. Afterwards, he moves back to his sitting position, his face taut and strained while he recovers slowly from his ordeal, unable to speak while he fights his jangled nerves and calms his strung-up muscles. It seems to be a matter of pride not to shout or scream when the terrible pains strike. I hear nothing more than muted moans and cries and imprecations.

The rest of the daytime is passed almost in silence, with only desultory conversation here and there. The afternoon heat and humidity smother the will to do anything at all. The men doze uncomfortably in a sweaty haze, the atmosphere thick with the odours of putrescent flesh and the filthy crude bedpan which is in constant use.

The bedpan is an insoluble problem. It is the lower half of a circular five-gallon steel drum, with a couple of strips of wood held in place across the top. It is the only one in a ward which has 120 men whose innards are irritated and scoured by grit in the dirty rice they have to eat, and by silt in the river water in which the rice is cooked and tea is brewed. There is always a queue to use it, mostly of some urgency, for loose bowels do not give much warning or allow much delay.

It is quite impossible to take it out to the latrine for emptying after each use – there simply isn't time between calls for it. The result is a build-up of muck which quickly gets so high that users find themselves in unpleasant contact with its contents. There is no facility for the orderly to flush it clean; the best he can do is scrape around it with a stick and swill it out with a pint or two of precious water.

There is only one light at night, a wick floating in a tin of coconut oil, the feeble flame emitting inadequate light for the orderly to work. When he takes the bedpan outside, the light goes with him and the hut is in darkness unless there is moonlight which, in the wet season, is not often.

Some – most – of these men have lived in these conditions, day after interminable day, for several months. Their stoic endurance is remarkable.

After a grim struggle, Ron has overcome his depression and is eating normally again, gaining weight and reviving his usual good spirits. Ted and the others are delighted, I carry messages to and fro. The fact that Ron has survived when so much was against him is encouraging to many who face the probability of losing a limb.

I am with Ron when his surgeon comes along to remove the bandages and check whether the stump is healing properly.

The suture line itself looks very good, it is an extraordinarily neat job considering that the amputation was done in twelve minutes flat – that being the limit of the available anaesthetic – with only a cut-throat razor, carpenter's saw, housewife's needle and cotton thread. The surgeon is very pleased but points out that the internal ties being ordinary household cotton and not surgical gut, they will soon start to rot and will start to work their way out through the suture holes. He snips away the outer threads and puts on a fresh dressing, a minimal covering because he can't afford to use more than is absolutely necessary. The bandages will have to be washed and go back into stock for reuse.

Ron's hut is for men convalescing from surgical operations. All of them were weak and under a death sentence when their operations were done, recovery is slow and there is no inclination to move around and chatter. The dozen survivors of amputations are at the far end, so the others must be appendicitis or similar internal operations. It is a quiet place, a little apart from the main camp, and if you ignore the familiar discomforts it is even restful.

Opposite Ron, on an ordinary sleeping platform (the individual beds being few and kept for new recoveries), is a man in his mid forties. We know little about him and there seems to be nobody from his regiment to visit him. He came in some three weeks ago in a state near to coma. He was a soldier in the Great War, and having come through all that he volunteered for this one and here he is, in the depths of Siam's forests, lying near-naked on uncomfortable bamboo slats. Occasionally conscious enough to totter out to the latrine and to collect his rice, he is out of our reach and does not respond to efforts to talk to him. Unshaven and long overdue for a haircut, he spends the days dozing. Sometimes he mutters to himself but we cannot catch the words – maybe a name, his wife? He wears an old and ragged green wool pullover, hand-knitted – a present from his wife on his departure overseas? – which he takes off in his waking moments. He picks lice from the seams, pops them between his thumbnails, puts it back on, and falls away into his own limbo.

We can do nothing but wait for his inevitable death; he has already surrendered his will and makes no response to any of us. Monday afternoon we feel that it is now a matter of days, and at three o'clock on Friday afternoon he stretches himself out straight and gives a long sigh. I fetch the orderly, who cannot find a pulse, and we carry him out to the small hut where the dead are placed to await burial.

It is odd how his death affects us. Tarsao's cemetery receives corpses almost every day, recently fourteen in a single day, and small processions of stretcher-bearers and chaplain can be seen all too frequently. There is even a permanent squad of grave-diggers, who try to keep a little ahead of demand with four graves always ready while they fill in over new occupants.

Although this particular death has been no surprise, and the hard fact of death is familiar to us, we somehow see it as special and out of the ordinary. Maybe he acquired some kind of Unknown Soldier status, this stranger brought into our community, being with us long enough to become part of our group but in his person not one of us, because we were never able to know him. A soldier of two wars, dying in total loneliness, put into a hole in this godforsaken spot which will never be visited by kith or kin – and we feel so impotent and helpless. The sheer futility screams at us – it has been so pointless, so aimless, no meaning or purpose to be found in it anywhere – and we are deeply disturbed, our protective mental armour fallen away. We have been reduced to men who mean nothing, who have no control over their own lives and who cannot give help of any real substance to anyone else.

This is a depressing attitude, and we must pull ourselves out of it. Our isolation from everything familiar in our old lives has been so total for nearly two years now; we may be at risk of drifting into acceptance of unreality as being normality. Sometimes I feel that we might have been transported to another world without realising it, but of course this is dream stuff – nightmare stuff? – and we are continually being reminded of where we are, and of the unpleasant facts of our lives.

A young man is hurriedly brought in and put on the vacant bed next to Ron. His eyes are rolled up, his mouth is wide open, his breathing is hoarse and ragged in his heaving chest. He has been brought in from an outside work party, severely dehydrated. Nothing can be done for him. In an hour his body gives up and he is dead.

We have noticed a number of new faces among the medical officers in the camp. The gossip is that our people knew there was a surplus in our Changi area, in Singapore, and asked the Nips to send up MOs and orderlies to help out with our massive numbers of sick men. We hear that seventy MOs have arrived with a number of orderlies, but no medical supplies came with them because the shortage in Singapore is as desperate as it is here. They have dispersed to various camps.

One of these newcomers walks up to our hut this morning to conduct sick parade, freshly turned out in a clean and tidy uniform, close-shaved, hair brushed to a shiny polish, moustache neatly trimmed and carrying a swagger-stick – a riding crop, would you believe it? – which he smacks against his leg as he approaches the hut doorway.

A small space has been partitioned off just inside, with a tiny bamboo table and a bamboo bench on either side, where patients can be seen by the doctor. We are all waiting in the central walkway, behind the partition, our wardmaster standing in the doorway in hospital tradition, putting on a bit of a show because word has reached us that Changi still works on army spit and polish, and the newly arrived MOs expect us to conform. Well, they'll soon find out that there's very little spit and no polish at all in this neck of the woods. We will try to let them down gently.

In this particular instance it takes only a few minutes! Most of the men in my hut are Australians, whose favourite pastime is taking the piss out of pompous Englishmen – well, any Englishman will do, but pompous and 'superior' types are much more fun. So the sight of this immaculate apparition has them all agog, their eyes brighten in anticipation, and they are not disappointed.

The wardmaster, wearing only a hat and fundoshi, brings his bare feet to squelching attention and salutes: 'Good morning, sir, ward ready for sick parade.' He doesn't get a proper salute in return, just a supercilious wave of the riding crop, a form of bad manners which has always irritated me and now prompts a flurry of subdued comment from the Australians, the mildest being 'Snooty bastard!' And then they hear his very English, university-accented, 'Thank you, wardmaster, shall we begin?'

Two strikes against him, and the poor fellow isn't even inside the hut!

The MO takes off his cap and lays it carefully on the bamboo table, his swagger-stick alongside, and seats himself. 'May I have the first patient, please, wardmaster?'

I really have no idea whether the first patient was elected by his fellows or came forward by pure chance. He is older than the rest of us, grey-haired and stocky with a face like a well-worn army boot, creased and indestructible. He had been a cavalry man in the Great War, served in Palestine, and thought the youngsters in this war 'might need a bit of a hand from an old-timer'.

Sliding his bowed legs under the table he sits down, leaning comfortably on his forearms. 'Mornin', doc, I got malaria,' in an affable voice.

The MO's reaction is extraordinary. 'This is a sick parade. Don't you know the proper procedure?' in an angry tone.

No answer, only a look of innocent puzzlement.

'You will stand at attention, give me your name, rank and number, and tell me your symptoms. Then I will tell you what is wrong with you! You will not sit down unless I give you permission! And you will address me as "sir"! Do you understand?' The MO is working up to a red-faced temper.

The Australian makes no move to stand up but remains sitting exactly as before. There is a noticeable set to his features and his hands tighten into fists.

In exasperation the MO shouts, 'Wardmaster! Can't you get some discipline into these men?'

Before the wardmaster can reply, the Australian's voice cuts in, still quiet but now with a gravelly edge to it: 'Like I said just now, doc, I got malaria. I've had thirty-two goes of malaria and this is the thirty-third. I know exactly what I've got, I've got malaria and I don't need you to tell me I've got malaria. So now we both know I've got malaria, don't we?'

Staring straight into the MO's disbelieving eyes he unhurriedly stands up. 'G'day to you, doc,' he says politely, nods to the wardmaster (who is having great difficulty keeping a straight face) and walks away down the hut. His mates make way for him, and break out into hoots of laughter.

The officer, furious with impotent rage, realises that he is beaten, puts on his cap with as much dignity as he can muster, picks up his riding crop and marches stiffly out. As he swipes the air angrily, he is followed by jeers and catcalls and sundry crude pieces of advice: 'What's the matter, mate, lost yer flamin' 'orse?' and 'Come back termorrer, an' 'ave another go!'

Shooting a pompous twit of an English officer down in flames this morning has delighted them all. The wardmaster, by the way, is not RAMC but a Volunteer from Kuala Lumpur and, like me, has little sympathy for medical officers who set their rank ahead of their duties. Thank heaven, they are rare.

We have often wondered what happens to the personal effects of men who die. There must be thousands of bits of this and that – mess tins, water bottles, groundsheets and blankets, hats, packs, maybe a few combs and toothbrushes – which have had to be disposed of. Many dying men, I know, tell their mates to help themselves after they have gone, but now an unpleasant scandal has become public knowledge.

Men who die isolated from their friends, such as in a 'hospital' like Tarsao, are simply carried away by medical orderlies, and their kit goes with them. We have always assumed that their possessions have been handed in to our own hospital authorities for distribution of useful items to those in need. Things of a more personal nature – wallets, letters, photographs and the like – would be destroyed, there being no possibility of preserving them for eventual return to the men's families. Some men have clung to wedding and signet rings for sentimental reasons, refusing to sell them even to buy food, and these (we thought) might be sold for the benefit of hospital funds.

Call it charitable thinking, simple-mindedness, naivety or trust in our fellows in these difficult conditions – whatever it was, we were wrong. In fact a number of orderlies have been helping themselves to dead men's belongings and selling them around the camp. This has been exposed by a soldier who held his dead friend's paybook. On the page 'Soldier's Will', which any soldier can use with full legal effect to bequeath his belongings, were listed specific items to be handed to his surviving mate. In his absence, his friend's body and kit were taken away, and by the time he was able to follow it up there was nothing but the body awaiting burial. He was able to identify several items in the possession of others, who all said, quite truthfully, that they had bought them from medical orderlies.

Our administration officers know nothing about it. There is no procedure at all to deal with dead men's possessions, and no thought has been given to the matter. The orderlies who removed the body were all affronted innocence, but if the officers were not prepared to do anything, the men were. A brief, no-nonsense interrogation elicited the truth, and the culprits were reported to the SBO. The word is that they will face a court martial on repatriation after the war. But who really believes that? It will be just another 'can't be bothered' fizzle.

The human body's capacity to repair itself is absolutely astonishing. Both Ron and I have only a few weeks ago been in such a shrunken state as to come very close to giving up hope of recovery. In spite of the miserable food – poor quality rice (and not enough even of that to fill a man's belly), a small quantity of soya beans (a new addition to our diet) and, very occasionally, an ounce of some kind of vegetable – Ron and I have improved quite remarkably, putting on weight and feeling much better in ourselves. Ron, of course, now being rid of the ulcer that was draining his life away, is also free of the dreadful unending pain that sapped his vitality. In my own case, I have no idea what it was that enabled me to escape from the deathly grip of beri-beri, finding my appetite just in time to avoid sliding over the edge. I think it was the rice polishings, coming at just the critical moment.

Growing up in circumstances of deep loneliness, Ron and I formed an exceptionally strong bond. I am quite certain that it was this closeness that enabled him to speak to me, and for me to hear him and respond, across nearly 100 kilometres of Siam's mountains. I am equally sure that it is our present togetherness that creates new strength which we share and draw upon to our mutual benefit.

In my mind there is no doubt that a large proportion of the men who died were simply spiritually suffocated by the smothering isolation in which we live. We could be on another planet, without any contact with our previous lives – no letters, no family news, no reliable news of the war. We do not even know what is happening in the nearby camps. Tomorrow could see us move elsewhere, we never know in advance where we are going or what it will be like when we get there. We have absolutely no say in our lives. We live like animals kept for work and nobody cares if we live or die. Each man has to rely totally on his own personal resources, with the support of close friends when he needs it, to cope with conditions under which familiar things have all but disappeared, leaving him with almost nothing in a grinding struggle to survive not only physically, but to retain sanity and a sense of humour.

While a man is in reasonable health it is a matter of passing through each day to the next. In time of serious illness there is an awful temptation to let go and have it all done with, and some are seduced fatally. As my own personal experience, in recent weeks, tells me.

In one of the surgical huts there is a Cockney lad who has become a kind of camp mascot. Typical of the inhabitants of the poverty-stricken East End of London, he has a sharp wit (despite a miserably poor education) and an irrepressible flow of lively chatter. What is remarkable about him is that he should, by any medical logic, be dead!

Thin almost to the point of being skeletal, his back and chest are crisscrossed with surgical scars. Nevertheless he sits upright on his bamboo bedspace, holding court every morning and evening with a little crowd of admirers, cracking jokes and tossing friendly insults in all directions, swapping tall stories and recalling his pre-war life at home and at the local pub. His obvious nickname is 'Sparrow', that perky little hop-around, and the Cockney form of this is 'Sparrer'.

I am told he has had thirteen operations, starting with a major TB problem and then repeated patching-up as something else went wrong. I have also heard criticism – not at all frequent – that too much (precious dressings and so on) has been given to one man while others have had to do without, but I cannot accept this. The medical officers have an impossibly difficult job – making decisions must be the worst part of it, because medical supplies become available at totally random intervals and must be put to best use in the circumstances at the time. Those responsible must be left to do as their consciences dictate. It is the only possible way.

To my thinking, however, the tremendous benefit of keeping Sparrer alive has been the almost miraculous effect that he has on everybody who comes to see him, which must include, as the weeks go by, just about every man who can get around on his own feet. He is living proof of the sheer toughness and durability of both flesh and spirit combining in determination to live despite adversity. To see the cheerfully grinning faces around him and hear the jokes and repartee bandied about give a hefty lift to my morale as it must surely do to others. Even the nostalgia which sometimes pervades the talk is good for us – we must never try to forget our real lives or give up hope that we shall eventually get back to them.

I have no doubt that Sparrer's continued presence amongst us more than justifies the resources which have been used to make it possible.

Ron has a setback in the healing of the stump of his right leg. As predicted by the medical officer, drops of pus have started to ooze from the suture punctures on each side of the scar where the flesh was sewn together. The scar itself has healed well; the pus is from bits of cotton thread rotting behind it, oozing out through the convenient tiny holes. There is no proper treatment available, no sulpha tablets to get at the internal infection and no way of reaching it from the outside. By the third day the stump is showing signs of inflammation, it is throbbing painfully and Ron is faced with the frightful possibility of having another three inches of his stump amputated. The surgeon is worried too, and my own feelings are nearing panic. The double row of tiny new ulcers has horribly unpleasant potential.

On the fourth day after the new ulcers appear the surgeon brings along a small bottle of carbolic acid and a splinter of bamboo. Saying that he is not sure if it will do any good but that he has nothing else to offer, he very carefully applies a drop to each puncture after wiping away the pus. There is an immediate tiny sizzling bubble as the carbolic sinks in, and the pus inside bleaches white. Despite taking the utmost care in applying each drop, the surgeon cannot entirely avoid touching the surrounding flesh.

Lying flat on his back, both hands pulling his stump upright for the surgeon to work on the underside, Ron cannot see what is happening, but the tightening of his fingers tells of the biting sting of each drop.

Every few hours the treatment is repeated, with a careful massage to push the pus towards the outlets and prevent it from working inwards. In a few days the cotton threads have rotted away completely and been expelled, the suture holes are cleansed by carbolic acid, and Ron's stump is back as it should be. It has been a close thing but it now seems to be over, to the relief of all of us.

On the far side of the boundary fence that runs past the ends of our row of huts the forest has not been disturbed, and tall trees stand amid the undergrowth. It is not true jungle as we know it in Malaya and in parts of Singapore, but more like a thick forest. Around Wampo the trees tended to be small, as if the soil did not provide much nourishment, and the undergrowth was lighter, so there was tussocky grass everywhere. Here the trees are altogether bigger, straight heavy trunks with foliage branching some fifty feet up, the ground in permanent shade with shrubby growth struggling upwards for sunlight, and no grass at all.

There is a full moon shining through the lace-patterned treetops, and the trunks are in silver-edged silhouette. Sitting on our bedspaces and chatting, we become aware of movements on the forest floor, glimpsed between the thin bamboo poles of the fence.

Then we see a group of small animals scampering around, leaping up to grip the tree trunks and galloping up without a moment's pause. It is so beautifully graceful, the lithe upward spring smoothly becoming a slickly coordinated pulling and thrusting climb that takes them, in seconds, to points just below the side branches. A quick look around and they push away from the trees, spreading broad 'wings' on which they glide swiftly downwards to the base of another tree maybe twenty yards away, where they attach themselves for a second or two before racing upwards again. The 'wings' look as if they are membranes between forelegs and body.

The performance continues for an hour or so, and the little creatures seem to be doing it for fun – running up, planing down, up again for another glide. There is constant motion, swift climbing and crisscrossing swoops in the moon-light, ribbed wings pale and stretched out taut. We think they must be some kind of bat, although they are a bit large – about the body size of a small cat.

And we have also had a visitor of a rare kind! Up in the roof, hanging upside down from the ridge-pole, is a large sloth making his seemingly weary way along the length of the hut. The interior is dimly lit by a couple of small coconut oil lamps, but we can clearly see its lean shaggy-haired body, long head and great curved claws gripping the bamboo pole. Poetry in slow motion!

No one saw it come into the hut, we leave it undisturbed and by daylight it has gone. How it crossed the fence to reach us, and how it will get home again, are mysteries to us, but we wish it well in its travels.

We have our human equivalent of sloths, in the next hut: two Dutchmen, plainly visible because our huts have no walls or side screens of any kind. During the day they are up and about, returning for meals but out of sight elsewhere most of the day. They do not appear to have much wrong with them – they certainly look in better condition than any one of us –

but at morning and evening tenko they are somehow stricken with a mysterious form of paralysis which makes them unable to turn out on parade.

While the rest of us troop out to fall in for checking by the Nips – who expect you to do so unless you really are incapable of walking – these two stretch themselves out comfortably, lying on their sides facing each other so that they can talk quietly and cosily while they wait for a Nip to come through, counting the bed-down cases.

As the bugle sounds for us to get to the parade area this morning, we see an unusual brownish heap on the bare earth under the sleeping platform in the Dutchmen's hut. Disturbed by the sudden stirring of so many men getting off the platforms and hurrying out along the central walkway, the heap uncoils to become an unusually hefty snake, stretching out to some ten or twelve feet and solidly thick in the body. The men in the hut do not see it as it starts to move. Fascinated, we watch it sliding under the empty slats until it reaches the point directly beneath the two recumbent Dutchmen. Here it stops and its head rears up, tongue flicking out. There is a gap between the bamboo slats. It shoves its head through (rather like a submarine's periscope surfacing), and stares into the face of one of the Dutchmen, only inches away, then switches round to gaze into the eyes of the other man.

There is a brief moment of frozen shock, then the two Dutchmen are off their bedspaces and sprinting down the hut like champions, followed by our cheers and laughter. The snake undulates rapidly to the fence and slithers through to safety in the forest.

The Big Australian doctor has certainly brought about some beneficial changes, all of which, it must be said, could have been initiated and carried through by the SBO who, as ever, prefers to spend his days fishing in the river.

The Nips allow the officers to have batmen, one each to lieutenant-colonels and one between three or four of lesser rank. These men visit their mates in the camp, so we have a continuing and reliable flow of news as to what goes on in their area. Some of the officers, of course, are older men for whom imprisonment must be a severe strain, and they take life as easily as they can. Between them they have a considerable stock of books which help to fill their time, and cards (by now somewhat tattered) for endless sessions of contract bridge. Their big problem is boredom.

All officers do get paid, however, and even after fairly hefty deductions from their pay for hospital funds (in addition to sums held back by the Nips) they still have a very useful amount to spend on themselves. What they can buy, of course, depends entirely on what happens to be available in the canteen, which until now has been very little and at irregular intervals. This looks like changing, however, under the Big Australian's vigorous efforts to improve our lot. But the minimum officers' pay is five times ours, which does allow them to buy important extra food – eggs, bananas, palm sugar and, occasionally, bottled and tinned stuff – and that treasured comfort, tobacco and the paper to roll cigarettes. Without the stresses of close daily contact with the Nips and heavy physical work, they should be able to keep reasonably fit, even if they are bored.

Men in the ranks, who also have deductions from their tiny pay, and are unable to buy supplements to their rice ration in any quantity, have had to perform backbreaking labour on starvation rations, put up with Nips at unpleasantly close quarters every day, and suffer diseases with little or no medical attention – all this without any means of relieving their tensions and strains except by the blessing of conversation with their fellows. There are few books indeed amongst us – I have one, which I will never sell even though there is a ready market in the officers' lines. Nor is there any music, of any kind.

You might think that the younger and more energetic officers would be sufficiently grateful for their privileged position to show it by taking some interest in the men. They could, with little effort, visit them in the wards, simply talk to them, read books to them, anything which showed sympathy. For if the officers are bored, how might the sick men be feeling, totally bereft of comfort and in many cases not even able to get out into the daylight? Sitting in wretched discomfort in the same spot, day after day, looking at other sick men in the same condition. And might it not take the edge off the officers' boredom if they were to involve themselves in the welfare of their men? It is, after all, one of their primary obligations in the holding of the King's Commission. Excluding the medical officers and administrative staffs, who have done sterling work in the face of unimagined difficulties, I have not seen any officer visiting the wards during my weeks in Tarsao – or, come to that, in any previous camp.

It is true that with the breaking up and dispersal of regimental units there may be officers who do not have any of their own men in their camp, but surely that is not an excuse for them to distance themselves (as they clearly have done) from soldiers of other units. We are, after all, still on active service, all of us together, and not in some state of suspension where rules no longer apply and basic human decencies can be suspended until things get back to normal.

Living and working in appallingly primitive and oppressive conditions, the men in the ranks have displayed an impressively high standard of tough stoicism, resilience and endurance. Treated by the enemy as cheap slaves of no consequence, bashed and humiliated constantly, they have still managed to come through with cheerful optimism, caring as best they can for sick comrades. They deserve better recognition from their officers, who have not had to face up to a fraction of these pressures.

There has been a suicide, the first that we know of in any camp. The body of a British soldier has been brought into the camp, the head severed and the neck badly mangled. Identification was immediate.

The man's friends say that a few weeks ago he slipped out to trade something with the local Siamese. On his return he told his mates that one of the village women had invited him into her hut, and into her bed. Never having slept with a woman in his young life he had thought himself lucky, especially as she did not want any money from him. Possibly she thought she was doing him a favour in his loveless life as a POW.

But it was not a favour, and there was a heavy price. The unpleasant symptoms of venereal disease appeared, which threw him into a deep depression, there being no possibility of treatment, and he began to talk of doing away with himself.

The position of his head and torso, when found, indicated that the method he chose was to lay his neck across a railway line in front of an oncoming locomotive.

Dear God, another sparrow fallen! Did you notice it? Amongst the thousands of others?

The Big Australian's driving energy and forceful personality have produced extraordinary results, in the strongest contrast to the lackadaisical attitude of his professional RAMC colleague (who is still his senior – unfortunately – and, as such, the senior British officer). Somehow he has got the Nips to agree to provide materials for men to make useful things for the camp; he has even managed to have these men classified as workers with the same pay as workers on the railway. More than that, there is to be half-pay for the sick who, officially, constitute the whole population of the camp apart from the medical, administrative and cookhouse staff. The benefit to morale of these small improvements is enormous, and the whole atmosphere has brightened.

There is no lack of talent in the camp, and the word has gone out not to throw away anything whatsoever, however poor its condition, but to give it to the hospital. The result is astonishing: carefully hoarded boots beyond any repair, bits of brasswork from webbing equipment, socks which will never be worn again, bits and pieces which had been kept simply because nobody threw anything away. Some men even have cut-throat razors, too blunt for shaving but having senti-mental value, which would have earned them a severe bashing had they been found in a search.

There are Australians splitting tree trunks along the grain, with an axe and wooden wedges, to form planks which in turn are split through their thickness to provide laths and strips suit-able for making crutches for amputation cases. Another group of Australians is stretching cattle hides over bamboo frames to scrape and cure them. Our rations of meat are scanty, but a single hide can produce a fair amount of useful leather for hospital straps and wooden-leg sockets. Ex-professional barbers have set up shop and visit huts in turn to give every man a shave; the soap (familiar yellow kitchen bar) comes through hospital funds. Some of the barbers have kept their old clippers and shaving brushes. Everyone gets a haircut too! Tinsmiths take four-gallon coconut oil cans and scribe outlines which they cut, trim, bend, roll, fold, tuck under and tap together into watertight cans and containers, invaluable in the hospital and cookhouse. Former instrument makers, accustomed to the delicate shaping of metals, make surgical instruments and small tools from scrap. Crude, maybe, but effective.

The legless men have been moved into the end section of a hut where they make bamboo brooms, cutting and splitting the stems and binding them into useful household items. They turn out a small stack of bamboo brooms every day, and attempts are being made at basket-weaving but not with much success because the right materials are not available. With the improving weather men are beginning to drift around the camp, and almost without exception conversations about brooms end up with, 'Well, I suppose making brooms keeps you busy?' So a sign has been put up: 'Yes, making brooms keeps us busy, and stops us being too bored'. Nevertheless, people still come up, read the sign and make exactly the same comment! Obviously, some brains are permanently woolly! Sheer, endless boredom – it loosens the nuts and bolts sometimes.

We don't know where all the brooms end up, for there are no floors to sweep in this camp and we are very careful about litter to keep the flies under control. Not that anybody really has anything to throw away! Maybe the hospital sells them to the boatmen?

To be doing something useful, utilising old skills and applying imagination, after so many deadening months of boredom, has had a magical effect, not only on the relatively small number of men involved, but also on every other man in the camp. At last something is being done, somebody is taking an interest in their wellbeing and not just leaving them to live or die, as fate will have it.

The payment of wages throughout the camp to men doing useful work not only points to a welcome change of attitude in the Nip command, but also makes life a lot easier for the men. The overall amount of money now in circulation is sufficient to bring in Siamese boatmen – who, I hear, have to pay our camp guards fifty-eight ticals per boat to be allowed to trade – and to provide useful contributions to the hospital fund. All wages have about ten per cent deducted, to enable the hospital to provide extra food for the seriously ill and, occasionally, to buy useful medications. So everyone's happier!

Ron's small suture ulcers have healed cleanly, and he is now with the twelve other amputation survivors. They are a cheerful, friendly lot; all have been through the same close-quarter fight with Old Man Death himself, forfeiting a part of themselves as payment for being allowed to live. In a secluded corner of the camp there are now buried 228 limbs, already rotting before being taken there to complete their decay and return to nature. It's a gruesome thought – why on earth did I think of it?

With Ron making up the lucky thirteen, I find myself included in a fascinating little group in which not one man is quite the same as any other. There are eight Australians and four British, in assorted sizes and shapes, and in no time at all Ron is taken into the circle. The Australians have a nickname for the British which, apparently, goes back to the bad old days of convict settlement in their country. The word is Pom or Pommies, of uncertain origin, and to be addressed as 'you old Pommie bastard' is a definite sign of friendliness.

I gather that most of these young men grew up during the grinding Great Depression of not too many years ago. Their schooling stopped at an early age because their parents couldn't afford to continue it and, in country areas, boys had to help out on the farm because no farmer could pay wages to outsiders. War broke out just when they were bored stiff and desperate for something active and interesting to do, and they swarmed to the recruiting stations just for the chance to break out of their dull existence – and to go abroad and see something of the world.

These men are all volunteers – there is no compulsory service in Australia – and I can visualise what a high-spirited and cocky lot they must have been – even in our conditions as POWs it shows. As new recruits they must have been a lively handful, impatient and full of real enthusiasm to get into the fight.

Their reward has been to end up in Nip prison camps, frustrated (aren't we all?) and a bit prickly towards us Poms in general because they feel it is all our fault. It's difficult to argue this point since they have been under our command throughout, and haven't we stuffed up one campaign after another since the war began? Except, of course, for the first brilliant successes in North Africa, against the Italians, but then our politicians stupidly threw all that away and we had to go back to square one. Churchill will have a lot to answer for, when the war is over, in our opinion.

Apart from Ron and myself and one other, the Poms are all from the British 18th Division, which arrived in Singapore too late to be of any practical use in defending the island. They come from Norfolk and Suffolk, Cambridgeshire and Lincolnshire, aged in their early twenties and part of the first fully trained and equipped division to leave Britain for overseas service, so they say. And all that was wasted when they were diverted from North Africa to Singapore, thrown into a situation already beyond hope, when they should have gone to Rangoon. There is strong opinion that the politicians hadn't the guts to admit that Singapore was doomed at that stage, and overruled military advice that the division be sent to Burma where it could have been far more effective. So, thousands of men suffer to save the face of incompetent politicians, and Burma was left with weaker defences than it could have had.

Our thinking is greatly clarified by our circumstances. There are no bars to hard objective logic and nobody to accuse us of (as the saying goes) causing alarm and despondency among the troops, nor do we have to be concerned with the tender egos of interfering politicians. In fact, we have a hard-earned right to criticise anybody who has failed us, as severely as we wish, and we take full advantage of that!

The senior Pom is a sergeant in the artillery, a battery of 25-pounders. Jack had started his first job as an actuarial accountant with an insurance company when he was called up, and he has an incredible ability to toss figures around in his head and produce answers without resorting to calculations on paper – very useful in his old job, but also as a gunner, because he could study an ordnance survey map and come up with ranges and elevations and other figures straight out of his head, in a fraction of the time taken by others to scribble measurements and angles and then sort them out. He has a girl at home, a serene confidence that she will wait for him to come back to her, but he is troubled by the thought that she might change her mind when she sees he has lost a leg – she might see him as disfigured.

Don is similarly concerned about the special girl he left behind, and he and Jack yarn together endlessly. Don has a very bad stammer, which kept him out of a frontline unit and in the Pay Corps, but didn't prevent him becoming a POW. He has suffered from this speech defect since childhood, and has never been able to overcome it, but says that in the last year he has definitely improved because he has been able to work on it free of the distractions of ordinary life. When he wants to say something, nobody becomes impatient or tries to hurry him along or say his words for him. He just takes his time to get them shaped and spoken.

Harry comes from the Middlesex town of Enfield, which gives its name to the army Lee-Enfield rife manufactured there. By coincidence, my grandparents have lived in Enfield for donkey's years, and I was christened at St Stephen's Church just down the road. Harry never had much schooling, worked as a labourer and in his spare time played soccer for Enfield Town. His muscular physique earned him a place in a three-inch mortar team, lugging bombs around to feed the weapon. Football was one of his two great loves, and he still hasn't got used to the fact that he will never again kick a ball on a field. He is simply reluctant to admit it to himself. His other great love is his fiancée (engagement ring and all the formalities), and he has the same worries as Jack that his girl might be put off by finding that he is no longer the vigorous young athlete she used to know.

Bert is the only professional soldier in the group. Serving with a regiment that provided battalions for overseas service, he was in the Singapore garrison when the Japs arrived. He is a bit less than average height and has wasted away somewhat, and wearing his Australian Digger's wide-brimmed hat while he hops around he has, naturally, acquired the nickname 'Mushroom' – or, amongst the Australians, 'Mobile Toadstool', if they want to annoy him.

Australians have always had a reputation as being tall men, and Arthur certainly fits the bill. He must be six feet four inches on his bare foot, and is so thin that from the side his beaky nose and prominent Adam's apple are the only notice-able parts of him. But he is a truly delightful man to know, with a lively sense of humour and a naturally kindly attitude towards others – a bit strained in the case of the Nips, but even then with a reluctance to admit that such dreadful people do exist. In peacetime he drove a heavy truck for a steel factory, and became an ambulance driver in the army, a role that was acceptable to his conscience.

Joe is another who will never be able to go back to his old profession, and because he loved it so much – it was his whole life – and never thought of doing anything else, he is inclined to brood for long periods, isolated in his sadness. He lived in South Africa conducting safari parties deep into the wild bush away from civilisation, sleeping rough for weeks on end. It was his strict rule that his expeditions were for seeing the country as it was and for observing the native peoples and animal life – no game was shot except as food for the party, or in self-defence. For people genuinely interested and prepared to put up with the simplest living conditions, it must have been a marvellous experience. Joe has a narrow strip of leopard skin sewn around his Digger's hat, and sits in his corner stroking this reminder of the old days, immersed in memories.

Dan and Rex are two country boys from the depths of New South Wales. When the war with Germany broke out they had never been in a township – in fact they seldom crossed outside the boundaries of their cattle stations, which are bigger in area than some English counties. Keen to go overseas they had not wasted a moment in packing their kit and catching a train to enlist. Nor do they regret it. Their present situation is simply part of the luck of being a soldier, and their thoughts are always on what lies ahead when this lot is over. Unfailingly cheerful and optimistic, they are a good pair to have around.

There are four other Australians, but I never get to know them for they keep themselves separate from the rest of us.

They spend their time in an empty space in the main part of the hut, on the other side of the partition, and we really have nothing to do with them. That's their choice, and nobody questions it.

This is the diverse group that Ron has joined, and with whom I spend as much of my time as possible. As English ex-public school boys we are at first regarded with some curiosity, being their first close contact with that mysterious world. Most of their officers will have been from similar schools, but they have been somewhat aloof because of their rank, whereas we are right amongst them. Apart from our education, which continued two or three years beyond theirs, we had been in the school's Officers Training Corps (OTC) and had passed War Office exams (both practical and theoretical) which would take us direct into training for officers' commissions in the army. Nearly all public schools have an OTC, affiliated to some regular army regiment and supervised by the Commanding Officer of a nearby military base. In the event of war these OTCs provide an invaluable call-up and initial training for commissions. On leaving school many of the boys join a territorial unit and thus add to their capabilities. All the boys who were at school with us would have joined the services when war broke out – we wonder how many will survive.

However, Ron and I are somewhat different from others of our background, having lived in the Far East apart from our years at school in England. They consider us as 'officer types' in the ranks, being private soldier and lance-corporal respectively, but then this would apply to nearly every man in the Singapore and Malayan Volunteer Forces – nearly 15,000 of us toting a rifle instead of being properly employed to make use of our abilities. We have university professors, scientists of many skills, pharmacists, managers in commerce and banking, managers of rubber estates and tin mines, engineers in power stations and the petroleum industry, lawyers, police, prison warders – in fact, a mass of men highly trained and competent in every aspect of a modern progressive society, all of them stuffed wastefully into the lowest levels of the army where their special talents are of no use to anybody.

This brilliant state of affairs was brought about by government in general and the Manpower Bureau in particular. The Bureau was set up after the collapse of France, in a panic about the shortage of manpower to defend the country, and every European male of military age was required to register. No man was permitted to leave the territory without permission, and conscription (with necessary exemptions) was introduced for part-time training.

Early in 1941 thousands of men were taken into the various Volunteer units, no consideration being given to any man's special skills or to his value beyond shouldering a rifle. That objective having been achieved, nobody seemed to think it necessary to provide the serious training and the level of weapons and equipment necessary to build an effective defence force. 'Paper' numbers were sufficient in themselves, apparently – actual fighting capabilities were of no consequence! The result was that these men, desperately keen to fight because they were literally defending their own homes and families, were sent into action almost totally unprepared and badly underequipped. Nevertheless they fought well, but always at a disadvantage.

While they were in the front line their wives and children were left – with no assistance from the government – to make their own escape or suffer internment.

There is a great deal of bitter, and wholly justified, condemnation of the bumbling and witless authorities responsible for the whole terrible mess.

* * *

Amongst the first to benefit from the Big Australian's drive to improve conditions are the amputation cases. Thirteen pairs of crutches, made to measure for each man, were brought to their hut a few days ago and have already knocked up astonishing mileages.

It took only a few hours for the men to acquire balance and the knack of stepping out, striding over the muddy earth in rain and shine to visit mates still immobilised in the old ulcer wards. After months of enforced idleness – because you simply cannot hop on one leg across rutted mud – there is tremendous exhilaration in being able to move around again. Some of these men have been confined to their bedspaces for five months, the first part in unending agony from their rotting limbs, a dreadful dragged-out ordeal that never eased until the crisis point of having their legs taken off, when new problems came upon them.

They have to build up strength in their good legs, weakened by prolonged lack of use, which now have to do the work of two, and in their shoulders, arms and hands gripping their crutches. I am fascinated to watch these men, so recently resigned to boredom and the slow passing of the days, swinging enthusiastically everywhere in the camp, whooping with pleasure at coming across a friend not seen for too long. They even get into the river, slithering down the steep bank and scrambling back up by their own efforts, cheerfully declining help from willing hands: 'Thanks, mate, I'd rather do it on my own!'

I try to find words to describe to myself this explosion of bottled-up high spirits and renewal-resurgence-resurrection of minds and bodies. For a long time we have been convinced, through our own observations, that there is a link of enormous strength between our mental and physical selves, that each reacts with and strengthens the other in times of need. What I am now seeing is the joyous celebration shout of victory over debilitating sickness and disease, despair and lethargy, death itself, and (always there in the background) the insidiously weakening poison of our total isolation from everything which used to be familiar to us and which we still hold dear. Did we ever have another life? Sometimes it seems so far back that it might never have happened. But now we have a bright faith in the future.

Despite their new mobility meals have to be brought to these men as you cannot use both hands to wield your crutches and at the same time carry a mug of tea and a mess tin of rice. The cookhouse orderlies bring the rice tubs and dixies of tea after morning tenko because it is more convenient, whereas we others eat before tenko. This means that I can cross the camp to join them at the start of their day, and swap cheery greetings such as, 'Hi there, you old Pommy bastard!' and other classic forms of 'Good morning'.

On this particular morning, not really different from any other, Rex suddenly comes out with an excited cry. 'Say, youse fellas, d'yer know what today is? It's the first Tuesday in November; it's Melbourne Cup Day! What say we have ourselves a race?'

Our ignorance draws some ripe Australian comments, from which we gather that it is a great horse racing occasion, a day of high-class races programmed around the finest horses in Australia – in fact, undeniably the best in the world, even if we dumb Poms have never heard of it. The betting money is colossal and the whole country shuts down to listen to the radio commentary. It is also the big day of the year for wealthy society to display itself in traditionally fancy hats and dresses, for the benefit of newsreel cameras and newspapers. We can't provide the fashionable ladies, but we can have a race! The idea flashes down our hut and leaps across to others, and within a few minutes there is a mob of excited men milling around the course, which is the open space between two rows of huts some 100 yards long.

At one end the thirteen starters line up, looking down the course to size up the best way to avoid sundry obstacles such as tree roots and twisting ruts in the mud. The horses are a mixed lot, from Arthur standing eighteen hands to Bert, who is about the size of a donkey, all pushing and shoving for a position to give them the easiest run down the course. In the noisy holiday atmosphere the excitable ones balance on their crutches and paw the ground with a hind leg, neighing and snorting, hooting with laughter and slinging insults at their competitors.

Have you ever come away from a racetrack swearing that all the nags you backed were three-legged and fit only for the glue factory? In this race *every* horse has only three legs – one at the rear and two crutches at the front – and every single one has only recently been desperately close to the knacker's yard. But you would never find a field more full of high spirits and determination to put on a show. In the midst of the hubbub men are shouting the odds. 'I'll put me dough on the tall one!' 'Nah, he's too skinny, lookit the condition on that fella!' 'Ten cents on Joe, who'll take it?' 'Give yer evens!' Big deal, ten cents all at once, but it's half a day's pay!

The starter bawls, 'Yer racin'!' and they're off. Arthur, cunning horse, has taken a position in the middle of the line and immediately sweeps his crutches out sideways and trips up the runners jumping off their marks beside him. Lunging forward, his height and long reach giving him a tremendous stride, he is well ahead of the mob, who chase him energetically while flailing their crutches in all directions to propel themselves forwards and throw their opponents. Arthur sprawls headlong over a rut, Joe get his revenge by holding him down with his foot on Arthur's rump as he charges past, while lightweight Bert has jumped on a spectator's back and is making good time at the side.

The whole pack stampedes over the finish line (wherever that may be, nobody is quite sure) in a scrambling heap, puffing and blowing with their mighty exertions. In the wriggling tangle of bodies and crutches it is impossible to declare a clear winner. And maybe that's the best result. The real prize is the quite extraordinary lift to everyone's morale, runners and spectators alike.

We are now well into November, and we pass on to the others the welcome news that the monsoon rains will end in a week or so, and we shall come into the winter months with brilliant cloudless skies, hot dry days and spells of cold snaps at night. Those who came to Siam last March and April have experienced only drenching rains pouring almost without cessation from a purple-black sky, the days and nights humid and sticky, stiflingly hot and sweaty, and the sun brassy and sullen when it broke through. Water from the river will be clear, our rice and tea free from muddy silt and grit, our scoured and abraded intestines will have a chance to heal and our bowels to dry up. We have survived nature's torments and the Nips' murderous speedo.

Together with the basic but so beneficial improvements brought to the camp by the Big Australian, we are now a very different lot from the sorry mob of only a few weeks ago. Our rations are very little improved (and still seriously deficient) but things are more readily available from the canteen. Medical supplies are still almost non-existent, but somehow more is being done to make life a bit easier for the long-term sick, with hospital funds able to provide occasional extras. We are still badly cramped for personal living space, and it is a year since we received our one and only piece of soap, so keeping clean is often difficult, but we can look forward to a shave and haircut now and again, which is good for our self-respect even when our only clothing is a grubby fundoshi.

We don't ask for much these days, don't expect it, for we have learnt that it is both pointless and disheartening to wish for improvements which never come. We still live much as animals inside a stockade, but nevertheless there has been a magical rise in morale. I find a few words creeping into my mind, from the Bible maybe? 'And all the dead bones stirred, and gathered flesh to themselves!' Something like that, very sharp-edged and potent in their meaning, and entirely appropriate to us. Whoever it was that spoke them might well have known a situation similar to ours, and I would indeed be proud of myself had I drawn such a powerful but subtle expression from my own mental resources.

A staccato bugle call rings out, seven notes on only three tones, unknown to us, but Bert's ears jump to attention immediately. The bugler repeats it excitedly, urgently, a dozen times – obviously it's something important.

'It's the mail call! Listen to it! A letter from Lousy Lou! A letter from Lousy Lou! Mail! Letters from home!'

Men are running out of every hut, my lot grabbing their new crutches and swinging along with the best of them. From the admin hut comes a party of men with two bamboo skips full of letters. They stop in the middle of the parade ground as a crowd gathers around, faces eager and eyes shining. Out come handfuls of letters, name/rank/unit shouted out. Lucky men dart forward to take their prizes, others wait cheerfully for theirs to come out of the skips. Some men are called back once, twice, several times; many never hear their names. It's so wonderful, and so unfair!

The skips are nearly empty. The unlucky men see their chances dwindle, and their smiles twist into disappointed creases. Tears start to roll down their cheeks. Those with mail have hurried back to their huts, so only the sad-faced group remains. 'There must be some more! Haven't you got another basket in the office? There must be something for me! Two years, and not a single letter!'

'Sorry, boys. The Nips only gave us this lot. We're certain they've got more, but they tell us that censoring them is difficult and we must wait. Maybe next time?'

Pleading voices, dejected shoulders, slow trudge back to the huts. The empty skips are picked up and carried away. Twenty minutes of excitement, delight for some and shocked disappointment for others, and when will next time be?

We have longed for letters from home, but now that some have actually reached us, let us look at the problems. Say there are 70,000 British and Australian prisoners (leaving out Indian troops, most of whom seem to have joined the Jap-controlled Indian National Army before we came up from Singapore), and two or three letters written to each one every week – scratch figures in the ground – thirteen million letters in all, to date. The whole lot sent (presumably) to Singapore, Jap Admin HQ, then on to our people at Changi.

At Changi they will have lists of the men sent to Siam. Most likely other big parties will have been sent elsewhere, all over the Dutch East Indies and French Indo-China, and they will have lists of these men too. But what records are there of men shifted repeatedly from one camp to another? Each camp will have lists of names, but with no central admin in Siam, who would have been able to keep track of each man's movements? There are some fifteen camps on the railway alone. Australians who started in Burma are now in this country, sick men have been transferred to hospital camps and sent away again. There will be camps in other parts of Siam, breaking up and dispersing, reforming elsewhere and, everywhere, men lying in graves known only to their mates who put them there.

It's a miracle that any letters have reached the right places for delivery – all credit to our admin staffs. And a black mark to the Nips for being so indifferent and unhelpful.

Everyone who has received a letter is more than happy to read out news of general interest. Those who were unlucky crowd around, eager to hear every scrap. But there isn't much, apparently. Only very brief letters have been allowed through and the news is nearly all personal. There is no space to spare for anything other than family events. One letter puts it plainly, even though it defeats its own purpose: 'Dear Son, I am only allowed to write 25 words, and have used them all up, so no news for now. Your loving father.' At least his Dad was alive then!

Other letters are lengthy, several pages in some cases, which suggests that most are not scrutinised by the Jap army censors so their excuse about delays caused by the need for censorship is not valid. News of war is not of much interest as these letters are a year and a half old and we have had a constant flow of rumours about the Allies' progress, some of which are obviously rubbish and some of which may be fact – it is difficult to sort them out sometimes. What progress was there, anyway, eighteen months ago? Everything seemed to be going wrong then.

Fathers lost at sea, brothers killed in action, sisters married, new babies, old folk passed away, weak beer hardly worth drinking, gin and whisky almost unobtainable – all the important things in life. Cigarettes rationed, eggs rare, the meat ration even smaller – dear me, isn't life tough at home?

Some news that possibly should not have been sent: 'Your wife has said she won't wait years for you to come back, if you ever do. She has sold everything and disappeared, taking the kids with her. We don't know where she has gone and don't want to know. Nasty bitch, why ever you married her we don't know. You wouldn't listen to us!' Such incredible insensitivity. What is the wretched husband, here in a POW camp, going to feel for the rest of his time in captivity?

Something written by a mum who obviously has no idea of our circumstances (well, how could she?): 'Your wife has moved in with an American air force officer. I can't talk her into leaving him. You should ask the Japanese for compassionate leave to come home and sort it out. You could promise to go back afterwards.' Such appealing naivety!

Much the same family news for the Australians, but with their relatively small population and the high proportion of men overseas or in the forces at home, their womenfolk are having to carry a big load of the men's work, especially on farms. There is no news of air raids such as on Darwin in the early days, which we heard of at the time, and this is a great relief. The Diggers know that at the time of the Jap invasion in South East Asia, their homeland was practically defenceless, all their forces being overseas.

An indignant letter from a brother: 'Here we are, stuck in what's left of Darwin. What a dump! Nowhere to go, nothing to do, and beer is five shillings a bottle rationed to six a week. You fellows don't know how lucky you are!'

The distribution of mail was a tremendous tonic. Now

that some letters have reached us, perhaps more will follow. Hope is everything. But now that the excitement has died down there is a reaction, a brooding nostalgia, a depressing sense of helplessness. Unable to comfort bereaved family and friends, or to take part in weddings, and what are the chances we shall ever see new babies? What should we feel, anger or resignation? Or just forget it?

'My mum tells me my wife has taken a man into the house. Thank God for that. I've been trying to think up some way of getting rid of her for years!'

'Here's an account from the Building Society. No one's paying the instalments. They say they'll take me to court. I wish they could!'

'Here's a letter from my wife. She's still nagging me for not apologising to her mother on our wedding day. Her mother's still very upset. Well, it looks as if she can go on being upset a lot longer. When I get home, I'll give her another earful. Nasty old bag, she is! One bloody good thing, she can't get at me in here – almost makes it worthwhile!'

Ron and I have five letters between us, all from Mum. She is in India, in the army's summer camp up in the cool mountains, at Simla. The barracks will be empty now that the army is too busy for peacetime holidays, and we suspect that it has been put to use as a kind of refugee centre for the thousands of civilians who fled from the Japanese advance without anywhere to go. At least we know that she was okay in June 1942, and she has been in touch with her mother in England. There will be no possibility of her travelling to England – it's too dangerous and she has no permit from the authorities. With Dad interned in Changi gaol, she will be very lonely. She doesn't mention having heard from him, but she did receive our cards from River Valley Road in Singapore. Life will be very hard for her, as long as this war lasts.

It's been a different day altogether – hopes and disappointments, homesickness and some laughter.

The new atmosphere which has brightened our lives has encouraged all kinds of enterprises, from making ingenious little contrivances for rolling cigarettes from paper and loose tobacco (selling privately for fifty sattangs), to looking for bits and pieces which can be adapted for use in the cookhouses or by the medical people.

One of these personal efforts has my admiration, for sheer cheek and brass nerves. One of our Volunteers from Malacca – a small group because Malacca is a sleepy small town – was a schoolmaster teaching English to the local children. A quiet man, he was sergeant-in-charge in a bomb disposal platoon which did a very good job in Singapore. Evidently he still has his cool nerves.

There has always been a shortage of containers to store water. Buckets and dixies bringing water from the river to the cookhouses have to stand, full, until the water is used before they can be refilled. There is no means of bulk storage, and water is always seriously inadequate.

Tony noticed a deserted Jap motor transport area fifty yards from our main gate. Checking that his hat and fundoshi were on straight and tidy, he marched smartly to the gate, halted, turned and threw up a stiff salute to the camp sentry. Startled out of his indolent daydreaming, the Nip pulled his rifle and bayonet into place and jumped to attention, bowing his head in response to Tony's salute. When he looked up Tony was heading for a stack of empty petrol drums. Heaving one onto his shoulder he was back at the gate within a few minutes – halt, salute, bow – and Tony was in with his booty.

While the same sentry was on duty, Tony repeated his

audacious theft nine times, presenting the ten 44-gallon drums to the astonished officer on duty in the admin hut. 'Just found them lying around, sir!'

These were the drums which had made the clothing sterilisation program possible, and also helped most usefully to provide boiling water for washing out bedpans and blanket foments.

Tony has, with typical modesty, not talked about this exploit. I heard of it from one of his friends who saw it all happen, but who was not allowed to help because, in Tony's opinion, it was a firing squad offence and not worth risking two men. The Nip sentry, he said, would never say a word because he would probably be shot for allowing it to happen. So all went well – quiet, unassuming, intellectual Tony!

Now mobile on his crutches, Ron comes with me to visit Ted and the others in the ulcer ward, Ted's big grin of welcome always being a good thing to see. His leg is improving steadily, he assures us, and the hospital fund has been able to provide occasional small helpings of tiny green mung beans to men on 'special' diets, and he feels they do a lot of good. Some days there is even a hard-boiled duck's egg.

All the men say the same – in fact there hasn't been an amputation since Ron's leg was taken off. Problems still remain, however. The total lack of exercise and the stress of constant pain over several months have left them listless and slack-muscled. Confined inside the hut, their skins haven't felt the touch of sunlight or clean rain for far too long. They look unnaturally sallow, and every man is wasted in his body. Eyes are sunk in shadowy hollows, teeth are dingy because no one has a brush to clean them, and they have not been able to move – all this time – from their hard and uncomfortable bamboo platforms. And every man in the hut, if he keeps his ulcerated leg, will be a permanent cripple for life, and he knows it. The long weeks of inaction have caused tendons and sinews to shrink, bending knees immovably. These men will never again walk truly upright, even though the Big Australian has introduced a new service – several men have been trained in basic massage and come to the hut every day to work on locked joints, trying to restore elasticity.

Success will be slow and painful, if indeed it comes at all, but the treatment can only do good. At last the men feel that someone is aware of them and is doing something positive to help.

I have found myself a place at the back of the usual little crowd gathered around Sparrer's bedspace. I have come only to listen and not to talk, because their background and home life are quite outside my own experience, and I do not feel I can contribute to the conversation bouncing around amongst his particular cronies. I am more than content just to look on and take it all in.

There is an argument over various London bus routes, specifically, which number bus service goes from here to there and places useful to know along the routes – such as pubs, shops, pubs, churches, pubs, parks, pubs, football grounds, pubs and so on.

Well, it is something to pass the time. New topics have long been difficult to find and boredom is a deadly enemy. Such is our situation: so completely insulated from the world as we used to know it by endless months of unnatural emptiness that even the most familiar details of the past can become blurred. Memory can lose its grip, even faces and names are recalled only with frustrating effort, and the past takes on a patina of unreality. Talk, more talk, persistent talk, is the only means of mental exercise that we have to stop our brains from turning into a sort of cold porridge. What is talked about is of less importance than the preservation of mental agility; the effort of recollection is essential to tuning up our intellect, and discussion and wrestling with problems keep the mind active just as physical effort is good for muscles.

Men who waited at the same bus stops at the same times of the day for years, catching transport to and from work or going to the local football ground, have become uncertain as to details and contradict each other vehemently. Even a mundane subject such as this can produce edgy tempers at times, but injections of good humour invariably soothe irritated feelings. Everyone knows of a pub frequented by colourful and dubious customers whose exploits are always worth the telling, and of little shops where there are friendly girls in the back rooms.

The argument reaches the stage where the buses are going round in such complex patterns that they might finally all disappear up each other's exhaust pipes. When everyone has had enough it is finally solved by – literally – the judgement of Solomon. I'm not talking fibs here. Elias Solomon is sitting amongst us listening to the contradictory chatter, and we all know he could have sorted it out right at the beginning, but nobody asked him to do so because then there would not have been any entertaining discussion.

Elias – known as 'Taxi!', shouted out loud – is a Cockney born and bred, and can proudly claim to have passed the dreaded examination set by the London taxi licensing authorities. Called 'The Knowledge', this exam must be passed by every applicant for a London taxi driver's licence, and it must surely be by far the most rigorous and unrelenting of its type anywhere in the world. The inquisition is in person and verbal, the applicant must immediately answer every question fired at him and no mistakes are allowed. He must know, with absolute certainty, the name of every street, railway station, hotel, club, place of entertainment, church, museum etc., and the quickest route from any one point to any other, naming streets, turning points and landmarks on the way, one-way streets, and even long-term deviations due to roadworks and so on. The vast amount of detail is incredible.

I listen with fascination as Solomon hands down his ruling. Without the smallest hesitation to collect his thoughts he smoothly unrolls a faultless description of every one of the bus services mentioned, from terminus to terminus, street by street (with locations of bus stops), and he even points out where to change from one service to pick up another for a particular destination. Here's one man whose brain is still firing precisely on all cylinders!

We all know of Sparrer's great devotion to his mum. An only son, his father died when he was a small boy and it wasn't long before young Sparrer learned the hard facts of a life of poverty. He found out that his mum was going without food because there was not always enough for both, and he left school at the earliest possible age to try to earn money to help out. Until he joined the army his life was a bitter struggle, and he gladly assigned nearly all his army pay to his mum. Now he's continually worried whether the army is still paying her, or has officially posted him as missing in the absence of advice as to whether he is living or dead. Just not knowing is a torment to him, as it is to thousands of other prisoners with dependants. Nobody knows what government policy might be.

The tough street urchin has a soft centre, and a deep and sincere love for his mum, which might earn ridicule in some circles but is wholly admired by us who know him. This afternoon he has made an announcement. Today is his mum's birthday, and he calculates that right at this moment she will be sitting at the kitchen table with a pot of tea, and maybe a kipper and toast. Before the war he would also have been there, giving her a carefully chosen birthday card, a big hug and a kiss, and a 'Happy birthday to the best mum in the world'. It was always a very special time for both of them, filled with warmth and happiness. When the shops were open he would walk round to the florist to buy a big bunch of red roses, his mum's favourite flowers, and however little money he had there was always enough scraped together for this special gift.

Sparrer sings us his favourite song, just as he used to sing it to his mum when he presented the roses to her:

> It's my Mother's birthday today!
> I'm on my way with a lovely bouquet.
>
> I'll greet her with a kiss,
> For that I know she yearns,
> And then I'll say 'God bless you,
> Many Happy Returns!'
>
> These roses will soon fade away,
> But she will know what they mean to convey,
> 'Cos it's my Mother's birthday,
> Today!

Hearing Sparrer sing it with his rich Cockney accent and intonation, a bit shaky in tone and with tears running down his pinched cheeks, I am so moved that I would weep with him. The song is sentimental, even corny, when played in a dance hall, but just now it is the deeply poignant expression of a sensitive man longing to have again the most important part of his life, the part that let him care for his loving mum. He doesn't even know if she is still alive, and she must be worried sick about him.

The song ends, his audience remains silent, then his face crumples and tears stream down his cheeks in a flood. Suddenly he cries out, 'Bloody Nip bastards, I won't never say happy birthday to my mum again, never take her any more roses! I won't, I know it. I'll never get out of here alive. I know it! I'll never be back home!'

He is rocking from side to side, hands to his face, frightened and angry, bitter and disappointed, his soul torn with the pain of his thoughts. He is beyond ordinary distress. The important little ceremonies marking the love which bound him and his mum together have been brought to a standstill and will never be revived. It is his mum's sufferings which worry him rather than his own, and he is distraught because there is nothing at all he can do about it. No more intimate talks, no more gentle touches, no more kisses to comfort, no more loving occasions to brighten his mum's hard life – he falls into a ragged mumbling, curled up tight as if back in his beloved mum's womb, incoherent and weeping.

His close friends try to ease him, but are helpless. One hurries to fetch the surgeon who has brought him through so many crises, but there will be no sedative to relax him. He will have to fight it out in his own dark pit of loneliness.

The rest of us drift away, subdued and shocked. The protective shell which each of us has built around himself has suddenly become vulnerable to deep-seated emotions springing up from within. It hurts, but at least we know we are still intact. In some way it is refreshing.

News of Sparrer's death comes to us, inevitably, during the next morning. We all know it must, but still it is infinitely saddening. The special circumstances of the last months of his life make his passing especially poignant, even to those of us who only knew him as the centrepiece of a group of imprisoned men determined not to give in to ill-fortune.

His slipping away was mercifully brief, leaving us the memory of an elfin sprite sitting in a bright pool of wit and humour, chirping happily right to the end. His gallant spirit gave up suddenly, fending off the creeping degradation which accompanies slow death in these camps. He was simply unable to struggle any longer. He would have preferred it that way, I am sure.

I know that I shall never forget him. What are your thoughts, God? Sparrer has fallen off his perch, although he really deserved so much to live and go home to his mum. Such a simple wish. Just one of too many sparrows for you to notice?

The rains are slackening and the sunshine is not only more frequent but far more kindly in the decreasing humidity. Instead of glaring at us with sullen and oppressive hostility through a steamy atmosphere, the sun is beginning to smile pleasantly on our bodies, and those of us able to help are carrying patients out of their gloomy huts to lie out on the drying earth.

Freed from the shadows and unwholesome stinks of their confinement, these men revel in the open space and fresh air. Even the nondescript surroundings of the camp are good to look at, and morale rises from simple dour refusal to die to high levels of optimism and confidence in the future. Men start to talk of the war ending and going home to their families, instead of uncomfortably wondering whether it would ever happen. And of Christmas now being only a few weeks away.

It's odd how the approach of Christmas can change

attitudes, inducing hopefulness and expectations of miracles, but it is a fact that it does. Even remembering that we had the same thoughts a year ago does not prevent us from looking at the bright side now, despite the truly dreadful months of disease and death through which we have passed. It is true that conditions have now eased, but the future is a blank and there is no real reason to contemplate it with optimism. We could all simply starve, for one thing.

Lurking in our thoughts is always the chance of being pressed into another major project, such as the building of a canal across the Kra Isthmus. We who live in this part of the world know that this has been an evergreen concept for years, and the completion of our railway will have removed all hesitation about the practicability of carrying it out. We have no doubt that the Jap government has been considering it, and can only hope that it will not give in to the temptation of using its massive (and cheap) labour force to get started on it. For us, the terrain and climate would be a lot easier there than here, but the possibility is disturbing. For the Japs, who have told us they will go on fighting this war for a hundred years if necessary (and we can all believe they would), the canal would shorten the sea voyage from Saigon to Rangoon by more than 1,000 miles each way, and that is a big inducement.

Anyway, the general rise in spirits is wonderful for our wellbeing, to which is most certainly linked the healing of our physical ailments. Logical or not, it is good for us!

This morning I was detailed to join a party to bring rations into the camp from the Nip store hut, which is just outside the main gate and, therefore, under the eye of the sentry on duty. It is the first time I do this, which accounts for what happens this evening.

The Nip quartermaster takes us out through the gate and into the store hut where the sergeant in charge of our work party counts out bags of rice and baskets of sweet potatoes and dried fish as each item is lifted on a man's back. I am one of the first, and am given a skip of smelly dried fish on my left shoulder.

Not able to see to that side I do not notice that the carriers in front of me have dumped their loads just outside the door, and I trot straight off through the camp gate directly to the cookhouse. The cooks seem a bit surprised to see me and none of the previous loads is in sight – I imagine the cooks must have moved them inside very quickly.

Back in the store hut I walk into a small commotion. Both our sergeant and the Nip agree with the number of items taken out of the store, but there is one skip of dried fish short in the stack just outside! They count, and recount, several times. We pick up the baskets and move them aside one by one but the answer is always the same – one short. Our sergeant is puzzled, and the Nip is building up a dangerous head of steam. It is too late for me to offer my simple explanation – it would only earn me a severe hiding – and I decide I will step forward only if it looks like the whole squad could be in trouble.

So we all stand around with innocent expressions until the Nip makes up his mind and orders an extra skip to be brought out. It can only be the fact that our sergeant's tally agrees with his own that has persuaded him that, somehow, they both made a mistake. As we carry our loads into the camp cookhouse, I breathe a big sigh of relief and feel that, by chance and luck, I will have done a small service to our sick men by providing 1,000 or so extra dried fish, for surely the cooks will hand over the windfall to the medical staff as extra food for those who need it.

Silly me! After evening rice two Australians with big smiles on their faces come walking through the huts, hawking dried fish at ten sattangs each from a familiar-looking skip carried between them. I know these two, they both live in my hut, an oily, smarmy pair of black market go-betweens who take no risks but collect commissions. The only beneficiaries from my little escapade have been these two shifty characters and the cooks who sold the fish to them.

There is nothing I can do about it; a complaint to the officers would bring only unpleasantness. They obviously regard themselves as being smart enough to grab an opportunity when it appears. I see it as despicable greediness – and myself as a bit of a simpleton. It upsets me that I have put 100 ticals into the pockets of these hyenas.

My precious toothbrush is holding up well. It is now nearly two years old and I have used it twice a day regularly – no paste, and tea is the only trustworthy form of water. Those men, and it is the great majority, who do not have a brush nevertheless seem to be remarkably free from dental problems. Maybe this is due to the high calcium content in the water, from rain soaking through the limestone hills – otherwise, would we have found abalone shellfish in the river at Wampo? Or possibly the almost total absence of sugar in our diet has spared us dental decay.

Despite daily brushing, I have trouble with two teeth, in the lower set, one each side just in front of the molars – bicuspids, I think they are called. Several years ago they both needed big fillings, which have now fallen out and the shells have broken up but are still bedded in the gums.

Tarsao is fortunate in having a dentist, presumably a New Zealander from the pyramid Boy Scout hat he wears. On this day there are thirteen of us who need extractions. He gives us a shot of painkiller in the gums and we wait for it to work. The major tells us he has had no experience of this stuff. The label says it is made in Shanghai and the instructions in English are hardly comprehensible. But there is nothing else available, and he has used a standard dosage – best of luck to us!

Never having had a tooth pulled out in my life, I don't know what to expect. It hurts like hell; the whole jawbone feels to be in danger of coming apart. All the other men have the same experience.

Waking up the next morning, my mouth is locked solid. I cannot open or shut it; there is no pain or any other sign of a problem, no swelling or bruising. Luckily my upper and lower teeth are fixed slightly apart, just enough for me to be able to suck rice out of my spoon, and to tip tea in carefully.

I find the other twelve men at the dentist's hut on sick parade, all of us in the same condition. The Kiwi major examines us in turn, very carefully, and is completely unable to account for what he finds. There is no sign of the immediate suspect, lockjaw, not the slightest infection or swelling, nothing at all that he can see – only the jaw locked rigidly at the hinge. Some men's teeth are clenched, which means they cannot eat and are barely able to drink, others' are slightly apart (like me), and two men have their mouths held gaping wide.

We are to come back tomorrow for a further check. We go back daily, but there is no change until the twentieth day, when every one of us wakes up with his jaw relaxed and normal. Every one of us, on exactly the same day! And nothing whatever to explain what happened, nothing to show for it, as if it had never happened.

The major is vastly relieved but still cannot account for it despite talking to every medical officer in the camp. We are all equally relieved, and thankful that the problem has resolved itself with no hangovers.

A week later I am back for the second extraction, and not looking forward to it at all. But I am in luck. Some genuine British Novocaine has been obtained, the injection works fine and the extraction is effortless and totally free of pain. Half an hour later, I wouldn't have known I had had a tooth out.

Fortune has favoured me again!

It is curious how the approach of Christmas has roused the old feelings of goodwill towards everybody, the desire to develop friendships and to give and receive gifts as expressions of love amongst family members and particular friends. And, of course, going to church, even if this is about the only occasion in the year!

Here in Tarsao we are frustrated in almost every aspect. The weather is all wrong – except for the Australians, for whom Christmas comes in midsummer – and there is not the slightest resemblance to frosty, snowy, dark nights, a church's stained glass windows glowing warmly and the cheerful rounds of carol singing. There are no family gatherings, no letters, and no cards with bright little pictures, no cosy evenings yarning over a friendly glass or two, no gifts.

And no love at all for our enemies – only contempt, hatred, loathing unlimited, world without end, *amen*! We long ago threw away any such concept, together with the teaching that, if thine enemy strike you, you should turn the other cheek. He just bashes that as well, and it's too painful and humiliating to bear with anything but deep-seated fury and a massive urging to strike back – all without showing any sign of emotion at all.

So we see the Roman Catholic padre pacing slowly in an

open space which ensures privacy (if you disregard the fact that it is in full view of anybody who cares to look), talking to a small group of our Eurasian lads. These young men are all Roman Catholics, staunch believers, and every single one of them has family in the hands of the Japanese, back in Singapore. So what are they discussing, with an earnestness which is apparent even at a distance? The sin of not being able to forgive their enemy? Of hating the Nips? Of disappointment that so many decent Christian men have died in squalor, broken in body and spirit, uselessly and without purpose? Offhand, I can't think of anything these boys can possibly have done to incur their God's displeasure. In our present circumstances, what sins can anyone commit (in a religious context, that is)? There are certainly no wives or oxen to covet, adultery is simply not an option, we do not steal from each other, and our lousy diet has made libidinous thoughts impossible because we have all become dried up. Would it be sinful to long to be once again with our batteries fully charged and looking for 'come-hither' signs from the girls? In my depleted condition it is difficult even to think about it!

The dentist has called me and the others back to check that we have no after-effects from the peculiar results of our gum injections. While waiting we watch – and thank heaven we were spared – while he drills a tooth.

The army provides a hand-operated drill for use where there is no electric power. It is a chrome-plated box held in an assistant's hand while he turns a crank handle, which is geared to rotate a long flexible cable ending in the drill at the dentist's end of the business. It is so clumsy that the assistant's best efforts to produce high revs are almost nullified as soon as the point of the drill touches the patient's tooth. We can hear the change in tone when the drill bites, the assistant is sweating as he labours on the crank, and the patient is squirming with pain.

At this point one of the Koreans stalks in, ordering the patient away and seating himself on the bamboo stool. Opening his mouth and pointing to his teeth, he demands attention. Such delightful manners these people have!

In the Nip army, we understand, medical treatment has to be paid for by deductions from the soldier's pay, so they come to us for free treatment expecting us to use drugs which we either cannot spare or have no intention of using on them, if indeed we have them at all.

The dentist takes a look and picks up his syringe. We hear him whisper to his assistant to fill it with distilled water, which he then injects into the Korean's gum. Sitting on the bench, waiting for the 'anaesthetic' to work, the Korean looks puzzled, poking his finger into his mouth. The injection doesn't seem to be having effect, and he grumbles, 'Damme, damme (No good, no good).' The dentist assures him the stuff is 'Nippon presento, Number One', which puts the Korean on the spot as he cannot deny that a Jap product is anything but the best. He has no choice but to submit while his tooth is slowly unscrewed from his jaw. Sweat springs out all over his face and runs down into his shirt, but (to give credit where it is due) he doesn't make a sound. Such is the Jap army discipline, which absolutely forbids the smallest cry of pain as being effete.

Watching all this, I think we are all sweating almost as much.

The British and the Australians are beginning to mix more freely than they have done in the past, when the Australians have tended to be a bit 'clannish' and kept to themselves. In this camp everyone is too close to everybody else, housed not by regimental units but according to your illness. There are a number of Dutch troops, not many, and they are mostly white colonial settlers with only a few Javanese and mixed bloods.

According to the Australians who were captured in Java, the only fighting to resist the Japanese invasion of the Dutch East Indies was done by themselves, some American artillerymen, and British RAF personnel who picked up their rifles and fought to defend aerodromes in Sumatra against Jap parachute troops. The Dutch commander-in-chief, recognising that no real resistance could be put up, ordered all troops to remain in barracks and wait for the Jap army to arrive and take over. Although all the Allied units had been placed under Dutch command, only the Dutch obeyed and this earned the contempt of all the others.

Well, how can you pass judgement in such a situation? The Dutch decision saved lives by accepting reality – after all, the British and Americans have just lost their territories in the Far East and the Dutch East Indies had no forces capable of putting up any real kind of fight. But the issue is, of course, emotional, and a matter of the soldiers' pride in themselves. So the contempt is widespread and frequently expressed, unfair and unkind as it may be, and the Dutch troops suffer from it. Basically, our people resent having fought in Dutch territory while the local troops 'lay on their beds reading magazines', as I have heard it put.

Trying to talk to the white Dutch, who all speak English to some degree, I have been told that the native troops were unwilling to fight and many threw away their uniforms and went back to their villages. Practising my Malay on the Javanese soldiers, I find that there is a strong dislike of their Dutch rulers, and when the war ends their first intention is to throw the Dutch out of the islands. And they sound as if they really mean it; there is an intensity in their eyes and voices. But they know that they will have to rely on the Allies to defeat the Jap nation before they can do anything for themselves, and their attitude towards us is most friendly and polite.

Because they do not speak English, they welcome the opportunity to talk to me as somebody who has some familiarity with the area and some ability with their language. They have grievances which, they are surprised to learn, do not apply in Singapore and Malaya, the most important being that they are paid so little for their work that they will never be able to escape from poverty. Because they are too poor to be taxed in money, they are conscripted to provide unpaid labour on roads instead, often for extended periods at some distance from their own villages. Working on the big estates – rubber, tobacco, tea, coffee – they have little choice but to spend their wages in the estate shops, which are owned by the estates and thus make a profit out of them. And, lastly, they say that the Dutch made no effort to resist Germany in their own homeland, so why should they be expected to fight for Holland out here? In their own country?

In Singapore and Malaya the native Malays are probably less than half the population, and are a peaceable community. I am coming to think that the Dutch, when they try to reestablish themselves in the Dutch East Indies after the war, will find the Javanese and Sumatrans far less easy-going than they used to be. The Japanese occupation period, however long it lasts, will provide plenty of time to brood, make plans, and build up a head of steam.

I have been contemplating my belongings, which are in fact my total worldly possessions at this moment and have been in use for about two years. They all show signs of wear but will have to see me through until the end of the war, however far off that might be. They are all irreplaceable – the Japs have not issued a single item – and therefore of great value as they are all essential. The loss of any one of them would be serious, especially as available substitutes are almost non-existent – in fact I can't think of any except bamboo chopsticks if I lose my spoon, and you can't use chopsticks with slops.

Hat: in my view, and most agree with me, of the foremost importance. We were quite extraordinarily fortunate when, back at River Valley Road Camp on the outskirts of Singapore's older suburbs, a small shipment of supplies from South Africa was handed to us by the Nips. There wasn't much released by the Nips, and the bulk of it was foodstuffs such as maize in sacks, all of which went to the cookhouse. Amongst the few personal items issued to individuals, however, were broad-brimmed hats made of a tough fur or felt, proof against the heaviest downpour as well as shading the eyes and back of the neck. No man could have survived through Siam's monsoonal rains and blazing sun without this protection. Sunstroke, blindness, frizzled brains – all these would have led to painful death. My hat is still in quite remarkably good condition, a tribute to the quality of the material and workmanship, and keeps my head comfortably warm in chilling rain.

Fundoshi: this skimpy bit of minimal clothing, not even a shadow of a loincloth, is yet essential to self-respect. Modesty is hardly a problem in our present circumstances, and the thin cloth does not really afford protection, but it does go some way towards satisfying an instinctive desire for a minimal degree of privacy. What we shall feel like if we have to appear amongst the local population, barefoot and wearing nothing but a hat and fundoshi, I cannot imagine.

Water bottle: holding one quart. This must surely be the most abominable creation in personal gear that was ever invented, an out-and-out disgrace to the British army. Its design must go back before the Crimean War. I can find nothing to say in its favour. Flattish and slightly curved to fit at the hip, it is made of thin sheet iron covered in some kind of dark blue enamel, sewn into a tight-fitting jacket and stoppered with a cork pushed into a narrow pouring neck. The cork has a hole drilled through from top to bottom, a short length of wire passed through and secured by a tiny nut and washers to seal the hole to prevent leaks, and a string from the top of the wire so that the cork won't get lost if it comes out of the neck. The bottle is carried in a webbing sling for attaching to a belt. The faults are that doubtful water cannot be boiled in it, the enamel is easily chipped off in the rough conditions of active service, the iron quickly rusts, the cork shrinks with age and is liable to fall out so that precious water is lost, and the metal bits in the cork are always rusty. Lastly, if the contents become contaminated, thorough cleansing is impossible.

The Jap soldier's water bottle is of aluminium with a screw-cap seal over its wide neck, shaped to be hung over a fire to boil the contents, and has a protective jacket which can be slipped off.

Mess tins: in pairs, a small one nesting inside the larger. The current issue is of aluminium, but mine are of thin sheet iron pressed into a rectangular shape and surfaced with a galvanised wash of microscopic thinness. Each pan has a fold-over wire handle which is intended to allow it to be carried when filled with hot food and to be used as a cooking pan. The handle is not fixed, and is unstable. It was never designed for carrying cooked or moist food when away from a kitchen, only packaged dry rations such as biscuits.

Without hot water or soap, I can clean my mess tins after a meal only by carefully scouring them with fine dust. The thin metallic wash has nearly disappeared, and I eat off a rusting iron surface. When holes develop, as they surely will in time, I shall have nothing whatever to replace the tins.

The Jap soldier's mess tin is of aluminium, in two halves sealed with lids, which means it can carry cooked and moist foods. Solid handles clamp them together and can be clipped firmly into place for use as cooking pans.

Spoon and mug: I have an ordinary dessert spoon. If necessary I could make bamboo chopsticks for rice, and drink vegetable water from my mess tin. The mug is enamelled iron, a bit chipped but holding up well.

Belt and pack: standard army issue, of strong webbing. In lengthy periods of rain the pack material lets in water freely, and the contents are soaked. In our wet monsoon, drying out is nearly impossible.

The Dutch have a strong waterproof canvas pack which can be put on wet ground in a heavy downpour and still keep the contents absolutely dry.

Blanket and groundsheet: army issue, but not issued to me by the army; both were bought for cash in Singapore, on the Changi black market, otherwise I would have had nothing. The blanket quickly wore thin, and the rubber coating on the groundsheet is patchy and in no way waterproof, but it helps a little to lessen the irritation of the knobbly bits in our bamboo sleeping platforms. Both items are of shoddy material.

Personal comforts: my toothbrush, a pair of nail scissors, and a comb. Small things, but quite extraordinarily helpful in maintaining self-respect. There will be very few indeed of these in this camp. I also have a pillow, which must be one of only two in Tarsao – Ron also has one. My only piece of loot taken from an empty house the day before Singapore fell was a pillow, and in Changi it was made into four compact pads shared between us and George and Wally. It makes so much difference in a night's sleep, far better than an army pack or a length of thick bamboo. Also, I have a singlet and a pair of underpants which I wear at night, which makes me one of the very few men who at bedtime can change out of their day clothes (what is the singular form of 'clothes', when there is only one item?).

And a book, which can be lent out in exchange for another book – by the oddest chance it is called *Siamese White*, about a Greek sailor named Phaulkon who ventured to Ceylon and further eastwards 300 years ago. He became stranded at Mergui, in southern Burma, where he was given the post of King's Harbourmaster. He is a historic figure who became fluent in the Siamese language and eventually was appointed as Chief Minister to the King of Siam in the old capital, Ayyuthya. From this book we know that there is a defined route from Mergui which must pass a little distance south of Wampo, to Siam's central plains. Useful knowledge, should we at any time need an escape route to the Indian Ocean – for instance, if the Jap government should decide to slaughter all POWs in Siam, which we see as a definite possibility.

All in all, I consider that I am better off than most men – officers excluded, for they are not in the same category – in Tarsao.

Religion, I have to admit, does not show up prominently in all this stirring of bones and quickening of spirits. I do not know of any daily services or prayer gatherings, although thinly attended services are held on Sunday evenings. Despite the sameness of one day to another, we have never at any time lost our grip on the calendar, and Sunday is still Sunday, as it ever was. I have heard of one man – and only one – who asked to be baptised, and another – again only one – who wanted to be confirmed, these being said to be prudent measures to ensure burial in consecrated ground in the event of death.

Consecrated ground? What does that mean, in these circumstances? Would a man who died be dumped apart from the others just because his parents had omitted to baptise him? Would our Church of England chaplain, or the Roman Catholic father, even think along those lines? And we have a number of Jews among us now; they do not have a Rabbi, but they die just the same, and their bodies are carried out to the burial site – what about them?

To accept what happens in blind faith, and not to seek reason for it, is not good enough. And if that is the only advice that an officer of any church can give me, I shall not waste my time – or his – by asking questions of him.

I would have thought that, if religion had any real value, it would have become manifest to us during these last two years. It has not happened, so where do I look now?

This is a real and great disappointment to me. If religion has not brought me a skerrick of comfort in all the miseries of these last two years, when will it ever do so? Everyone needs a religion, even if only to keep him in his proper place on this earth and to give him a code of behaviour to live by. I think I have these qualities, as an ordinary human being, but I cannot feel that they are due to religion. They are there by instinct, and I value them because I think they are worth having. I do not need mystic rituals and symbols to convince me of their truth.

I wish it were not so. Deep down I know I am missing something.

When the war started in September 1939 there was, amid all the apprehension, a feeling that now that the Allies had stopped dithering and declared war, Germany would come to its senses and realise that it could no longer get its way by being a big bully. Problems would be sorted out sensibly and our men would be back home by Christmas. Why is it that Christmas, which has nothing to do with the circumstances of war, has such a powerful effect on people's thinking? My parents told me it was the same in the Great War, and when the first Christmas passed without any relief it was going to be over by the next Christmas. And so on, year after year.

It is the same in this war and we are now, in 1943, celebrating the fifth Christmas since it started. Despite the fact that with every passing year things have become worse, the war more intense and human suffering increasing dreadfully, we, in this squalid camp where we live like animals in a compound, still feel the urge to look around us with optimism and cheerfulness. This, surely, must be our last Christmas as prisoners of the barbaric and uncivilised Japs, our Christian brothers outside must soon triumph and bring us back to our families.

So we move around the camp, on this our personal second experience of a POW Christmas, with genuine smiles of welcome and goodwill towards everyone. Groups of men sing carols all over the place, the well-loved words and tunes clear in our memories, and the cookhouse has managed to produce savoury fried riceballs for breakfast, so we are, at least for the present, comforted in spirit and body. There are no other Christmas trimmings, and nobody has presents to give or drinks to offer. Never mind, the atmosphere is here – a bit wan-looking, perhaps – and we are doing the best we can.

Somewhere the Christian ministers are blessing their small congregations. The Nips have not allowed the construction of chapels; the services are gatherings of the faithful in spaces where the ministers choose to stand, prominent in their robes of office.

In recognition of our special day, the Nips have waived the usual morning and evening tenko. We shall all be here tomorrow; no one has anywhere to go.

In a quiet way, it is a tonic to all of us and therefore welcome. We just accept it as it is.

Life is quiet in Tarsao. Aside from each man's personal problems, daily life has settled into a smooth routine now coming close to boredom for those not actively engaged in some kind of productive work. Improvements introduced by the Big Australian have resulted in quite astonishing progress in the men's health. Of course, the seriously ill and the long-term sick are still with us – and receiving better attention than previously – but those who at one time were supposed to be convalescing, but in fact were not getting on as well as they should, have now begun to look distinctly better, so much so that in any working camp they would have been back at work. There have been no more amputations since Ron's leg; that desperate last hope of saving life has been pushed away by new possibilities of healing.

I am more than ever of the opinion that physical and emotional conditions are closely bound to each other, and that the recent physical improvement is due as much to boosting of morale as to the hygiene measures now in place. The Big Australian is to be seen everywhere; after a strenuous day's work he is often in the wards during the evenings, talking to patients and looking critically at everything, infusing his confidence and good humour into everybody. Another factor is the sunny weather which has settled in, lessening the shabbiness of the camp. Well, it doesn't really fool us, but during the wet monsoon it was an awful depressing place, gloomy and sodden and a weight on our spirits, and the brighter aspect undoubtedly benefits us.

Tarsao's population has steadily increased with parties of sick men coming down from upriver camps. Some of the men are in a shockingly weak state. The completion of the railway in mid October has provided transport to bring these poor fellows down from those terrible camps which were far worse, we now hear, than those which we were in, and they were bad enough. There are so many of these men that trainloads have gone past us to Chungkai, where the food is rumoured to be better than here because it is nearer to the growing areas around Kanburi.

With the big railway job finished and requiring only maintenance gangs to keep it in repair, no doubt the not-so-sick men will follow. We shall have to make the most of this interim period, before something new is found for us, to pick up as much strength as possible.

We think the Nips must have been given a big 'thank you' for getting the railway completed in a little over a year, because their attitude towards us is now quite different. Apart from morning and evening tenko we seldom see a Nip inside the camp, which is a considerable relief and allows us to relax. They are probably glad to be able to stay outside as Nips have an unreasoning fear of catching diseases and often wear a cotton pad taped over their mouth and nose as protection when counting bed-down patients in the wards.

Conversation is a pastime of major importance, but unfortunately the average British soldier is not accustomed to talking about much beyond sport and his favourite hobbies at home. So there are endless discussions about ancient football matches and racing pigeons, with heated arguments over obscure details, to fill in time. Subjects of interest are soon exhausted, the talk shifts to minor issues of diminishing significance which are chewed over to extinction. The more trivial the point, the greater is the heat and irritability stoked up by futile argument. No matter, the talk's the thing!

So it is that the welcome benefits of the shedding of apathy, the quickening of pulses, enforced idleness (what was that, again?) and boredom have together created a new atmosphere of restlessness, which has its own problems. Whoever would have anticipated that, a few months ago?

The memories are pleasant, but the blood doesn't race around with desire, our miserable diet of tasteless and inadequate food over such a long period has worn us down to low-revving neutrality. Overheard in the breakfast queue: 'If a beautiful girl, you know, one of them film starlets, absolutely naked, appeared right now and threw herself at you, what would you do?'

'I'd tell her, sorry, luv, you'll have to wait a few minutes until I've had my rice!'

But it is, in fact, a matter of serious concern, for the word has been around for a long time that if our starvation rations continue much longer, our sexual powers may well be damaged beyond recovery. Something to do with those newfangled vitamins – nobody really knows how long the body can be deprived of essentials before it suffers permanent damage. Most of the men are young virgin bachelors, and it is a dismal prospect to think that, even if you survive and eventually get home, you may never have kids – may never even be able to settle into a contented marriage. Our married men don't seem to want to talk about it. Some of them, I know, are worried about whether their wives will be waiting to welcome them back. Overlong loneliness and endless worry can be fatal. And if they are welcomed back, will they be able to perform as they used to?

There is so much uncertainty, and no answers. If you think about it all too much you will shrivel up inside, but if you deliberately keep your thoughts away from it you are depriving yourself of a source of comfort. It's a real bugger of a situation.

There are other things, too, that contribute to the oppressive load on all of us. The heaviest, I think, is the absence of outside news, in particular letters from home and the fact that we cannot write letters to loved ones and friends. The sense of isolation from our old world is numbing. It creates perceptions of not being really alive, as if we have passed in Alice-in-Wonderland style into another existence where everything is the same but different, and the differences cause no surprise, and our old world can still be seen in slightly misty outlines somewhere in the distance. In these hills we see no signs of civilised communities, no houses or other buildings, no shops or restaurants. We have not turned on a tap or switched on a light for nearly two years, nor have we opened a door, or sat on a chair, or had a proper floor under our feet, or a roof over our heads that didn't let the rain in.

Most of all, what offends us more than any other single thing is the primitive hygiene we are forced to endure. With no water supply in any camp, no soap, no disinfectant of any kind, personal cleanliness is only what can be managed with limited access to the river – and even that, in the cholera season, has been out of bounds. You do get rinsed off by drenching rain, whether you want it or not, every time you go outside your hut in the wet season, and luckily the rain is warm, because there is nothing to dry yourself with and you simply stay wet for a time.

There is nothing more depressingly miserable than having to squat over a narrow trench (with crumbling earth sides) while rain streams over your naked body and pains stab through your guts. Stinking vapours rise from the maggot-seething muck below, and a few feet from your nose another man's rump is spurting out his contribution. It doesn't seem to matter which way you face, you cannot avoid the sheer unpleasantness of this basic function. We have never been issued with toilet paper, that simple necessity of civilised life, and there isn't a leaf within reach of the ground – anyway, most leaves are uncomfortably harsh and unsuitable.

We have long ago learned to disregard the disagreeable aspects of our lives, just as we cannot let ourselves grieve over the deaths of so many fellow soldiers. That is not to say that we no longer care – we do care intensely – but if we did not make these tribulations slide past us, we would all give up and die. I am sure that many men have already let themselves slip away, overwhelmed by the sheer weight of loneliness and lost hope, and stresses beyond their personal endurance. To out-siders we who have survived this far would surely appear to be insensitive, blunted in our sense of decency, but this is definitely not so. We have, out of necessity, grown a protective skin that we shall be only too glad to slough off as rapidly as possible when we have been set free. We are still the same men inside, but if our captivity goes on too long, we may need time to sort ourselves out and fit into normal society again.

Meanwhile, we roundly curse the politicians who dropped us into this mess through their abysmal incompetence.

This past year has changed all of us, unavoidably and, surely, without exception. The onset of the rainy season last May, bringing its own horrors of cholera to oppress us, the murderous 'speedo' which killed so many thousands of our men and scores of thousands of hapless Asiatic labour conscripts, and the total indifference of the Nips to the most ordinary human health needs, all these took us down to the lowest depths of misery and squalid living. We who have survived are the fortunate ones, no more deserving to live than were our friends who died – we are just lucky, and we know it.

Our dead are still so close to us. Nearly all of them are young ghosts of less than a year. The few we knew personally and the thousands whom we never met, they are all indissolubly our kith and kin. They crowd the atmosphere around us, waiting patiently to be taken to their final rest. We are keenly aware of their presence; they brush softly against our hearts. We must never forget them, however long we live. Our remembrance of them, their faces and names, is our only way of honouring them and of showing our thankfulness for our own deliverance. For me this is an intensely personal and private thing, without any shade of religion in it. Any attempt to draw upon religious faith, to make sense of it, collapses weakly and fails totally to ease distress. Nor does it offer one iota of encouragement for the future.

We must now fortify ourselves to face that future. Unpleasant as it is to know, nothing whatever in the news and rumours holds out the smallest hope of early release. There will certainly be another wet monsoon to endure, and we have not the slightest idea where we shall be at the time, but it will be uncomfortable – maybe not so bad as last time, but there's no telling. We cannot look for any improvement in the attitude of the Nips – their civilisation is still bogged in medieval sludge and they will not change, nor will the outside world be able to penetrate their callous rejection of decent human values and send in medical supplies.

* * *

We are warned to stand by for moving out of Tarsao. The Nips are intending to empty the camp since it is no longer needed as a main base for the railway. The fit men will go first, to a new camp 'somewhere the other side of Kanburi', and the sick will follow, to a new hospital camp beyond Ban Pong – that hated place. It is rumoured that the International Red Cross has had some influence in the construction of this camp, so maybe our sick men from all the length of the railway will have better accommodation than the squalid slums so far endured by all of us. It is something to hope for. Any cheering rumours are welcome – we just have to cross our fingers that there is some truth in them, and at the same time be a little cynical so that the reality will not be too disappointing. Optimism is a wonderful uplift, but we have learned from experience not to actually expect anything from the Nips.

There is a sudden flurry of shouting, Nips and our people dashing around the huts, the camp bugler tooting 'Fall in A, fall in B, fall in every companee!' In minutes we grab our kit and sort ourselves out for tenko. Everything is 'speedo', the train is nearly here and we have to be at the railside as soon as possible. No time for leisured farewells, just shouts of, 'Bye, see you again,' as we are rushed away. Ron and I are separated.

We have hardly cleared the camp area before we come to a sudden halt. The Nips have stacked up a great heap of their gear, heavy cast iron kwalis from the cookhouse and big earthenware jars, bundles wrapped in straw matting, wooden boxes of rations, a whole mass of stuff. We are to be their porters, and groups of our men are directed to pick up as much as they can carry.

I find myself loading a kwali and several big jars onto a small flat cart. It has shafts for a small horse, or perhaps a donkey, big wooden wheels reinforced with a steel band for a tyre, and a straight-through steel axle without any springing.

We last saw these in Singapore, when we were carting sawn timber, and they were clumsy vehicles even on tarmac roads. On our bush tracks, as we soon find, they are sheer hard work even with a dozen men pulling and pushing. The narrow wheels sink in the mud and the shafts jerk and twitch at every rut. There are no ball-bearings in the hubs; the axles sit in plain steel bushes, so a lot of effort is needed simply to keep moving.

And these carts were, in fact, the Jap army's idea of ambulances! Their wounded were piled on and dragged away for treatment, a slow and agonising trip for men already in severe pain. We heard about this from one of our armoured car officers who had been allowed to join the Argylls when they formed a similar unit. Cut off during the fighting in Malaya, he and a body of Highlanders had followed up behind the advancing Japs, harassing them until they, too, were captured. They had watched Jap troops cleaning up after an action, loading the carts and tossing bodies onto big fires. Those of their own men too badly wounded to be of further use were finished off with a bullet before incineration, while our wounded were thrown on the fires while still alive.

Cursing and sweating while we manhandle our lumbering monster, we notice that the big wooden plug in the neck of a jar has been jolted loose. A quick dip inside finds thick slices of dried beef. Other jars have flat cakes of palm sugar and pickled vegetables. Swift distribution of a reasonable quantity of loot – not too much! – makes us all feel a lot better.

It takes us a couple of hours to reach the railway, laid here on a low embankment snaking across rocky ground, with trees growing wherever they can put down roots. It is typical scenery for this area, pleasant enough to look at but not very comfortable for a bivouac.

We sit down to wait. Hours pass. Expecting an immediate

pick-up, the Nips have brought no rations or water for themselves or for us. There are no spades to dig latrines, and men are walking a couple of hundred yards into the scrub to relieve themselves. We hadn't been allowed time to fill our water bottles before leaving Tarsao, though some men have a little tea left over from our last meal.

Darkness falls, but luckily it is a fine night with enough of a glimmer from the night sky to allow men stumbling around amongst the rocks and trees to see a little. We eat some of our loot; the pickled vegetables are tasty, vinegary, tart and sweet, but they only stimulate our appetites. Making ourselves as comfortable as we can in the lumpy rocks, we sleep.

By morning it is twenty-four hours since our last rice. The Nips don't know what to do – will the train come soon or not? Sending a squad back to Tarsao for cooked rice will take hours. Supposing the train comes in and the party is short so many men? There are, I think, some 400 men in the party, and it will take a good number of men to bring back sufficient rice.

There is a telephone line strung on poles alongside the track, but no means of using it. One of the Nips is sent off at the double back to Tarsao. The sun blazes down on us, and we shift around to try to stay in the scanty shade patches. Without water we cannot allow ourselves to sweat more than can be helped.

Mid afternoon a couple of carts, pulled by our men left behind in Tarsao, bring us a few tubs of rice, about half a pint each and not nearly enough to carry us through another night. The Nips tell us nothing; maybe they just don't know anything.

Our second night is a repetition of the first, followed by another hungry dawn. We daren't eat our bits of dried meat without cooking them, which is impossible. Another messenger to Tarsao – don't they know there what is happening here? They do have telephones at Tarsao – and, later, another load of rice – inadequate, but welcome.

Our third night, and we are getting really fed up. We are bored and uncomfortable, apart from being hungry. So far no water has reached us and some men are showing signs of distress, which will be really serious before much longer.

We are having to walk further afield to relieve ourselves and at night this is tricky, picking your way – in bare feet – through the little heaps of uncovered ordure, and we are being bothered increasingly by flies. We have no shovels to cover up our droppings.

Good news. Someone, exploring round a curve in the track without being seen by the Nips, has found a small bridge carrying the lines over a gully with a clear steam at the bottom. The Nips are as pleased as we are, and our bottles are quickly topped up.

Early afternoon. Our somnolence is pierced by a loco-motive's whistle from the north. Our train is only three days behind schedule, and the Nips didn't even know it was going to be late!

There is to be no luxury in this ride. We scramble onto flat wagons, the kind used for carrying thirty-foot steel rails, no sides and no roof. Perched on and amongst the baggage we are badly crowded, and with nothing to hang on to we shall have to be careful lest we fall off when dozing or during the night if it takes that long.

In half an hour we are in familiar territory, crawling along the ledge at Wampo North, with its bridge across the split in the cliff face and its buckled rails beyond. We come to our pride and joy, the great viaduct at Wampo South. We see the excavation pits which we dug to build the embankment leading to the viaduct, the drilling channels for dynamite in the bluff, the monkey cave where we rested during the day, the

Kwei Noi – clear again in this dry season – the round bulge of the great boulder sitting in the river, and the magnificent southwards view through the diminishing hills. And we think, nervously, of the shoddy concrete and timber which we put in beneath our rumbling wheels!

Beyond the Wampo camps it is new territory, but the rough signboards at the sidings and 'stations' are familiar from what we heard back in those days a year ago. Aru Hiru, or Arrow Hill (which name is derived from the other?), Takilan, Ban Kao, Wan Tow Kien, Wan Lan, Chungkai (a big 'hospital' camp near here), and amongst these a deep, deep cutting through a small mountain, done with picks and shovels and wicker baskets and causing the deaths of hundreds of men.

Beyond that is the multi-span steel girder bridge built by our men on concrete foundations in the riverbed, at Tamarkan. This river is not the Kwei Noi, alongside which (on its eastern flank) the railway has been built. The name I heard for it, in Tarsao, is something like Mae Klaung. It must be this river which we crossed, somewhere upstream, during our march from Kanburi to Tarsao – the unforgettable point where that British major told us (quite correctly, as it turned out!) that our lives were worth nothing on that side. The Kwei Noi, we worked out, runs into the Mae Klaung some distance to the south.

Trundling over the Tamarkan Bridge, we remark on what an outstanding target it will be for our bombers once they are within range. Downstream we can see a timber bridge which will have carried trains across while the steel bridge was being put up, and which will no doubt be back in use after the bombs come down!

From Kanburi it is an easy run across flat country, some forty-five kilometres we reckon, to a station labelled Tamuang. Here's where we get off; a track leads us south for a couple of

485

kilometres until we reach a metalled road. It looks familiar – it's the road from Ban Pong to Kanburi, along which we marched a year and a half ago through 'a land of milk and honey', to the tragic deaths of so many thousands of good men.

In front of us is that same magnificent flame of the forest tree, flaunting its bright scarlet crown, which caught our attention on our march through. Behind it, 100 yards along a track leading off the road, is a Nip guardhouse and the usual bamboo and attap huts, amongst great trees.

11

Tamuang Camp

MARCH TO JUNE 1944

We wait a while before crossing the road, to allow the rest of the party and the baggage to catch up, and look around us. It's all so *different* – the flat countryside spreads itself around us, rice paddy fields in a neat pattern formed by their surrounding low bunds or earth walls, little groups of trees and villagers' homes. A broad scene of rural peace, with here and there a Buddhist temple glowing warmly in the afternoon sun, its elegant roofline and orange tiles banded with dark green, pleasing to the eye and promising comfort to the faithful – everything we see is conducive to a relaxed and contented life, everywhere a soothing calm.

Our spirits instinctively respond, sloughing off the protective scales which we had acquired during our year and a half in those gloomy, confining hills, and stretching our eyes into far distances. I am almost light-headed with an intense feeling that life is no longer something to be clutched grimly but is here to be enjoyed. I don't have long to indulge myself. Our pestilential Nips are soon yapping at us to cross the road and move up to the guardhouse for tenko. This is a formal affair; the guardhouse itself is far bigger than those in our jungle camps, with one man on a chair out in front and the rest of the guard seated in a row behind him under the roof, the sergeant-in-charge perched higher, behind a table in the rear. We form up and number off, there is a flurry of barking and saluting, and surprisingly quickly we are through.

There is another brief parade inside the camp area, this time for our own officers to receive us and point to the huts allocated to us. We are told that we shall find things much improved over our old working camps, but to be careful in our behaviour because we shall be working mostly inside the camp under the close supervision of the Nips. Being in the midst of the local Siamese people, as distinct from our isolation in the hills, we will find the Nips much more alert and we must keep well within the camp area. The river is some 500 metres to the south, and out of bounds except in organised parties. There are no fences or defined boundaries as yet, so we must stay in close and avoid trouble.

It is thought that the camp is to be developed to take in up to 10,000 men, and we early arrivals will probably be building huts to receive them. Discipline is not unreasonable – behave sensibly and keep it that way! The rest of the day is ours.

The huts are not new but are in better condition than those we have been living in and are blessedly free of bugs. We are at the edge of a belt of trees extending to the river; the cookhouse staff has to carry water all the way, which is heavy physical work. As usual, there are no facilities to store water so there is a constant procession to and fro to provide sufficient for tea and rice, and none at all to spare for washing.

Around the cookhouse is a grove of dark green-foliaged trees of quite magnificent proportions, reminding us of English oaks. The leaves are speckled with thousands of tiny green fruit the size of a finger joint, and the ground beneath the massive branches is littered with them. Mangoes, tiny in their early growth but perfect in their shape, with the characteristic upturned tip, giving out their delicious scent when pierced with a thumbnail. As children in Shanghai my brother and I used to love them. They were brought by sea from the Philippines and have always been a favourite fruit, and now their perfume stirs my memories.

The flat open ground is dotted with shrubby bushes which our agricultural scientists identify as castor oil plants. They will pass this on to the medical officers as the nuts may be useful in providing oil for massage and dressings. We cannot afford to overlook anything that might be of value in our deprived circumstances.

There are several hundred men already here in Tamuang – not more than 1,000, I think – and all of them look to be in far better physical condition than we are. And, looking at them and then at each other as we talk, something else becomes noticeable – we have all acquired a withdrawn, almost haunted look which has become apparent only now when we mix with men who have not worked on the railway.

By good fortune, pure luck of the draw, they were put to work in the Ban Pong/Kanburi area on their arrival in Siam and have remained there since. While their rations have not been generous they were sufficiently better than ours to keep them in reasonable health. Most important of all, their workload has not been nearly so demanding and they have not had the severe stresses of our 'speedo' time. They have heard rumours of our hardships but did not know what to believe. The sick and dying men brought down from upriver have gone to other camps and we are the first real evidence they have seen. And what we tell them is a shock to them.

We all know that the big problem in bringing supplies to camps in the upper reaches of the Kwei Noi is the fact that the river was the only practicable line of transport until the railway was completed. For much of the dry season the river's shallow patches and sandbars make it difficult or impossible to bring boats up. In the rains the river is navigable to laden barges, but they are of small capacity, and sometimes the current racing through the many narrow gorges is beyond the power of the towing pom-poms. The so-called road, running in support of the railway, was never more than a muddy track, frequently impassable even to infantry on foot – and anyway, I don't think the Nips ever had sufficient motor transport to allocate any to our camps. So the Nips had first pick of whatever inadequate supplies did manage to reach the more distant camps, and our people had to make do with what was left – and that was often spoiled or rotten from the length of time in transit, and from exposure to the weather.

We are now in the vast food-growing central plain of Siam, where transport is not a problem and the only obstacle to decent rations is the bloody-minded attitude of the Nips responsible for feeding us. It would not surprise us at all if crooked Nip quartermasters were doing deals with rice suppliers to put money into their own pockets by issuing us with inferior rubbish, in inadequate quantities. Or, of course, it may be deliberate policy to feed us inferior rubbish!

Weeks have passed since we came to Tamuang. The winter weather has stayed true to form – dry, hot and sunny, the air crystal clear. We get down to the river to bathe every day, after putting in the hours erecting bamboo and attap huts for the steady flow of men coming in from the railway camps. It is easy and pleasant work, the Nips are not excessively officious, and we are sensible enough to keep ourselves busy and thus encourage them to leave us alone as reliable workers not needing supervision. All these small things help to make life easier, and since what we are doing is for the benefit of our people, we are altogether in a far better frame of mind than hitherto.

There has been an incident, however, which really should have distressed us but, in fact, gave a good deal of satisfaction. After the routine morning tenko one day, we are divided up into work parties and find, to our complete surprise, that one of our own officers is to accompany us. Apparently it is a complete surprise to him too, because the first thing he says to us is that this is the first time he has ever joined a working party, and he would be glad if we would show him the ropes as we go along. He has not had any dealings with the Nips and isn't at all sure what he will have to do. In fact, although he has been with us in Wampo and all our camps to Kinsayok, the first time he has actually seen the railway was when he had to travel on it, from Tarsao to Tamuang, with us.

'And I must say,' he beams at us cheerily, 'you fellows seem to have done an extraordinarily fine job in the face of so many difficulties. I really must say so! Now, would you be so kind as to tell me what happens next?'

We all know this officer, he is – I'm truly ashamed to have to admit it – in one of the Kuala Lumpur Volunteer units. He came up with us from River Valley Road Camp in Singapore, and from then on we completely lost track of him. So adept was he in keeping out of every activity, and out of our sight, we did not know that he was with us all this time. And now, after nineteen tortured months in Siam, he has the bloody nerve to chirrup away about his first sight of the railway and his very first experience of a working party! And, in addition, he has the sheer condescending effrontery to congratulate us on building that accursed railway 'in the face of so many difficulties'! All those thousands of men murdered by starvation and disease, and thousands more broken in health for the rest of their lives, all those dreadful sacrifices to the railway, the sweat and agonies, are dismissed by him as 'so many difficulties'! And in such a light-hearted casual fashion!

He is in his forties, a captain – quite possibly because of his position in KL's civilian society rather than due to any marked military skills – and, like all of us Volunteers, by no means properly trained or equipped for war when it burst upon us. Nevertheless, the pips on his shoulders place obligations on him to look to our welfare to whatever extent it may be possible, and by his own carefree admission he has deliberately avoided those obligations. Corpulent, pale and flabby, he is a prime example of the idle layabouts whom we so despise.

Our contempt for the mass of our junior officers is now instantly crystallised by this man's attitude, his sheer selfish complacency. There used to be a tiny whisper in the back of my mind that, well, maybe we were being a bit harsh in our condemnation and, well, maybe we were expecting too much of them, and so on. But now my judgement is hard and unforgiving. This despicable man with the backbone of a sponge is typical of all of them.

We must all be having the same thoughts as not one of us has a word for him. We all stare at him in stony shock as his little speech sinks in. His friendly smile starts to warp before it slides off his face and puzzlement takes its place. He cannot understand our cold hostility – after all, he has only been trying to put us at our ease, commissioned officer talking pleasantly enough to men in the ranks, what?

Our Nip turns up to collect us for work and we immediately move off with him, ignoring the plaintive voice crying after us, 'Hey, you men! What's the matter? I asked for your help! Wait for me!'

The work pattern has settled during the past weeks into a routine, the same groups with the same Nips every day, working on the previous day's site. Our work party consists of twenty Volunteers and five men from the 9th Coast Defence Gunners, these last being a tough bunch of insubordinate rogues quick to take advantage of any weakness in authority. In the early days of our acquaintance we didn't get along with them at all well, but now we know you couldn't have better mates – just be careful not to get mixed up in some of their antics!

We are left in no doubt that these men hold the same views as we do. Their comments, deliberately loud enough for our captain to hear as he puffs and pants to keep up with us, are heavily manured with army barracks slang. I can almost hear the rasp of a grindstone as they put an edge on their bayonets, especially sharpened for him. And the opportunity comes, at a ten-minute smoko break. Our Nip – not a Korean, but Japanese regular army – is a strict disciplinarian and not unfair. Do your work properly and he leaves you alone, try to be funny and you get your face warmed up. He is an unusual type amongst the Nips, and we respond appropriately, and thankfully.

So, after smoko we are back lashing bamboo poles into place when the Nip comes along to count heads. Five short! He bawls for the 'shoko' (officer) who is, of course, our ignorant dolt who is about to pay for his careful avoidance of working parties. He doesn't even know that 'shoko' means him! And we don't intend to warn him – let him sort it out for himself.

Nip sergeants fly into a rage if there is no proper response within a split second. Glaring around, he sees our captain sitting in the shade of a tree, oblivious to the approaching storm. As the Nip stamps over to him he looks up innocently, points to his chest and, with a cherubic smile, asks, 'Do you want to speak to me?'

One of our fellows, too soft-hearted (and soft-headed?) to stand it any longer, shouts out, 'Stand to attention and salute him!' He does so, scrambling to his feet just in time to avoid being booted in the ribs, catching it on his rump instead.

The Nip extends his right arm rigidly, his hand just above the ground, his body bent. Our captain leans forward, peering down as if the Nip is pointing to something on the ground. The Nip snaps himself upright, his right arm coming up with all his substantial body weight behind it, his stiffened hand catching his victim neatly on the jawbone. I see several inches of clear space under our officer's feet as the blow lifts him bodily before he falls flat on his back, knocked out cold. It is several minutes before he comes to. It would be suicidal for anyone to try to help him under the eyes of our enraged Nip – and that's a very good excuse for us to leave him lying there. He will find no sympathy amongst our lot.

I wonder what the captain's version will be when he returns to his friends in the officers' hut. What will he say about us? We don't really care. We have huts to put up for our own people coming in, and we get on with our work. We have seen punishment handed out in unpleasant form, and although as far as the Nip was concerned it was simply a disciplinary matter, to us it has been a kind of rough justice finally catching up on a gutless slug. It is ironic that we could not have done any such thing ourselves – it needed a Nip to do it for us!

The five gunners rejoin us. 'Had to go for a piss, took a little longer than we expected.' A frank smile. 'Pity, eh?'

There has been an incident in the camp area, in itself of no great consequence but pointing up starkly a wide difference between the outlooks of Australian and British soldiers. With both comic and shabbily mean aspects, it has Australians in fits of laughter as they tell us about it, while our men listen with stony faces and mutter 'Dirty trick' and 'Shithouse thing to do'.

The story seems to be consistent in its details as related all over the camp. It happened in an outlying area of the camp, the boundary not yet defined and bushes not yet cleared and providing good cover for men wanting to meet Siamese traders. An Australian soldier was haggling with a Siamese over the price of a live chicken and, not being able to beat the price down, the Australian snatched the chicken and ran off. The enraged shouts of the Siamese were heard by a Nip camp guard and the two of them took off after the fleeing Australian, still in sight in the distance.

The Australian swerved into the cover of the shrubbery and came across an English officer strolling along. Realising that he might be caught, he ran up to the surprised officer and thrust the squawking chicken into his hands, saying, 'Present for you, sir, hope you like it!' The Australian vanished, leaving the bemused English officer to be confronted by a very angry Siamese and a furious Nip, with the chicken clutched to his chest.

This account has been delightedly put around by Australians as showing how quick-thinking and clever their man was in grabbing the chicken without paying for it and, when things went wrong, getting rid of the evidence and escaping. The really funny bit is that it was a Pommy officer, no less, who was left holding the baby, so to speak! Not just anybody, but some stuffy prick of an English officer who actually said 'Thank you' for the unexpected present. 'Jeez, what a laugh! Ain't that really rich?'

We see this as a despicably mean act by a petty sneak-thief who had no hesitation in trying to make an entirely innocent man pay the penalty for his crime. To make it even worse, the victim was one of our own people being handed over to the enemy for punishment of a quite unpredictable degree of brutality.

The instant ill-feeling which has flared from this unpleasant event is relieved only by later news that the Siamese immediately realised that the English officer, in uniform displaying badges of rank, could not possibly be the near-naked thief. Retrieving his chicken, he was able to hold the Nip off from bashing the stuffing out of the officer. But a nasty taste has been left. We British have our own petty crooks, no doubt about that, but we do like to think that not one of them would try to save his own skin by betraying one of his own men to the sheer savagery of Nip discipline.

It is curious how the one happening can be seen in quite opposite lights! There will be many Australians who agree with us in regard to this particular affair, but those who put the story about have left the clear impression that they are, one and all, having a great big laugh over it.

These last weeks have been of tremendous benefit to us, and our bodies have made the most of it. The warming sun, the pleasant work duties, the expansive surroundings of the open countryside, the improved rations – all these have made new men of us in both body and mind. The mere fact that we are again living in the midst of a civilised community, even though we have no contact with the people, is stimulating. We can feel that the depressing gloom of the forested hills has at last been shed from our souls, and buoyant optimism is once more a natural part of our outlook.

The rainy season is due, but we know that it will not be nearly as bad here in the plains. We are not bothered by the prospect, our hides are so thoroughly weathered and we are mentally toughened and will easily cope with whatever comes.

I do have one problem, however. My one and only fundoshi is wearing thin and doesn't provide even minimal modesty. I am not the only one in this situation, there are scores in worse condition, and while it does not matter much inside, I would feel distinctly awkward if called upon to go out of the camp on a ration party. We are all hovering on the edge of bare-bottomed poverty – literally – and although we have come to accept hard-edged realities, we do still have a hankering to keep up some tiny degree of respectability. Of course, once a garment is actually hanging in shreds and quite beyond repair, you are faced with the fact that you will soon be totally naked (except for your hat!) simply because there is no possibility of a replacement. Even your friends can't help – by now nobody has a spare of anything!

Passing by the Nip huts I see a long bamboo rail with various bits of clothing drying in the sun. Nothing I can pinch, it is all recognisable as Nip army stuff, but right at the end and out of sight of the huts is a hessian sack. A quick diversion and lightning snatch, and I have a complete new wardrobe! It turns out to have a multicoloured floral design on one side, the trademark of a Canadian supplier of high-grade chicken pellets, which means that I shall have to be careful to wear it with the colours inside in case some Nip should recognise it. A pity, it would have given me such a jaunty look, flowers rosily glowing on my bum!

It happened just in time too, for I am to be in a party to go to the new hospital camp at Nakhon Pathom, which has been built under some degree of supervision from the International Red Cross office in Bangkok. Ron is already there, and someone in admin has been thoughtful enough to include me in the move so that I can rejoin him.

Tamuang now has, I think, some 3,000 men. The evening tenko forms up in blocks of 100 so that even the Nips can get the count correct first time. On the day before our move we are shifted to new huts on the far side of the camp, to be ready to set off early next morning. As soon as tenko is over in the main camp a swarm of our men comes rushing over to us, with exciting news.

The Jap commandant, who has seldom attended tenko before, appeared in his ceremonial uniform and announced that news had come, by radio, that British and American forces had made a landing in great strength in northern France, and had established a firm bridgehead. He thought we would like to know that. Indeed we would, thank you! The commandant is our old friend Lieutenant Tanaka, from Wampo. How extraordinary that he should give us this momentous news of the progress of the war, when they have always made so much effort to keep us from knowing anything.

Next morning, early (usual panic at moving time) we are fed and counted, waiting with our scanty personal gear to march out to the railway line for Nakhon Pathom. I am approached by an elderly officer who asks me if I will carry his suitcase to the railway and, at the other end, to the camp. He apologises for having to ask for help, he has stomach ulcers and is not so young as he used to be, and cannot manage it himself. I look at his grey moustache and tired, lined face – at his age he should not have to live under our straitened conditions. Yes, of course I will, where is it?

Gripping the handle I find I can barely lift it off the ground. It's a bit heavy, he says, sorry about that, it's full of books, about sixty of them. How the hell am I going to lug this bloody thing two kilometres to the line, then God knows how far at the other end?

The Nips start shouting to us to get started, there's no time to argue, and anyway the officer has already moved off with his fellows, leaving me to cope, and I can't just leave it behind.

Luckily, young Hughie has seen me struggling. Grabbing a length of stout bamboo left over from hut-building, he shoves one end through the handle, and together we start to catch up with the others. Swinging and sliding on the pole it is a clumsy and awkward load, and putting a hand on it to steady it means walking in a twisted sideways crouch, tiring and ultimately painful. By the time we reach the railway we don't have even the wind to curse it. Hughie and I are both streaming with sweat and rubbery at the knees.

By some extraordinary luck the train is already here waiting for us. We dump the suitcase in the goods wagon reserved for just a few officers – who did the space allocation? – while the rest of us cram into the other wagons. The Nips always do their arithmetic the wrong way round; instead of saying that at so many men per wagon we shall need so many wagons, they wait until the train arrives, count the wagons – then tell us how many men will have to be stuffed into each, and leave us to sort ourselves into squads of the right size. It never works out in our favour.

We take a professional interest in the track. This is the first stretch to be laid, from Ban Pong westwards to Tamuang, Kanburi, Tamarkan (where it crosses the Mae Klaung on the big steel and concrete bridge), then on to meet the Kwei Noi at the Wampo South viaduct and continue upriver.

The terrain is, in our view, ridiculously easy, flat as a pancake and requiring only a low embankment as protection against flooding. There are only a few small bridges over drainage ditches, no obstacles, and after some twenty or more miles we are passing by that disgusting slum on the outskirts of Ban Pong. From here we are on the well-built international track, coming from Singapore 1,200 miles to the south, running east to Bangkok and then curving south to Phnom Penh and Saigon.

Beyond Ban Pong we come to an array of several parallel tracks with a very large hutted area to the left. This must be Nong Pladuk, a major railway focus and stores dump, with a big camp of POWs and Jap base workshops. Locomotives and rakes of goods wagons stand on the sidings.

Ten or twelve miles further on we stop at Nakhon Pathom, a proper station (like Ban Pong) with platforms and buildings and signals. We don't see much of the town; it looks very ordinary except for one outstanding feature – an unusually large Buddhist temple, with its typical Siamese curved dome rising to a slender spire.

Hughie and I, with some reluctance, take our bamboo pole to the officers' wagon and pick up our suitcase of heavy reading. Thankfully, it's not very far to the camp but far enough to have us cursing it roundly. At the camp entrance the guard has gathered to see us come in, scrutinising us intently as if looking for something in particular, and their eyebrows all shoot up together when Hughie and I come up. Whether it is the sight of two supposedly sick men staggering with bent knees under a heavy load, or suspicion as to what the suitcase might contain – a machine gun and ammunition? – I don't know, but I'm relieved when they giggle and turn their attention elsewhere. Maybe it was my chicken-feed kilt?

The camp is laid out with a broad raised-earth roadway down the centre with huts on each side and smaller roads running at right angles. As we form up for tenko, a mass of purple clouds races towards us from the west, and just as the count is completed the storm bursts on us. The Nips wave us into the huts; we dash in and immediately look for leaks in the roof so that we can stow our kit in a dry spot. The rain thrashes down in a torrent, but to our amazement the hut remains dry! More than that, the sleeping platforms are timber, not knobbly bamboo, and the side walls are high enough to prevent rain from blowing in. Such luxury – we are simply not used to it!

We claim sleeping spaces and when the rain stops everyone goes out to explore the camp. I go out to look for Ron and the other amputees.

12

Nakhon Pathom 'Hospital' Camp

JUNE TO NOVEMBER 1944

I quickly find out where the amputation cases are and walk in on Ron and the rest of the familiar gang. It is a happy reunion, and already our news of Allied landings in France has spread throughout the camp. The whole place is buzzing – this being authentic news from a Nip officer, there is no need to talk about it with a wary eye open for loitering guards.

This is a lively camp, with a busy hum of talk in the huts. All these men are here in this camp because, only a few months ago, they were in the shadow of death, their eyes dull, their bodies shrunken, and their spirits under dreadful stresses. To me it is miraculous that they have recovered so well, having pulled themselves out of the pit by sheer determination and refusal to die.

Medical resources are still miserably inadequate, but there is easier access to supplementary foodstuffs from outside, and that makes an enormous difference both to physical health and to morale. It is even possible to buy tasty snacks from the Dutch hut, cooked Javanese style – I think there may still be a connection with the original Dutch rail-laying gangs, with their privileged access to Siamese traders, who can bring in supplies for their mates to cook and sell. Our enterprising lads found out a long time ago that Nip soldiers are as ready as any others to take bribes to help things along!

There are, of course, hundreds of men still in a bad way and desperately needing all the help that can be provided, but now at least there is a chance of keeping them alive until the war ends and they can be taken home for proper treatment. A few months ago this was not even a hope. Circumstances do change, sometimes for the better.

As a 'hospital' camp for seriously ill men, however, this place is still woefully inadequate in the most ordinary facilities. There is no water supply inside for cooking, for personal hygiene or for hospital use; there is no electric power, which means no proper lighting for surgery or emergencies; there is a total absence of disinfectant and soap. The old trench latrines, however, have been replaced by wooden tubs placed under a platform with squatting holes, and the tubs are removed daily and replaced by clean ones. Probably the contents are sold by the Nips to local farmers for their crops, as is done throughout Japan and China. Waste not, want not, as the saying goes! Or, in a roundabout way, you might term it 'Getting your own back'.

There is, however, one quite marvellous innovation: a blood transfusion service. The methods are unavoidably some-what crude, the Nips providing no assistance whatsoever, but the results are wonderful, even if not always entirely successful because of the absence of proper equipment. Ron was given blood, from a Dutch soldier donor, before his leg was taken off, and I feel strongly that I should see if I can repay this gift.

Walking into the blood transfusion hut I wait for the officer in charge of administration to deal with me. He looks familiar, and although it is five and a half years since we met, we recognise each other. He was one of a group of officers taking up appointments in Singapore, on the Blue Funnel ship *Aeneas*, and our family shared a table with him and his delightful wife in the dining saloon. Swapping memories of that happy voyage, I tell him how, when the ship was tied up at the wharf in the scrubby and smelly mangroves at Port Swettenham, the last call before Singapore, his wife and I were leaning on the boat deck rail at sunset. Below us an empty steel lighter was snugged alongside and, as we talked, the Tamil boatman came out of his tiny cabin carrying a bowl of rice and curry, the savoury odour drifting up to us. Finishing his evening meal the Tamil rinsed out his bowl, unrolled the top part of the sarong wound around his waist, and pulled it up to cover his upper body and head. Stretching out on a straw mat he went to sleep, protected from mosquitoes and the cool night breeze.

'Ah,' said the man's wife, 'look at that. A simple life indeed! Maybe we are too sophisticated in the way we live, changing for dinner and other such rituals which are really unnecessary.'

My anecdote pleases my friend, who is happy to meet someone who can recall a casual conversation with his wife so long ago. He comments, rather sadly, 'Well, now that we've tried it for ourselves, frankly I'm all in favour of life the way we knew it then!' Too right, as the Australians say.

He can't stay to talk any longer, he has duties to attend to, but we will meet again to yarn further. At least he managed to put his wife on board one of the ships that had brought in the 18th Division late in January 1942, and can reasonably hope that she was taken away to safety. He congratulates me on the way Ron and I had news of Mum's escape, and hopes Dad is coping well with being interned in Singapore.

The requirement for being acceptable as a blood donor is simple: no malaria for three months and no current disease of an infectious nature, and I qualify. If the specification were any more complex than that it would be nearly impossible to find donors, but with so many convalescent men in Nakhon Pathom who are now free of malaria, the blood transfusion unit is functioning well. Two months between donations is the minimum period.

There is no shortage of men willing to give blood to their mates. When the word goes round that blood is needed, a queue forms rapidly. The problem is the insufficient facilities; every piece of equipment used is makeshift.

There is no method of testing and matching blood, so Group 'O' is most in demand as it is generally compatible with other groups. If a man's blood group is definitely known, a match between patient and donor can be tried, but it doesn't always work properly as other factors, which are not ascertainable with our crude equipment, can intervene.

I am selected for a particular patient, one of the Singapore Volunteers as it happens, who cannot digest rice and has suffered from dysentery persistently for over a year. The needle from a syringe is pushed into the artery in the crook of my elbow; blood flows through it along a length of tubing from a stethoscope and into a coffee tin containing a citrate solution.

The medical orderly stirs the blood constantly with a glass rod to prevent clotting while I watch the level rise in the tin. He tells me that when there is sufficient he will take it straight to the patient and plug into his arm, letting the blood run in by gravity. If I want to I can come and watch, but he thinks that a walk outside in the hot sunshine would not be a good thing. Better I rest for half an hour, and have a mug of tea.

That sounds like a good idea, and while I'm chatting with the other donors – being in no hurry to leave – the orderly comes back. The transfusion has been completed successfully, by which he means that the patient received my blood without any discomfort. On two previous occasions he had suffered a shivering rigor during transfusion, but this time all went smoothly. The orderly hopes that I shall be available again to give blood to this patient, when wanted, and I tell him I shall be happy to oblige. Something really useful achieved!

I am given a hard-boiled duck egg to help replenish my blood supply, and walk through the hot sun to Ron's hut. I am glad I didn't try it earlier – the heat and glare have quite a dizzying effect, and I feel a little flow of satisfaction that I have been able to do some positive good in this poverty-stricken dump. I really don't think I have the stomach to be a medical orderly in these conditions. I have often thought of offering to help but decided against it – it would upset me too much. But donating blood is no problem.

We all have our own degrees of personal stress and have to cope with them in our own way. Adding to them can well make the burden intolerable. I have the greatest admiration for those men who, with no previous training or experience, willingly work in dysentery and ulcer wards with the simple desire to help their fellows, amid dreadful stenches and sights.

It is not just a matter of spending the days and nights in physically nauseating conditions, it is the intimate contact with so much pain and suffering without even the most elementary means of alleviating it – this is what would defeat me. Put simply, it would all combine to be unbearable for me. It seems odd, the genuine sympathy is there but it is not tough enough to take on the strain of being put to practical use. I feel uneasily that it must be a weakness in my make-up, but I have to accept myself as I am. There must be thousands of men in the various camps who have had similar thoughts, since everybody knows that help is needed and so few actually volunteer their services.

There was a wonderful man in Tarsao, who worked all hours in the dysentery wards, his days and nights filled with filth and unpleasantness, and so much pain and torment, until – inevitably, as he well knew it would be – he picked up the disease himself and died, uncomplaining and only regretting he could no longer help. We all knew of him.

Really, I don't give a damn for the church's technically pure saints. It's men like that who deserve haloes.

Golly is a young Eurasian lad in our Singapore Volunteers – in fact he is far too young to be amongst us and should never have been allowed to enlist. But, like many others in his group of friends, he saw the Jap army's drive down the Malayan peninsula as a direct threat to his family and home. So, although they were all well under age, they joined up and, such was the blind, panic-stricken state of the authorities who controlled our destinies, they were taken on our strength. This despite the very obvious fact that there were no weapons to arm them with, and no possibility of training them to become effective soldiers.

These boys should have been turned away so that they could remain at home to support their families, but now, for no good reason whatsoever and never having had a chance to fight, they have become prisoners of war, and their families are at very real risk of execution simply because they have someone in uniform. There is no possibility of even the smallest snippet of news passing in either direction about the fate of any one of them. Nevertheless, with these awful uncertainties hanging over them, the Eurasian lads have always been cheerful and borne their share of work and pain without complaint. Their good morale impresses us who have lived in Singapore and know their problems, and I have just become aware of an outstanding example of their high personal standards.

During Tarsao's dreadful months of steady deterioration to the status of a squalid death camp due to the weakness and lack of will of its senior British medical officer, and before the Big Australian pulled it out of its morass, Golly developed tropical ulcers on both feet. The ulcer on his right ankle rotted away the Achilles tendon and other ligaments, so his foot was more or less hanging loosely at the end of his leg. Skin was taken from his chest and grafted successfully to both ankles, and the shocking messes were at least covered and given a chance to heal – it was a triumph of his body's recuperative powers and a tribute to the surgeon's skill under such difficult circumstances.

But an unkind fate was not going to let Golly off so lightly. A sudden outbreak of cholera – probably from a man who carried the bacteria without knowing it – was dealt with immediately, but seized a few men in the hut. Golly was one of them, and while in the isolation compound the whole of his painfully acquired new skin sloughed off. Surviving the cholera attack – fortunately only mild, but most unpleasant – Golly was brought back to his old ulcer hut, his ulcers again raw and getting visibly worse.

The medical officer, knowing what Golly was going through, set aside a number of M & B 693 sulpha tablets for him, in itself a sure sign of Golly's desperately weak condition. M & B 693 tablets are so rare that any man given them knows full well he is so close to death that the tablets are his very last hope of keeping a hold on life. This highly disturbing mix of fragile optimism and despair can either strengthen a man's determination to fight just a little longer, or it may induce him to give up, seek relief from his never-ending pain, lie down, and let himself die thankfully.

After a few days the medical officer commented that

Golly was not showing signs of improvement as expected, and he was puzzled because he was certain that Golly would never have thought of letting himself go. His round of checking patients concluded, the medical officer was approached by the man who slept next to Golly and was told that Golly had been giving his tablets to the man on the other side of him because, Golly had told him, 'He is in a worse state than I am, and needs them more than I do, and anyway I am going to die and they will be wasted on me and he might live.'

The medical officer gave Golly a friendly pep-talk, and thereafter Golly took his medicine on schedule and is alive and limping around here in Nakhon Pathom.

Those who have skills of one kind or another are busy all day long, shaping bits and pieces of scrap into useful articles for improving the lot of our sick men. Bamboo backrests for beri-beri patients who cannot lie flat for fear of the oedema in their bellies creeping to their hearts and stifling them, artificial limbs with knee joints, leather straps and supports, tinware for the medical officers to use. Even painting materials have been procured for a couple of artists, who (in the absence of cameras and film) depict obscene ulcers and skin disorders, emaciated men and the huts in which we live. These paintings will be solid evidence when the war is over, to show people who will otherwise not be able to believe what we shall tell them. And, perhaps – we hope – will assist in bringing retribution on senior Jap officers who allowed it all to happen. Never mind the Geneva Convention rules, which they have told us they do not recognise – there are rules of human decency.

It must be awful for an artist to have to stare at some foul ulceration while he meticulously copies it all onto paper. I have seen some of their work and it ties knots in my stomach. What will it do to anyone coming across it for the first time?

There is a large pond in the camp, home to a flock of ducks which are strictly the property of the Nip guards, and we are not allowed to wash ourselves in it or draw water out of it. I wouldn't be too keen to do either of those things – the water looks to be of doubtful quality – but in the absence of any other water source in the camp, it would be a temptation to many men.

There is a squad of our men who look after the ducks and – in theory, at any rate – prevent us from stealing them, but both the ducks and their eggs are impossible to count, and I understand that duck soup and eggs occasionally find their way into the avitaminosis hut.

Towards the end of July, a bright sunny day with a cloudless blue sky despite it being in the middle of the wet monsoon, Ron and I and a few others are enjoying the unexpectedly pleasant weather, strolling along the shore of the pond. Suddenly a chill descends on us and the sunlight weirdly diminishes. A quick upward glance tells us that an eclipse of the sun is just starting. We all have the sense not to stare directly at the sun, but have an excellent view of the event reflected in the brown surface of the pond. Not so one of the Nip guards who has been mooching around nearby – he is obviously frightened and has no idea what is happening. Even the ducks are quiet.

As the shadow spreads across the face of the sun the Nip becomes more and more agitated. He starts gibbering to us, pointing up as if he cannot understand why we have not noticed what is going on up there. The air temperature falls, the darkness intensifies, the Nip's alarm is comic to watch. We put on our stupid faces. It would be distinctly unwise to let him think we understand more about it than he does – far better he should decide we are simply too ignorant to have noticed anything, just staring at the pond!

When only a tiny part of the sun remains, the shadow begins to recede. By now the Nip is in a state of abject terror, on his knees with his hands stretched upwards, trembling and mumbling, rocking back and forth as if in urgent prayer to angry gods – altogether an interesting example of the power which can be exerted by a celestial event on a simple intellect – in only a few minutes this unschooled peasant boy has been reduced to an unnerved jelly!

The sun's brightness and genial warmth come back to us, but the Nip needs a few minutes to recover his poise before he can break out of his trance and gather himself for a stumbling dash to his mates in the guardhouse on the far side of the pond.

We are intrigued by his behaviour. There must be more to account for it than simple panic brought on by the unexpected occurrence of this strange event. Then it suddenly strikes us – it may be a bit fanciful but most certainly not beyond possibility – did the Nip, knowing nothing of the mechanism of eclipses, see the extinction of the mighty sun as an ill omen for his Emperor, and consequently for Japan? A warning of disasters to come, even the end of the nation? This is not too far-fetched; the Japanese people believe their Emperor is a divine being, descended through a long line directly from the Sun God. It is an unquestioning belief inculcated into every child from birth, flaunted in their national flags, and the background to every person's individual and family life.

What a stunning thought! Will there be a collapse in the morale of Japan's fighting troops? Will those in this area, where the eclipse has been seen, believe in their ignorance that it covered the whole vast area of Japanese operations, and thus will have affected everyone? It is certainly an absorbing speculation to debate, and as we continue our stroll along the edge of the pond we notice a gathering of Nips near the guardhouse. Just about every Nip in the camp must be there, all chattering in nervous, highly strung voices. Newspapers are held up, everyone is talking at the same time, and the air is charged with tension.

Drifting closer, we cannot read the headlines because they are, naturally, in Japanese ideographs, but loitering around in the excitement and listening to the voices we are able to catch a few recognisable words such as names of Pacific islands where, according to news rumours, the Americans are operating. But there is too much confusion, the tension is building up and we think it prudent to slip quietly away.

There can be no doubt that something has stirred them up, and with luck it will be some time before the eclipse is explained to them. The longer the rot eats into them, the better. We are quite convinced that we have hit upon a truth, which accounts for the obvious dismay amongst our camp Nips, taking into consideration their overall lack of general education.

I have met a most unusual man in the British 18th Division, quite outside my previous experience. Like all the men in Nakhon Pathom, he came close to death on the railway but has been fortunate enough to recover. It continually amazes me how the human body not only fights back from death, given half a chance to do so, but also restores itself to its original form. Wasted muscles do not just get back into working condition, they resume their original shapes, and tissues rebuild where they used to be. My friend, known to his mates as Tiger Tim, has regained the cat-like sinuosity and fluid movements which earned him his nickname.

I have been helping admin by writing down details about men in my hut – maybe they thought a non-smoker could be trusted with a few sheets of paper! – and Tiger Tim confessed to me that he could hardly write his name. Would I help him to learn to read and write? His formal schooling had ended when he was eleven, and had been a bit patchy up until then – he had never been able to catch up. His father had been a professional boxer, and from a very early age Tiger Tim had been in a travelling circus in which his father operated a boxing booth. Taking on all comers with a prize of ten shillings to anyone who could knock him out, Tiger Tim's father had become a battered lumbering hulk, pickled in beer to ease his bruised body and his shattered ego.

Not knowing any other life, Tiger Tim had taken over boxing in the booth at the age of sixteen. His years with the acrobats and strong men of the circus, together with the heavy work involved in daily circus activities, had built him up to a condition of strength and agility so that he had no problems fending off challengers who were trying to show off in front of the girls, or who were foul-tempered and aggressive from booze. 'Keep moving, dodge around fast, and get the first punch in. That's the secret,' he tells me, with his disarmingly big smile. His perfect teeth are proof that his system works. In several hundred fights, very few punches landed on him.

I am told that he has never been known to lose his temper, and never drinks more than a pint or so – he remembers his father too well. Nor does he retaliate when some young tough tries to pick on him. He simply spars defensively until his assailant gives up in frustration. He is, in fact, a natural fighter, easy-going because he doesn't have to prove anything to himself or to anybody else.

In return for a couple of hours' tuition in the afternoons, he keeps me laughing with tales of circus life – the bearded lady who was no lady (and he refused to explain just what he meant by that!), the clowns, the family with a troupe of trained dogs, the prima donna trapeze group – all fascinating people. Tiger Tim may not know how to read and write, but he can tell stories with quite surprising fluency and vocabulary.

I cannot do much about writing since there is no paper available, but we draw outlines in the dust and my treasured book has the words for him to study and recognise. It is a shame that he had no real schooling, for he is sharp and intelligent and very keen to learn – a most rewarding pupil.

What I gain from him is worth as much to me as my teaching is to him, and we both enjoy ourselves immensely.

At tenko yesterday evening the Nips announced that there would be an issue of food, clothing and footwear for each man. This morning these goodies – presented to us in the name of the Emperor, to whom we must be properly grateful – are distributed. We have no idea what to expect – certainly not generosity! – and when the evidence of the Emperor's lavishness makes its appearance, we don't know whether to laugh or cry.

The food consists of a cardboard box of pepper, fine ground white, about a pound in weight. The box is plain brown, with a white label proclaiming 'NOTE, THE PAPER CHANGE BECAUSE IN THE MARKET. TIME.' Just like that. The quality is excellent, and we shall make the most of it to flavour our depressingly tasteless diet. But a whole pound of it?

The footwear is a pair of wooden sandals, flat on top and rounded underneath, with a hoop of bicycle tyre nailed across the toe end.

The clothing, in my case, is a black cotton fundoshi of such small size that it would fit a child if he were lean enough. Is black this year's fashion colour?

Our gratitude to the Emperor is beyond words, despite efforts to think of some!

The nervous demeanour of the Nips persists, but it seems significant that they are not trying to take out their feelings on us. In fact, apart from tenkos we seldom see them in the camp. No longer do we have one or two of them drifting around with their eyes flicking everywhere and expecting to be saluted as they pass by – in our view a kind of 'unobtrusive' patrol looking for illegal activities and, in particular, signs of wireless sets. We think it very likely that these Nips may have some understanding of English, sufficient to eavesdrop on conversations in the hope of picking up evidence of recent news being discussed.

We have been warned to be very careful on this point, because our news bulletins have been more frequent recently, and certainly more up-to-date – we know, for instance, that the Fourteenth Army in Burma has gone on the offensive and, last August, recaptured Myitkina in the north. We are confident that momentum will now build up rapidly, which will most certainly raise unpleasant questions about our own situation when defeated Jap troops start coming out of Burma down 'our' railway. Decisions will be extremely difficult, especially in camps such as this where, should we fitter men take off into the countryside, our sick would be left helpless to be slaughtered. If we were to stay, though, we would still not be able to protect them and would simply be knocked off with them. Killing so many of us would, of course, be beyond the capability of our relatively small camp guard as we would easily be able to overwhelm them, so it is obvious that local army units would have to be called in to ensure a quick job.

The attitude of the Siamese army is a matter of conjecture. Even if they come in on our side it would be all over and done with before they could intervene. The civilians, we are sure, are our friends.

Not a cheerful prospect, whichever way we look at it.

During the night there is a big stir-up, about 3 am, Nips dashing around screaming 'Tenko, tenko,' hurricane lamps like yellow fireflies flittering everywhere. It is raining steadily, near-naked bodies glisten in the feeble lamplight as we try to form up in our usual places, shifting and shuffling around as each Nip tells us to stand here, stand there, go over there, come this way, and become more excited as the confusion grows.

Things only get sorted out when we all decide to ignore them and find our own places. Standing ten deep and twenty along the front, 200 men in a block, we fill the main roadway. There must be some 5,000 men in the camp, and in the moonless dark the Nips, by now in a real panic, cannot get the numbers to add up, what with us outside the huts and sick men inside, too ill to move, and sundry medical officers and orderlies trying to attend to patients, admin officers being shouted for hither and thither and, always, men hurrying to the latrines and coming back from them, being counted twice or three times or missed altogether.

Some of this is deliberate on our side. It is known that a number of men are outside the camp, to get news, make contact with the Siamese, try to locate medical supplies to buy, or to sell such few signet rings and other valuables as are still available. The more that tenko can be prolonged, the better their chance of getting back in to be counted.

Four hours later the sky lightens and a final count is possible. The Nips are hoarse and ragged, squelching around in soaking uniforms while we have remained in formation, chilled but unperturbed, chatting quietly, waiting to be dismissed. We have been standing all this time, rivulets of rainwater sluicing over our bare feet in the stony gravel, our painfully acquired self-discipline keeping us even-tempered and philosophical.

Back in our huts we find there is no morning rice, the cooks having had to turn out for tenko. There is no possibility of a meal now; fires have to be stoked up for midday when, with luck, there will be a bigger ration of rice and pepper!

Rumours start to get around. One is that the local Jap army police, the horrific Kempei-tai, saw some of our men in the town and ordered an immediate count. This has been expanded by whispers from the officers' batmen that the Kempei-tai discovered some funny business going on in the Nip administration. Our people produced a set of figures for the camp population and steadfastly refused to alter them. The Nips showed higher figures and are suspected of having falsified them – for example, not reporting deaths and outward transfers of men – enabling them to draw pay for these non-existent men and put it into their own pockets!

With the coming of daylight (and our ranks filled to what they should be) the Kempei-tai have had to accept our figures as correct. If this is indeed the case, our guilty Nips are in for a very rough time!

* * *

517

Today we have witnessed something so unutterably foul, so obscenely destructive of human decency, that our senses have been numbed. This evening, back in the comforting presence of our own people, we can describe what we have seen only in subdued voices. It is necessary for us to talk about it, even though just saying the words makes us shudder. It is the only way we can cast out the horrible demons that lay in ambush for us at the railway sidings.

The Nips have called for working parties now and again, when stores are to be shifted or rations brought in. Nobody minds being sent out of the camp – the work is light and it makes a change to be amongst ordinary people. The townsfolk pay little attention to us, and usually we are allowed to buy bananas and eggs.

There are parties of Jap army men carrying boxes and rolling petrol drums here and there, while our job is to hump bags of rice into trucks (though not for our use – it is far too good in quality to be issued to us). We have just finished when a long rake of goods wagons rolls in on the line where we are working, and stops close to us. They are closed steel wagons, roofed and with a sliding door on each side. They are the same type that brought us up from Singapore, and we know well just how uncomfortable they can be, crammed with thirty men, on a five-day journey under the tropical sun. We look at them without much curiosity until the doors, only partly open until then, are pushed open in uneven jerks. Either they are very stiff or whoever is trying to open them is finding it beyond his strength.

A few arms appear, straining to open the doors further, then a few heads, turning to look at the surroundings. All movements are slow, lethargic; the clothing tells us the men are Japanese army. And they are all filthy. It's not just the grime of a day or two – this dirt looks as if it has been there a long time. The men are exhausted, nearer to death than life.

When the doors are opened wide enough, men start to come out. Sitting on the floor they dangle their legs and drop out. Not one of them can land on his feet – every man collapses in a heap, lying still and moaning softly. Uniforms are in rags, and we see exposed skin crusted with blood and oozing pus from infected wounds and sores.

Then the awful smell, the foul stench of decaying flesh and gangrene, blood, faeces, putrefaction and thick sweat, pours out of the doorways. All the offensive stenches of those terrible ulcer and dysentery huts at Tarsao, concentrated in an overwhelming, nauseating, heaving wave that wraps itself around us, clinging to our bodies and pushing into mouths and noses, sickening, revolting.

As the doors open more men slowly emerge, stiffly and painfully, falling to the ground over the inert bodies already there. In the shadowy interiors of the wagons the air is scarcely breathable. Men and their kit are piled all over the floors, vomit and excrement spattered profusely everywhere. Many of the men look to be dead, with flies circling lazily in and out of open mouths. Others are barely alive, their eyelids closed or fluttering, and flies in thousands crawl in dense layers over filthy faces and exposed wounds, over foul dressings. Their buzzing reverberates inside the steel casing of the wagons.

Enemy soldiers they may be, but no human being deserves to be reduced to such helplessness and degradation. We have to help, and turn to our Nips for permission, but they are deliberately facing away. Jap troops nearby look on for a moment, then resume their duties, totally indifferent. There will be no help from their own people for these dying men.

What can we do? We have nothing we can offer, except determination to try to do *something*. The first need is clearly for water – the Japanese word 'mizu' we can just distinguish among the moaning – but there is no supply at hand. A dash to the station platform, tip sand out of fire buckets, look for taps, hurry back, shout at hawkers selling fruit and tea, adding our own tiny contributions of tobacco and hard-boiled eggs. Our Nips make no attempt to interfere or bring us back to the work we came to do – they won't help their own wounded but at least they don't try to stop us. What sort of people are these, the Japanese? What motivates them?

There are maybe thirty freight wagons in the rake, and groups of our men are dotted along the length trying to help. The problem is huge and our resources so pitifully inadequate. We cannot even reach most of those inside, and even if we were able to, there is really nothing we can do for them. Some of the Siamese hawkers give us limes which we squeeze into the buckets of water – it will help to freshen up mouths gummed up with dried saliva. We cannot pay for anything, none of us has more than a few sattangs, but the fruit is pressed on us. Thankfully, the flies stay inside the wagons – they probably prefer the semi-darkness and the awful stench.

It is so frustrating, so much to be done and we cannot even wash faces. Sips of water are taken, small movements of hands and tired smiles show their thanks. Their exhaustion is such that even the effort needed to make these tiny gestures is too much for them. The hawkers pass cigarettes to us – we have to put them between the men's lips and light them, and a few puffs is all they can manage before the cigarettes fall away.

The sufferers inside the wagons do not move. If they see that those outside are being cared for it seems to be beyond their strength to make any effort to struggle out. And there is absolutely nothing we can do.

Some of the soldiers try to talk to us – their voices are croaky and the words are forced out with difficulty – but with our bits of Japanese and their scraps of English we gather that they are from Booruma (Burma) and have been on this train for thirty-six days! No food (meishi nai), no water (mizu nai), and (pointing at nauseating dressings) no treatment for wounds during all that time. We can believe it; we have had the same sort of treatment. In the Japanese army nobody is interested in you if you are unable to fight; nobody will allocate scarce resources to feed you or to heal your wounds or sickness. You are cast adrift with nobody responsible for you – fend for yourself, live or die, who cares? With us it has been 'no work, no food' and never any medical supplies, but these are their own troops who were wounded in action. A ruthless philosophy, devoid of human feelings.

We can imagine that terrible journey from some battlefield in Burma, shunted into sidings while priority traffic passed through, foraging for food and water whenever they could get out of the wagons, then, as they weakened, becoming less able to care for themselves, pushing the dead out through the doors, relapsing into a coma as the sweltering days and cold nights passed, the interiors becoming more and more foul until life came almost to a standstill. Here, right here, at Nakhon Pathom. How far to go? The 1,500 miles to Saigon?

They cannot have much life left in them; nobody is going to come to their rescue. When someone eventually notices an awful stench from wagons abandoned in a remote siding, they will be shovelled out and obliterated in blazing petrol. All this suffering for nothing, no purpose at all. They will simply be Jap army rubbish.

Our Nips shout for us – time to go back to camp. We are distressed at having to leave, but at the same time glad we cannot stay. It has been a severe strain on us, as we begin to realise, to be confronted at such close quarters with such abysmal suffering while being unable to do anything useful.

Our emotions are in a mess. We have not been on the spot long enough to adjust and now we have to sort ourselves out, get back to normality. There is little talk amongst us as we walk away. Each of us has his own emotions to deal with, and we all need to unwind.

The bugle sounds lights out, not that there are any candles or coconut oil lamps because it's a brilliant moonlit night and we don't need them. Lying on our hard timber planks in the soft illumination we become aware that the moonlight has attracted others – a faint growling in the distance grows steadily louder and we all know what it means.

Moving quickly outside our huts we watch our bombers come into view, not flying in neat formation but in loose groups, swiftly swarming over from the east. The spire of the great Buddhist stupa in the town points upwards starkly, and no doubt the glazed tile surface of its great dome makes a brightly gleaming landmark for the navigators and pilots. The bombers fly low, jet black silhouettes edged in silver. We can even see tiny sparkles from moonlight striking off windscreens and propeller blades as they head west towards Ban Pong and our own railway. Are they returning home from a raid on Bangkok? If so they would surely be flying higher. Or are we at the business end of it?

The big railway yard at Nong Pladuk isn't very far away, and almost immediately we see the arcs of tracer and anti-aircraft shells rising and bursting in red flashes. Then there are great flaring incandescences. The ack-ack shells no longer appear, and the heavy rumbling of exploding bombs reaches us. Somewhere has had a pasting. It must be Nong Pladuk, and we wonder about the big POW camp which we saw along-side the railway sidings. Bombs do not discriminate between friend and enemy, and a ringside seat can be uncomfortable.

We hear more aircraft engines coming from the east, and spot a group of three. Maybe their job is to have a look at the results and do some tidying up. But they dip suddenly, even lower than the first lot, and drop their bombs not very far away. There is a sudden whooshing flare, and we think of the petrol dump where the Japanese soldiers were rolling drums this morning in the railway sidings. And we also wonder about those wretched soldiers from Burma. Lying comatose under the seething flies, waiting, endlessly waiting, for an end to their suffering. Did that end come tonight, in the fires of hell?

Last night's air raids are a keen topic of conversation this morning. The bombers were bigger than any we had seen, our knowledge being as badly out of date as the obsolete aircraft available during the Jap attack on Malaya. But men of the British 18th Division say they were Liberators, four-engined and with twin rudders, capable of carrying big loads over long distances. Now that they have appeared as far east as Bangkok, we can expect to see more of them. Further thought suggests that we may have captured the Andaman or Nicobar Islands, which would possibly be their operating bases. We have a fair idea of distances in this part of the world, and it is interesting to toss speculations around and see if they fit into a pattern.

There is another side to the raids. A convoy of trucks comes through the camp gate, and there is a call for all those fit enough to hurry over to help in carrying bombing casualties into the huts. I find myself holding a corner of a stretcher (British army type) with a man whose left leg has been taken off near the hip. There are several amputation cases, and scores of other casualties. It is immediately noticeable that their bandages and dressings are fresh – the

Nips at Nong Pladuk must have released brand new stocks.

These wounded men can give us first-hand news. There were at least three trains in the yards at the time, and some must have been carrying ammunition from the way they exploded and burned. The anti-aircraft fire was from batteries manned by Indian troops, formerly British units which had gone over to the Japs in the Indian National Army. Supply huts and dumps were also hit and severely damaged, but two sticks of bombs fell across the camp. Our casualties were heavy – British, Australian, Dutch. Around 100 are thought to have been killed and several hundred wounded. The camp itself has one fence bordering the railway sidings and there is no protection – not even trenches – so casualties are inevitable in the event of a raid.

Casualties amongst Jap troops must also have been considerable, for this is a major supply base for stores sent up from Saigon and Singapore for the Jap forces in Burma, and the whole area is swarming with admin troops, engineers and transport units. There are also workshops equipped to make and repair material for the railway which, we hear, has been taking a pounding now that the whole length of it is within reach of our bombers.

Clearly, we are happy that the Allies are now showing visible evidence of being on the move in this part of the world, although our position in the overall pattern could easily be somewhat dicey. A soldier is always aware that he may become a casualty – wounded or killed – in action, but there is something distinctly unnatural in being placed by an enemy under your own side's bombs.

As POWs we do indeed have unique stresses, strains and emotional pressures imposed on us, to which each man has to adapt in his own way. Completely isolated from our own world, and from civilisation as we know it, we have to rely on our own internal resources and – absolutely essential – our comradeship with those in the same boat with us. Holding us all together is our total contempt for the Japanese – more powerful than mere loathing.

Despite being made of new timber our sleeping platforms have already started to develop colonies of bugs. These little brown horrors lodge in tiny crevices, between the boards and underneath, and crawl out in scores to suck blood through your skin. The irritation is intense and when you swat them their squashed bodies give out an incredibly nasty stink. In the river camps we used to keep their numbers down by passing a flaming bamboo torch underneath, but that's not possible here.

So some bright boy has sprinkled some of his pepper ration between the boards, to kill them off. Now, in his part of the hut, every time anyone turns over in his sleep everyone goes into fits of sneezing. The resulting language is educational, but not really appreciated in the small hours of the night.

And the bugs are still there, in apparently undiminished numbers. Maybe they like their meals well seasoned?

Nakhon Pathom is just about full. We are told that there are still many very sick men to be brought in, some of whom were too ill to be moved earlier and are in desperate condition even now, but camps upriver are being closed and they have to be moved. So we fitter men will be shifted out, back to Tamuang, and this will include me. I cannot ask to be allowed to stay, in order to be with Ron, if it means keeping a sick man out. I have just made a second blood donation to my special patient, so obviously I am one of the healthier men. I must be thankful for that, and accept it as balancing the need to move. Fate was kind to me in letting me rejoin Ron, twice; maybe it will happen again. In fact, every aspect of our lives is a matter of chance. Every man has to accept whatever happens as philosophically as he can, then simply make the best of it. Prediction is not possible, bad beginnings can turn out well and hopeful moves can prove disastrous.

And now, after surviving thirty-two months of captivity – having made the spirit-breaking adjustment from being proud soldiers of a great empire through shameful defeat to becoming slaves of no value – we are at risk of being killed by bombs dropped by our own people. We have endured un-believable hardships to our bodies and humiliations to our souls, and seen the squalid deaths of thousands of our fellows, only to come to this situation. Always, at the back of our minds, the certainty – no one fools himself enough to see it as only a vague possibility – of being killed off by the Nips when things become desperate for them.

More oppressive than anything is the deep feeling that none of this has resulted from our own deficiencies, or lack of fighting qualities, or determination to face the enemy. The blame goes back to our piss-begotten politicians and military muttonheads, who not only did nothing but prevented any-one else from doing anything, refusing to accept or permit modern thinking and developments in armaments. If curses have any power these men will be thoroughly scorched by our hostile thoughts. In our circumstances we are free of con-ventional niceties, and our brains work very clearly and logically. Criticism is hard-edged and penetrating – we don't have to worry about personal reputations and can disregard propaganda and official whitewash, and think our own thoughts; there is nobody here whose feelings might be hurt.

Without the usual mad panic to move out, we are told in the evening to be ready next morning. There's time to go around saying goodbye, but no emotional displays since we have all long since learned to be cheerful on these occasions. But the feelings are there, nevertheless, for who can say if we shall meet again or even survive the war?

Our party hikes through the town, not in any precise army formation but closed up and disciplined, to the sidings area beyond the railway station. Some hawkers approach while we wait for our train and the Nips allow us to buy, but there isn't a lot of choice. I show a hawker what I can spend, twenty-five sattangs, and he hands me two big bunches of magnificent ripe bananas, big and golden yellow. It's a bargain, he is generous.

A rake of flat wagons is shunted along; we climb aboard and settle down. It's a fine day and we have an excellent view of the pleasant countryside. We look for damage from the recent air raid, but the yards have been tidied up and the only evidence is some fire-blackened rubble. Nong Pladuk, however, shows its scars. Burnt-out wagons, twisted by heat, have been shoved aside, too badly damaged to be towed away. Obviously new rails and sleepers have been laid over filled-in craters. We cannot see into the POW camp area, and anyway the flimsy huts can quickly be repaired. What must be Jap army workshops or store huts, grouped around spur lines, have not been rebuilt. Both here and at Nakhon Pathom the bombing was remarkably accurate. What damage can be seen is all in the target areas.

The way this train is creeping along we shall not reach Tamuang until early afternoon. We have not brought any lunch rations with us, so I start on my bananas. Thirty-two of them, all eaten comfortably in a leisurely meal, sitting in bright sunshine cooled by the breeze of our movement. It really is extraordinary how so many months of privation and near-starvation have given us the capacity to absorb incredible quantities of food when it becomes available, without any sign of bloating or indigestion. I am not the only one; all the others have tucked into their purchases from the hawkers, with only a few appreciative burps to show for it.

Familiar scenery again, the small siding where we get down from the wagons and head off for Tamuang Camp, the brilliant flame-tree and the sullen-faced Nips at the guardhouse.

A quick, even offhanded tenko and we are back to knobbly bamboo slats and leaky attap huts. Just like coming home after a few months' holiday!

13

Tamuang Camp

NOVEMBER 1944 TO MAY 1945

The camp itself looks much the same as when we left it last June, except that there are many more huts. The population is now about 8,000, around that of a modest country town with the difference that all the inhabitants are men, crammed into a few acres of land, with no civic amenities of any kind. The parade ground is big; it has to be in order to have room for so many men at tenko. On the south face a wooden stage has been built so that whoever is in command at parade times can be seen and heard by those at the back and sides.

The standard hut accommodates 160 men, so already there are some fifty huts plus cookhouses and a few small huts for medical and admin use. There is a hospital area, but not many patients since this is supposed to be a camp for fit men held ready to send out to other areas that need a labour force. Any man with long-term illness is sent down the line to Nakhon Pathom.

It seems that still more men are expected to come in, for new huts are under construction. Apart from this there is no real work at the moment, except for work parties necessary to keep the camp functioning. Firewood for cooking is no longer a simple matter of going into the surrounding forest and chopping down bamboo – the local countryside provides none. Food supplies, however, are plentiful all around us, and although the Nips are still parsimonious in what they give us, at least our camp canteen is able to carry reasonable stocks of fresh items such as eggs, bananas and limes, which are so important to our health. Even a few luxury items are available at prices within our scanty finances, bottled chilli sauce and cooking fat, sun-dried fish pieces, and rank tobacco.

As always, there is no water supply in the camp. The river, no longer our familiar Kwei Noi, is some 500 yards to the south, and water-carrying parties are constantly trudging to and fro. There are no storage tanks in the camp, and not nearly enough pails and containers. The quantity required daily is enormous, and so is the sheer physical effort of lugging it all the way from the river.

There is in fact a well, only some three feet in diameter and presumably the relic of a sometime village because it has a stone parapet and inside facing. The clear water is brought up in a bucket on the end of a plaited rawhide rope made by Australians in the camp. This well happens to be near the hospital huts, and its water is strictly for their use. The supply is not generous – the well empties quickly and refills slowly. Its depth below ground level is indicated by the rope, which would stretch the length of a cricket pitch. But the water is cool and drinkable without being boiled, a great boon to malaria sufferers.

There is such a great change in the physical condition and cheerful faces of the men, that I have to remind myself that they are the lucky survivors of those dreadful death camps along the railway, and were themselves little more than warmed-up corpses only a year ago. The lifting of the crushing stresses of slave labouring, the move from claustrophobic hills and gloomy rain-soaked forests, the small improvements in food – all these have contributed to a lightening of spirits and easing of bodily oppressions. Open sores have healed, fevers are less severe and not so frequent, bowels have dried up and normal functioning has returned. It is truly remarkable how the human body and its intrinsic mental processes can endure the most damaging hardships, and then repair themselves. Not always, of course, to their previous health level, but nevertheless to a degree which many of us had not thought possible. We can only hope that this progress will not be interrupted or set back by some new project which the Nips might think up.

There is one new thing in this camp, nearing completion when we arrive, which might be symptomatic of a changed Nip attitude towards us. It has been nicknamed The Palace, and the fact that it is only a latrine understates its importance in our view of things. Our lives so far have been dominated by the more unpleasant, unattractive, and downright repulsive aspects of latrines. Everyone's bowels have to move frequently, there is no avoiding it, and in our living conditions this has meant squatting over a trench in a camp or a hole scratched in the forest. Every occasion has been unpleasant, and resignation does not lessen any of the stench, the sickening fumes welling up from the mass of seething filth and crawling maggots, the continued erosion of personal dignity caused by the total absence of privacy, not only your own but that of the man crowded up close to you. And the flies, big and shining iridescent blue-green, buzzing fatly around to encourage you to finish and get away as soon as possible.

Never before have the Nips allowed us to use men and tools to dig new trenches when they were needed. Overused, the contents flood out in the rains and swill through our sleeping huts, and old trenches are not filled in because we are not allowed time to do it, thus they become breeding pits for even more flies. The Nips are known to be fanatical about personal hygiene – their own, not anybody else's – but they know bloody nothing about field hygiene. They have not been able to grasp the simple fact that flies in our camp are also a menace to them in theirs. Maybe they live like that at home.

So now we have The Palace, an enormous rectangular pit dug into a low mound, roofed over with attap to keep out the weather, and floored across the top with bamboo poles. Rows of bamboo benches enable you to actually sit instead of crouching on your heels, and every hole has a wooden cover which drops down when it is not in use. Apparently the sawn timber came from Nip ration boxes; we haven't seen any for years. Our people have even managed to scrounge old sacks and sump oil, so that smouldering bundles can be suspended in closed-off sections to prevent flies from breeding.

The Palace stands as a symbol of hope for a better future. Is that incongruous, or stupid, or comic? Could we expect an outsider to have any understanding of how we see it? To us it is quite simple – the product of circumstances, not to be considered with undue seriousness or to be given more weight than a sly poke at Nip mentality but, nevertheless, it is new, different, and a definite improvement in our circumstances. Maybe, like the Statue of Liberty, a symbol of hope – no disrespect intended.

A new work project has started, some 200 of us digging a great pit which leads to all sorts of speculation about its intended use. The earth here is soft clay, easy to handle, and the excavated soil is piled around the circumference in a thick wall. A broad column of earth is left in the centre and this provides a support for hundreds of coconut palm trunks brought in from outside and laid crisscross to form a solid roof. There is a single entrance via a down-sloping ramp, and no ventilation is provided.

From a few hundred yards away we bring earth from a small hillock and spread it over the palm trunks. The banana trees which crowned the hillock are now carefully replanted in this new location and, by enormous prolonged effort, watered in to give them a new start.

It is a mystery to us. Camouflaged from the air in military style, it has no gun ports to make it a defensive bunker – although these could be cut out without difficulty – and its depth is such that no man standing on the floor could use a weapon above the outside ground level. It is also clear that the entrance ramp would, in the rainy season, act as a chute to bring in floods of water as there is no overhead roof and we have carefully sloped the sides to collect as much rain as possible.

So there it is, on the edge of the camp area, built to definite specifications – which would indicate some formed intent – but serving no useful purpose for the time being. And declared to be strictly out of bounds.

At tenko this morning a group of Nips went around pulling men out to stand away to one side. There must have been more than 1,000 by the time the selection was over. They are marched away to a distant area of the camp. We are told nothing, and disperse as usual in working squads to our various jobs.

At evening tenko all is revealed. These men are being sent to Japan, where they will be privileged to work assisting the Japanese war effort! Other parties will follow later. They will be kept separate from us, a barricade will be erected, and although we may talk across it we may not mix, as the men are in some kind of quarantine and, therefore, isolated.

It is a couple of weeks before we are able to cross over to the group of new huts where the Japan party has been sent. The 'barricade' is nothing more than a single rope strung along a line of bamboo wands stuck in the ground, but in the Nip army that is enough to signal 'STOP' as effectively as a true barrier.

The men seem to be pleased with their situation. They have been told that they were selected as being in good health, they are being fed greatly improved rations and heavens above! – they have each been given a toothbrush! They have been urged to make themselves strong and healthy, so that they will be able to work well in Japan and be a credit to His Majesty The Emperor! Within a week they will be taken to Singapore or Saigon to board a ship. The prospect doesn't seem to alarm them; they grin cheerfully as they tell us the news. Maybe they are tickled by the big joke that immediately circulates: with most of its men overseas, Japan is bringing them in as stud stallions to be available to their womenfolk, to improve the home breed! Otherwise, why all this issue of toothbrushes and extra food, and the selection of the fittest men? Even soap has appeared! What next?

But serious thoughts surface amongst our chatter about this new development. We reckon that the distance by sea to Japan must be at least 4,000 miles, and recent news/rumours tell us that the Allies have been sinking Jap shipping everywhere. So it could be a risky voyage. And we know something about Jap ideas of transporting troops by sea, from those Australians shipped from Java to Singapore and up the Burma coast. The thought of enduring such privations over several weeks is not to be dismissed. And, more important even than that, the totally random selection process has separated men who have kept together and supported each other closely all this time. It is a tremendous wrench to be treated in this callous way, and no time has been lost in seeing what can be done about it.

The opportunity comes with a Nip order to our admin people to compile a list of names of the men who will be going, which results in a good deal of name-shuffling – some don't want to go and others are willing to take a chance, some in the party will swap places so that friends can go together, some want to stay back with mates and need a voluntary replacement. The roll of names is finalised in time, no last minute changes can be considered, and men slip quietly under the tape in the dark hours of the night. The rest lies with fate.

It is now winter in Japan, far colder than any of our men will have experienced. We can only wish them well.

There are now over 10,000 men at Tamuang, and tenko has become an exact art to get us all crammed into the parade ground. The area has been paced out and pegged to show the position of the right-hand men of the front rank of each block of men. We have a warrant officer with the most powerful voice I have ever heard, a true replica of the ancient Greek herald Stentor, who calls out first the front markers and then general 'fall in'.

All of us, standing around in readiness, quickly form up in our appointed places amid a low roar of chattering voices which cuts off instantly to absolute silence when we are called to attention. We are now formed with geometrical precision into some forty groups of 250 men, each ten deep on a front of twenty-five. There is no room to spare, but the counting is simplified and even the Nips can get it right first time.

Up to this point the parade has been conducted by our warrant officer, who reports 'Parade present and correct' to

ONE FOURTEENTH OF AN ELEPHANT

our colonel. This officer has earned himself a tremendous reputation amongst us, and he is supported by our old colonel from Wampo, for whom we all have the greatest respect. The tight discipline at tenko is due, I am sure, to our regard for these two senior officers, as is also the personal bearing of each man, so noticeably improved in recent months.

The parade is then handed over to the Nip duty officer, and from then the formal commands, which were drilled into us way back in Singapore and are now second nature, are in Japanese. The count is quick, the Nips return the parade to our officers and we are dismissed. In a split second – as if a switch had been turned on – the roar of conversation resumes.

Looking back at the somewhat casual attention paid to army 'bull' that had become the norm in the railway camps, I suddenly recall a particular evening tenko before I was transferred from Tamuang to Nakhon Pathom last June. We had drifted into tenko formations in our customary lack-adaisical style and were given a blistering dressing-down by our colonel. He told us, loudly and forcibly, how this attitude was understandable in the grim days on the railway, but was totally unacceptable in this camp, under his command. We were soldiers of the King, not small school-boys on an outing, and our slovenliness disgusted him! Now that things were easier we should pull ourselves together and act like men! He was ashamed to be in command of such a shambling mob, and he expected an immediate smartening-up. He greatly regretted having to speak to us like this, but it was necessary. Circumstances prevented him from taking disciplinary action – and anyway, he didn't want to have to do so – therefore it was up to us to take a good look at our-selves and DO SOMETHING ABOUT IT! He looked for improvement and hoped he would not have to speak to us again! He was confident that we would remember that we were still soldiers belonging to proud regiments, and would conduct ourselves accordingly.

There could be no doubt about the colonel's feelings. Anger, disappointment, concern for his men, his powerful appeal to us to see how we had dropped our standards, and to recover our self-respect – all these emotions came through to us in his voice and in his words.

Self-respect, that was the nub of it! The angry buzz of protest which followed dismissal gradually gave way to thoughtful consideration. The man was *right*! We *had* let ourselves drift downhill, but that was unavoidable under the stresses of the railway camps, and now it really was time to buck up and be ourselves again.

The men's conduct on parade nowadays is proof of the new attitude. The absolute silence observed during the formal part of the parade commences only when the exact moment requires it, and finishes the instant it ceases to be necessary. We stand rigidly at attention, even those in the midst of the formations who can't be seen, while the count takes place. We have recovered our pride as soldiers, at the same time asserting our individuality. And we feel a lot better for it, within ourselves.

If the colonel should call us to attack the Nips bare-handed we would do it, because of our respect for him. Such is the change in our attitude. What an inspiring man! Maybe he can put some backbone into the mass of layabouts in his junior officers. There can be no doubt that their disinterest in our welfare, their total lack of concern, their near invisible presence in our camps – all these were definite contributors to our slipping standards.

* * *

Today has been a pleasant change, and I hope there will be more like it. It is entirely a matter of luck as to which work party you find yourself in, and this morning we are taken down to the river to two wooden barges and a pom-pom towing launch. Our Nips, of course, park themselves under the pom-pom's canopy, leaving us to relax on our own.

We idle along downstream for half an hour or so. The river is already well down after only a few weeks of the dry season. The somnolent countryside slides past in the clear sunshine – I could happily take a lot of this!

We approach a fifty-foot cliff on our right, and the pom-pom goes into a wide turn to come in facing upstream. At the foot of the cliff is a broad table of smooth stone which would have been submerged in the rains but now stands out dry and provides an easy landing place. A swarm of Siamese children fringe the top of the cliff, waving a welcome as kids do everywhere.

There is a sort of goat track up to the top, and we find ourselves on a large area of flat ground between the timber houses of a small village and the river. The whole of this space is taken up by stacks of firewood – tree branches, not split logs, held in between upright stakes driven into the ground. Evidently, these are made up in measured quantities, two metres long by a metre wide by one and a half high.

Our Nips disappear into the village, presumably to dicker about quantities and prices over coffee and banana fritters while we are left to amuse ourselves getting to know the friendly but somewhat shy children. The womenfolk keep a wary eye on us to start with, but soon decide we can be trusted and shortly after bring out trays of fruit and little bowls of cooked rice, fish, omelettes and vegetables. We have a little money, but they wave it away with broad smiles. The kids are everywhere, playing amongst themselves, occasionally staring at us as if we were new in their experience. And we notice that a number of them have distinctively different features, fair to auburn hair, blue eyes and a lighter skin tone, indicating fathers from overseas countries. They all play together, with no sign of anything but comfortable friendliness.

There seems to be no hurry, no one is supervising us, but we are sensible enough to behave circumspectly and not do anything stupid such as try to approach the houses. Some of us wander down to the river to cool off in the water; we can get back in a few moments if necessary.

A bird appears from downstream, flying slowly with its head turned down to search the river. Suddenly it goes into a vertical dive, wings thrashing at full power and then held in tight a split second before hitting the water, so that the bird disappears below the surface with only the smallest splash. Moments later it reappears, floats for a few seconds, then flies up for another dive. Several times it spears into the river before emerging with a fish held in its long beak, then it disappears over the far bank to settle down to lunch. Which reminds us that, thanks to the generosity of our Siamese hosts, we haven't yet touched the rice ration which we brought with us. It would not be good manners to bring it out now, so we keep it to eat on the way back to camp.

Our Nips show up, obviously in good humour, well fed and well boozed and probably a happy bit of jig-a-jig thrown in, which should give us a trouble-free afternoon. Red-faced from their lengthy lunch and exertions, they can hardly pull themselves together sufficiently to point out which stacks of firewood we are to toss over the cliff and then load into the barges. However, all is soon done and we perch ourselves on top of the firewood, moving slowly upstream to the waves and shouts of the children and their mums.

With their extra depth our loaded barges catch on sandbanks here and there on our trip home, but it is pleasant to drop into the water and shove them clear. Pulling in to the bank we are surprised to find a work party waiting to unload the firewood and carry it up to the cookhouses. What a perfect end to a happy and unusual day.

We haven't spoken to children, or watched them playing together, for two years, and it has had an oddly softening and humanising effect on some of us. We still have our feelings and sentiments underneath the case-hardened shell that we have all grown to protect our vulnerable personalities, and for that I, for one, am truly grateful.

Christmas is once again in the air and looks to be a far happier time than it was last year at Tarsao, when the preceding eight months had seen so many deaths – counted in thousands – and every man in the camp was either sliding into death or grimly dragging himself out of the pit, and nobody could tell with any certainty which way it was going to be, for himself or for his mates.

The camp canteens – with 10,000 men in the camp we need more than one – are thriving marvellously. The Jap authorities have not introduced their own worthless paper money in Siam as they did in Singapore and Malaya, and only official Siamese currency circulates. Our daily pay is equivalent in sterling and Australian currency to about threepence and fourpence, but multiplied by 10,000 it is sufficient to interest local suppliers of duck eggs and other goodies. For the first time we have a continuous supply and can use our pay when it comes in and not have to wait until something turns up. With adequate supplies of cooking fat, the canteens can provide hot snacks, which is important because we now do not have access to firewood for individual cooking as we used to have in the forest.

The favourites are deep-fried banana fritters, and duck eggs fried in several inches of bubbling fat. The eggs are cooked in seconds and are like a sandwich, with the yolk wrapped around and sealed in by an envelope of white. It makes it easy to eat, and sometimes you can be lucky enough to get a piece of rice 'toast' to go with it. This toast is the hard skin of baked rice formed on the wall of a twelve-gallon kwali when rice is steaming off, and the cooks lever it off in sheets when cleaning up. There is also 'coffee' made from the same rice skin when it has gone beyond being baked and has charred black. My goodness, we *are* becoming civilised! But these extras do make such a difference, not only to our wretched diet but also to our mental outlook. We have been deprived of so much for so long, every little thing is appreciated and valued.

The canteen utensils are not purchased from outside or supplied by the Nips, they are made in the camp by tinsmiths from scrap bits and pieces scrounged from the Nips, who now seem to be less obsessive about keeping for themselves every empty container. It's surprising how much apparent rubbish can be cut up and reshaped into something useful.

The hospital fund has also been able to buy in and accumulate extra foods for the cookhouses, with the consent of the Nips, who scrutinise all purchases – and probably get a rake-off from the traders. They say that they recognise Christmas as a special celebration for us, and in the goodness of their hearts are happy to allow us to buy extra supplies. There's no point in sarcastic thoughts such as 'How kind of them', for they can shut everything right down if they choose to do so with no explanation required.

Christmas Day is a holiday. There is no work except for the cooks, who have been working all night to prepare a special breakfast. The shortage of every kind of equipment has required the most careful planning and timing of cooking and serving, because there is nowhere to hold batches until all are ready, and no means of keeping anything hot. But everyone is good humoured and patient, understanding the problems, content to just wait in happy anticipation of a good feed. And that is exactly what it turns out to be. As much rice as you want, a thick slice of fried pork, a fried riceball with something savoury in it, a solid hunk of something like bread made from ground rice, and plenty of tea. We retire rapidly to our huts to settle down to it.

Nobody has a knife or fork – what can't be managed with a spoon has to be tackled with fingers and teeth. The appetising smell is marvellous, and as I inhale it luxuriously I feel the first uneasy twinges in my stomach. It's not the food. I'm feeling chilled, dizzy and nauseated, and I'm beginning to shiver. My mouth dries, my eyes are hot, my ears are ringing and I'm not sure if I can stand up without falling over. There's no doubt about it, I am starting a full malarial rigor. I can't eat my first decent meal in God knows how long.

I can hear myself crying and protesting at the unfairness of it, pumped up with frustration and indignation, helpless to do anything but put my mess tin down on my bedspace. My mate Jimmy says consolingly, 'Never mind, it won't be wasted,' and picks it up so that I can stretch out under my blanket. My shivering develops into the usual trembling and shaking, my head aches and the bamboos rattle underneath me as the rigor intensifies. There is really nothing my friends can do for me, so they all get on with their interrupted breakfast. Later, when I have calmed down, they will get me into the hospital, but meanwhile there is no point at all in letting their pork slices spoil.

The fever breaks during the morning. I sit up and

gratefully pour a mug of hot tea down my parched throat. My stomach rumbles with emptiness while my well-fed mates burp contentedly. As my head clears I become aware of voices singing hymns outside the hut, an informal group – I cannot see a chaplain – come together to enjoy proclaiming their faith. They really mean it; the singing is loud and rings with sturdy confidence that someone is listening to them. All the old favourites swell up to the sky, ranging through the happy verses of 'Oh Jesus I have promised to serve thee to the end' to the more solemn invocation of 'Abide with me'.

The loudest voice is pure Cockney in its accent, not very melodious or true on the notes, but filled with sheer enthusiasm and carrying the rest of the circle of singers with it; they know all the words, there are no written slips of paper in their hands, and the hymns are followed by Christmas carols familiar to us from our childhood days. Days that in reality are only a few years back for most of us, but now are smothered in mists of suffering and the heavy shadows of loneliness and so many deaths.

The joyful exhilaration of the fervent voices brings men out of nearby huts, some to listen and look on while others join the group to sing. In close to two years as prisoners we have not heard anything like this. The few formal services have been poorly attended, and the voices have been subdued as if the singers were frightened to be heard. I think *'timid'* would be a good description.

And this reminds me of an incident during confirmation classes during a school term, when our chaplain invited questions. On being asked why the church taught that God could be approached only through a minister and not directly while, say, walking through the fields and wanting to give thanks for happiness, our worthy chaplain flew into a rage. The question was improper and totally disgraceful, and he would not answer it. We should accept unquestioningly the wisdom of the church's ruling.

I have waited until now for an answer to that question, thanks to a Cockney soldier and his fellow believers. *Amen.*

On New Year's Day 1945 – also recognised by the Nips as a special day for us, and so permission is given for extra rations to be purchased (they must be getting soft!) – my friend Jimmy goes down with malaria. It was he who ate my pork steak on Christmas Day, and I am delighted to return the favour today.

The first day of 1945 has a cloud hanging over it. There is a particularly nasty Nip officer who was duty officer yesterday, and in this role he has always been especially obnoxious by making his presence known to all of us. Usually the duty officer does not bother himself unduly with the daily life of the camp, being concerned with manning the guardhouse at the entrance and occasionally doing the rounds of the camp limits. But this particular character is always immaculately turned out, sword and pistol exactly in place, and an intimidating scowl on his face. His men are as tidy as possible in their patched and shapeless uniforms – how they must hate him! – and a squad of four actually marches in step behind him as he zealously patrols the whole of the camp area. He speaks good English and often stops to tell our men how deeply he despises us for allowing ourselves to be taken prisoner. He is ashamed beyond words to be compelled to associate with us, and would much prefer to be with a fighting regiment in the front line – well, we too wish he were somewhere else where he might stop a few bullets.

Last night there was a good deal of commotion after lights out, with Nips running around and shouting to each other. The boundary line on the north side is marked by bamboo sticks in the ground and a single strand of rope – in no way a physical barrier but a quite definite marker. For over an hour the sound of running feet and hallooing continues. Obviously they are on to something and we all know that some of our men were going out to try to buy hooch for New Year's Day. Stupid and dangerous, but there are always men willing to have a go. The tension builds up.

Suddenly there is total silence. We hear the officer shouting in English, just a few yards from our hut – the rope is only a short distance beyond the doorway at the end. In the starlight the men living at the rear of the hut can make out a group of figures, four Nips with bayoneted rifles pointing to a man lying on the ground under the rope. The officer stares down along his outstretched arm, and then comes the simultaneous flash and report of his pistol.

The Nips sling their rifles across their backs and pick up the body, the officer holsters his pistol, and they head off towards the guardhouse. In their view a prisoner who was found outside the boundary has received proper punishment. In our eyes, murder has been committed.

For the rest of the night armed Nips roam the camp, walking through the huts, flashing torches around. It is best to lie quiet and still – too many nerves are on edge.

What a happy and unexpected surprise! A small party has come into Tamuang and prominent amongst the group of men, swinging along on his crutches, is Ron. They have come from Nakhon Pathom for a special purpose, namely, to make up a list of names of the Allied POWs who have died while working on the construction of the railway. Someone who could use a typewriter was wanted, and Ron promptly applied for the job.

This seems to be a typical piece of Nip staff work. The lists of names kept in every camp by our own admin officers are in Tamuang, held by the officers who helped to write and collate them. So, instead of sending a few officers and a sack of paperwork to Nakhon Pathom, they have brought a squad of some twenty soldiers, shown in the records as 'clerical workers', to Tamuang to sort out the records. And a tricky job it has turned out to be, which is not surprising when the circumstances are considered.

Men have died in thousands, all over the place – some in the big camps, some in smaller groups such as the fifteen-man sawmill camp out of Kinsayok where I spent a few weeks, and unknown numbers died on the brutal marches from Kanburi up the railway track to the farthest camps, starved and bashed, never out of the torrential rain, staggering on bare feet along that morass called a motor road through the lifeless forests and mountains. Men died where they fell. The names of some were carried in the hearts of friends in the hope of having them properly recorded, and some of those friends also died with their messages undelivered. The Nips made no effort to keep records at all. They were simply not in the least interested – life or death amongst us has never been of any significance whatsoever. So there is an incredible amount of sorting out to do, piles of paper in exercise books, loose sheets of all sizes, scraps from anywhere, over-written pages from books, some readable but others smudged and mouldy, damaged by the weather and poor storage, written in makeshift inks with worn-out pens and bamboo splinters.

Making up lists of names cannot even start until this sorting is done, and then there are further complications – nationality, misspellings, absence of details such as regimental number/rank/unit, duplications, causes of death and where death occurred. There are endless problems building an accurate list and dividing it into nationalities in the first place, then trying to identify units for men with similar names, and so on. And the sheer numbers! We all know that thousands of men died during that dreadful rainy monsoon from May to November 1943, and hundreds more have succumbed since that period from the privations they endured, but the tentative count, when some kind of estimate is possible, is staggering. Ron tells me it could be as high as 24,000 – certainly somewhere near that awful figure, especially if permanent disablement is included in the 'casualty' definition.

It will take weeks to write up lists ready for typing, and even when completed as well as circumstances allow, it will not be more than reasonably accurate. Something of this nature has to be attempted, though, and the surprising aspect is that the Nips have not only agreed to having the work done, they have even found a typewriter and sufficient paper. The men are keen to work, especially as nobody knows when the Nips might decide that enough time has been spent on it and cut it short. They are totally unpredictable, and do not have to give reasons or listen to any request from us.

One mystery, however, has been solved. At the end of each day's work two Nips come to the hut where the work is being done and solemnly escort two of our men while they carry the typewriter into that massive bunker which we recently built in a far corner of the camp. There it is placed on a newly made bamboo table, in solitary splendour like a religious statue, and the Nips padlock a new bamboo gate at the entrance. It is always instructive to learn the true value of ordinary things!

There is no such concern for the papers which carry all the information. They are left with the working party who willingly continue as long as daylight lasts, searching the lists and trying to answer dozens of queries from men seeking news of mates from whom they have been separated. Too often, the answer is a regretful, 'Sorry, he died in August '43 at Hintok,' or some such sad outcome.

It's good to have Ron in the same camp again, and I spend as much time as possible with him. He certainly earns his twenty sattangs a day, typing solidly as new lists are passed to him. A typewriter mechanic has come forward, and even without any tools he has been able to improve the machine's performance so that it runs reliably most of the time.

My working hours are now taken up with a new project which, I think, must have absorbed nearly every man in Tamuang. The original Japan party has long departed, and two more have followed, so the camp population has fallen.

The new project is a great ditch, to be dug along three sides of a rectangle. The fourth side is to be a tall bamboo fence across the space between the river and our huts, which means that access to the river will only be through a gate in the fence. If the gate is kept closed we shall have no water for cooking or for personal hygiene. The object of the trench is explained to us at evening tenko, the day before work is to start. We are told that the local Siamese people are becoming hostile to our presence and might wish to do us harm, and the trench is to provide protection for us and will enable our camp guards to defend us effectively from attack!

We, of course, see this as bullshit. Our view is that the Nips are worried that the Siamese army may invade the camp and kill off the Nips, releasing us to be taken into their own service as technical instructors in artillery and other weapons. Our first day at work proves us right. The trench is to be three metres deep, a metre wide at the bottom and three across at the top. The inner wall is to be vertical, the outer to slope to three metres at the top, all the excavated earth being piled on the outer side to form an embankment with a smooth sheer face from the top edge right down to the floor of the trench. Obviously the intention is not to stop anyone coming into the camp, but to make it difficult for inmates to get out.

At each corner we are to dig pits which, coincidentally no doubt, are just the right size for machine-gun crews to fire along each leg of the trenches. Somewhat belatedly, after digging has begun, the Nips wake up to the fact that these guns would fire straight into each other, and the alignments are hastily adjusted so that the trenches are slightly angled towards the midpoint on each side. The machine-gun posts are now obscured from each other, but can put a massive hail of bullets into the trenches should a breakout be attempted. And, of course, the top of the embankment will provide a perfect viewing platform for infantry to look down on the whole of the camp ground, and to shoot anyone inside, where there is no protection of any kind.

We are always looking for significance in any new event, and try to piece things together to form logical patterns. We know that the 14th Army in Burma captured Rangoon several months ago, which means that the Jap armies there have lost their major supply route by sea, which will be devastating for them. By now they will have used up most of their reserves, and the only route for replenishment will be through Siam, and here the critical – and weakest – section is that bloody railway we built for them.

There can be no doubt that the Japs are preparing a new defence area in Siam, bringing back such troops as they can from Burma and relying on the mountains running down the Burma–Siam border as a natural barrier to invasion from the west. (Our personal experience of those mountains can testify to this.) They will not want to have tens of thousands of Allied soldiers amongst them, all trained men looking for an opportunity to turn on them. Long ago we accepted the fact that, as the war starts to go badly for them, the Nips will not hesitate to kill us off, and now this possibility is becoming a definite and specific risk. Our new trench, no doubt being constructed in other camps too, is a clear pointer to how things are developing.

We know the Siamese are reluctant and uncomfortable partners with the Japs. One or two of our Volunteers who used to conduct business with Siam, and who speak the language, have been outside the camp and in their opinion an invasion by the Allies could in all probability see the Siamese army coming in on our side. Whether it would be in time to save us is doubtful – the Nips have all the advantage of proximity and ready-laid plans, and we would simply have to keep our eyes open and jump smartly off the mark. There would be no possibility of us protecting our sick and disabled, it would be suicidal even to try, with no chance of success. A breakout to join the Siamese army would be the only positively useful course to attempt, and that would have little enough hope of success. I think of Ron and all the others, and am filled with gloom, for much as I long for an Allied victory I can see that, for us personally, it could well be disastrous. It is a cruel choice, to be forced to abandon helpless mates or to stay and die uselessly.

At evening tenko we are told that all our officers – even the junior ones – are soon to be moved out to a new camp, where officers from everywhere will be brought together. This is said to be so that the officers can be accommodated and treated in accordance with their rank. Again, we do not accept this explanation – we believe its purpose is to remove our leaders and thus keep us ineffective, the assumption being that Jap soldiers are lost and useless without their officers and that we would be similarly affected.

By now our opinion of our officers, except for the relatively few – mostly of senior rank, but not all of them by any means – who have stood up to the Nips, is such that we couldn't care less. We have done without their help so far and it can continue that way. In any case, if the crisis does arise there will not be time to organise units under the command of officers. It will be a situation for small groups and individuals reacting instinctively, and very fast, to circumstances as they happen.

We must be clear-headed and realistic about this. We must not expect any earlier warning than the time between the rattle of machine guns, and bullets smacking amongst us. Plans, of course, are not possible in even the loosest sense as there is not a single thing that can be predicted except a night attack when we are conveniently closely packed in our huts. We can only watch for the smallest signs of impending trouble, and we discuss what these might be. The removal of our officers is simply another pointer that something is planned, and we must be on the alert and ready to move instantly.

We have a particularly nasty bastard, a Korean, known to us as the Mad Mongol. He even looks the part: his right eye swivels loosely and his torso is slightly twisted so that his shoulders are uneven. He is unusually dark in his features and permanently scowling, with a vicious temper to match. Altogether he looks, and is, a thoroughly evil fellow, and he has been with us from our Wampo days, to our disgust. Bashing us is his favourite pastime.

While at Wampo he reported sick to our medical officer – a frequent occurrence since in the Nip army soldiers pay for their own treatment – and demanded drugs for his syphilis. Our MO was able to slip a fresh dab of dysentery faeces down his throat while examining him, with the result that his own people sent him to their military hospital where, no doubt, they discovered his syphilis. But in a disappointingly short time he came back to us, illness being no excuse for avoiding duties. It is probable that the syphilis is corroding his brain – his what? – and is the basic cause of his foul temper, which in our view approaches clinical madness. However it may be, we all loathe him with the deepest intensity.

He has gone too far this time. In a fit of gibbering rage he has felled one of our men with the blade end of a changkol, fracturing the skull and bringing the victim close to death. Even the Nip commandant has had to agree that, there being no speedo or urgency in camp works, such an attack was out of all reason.

A curious situation now arises. The Jap commandant has to agree to the argument of our people that the Mad Mongol must be punished but, to save face, he will only go as far as to say that he will be arrested and charged in the event that our man dies. Otherwise, his action will be regarded merely as a disciplinary measure against our man in the ordinary course of events.

Our people say that our man will definitely die if his skull is not operated on, by surgical lifting of broken bone pressing on his brain. We do not have the necessary equipment to do this, although we do have capable surgeons in the camp. If the Jap commandant does not provide equipment the man's death will be his responsibility and he will also have to order the Mad Mongol's arrest. Even with the equipment our surgeons cannot guarantee success, although they will do their

552

best. The skill with which our colonel and the doctors have pressed this argument deserves the greatest credit. In an extremely difficult and touchy situation they have pushed the Jap commandant into a corner – a singular achievement in itself – from which he must extricate himself. The matter is urgent, and he must make an immediate decision.

His way of slipping out of his corner is indicative of a distorted and suspicious mind, typical of Nips as we have seen them even in matters of a trivial nature. He has been told that the operation is extremely delicate and dangerous, that even with adequate facilities the patient's death is quite possible. So he produces anaesthetic, bandages and antiseptic and orders the surgeons to perform the operation. But – and this may seem incredible to those who have no understanding of the Japanese – he and his officers will attend the operation to watch that it is done properly, thus ensuring that we do not deliberately kill the patient, or let him die, with the object of revenging ourselves on the Mad Mongol by securing his arrest and date with a firing squad.

We might have dismissed this as spiteful and fanciful rumour had not the Nip officers presented themselves in ceremonial uniform and face masks at the hospital hut. We hear that the sawing open of the skull, exposing the brain while chips of bone were picked out, was too much for some, who had to retire with green complexions. How could they imagine they could monitor such a complex and highly technical procedure?

All seems to go well, but it is several days before the surgeons can say that the patient has a good chance of recovery. The Mad Mongol reappears in charge of work parties, much subdued and downcast, so maybe even he has realised he owes his life to enemy doctors, a most difficult thought for him to accept!

As a display of the mental processes of which educated Japanese are capable, this has been an eye-opener, but not altogether a surprise. It has merely crystallised suspicions which we have developed about the sheer barbarity and brutality which are part of their individual natures and national culture.

It is simply the way they are.

Our trench has been completed, its sides neatly sculpted in the hot dry sunshine with the outer face rising smoothly from the bottom of the ditch to the parapet. Supposedly unclimbable from inside the camp, the soft light clay will crumble and slide down in the first downpour of the rainy season. We can only hope that nothing will happen before then.

Belatedly, the Nips have woken up to the fact that if men are to be able to move in and out of the camp, there has to be a bridge across at some point. It is provided in the north-west corner, near the guardhouse. At least this indicates that they were not thinking of boxing us into a pen, to be shot at like rabbits – not immediately anyhow!

Maybe we are too valuable as labourers to be disposed of any earlier than necessary, and we are to be kept for use for as long as possible. It's nice to know that someone is thinking of our welfare!

We were right, a new job has started. Several hundred of us form up between the guardhouse and the tarmac road, and are marched off westwards through the tiny village of Tamuang. We reckon we have covered twelve kilometres when we are turned off into the bush on our left, to find ourselves coming into a group of huts with several Jap army trucks parked under the trees and soldiers lounging around, apparently waiting for us.

Our camp Nips disappear and we are taken over by Jap soldiers who seem to know exactly what is to be done. They sort us out into work parties and take us to pegged-out sites where we are to build huts of bamboo and attap. It is clear that this is to be a large permanent encampment, the huts located not in rows but dotted around where trees and the contours of the ground provide cover from observation by aircraft personnel. No trees or shrubs are to be cleared except where necessary.

Being themselves obedient soldiers who would never think of disobeying an order or slacking, the Japs start us working and leave us to get on with it. This, and the cover provided by undisturbed bush, allows some of our more adventurous fellows to slip around and make contact with the local Siamese, to arrange for future trading. There are still a few gold wedding and signet rings hidden away amongst us, fountain pens and propelling pencils, watches and sundry knick-knacks, all of which have a value these days while Siam is cut off from all overseas trade.

We don't have a set task to complete but are sensible enough to do sufficient to make a show of it. It is pleasant to be in the shade while we work. It is easy labour and – best of all – there is not a Nip face or voice to be seen or heard. We stop to eat our rice, drink a mug of tea, get back to work – it is marvellously peaceful.

Mid afternoon our Jap soldier turns up, looks around and smiles happily, says something in a pleased tone of voice, and we rejoin the others. We have a comfortable twelve-kilometre hike back to camp; the tarmac is by now hot for our bare feet but not troublesome. Almost a picnic day – we hope it continues.

And it does continue. Maybe our new bosses have asked for us as being good workers, for the same men march out for the next month or so. More than that, after a couple of days we are taken there and back in trucks, to avoid wasting time.

Our comfortable life is unexpectedly improved by the distribution of Red Cross parcels. We know that some must have arrived because our Nips are seen smoking cigarettes from American-branded packs, but we had not seen any actual boxes because nobody from the camp was involved in bringing them in. But here they are, one parcel between thirteen men!

For one man, as the Red Cross had intended, a parcel would be a treasure chest – tinned milk, cheese and meat, some chocolate, cigarettes, cotton shirts and socks, even toilet paper. For thirteen men equal distribution is impossible – there is not enough of any one item to divide it up or share it out at meal times. Nevertheless, we are delighted. The evident change in attitude in our Nips is just as important as the goodies themselves. Some high-up Nip officers must be thinking it could be a sensible idea to improve relationships with us.

Nobody has worn a shirt for ages, and nobody wants to wear one now during the daytime – it would simply be pointless; with no laundering facilities, a shirt would last only a few weeks before falling apart. But they have a definite value to the local Siamese, and a few dollars to spend at the canteen is really attractive. The opportunity to trade is inviting, and it is easy to hide a number of shirts among the packed bodies in our trucks.

One of the Gordon Highlanders wears his customers' shirts, one on top of the other. It's a bit warm, but the journey takes only a few minutes and then he can slip away into the bushes to meet his buyers. It's in his interest to haggle for a good price, for he charges forty per cent for his service – he does take all the risks, after all – although if he is caught and the shirts confiscated, it will be a write-off for both parties, with Jock's ears swollen and ringing for several days afterwards.

This morning the trucks do not turn up, and we are ordered to march. It is a sweltering hot morning, even at that early hour, and Jock – wearing his seven shirts – is soon glowing and steaming uncomfortably. There is a Nip who persists in walking alongside us, and we cannot shake him off by slowing down or stepping along smartly, so Jock cannot strip off until we reach our worksite.

It happens that the shirts he is wearing are of several different colours, and Jock is unable to spend time haggling because our busybody Nip is hanging around. So he is nipping off and selling one shirt at a time, having to be content with quick sales at low prices but hoping for better offers each time. Our Nip begins to look distinctly puzzled because every time Jock reappears he is wearing a different coloured shirt, but luckily the Nip does not work out what it is that's bugging him.

We have a quite extraordinary experience while working at the new Jap army camp. It is a hot afternoon, somewhere over 100° F, and the atmosphere is brilliantly clear, which is not unusual at this time of year. Quite suddenly, over to the east, a mirage appears in the sky. There is no gradual apparition but an entirely instantaneous picture, clear and so sharp in detail that we recognise it at once. It is our camp at Tamuang. Everything is inverted to be a mirror image with huts and trees upside down! Everything is so pin-sharp that we can even see, clearly, men moving about and can identify individuals. There is our cookhouse, men carrying firewood from the stack, and

– a sight which makes everyone exclaim – the sergeant-in-charge sitting under a tree rolling a cigarette.

Tamuang Camp is twelve kilometres away, the picture hanging upside down is full-sized, all colours true to life – even the attap thatch shows up sharply. The great mango trees are there, tiny green fruits speckling the dark green leaves. It really is truly amazing. All work stops while we stare at this marvellous sight, which is not only extraordinary in itself but made more so by the fact that it is our own camp which we can see! And at such a distance! And so perfect in every detail!

I don't know how long the vision holds our mesmerised gaze, but it is certainly for several minutes. Then it switches off as suddenly as it appeared. The sky is an unbroken blue, with not even a shimmer in the atmosphere.

Back in camp we tell others of our incredible mirage. At first there is disbelief, but so many of us have the same story that it is obvious we cannot have made it all up.

Did Abraham and the ancients see images in the desert, to inspire their thoughts?

Nobody has a watch nowadays, but we really have no need for any kind of mechanical timepiece. We have become so attuned to the natural rhythms of daytime and night that we – most of us, anyway – know what the time is with reasonable precision throughout the twenty-four hours of the day.

At this latitude – fourteen degrees north of the equator – the sun is to our north and overhead for some three months of the year, and down south for the rest. The compass points are second nature to us.

The hours of sunrise and sunset do not vary much. The dawn lightening of the sky and the sunset fading are brief, and during daylight the altitude of the sun is a good indicator of the passing hours. Except, of course, during the rainy monsoon months, when we may not see the actual sun for days on end, although even then it is usually possible to discern a slightly paler patch in the sodden clouds, moving slowly from east to west to mark the day's progress. It's odd to think that, above that thick indigo blanket, the sun continues to shine in all its brilliance.

We sleep lightly, as dogs do, with an ear cocked for the faintest sound of trouble, and the moon's phases are as good as any clock. An eye opened for a few seconds is enough to note whether the moon is up or already set, or still to rise, depending on the stage of its cycle. I do not have to work it out; the comprehension is simply there instantly when I need it.

And nowadays, with the increased certainty that the Nips may decide to slaughter us without warning, a wary sensitivity during sleep is essential. It may not prove to be of much practical help when the fireworks start, but it is our only hope of survival – a very slim one indeed! – with all the odds so heavily stacked against us.

So it is that the whole camp stirs in the last few dark minutes of the night, and by the time we have walked out of our huts in readiness for morning rice, the eastern sky is beginning to brighten. And to the west, where shadows still linger, we hear the deep growl of approaching aircraft.

They must be ours, we haven't seen a Jap plane for ages, and the distant rumble of bombs confirms it! The target must be the steel and concrete bridge spanning the river at Tamarkan, some thirty-five kilometres from here. We are close enough to hear bomb explosions but too far to tell if there is any anti-aircraft fire. The timing of the raid would have given the crews the first glimmer of daylight for sighting their target and, we hope, caught the Jap gunners off guard.

Within a few minutes the whole sky is light and

suddenly, as we stare towards the sounds, we see them! Coming straight at us in line astern, we count ten big bombers, the four-engined type which we had recently seen black against the full moon over Nakhon Pathom. Flying low, not more than 1,000 feet up, we reckon, the leader dips and we hear cannon and machine-gun fire. All the other planes follow suit; the leader picks up altitude and circles to fall in behind the last aircraft. For several minutes there is a continuous procession of these big bombers, dipping and firing, swinging up and around for another run.

The only target we know of in the area is the Jap encampment on the far side of Tamuang village, where we have been working for the past few weeks. Thank heaven the RAF decided on a dawn attack – not a daytime one, when we would have been working there!

By now every man in the camp is out in the open space of the parade ground. The bombers break off their shoot-up and head directly towards us, very low indeed, less than 500 feet up. It doesn't occur to us that we may be mistaken for a Jap camp and become targets. We are all looking up and waving like mad.

The planes edge downward until we can see the pilots clearly as they look down at us, gloved hands raised behind the cockpit windows to show that they know who we are. All ten of them, acknowledging our wild waving and close enough for the crews to see our open mouths cheering.

The bombers turn away and start to gain altitude rapidly as they recede to the south-west. Suddenly we see another air-craft, circling in the distance, high up, and our bombers home in and make formation on it. It is a huge machine, far bigger than any we have seen, looking like a mother hen with a brood of chicks as they fade out of our sight. Can this be one of those fabled Fortresses, the B29s which we have had described to us by men of the 18th Division? We remember seeing B17s on newsreels nearly three years ago, and this new plane, as far as we can tell at long range, appears to be similar.

Our Nips appear, looking somewhat sheepish. While we have been out in the open watching the spectacle, they have had their heads down in the slit trenches near their huts. Just as well, we think. If they had shot at the bombers with rifles and machine guns, we could well have been caught in retaliatory fire.

The Nips remain subdued, which is a good sign – we could have expected an orgy of bashings and unpleasant disciplinary measures while they worked off their hostile feelings on us. It is a great day for us, a great big lift to our morale.

Three things come out of this raid. One is news that bombs fell in or near our camp at Tamarkan, which accommodates the men who built the steel and concrete bridge and the subsidiary timber bridges which preceded it and, after its completion, were kept for use as bypasses should the steel bridge be damaged. There are no exact figures, but the casualties seem to have been heavy.

The second is that it was indeed the new Jap camp which was shot up. We shall not be sending working parties there any more.

The third is that, with no requirement for that work, we are for the time being unemployed until they think of something new for us to do. To fill in time a squad of us is detailed to tidy up outside the Nip huts, sweeping up rubbish and so on. Amongst all the tossed-out bits and pieces we come across an aircraft recognition booklet, the standard type showing silhouettes of Jap and Allied aircraft. The text and notations are in Jap ideographs and therefore meaningless to us, but to our surprise all the performance details are in English! Not only in metric, which is the system in use in Japan, but in imperial measures, so we now have an up-to-date information sheet which shows new Allied aircraft that we have not even heard of! Fascinating! And what cheers us enormously is the fact that all our new aircraft are so superior to their Jap counterparts in every respect – speed, range, bomb loads, armaments, operational heights and so on. How accurate their figures are for new Allied planes when wartime secrecy is considered, we cannot know, but surely they must have some kind of reliable basis to be put in an official publication.

And another thought. The news which we find so exciting must have just the opposite effect on Jap soldiers who study them! Identification silhouettes are necessary for ground troops and warship crews to recognise friendly or hostile aircraft, but do they need to be told that enemy planes are so far advanced beyond their own? How depressing to be told by your commanders that your fighters cannot catch their bombers, and that your own bombers are easy meat for their fighters! Unimaginative bureaucracy at its best!

We know the feeling very well. We weren't exactly told that our aircraft in Malaya and Singapore were obsolescent, inadequate and no match for the Japs, but it became obvious bloody soon. And while those responsible for that state of affairs are, no doubt, smugly drawing retirement pensions, we are stuck with the consequences of their unbelievable incompetence. We take this very personally; we do not accept that it was unavoidable but are in fact convinced that it need not have happened. There was too much complacent political fooling around and refusal to look at facts, too much wishful thinking instead of determined resolve, in the years before the war. And too much irresolution and plain disastrous strategy after it began.

We are not in any way feeling sorry for ourselves, we're just angry as hell about the colossal wastage and suffering that has resulted. We who lived out in this part of the world, and represented by our presence the British empire, feel very keenly our failure to protect the civilian populations in whose territories we lived and traded. It is a moral shame of incalculable extent, and if we are never forgiven, and not welcomed back after defeating Japan, who will carry the stigma? Not our politicians tucked safely away in Britain!

There is a small commotion at evening tenko. That nasty little creep, the officer who murdered one of our men on New Year's Eve, struts onto the platform to conduct the parade and gets his feet tangled with the samurai sword which is his pride and joy. Either he is too short or the sword is too long – whichever, he usually has his left hand on the scabbard to keep it clear of the ground while he swaggers about. So he trips and does a nifty little dance to recover his balance. It says a hell of a lot for our newly found personal discipline that not a man laughs amongst the thousands on parade, but it puts Billy the Kid – that's his nickname – in a foul mood.

It's sheer bad luck that at this moment one of our men suddenly breaks into a severe malarial rigor, which throws him forward off his feet. Even worse luck is that the man is standing in the front rank immediately below the saluting platform. In an instant Billy the Kid explodes, bawling an order to his men which sets two of them to a brutal bashing of the sick man, and shouting to us in English that the Emperor has been seriously insulted by this soldier who did not stand properly to attention.

There is a long drawn-out minute or so when things seem to be poised on a fine edge. Billy is gripping his scabbard and sword as if he is about to go into action. Everywhere is an absolute silence except for the thumping fists and boots, while Billy gets himself under control again.

What is stopping him from whipping out his sword and performing an execution on the spot, which is clearly what he would like to do? What makes him tell his men to stop punishment (for they will keep on with it until told otherwise)? Can he actually feel the tremendous rage and contempt of several thousand prisoners, focused on him as heat through a burning-glass? And if so, has it been sufficient to restrain him? Surely there must be some kind of power, intangible maybe but nevertheless effective, in our intense hatred of this barbaric Nip, able to penetrate even his megalomania? It's an interesting speculation. I don't for a moment think he is afraid of us. I am quite sure he would happily die slashing at us if we were to break ranks and charge at him. Something held him back, and it wasn't any kind of human feeling – which he would consider to be contemptible weakness.

One of the camp Nips has died, cause of death not known. Our colonel announces the event at evening tenko, adding that as a mark of respect for a fellow soldier the canteen will have a half-price day tomorrow. The cheek of this announcement, delivered in the presence of the Nip commandant, astonishes us. But all is well: we are thanked for this sensitive reaction to the death of an enemy soldier – it proves that fighting men can respect each other even under difficult circumstances, etc.

Our colonel accepts this with a straight face, all formalities are observed and we are dismissed. Half price actually starts immediately, so we all sleep on satisfied stomachs. The subtlety of the joke is as delicious as the canteen's banana fritters!

* * *

Ron and his clerical party have all gone back to Nakhon Pathom. The typewriter may still be sitting in solitary splendour in its bunker. We have not been informed of the results of their efforts. The lists which they have produced will be invaluable documents in building up official records after the almost total blank from February 1942 onwards. Have family dependants been paid all this time? Will refunds be demanded by stuffy bureaucrats if it is found that payments should have ceased when a soldier died? What has happened about mortgage payments, and other personal arrangements, which will have lapsed during these years? There's no point worrying, but the questions are asked.

My particular friend, Wally, who came out to Singapore on the same boat in March 1939 on his first contract with a firm of accountants, has spent three interesting days in the camp admin office. There is a problem that might well become extremely dangerous, and Wally's special skills in auditing accounts are in demand. Not, as he first thought when called to help, to check that figures were being properly kept, but to find ways of cooking them to conceal things that our people don't want the Nips to know. This is not to suggest that Wally is a crooked accountant, but the fact is that his training included thorough examination of the scores of methods and ruses used by people and businesses to avoid showing a true picture. How to hide funds, cover up revenues, convert profits to apparent losses, divert attention from improper movements of cash – Wally is an expert on all these tricks and his job was primarily to ferret them out.

The Nips have become suspicious about the amount of cash circulating in the camp. They know, of course, how much money they hand out as pay to us prisoners, and they also know – because it is done under their supervision – how much is spent by our flourishing canteen and by our medical officers on purchasing supplies from the local Siamese. What they are asking is, how is it that these purchases exceed the funds officially available to us? There must be money coming in from outside, either by donations from Siamese – or the Red Cross? – or from prisoners selling personal items outside the camp, either of these sources of money being strictly illegal. The Nips can understand that the edible contents of the recent issue of Red Cross parcels will have been consumed, but what about all those shirts? Why is nobody inside the camp wearing a shirt? Remember that man caught on New Year's Eve, trying to slip back into the camp? Obviously he had been out for some private trading.

There can be no simple or easy answers to these questions; the arithmetic is there. So Wally and a few other experts have been applying themselves to faking the books and shuffling sums in all directions, to confuse and baffle the Nips and at the same time make it all look correct and convincing. There is a neat little bit of psychology here. The camp Nips do not really understand anything beyond simple arithmetic, but they don't want us to realise that. They are certain – quite rightly too! – that something is going on, but can't prove it. They don't trust our book-keeping, but don't know how to challenge it. They can't call in outsiders, because by doing so they would be admitting their own incompetence. They try to bluff us that they understand our explanations when they don't but can't admit it. Having accepted such explanations they can't argue against them. It's all a matter of 'face' concealing ignorance.

Our people are polite, earnest and smilingly helpful, patiently dealing with every query, and steadily pushing the Nips into retreating into a box of their own making. Eventually the Nips have to declare themselves completely satisfied and the matter is closed. We have the satisfaction of knowing that it will go no further – if it did, our Nips would lose face on an unacceptable scale.

Wally, as a staunch member of the Church of Scotland and thoroughly imbued with its traditions of honest dealing and upright character, prays for forgiveness in his deliberate sinning, relying on the particular circumstances to support his prayers. But he confides to us that he is absolutely delighted with the success of his – and his colleagues' – efforts. Marvellous practical training! As he puts it, with a happy grin, the camp books have been audited, all matters duly examined, and the accounts have been found to be 'incorrect' in all respects!

It was a tricky business, and could easily have gone wrong.

Still on the easy-going work routine that is intended simply to fill in the day, a few of us are sweeping up leaves at the rear of the big guardhouse. The low attap wall which allows free movement of the breeze through the shed also gives us a view down the gravel track leading up from the main east–west road from Bangkok to Kanburi. There is not much traffic, and most of that consists of Jap army trucks – we imagine that petrol is not available to Siamese civilians in any quantity.

Out of mild curiosity we take a look when we hear a vehicle passing, the sound of its engine breaking through the bored chatter of the Nips perched on a long bench in the guardhouse. Upfront is a solitary Nip sentry, seated behind a small table, and he calls the guard commander to deal with a visitor.

So we are idly watching when an army truck packed with soldiers standing shoulder to shoulder slows down and turns into our approach driveway. The effect of this is astounding. Simultaneously, the light chatter turns to cries of alarm and the sentry half rises and turns towards the others, pointing back at the approaching vehicle and stuttering incoherently, unable to form words. In the sudden babble we catch the word 'Kempei-tai' several times, and after a few frozen moments there is a panicky twisting and turning to and fro, as men might do when suddenly confronted with a totally unexpected but fearsome threat.

Even the gunso's sharp barking takes a few seconds to bring them to attention, by which time the truck has pulled up and its occupants are speedily forming up in a straight line facing the guard. An officer steps down from the cab, and our gunso is only just able to be there in time to meet him. Nevertheless, he gets what is clearly a haughty reprimand for being slow, and slovenly in his appearance. The men of the guardhouse, standing in trembling paralysis, are treated to an agonisingly slow appraisal accompanied by sneering words and looks.

Prudently, right at the start, we sidle away so as to be inconspicuous, but we can't miss watching what's going on – it's too interesting! The Kempei-tai men really are something different. They are all in immaculate uniform, caps held in place by taut chinstraps, gaiters and harness polished. They have no rifles but each man has a short sword and holstered pistol. But it is their faces which seize our attention – grim, stony, glaring with implacable malevolence, fearsome in their brooding violence. Surrounding these motionless figures is an almost tangible aura of savagery so powerful that it leaps instantaneously through the guardhouse to us at the rear, setting our nerves aquiver. With it comes the queasy odour of fear, bodily emanations from our terrified Nips. There is something uncanny about these awful men, something so evil that it chills the air around them and reaches out to touch others. I'm not exaggerating. I swear that the temperature plummets twenty degrees – I'm shivering.

Without a word of command the Kempei-tai officer doubles off towards the Nip admin huts. His men immediately take off after him, in total silence except for the thud of boots – a pack of hunting dogs looking for victims, intent on a brutal killing. Their departure breaks the spell. We relax and look at each other; we have all been affected. But our camp Nips are slow to recover. They are talking disjointedly and mopping the sweat streaming down their faces, grinning weakly as they pull themselves together. They have been severely shaken.

Those thugs must have been carefully selected for personal depravity and specially trained to create a feeling of terror and helplessness by their mere presence. We have just seen it work on soldiers of their own army, who are not weaklings in any normal sense of the word. We British have never experienced anything like it, nor have we ever imagined an army might have such a unit. Maybe this is the image behind the Dark Ages thinking of the Christian church, when they wrote about the torments of hell that supposedly awaited those who misbehaved or lacked unquestioning belief.

We return to our sweeping, but not for long. All men are recalled to their huts for a search to be conducted by the Kempei-tai for radios and other illegal items. We have had searches in the past; surprisingly, there has always been a quiet warning in advance which has given us time to hide our bits and pieces. It is not necessary for something to be illegal. If an object takes a Nip's fancy he is liable to pocket it and there's no hope of getting it back. Every item, nowadays, is so valuable to us that we cannot risk having it taken, so our kits when laid out for inspection are about as interesting as Mother

Hubbard's cupboard. The attap thatch, however, will be stuffed with oddments such as pencils and penknives, family photos, or an occasional cut-throat razor which used to belong to Dad. Anything which might be an aid to escape – such as cash or valuables, a weapon (the razor would qualify), or canned food – is illegal, but other things have personal or sentimental value.

These searches have been somewhat perfunctory, and a casual display of photos of young children would usually bring a Nip to a halt, to gossip in broken English/Japanese, for most of them have a soft spot for family life. Like us, they have all been away from home for far too long, and no one can see any hope of getting back, not for a long time.

This time is very different. Quite suddenly there is a ghoul standing in the entrance to our hut, eyes everywhere. Standing on the sleeping platform he reaches up and tugs at a bamboo rafter, shaking it vigorously, and down comes a shower of small objects. We are all standing to attention along the central gangway, at our bedspaces, staring in front with our best wooden expressions in place, waiting for a horrific bashing to start. But nothing happens, except that two of our men come into the hut carrying a large vegetable basket from the cookhouse. The Kempei-tai indicates that we are to pick up every item and drop it into the skip, and he watches while we do it. When all is done he orders the skip to be taken to the guardhouse, presumably for confiscation.

Obviously he hasn't dealt with prisoners before, because he seems to think that his orders will be obeyed without question. Off he marches, having done his duty, to the guard-house, and half an hour later the truck grinds off with him and his unholy mates.

Our skip, with all the others, is tucked out of sight amongst the bushes, and after dark we all have our precious possessions back in our hands. Maybe our camp Nips were not told to seize the skips, or quite possibly their hatred of the Kempei-tai is such that they deliberately forgot all about it. We wouldn't be surprised either way. They can be a funny lot, sometimes, and unpredictable.

A large party has come into Tamuang, several hundred men including a big group of Singapore and Malayan Volunteers, and they have just survived a dangerous air attack.

When we, and thousands of others, were brought out of the hills to Tamuang and other camps on the central plain after the railway was completed, parties were kept on to carry out maintenance work. Damage from increasing bombing attacks added to other problems such as washaways and slipping earth in cuttings. Timber which had been used in bridges only a few days after being felled in the jungle, green and untreated with creosote, dried out and fed armies of termites. The work was constant and the men were frequently shifted from one place to another as and when they were needed.

So it was that they were trundling northwards beyond Takanun in steel goods wagons late in the afternoon when those perched in the open doorways saw three Allied bombers coming towards them out of the sun. They flew in line astern, making two circles around the train as if the crews were sizing it up as a target. Then they drew off to the west some distance, apparently not having observed the frantic waving of our men in the dark openings along the rake of wagons, for they suddenly reversed direction, their bomb doors opening as they headed in a shallow dive at the locomotive.

The engine driver slammed on the brakes and jumped down from his cab, racing for the cover of the trees alongside the track. Everyone followed, from both sides of the wagons, running like mad for protection. Except for a Dutch soldier, who ran up the line in front of the locomotive, pulling off his shirt to wave a signal. The first cannon shells tore him to pieces, the first bomb shattered the locomotive, and the wagons were systematically bombed and shot to total wreckage. Amongst the trees our men stood behind the stoutest trunks they could find, only to be sprayed by the tail gunners as each bomber swept past. Not that the trees gave any real protection anyway, the heavy rounds passed through them easily.

Casualties were heavy, more than eighty killed and many wounded, but not a single Nip was even scratched. And no doubt the crews of the bombers were back at base in a few hours, enjoying a shower and a hot meal with a few beers, telling their mates how they had just knocked over a Jap troop train and sprayed the jungle trees where they ran for cover.

Gathered together after the planes had left, the Nips were totally demoralised and helpless. It was one of our sergeants who got them sorted out, sending Nips up and down the line to find an army post and get help. Meanwhile, night was falling, there were wounded to be cared for and bodies to be buried, personal belongings and cooking stores to be salvaged and put to use. A lot of the men's kit was useless, slashed through by shells and bomb splinters, and none of it would ever be replaced.

It took three days for a relief train to arrive, by which time our men were suffering badly from thirst. Hunger too, but that was easier to bear because they were used to it.

Our admin staff at Tamuang has done its best to replace essential items such as mugs and mess tins, but really there is very little available.

* * *

There is a natural open-air theatre on the edge of the camp, just outside the big trench, and we have been allowed to have an occasional concert there. The stage is in a hollow which has a sloping bank rising in a half-circle to provide sitting space for 1,000 men or more. On each side of the hollow are several big trees – the army term when describing this landscape would be 'bushy top' – and the whole array is both practical and attractive.

There is no music, but any number of men – some with peacetime professional or amateur experience – willing to stand up and sing, or tell yarns and jokes; some of them have real talent. There is a sexual slant to most of the jokes, which I suppose is to be expected, but it is all inoffensive and there is nobody in the audience whose feelings will be hurt.

We have a regimental sergeant-major, a bellowing bull of a man and martinet on the parade ground, who sings 'Phil the Fluter's Ball' in a high Irish tenor which dances lightly to the sprightly tune. Irish folk songs are his favourite, and he seems to know all of them. In contrast, a quartet sings the aria from *Rigoletto* and even those who have never heard it – most of the audience, that would be – cheer enthusiastically.

What does not go down well is the Dutch contribution. There is only a small group of Dutch soldiers, mostly white but with a few Javanese Eurasians amongst them, but they must have their turn. One of them tells a yarn that goes on and on, the narrator stopping to laugh and cackle at the funny bits, and it's all in Dutch and totally incomprehensible to all except those few. After fifteen interminable minutes the crowd is restive. Five more minutes and there's a shout: 'Gottverbloodydommert, man, get on with it or shut up!' The speaker stops, stares round at the interruption, and continues

exactly as before, monotonous and by now not even entertaining his fellow Dutchmen, who look bored and glum. So a
new bunch gets together and starts to sing, drowning the
Dutchman who, nevertheless, plods on defiantly.

The Nips have introduced a new irritation into our lives:
sending men into our huts during the night to conduct head
counts which, of course, disturbs our sleep. Although this is of
no great consequence in our current relaxed daily schedules,
the Nips can never get the figures right and this both irritates
them and keeps us awake and bored.

The reasons for the numbers not coming out as they
should are simple. With the camp's big population there are
always men out of their huts, usually visiting the latrines
or maybe preferring to sleep in the open to escape bugs, or
simply wanting to be alone for a time. Our huts are still built
on the basic measurement of twenty-two inches sleeping space
per man, and it is pleasant to stretch out occasionally on the
ground where you can have some clear space around you.

So the Nips walk through the huts with a hurricane lamp
or feeble torch, counting sleeping bodies and empty spaces. It
doesn't add up, so they go round again and in the meantime
men have come in and others have gone out, and the count is
different from five minutes earlier. Then they wake everybody
and get them to stand in the central passage for another tenko,
which brings in the outside sleepers to confuse things further.

Obviously they are trying to find out how many men
have sneaked out of the camp to meet the local Siamese, and
we have to admit that they have good reason for this. Despite
the enclosing trench, the word is that some twenty men go
outside on any night of the week, which might be put down
to the general easing in our lives and the slightly improved

food, which have produced better health and livelier spirits, and a degree of restlessness. Surprisingly, this has not resulted in the foul-tempered bashings and punishments that we would have expected six months ago. We do get snippets of news about our progress in the war, largely from our more enterprising people who slip out of camp and listen to wireless sets in Siamese houses, and it could be that the Nip officers are aware that things are going badly for them, and this may have induced them to be more careful in their treatment of us.

So instead of slapping us around they have decided to make us accountable for keeping close watch on our numbers. At one end of each hut, in the doorway, is hung a small notice-board showing the total number of men in the hut, and on each doorpost is a section of hollow bamboo, one of which has a number of tally sticks. The system is simple. Every man going out takes a tally from one bamboo and puts it into the other, replacing it when he comes back. Foolproof. The Nip counts the actual bodies, adds the number of 'out' tallies, and there's his total.

Well, it may be foolproof but it does not cope with some of our thickheaded soldiers. The latrines are near the far end of the hut, and if you're in a hurry there isn't time to walk down the hut and back again – and a jolting run to save time can be disastrous for straining bowels. And, of course, some idiots will take a tally out of the wrong holder, or someone will shift a tally while the Nip is actually counting. Nothing is so simple that it cannot be complicated hopelessly.

The next step is to have a man from each hut standing in the doorway, and *he* will move the tallies as men go in and out. Any mistake in the count will result in him being held responsible and punished accordingly! Now the Nips can make a faster check by counting empty spaces only, which should agree with the tally. But then they always have one man not shown by the tally, and it takes a lot of explanation to convince them that the watchkeeper's bedspace would be counted as empty, but there would be no tally because the man is still inside the hut!

It is too much for them to grasp. After a fortnight they give up and leave us in peace.

It is 29 April 1945, the official birthday of His Imperial Japanese Majesty, the Emperor. In 1943, at Wampo, it was celebrated with a sports day and dynamiting the Kwei Noi for fish. It was missed in 1944. Now it is to be a holiday, the Jap commandant exhorts us all to remember that we are alive only by the grace and goodwill of the Emperor, and to be thankful, and to behave ourselves in a suitable manner so that as many of the camp guards as possible may be off duty to take part in their own celebrations. Thank you for your kind attention!

But it's not to be a quiet and lazy day for us, although it turns out well. By some mysterious means our small group of Singapore Volunteers has been selected to assist in the preparations. I think our usual work party Nip is responsible for offering to employ us on a special little job. He comes for us after tenko and takes us to a brand new small hut with a charcoal brazier in the middle and sacks of rice flour and white sugar leaning against the attap wall. There is also a Javanese soldier with a large shallow frying pan and a four-gallon can of vegetable oil, and a wooden tub of duck eggs. The Javanese speaks Dutch and no English, but we are Singapore people and can talk to him in Malay. He is there to cook special ceremonial pancakes, eaten only on such occasions, and why this is going to need him and four of us we cannot imagine.

Anyway, he gets to work and there is nothing whatever for us to do except look on. Fanning his brazier, he heats the pan and wipes oil around the inside. He has made a batter of rice flour, eggs and sugar, and pours in enough to cover the bottom of the pan. When it sets he flips it over, cooks the other side, then carefully lifts it out onto an enamel plate. To us it looks perfect: pale yellow with lovely brown speckles, most appetising.

Our Nip beams happily and hurries off to his hut with the sample. Minutes later he is back. The pancake is not right, it is too dark. It must be pale and unmarked – this is necessary.

The Emperor's birthday must also be 'Be Polite to Everybody Day', because our Nip goes to endless trouble to get us to understand exactly what is wanted – not easy when there is a language problem. Yesterday he would have ranted at our ignorance, and probably warmed our ears, but today he is all gracious smiles and soft words. But 'Be Polite Day' doesn't apply to us, so there's no reason why we shouldn't grab the opportunity to acquire a little loot.

While the cook is experimenting with stove temperatures and so on, producing several more samples for inspection, we have a little discussion. In our generous opinion – weren't we asked to be kind and thoughtful? – we decide that, since the Nips have provided the ingredients, we will let them have three pancakes out of every five. That is, two in five will be carefully browned just enough to disqualify them for the Nips but remain pale enough to look as if we really have tried to get it right. We can always fry them a little more later on to the colour we prefer. Fair enough? We think so.

Having got his recipe right the cook is turning out pale pancakes at a steady rate and our Nip trots back and forth with platefuls. There is no indication as to how many are required, so the process simply goes on. Nor is there any count of how many are actually cooked, so there is no difficulty in helping ourselves. And no one is bothered about how much of the stock of ingredients has been used to produce the quantity of pancakes supplied.

It is 'Generosity Day' for all concerned. At midday rice we fill our mess tins with pancakes for our friends – there is enough to go around all of us. In the middle of the afternoon we are told that another twenty will be sufficient for the Nip celebrations, so we speedily cook up a last batch for ourselves and a plateful for them.

Smiles and 'Arigato', and we walk to our hut with full bellies and clear consciences.

Momentous news – or is it just another rumour? – Germany has surrendered!

It could well be true. Recent occasional but persistent news and/or rumours as to the war's progress could indeed have been leading to Germany's final collapse. A date is part of the rumour, 7 May, and it is intensely irritating that the genuineness of something of such importance should be uncertain. Germany's defeat must come some time – it must surely be nearing absolute exhaustion.

In a combination of probabilities and wishful thinking we are inclined to accept it as true. In which case our own situation will see considerable change. Renewed hope of our rescue is suddenly made fragile with the uncertainties and dangers which we have long foreseen, and which now spring into focus.

We can only wait, alert for signs and ready to react.

Somewhere to the east of Nakhon Pathom there is an airfield. While I was in that camp we used to see an occasional plane spiralling upwards, an antiquated biplane similar to a model

Siskin Fighter which I made in school: a single radial engine with exposed cylinders sticking out all round, the top wing broad and long and the lower much narrower and shorter, it was a distinctively shaped aircraft but not much of a performer. It must be a Siamese air force plane.

We are all looking to the east, towards Bangkok, from where we can hear the faint growl of powerful engines. Just as we are able to pick out the black specks coming towards us we see our old Siskin type friend flying towards us and wearily climbing in a wide spiral. It is immediately obvious that the great bombers and the tired old fighter will meet almost overhead if they continue on their present courses. It's a fascinating sight. The pilot of the labouring fighter cannot have noticed the approaching bombers, and it is doubtful that the bomber crews will have seen his tiny shape against the ground.

The bombers are low, maybe 2,000 feet up; the fighter is still straining for altitude when the pilot, as he turns, must surely have seen the bellies of the bombers filling his windshield. Just in time he performs a frantic flipover and heads for home in a long downward swoop. The bombers – they are B24s, Liberators – steam majestically overhead, close enough for us to see their outside details clearly. Going home, back to base, while we are stuck here. Such a short distance between them and us, and they are free and fighting while we are prisoners and passive.

There is a big move in the wind, and our lot has been picked to be part of it. It seems to be the policy of our admin staff to keep men together where possible – not in army units, because they were irretrievably mixed up long ago – but in the labour battalions in which they worked in one camp after another.

This is an excellent idea; faces have become familiar and it is very important to have them around when you are shifted into unfamiliar surroundings.

One result of this is very noticeable to us Volunteers. The original party of 1,600 men which was sent from Singapore to Wampo included a big contingent from the 7th and 9th Coastal Heavy Artillery, the men who manned Singapore's big guns. We had been told that every man in these two regiments had a criminal record, either civilian or military, and that being posted to them was a definite punishment following gaol or detention. I really do not know the truth of this, but the men were indeed as tough a bunch of roughnecks as you would find anywhere, and they viewed us with suspicion just as we looked askance at them. We did not mix.

A great change came when the train was bombed and shot up at Takanun. The sergeant who took over control of the whole unhappy disaster was one of our fellows, a former schoolmaster from sleepy Malacca, a quiet, intellectual man who nevertheless commanded a bomb disposal platoon which dug up and dealt with more than thirty unexploded bombs in Singapore city. And, incidentally, helped himself to all those empty petrol drums from the Jap transport unit at Tarsao.

In his quiet way, Tony is a man of courage and determination, and his actions after the destruction of the train, taking control of the demoralised Nips and seeing to the dead and wounded, earned enormous respect from the gunners. Almost imperceptibly they began to approach us, asking us to settle arguments amongst themselves and joining in conversations and discussions. It has been a most interesting transition from wary aloofness – on both sides – to genuine liking and friendship. Most of them joined the army to escape poverty and the dreariness of life at home, for the certainty of regular food and some kind of a future, and a weekly pay packet. The 1930s were a miserable decade of hardship and hopelessness for millions of people in Britain, something I had never realised but now hear of at first hand.

Beneath their toughness these are decent men of solid human values, totally reliable as friends and with genuine sympathy for others in difficulty. Helping out is an instinctive reaction, born of their own deprived childhoods, but only to their own kind who so badly need help. Their so-called crimes, freely admitted and discussed, were petty and understandable – stealing for the sake of a few shillings in the pocket, irritation with the army's stupid disciplines and bullying NCOs, drunken sprees driven by sheer boredom, the loss of personal pride and initiative which is the lot of a professional soldier. We learn a lot, a hell of a lot, which is absolutely new to us. So it is with pleasure that we find the gunners will be in the party moving out.

One benefit of our new friendship, incidentally, is that petty thieving has stopped abruptly. There is always a pair of these lads at each end of our hut, and the suspicious characters who used to roam through furtively eyeing our kits are now firmly turned away with a threatening fist bunched up against their noses! As they say, it takes one to know one, and we are duly appreciative. Nothing is said, there is no need for words, but we all know what is happening.

As a matter of interest, a thief was caught some months ago stealing from the cookhouse. A serious crime, the Nip commandant heard of it and, in accordance with Jap army rules, wanted the man to be stood in front of a firing squad with the whole camp viewing the execution. 'Bloody right too', was the only opinion I ever heard.

But our senior officers (this was before all our officers were shipped out to a camp of their own) were reluctant to have a disciplinary matter of this kind handled by the Nips, and it was agreed that we would deal with the culprit. What happened? In a small open space the man – a former footballer with Tottenham Hotspurs, my grandfather's favourite London team – had to dig three holes. Then, using a small wicker basket, carry the excavated earth from one hole to fill in another. He repeated this endlessly for three days, working strict hours supervised by two sergeants who lolled in the shade of nearby trees. Every fifty minutes he joined them, to relax with a mug of tea and a smoke for ten minutes. He worked at his own speed, just so long as he didn't stop.

And this was supposed to be punishment? For a crime which, in our circumstances, was serious? It would be laughable if it were not so utterly fatuous. Tens of thousands of us, completely innocent of any misdemeanour, had worked routinely, for months on end, a bloody sight harder, and in foul conditions. The unrealistic mental processes of our officers is beyond belief! Maybe it is because they never attended our worksites, so have no real concept of what we endured.

The incident reminds me of another farcical incident, although quite different in character, back in River Valley Road Camp, about July 1942, when we had been prisoners for some five months. We were closely interested because our legal man, George, was requested to act as Prisoner's Friend at a court martial. The whole affair was ludicrously wrong. There was no officer of sufficient rank to call a court martial, but nevertheless it was decided to go on with a rider that the trial was required to establish facts which could be presented at a formal, full dress court martial in London after the war. In consequence the accused would have the 'informal' proceedings hanging over his head for the full duration of his captivity – and who could know how long that would be, beyond a minimum of two years? – at the conclusion of which he would be shipped home under close arrest to face trial.

For sheer pompous, thoughtless inhumanity and mental cruelty this was beyond all reason, and George told the officers of the court that he, as a practising partner in a legal firm run by his family for a century and a half, intended to lodge a complaint in the strongest terms at the first opportunity. George is a sergeant in the Penang Volunteers, and as such was held to have little standing. He was told to shut up and do his job.

What were the circumstances? A private soldier, working in our cookhouse, had handed a quantity of cooked rice to a Chinese child over the single strand of barbed wire which marked the camp boundary. The child was skinny, obviously underfed, and starving. The crime, which merited a full-scale court martial in the eyes of our senior officers (lieutenant-colonels), was 'Stealing Government Property'. Simple as that.

George pointed out that the rice was Japanese property, not belonging to the British government. That stealing implies personal profit from the deed, and there was none. That the rice was surplus, all men having been fed, and would have been thrown away. That, in any event, the quantity was so small that its 'theft' – which had not in fact occurred – should have been assessed only as a minor disciplinary matter, not a court martial offence. That it was an act of ordinary decency to give food to a starving child, food which would otherwise have been dumped and was a loss to nobody. Having totally dismantled the charge in every respect, and shown the officers of the court to be idiots, George was told to sit down and keep quiet. A verdict of 'Guilty as charged' was pronounced.

This was too much for George's Irish temperament. He told the officers that they were a bunch of vindictive ignoramuses, without enough intelligence to consider simple facts. They warned him that insolence would put him on a serious charge. He reminded them that it was they who had appointed him as Prisoner's Friend, and as such he was immune and free to say whatever he thought about the case. Hostility on both sides was at boiling point, and George was asked to leave, his role concluded.

George never heard what happened after that. For a bench of colonels to be so severely reprimanded by a sergeant – from a semi-military unit at that – would certainly be something for the record.

We have no idea what happened to the man who was so wrongly accused. Maybe he has died on the railway, a hurt and troubled man, guilty until proved innocent at some unknown point in the future of a 'crime' which had never been committed! But would a full court martial vindicate him? Or would it uphold the original verdict, with all its inaccuracies and its unsound basis, 'in the interest of good army discipline'? We have discussed it occasionally, but cannot reach a conclusion. Was there any hope that the colonels would be reprimanded for their so obvious stupidity?

There is a buzzing of small new activities throughout the camp, a result of all-round easier living, revived spirits, and the urge to do something different. Our small group has bought palm sugar, ginger and garlic, chilli sauce, salt, limes, bananas and a pomelo (a sort of oversized grapefruit), and a bottle of tamarind sauce which is new even to us. All this has been stewed into a flavoursome concoction which goes well on our rice. When we are out of stock there are numerous offerings available from other groups, who make enough to sell around the camp. For a few sattangs we have a wide choice, a favourite being what the hawkers call mango chutney – well, it has to be called something, doesn't it?

* * *

Early in the morning 850 of us gather, ready to move out. As usual, we have no idea at all where we are going or how we are to get there. Our people call our names – this has never been done before – and one by one we fall in for tenko.

The Nips check numbers and tell us we are to be searched, another new procedure, presumably to make sure we are taking nothing illegal with us, such as a radio or parts. The method seems to be foolproof. The front rank steps forward twenty paces and all kit is laid on the ground, haversacks empty, together with hats, belts and fundoshis. Then, absolutely naked, we walk forward another ten paces while the Nips move along the row of our possessions, checking inside haversacks. It doesn't take long – there is very little to inspect.

The front rank comes back to pick up their belongings, and moves fifty paces away to repack while the procedure is repeated rank by rank. When we are all proved to be clean we march off past the guardhouse, cross the tarmac road and walk on to the railway to wait for a train.

The search didn't bother us. Two of our men are detailed to act as servants to Billy the Kid, who has been provided with a truck and driver to take him direct to our destination. Our men pack his belongings into the truck, and with them a radio receiver concealed in an oversized Indian army water bottle. They will travel in the back of the truck, Billy in front with his driver, and take their own gear with them. When they arrive they will unpack the truck and tuck the radio away somewhere safe. It's a pleasure to think of that arrogant bully being fooled in such a simple way.

14

Nakhon Nayok Camp and the Long Hike

MAY TO AUGUST 1945

Our train arrives almost immediately – what went right? Did they telephone Kanburi to say we were on the way? Such efficiency is not the usual thing.

Our officers having been withdrawn, we are under the command of one of those oddities in the British army, a master gunner. This rank is superior to those extraordinarily fine and competent men who reach the top of the warrant officer grade, regimental sergeant-majors, but it does not carry the King's Commission. It is awarded on technical merit alone, and there are few master gunners in the army for the man must know everything there is to know about every weapon in use, from the fifteen-inch heavy coastal cannon to the basic revolver. It takes a technician of unusually high competence to carry this special rank, and this in fact is the first occasion I have even heard of it. Our friends in the 9th Coast have the greatest respect for him, and are proud to introduce him to us when he comes along to inspect his troops. Did any officer, other than the doctors, ever do that in our many moves in Siam?

We are a little surprised when we meet him. He is the most unsoldierly man amongst us in appearance – more like a middle-aged kindly schoolmaster getting to know his boys – and he is in charge of this party simply because of army protocol with regard to seniority in rank, because he will have had no experience of command responsibility during his thirty-something years in the army. We hope this will not create problems with the Nips, who tend to despise anyone who is not case-hardened with military bullshito. Wish him luck!

We have reached Nong Pladuk, heading east towards Bangkok, when the train stops. We are ordered to disembark, and the train pulls away. Is this our destination? We could have walked this far without any real effort.

Ah, there it is, faint aircraft engine noise to the east. We turn to one of our Nips: 'Hikoki-kah (Aeroplanes)?'

He tries to make the best of it: 'Nippon hikoki.'

There is a lengthy rumble of exploding bombs. 'Nippon boom-boom-kah?'

He looks thoughtful, a big struggle. 'Hai, Nippon puractiso!'

Give him full marks for trying. We know the planes are coming our way and wait for the look on his face when he sees the big bombers with Allied markings. It should be interesting.

Here they come, spread loosely all over the sky; the powerful throb of hundreds of engines, growing louder, makes the air vibrate. They seem to extend from the north horizon to the south, heading west, homewards, purposeful and majestic, low enough for everybody on the ground to see and identify them. There is not a Nip plane, not a gun fired, against them. Some of us saw more than seventy, others nearly 100; they moved too fast and were too scattered to total accurately. And, excitingly, something new! A type of aircraft none of us has ever seen before, but nevertheless it has lines which are familiar to some of us! We worry at our memories –

ten years back, maybe less. GOT IT! The London to Melbourne international air race – when was it, 1936? Won by Scott and Black, flying a De Havilland Comet, a small, low-winged monoplane, two in-line liquid-cooled engines and a high tailfin. A real racer, and this could be a direct descendant! Also in that race was a Douglas DC-2, an American-built passenger plane, entered by the Dutch KLM airline and flying with full complement of crew and passengers, as if on a regular commercial flight although this was the first time it had travelled on this route – a most creditable performance.

Of course, we exhaustively analyse everything we see, especially something new. The Comet's engines, weren't they developed from the Schneider Trophy seaplane that won the world record in – August, was it? – 1931, the month after my family arrived in England from Shanghai – Ron and I to go to school, and so a big landmark in my life. Every boy in the school was a keen follower of all types of aircraft, and Ron and I lived our last three years of holidays at Felixstowe, where we spent hours standing outside the fence at the RAF's experimental flying boat base. The ramps into the sea were only fifty yards away, and we knew every type of flying boat in service, even saw autogiros on floats being tried out. And we saw the early Empire flying boat fitted to carry a small, high-speed aircraft on its back, to carry fast mail to New York. Stimulated like this, we spotted everything that flew. And at school in Suffolk we were near the RAF experimental station at Martlesham, even went there for a day's outing when the station was open to the public, and watched a Spitfire going through its paces.

So the appearance today of a new, smallish, very fast bomber flying with the big Liberators was a special treat. It must operate from fields within range for its size, which suggests the Nicobar Islands, a little closer than the Andamans and possibly making a big difference to their capability to strike as far east as this. And this aircraft is so new that it does not appear on the identification charts which we recently acquired.

Our Nip has disappeared while we were watching the pageant; he must have felt too discouraged to face us.

The skies clear and our train chugs back to us, we climb aboard and move off. Remembering what happened recently near Takanun, and with the show just concluded, most of us climb up onto the steel roofs of the wagons, disregarding the shouts of our Nips. There are no proper handholds so we shall have to cling on as best we can, but it will certainly be far quicker to jump clear from up here than from inside, and that's the important thing! And also, the breeze as we roll along is very pleasant, and the view is much better. And very pleasant also. The farmland is dotted with groups of trees with houses showing through, and the inevitable Buddhist temple glowing warmly with its green-edged golden brown tiled roof. There are numerous houses on either side, closer together as we come to Nong Pladuk, then the township of Nakhon Pathom. We cannot see the camp, but the great temple – the biggest in Siam, we think – stands up prominently.

Late afternoon we reach a river. The steel arch bridge has been broken up by bombs, which is possibly what we heard earlier this morning. We are off-loaded on the riverbank, and watch the local population picking their way across on wooden planks lashed to the wreckage of girders. Groups of Jap soldiers are working here and there on the damaged structure, but we see no signs of organised and efficient repair work, only small-scale pottering around.

We camp where we are for the night. Not having arrived at our intended destination there are no arrangements to feed us, and this will be the situation tomorrow as well.

At daylight we are first across the river, all 850 of us. The timber gangplanks are as shaky as they looked to us yesterday afternoon, and there is a good deal of hauling ourselves from one level to another. The damage to the bridge is such that much of it has collapsed into the river, putting the whole structure at odd angles; the planking has to fit where it can.

We are pleasantly surprised to find the local people not in the least angry about this disruption to their lives. On the contrary, we receive cheerful shouts and smiles, and waving of hands. We can only hope that there were not many casualties. Looking around, the bombing seems to have been very accurate – there is very little damage outside the target. But this bridge would have needed only a fraction of the bomber force which we saw. There must have been other targets as well.

The railway line comes to a dead end on the west bank of the Chao Phraya, the broad river which flows through the city of Bangkok. Luckily there was a goods train available for us after we crossed the bridge, which would now run, at least for the time being, only on the short stretch to the city and back again.

On our left, just a little way upstream, is the large bulk of Bangkok's Chulalongkorn Hospital, identified by our travelling businessman. Barges and pom-poms are waiting, and soon we are chugging steadily downriver. On our right is the sprawl of the ancient city called Thonburi, and on the far side is the more modern Bangkok. The river is very broad; it must be all of a mile across, flowing muddy and strong and only a couple of feet below its banks. There is a constant scurrying of small craft to and fro, ferries carrying people across, for the only bridge joining the two cities in all this densely populated stretch is some way downriver.

The Thonburi shoreline is alive with activity: barges at warehouses which lean against each other, their undulating roofs showing their age. Women and children paddle and steer long narrow canoes up and down the many canals running into the main river, bringing shops to housewives in their stilted houses perched over the water. Everywhere are brilliant colours, flowers, fruit and vegetables piled in the canoes, and the cheerful sounds of people shouting and calling to each other. In the background is the pulsing pom-pom-pom-pom of hundreds of boat engines – the air vibrates with the sound. A scene of great animation and human busyness, it is our first contact with ordinary people living their own lives since we became prisoners, and we find it very pleasing.

Now here's something of considerable interest: a ship-builder's yard with a dozen hulls under construction, sterns to the water. They are far bigger than riverboats, and made of heavy timbers with a propeller jutting out of the stern – obviously intended for ocean travel. Surely no civilian shipowner is building new boats of this type nowadays? That can only mean that the Jap government has ordered them. Who else could provide marine engines? Have the Japs lost so much shipping that they are driven to this? We hope so!

The light is failing; the western sky is turning from dazzling sunset hues to unbroken blood-red, deep in the west and shadowing to the east. The Thonburi skyline stands in jet black silhouette, the slender tower of the Temple of the Dawn, Wat Arun, points blackly upwards, and we are about to move under the steel traffic bridge which spans the river. One section has been torn apart by bombs and the decking has collapsed into the water.

An hour or so later our barges are tied up at a concrete wharf, well down below the city amid mangrove swamps. There is a cookhouse, staffed by British prisoners who look fit and happy as they ladle beautiful snowy rice and thick vegetable stew into our mess tins. Anyone for a second helping? When did we last hear that? The vegetables are just scrumptious: sweet potatoes, greens and eggplant, not just a few bits swimming in hot water but a solid pack, and fried at that! A little bit salty, because the water supply is brackish, but who cares? And tea unlimited.

There is enough light to see that the concrete in the wharf is new; the sheds are steel stanchions with corrugated iron roofs. No walls, so apparently building was stopped at that point. There are three sheds, and all have been damaged by bombs. The cooks say it happened a few days ago. They lost two men and were very lucky the casualties weren't heavier, for bomb shelters cannot be dug in a mangrove swamp. They took cover under the concrete decking.

We look for places to sleep and settle down. We perch ourselves on a big pile of sandbags sodden with rain, the roof above being torn where bombs fell through. Not quite so hard as bare concrete.

For three days we laze around and stuff ourselves with food. The cooks say that a train will turn up eventually and cart us away. There have been a few parties before us, but where they all went is not known.

There is a great pile of empty cooking oil tins, the standard rectangular four-gallon type. Nobody seems to be interested in them, our Nips have disappeared, so gradually we have helped ourselves to as many as we need – and the pile is hardly diminished. Borrowing some tools from the cooks, and finding odd bits of wood and wire, we now have useful water containers with handles. This is indeed a good place to be! But on the fourth morning we hear a train whistle approaching, and get ready to move. The engine driver is Siamese, and when he sees us heaving our kit inside the goods wagons and starting to climb on the roofs, he becomes all excited, waving his hands around. Nobody can understand his language. We continue to climb up and he gestures in disgust. He gives up trying to tell us something – he's done his best.

Our cooks tell us something, though, before we pull out. 'Those holes in the roof, the bombs that made them went through the floor without exploding. They are still in the swamp, underneath the pile of sandbags. They've been waiting to go off for the last week or so!' Big smiles and waves as we depart, and calls of good luck which we return, for if those bombs do explode, they could all be killed.

We trundle upriver and are soon in the outlying areas of Bangkok. It's pleasant sitting on the roof in the morning sunshine, looking at the local population going about its daily business. Looking out to the sides we do not see the hazard in front but react quickly to urgent shouts of 'Heads down, lie flat!' from the wagons ahead of us. Just in time we sprawl flat as the train runs under the steel cross-girders joining the side arches of a bridge. This is what the engine driver had been trying to tell us! The undersides of the trusses spanning the railway lines are only eighteen inches above our flattened bodies. Had it happened in the dark every man would have been dragged off, badly injured.

Of course, we cannot move down inside the wagons, and now forget the scenery and watch our front. There are many streams running into the river somewhere over to our left and every one has to have a bridge so we are frequently ducking down until we roll into the big railway marshalling yards on Bangkok's eastern flank.

This is a disaster area. It must have been a recent target – possibly of those Liberators we saw a few days ago – for the torn steelwork of locomotives and sheds hasn't yet rusted. There is bomb damage everywhere, locos torn apart and over-turned and rails twisted and pointing upwards. We pass a roundhouse, shattered and buckled. The locomotives inside are wrecked and the turntable at the hub has been destroyed. The engine standing on it at the time now lies on its side down in the sunken pit, on top of the wreckage, itself a heap of twisted metal.

Some tracks still run through, however, for a few move-ments can be seen amidst all the rolling stock which will never run again. It is a vast area and must at one time have been very busy, for this is the focal point of the main lines from Chiang Mai in the north, from Singapore down south, and from Saigon in French Indo-China.

Our train comes to a halt and we are ordered to dis-embark. Waiting for us is a white-coated group of Jap civilians, standing behind tables on which there are cardboard boxes full of glass test tubes and rods and cotton wool. It is explained to us in good English that we have come from a cholera area, and must be tested before going further. This procedure involves us slipping off our fundoshis and standing in rows, bending forwards and holding the cheeks of our bums apart while a glass rod is slipped in to pick up a specimen, which is then dropped into a test tube with a plug of cotton wool.

A bit undignified, but to us it is appropriate to have an official opportunity to present our bare arseholes to the Japs. With some advance notice, we might even have been able to conjure up a sweet, if toothless, smile! The idea tickles our sense of humour.

The medical Japs are in a hell of a hurry to get this inspection done; they are nervous and try to rush things. Soon we know why: the air raid sirens start to wail, and in a split second the white coats are dashing off out of the yards. In moments we are alone in the middle of empty space – maybe our particular Nips have never heard warning sirens before and haven't caught on to what they mean. Then the penny drops and, without allowing us time to collect our precious kit from the wagons, they hustle us away. A road runs past the yards, and in a few minutes we turn into a gate set in the brick wall of a neat garden of fair size. A colonnaded building fills the opposite side, and here we are, 850 nearly naked men on the lawn of a Roman Catholic convent, with saintly statues looking down on us, no doubt with disapproval.

The 'all clear' sounds in an hour or so, and when we emerge from the gate there are hundreds of interested Siamese waiting for us. We are dressed in nothing but a hat and diminutive fundoshi, and instinctively bunch close together as we start walking back to our train. The crowd, increasing in numbers, surrounds us, walking with us and chattering. There is anger in their voices, women gesticulating, the tone rising, but none of this is directed at us. We sense only sympathy, and comment quietly to each other as we move along.

And then it happens. A big black car with Jap army pennants on each front wing comes up behind, hooting arrogantly at everybody to get out of its way. It has to slow to a crawl because nobody moves aside; in fact the crowd around us suddenly breaks up and runs back to surround the car, forcing it to stop. Siamese men and women press around it, screaming, shouting at the officer inside, ripping the pennants off. The officer and driver sit bolt upright, staring ahead as if they can't see the mob. The car is rocked and tipped from side to side. Our Nip escorts are struck dumb, not knowing whether to try a rescue or to stay with us, hesitating and staring around while we look on. Prudently, they decide their duty is to get us back to the train, where we find everything as we left it. The air raid must have taken place elsewhere – we have seen and heard nothing.

Our train pulls out eastwards while we perch on the roofs, hungry but philosophical, and with something new to talk about.

The great glittering pattern of stars in front of us slowly swings over to our right. We have, of course, taken a long curve to our left, northwards; it is a magnificent sight in these open plains, millions of bright sparks in the deep spaces of the night sky. Away over westwards, in the mountains, there could well be the first shattering rains of the wet monsoon, and we are truly thankful that we are out of that area. On the wagon roofs the view is perfect.

We pull into a real station, with roofed concrete platforms and small buildings, not like the gloomy sidings with a name board on 'our' railway. We come to a halt, and on the next line is a stationary passenger train headed towards Bangkok. It is crowded with local folk; scores of people sit on the carriage roofs and the interiors are packed. They start to call across to us in friendly voices, but we cannot understand them until someone speaks in French. A number of us have sufficient schoolboy familiarity with that language to be able to exchange a few sentences, but one of us has a French mother and is fluent. These people are from the provinces of French Indo-China, and learn French at school from their early days. Like the Siamese they regard the Japs as intruders, and maintain an independent attitude which is fortified by an intense dislike of everything Japanese.

In no time at all we are brought up to date on the progress of the war, encouraging news to us, and we hear that there are thousands of our people working at the docks in Saigon, and on airfields and in other places such as Phnom Penh. As their train starts to move away we are showered with gifts: parcels of food, fruit, hard-boiled eggs and even cigarettes, to a chorus of good wishes to us and imprecations to the Japs.

It is curious and interesting that we, as representatives of white colonial powers who failed to defend them from invasion, are so popular and find such friendly attitudes everywhere, while the Japs, who are an Asiatic nation, are hated and despised with great intensity. The answer must lie in the bullying and arrogant way of the Japs towards every other nation, compared with the benevolent and easy-going rule of the British and French – not perfect by any means, but at least tolerant and respecting the dignity of others.

The railway swings back eastwards, and mid morning we stop in the middle of nowhere. Apart from the snacks tossed to us during the night, we have had no food since yesterday morning at the riverside wharf. Our stomachs are rumbling and our bowels ready to burst, our bladders having been easier to relieve from the train. There is a small group of bamboo and attap huts, to which we are directed. This seems to be an encampment set up to feed bodies of men in transit. We are to be here all day, and will march all night to another such point. We are fed reasonably well, there is enough water for a wash, and we stretch out gratefully to sleep the day away.

For the next three nights we march across flat country. There are no villages to be seen, and no kind of path either. A Jap soldier from each encampment is our guide to the next stop; he must know the ground well enough to take us straight there. We estimate we march twenty-five kilometres or so at each stage without difficulty, carrying only our personal gear. The nights are cool, the stars a sheer pleasure to look at.

The last stretch brings us to our destination, Nakhon Nayok Camp, just after daybreak. It's the usual collection of bamboo and attap huts with the usual bunch of surly-looking

Nips at the guardhouse, bad-tempered, no doubt, as a result of having had to keep the dogwatch. We fall in for tenko, and one of our Eurasian sergeants is in charge. After the initial courtesies, sullenly acknowledged by the scowling Nips, he shouts out the order to 'Number'. But instead of 'Bango!', he nervously comes out with 'Benjo (shit)!' There's a moment's silence. The Nips could easily take it as an insult, but suddenly they all burst into howls of laughter. It's the best joke they've heard in a long time, and from then on everything runs smoothly.

There is nothing spectacular, or even picturesque, about the countryside here. The camp sits, isolated, on a flat plain dotted with little pimply hillocks and patches of shrubbery. There are few trees in sight, and neither cultivation nor village life. A line of hills stretches across the northern horizon.

Apart from the resident guards, the camp is empty. It's much like the other camps we've been in, except that one most important thing is different: we discover a constant supply of clean drinking water only a few feet down. We dig a square pit some twenty feet each way, and it immediately fills with clear fresh water, ready to use without being boiled. This is near the cookhouse, and we locate the latrines over on the far side of the camp area on a slight rise. The pit replenishes itself as fast as we draw water out, for all 850 of us. A second pit is dug for personal ablutions, well away from the first to avoid contamination. It is quite marvellous to have drinking water 'on tap'; we don't want to risk spoiling it.

The Nips, who seem to have been getting by on a limited supply coming to them by tanker truck, are admiringly amazed by our ingenuity, and it does a great deal to set up good relations between us.

There seems to be nothing urgent for us to do. We are allowed a few days to settle in before work parties are called for, and the rations improve noticeably. With the war obviously nearing a critical phase, at least in this part of the world, we feel that this camp, tucked away in the backwoods, may be as good a place as any to be for a few months.

On our first turnout for work we are handed over to Jap army troops, and our Nips disappear back to camp. These are frontline soldiers, quite different in their bearing and businesslike approach to the second-rate slobs who have been in charge of us all this time. These men must come from a camp in the neighbourhood; there is a fleet of trucks parked in the scrub. Some of them speak understandable English, and are keen to improve their knowledge. Joining us for impromptu conversation, asking us to explain words, seems to be more important than getting anything done. It suits us; we can be as lazy as they like!

What they want us to do is dig emplacements in the sides of the hillocks, where trucks and fieldguns can be parked and remain protected from aircraft. The soil is easy to work; the loose earth which we shovel out is formed into walls, and embankments to provide additional cover. There is no set task for the day – as long as we keep at it steadily, the Japs are happy; we don't have to exert ourselves unduly.

This seems a bit odd to us. Without any doubt we are helping to construct defensive positions for the Jap army in Siam, ready for an Allied offensive which can be expected to follow the Jap withdrawal from Burma. But there is no atmosphere of concern, no hurry to get things done – it's all quite leisurely. We can only surmise that the High Command must be fully aware of the situation, but does not want to cause any alarm by ordering a speedo schedule, and therefore is proceeding quietly with its defence works.

Also, in our view, this will not be a priority area for an Allied invasion. Firstly, our real objectives are Malaya and

Singapore, and north-east Siam can simply be left isolated. Secondly, there is no access across the Siam–Burma border for a modern army with tanks, except way down south in the Tenasserim area, where the RAF used to have an airfield at Victoria Point. More likely, however, it will be further to the south, on the Malayan coast itself around Malacca, perhaps, for the Jap navy must now be almost non-existent in the Indian Ocean and the Straits. So the building of fortifications – if what we are doing can justify such an expression – is a bit casual. It looks like something is being done, and it costs them nothing in manpower.

It's not long before the Japs discover that I visited Japan as a child, whereupon all work stops for coffee and cigarettes, biscuits and bananas, while we chat together about life in Japan and in England, and their experiences in the great Japanese invasions of 1941–42. I carefully don't tell them that I lived in Singapore, and that my father is interned there, and that I have a brother in Siam. There is always a risk that something may trickle back to the Kempei-tai, and that could be most unpleasant.

In a couple of weeks we have used up all the local space suitable for defence works and are taken by trucks to work further away from camp. We are now able to see that the whole area is swarming with troops with the usual extras such as field workshops and supply dumps. We see a couple of squadrons of tanks – about fifteen tons, we reckon – armed with a medium-sized cannon and two machine guns. They rattle noisily and put out an undue volume of exhaust smoke, suggesting a lack of spare parts and maintenance facilities.

Humping bags of rice and supplies for an extensive cook-house we see a large blackboard on which are chalked up in Japanese characters what must be the names of the units supplied. Alongside, in Roman numerals, are the requirements for rations on this day – that is, the numbers of men to be fed at each unit; the total for which this cookhouse is responsible is shown as 12 792, which accounts for the rows of steaming kwalis and baskets of vegetables, and the overall hustle and bustle.

The Jap army seems to use Roman numerals instead of their own symbols, just as in the aircraft identification leaflets we picked up a few months ago. I wonder why. A further thought: they must use the English alphabet for all Morse code signals, which build up letter by letter and could not possibly be done with their own form of writing.

We have a happy day at the cookhouse, rendering down big slabs of pork fat with the rind still on. The cooks want the oil but are not interested in the rind – frizzled up to a high temperature it is delicious, and they even give us salt to sprinkle on, and empty flour bags to take back to camp what we cannot stuff into ourselves! Beautiful pork crackling, and they have no use for it. Great heaps of it! Rich, oily, crunchy and crisp – wonderful stuff!

The Jap soldiers where we are working – not our camp Nips – greet us with beaming smiles and obvious signs of great satisfaction. Something must have happened which they think is of major benefit to them, and they are bubbling over with eagerness to tell us what it is. Do we know that Germany surrendered two months ago, that Roosevelt died before that, and that Churchill is 'no more Number One in Ingerandu'?

They have enough English amongst them to explain that these two warlike men – pantomime of gnashing teeth and fearsome grimaces and menacing fists – have been 'orru one-time': responsible for keeping the war going. Now that they have gone and Germany is 'finishu', there is no reason for us to go on fighting Japan. We shall all be friends again, as we were in the last boom-boom! So, 'orru boom-boom quicku finishu, orru Ingerishu go home' – presumably leaving Japan in her occupied territories. Their cheerful and confident optimism leaves us in no doubt that this is what they expect will happen, which means that they have no understanding of how badly the war is going for them. For which we must be thankful, otherwise their easy-going treatment of us – bedded in their feeling of superiority over us – might become very different.

We thank them politely for telling us all this, not showing any reaction or offering any comment. They grin at us with an air of condescension, taking our silence as concealing the shocking hurtfulness of this news, which would have been their own response to similar circumstances. On the contrary, our first thoughts are that our part of the world, deliberately and cold-bloodedly betrayed, abandoned and cast adrift by Churchill in 1941, might now be given its rightful and proper attention! Discussion in camp tonight, when we bring in our news, will be most interesting. It may not be good manners but we have no intention of repaying our hosts with any sign of appreciation – they already owe us far too much.

Helping to wash down trucks, normally the job of the driver's mate, we take a look under a bonnet. The engine and its accessory parts are, according to our expert who ran a major vehicle business in Singapore, similar to American truck engines of the mid 1920s, simple but hard-working and not requiring a great deal of mechanical know-how to maintain. The driver's mate is astonished that all of us are familiar with vehicles, because there is such a shortage in the Jap army that any man who can drive is treated as a semi-god, and has a mate to do all the donkey work for him.

He is amazed to see us check dipsticks and radiators, batteries and belts, just as we are surprised to find that all parts are known to him by English names. Well, more or less, that is. Engine block is enjinu brocku, petrol pump is petrooru pumpu, the real prize going to flywheel housing which comes out as frywheeruhossingfu! Doesn't the Jap language have its own names for these things?

He is happy to go off and join his mates while we attend to superficial checks, so he does not see wheel hubs being opened up and packed with grit. The bearings will crack and break up a long way from us, thus avoiding suspicion falling on our innocent heads.

I would have thought that the stresses and strains of our existence might well lead to short tempers and abrupt explosions of fisticuffs now and then, but the fact is that I have never yet seen anything like that happen. Wordy, shouted arguments and threatening attitudes, yes, but even those don't happen very often, and they are always smoothed over by someone standing by. We have quite enough to put up with from the Nips without adding our own personal squabbles – everyone knows it and, deep down, is glad to be drawn out of these moments of flaring temper. Besides, injuries will get no treatment and may turn nasty.

So, late this afternoon, we are surprised by a commotion in the hut opposite ours, the end doorways separated by a small space. Amid cheering and shouting two men burst out of the opposite doorway, slugging at each other as they try to find a footing. The smaller one catches the other a solid punch on the cheekbone and we hear the distinct sound of cracking bone, followed by a howl of pain and whimpering as the bigger man falls to the ground, hands to his face. Jubilant shouts spill out of the hut, and the big man's haversack and personal belongings are tossed out around him. The victor is led back in; there's a great deal of shouting and back-slapping.

What has it all been about? We are told that the big fellow has been a bully and overbearing bastard since arriving in Siam, using his fists freely on anyone who annoyed him. No one has been able to deal with him, or avoid his unpleasant attentions, during all that time. This afternoon brought matters to the point where the smaller man, normally quiet and inoffensive, was being picked on and suddenly lost his temper.

So the wicked giant has been driven out by the smaller hero, just as in a fairy tale!

We are all gathered near the camp guardhouse, waiting to be collected for the day's work, when a Jap army car flying a pennant drives in, to the consternation of the duty sentry who has not seen its approach, having had his back to it while lazily pissing against the fence. An officer dismounts, his insignia of rank visible above a white surgical-type gown draped over his uniform to indicate, presumably, that he is a doctor. Some panicky shouting and screeching – everyone caught by surprise – and a group of men in various stages of undress hastily lines up for what must be a sick parade.

The officer, obviously bored with such a trivial matter as the health of the troops, lights a cigarette and carefully blows smoke into the face of each soldier as he presents himself to be examined. With neither stethoscope nor thermometer to aid him, he languidly checks his patients, listening without the slightest show of concern to their symptoms, peering into an open mouth and glancing casually at their bodies, but not touching them to test glandular swellings or stiff joints.

As each man is dismissed he says a few words to the gunso in charge of the squad, presumably instructions as to treatment. Last of all is a tall young Korean, who points to a greyish patch on his brown chest, pinching and poking it and apparently explaining that he cannot feel anything. The area is slightly raised and the surface looks roughened, which prompts a remark from our pharmacist that it could indicate leprosy, which he had occasionally seen when running his dispensary in Penang before the war.

From the sudden look of alarm on his face and his quick step backwards, as if to distance himself from his patient, the doctor must have reached the same diagnosis. He has just lit a fresh cigarette, and leans forward to press the burning tip firmly against the pale patch of skin, which blisters and sizzles and sends up a wisp of smoke. This subtle technical test is repeated in three places. The Korean remains stiffly at attention. He hasn't flinched and that seems to convince the doctor, who resumes smoking his tainted cigarette. A casual wave dismisses the Korean, the officer puts on the faint, superior smile of a learned academic as he says a few words to the blank-faced gunso – maybe they are words of wisdom, or just, 'He was right, you know, no feeling at all in that area'.

The Korean, as he turns away, faces us directly and we see his face tighten in a black grimace as he glances down at his mutilated chest. He looks at us and mouths something full of hatred, a simmering and malevolent curse as bloody and raw as his wounds.

Sick parade is over, the officer has fulfilled his duty and drifts back to his car to be driven away. In the Jap army, of course, a Korean is less than nothing, but we, who have long since ceased to be surprised by Nip brutality and callousness, cannot find words to express our disgust.

* * *

A small group of Americans has come into the camp, about forty men in all, we think, and while walking to our spot for digging we fall in with them. I start talking to a young fellow about my own age, and find that he is a sailor from the USS *Houston*, an eight-inch gun cruiser which was sunk with the Australian HMAS *Perth* in the Sunda Straits. His name is Elmer, and he is the only sailor in his group, the others being Texas artillerymen captured in Java. They stick very much to themselves, not talking to us and not inviting us to approach them.

Nevertheless, after some hesitation Elmer joins freely in conversation. Maybe he is glad to talk to new faces. He joined the US navy as a volunteer before the Jap war started, because he was certain it was coming and thought it better to be a trained sailor when it did start, rather than be drafted in and, maybe, have to fight as a rookie. Very sensible of him!

On the walk back at the end of the day's work he comes up to me and asks how much we paid for eggs from the local traders during the lunch break. I tell him five cents each, it is the regular price and everybody paid the same. Apparently not. Their master sergeant, who had collected their money and done the buying, brought eggs back to the men and said they had cost eight cents apiece, which means that he cleared three cents an egg, and bought eggs for himself with the men's money. Which was theft, deliberate, bare-faced. Elmer goes back to his mob, looking very grim.

We haven't seen the Americans since then, so I don't know how the matter was resolved.

A tremendous squall of high velocity wind hit us last night, just after dark. We have had no previous experience of such a wind. In the mountains the rains were trapped but we were protected from the monsoon winds which brought them in. Here, there is far less rain but the countryside is flat and open and, as we find out, the wind can scream across unimpeded.

It is all very sudden. In the darkness we can see no warning in the sky and the gale strikes at full strength in just a few seconds. There we are, sitting on our sleeping platforms in groups, talking about this and that, when we become aware of a distant moaning sound. Before we can think what it might be it changes to a peculiar whistling roar. The whistle is the angry screech of the squall, the roar is the rolling drumbeat of a massive torrent of rain.

In an instant all our belongings are swept off the platform, for our open-sided huts provide no protection. The pelting rain sweeps horizontally through, and the attap roof starts to undulate and flex as air pressure heaves up from underneath. The whole structure is twisting in all directions, and in the dazzling brilliance of lightning flashes we can see that the upright poles are beginning to work loose in the ground. The roofing thatch suddenly reverses itself, the attap panels rotating upwards. It takes a lot of strain off the roof by allowing air to pass through freely, but it lets the rain pour in even more heavily. Not that that really matters much!

Every man in the hut is clinging to the vertical bamboo poles that support the roof. Even with our weight holding them in place we can feel the whole structure distorting and trying to pull itself out of the ground. It comes very close to succeeding – we are sometimes lifted bodily so that our downward pulling is almost ineffective, and only our weight prevents the hut taking off like a giant kite. It lasts more than half an hour, and leaves us chilled and soaked, shivering in the sudden cold. We are exhausted with the sheer physical effort of holding down the roof, for it is difficult for a dozen men to get a useful grip on a single pole, some squatting at the bottom and others leaning over them awkwardly. It has been a near thing; we were close to having to give up.

When calm returns we search around to retrieve our belongings, which became entangled amongst the bamboo stumps supporting the sleeping platforms. We notice one thing that earns our admiration. These huts are held together by ragged strips of tree bark, stringy stuff which is used to lash every joint and bind down every slat and crosspiece. We have always considered it to be primitive material, but it has just proved its strength without any doubt. There is not a nail or a piece of conventional timber used, or even wire – everything depends on these tough little strips, and there has not been a single failure as far as we can see.

All our huts have survived, but the Nip guardhouse, not having sufficient manpower to hold it down, has been ripped out of the ground and lies in a collapsed heap fifty yards away.

Another move is announced. We are to evacuate Nakhon Nayok to work at another place and the empty camp will be filled by a new party. This is inexplicable to us. Why doesn't the new party go direct to where we are now to go? The logic escapes us but, as they say, it is not for us to reason why but only to do as we are told, and as usual there is no hint even of which direction we will march.

An advance party of 250 men moves out, to set up camp at a destination where we will join them in a week or so. Our lot of 600 men has an escort of thirteen Nips presided over by a nasty little nineteen-year-old Jap lieutenant, rather like Billy the Kid, but more of a spiteful adolescent with too much power and wanting to use it.

We follow a tarmac road which is soon uncomfortably hot for our bare feet, especially as we are lugging cookhouse kwalis and sacks of rice, clumsy loads which swing about in a most annoying fashion as they hang from shoulder poles. There is no way of controlling them, and they add a lot of stress to the men carrying them; they can only stand it for half an hour at a time.

We bivouac for the night in a fallow paddy field, after some twenty kilometres in hot sun and high humidity. It is a convenient spot for the Nips to watch us, confined by the narrow bunds of earth which separate the fields and control their flooding during the growing season. But we're not too happy when the humidity turns into a thrashing thunder and lightning storm, totally exposed as we are with nowhere to put our kit out of the rain. Having completed the day's march by digging latrines in our field, finding firewood and water and setting up the kwalis for evening rice (there's nothing else), we are not in a good mood. The Nips are under cover – we carried their tent for them – and that doesn't improve our feelings.

We are quite fascinated to watch the Nip sentry plodding on his beat along the top of the bunds. He carries his rifle, with bayonet fixed, slung upright over his shoulder. He is by far the tallest object in the flat landscape, and his bayonet is an inviting lightning conductor, but the lightning zigzags everywhere else but on him. How disappointing – we have been hoping for a spectacular display of barbecued Nip!

We have been on our feet for eighteen straight hours by the time the storm passes, and if we want any sleep it will have to be while lying down in a muddy slop. And tomorrow is another day, probably the same again.

Early in the march we are joined by a dog, a muscular young animal of several breeds. Where he came from we cannot guess, for we haven't seen a house or people, but he is content to trot along with us. Some of the men talk to him, even find spoonfuls of rice at the midday halt, and during the afternoon it is noticed that his paws are bleeding – the hot tarmac, over so many kilometres, has been too much for him. The men, who do not have dressings for their own sores, produce scraps of rags to bandage the dog's feet; such is the sentimental streak in British soldiers. During the night he disappears, presumably to return to his home.

On the third afternoon we camp in an open space on the outskirts of the town of Sraburi, and our Nip lieutenant disappears. No doubt he is reporting to the local command that we are here and ready for work.

Our advance party rejoins us the next day. Exciting news! The work scheduled for us, on the far side of the town, has been cancelled. There has been a lot of Allied air activity in the last few days – no bombs, but millions of leaflets showered on the local population. One side is printed in Siamese, the other in English and Japanese, saying that the Japanese army, navy and air force are being beaten everywhere, our aircraft fly where they like because the Japs cannot stop them, this time it is leaflets but next time it could be bombs, tell the Japs to get out of your country! In their naive fashion our Nips tell our men to pick up every leaflet they see, but they are not to read them! How stupid can you be? And, of course, they are good for rolling cigarettes.

We hang around in our bivouac for a few days, fed from some nearby Jap army kitchen which sends along a truck once a day. It's a lazy life – we don't object at all. Most of our escort Nips seem to be on leave in the town, and the odd few on duty allow us to buy from hawkers, no doubt getting their usual 'commission' for permitting it. Contrary to our expectations, our pay has always been handed out at the prescribed ten-day intervals, and being out of camp we receive the full amount because there are no hospital deductions. We have never grudged these contributions to improve the lot of the sick – haven't we all had occasion to be thankful for small extras? – but it really is astonishing how much difference it makes to have an extra fifty cents when payday comes around.

Ready to move off, we collect wooden carts from the local army store. The kwalis and other heavy gear are piled on, the Nips even add their rifles – which leaves them unarmed and their weapons within our reach! But they trundle smoothly along the tarmac road heading northwards, the weather is fine and not too hot and we take things easily. We have brought rations, and camp at night – life is not at all bad.

The fourth morning takes us to Lopburi, where the events at Sraburi are repeated. Nobody wants us; we are given rations for five days and move out. After an hour or so on the good road we turn off onto the grassy earth, and those who scrambled for the easy job of pulling carts suddenly find they have to work a lot harder. It gets worse. We come to a steeply sloped embankment with a railway track on top, and the carts have to be unloaded and everything dragged to the top where it all has to be put together again. Dragging the carts over the sleepers, which happen to be spaced as inconveniently as possible in relation to the wheel diameters, soon becomes physically exhausting. The wheels fall heavily between the sleepers and the cart has to be bodily hoisted onto the next sleeper, only to fall again. It is not possible to develop a fast run and skim from one to another, and the solid jolt-hoist-jolt tears at shoulders and every other joint in the body. We all muck in to help, but it makes no difference except to half-kill everybody.

Then an axle shears, and even the Nips have to admit that we cannot go further like this. We are knackered and making no progress. We shall have to off-load every cart, run them down the embankment into thick scrub, and resume our march down there. The load from the broken cart is distributed over the others and the wreck itself is dismantled; the pieces must be carried to the next Jap army store – two wheels, steel axle, and frame with shafts. Nothing can be thrown away in this army; all bits and pieces have to be handed in, inspected and accounted for!

By the time we reach Nakhon Sawan we are dead on our bare feet, and the air around us is a blue haze from our cursing and swearing at the carts and the Nips in general. Everything is thankfully handed in, and we bivouac for the night. This is a fair-sized town, with a broad river flowing through it from north to south. To get from our camping site to the Jap food stores where we are sent to work, we simply wade across, about chest deep. Nowadays this is not regarded as an obstacle but merely a part of the day's activities.

Working in the Jap quartermaster's stores is not only easy but profitable. We are told what to do and left alone to get on with it; so many bags of rice – beautiful stuff, Siam No.1 it is called in Singapore, where it has always been the local favourite – to be lifted off the stack here and piled over there in readiness for army unit trucks to collect. Jap soldiers do not need to be supervised, simply because it would not occur to any of them to disobey or misbehave, and nobody keeps a check on us.

The first thing to establish with the gunso in charge of the store is whether we can keep the rice spilt on the dirt floor from broken bags. He looks surprised at our request – maybe Japanese soldiers are not expected to eat dirty rice – and he indicates we may sweep it up and fill our haversacks. So we make sure that the odd bag or two suffers a mishap to provide plenty of rice all round, the clean stuff is put away first and a dusty layer on top, and tucked away in the middle are cloves of garlic, knobs of ginger, and a few chillies. They owe us far more than this anyway.

Having got rid of our cumbersome kwalis we are now cooking for ourselves, so the system works fine. The tins which we acquired at the wharf downriver from Bangkok are just what we need for holding water, and cooking rice and making tea, in the groups of six or eight which we have now formed for convenience in taking turns at our various chores.

For the first time in well over three years we have full bellies and food worth eating. By pooling funds we can afford cooking oil, garlic, little purple onions, eggs, palm sugar, chillies and fruit from Siamese hawkers. Daily tenkos, morning and evening, are quickly over, and smaller working parties are called for so that many of us stay in camp all day and can collect water and firewood, and have hot food ready when the workers return. Nobody hassles us, and we have discreet contacts with hawkers, who sometimes pass us encouraging messages from the townsfolk. Things are looking up!

It has been a long and tiring day, busier than usual at the Jap store, and we are kept at work well beyond the normal time to knock off. We are back in camp just in time for tenko before sunset and as we stand there being counted it starts to rain. Thankful for a hot meal waiting for us, we eat in the dark and keep the rain out of our mess tins as best we can, but out in the open there is no shelter of any kind.

The rain drums down more and more heavily, and a chilling breeze comes with it. We cannot lie down on the saturated ground but have to stand about, holding our kit clear of the puddles. The rain is cold, almost sleet, and our feet start to go numb. Stamping them doesn't help – it only splashes muddy water everywhere. Not that that makes any real difference, but somehow it adds to our discomfort.

In the pitch darkness we can hardly see even men standing close to us. Wearing only a hat and a fundoshi, our bodies smart from the stinging rain, coldness spreads from hands and feet into our bodies, and it becomes an effort to think. Nobody moves much. Instinctively we huddle closer together for whatever mutual warmth may be available, our backs to the bucketing rain – now heavier than ever – and the penetrating wind which wraps itself around each of us. Someone starts to sing, a few join him, but the sound is miserable and does nothing for our low spirits. The voices trail off and there is silence except for the thumping rain and sloshy gurgles of shifting feet.

Midnight comes and goes. We still stand like cattle in a field, presenting our rumps to the wind and rain, waiting, waiting for them to stop. They keep on, with no easing in intensity. We have started a routine which, at intervals, moves the men in the centre to the outer fringe, where there is least protection, to allow those who have been most exposed to come into the middle of the group for at least some relief. It also keeps us moving now and again, which is necessary because tiredness and persistent cold have left us almost asleep on our feet. We keep ourselves upright by some trick of involuntary balancing, for we are so chilled that deliberate effort is near impossible. All we can do is wait, either for the rain to stop or for dawn and some lightening of the sky.

We are wrapped in streaming blackness, numbed and stiff with fatigue and cold, hardly noticing that the wind has dropped and the rain lessened. A watery glow appears in the east, the clouds are clearing and the yellow crescent of the moon appears, just above the horizon. We know it is in the last stage of its waning phase, so we have been on our feet for nearly twenty-three hours continuously, half of it near frozen, and without sleep.

We start to move slowly, as if coming out of anaesthetic, aching to lie down. I spread my sodden groundsheet, useless for keeping water away but providing some sort of bedding, wrap my thin blanket tightly around me and stretch out gratefully, my body and limbs relaxing and some warmth beginning to flow through me. Water from the sodden earth under my groundsheet seeps up into my blanket, but there's nothing I can do about that. Simply lying down is a dreamy contentment.

But I am not going to be allowed to doze off. Some annoying little creature starts to crawl into my blanket, over my feet, and brings me sharply back to full consciousness. It's not a snake; it has feet, dozens of them, making their way to my ankle and up my right leg. The front end reaches the calf muscle, the rear end is on my ankle bone, so it is some eight or nine inches long – it's too wide to be one of those harmless little millipedes, for I can feel its moving feet quite distinctly.

What the hell is it? I run over in my mind's eye some of the numerous species of crawling insect and other creatures which we have come across. Hell, it can only be one of those nasty centipedes, brilliantly coloured in alternating red and yellow segments, with sharp pincers sticking out in front – and they bite!

It has reached the side of my knee joint and is working its way along the inside of my thigh. I can't open up my blanket without a great deal of flurry and movement, my arms are inside it and strapped close to my body, and that bloody little monster is still creeping forward! I have to do something immediately, before I find myself seriously damaged – there's no avoiding pulling my arms free and opening up my blanket.

The sudden upheaval must have frightened the centipede. Before I can bring my hand down on him I feel him bite, like red hot needles thrust into my skin. In the bleary moonglow I inspect his crushed body and find that I had guessed correctly. Poor little fellow, he had only been wanting to get out of the puddled ground and must have thought he was lucky to find a soft warm place to curl up for a nap. And I had no wish at all to kill him; I would have picked him off my leg carefully, had I been able to do so.

There is a lump in my thigh, hard as a bullet, and the pain is intensifying as the venom spreads. It seems logical to sit up to lessen the risk of it moving up into my abdomen, and all I can think to do is to scoop up cool wet mud as a soothing plaster. It doesn't have any effect, but at least I feel I am doing something.

The others sleep on. I cannot bring myself to wake my friends. They need their rest, and would not be able to help in any case. Kept awake by my throbbing leg, I can only wait for daylight when the camp will rouse by force of habit.

At tenko I show the Nip my crimson lump, which is oozing a little fluid from two punctures, and show him the carcass of the centipede. He is sympathetic and says, 'Okay, campo,' which means I can remain in camp. Fortunately the venom stays in the leg, and the pain and swelling start to ease over the next three days. Still, I wouldn't like to try marching on it, not just yet.

Trying anything available, I find that the moist inside of a banana skin held against the lump does seem to take out some of the burning. We have no medical supplies of any kind – I shall just have to wait for the swelling and burning sensation to disappear.

We're on the move again, with no excess gear. We will each carry five days' rice and nothing else, so we make the best of our last day in the Jap store to help ourselves to extras – we even find some dried and salted fish. To our great relief we are back on a tarmac road again, heading north. It's a curious situation: nobody wants us and the local military command just gives us rations and tells us to move along to someone else's territory. Presumably there have been telephone calls in all directions, and the end result is to get rid of us. Suits us fine!

When we halt to set up the night's bivouac we observe that there is a group of Siamese huts a few hundred yards away, standing amidst fruit trees. Our master gunner gets permission for a purchasing party; ninety-one of us are escorted by a couple of Nips.

On arrival one of the Nips disappears amongst the huts and the other watches while we buy bananas from the villagers. He then wanders off into the huts, and the first Nip returns to find us all standing around holding bunches of bananas. Immediately he explodes in a rage – he hadn't given us permission to buy and it's no use trying to explain that the other Nippon heitai (soldier) had said we could. Lining us up in a single rank he starts to whack every man on the head with a lengthy piece of bamboo, a two-handed swipe which lands with a loud thwack.

Four men jettison their bananas by discreetly flipping them into the long grass behind us, and they are meticulously excluded. Eighty-seven of us receive a head-ringing thump. My skull seems to swell and deflate in turn as we march back to our camping area, still clutching our bananas. Perversely, I am pleased with myself that I was bloody-minded enough to hang on to my bananas, though they don't taste any better for it.

The march to our next stop is easy going, only some twelve or fifteen kilometres a day. We think that we have been told to take five days to get there, and this regulates our daily stretch. The routine is simple: cook sufficient at daylight for breakfast and midday, and when we bivouac in the afternoon, collect firewood and find water for evening rice and the next day. Our four-gallon cans are invaluable – without them we would have had real problems. When full of water they are awkward to carry, but the marches are brief, almost leisurely, and we never know if there will be water at the next night's camp. And indeed, on one occasion the only water available is in a buffalo wallow, which doesn't taste too good to those who couldn't be bothered to carry their own supply. It's one way to learn!

Occasionally we come to a village, sometimes quite large, and all the inhabitants turn out to line the main street as we pass through. Always there are groups of saffron-robed Buddhist monks who call out benedictions and make goodwill gestures, and throughout the crowd are many who speak English and shout snippets of war news and friendly remarks. It's all very encouraging.

We have not seen telephone wires by the road, but these people are always there, waiting for us. Maybe it's due to the garlic which we have all taken to using generously in our meals and even chew raw during the day – perhaps the wind carries our presence ahead of us! Our garlic consumption started in earnest when our knowledgeable fellows remarked that since Roman days it has been considered in most of Europe as an excellent preventative against fevers, and as an internal disinfectant. In fact, the ancient Egyptians used it extensively, as is shown in their wall paintings. Whatever the facts, we have not had so much as a cold amongst us during our recent exposure to the weather.

And any kind of flavour is welcome; our rations are so insipid. Such is our longing for flavour in our food (after some 3,700 consecutive meals of tasteless slop) that I really cannot find words to adequately describe our tremendous enjoyment in cooking our own meals individually. Using the rice which we carry with us – the top quality rice filched from Jap army stores, that is – we are able to add bits and pieces bought at the roadside. And packets of spices are frequently pressed on us, with no payment expected, by the friendly and generous local people. Our Nips cannot help but see this going on, though they pretend not to, which we take as a favourable sign of the times.

Henry is a Singapore Eurasian in our group of six, and when his first turn comes to cook our evening meal, even I find his curry a bit fierce. Someone asks how many chillies he has put in and he replies, 'Only six.' 'D'you mean for all of us?' 'No, six each!' It's surprising we haven't all suddenly become curly-headed.

There must be something in chillies that produces an all-over feeling of wellbeing – quite definite but elusive to identify. I used to love strongly flavoured curries and Chinese dishes, and am now finding the pungent bite of chillies almost addictive. Occasionally we come across chilli bushes growing wild along the roadside and I am able to pick chillies off the bush and pop them straight into my mouth, crunching up the seeds and skin. Once I get past the heat – with a few hiccups – there is a distinct flavour, fresh and clean, which I find very pleasant. Afterwards, there is a quite definite feeling of having been in some way refreshed and cleansed throughout, almost a purification, and to round it all off my digestion is in perfect equilibrium. Even to me this seems strange, but that's just how it is.

Some of these chillies, by the way, are the short stubby varieties which Malays call 'chilli pedas' – *hot* chillies – the ordinary long red or green kind being 'hardly noticeable'! So the short ones really are powerful, and it is these which cause me a few hiccups. From the most informative book (*The Chemistry of Nutrition*) that I was lucky enough to study back in Wampo, I know that chillies have a higher concentration of vitamin B1 (anti beri-beri) than any other edible plant. So, as a nutritious food which also flushes out my internal plumbing very thoroughly, they are clearly beneficial as well as pleasing to the taste buds.

These improvements in our daily lives have profoundly benefited our personal outlooks. Leaving behind our repressive camp life with its irritating disciplines, we now have relaxing days (for the weather is kind to us) filled with easy marches through changing scenery, contacts with local people who call out encouraging messages, all contributing to a lifting of our spirits out of the great bog of forty months of grim hardship and repression. And our good, satisfying meals top it all off.

We have acquired a buoyant optimism, almost akin to being free men again, which feels marvellous, but we must take very great care not to allow it to be noticed by the Nips. We do not want to risk provoking an outburst of the brutality which is part of their nature. Life is good just now, and must not be spoiled by some foolhardy piece of cocky behaviour. How long this will last we can have no idea. We can only ride along with our happier fortunes, and hope that they will continue.

For some reason not made known to us, we have not made camp for the night after cooking our evening rice but have been told we are marching on in the dark. The Nip officer heads off cross-country at a fast pace, almost a jog-trot, and we have no choice but to keep up with him.

We start to straggle, and in the darkness and occasional

brief downpours we are not always sure that we are on the right track. It is easy to lose sight of the men in front, and even when you can see them you can't know for certain that they are in touch with those ahead. We might all be veering off to one side or the other, for there is no defined track to follow.

The rain and the wet ground keep us cool, although we cannot see clearly where we are putting our bare feet and can only hope there are no snags. The rain stops and there is a feeble waning moon when we catch up with the leaders. We are on the right bank of a broad and swiftly flowing river.

The Nip officer has said that a big bridge is being built somewhere upstream and he has taken a party of our men to see if we can find a boat to get us across. We stretch out on the soaking ground and wait. Eventually a pontoon raft appears with our men aboard, and is poled in to the bank. It is to be used for taking non-swimmers across, and the Nip guards with their gear.

The first crossing commences; the current seizes the raft and starts to carry it away. The steersman thrusts with his pole towards mid river, and suddenly they are in a deep channel and the pole cannot find the bottom.

I am with a group of swimmers who have waded out, holding on to the raft and pushing to help it across the current, when suddenly we find ourselves swimming. It's a long crossing, cutting diagonally across the fast stream to a footing in the shallows on the far side, and then a long haul up against the current to our intended landing point opposite where we started, where there is a clearing in the trees. We hold the raft in place while everyone gets ashore and quickly disappears into the trees, leaving us swimmers to push the raft well upstream and make the crossing back to the other side.

Those who can swim now wade in and get themselves across, and we dummies who made the first crossing are left to cope with all the non-swimmers, who are waiting for their turn on the raft. We are the only men available to do this; everyone else who can swim has gone. It is not a big raft, and it takes six more round-trip voyages to get everyone over. It's raining heavily again and we can hardly see where we are going. By the end of the last trip we are in a thoroughly bloody-minded mood, not to say tired.

We abandon the raft; it can go wherever it wants to go. There is only one path out of the clearing, as far as we can see, and nobody has thought to wait and guide us, so we take it. Half a mile along there is a great glare, and we come into our camping area where several enormous bonfires are blazing. There is a small shack, occupied by our Nip guards. From the look of the area it was in the process of being cleared. Whole tree trunks are piled with masses of brushwood, and it is a number of these which our men have ignited, the flames roaring skywards and throwing out heat all around. Even the rain disappears in steam before it can reach the ground.

I find the other five in our group of six. They've been waiting for something to eat – it's my turn to cook, they're hungry, where the hell have I been all this time? Muttering imprecations I find a long bamboo spear, dangle our four-gallon can from a notch at the end and hold it in the side of the furnace. If it weren't for the rain pouring over me I wouldn't be able to stand the heat, despite my being well clear with my long pole.

The water comes to the boil in thirty seconds; the rain keeps the pole from catching alight. I have to juggle the can's position to prevent it from boiling over, the heat is so fierce. When I guess the rice is cooked I take the can off the fire, plugging my hat over it to keep the rain out. A few minutes to steam off, and it is perfect – a triumph under such difficult conditions. We share it out, break an egg or two into it, and feel the warmth spreading inside.

'Congratulations to the cook!'

'Ungrateful buggers!' is my reply.

It stops raining; the moon is with us again. The party which went to find the pontoon has an interesting story. There is a part-built concrete bridge, the foundations on either side of the river nearly completed. Work stopped two years ago because the supply of cement and steel dried up. Since then the four Swiss engineers have lived in a nearby Siamese village – they can't leave but the Siamese government pays them enough to live on, and they are enjoying an idyllic life with the local village maidens to keep them company. Our men listened to BBC news on their wireless sets, and the war is now going well on all fronts.

While this news is being passed around we hear an aircraft approaching; we see it coming straight at us at a low altitude, as if using our great conflagrations as a guide. Our Nips start to scream hysterically, apparently telling us to put the fires out, although the nearest water is the river, half a mile away. How significant is it that any plane is assumed by them to be ours, and not theirs?

The plane banks to its right, flying very slowly, and dips even lower until we lose it behind our ring of trees. The two engines seem to be barely ticking over. It is a low-wing monoplane and its underbelly silhouette is plain as it tilts to make the turn.

'It's a Nip bomber, like those we saw over Singapore.'

'No it isn't. With the Nip bombers the leading edge of the wings was swept back, the trailing edge at right angles to the fuselage. This one's just the opposite; the leading edge is at right angles. Remember those silhouettes in the Jap identification leaflets? I'd say this is what they showed as a C47.'

The aircraft must have passed right over the bridge; it was certainly in that area when it disappeared. We don't see it again for another chance to observe its shape, but there can really be no doubt that we have identified it correctly; the differences are too marked and were spotted by several of us, so no mistake can be possible.

Was it dropping weapons, or bringing in men by parachute? We are all most intrigued, and agree that we must be ready to act quickly if we are suddenly confronted by something of this sort.

We have stopped for the night in a pleasant area. Trees provide firewood and there is a broad stream for a bathe and fresh water. The Nips have designated the point we can use on the bank of the stream – downstream from their area – and there is a general hum of talk and snapping twigs as we settle down for the evening meal. Suddenly there is an outburst of angry Nip shouting; one of our men is being bashed. All sound is abruptly switched off; there is a blanket silence while we all stand up to see what is happening. How are these spontaneous events triggered off, so that every man in our crowd behaves in exactly the same way at exactly the same moment?

The Nip becomes aware of 850 pairs of eyes fixed on him, and is immediately unsettled. He stops the bashing, looks around uneasily. Clearly nervous, he starts to walk to the patch where all the other Nips are grouped for the night, but his path takes him right through the middle of our area. Putting on an air of bravado he swishes his towel around and starts to swagger. He is still nailed by our stares, hostile and steady, unblinking, and in a dozen yards he starts to speed up, walking fast.

Sweat springs out on his face. He is within touching distance of us but makes no attempt to push us aside, or to shout at us to move out of his way. As he turns aside to go between us he meets more and more glowering eyes. His head twitches from side to side and his eyes start to bulge – the strain is becoming too much for him.

His nerve crumples, he lets out a high-pitched scream and breaks into a trot, then into a run, and finally a panicky dash. Our eyes meet him and follow him – he must, surely, feel them pricking his back – and when he is clear of us the laughter starts. An initial chuckle here and there soon swells to a great rumbling chant of victory, won over a despised enemy by sheer willpower and force of character. The Nip's humiliation is mighty and it spreads to his mates – in the Japanese philosophy they all share in his disgrace, cannot escape it. And by doing nothing to retaliate, they have accepted it as a defeat.

It could not have happened even a couple of months ago – there would have been instant reaction of the violent kind which is all the Nips understand. There must be some subtle change in their perception of us. Have they come to know that the war is now going badly for them, and are they starting to feel uncertain about us? If there has been such a change in them, have we sensed it and responded in our visible outward appearance to them?

Tenko in the morning finds our Nips subdued and in a hurry to get it over and the march resumed. They do not face us squarely and do not say a word, turning away and waving a hand at us to get moving. Things are indeed changing!

We reach Raheng, also known as Tak City – an odd name, surely, for Siam? – and our first view of the place is a real surprise. We head off our tarmac road onto a concrete road running westward and come to a tall monument around which the road circles to continue between modern style two-storey shophouses built of concrete. All totally out of character with any town we have yet seen, and totally devoid of people. There is nobody in the buildings, not even a bicycle on the street. It is only a small area, and then we pass through what look like ancient city walls of brick and earth. The builders do not seem to have learned how to build a round arch, but used a chiselled block of stone across the top of a doorway or passage through the wall. We bivouac in the grounds of an old temple, the ruins of the central building being propped up to prevent collapse. It must be a place of some significance, to have such trouble taken to preserve the remnants.

It starts to rain again, heavily – after all, this is well into the rainy season – but it is nothing in comparison to the incredible downpours which we experienced in the hills to the west.

There is no comfort here. The ground, which used to be courtyards, is layered with bricks and rock slabs, there is no shelter from the weather, no water supply, and we have to dig a small latrine in a far corner to avoid damage to the temple grounds. Lighting cooking fires, with wood brought in by us, is unavoidable. We can only keep to using stone slabs which can be cleaned up afterwards. We wonder if the local people object to this use of their historic places.

Well, maybe they have complained, for we have moved to another site on the outskirts of the town. It is an open area of grass with a narrow tarmac road running along the longer north side, and at the eastern end there is a footpath from the road towards the town. The road and path are busy all day long with people on foot and riding bicycles. They wave and smile at us cheerily as they pass, calling out in Siamese and, occasionally, English.

There is a dense thicket on the far side of the road, and in order to allow us some privacy we have been permitted to dig latrines out of the public gaze amongst the bushes. The attitude of the Nips has certainly changed – they have never before shown any sensitivity towards us. Even more puzzling, it must be happening with the approval of that jumped-up twerp, our Nip officer.

The latrine site means, of course, that we have to cross the road to use it. A Nip stands on duty to give permission to cross over, and to see that we don't have contact with the Siamese, but he soon finds it impossible to oversee the constant comings and goings of 850 men. He gives up and disappears.

In no time at all the local traders set up their mobile food stalls and charcoal braziers in the shrubbery. Everything is remarkably cheap – would this be another way of showing friendship?

Then we have electrifying news. A short length of bamboo is tossed in amongst us. Inside is a rolled sheet of paper with a message written in clear English: 'Do not try to escape. The war must end soon. The Allies have dropped what they call an atomic bomb on Japs. The casualties are enormous. We will give you more news later.'

What is an atomic bomb? How powerful is it? I recall our physics master at school saying that if all the energy in the atoms contained in a single pound of coal could be utilised and released under control, it would be sufficient to drive the *Queen Mary* across the Atlantic and back. If it were released without control, it could destroy the earth. I pass this on, for what it is worth, and it provokes animated discussion. Our professor of mathematics confirms that there was a great deal of research during the thirties – the atom has actually already been split in laboratory experiments, so maybe a form of bomb has indeed been built.

That night a group of thirteen men slips out of our bivouac unobserved. The men are out only a few minutes when they are intercepted by soldiers of the Siamese army, which has apparently been keeping watch on us since our arrival. They have had a standing force nearby, in readiness to intervene if the Nips start anything unpleasant such as a massacre.

Our men listened in to BBC news broadcasts, and the note which we were given about an atomic bomb is correct. It is expected that Japan will soon have to sue for peace. It was then decided that one of the thirteen should return to tell us exactly how things stand, as events might now move very fast and we must be ready to scatter. The remaining twelve decide to stay with the Siamese army, which must have been a most difficult choice to make.

All this took place during the hours of darkness, the Nips apparently being completely unaware of any movements. At tenko just after sunrise, our master gunner decides it would be politic to inform the Nip officer that we are twelve men short, before they find out in the counting.

As expected, the officer explodes in a fearsome rage, screaming and shouting and even slipping out his Samurai sword and slashing the air all around our master gunner's body and head. To his enormous credit, our man, who is elderly and has never been a fighting soldier, stands calm and unmoving while the razor-edged sword hisses around him. A single move and the officer in his madness may well slice him up.

It is some time before the Nip runs out of steam – long enough for us to become decidedly strung up as we look on. His soldiers are also edgy, fingering their rifles and eyeing us nervously, not knowing what to do while their officer rants on. It is a highly dangerous situation, unpredictable, and unsteady nerves on either side could precipitate violence.

Quite suddenly the officer calms down and sheathes his sword. He demands to be shown where the men slept, and he is shown their personal kits still there. Maybe they have not escaped, just gone into the town? We don't know. All we know is that they were not there at daylight, and not across the road at the benjo, so we reported their absence 'as is our duty'. The master gunner's face gives nothing away.

We are ordered to stand where we slept, and the five men on each side of the missing men are made to stand out front where they will be under special guard. They should have known of their comrades' intention to escape, and stopped them from doing so. They may be executed for failing in their duty. No one may move away for any reason. The Nip officer's fluency in English surprises us. There is no doubt he knows what he is saying and means it. Misunderstanding will not be an excuse.

We wait and watch. The sun climbs into a cloudless sky – it's going to be hot. The officer distributes his few men on all sides of our patch and sends one off at the double, presumably to report the event to the local HQ.

An hour passes, a Jap army truck rolls up and stops. A Kempei-tai officer gets out of the cab and waits for our officer to approach him. It is very obvious who is boss, and that our man is up to his neck in trouble, by the way he bows much lower, and holds the position far longer, than the Kempei-tai officer. He is in disgrace, and knows it! We don't have any sympathy for him, but the appearance of the Kempei-tai, rather than the army, is alarming. These troglodyte horrors would chill anyone's blood just by their frightening presence, and without waiting for orders they have positioned themselves all around, automatic guns on the ground with magazines fitted and the gunners lying on their bellies behind them, ready to open fire.

The discussion is terminated abruptly; our Nip officer is marched off with a Kempei-tai trooper on either side of him, obviously under arrest. An arm is waved and in seconds they are back in their truck, and leave.

Nobody knows what to do. We start to relax and pick up water bottles, but these small movements bring angry shouts from our guards. It is not until the Nip warrant officer – equivalent to our regimental sergeant-major – walks up to our master gunner and talks to him that shouts of 'Yasumi' and 'Stand easy' tell us that we are back to normal.

The Nip WO is, we understand, a professional soldier who has spent all his life in the army. We have noticed that he wears a purple decoration on his shirt, and this must be of a particularly high order because officers have been seen to salute him and bow. We hear that this is a rare decoration bestowed only by the hands of the Emperor personally, for highly meritorious service, and for that reason it demands respect from all ranks, even senior officers. Don't ask me where all this kind of information comes from – it simply circulates, and in this instance fits in with our own observations, which are very keen and don't miss much at all.

Maybe his decoration imposes a personal dignity on him, but we have found this Nip WO to be even-tempered, a disciplinarian but very fair, all through this march. We are happy to have him in charge of us instead of that temperamental twit of an officer. He seems to know of our master gunner's special standing in our army, and there is a mutual respect and understanding between them, which is a good thing.

A few days later another short piece of bamboo lobs in, with another message telling of a second atomic bomb. The first city is named as Hiroshima, which we haven't heard of, and now Nagasaki, which is familiar to all of us. The devastation of these two cities, and the loss of life, have been terrible. The note adds that it is rumoured that the Japanese government has put out peace feelers.

Our guards don't seem to have been informed that their homeland is being destroyed – their attitude towards us is unchanged. We, on the other hand, are beginning to fill with growing excitement, but are sensible enough not to allow it to show to them.

Three mornings later all is speedo, pack up and be ready to march in half an hour. This is not difficult. We fold up our blankets or whatever we have, stow it all in a haversack or pack, and we're ready. It takes about three minutes. We move out early, but not too soon for hundreds of Siamese to gather and watch. This time there is frank cheering and hand-clapping, much to the puzzlement of our Nips.

We haven't had time to eat but we stop by the roadside a few kilometres out to cook up some rice. Again we carry five days' rations and head north, marching comfortably on tarmac in pleasant weather. We arrive at a road junction with a signpost in Siamese script. Grandpa Bill, one of our older men who has traded in Bangkok for years, is able to decipher the names – Lampang to the north and Pitsanlok to the east. The Nips dither for a bit, then decide on Pitsanlok which, of course, they cannot read on the signpost.

That afternoon we turn off the road to bivouac in a fallow paddy field. Down the road we see a village, and the Nip WO agrees to letting a small purchasing party go to the shops to see what's available. The squad moves off with a couple of Nips as escort while we settle down to dig latrine trenches – always the first thing to do – and prepare the evening rice.

The purchasing party comes back with wonderful news. On reaching the village general store the proprietor, a Chinese man, sat the Nips at a table in the corner with a bottle of hooch to keep them quiet. Disappearing out to the back of the shop, he returned wearing a coat over his grubby sweatshirt. Opening the front of the coat he displayed a sheet of paper pinned to his shirt: 'THE WAR IS OVER. THE JAPS ARE DEFEATED, AND HAVE SURRENDERED'. Off he went again, and came back minus coat and paper. All smiles and chuckles, he piled sugar and tobacco, fruit and eggs into a basket, and waved our men off. The Nips, now half-sozzled, lurched out in pursuit.

So here we are, in a bare paddy field miles from any-where, in a countryside thick with enemy troops who don't know they have been defeated, and with a miserable bunch of Nips to protect us.

We eat our evening meal, the sky is yellow and scarlet with the setting sun, and we hear an aircraft coming from the west. It is flying low, not more than 1,000 feet above us, we think, and it is all lit up. Navigation lights are on, and the cabin windows bright. It is smallish and has twin tailfins and two engines – it looks like the familiar old Lockheed Hudson.

Flying low with all lights on, and from the west where our people are! There can be only one explanation: it must be carrying our representatives to Bangkok to receive the Japanese military surrender! Is that a leap of imagination? Or is it clear thinking? We are buzzing with chatter, going over every detail.

Eventually we settle down for the night, but before we doze off a string of Jap army trucks comes to a halt where we are camped. An officer dismounts and our Nip WO has what looks like an earnest conversation with him. The trucks move on, and our Nip WO calls his men together and addresses them. There is a lot of peering towards us and quiet muttering; the sentry resumes his beat.

At morning tenko our master gunner takes the initiative. Having called us to attention he walks up to the Nip WO and speaks loudly enough for all of us to hear his voice: 'The war is over, finished. Japan has been defeated, beaten, lost the war. There are twelve of you and 850 of us. What are you going to do?'

The master gunner really is a marvel. With only bits and pieces of each other's language and, most importantly, patience and goodwill on both sides, he and the Nip WO work out an arrangement which he announces to us while his opposite number speaks to his own people.

'He knows that the war is over, and that Japan has lost. However, he has been ordered to take us to the next town, Pitsanlok, and he wants to do that. He is responsible for our safety, and this area is full of armed Jap troops who may be very angry. On our own we might all be killed, but if he stays with us we will reach Pitsanlok. He understands that his men must not touch us, no bashings, and I have said that you will all behave properly. It is a sensible deal, and I want all of you to back me up. No fooling around, keep your discipline for the next two days, no arguments or provocations. Be ready to march as soon as possible.'

The change in circumstances is enormous, but the outward appearance of our march shows none of it. Except that we stay bunched up behind our MG and the Nip WO, who march side by side while the Nips take up station all around, whereas we usually string ourselves out in a long patchy line. The wisdom of our new arrangement very soon becomes apparent.

Fallen out at the side of the road across a wide bare plain is a company of Jap troops, about 100 of them. As we approach, they rise to their feet, rifles at the ready. Their attitude is uncertain but could well be hostile and touchy. Our Nip WO immediately marches up to their officer, who notices his purple decoration and snaps to attention, saluting. A few words and the Jap troops relax, settling down to rest on the grass verge.

Standing there and looking on, wondering what might happen, we recognise the Jap officer. He is the one we met on a work party at Nakhon Nayok, who assured us that no Japanese soldier would allow himself to be captured but would rather kill himself. And amongst us we have to have a brainless humorist who steps forward and points at him, saying, 'You're the fellow who would rather kill himself than be taken prisoner. Well, we've won the war, you've lost! Can I lend you a knife?'

The utter stupidity of this smirking nitwit handing out such a gratuitous insult appals us. At this moment, after all we have been through, we are put at risk of instant death by the unbelievable inanity of one of our own men! What's the matter with him? Does he think that, now that the referee has blown his whistle for the end of the game, it's all over and we can toss friendly insults at each other?

After a frozen moment the Jap WO speaks sharply to the officer, and our MG shouts, 'Bring that man to me!' An angry dressing-down – and soothing words in Japanese, in full view of all – brings calm. We are extremely lucky that, although the Jap officer understood what was said to him, his men did not. Had they done so, I doubt that the situation could have been controlled. And only our Nip's purple ribbon kept the Jap officer in check. Without it he would have been brushed aside.

We resume our march, and our idiot is going to have his

arse thoroughly kicked when we camp tonight. In the meantime every man will give him a large piece of his mind.

We bivouac for our last night on this march; tomorrow we reach Pitsanlok, if the gods allow it. What awaits us there we have no idea at all.

Just as it did on the first night of this march, the heavens open on us, thunder crashes with almost physical impact and lightning stabs into the land all around us. There is no Nip sentry pretending to be a lightning conductor, and we get no sleep in the roaring, dazzling downpour. But who cares?

We step out briskly, full of energy, and reach Pitsanlok before midday. Not the town itself, but a large hutted camp capable of holding thousands – evidently a permanent Jap army base, now deserted.

It has a pole and barbed wire fence with a formal gateway, and lined up outside it is our reception committee. It is quite astonishing; we had never expected anything like this: a row of seven senior Jap officers in full parade uniforms, polished and immaculate. As we approach they spring to attention, and when we are called to a halt there are formal salutes all round. It looks as if this is to be a sticky bullshit affair, until our Nip WO marches up to them. Again his purple decoration has its effect. And these are senior officers – we recognise the colonels' badges of rank, but some are evidently senior to that.

Immediately the severe expressions break into welcoming smiles, and the group loosens. In fluent English we are asked, 'Is there anything you want? What can we do for you? Please tell us if you need anything. We want to help you in any way we can.' No sign of reluctant acceptance of our reversed positions. Privileged guests being met by the entire management of the Ritz hotel could not wish for a more amiable and helpful welcome.

There is plenty we want. We are shown the camp food stores and cookhouses and invited to help ourselves, and by mid afternoon a small convoy of trucks brings us waterproof groundsheets, blankets (of quite magnificent quality, no doubt intended for senior officers), dressings and other useful medical supplies. Also toothbrushes and toothpaste, soap, towels, cotton singlets and shorts, shirts. But no razors – Japs don't use them.

Except for our party the camp is empty. We settle down to enjoy our new style of living while our master gunner tries to find out what is happening amongst our own people about bringing us all together from all over Siam. It will take a few days, for the Siamese telephone system was not up to much, so I'm told, at the beginning of the war, and will surely be a lot worse now. Maybe our Japanese hosts will help through their army system. Meanwhile, our various sores are healing up, and we are soapy clean for a welcome change, and altogether spruced up.

It's a lazy life. No tenkos or parades, for we don't need to be counted – nobody is going to be outside the camp when transport is found to take us south back to Bangkok, or wherever we are to assemble for repatriation. Repatriation, going home – the magic words!

We calculate we have walked nearly 800 kilometres to get here, barefoot all the way.

15

Going Home

AUGUST TO NOVEMBER 1945

It is several days before the news comes. We are going back to Sraburi, which we passed through at the start of the hike from Nakhon Nayok. It seems that the Jap local command expects us to march all the way there, and when asked about trains our MG is told that very few are running.

In fact, there are only thirteen locomotives in service in the whole of Siam. When is the next train due into Pitsanlok? Day after tomorrow, but it's full of Jap troops going through, not stopping. Well, bloody well stop it, get the troops off and into this camp and we will have the train! Surprised stares, recovery from shock, and the train is ours – all apologies, smiles and bows!

Midnight comes and I click into my twenty-fourth birthday. My twenty-first was in River Valley Road Camp, in Singapore. It happened to be a yasumi day, and all my friends contributed to a surprisingly good curry. One of my precious memories!

It's a long drag through the dark hours and morning, but we finally reach Sraburi. The local population turns out to cheer as we hike off to what was once a POW camp, and now is a main centre for gathering our men from all over the country. There are still some men on that accursed railway, and others working on a lorry route through similar country from Mergui to the interior. All over Siam there are working camps, some not known to our senior officers, and information is slow in coming in.

Arriving at Sraburi Camp we are met by medical officers. Have we had any illnesses, casualties on our march? No casualties, but four men with pustulant skin eruptions. An immediate examination – chickenpox or smallpox? Can't tell for certain. If it's smallpox the whole of the POW evacuation planning which is now in progress will have to be reviewed, maybe even cancelled. We are herded into a far corner of the camp, in quarantine. The possibilities are too serious for leniency and taking chances. A wire is strung along a row of stakes, sealing us off, and it will be three weeks before we can be let out. Three weeks! Behind barbed wire again! Everybody will be gone by then, we shall be on our own!

A new cookhouse is set up inside our area. There will be food on tap to keep us happy. It doesn't succeed in doing that, but the rich pork chops and steaks do bring us all out in irritating pink rashes, which fade as our systems adapt to cope with all this food.

In the old camp the Nips had a duck farm with a pond, so we have drums of duck soup – the meat is too tough, even for us – and there are feathers everywhere. We shall be happy enough eating our way through quarantine.

Two squat little vehicles roll into the camp. We have never seen anything like them. The crews tell us they are called Jeeps. One has radio equipment and Signal Corps men; the other has four of the most impressive soldiers imaginable. Hefty fellows armed with Tommy guns, Webley forty-fives, knives stuck into leggings, hand grenades all over them – and two machine guns mounted on each vehicle.

The signallers are in contact with Rangoon within minutes. The commandos have discussions with our people – we need a couple of trucks and the local township cannot supply them. No trouble at all. A Jeep whizzes off to the main road and waits for a Jap army convoy to show up. There must be plenty of these moving over the roads, for they will be bringing in their own troops to concentration areas where the Allies can disarm and watch them. In two hours they have stopped a line of trucks, turned everyone out of the first two, and brought the trucks back to us.

The signallers report to Rangoon that our men, as POWs, had nearly completed a runway for the Jap air force, and it is now ready for Dakotas. Rangoon, HQ 14th Army, will fly in Dakotas with uniforms and other supplies at notified intervals. The trucks will take out twenty-four men for Rangoon, and bring back the supplies to camp.

Our evacuation program will be drawn by lot, so everyone has a fair chance of getting out early. Except for us, bored, itching, and envious watching two or three truckloads departing daily. It's just as well men are being taken out, for more are still coming in and the camp stays full.

We have been told that the Jeeps were brought in by glider, which opened up for them to be driven out ready for action. The army has indeed pepped up its imagination since our day! It's going to be interesting to catch up on it all. Meanwhile we must wait patiently. We have become very good at that – waiting patiently!

We have a visitor – not a welcome one, but we find we cannot turn him away. The Mad Mongol, that twisted mistake for a human being, has been brought to the camp gate by another Nip who speaks a little English. He has been severely bashed and, in addition, his nose and ears have been hacked off, leaving his head bloody and gory from his raw wounds. His companion manages to tell us that the Mad Mongol has always had a bad reputation for ill-treating the Siamese womenfolk everywhere he has been, and the villagers have taken the opportunity to punish him. He has asked to be brought to us for medical treatment, because his own people cannot treat his awful mutilation.

Our medical officer has been pestered by this dangerously mad savage in one camp after another, and has been bashed several times for not giving treatment when demanded. The fact that we had no medicines didn't satisfy the Mad Mongol, who took out his maniac rages on everyone who displeased him.

Nevertheless, our MO does not reject him. We now have sufficient medical supplies, and the MO patches him up as well as possible. We agree that he is right to do so, despite a hard edge of hostility that says the Mad Mongol has only got what he thoroughly deserves. The manner of it sickens us, but some kind of severe punishment was certainly due.

The Mad Mongol is escorted out of the camp area, to find his own way back to his people. We understand that they are in a Jap barracks only a few kilometres away, confined to their huts on pain of being shot by perimeter guards if they come outside. We hear that a number of Australians, waiting for ships to repatriate them, have offered to do such camp guard duty, in the hope of picking off a few old acquaintances!

A couple of days before our quarantine is due to end we have another visitor, totally unexpected and just dropping in without any fuss: Lady Mountbatten, in Red Cross uniform with

badges of high rank. Welcomed enthusiastically with prolonged cheering, she charms all of us with her friendliness and
bright personality. She is the wife of Lord Louis Mountbatten,
commander-in-chief of our side of the Japanese war, and tells
how repeated requests for us to be allowed to receive Red
Cross parcels, and to write and receive letters regularly, were
flatly rejected by the Japanese government throughout our
period of captivity. Also, now that they know how we were
treated, and how many men died, those Japanese officers and
officials who were responsible are being rounded up, to stand
trial.

Suddenly she spots our lot, standing behind a strand of
wire separately from the others crowding around her, and
wants to know why: 'Surely they're not all defaulters on a
charge, are they?'

There's a burst of laughter, and the camp medical officer
explains. A senior MO flew in last week to examine all of us
and still couldn't be certain whether our four suspect cases had
had smallpox infection or not, so we are still in quarantine as
a precaution, for two more days.

Declaring that if nothing had shown up and there were
only two days to go, Lady Mountbatten asks that we be
released from quarantine. In moments we are swarming
around her, and she is talking freely to us, asking questions
and giving us news from home. She has to leave, saying she is
so pleased to see us all in such good spirits. She has only a
single officer as escort, and her black American limousine is
driven by a uniformed Japanese soldier, impassive and facing
rigidly to his front. A wonderful lady!

Now that we are able to roam around we head for the
truck to take us into Sraburi. We have all been given enough
Siamese money for an evening out, and we are dropped off
where the food stalls and small shops are. Starting at one point

we visit every stall in turn, buying something different at each one and picking up a bottle of rice wine to go with it. This hooch has a Siamese government distillery label on the bottle, guaranteeing purity and quality. It's pleasant stuff to drink and not very potent. Which means that by the time we catch our truck back to camp we are full of both good food and warming wine, in a happy state and ready for a night's sleep. It's an absolutely marvellous feeling; our present is contented and our future is assured.

The mayor of Sraburi presents us with a battery-operated wireless receiver, and when we tune in we catch an Australian program beamed especially to all ex-POWs in Siam. A gloriously rich voice overwhelms us, a soprano whose name is known to us – Joan Hammond – may God bless her for reaching out to us at this particular time from across the seas.

It is an emotional time, two great ladies in one day, the first women's voices speaking English we have heard for nearly four years. We start to give real thought to what we have been missing, suppressed during our captivity to avoid unbearable homesickness, and now we must think how to bring ourselves back into the world we used to know. We are all older, in more ways than just years, and we have been so isolated that we might have been on another planet. We have to ease ourselves out of years of restraint without jumping off the rails. We shall be back with men and women who fought the war in conventional ways; we have had our own unique experience of war, and we do not know for certain how we shall be received by the others or how well they will understand the oddities which we must surely have developed. Or, indeed, if we shall be able to understand theirs!

But for now, the truck has brought us back to camp, we hand the wireless set in at admin, and sleep is our first requirement.

* * *

Days pass, and the chosen squads are waved happily out to the waiting Dakotas as their numbers come up. While we were in quarantine our names were not in the draw, but it matters not to us. The great move is under way. It is an enormous program made more complex by the fact that all the 14th Army's planning had been for a seaborne invasion of Malaya, and had suddenly had to be reshaped, ships and aircraft redeployed, for a peaceful occupation and for bringing out tens of thousands of prisoners for repatriation. We are told that the men of the 14th Army have voluntarily taken a cut in rations, so that we can be supplied with foods that we have been deprived of for so long.

We are not in disgrace for letting Singapore be captured so easily, as we have feared we might be. Possibly it is now accepted that we were never given a chance to fight properly, never had the weapons and support which we should have had. To that we would add that political interference and ineptitude, coupled with military incompetence at high level in certain places, is a combination which the ordinary soldier cannot overcome. All he can do is fight and die or, as in our case, become a prisoner, while those responsible retire on undeserved pensions.

Surely the truth will come out some day, when the stringencies of war have gone and guilty men can be named in public. We can wait, as we have been forced to wait for far too long. Our time will come.

Our squad number is called. We have been watching for it since yesterday's last party rolled out, and we are ready packed with more belongings than we have had for years. Our Jap army truck badly needs maintenance; it belches and staggers but finally gets us there. This is the airfield which our people were constructing for the Jap air force but had not completed when the war ended. It was finished off by our own men, helped willingly by the local townsfolk.

The Dakota is parked at the extreme end of the grass runway, its crew standing under the nose with big smiles of welcome and shouts of, 'Hello there, glad to be here to take you home', and suchlike. The pilot looks us over and his eyebrows go up. 'Say, you're the first lot of ex-POWs I've seen and I expected a bunch of skinny skeletons, but you all look to be in pretty good shape!'

Indeed we do, stunningly suntanned and, by now, reasonably fleshed out, clean-shaven and in fresh uniforms. Something has to be said to put the pilot in the picture without hurting his feelings, and my mind scrabbles for suitable words. I find myself saying, 'We've had six weeks of good feeding. You should see the 20,000 buried alongside the railway – they don't look too good at all!' To my relief nobody takes offence at my almost involuntary response.

Smiles change to red-faced embarrassment, apologies are stammered out, but in a few seconds all is smoothed over. We ask the pilot if we will be flying over the railway – we would like an opportunity to shit on it from a great altitude, as the saying goes. Afraid not; we have just enough fuel to get back to Rangoon by the shortest route.

Takeoff is towards the camp. Men wave, their cheers soundless as we roar low overhead then swing towards Rangoon. The pilot gives us a special treat by circling the great Shwe Dagon Shrine, Rangoon's world-famous landmark, its gilded dome glowing in the sunlight – a sight to remember.

As we aim for the landing strip, losing altitude, we can see through the pilot's windscreen that there is a Dakota finishing its run at the far end. There is little space to spare, for each side of the strip is lined wing-to-wing with scores of Dakotas parked facing the runway. All the aircraft have a flying horse symbol painted on the nose, with the word PEGASUS.

As we touch down there is a rattling clatter; the surface of the runway is carpeted with steel plating locked together. As we wheel off at the end of the runway we look back to see another Dakota touching down. A busy airport indeed, to us who have never seen more than twenty-seven planes in a formation, and those were Japanese bombers at that!

An army truck is backed up ready when the aircraft door is opened. We pile in with our kit, and our Indian soldier driver zooms off, a veritable Jehu. Nearing the city we stop at a military police checkpoint. A sergeant peers in, counts us, shouts out, 'Welcome back, lads,' and gives the driver a chit. He has a record of available beds in the military hospitals in Rangoon, and has directed us to one of them. I'm thinking, if there's more than one hospital, how the hell am I going to find Ron? If he's here, that is, and didn't end up in Bangkok.

We swing in through the big gates of the General Hospital, round a circular bed of flowers and shrubs, and keep moving past the front steps. At the top, amongst a group of legless men on crutches, is Ron! I bawl out his name, waving frantically to catch his attention, and leap out of the back of the truck. Just in time. They had paused only to decide which way they would stroll up the street – in another few minutes I would have missed him.

We quickly learn that efficiency is the watchword in the 14th Army. The first consideration is 'Get it done!', paperwork can follow and even then, only if it's unavoidable. We are checked in rapidly, led to our ward, allocated beds, introduced to the nursing staff and given leave tickets to walk out until sunset, all in a few minutes.

In the morning there is an overall medical inspection to see whether we have any infections or need immediate treatment. And also to judge if we are fit to travel to England, for at the beginning of the repatriation program a lot of seriously ill men were flown home by RAF ambulance planes. Despite skilled nursing on the way, many died, too weakened by years of privation to survive the journey, and now all passages are to be by sea, but only if you are reasonably fit.

Ron and I have a problem. Our last message from Mum was dated July 1942, more than three years ago. She was in India then, but where is she now? And Dad, last seen in May 1942 working as a civilian internee on the Singapore docks, is he still alive? Does he have news of us, and does Mum know we are still alive?

There is a table in the hospital lobby, staffed by a lady in Red Cross uniform; we will talk to her. She listens to us and will be delighted to help. She takes our details and asks us to call back in twenty-four hours. We do so, and she can tell us that Dad is alive and well in Singapore, and that he has been told that we are in Rangoon. The Red Cross in London has cabled that Mum is back in England and is registered with them, they have an address and will contact her. Come back tomorrow, there should be more news then. How incredibly efficient!

Next morning our lady has Mum's address. She has been told that we are in Rangoon awaiting repatriation and are both well, apart from Ron losing his leg. Now that we know where she is we will be listed for a ship to England. And she has heard that the amputation cases will be on the first draft to go, and she will ensure that I will be in the same draft to travel, being Ron's brother.

We are bursting with thanks, but she smiles modestly and says it's all part of her job. We will have a week or so to wait for sailing day, and we must be sure to come back to her if we have any problem. As a parting gift she gives us telegram forms for free – priority! – telegrams to Mum in England and Dad in Singapore!

Really, there is a palpable atmosphere of victory in Rangoon, an electric tingle that we breathe in and see in the faces and bearing of our 14th Army men, both British and Indian. It's a tails-up, cock-a-hoop attitude, coming from a tremendous victory after years of grim adversity, and we see it everywhere. There are hundreds of posters put up for public viewing. People who are wanted by the 14th Army, such as Subhas Chandra Bose, an Indian politician said to have collaborated freely with the Japanese, and who was influential in persuading tens of thousands of Indian troops to defect and join the Japanese army as a new Indian national army. And people to avoid: a list of notorious prostitutes in Rangoon who had infected scores of servicemen with venereal diseases.

And we are provided with hours of films taken during the war, life in England and America, battle footage in the Pacific Islands and in Burma. We do not like the grating, hate-filled voice of an American commentator when Jap soldiers stagger out of a bunker, burning head to foot as flame-throwing tanks hurl fire at them. 'Burn, burn, let them burn, let them roast!' He goes on and on, turning our stomachs – we, who hate and despise Japs as much as he ever can, find this venomous commentary totally beyond acceptance.

We see the ruins of Hiroshima and Nagasaki after destruction by atom bombs, and a film of Tokyo after the fire raids last March, when the civilian casualties were actually higher than in the atomised cities. But we catch the point immediately; the atom bomb requires only one bomber to get through, whereas the Tokyo raids needed hundreds. We all admit to each other that we are physically chilled at the implications, for there has never been a weapon of war developed by one nation which has not been improved upon – can that be the right term? – by others, and used against the originators. Will we be next to be atomised? These must be the bombs we heard of at Raheng.

And there is film of campaigning in Europe, the shattered monastery at Monte Cassino. Was that necessary? Or was it just the barbarism and insanity of war? And shambles of German cities – well, they started it, didn't they? – and dreadful scenes in Auschwitz and Dachau. Trenches filled with corpses, a British army bulldozer the only way to move thousands of bodies lying in the compounds, for mass burial. Even the Japs didn't do that sort of thing! We are shaken, disgusted, frightened – all this was happening while we were dying slowly on that accursed railway, and thinking we were having a hard time! Well, we were, but look what was going on in other places: atrocities energetically carried out by nations we used to think were civilised and, indeed, almost our kith and kin!

What sort of world are we coming back to?

We have been told that the amputation men, with me in the party as general help for them, will be in the first draft to sail aboard the troopship *Worcestershire* in a few days' time. It is, in fact, the first troopship to be allocated for repatriation. Meanwhile, we are required to fill in a couple of forms which will be lodged with the 14th Army legal eagles for studying. The first asks for the names of Japanese and Korean troops who were responsible for any kind of atrocity or brutal behaviour towards us. The second is for naming any of our own people who collaborated improperly with the enemy or who actively worked with the enemy. We are told that we shall not be allowed to leave Rangoon until these documents are completed.

This raises all kinds of queries. Atrocities are one category, but brutality was simply a part of Japanese army practices, and we came to regard it – after the initial shock – as routine and only to be expected from savage barbarians. And there is a very wide range of brutal acts, from relatively mild to severe beyond any justification, and occasionally done just for the pleasure of doing it! We saw that frequently.

And as for our own people, we know of no soldier who actively collaborated with the enemy. But should we include officers such as the colonel at Tonchan, who could not bring himself to speak to Staff-Sergeant Furobashi, The Tiger, and thus did nothing to try to ease the lot of his men in the interests of preserving his personal concept of dignity? Would he have been able to achieve anything worthwhile if he had 'lowered' himself to try? Maybe not, but he would have had the respect of the men in his charge. Do we mention him?

Or do we complain about the professional RAMC colonel who watched the dreadful deterioration at Tarsao 'Hospital' Camp without even speaking to the Nips? That's the way we saw it.

In both cases literally thousands of men saw it the same way. Whether or not some improvement might have been achieved, the whole point in our view is that those officers should have suppressed their petty egos and *tried*, and *tried* again. There were many senior officers who, to their eternal credit, had the moral courage to keep their men's welfare in constant consideration, and who performed miracles large and small. And had their faces walloped in the process.

How does each of us, individually, assess hearsay and

only brief personal experience with particular cases? Do we complain about the great general body of officers of the rank of major and below, who almost to a man completely ignored our existence and concentrated solely on passing the tedious days with as little discomfort to themselves as possible? Who did nothing to help the sick in ways within their reach, such as reading to them – the officers had stacks of books – or simply holding conversations, the very ordinary doings of people helping each other in difficult times? It was their duty as commissioned officers, and they failed shamefully.

As our medical officer put it: 'My patients would have their misery considerably lightened if the officers would get up off their fat lazy arses, and DO something to show interest.' Pungent words, said deliberately loudly, in the hearing of all around, and repeated frequently, but with no real result.

But neglect of duty will not be in the categories specified in the hunt for war criminals, so we have nothing to write about in these accusatory forms. As for the Nips who ill-treated us, we seldom knew their real names but labelled them with insulting nicknames.

If we leave the forms blank will it be said, 'Why, they didn't have such a bad time after all'? So we do what we can to avoid giving such an impression, using general terms and nicknames, nothing which we can really report about our own people, even though there are things that should be made public under other headings.

The days pass, we are issued with a note informing services personnel and civilian officials that we are RAPWI and, as such, are to be given all possible consideration and assistance. The initials stand for Returned Allied Prisoners of War and Internees. Someone has been having kind thoughts for us, to help during the next few months while travelling and finding our feet at home.

And there's our ship, HMT *Worcestershire*, lying in the broad reaches of the Irrawaddy River, waiting to take us away.

Naturally, all the men with me are looking forward to going home – that is, back to the United Kingdom, which is where they spent all their lives before being sent out to this god-forsaken part of the world. But for Ron and me England is not our home, we have always lived in the Far East apart from some seven years in England for schooling, there being no suitable educational facilities for boys of our age in Shanghai. So we, alone in the contingent of 1,500 men assembled in huts on the banks of the Irrawaddy, will in fact be sailing away from our real home, not knowing when we shall be able to get back or what the situation will be in Singapore when we are eventually able to do that. We know nothing about our home and all our personal belongings which we had to abandon, whether anything survived the Japanese occupation or, indeed, the Allied reoccupation which is now taking place. Accommodating the mass of the 14th Army will demand every bit of available space including, no doubt, our house, and whatever might still be in it will be at the mercy of the new occupants.

The amputation cases are to embark a day ahead of the rest, to give them freedom to settle in and find their way about the ship unimpeded, which is a kind thought from someone in the admin office. The *Worcestershire* is a former passenger/cargo liner of the British India Steam Navigation Company, converted to a troopship and now a seasoned veteran of six years of war. The crew tell us that she normally carries 3,000 men, so at half that number we shall be relatively well off.

Our party is exactly fifty including myself, and I shall be required to keep and produce such paperwork as may be necessary. The reason for this precise number of men is that the dormitory space normally occupied by warrant officers has exactly fifty bunks (two high, with mattresses and sheets and even pillowcases) and this has been allocated to the one-legged men. The rest of the rank and file will sleep in hammocks slung way down below in the hold spaces.

Following instructions from our crew member guide, I dump my kit on one of the beds, and we all go to the warrant officers' mess for lunch. The duty officer spies me walking on two legs and says he will allow me to eat in this mess until the others come on board tomorrow, after which I shall feed with them. This sort of army claptrap irritates me, but there's no arguing with it.

Big, thick pork chops with roast potatoes, carrots and peas followed by tinned peaches and custard! Our first civilised meal for nearly four years, served on good china with a proper set of cutlery and glasses of water! After close to 4,000 mess tins (battered and rusty) of dirty, gritty, low-grade rice and plain tea in a chipped enamel mug, someone has to declare, in an aggrieved tone, 'My bloody chop isn't cooked right!'

The ship fills up and I take my meals down in the dungeons but still sleep in a luxurious bunk up in the warrant officers' quarters. On the third day I receive a quiet word to shift my kit down below as there is to be an inspection due to some irregularity in our numbers, but, to make sure that nobody is put into my vacant bunk there will be some stuff laid on it so that it will appear to be occupied.

I spend two nights in a hammock slung above the mess tables before someone tells me I can come back upstairs. It's far more comfortable, light and airy – which I am accustomed to! – compared with the stuffy, hot and almost airless hold space which vibrates with the thump of the ship's engines.

And I do dislike being slung up high with my face a foot below the deckhead.

I am called to the admin office to provide a list of names of those in my party. Is my strength forty-nine plus one? Or fifty plus one? There is a discrepancy which they cannot resolve. I assure them that there are forty-nine amputation cases – there are the names – and myself. Total, fifty. I offer to take a clerk with me to check every man individually against the list. No mistakes, but they are still puzzled, because they have a total of fifty-one and can't find an error.

The weather is absolutely perfect, the sea flat calm and blue, the sunrises and sunsets dazzlingly beautiful. We have plenty of deck space – no chairs to sit on, but that's of no consequence. We mooch around in the sun, in the shade, chatting endlessly, quite happy to let the days go by at their own pace, lazy, dreamy days, heading home with every pulse of the engines.

Only part of the ship is ours. All the internal cabins and saloons are reserved for officers and a group of ladies in green uniforms, and parts of the weather decks are also roped off to keep us separated. We couldn't care less; we don't even know if they are ship's personnel, ex-prisoners, or simply on transfer back to Britain. They don't speak to us across the ropes, and we don't encourage them. We note several officers slithering around, jockeying to be near the women, and looking petulant when they are in turn displaced. It's a bit of a giggle and it helps to pass the time, watching their little games.

The women do seem to be more interested in us than in the officers. They stare across at us sympathetically, and talk quietly to each other as if discussing us. Their green uniforms have a badge with the letters WVS, new to us but we hear from the crew that this means Women's Voluntary Services, and they are part of the ship's establishment, concerned with the welfare of the troops on board. Are we troops, or not?

On the third day it is announced over the Tannoy system that a sweep will be run daily on the distance covered by the ship from noon to noon. Tickets on which you can write your guess are threepence each; prizes will be a percentage of the pot with the rest going to welfare funds. This gives the WVS ladies an opportunity to talk to us, for they run the sweep. They tell us that the commanding officer, who has been OC Troops for most of the war, is a bit of a disciplinarian and has told them not to mix with us, because he is uncertain as to how we might behave. He seems to think that after four years without even speaking to a woman, we might get out of control and rape all of them! He might have asked us!

The ladies, it seems, politely told him to shut up as they were confident that we would behave properly, and they intended at least to talk to us across the ropes! And they are doing so, and that's all right with us, isn't it? We thank them politely for standing up for us, and amongst ourselves we begin to wonder what sort of attitudes we are going to encounter in the future – questions which have never before occurred to us.

Right from the start of this voyage there has been an irritant in the background. At first we ignore it, then tolerate its sheer persistence, then hate it. Of necessity the ship has a Tannoy system, broadcasting to all decks and spaces where men might be so that routine orders and emergency instructions can be made known everywhere immediately. The problem is that some brainless clot in admin uses the system to saturate us with so-called music, playing records all day long with, presumably, the idea that an unbroken stream of music soothes such savage breasts as ours.

Now, the last popular music we heard was back in 1941, since when the same tunes and songs have been hummed and sung until we have all become thoroughly sick of them. Surely, at last, we shall have fresh songs, new tunes, maybe even a new style of music to enjoy? And new singers? But all we get is the same old ancient rubbish, endlessly repeated all day long because there are only twelve records, and they are worn out, scratchy and almost tuneless. It seems that some kind of noise, any kind, is preferable to silence.

Nobody has asked us whether we want this awful trash thrown up at us from daylight to lights out, and on the third day we have had enough when the cycle starts again for the ten thousandth time. A small group walks into the broadcasting shack and seizes all the stock of records, chucking them over the lee rail of the ship into the sea. One of the vocalists is some new fellow named Sinatra – God, he's awful!

And blessed peace enfolds us.

The coast of Ceylon shows up on the horizon and the OC Troops announces over the Tannoy that we shall moor in Colombo harbour towards sunset, staying for twenty-four hours to take on supplies and mail. There is no mention of whether we shall or shall not be allowed to go ashore. We have no idea whether we have any entitlement. The flaring red and orange sun dives into the sea just as we complete tying up to a buoy in the harbour. We are the first ship to arrive with former POWs being repatriated, and the welcome we receive is tremendous.

The port is full of merchantmen and warships, and every siren and hooter is blasting away, rockets zoom up everywhere, searchlights form 'V' for Victory signs, signal lamps flash – in all there is half an hour of enthusiastic bedlam to welcome us back amongst our own people. It's an emotion-filled time for us. These ships and the men and women in them have fought to win the war and bring us home. They are glad to see us and we are enormously grateful to them. And we don't forget the army and air force people also there, who have no sirens and rockets to sound off, but we think of them too.

With the ship at a standstill and the Ceylon night hot and airless, we all bring up our bedding to lay out on deck. The CO's minions come along to tell us we can't do that, the CO won't allow it. We tell them to get stuffed and lie there, immovable. There must be 1,000 or more of us, and they give up. For the rest of the night we are undisturbed, and before sun-up we clear the decks ready for hosing down by the crew. We have our own disciplines and do not care for stupid and pointless regulations, especially when they cause needless discomfort. We have had more than enough of that during the past few years, thank you.

Early morning we are up, shaved and dressed well before breakfast, hoping to see boats leaving the shore to collect us. Nothing happens. We are called for porridge and bacon, bread, jam and tea. Back on deck we stare around the harbour; there is nothing else to do.

A water-tank craft comes alongside and starts to pump fresh water, and a barge with fresh vegetables, towed by a launch, comes to the foot of the gangway; a few of our officers wander down to talk to the supply officers on the launch. To their exaggeratedly obvious surprise, they find themselves being taken to the shore, caught unawares during their conversation! The sheer childishness of this manoeuvre makes us roar with laughter and call out rude comments, causing embarrassment to other officers amongst us who were not clever enough to join them – embarrassment because they can neither reprimand us for insolence nor escape our criticism of their fellows.

Boredom settles down on us for an hour or so. The morning is sliding away and our chances of going ashore diminish accordingly. Then a large launch puts out and heads towards us at speed, froths to a stylish halt at the foot of the gangway, and it is immediately apparent that something is about to happen. A formidable-looking lady in WVS uniform, resplendent with badges of unmistakably high rank and campaign ribbons, treads resolutely up the steps, followed by a covey of ladies in similar uniform. There is no doubt that she is severely displeased about something and is going to make sure that some unfortunate person will soon cop the benefit of it.

The duty officer welcomes her aboard with a smart salute and a polite, 'Good morning, Ma'am,' but she has no time for him.

Without returning his salute or greeting – in itself a studied rebuke – she barks at him, 'Where is the OC Troops? I wish to speak to him.'

The duty officer recovers his poise: 'Certainly, Ma'am. If you will follow me I shall be happy to conduct you to his office.'

'You will do nothing of the sort! You will go to him at once and tell him that I wish to speak to him. Here! And I do not expect to be kept waiting!'

We do not know the protocols of this skirmish – the lady's rank is new to us, as is her status in the military world, but the duty officer takes off very rapidly, without a sign of protest. In a moment the situation changes. The fire-breathing dragon is transformed into a charming woman, all motherly smiles and easy conversation, asking after our health and wellbeing. Her ladies are the same, mixing with us, shaking hands, telling us they know we have had a rough time and expressing admiration for our coming through it all. In just a few minutes our morale gets a marvellous boost.

The duty officer reappears, leading the OC Troops. It's the first time we have actually seen him, and also the first time we have seen an officer of his rank hurrying in answer to a summons and with an apprehensive look on his face. By the time he comes to a halt the lady's battleaxe is swinging, his snap salute is ignored, and there is no doubt as to who is boss.

'Colonel, I want to know why these men are still on this ship!'

'Ma'am, I wasn't sure how they might behave –'

'It's gone nine-thirty –'

'They haven't mixed with young women for –'

'And my ladies and all their staffs have been waiting –'

'I thought it better not to risk –'

'Since seven o'clock, with breakfast laid on and parties organised to –'

'Using my best judgement –'

'BE QUIET, WILL YOU! DON'T INTERRUPT ME WHILE I'M TALKING TO YOU!' Imperious, formidable, the colonel is no match for her.

There is a pause while the colonel tries to recover his composure. He has been dressed down unmercifully in front of us. He is humiliated and off balance. There is more to come.

'I wish to see every man off this ship and on shore within an hour.' And the knockout punch: 'I shall be in conference with Lord Louis Mountbatten tomorrow morning, and he will be keen to have a report on the reception of these former prisoners. You have very little time to act if you wish to escape an adverse account from me!' There is no mistaking this calm and deliberate reprimand – and threat.

The OC Troops excuses himself, his dignity in shreds. The dragon turns a beaming smile on us – I think we must all be looking a bit dazed – and says in a conversational tone, 'Well, now that that's all arranged we shall look forward to seeing you ashore in an hour or so. You deserve to have a bit of a fuss made over you, and the WVS and Wrens and all the other services have organised all sorts of things for you. So, just relax and enjoy yourselves!' With a wave and bright smiles all round, the ladies troop down the gangway to their launch, with more smiles and cheery calls as they head towards shore.

'Chee-suss, that was something, wasn't it? She must be on Mountbatten's staff, head of the women's services or something, to be able to use his name like that!'

The OC Troops must have moved fast in getting signals to his people on shore. Already there is a small swarm of launches, towed pontoons and barges, heading out our way.

We have been given pocket money to spend, but there is really no need for it unless we want to buy knick-knacks or small presents in the local shops to take home. We are made welcome everywhere – canteens and messes are open to us for something to eat or drink, trucks and Jeeps (those funny little vehicles we have seen only once at Sraburi) are available for sightseeing rides around Colombo and the countryside. And the girls, in WVS green and Wrens sparkling white, eager to talk to us, wanting to know what it was like under the Japs – it's all a bit overwhelming. We notice that they look puzzled when we are asked questions and reply in matter-of-fact tones: oh yes, we reckon about 20,000 died on the railway. No, we never had enough to eat. No, there was never any proper medical attention. Yes, I had fourteen attacks of malaria. And dysentery, on and off. Beri-beri, yes, pretty well every man, some not too bad but hundreds died of it. Yes, some men became insane, couldn't take the stresses. Yes, we were beaten up, some men died as a result.

We speak quietly, not showing emotion as we tell of deaths, crude amputations – Ron and the others are there, on crutches – brutalities and deliberate cruelties, the ever-present strains and humiliations, the shocking conditions under which we lived and worked, the total indifference of the Jap officers and senior command (who were responsible) as to whether we lived or died. The girls want to know it all.

We know that we are giving an impression of callousness, of being unfeeling, but cannot lift ourselves out of it. For too long we have had to seal off our normal sensitivities in order to stay sane, and we haven't yet had time to loosen up.

One of the girls says, 'You know, you all have a kind of faraway look in your eyes. Here you are, talking to us easily and freely, but you seem to be holding yourselves off, at a distance, as if you're not sure about making real contact with us.'

I tell her: 'We have all been so isolated from our old world, so totally cut off, for so long, we might have been on another planet. It's so strange to be talking to normal people again. You're the first, and we've just not yet got used to it, to being back on earth. We're still unwinding, I think. It's going to take time – maybe, for some of us, a long time.'

She looks thoughtful: 'It must have been unbelievably tough for all of you. But you've come this far, and you'll pull through all right, you must do.' She leans forward and gives me a soft friendly kiss on the cheek. 'Goodbye, and the best of luck to all of you in your futures.'

It's time to be getting back on board. Already I can feel that little warm and comforting glow on my cheek beginning to thaw me out.

* * *

There is a dreamlike quality about our shipboard life, sitting on the teak deck in the warm sunshine while the breezes of the Indian Ocean curl soothingly around us. The deck vibrates almost imperceptibly with the thrumming engines below us, and men's voices buzz vaguely in the background – it is easy to relax and doze away the hours between meals.

For some of us it is a time when thoughts start to drift into our consciousness, seeping in from the outer haze and gradually massing until they acquire sufficient weight to demand attention. It is, I feel, a natural instinctive urge, reminding us that we are going home and have to do some careful thinking about ourselves. How much have we changed, how much has our old world altered, what adjustments must we make in ourselves? The questions themselves are simple, but the answers seem to become ever more complex as we start to peer into them. Nothing is complete in itself; every thought opens up links that run off in all directions to others, continually expanding the puzzle.

The process has been triggered by our brief visit to Colombo, when the extent of our withdrawal into ourselves became apparent, not only to ourselves but also to those who talked to us – our very first real contacts with normal people in nearly four years. In those few hours a perception was created, in the recesses of our minds, that the relaxation and unwinding process must now be directed to focus on some practical ideas about returning to normal human society. We must each do it on our own, for although many of the problems are common to all of us, we are individuals who must make the finer personal adjustments entirely on our own. And we now have a matter of three weeks to do it before we reach Liverpool and lose the comforting comradeship of this ship and are scattered amongst families, friends and the wide world in general – people who will have no concept of what we have been through.

There are important questions that must be faced and dealt with. Every man has been changed by the last few years – no one can have escaped except those who died, may they rest in peace! What have we become? To what extent can we regain our old selves? Are some changes to be permanent? How are we going to cope? I see two possibilities. According to our individual personalities we may or may not have a free choice – we may have to accept the effects imposed on us by our natures, but the outcome is of great importance in our personal development for we are all young men who, over a period of several years, have been subjected to physical and emotional stresses so severe that a number of men blew their fuses and retreated into insanity. We all carry, unavoidably, feelings of hatred and contempt for our captors, and of resentment towards our own people who were responsible for the shameful acts which led to our captivity. These feelings are bedded deep, and will always be with us.

So, what burden will each of us carry when we return to our own people, and as the years pass? Will it be a sack into which each poisonous snake was stuffed as it attacked us, and will that sack always be full of writhing hatreds ready to uncoil and strike? Or will it be a kitbag into which each problem has been stowed away after being met, wrestled to a standstill and laid to rest? A kitbag which, at some later time, it may be possible to unpack, item by item, to be considered calmly as a major part of our personal histories, to be reviewed in conversation or to illustrate a point. We may never reach the bottom of the kitbag; we may not have the nerve to fossick too deep, we may simply prefer not to rediscover what is there. Nothing can ever be discarded, but I suppose it might be blotted out.

But, surely, we owe it to our dead to remember, to keep alive the fearsome circumstances under which they perished, helpless and innocent sacrifices to the incompetence of others. Remembrance, in private and in public, must be our outward sign of thankfulness for our deliverance; we were not more worthy than they, just luckier. Nor did they deserve to die in such interminably drawn out squalor, degradation, suffering and infinite loneliness, far from families and friends. No doubt we shall be told to forgive and forget by those who were not there and who cannot – will not wish to – comprehend. To do so will be a betrayal of our dead friends, and even now I know it will never be possible for me.

When Singapore capitulated, late in the afternoon of Sunday 15 February 1942, our lives were split into two with the brutal finality of a guillotine blade. It could not have been more abrupt, more complete, or more destructive to our personalities, and it was – despite the defeats of the two months leading up to it – a devastating surprise. It had, simply, never been acceptable – we believed it could never actually happen.

We had been hearing of Japanese troops advancing all over the island. Places familiar to us who lived there, residential suburbs where our homes stood, were named as overrun with little apparent opposition. It seems that our defences were so full of holes that the enemy simply moved through wherever he wished, and no attempt was ever made to destroy or eject him. How could this happen when we had so many thousands of soldiers packed into such a small area? Surely gaps were not possible in such a solid mass?

We had all been waiting for an abandonment of formal military tactics, falling back and regrouping, counterattacking, all that sort of thing. There was nowhere to fall back to, no regrouping necessary because we were already stuffed tight together. What we were expecting was an order to fill haversacks with ammunition, fix bayonets, and get in amongst the Japs, man to man, hand to hand, where their artillery and aircraft could not be used against us, and kill every damned one of them, all over the island. Unorthodox, but everything else had failed dismally.

No such order was issued. Instead there was a special Order of the Day from our commander-in-chief, telling us that Singapore had capitulated. Tame and meek, just like that! Every man was to remain where he was, no attempt to escape was permitted, no weapons or other materials were to be destroyed but must be handed over intact. But isn't it every soldier's duty to try to escape after capture? Or was all this in the terms of capitulation, laid down by the Japs? And to attempt to escape would be disobedience of our commander-in-chief's Order of the Day – mutiny, nearly!

The enormous shame of the surrender was a fearsome blow to our self-respect. We had been on Singapore Island, as part of its garrison, during the whole of the Malayan campaign and, rightly or wrongly, we had seen the whole affair as bungled, ineffectual, always on the wrong foot, and always enfeebled by irresolution and bad judgement, the civilian government being as much to blame as the military chiefs. And on top of all these weaknesses, the clumsy dithering inertia of the controlling councils in London, overwhelmed by the problems closer to their home and blind to our circumstances, planning – when they could bother to spare us a thought – on the basis of wishful thinking.

And the consequences of this colossal disaster were dumped squarely on us. Up until the moment of surrender we were part of a fighting army supported by the imperial forces of a great empire, linked firmly together and mutually supportive. Then, without even time to think about it, our

framework was shattered, our leaders made themselves power-
less, ourselves helpless and put into the hands of a totally alien
nation whose barbarities – in China over the past decade –
had been beyond belief.

A further heavy burden for husbands and fathers among
us Volunteers was the capture of wives and children, awaiting
internment in utter loneliness, frightened and deprived of the
comfort of their men. They were innocent victims of
the Governor's persistent refusal to consider their evacuation
when it would have been possible – may his soul slide down
to hell and burn forever!

We put our trust in all these people, and they failed us
abysmally. As is the way of things, they will personally largely
escape the consequences of their incompetence, while those
who were let down by them will have carried the great mass of
misery that gathered over our heads, a crushing spiritual and
emotional blackness. All this, and the horrors of the
Siam–Burma railway, we have endured, our ranks sadly
thinned by death and – as the Bible somewhere puts it – the
travails of the spirit, until the war ended. *We* know where
the blame must fall.

It is now time to make repairs and move forward. We
must draw some benefit, find something worthwhile, from
those terrible years, for to fail to do so will be an admission
that we were defeated in ourselves. And that is something we
can never allow. We must prove to ourselves, and others, that
we have come through intact – changed somewhat, but whole
in ourselves.

The years have passed, and our experience of living them
must not be wasted – that would indeed be an unthinkable
tragedy. But we must not let our thinking be poisoned by
hatred. We must remain civilised, which does not in any way
mean that we should forget the actual realities, or forgive those

who perpetrated them – or those who were responsible for our having to endure them.

In the company only of men, tens of thousands of them always crowding around you, it was possible to feel desperately and unnervingly lonely. And yet, at times you could curse their unavoidable nearness and yearn for a time and place of solitude. There was never any choice, of course – whatever your longings of the moment you simply had to adapt and make the best of it. But, *always,* you needed the closeness and support of friends; no man could survive on his own. I am totally convinced that many men who died just gave up because they had become separated from their mates and couldn't face all the problems on their own. The feeling of being *totally alone* can destroy a man.

Adapt, alter, redirect thoughts, suppress emotions, control temper, twist and distort your personality to accommodate circumstances forced upon you, to create a defensive shell, to be part of a bond of *togetherness* with those around you. For it was that bond, loyalty *to* each other and concern *for* each other, that forged a tough shield of mutual protection. Without it you were too vulnerable – you could simply fall apart. There was a subtlety in this shield. Nobody actually had to ask for help; watchful mates saw when it was needed and there it was, in place, unobtrusively. But if you had no mates near you at a bad time, you could die almost unnoticed.

These last thoughts have made me pause. They seem to be to some extent contradictory and I must ask myself how that can be for they are undoubtedly true. There must be a reconciliation between the existence of compassion for everybody, and yet seeing men die in sheer loneliness.

I see the answer as lying in any man's capacity for sympathy towards others. There is a limit to how widely he can stretch his natural feelings, and every man has his own limit. He must, firstly, look to his own being – otherwise he will surely be so open to stresses that he will die, even if others try to help. Secondly, he will care for his immediate group of friends and all in that group will help the others. Thirdly, he will be part of his army unit and, probably, of other units linked to his – in our case, we Singapore Volunteers had an affinity with men from up-country Malaya, whom we may not have met before but who had led similar lives to ours, and who also had wives and children interned in Japanese hands.

Beyond this larger group individual men were strangers, even though they were part of our wider 'family' and therefore were friends entitled to support. But at this point a man's capacity for sympathy has become thin, his personal problems absorb much of his pool of generosity and his friends take up most of what is left. In actual fact there is little he can do, in practical terms, for himself or his close mates, and spiritual comfort is all he can offer to others. It is indeed there, but sometimes not strong enough to be of real help – or, simply, it may not be what is needed at the moment.

So to the outsiders we shall be meeting in a few weeks, we may appear to be insensitive, even callous, but that would be a totally incomplete – even wrong – impression. That girl in Colombo who kissed me and offered words of encouragement, she had some understanding, and we may hope that others will when we get home. Meanwhile, we must take ourselves to pieces and polish all the bits, and reassemble them into ordinary human beings.

There is, of course, another problem hanging over us, and it is somewhat upsetting to recognise that we have no way, at present, of knowing its extent. Indeed, it may not even exist, for although it has been in our minds from our first days of work on the railway, it is how others see it that will matter.

There is no getting away from the fact that we built a railway for the enemy, who used it to transport men and war materials to his armies in Burma, for use against our own people. What difference this may have made to the war in Burma we can have no idea. How much was destroyed by the RAF, and how much of our war effort had to be diverted from the fighting front to deal with it, we have no way of knowing. But these considerations are not in fact relevant. The point is that we constructed a major war asset for the Japanese, and that alone may be held against us. It is worrying, extremely so.

Of course, our welcome in Colombo was exuberant and genuine, but then the war had just ended in a magnificent victory, everyone was elated and we – as the first draft of ex-POWs going home – benefited from all the excitement and kindnesses released by our arrival. The authorities at home, detached by distance and not personally involved, will have had time to think about it and may well have different opinions, and these are the people – chilly bureaucrat types – who may feel they need to probe and pick things over.

We had no choice in the matter, our senior officers in our camps told us to comply – what choice did *they* have? – and the railway was built in the incredible period of some twelve months, at a truly dreadful cost to our men. We suffered intensely while we laboured, both in body and in spirit, starved and sick, and without even the most basic amenities, deprived of even the smallest human decencies except for what we managed to find for ourselves.

And from that we developed a reluctant pride, a special and personal pride in our achievement against ferocious odds. We came through as whole and sane human beings, and that is where our pride is justified. That we built a railway for the enemy is a separate and distinct matter, and we must hope that others will consider the circumstances when they come to a decision.

We have a daunting task ahead of us, may the gods smile on us when we need their help. I think we deserve that!

For the time being the gods really are smiling on us. Never have I experienced such perfect weather, day after day, in all my many sea voyages between England and the Far East, via Suez and America before the start of the German war. The ship steams serenely over calm seas under the bluest of skies, while pleasant breezes keep us cool. It does wonders for us, soothing and healing our souls and bodies.

Not for everybody, though. A young fellow who must have been only eighteen or so when he joined the army has, quite suddenly, lost his reason. One of the tattered paperbacks from the ship's library has a picture of a smiling girl advertising a brand of toothpaste, and he has identified her as his sweetheart from before he became a POW. Somehow, he has had a message to say that she has married another man, and the disappointment is too much for him. Broken-hearted with unhappiness, weeping convulsively, he has poured out his story to his mates, who know well that he is making it all up. They tell him that the girl in the advert is not real but exists only in his imagination. He won't accept that – she really is his girl and he lived through the last years only to come back to her. Now he wishes he hadn't, she wasn't worth it. The medical officer is called and removes him to the ship's sick bay.

I wonder, if we had been having overcast skies, heavy seas and violent, pitching gales and rain forcing us to stay below in the sweaty holds, would we all now be in a state of seasick depression? I can believe we would be, sick unto death, literally.

Thank you, gods, for your kindness!

* * *

I have had another summons to the admin office, where they still cannot make the figures for my party add up. They insist that there are fifty-one, including me, and I am equally sure that there are forty-nine plus me. Once again we check every detail. The answer is so obvious, but they cannot see it. I would be inclined to tell the sergeant clerk what it is, but the pipsqueak officer in charge is so childishly petulant that I let him stew. It can be sorted out on our last day, before we berth at Liverpool. Obviously they have counted fifty occupied beds in the warrant officers' dormitory as all legless men, plus me in a hammock down below, total fifty-one. Stuff them!

The peace and calm of this leisurely voyage, the beautiful weather and solid troopship diet – they gave up serving rice puddings after the first few days as nobody would touch them (except me!) – have done wonders for us. The steady mending of our bodies and the soothing effect on our mental processes have allowed instincts and urges, long dormant through starvation rations and lack of opportunity, to awaken.

And this has raised an uneasy thought as to our future. The question is plain, but there is no definite answer and this is beginning to bug us. Are we going to find, when we are again mixing with girls and wanting to get married, that we might well have been made infertile by malnutrition prolonged over so many years? We discussed this with our medical officer back in Wampo, when every man showed signs of deterioration and another six months could have seen us all dead. The MOs had talked about it amongst themselves and could not reach a definite opinion – there was no published medical history to call upon. The relatively new science of vitamins and other necessary, tiny, food essentials had indicated all sorts of possibilities, but not enough was actually known to permit conclusions. Medical researchers knew that their explorations had only just begun, that there was still an enormous amount to be discovered, and who could forecast the findings?

Altogether, the situation is such that there is plenty of doubt, which might turn out to be unnecessary, but equally might not – there is nothing to reassure us. And this raises an ethical question which, it must be said, we are not too keen on facing. Will we be able, in good conscience, to propose marriage to a girl – with all that implies about having children – when we are in doubt as to our ability to be fathers? Should we tell the girl and give her the opportunity to back away? Or should we get married and hope for the best? We just have no way of deciding right now. Maybe the dilemma will resolve itself when the moment comes – it could be that we are worrying ourselves unnecessarily. The powerful emotions of love between two people may sweep it all aside in the simple desire to be together and leave the rest to happen as it may. And the sooner that happens, the better for all of us. We have been deprived for far too long of this most ordinary, and most magical, aspect of human life.

As our ship ploughs steadily homewards, our spirits lift as we push our worries aside and begin to develop a positive attitude towards our futures, a growing confidence that we shall be able to merge back into our own people. Most will be going back to welcoming families and friends from their past. Ron and I will be reunited with a mother who has endured years of dreadful stress, and a father fresh out of Japanese internment camps. Except for her own mother, our mum has not had a word of interest, or support, from any single one of our numerous uncles and aunts!

We shall have our own problems, I can see that!

* * *

Halfway through the voyage we reach the top end of the Red Sea, where we come alongside a wharf at Port Tewfik. Half the troops go through the immense army stores depot to be kitted out for the cold winter ahead of us, while the rest pile into coaches down to a perfect stretch of beach. Here a group of West African troops, splendidly muscular in their bathing trunks, takes our legless men pickaback racing along the sands and plunging into the sapphire sea. Huge men they are, with beaming white smiles and gentle hands, full of fun and energy, and bursting with goodwill.

After lunch back on the ship, we find ourselves in the cavernous depths of the colossal supply dump. We have never seen anything like it – all the stores that there ever were in Singapore could disappear from sight in this mass of army material. The counters are stacked with piles of clothing in various sizes; a clerk takes a quick look at each man and directs him to a particular pile. We pick up a kitbag and, with a sweep of the arm, fill it with all we need. The whole procedure is so quick that we have an hour or more to wait for our coaches to return for us.

We find a table in the canteen for a mug of tea, and a young woman in WVS uniform joins us. She is English but grew up in Brazil, and when the Hitler war started she and all her friends took a ship to England to join up. Conversation is easy, but she tells us that we all seem to have a distant look, a kind of withdrawn attitude akin to a wariness, almost as if we are functioning on two planes – talking freely, but still not making real personal contact with her.

We tell her that her colleagues in Colombo had the same impression of us, and we explain things as best we can. She has no difficulty understanding our problem, and offers sympathy and best wishes towards sorting it out. This is very encouraging! Other people can see that we are still partly in the shadows and can at once understand how it is, while we know that we are making progress towards open skies and our old selves. We need a little time, but it will all come out right. Undoubtedly there will be some spiritual scars, but we can live with them.

Back to the ship for a day through the Suez Canal – my fifth transit through this waterway, and by far the most significant for it must lead to a renewed life in a world which has changed in so many ways.

The dreamy voyage continues, broken shortly after clearing Port Said by the ringing of alarm bells for Action Stations. The Tannoy tells us that only the crew are to move, passengers to remain where they are. The ship slows as it comes up to something floating in the sea, possibly a mine – there are still plenty of these drifting around – but on closer inspection it turns out to be a damaged lifeboat, waterlogged and with bits of clothing and rubbish inside. It is a saddening reminder of the deadly side of the war just ended, from which we as POWs were excluded. Although we did have our own casualties, of course, from the treatment dished out by the Nips and from our own bombers, just different – that's all.

The flotsam is hauled on board for examination, and the ship builds up speed again. We cruise smoothly the length of the Mediterranean, halting at Gibraltar for mail and stores, then push out into the Atlantic. Amazingly, the seas are still flat and the sunshine comfortably warm, all the way northwards into the Bay of Biscay. Then the temperature drops and a light sea mist forms. We are glad of our warm clothing, for some of us – Volunteers and regular garrison troops – have been in the tropics for six years and more.

Three days before we are due in Liverpool we wake up to find the ship crawling along. Word goes round that the dockers in Liverpool have gone on strike and consequently the berth allocated to us will not be vacant as expected. Meanwhile, as long as the strike lasts we shall dawdle around to waste time, and no date can be given for our arrival. This just makes everybody bloody angry. Immediately we think of the Liverpool Irish stokers on the *Empress of Asia*, one of the five ships bringing the 18th Division into Singapore towards the end of January 1942. These stokers demanded danger money while in Singapore waters, the captain refused and the stokers went on strike. The ship fell behind the others and lost the overhead protection which the RAF had managed to scrape together. Pounced upon by Jap bombers, the *Empress of Asia* burned and sank, all her precious military armaments being totally lost. To make matters worse, some of the troops who got ashore from the wreck – and a few weeks later were in prison camps on Singapore Island – saw these stokers at large in the city streets. The stokers waved their neutral Irish passports at our men, laughing and shouting taunts and insults.

So the linking of Liverpool Irish dockers and stokers kindles a great flare of anger on our ship. Within a couple of hours a letter, signed by every man on board, is handed to the OC Troops to be forwarded to the authorities in Liverpool. It declares that every one of us is prepared to unload ships – particularly those carrying food supplies – and to work as long as may be necessary and to delay our return home accordingly. We haven't been told whether this message has been transmitted or not – we haven't seen the OC Troops since his humiliation at Colombo – but we hope that he will think he should keep on good terms with us. In any event, during the afternoon the ship picks up speed again and brings us on schedule to a berth opposite the famous landmark, the Liver Building.

Leaning over the rail looking down on the main

gangway, we idly watch a procession of officials come on board. Bringing up the rear are two very burly military police, and twenty minutes later they reappear, tramping down to the wharf. Between them is an officer, evidently under arrest, and to our surprise we recognise him immediately. In charge of a labour camp back in the very early days on Singapore Island, we heard talk of complaints about his behaviour – sucking up to the Nips, turning men out to work when the medical officer had exempted them (it was possible to do that, in those days) and sundry other objectionable habits. We saw him briefly, taking a party of the ill-fated 'F' Force through Tonchan South, and the men in his care told us more about him.

Evidently, the forms reporting such misdemeanours that we filled out in Rangoon had contained allegations which had reached London ahead of us, and his arrest is the consequence. We see him seated in a Jeep, an MP on either side, before being driven off the wharf to face his future. He is not the senior British officer at Tonchan, who considered it beneath his dignity to try to discuss his men's privations with a Japanese coolie – that officer died of illness a few months before the war ended and so escaped justice – what a disappointment! I have no idea what happened to the soldier who wanted to have him publicly exposed, but I very much doubt that he survived – or any of his thirty-one fellows.

There are hundreds of civilians on the wharf, waving and shouting welcomes to us. Some have banners, some hold up sheets of cardboard with names on them but as far as we can see they are out of luck – no one responds to them.

The day darkens as grey November clouds build up, and a chilling rain starts to fall.

That clinches it – we have definitely come home!

Afterword

I know that my experiences on the Siam–Burma Railway were in fact only a tiny part of the staggeringly immense tally of suffering and death of innocent people, military and civilian alike, which the Japanese (also military and civilian alike) spread like a foul disease everywhere they went during the years of the war that they started. I have no doubt that the atrocities described by people who endured them did happen, and countless more also happened but left no one alive to talk about them.

Long before the Japanese war ended on 15 August 1945, some 700 million people living in Asia and adjacent territories – Manchuria, China, the Philippines, Borneo, Papua New Guinea, French Indo-China, the Dutch East Indies, Siam, Burma, Hong Kong, Malaya, Singapore, and in numerous islands in the Pacific Ocean – had had first-hand or unpleasantly close experience of the sheer brutality and barbaric savagery which were a habitual and daily part of the Japanese invasion of their peaceful homelands. By the end of 1945 many more millions of people who had not been directly involved – in Britain, Australia, America, Canada and France, in particular, and in the rest of the world in general – also knew. Personal accounts poured in from those who had suffered, including non-combatant nationals who had been trapped in Japanese-occupied territories, as to how the Japanese (government, civilian, military) had carried out their methodical programs of massacre, rape, torture, looting and repression. Japan's reputation became an abomination throughout the civilised world; the nation was seen as a foul blot on the earth.

In the face of this enormous mass of undeniable evidence *only one nation* in all the world – Japan itself – did not show the smallest sign of recognition. The Japanese government of the time simply refused to admit that anything of the kind ever happened, insisting that accusations were fabricated lies, and that there was nothing requiring even an expression of regret let alone an apology.

The word 'apology' is almost impossibly difficult for any Japanese to pronounce, however shocking the circumstances, especially to any non-Japanese. Over the fifty-plus years which have gone by since 1945, Japan has never showed the smallest sign of changing its attitude – successive governments have continued to present an implacable stony indifference. There has even been a sense of irritation that anyone should be so impertinent as to persist with questions and accusations in the face of official Japanese denials. In my view – and surely it is shared by countless others – this attitude only increases the shame which stains Japan's international reputation.

It also makes it all the more necessary to remind the rest of the world of what happened – frequently and with a deliberate intent to trouble her national conscience.

The Dilemma of Forgiveness – Thoughts of an ex-prisoner of war

'Forgive!' saith my God.
But he who offends must first
Earn my forgiveness.
Wanting to forgive,
My spirit is baulked by those
Who do not repent.
There must be exchange,
Stricken conscience seeking peace
Will find forgiveness.

Horrors lie hidden,
Sealed, in my memory cells,
Sights my eyes have seen.
They are all brought back
In vivid flashes – a smell,
A sound, some small thing
Lying quiet – as
Might mines waiting to explode
On unwary thoughts.

My heart is torn, weeps,
Heals again, a new small scar
Pale as death itself.

Years pass, thoughts stay fresh,
Memories are the headstones
Of sacrificed dead.
How can we, who lived
By the whim of heedless gods,
Forget those who died?

And, in their ghostly names,
Not revile those brutal men
Who stole their old age?

The Japs repent not,
Forgiveness would be pointless,
Ineffective, void,
False comfort to me
And not even known to them,
Totally wasted.

Forgiveness will meet
Repentance. Without these – both –
Is either soul free?

It has to be thus!
The first move must come from them.
I wait. So be it!

Let us never forget, and forgive when called upon.
You should keep this in mind – always.

Picture Credits

Publisher's Note: There are occasional discrepancies in the recorded spelling of the names of some of the camps along the Burma-Thailand railway. Our intention has been to match the picture captions and credits with the names as they appear in the text.

London; POWs at Nakhon Pathom: AWM P00406.005; pen-and-ink drawing by Ronald Searle, 'Cholera': IWM ART 15747 (99), copyright © Ronald Searle 1943, by kind permission of the artist and the Imperial War Museum, London; cholera block, Kanyu: AWM P01087.002.

Clockwise from top left: battle of the bridges: IWM C4987; railway at Hintok: AWM 122309; pen-and-ink drawing by Ronald Searle, 'Planes dropping off pamphlets announcing end of war, over Changi gaol camp, Singapore': IWM ART 15747 (195), copyright © Ronald Searle 1945, by kind permission of the artist and the Imperial War Museum, London; graves at Lower Kanyu: IWM HU 4636.

Ex-POWs with a nurse: AWM P00761_015; ex-POWS with Lady Mountbatten: IWM S.E. 5182.

AWM = Australian War Memorial, Canberra
IWM = Imperial War Museum, London

GWEILO
Memories of a Hong Kong Childhood
By Martin Booth

Martin Booth died in February 2004, shortly after finishing the book that would be his epitaph – this wonderfully remembered, beautifully told memoir of a childhood lived to the full in a far-flung outpost of the British Empire . . .

'Triumphant . . . one of the most original and engaging memoirs of recent years, all the more telling because it is so personal, witty and true'
The Times

'Wonderful . . . it has such pace and power. The theme of good fortune may be ironic in the light of his death, but his memoir is, above all, a celebration of an enviable start in life . . . The portrait of his parents is particularly fine. There are some great comic moments too'
Sunday Telegraph

'Highly evocative . . . as a sharp-eyed, sensitive child of a vanished Hong Kong, Booth earns his nostalgia . . . his family are not the only ones who will enjoy the book'
Daily Telegraph

'The best autobiographies are written by observers rather than participants, evoking memories and emotions familiar to us all . . . *Gweilo* is admirably evocative of the noise and bustle of Hong Kong half a century ago . . . One longs to learn what happened next; but, alas, we never will'
Sunday Times

'Booth must rank as a giant of modern English letters . . . *Gweilo* is alive with delight in the new . . . this sunny, luminous account of a very special time and place will have to serve as an epitaph . . . ensuring that he will remain forever young'
Time magazine

'His finest work. Full of local colour and packed with incident'
Evening Standard 'Pick of the Year'

0 553 81672 1

BANTAM BOOKS

UNDER THE WIRE
By William Ash

Bill Ash was one of a rare breed – an American prepared to sacrifice his citizenship and risk his life to fight the Nazis at a time when the USA was still neutral. He joined the Royal Canadian Air Force and before long found himself in England and flying Spitfires in combat.

Then, in March 1942, Bill was shot down over the Pas de Calais. He survived the crash-landing and, thanks to the bravery of local civilians, evaded capture for months. He made his way to Paris only to be betrayed to the Gestapo. Tortured and sentenced to death as a spy, he was saved from the firing squad by the intervention of the Luftwaffe, who sent him to the *Great Escape* POW camp, Stalag Luft III. It was from there that Bill began his extraordinary 'tour' of Occupied Europe, breaking out of one camp, being dispatched to the next – in Poland, Germany and Lithuania. Bill became one of only a handful of serial escape artists to attempt more than a dozen break-outs – over the wire, under it in tunnels, through it with cutters or simply strolling out of the camp gates in disguise. These were years of extraordinary hardship, frustration and brutality – each time he was recaptured Bill's punishment was a long spell in solitary: he was a real-life 'cooler king' – but through it all he maintained not just remarkable courage, but also an anarchic sense of humour, great humanity and an unstoppable desire for freedom.

From its honest, funny and exciting reflections on life in wartime Britain, to the vivid, compelling, sometimes poignant recollections of his time as a POW, *Under the Wire* is more than just another memoir. It stands as a tribute to the bravery and resolve, not only of Bill Ash, but of an entire generation.

0 593 05408 3

NOW AVAILABLE FROM BANTAM PRESS

BANTAM PRESS

WITNESS TO WAR: DIARIES OF THE
SECOND WORLD WAR IN EUROPE
Everyday accounts by the men, women
and children who lived through it
By Richard J. Aldrich

From the moments of unbearable tension as Europe waited for the
coming conflict in 1938 to its tragic dying embers in 1945, the
Second World War changed millions of peoples' lives. It was
the greatest tidal wave of destruction and displacement the world had
ever seen. For ordinary men and women, it was a cataclysm they could
have never before imagined. Here is their extraordinary collective
testimony, an alternative history of a world in motion.

Most of these diaries involved a degree of danger and secrecy. In
occupied Europe a captured diary could betray friends and relatives to
the enemy. Some were downright illegal, such as those kept by soldiers
on the front line. Here, rare material from figures such as Joseph
Goebbels, Jean-Paul Sartre, Evelyn Waugh and Noël Coward has been
unearthed along with the insights of those close to Winston Churchill
and Adolf Hitler.

Witness to War is the innermost thoughts of people from every walk of
life. Their daily terrors, their fears and feelings, scribbled down and
secreted away, are revealed for the first time. Previously undiscovered
diaries have been brought to light to reveal an eye-opening, immediate
and intimate glimpse of a different kind of war.

'STANDS HEAD AND SHOULDERS ABOVE ALL THE
OTHER [WWII] BOOKS FLOODING OUT TO MEET THE
60TH ANNIVERSARY. [ALDRICH] GIVES AN EXCELLENT
PICTURE OF A WORLD IN AGONY'
Spectator (Books of the Year)

0 552 15108 4

BLACK SWAN